DEDICATED

To my wife Nancy who helps in every way and so patiently allows me to pursue my interest in plants. To my parents who afforded me the opportunity to be interested in rhododendrons. To the late Willard and Margaret Thompson whose love of rhododendrons gave me and many others the desire to excel in plants and whose new rhododendron 'Dad's Indian Summer' is featured on the book cover. Their interest and hybridizing skills continue today in two people who are very special, their son and daughter-in-law, Roy and Evelyn. To the late John Eichelser whose love of rhododendrons and inspiring image I will never forget. To Bruce and Doris Briggs whose desire to further rhododendrons is unending and who have produced thousands, or more likely hundreds of thousands, of rhododendrons world wide. And lastly, I dedicate this book to all of you I have had the joy of meeting, or may not have yet had the opportuntity to meet, whose love of rhododendrons has made it one of the most popular genera.

R. 'Extraordinaire'

Greer's Guidebook to Available Rhododendrons Species & Hybrids
by Harold E. Greer

R. 'Plum Beautiful'

Acknowledgments

To put a book together takes the efforts of many people, and hundreds of hours. This book, in its three editions, has had the help of countless people and I offer them all a special thank you. I especially thank Carol & Diane Johnson for their assistance in getting out the first edition. In this edition special thanks go to Suzanne Seip for hours of editing and proofing, Sara Leininger and Eileen Osborne for research and writing. Thanks also to Linda Rain for the layout of the color pages and for the original art work in this book.

By Harold E. Greer
Editor Suzanne Seip
Artist & Designer Linda Rain
Photography by Harold E. Greer

Offshoot Publications
1280 Goodpasture Island Rd.
Eugene, OR 97401-1794

Library of Congress catalog number 95-067367
First edition 1982
Revised second edition 1988
Revised third edition 1996
Copyright 1996 by Harold E. Greer
All rights reserved. No part of this book may be reproduced without permission of the author.
Printed in Thailand by Eastern Printing
ISBN: 0-910013-05-5 (*softcover*)
ISBN: 0-910013-06-3 (*hardcover*)

R. 'Hallelujah'
(Pictured on facing page)

R. strigillosum

R. strigillosum

R. strigillosum

R. proteoides

INTRODUCTION

This book was not written for botanists, but for laymen who want to know something about rhododendrons and how they relate to each other. I am thankful to botanists for the work they do, but there will always be a conflict between botanists and horticulturists. For example *R. metternichii* had its name changed by some botanists to *R. japonicum*. But wait, the horticulturist says, there is already a plant that does not even look similar to *R. metternichii*, that has been, and probably always will be known as *R. japonicum*. I neither agree or disagree with either side, and both are doing their best. Horticulturists don't agree with other horticulturists and botanists don't agree with other botanists. So what are gardeners to do if they wants to know a little more than the fact that they have "just a rhododendron" in the yard? I don't have the answer, but I hope this book will be able to provide some valuable information if you desire it, and yet not confuse an already confused situation.

The old Balfourian system of classification that is so familiar to us was meant to be a temporary system of rhododendron classification, but with the publication of The Species of Rhododendron by J. B. Stevenson, it became firmly entrenched in the thinking of rhododendron enthusiasts. It became widely accepted and is still accepted by leading rhododendron authorities today. In fact a recent series of books on rhododendron species was published using this system.

With regard to species, this book makes an attempt to compare the two systems of rhododendron classification. It should be understood that changes in the way the species are classified are being made daily, and only time will decide the "right" answer.

Now a few words about RATINGS. My pet peeve is the customer who comes into the nursery wanting only to buy a plant rated 5/5/5. I still have favorite rhododendrons that are rated 2/3/3, and a plant that is rated low in one part of the country may be excellent in another area. Remember, ratings are personal opinions (some of which are mine)! You may have planted your R. 'Jean Marie de Montague' in a dry or poorly drained spot, and your rating for the plant would be 2/2/2. Another person in the same climatic area might have planted it in the "perfect" spot and rate it a 5/5/5. And this true scenario does not even take into to account the differences in how well a plant will do in different climate zones. Don't ever consider ratings to be Biblical truth.

The word "AVAILABLE" in the title of this book does **not** mean available everywhere or all of the time. We have tried to include rhododendrons that are most likely to be propagated for the gardening trade. But remember, some of these are plants that are grown elsewhere in the world and may not be available for your garden. There are thousands of rhododendrons out there and we have tried to include those that you as consumers around the world are most likely to find; but as hundreds of new rhododendrons are hybridized each year, it is harder and harder to keep up with all these plants. We apologize if we missed your favorite!

INDEX OF COLOR PHOTOGRAPHS

Contents

SPECIES

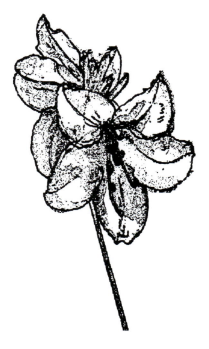

RHODODENDRON FLOWER & LEAF SHAPES

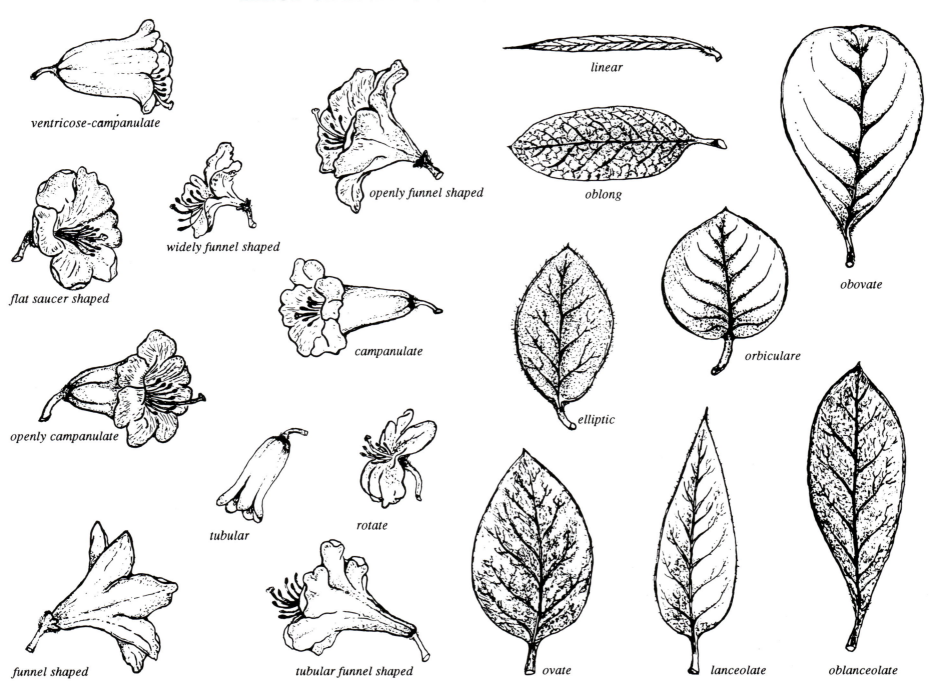

ventricose-campanulate

widely funnel shaped

flat saucer shaped

openly funnel shaped

linear

oblong

obovate

campanulate

openly campanulate

elliptic

orbiculare

tubular

rotate

funnel shaped

tubular funnel shaped

ovate

lanceolate

oblanceolate

BOTANICAL AND HORTICULTURAL TERMS

Plant names do not just "appear". To put some order in what could easily become chaos, the International Union of Biological Sciences helped create The International Association for Plant Taxonomy, which in turn initiated the International Code of botanical Nomenclature and the International Code of Nomenclature of Cultivated plants. The purpose of these organizations is to set up and oversee rules and guidelines to identify and name plants.

I. International Code of Botanical Nomenclature

The Botanical Code is the botanists' code. It is concerned with the classification of all plants, past, present, and future, from the top of the botanical hierarchy down through species, subspecies, varietas and forma.

Species -

A. The following three conditions must be met to have a species.

1. Species must differ from their closest neighbors in at least two characteristics.
2. Species must differ in geographical distribution.
3. Species must differ in ecological distribution. (Example: sun, shade, wind, etc.)

B. Species are usually considered to be a group of organisms (population) that actually (or potentially) interbreed and are reproductively isolated from all other such groups. (Example: *R. macrophyllum* interbreeds with *R. macrophyllum* and the resulting offspring remains *R. macrophyllum*.)

Subspecies -

A. Generally speaking, a subspecies does not fulfill all three of the above requirements, but will differ in one way or another.

B. A taxonomic sub-division of a species, usually defined as being different from the species as a result of growing in a separate geographic area.

Varietas - (pl. Varietates, abbr. Var.)

A. A sub division of a species which differs as a group in some minor definable characteristic(s) from the rest of the species.

B. A plant that differs or varies within a geographical and/or ecological unit, generally not deter mined simply because a group of plants are a different color.

Forma - (pl. Formae)

These are plants occurring in the wild as occasional individuals showing some peculiarity, such as a color variance. They may or may not breed true, and many are sterile.

When using the definitions, it must be kept in mind that they are not all precisely and unanimously agreed upon, though the ones given seem to be generally accepted.

II. International Code of Nomenclature of Cultivated Plants

The Cultivated Code concerns itself with plants of horticultural importance, beginning where the botanists end. It seeks to regulate horticulturally important clones, cultivars and groups.

Cultivar -

An assemblage of cultivated plants which is clearly distinguished by any characteristics, and which, when reproduced (sexually or asexually), retains its distinguishing character.

Variety -

This word is synonymous with Cultivar in the Cultivated Code. Many prefer **cultivar** and have dropped the use of **variety** because it is too easily confused with the Botanical Code's Varietas.

Clone -

A genetically uniform assemblage of individuals derived originally from a single individual by asexual propagation.

Cultivariant -

A plant which appears different in habit or foliage from its vegetative parents as a result of propagating from other than typical type foliage. It is also commonly called a "sport". This term has not as yet been accepted by the Cultivated Code. However, since it is being used frequently, and since it more precisely describes a large number of horticulturally important plants, it is almost sure to be suggested for adoption.

"THERE ISN'T SUCH A WORD!"

Often we hear the word **specie** used when someone is referring to a single **species.** There isn't such a word, at least botanically. The word **specie** means "payment in hard currency, such as gold". The word **species** is a botanical term and is **both** singular and plural. Therefore, don't make the very common error of referring to that one plant of *R. decorum* in your garden as a **specie**; even if there is only one, it is still a **species.** To state another common error, it is **not** the Rhododendron **Specie** Foundation. It is the Rhododendron **Species** Foundation!

A COMMON QUESTION

What is the difference between a rhododendron and an azalea?

All azaleas are rhododendrons. They belong to the subgenus Pentanthera (deciduous) and the subgenus Tsustusti (mostly evergreen) by the revised classification, or to the Azalea Series by the Balfourian System.

All azaleas are elepidotes (they never have scales).

All Azaleas have five lobes to the flower.

Most (not all) azaleas have only one stamen for each lobe of the flower, meaning they have five stamens, while most other rhododendrons have two stamens for each lobe, meaning they have 10 or more stamens.

Azaleas tend to have appressed hairs (hair that grows parallel to the surface of the leaf). This is particularly true along the midrib of the undersurface of the leaf and is easily seen in the so called "evergreen" azaleas.

Azaleas have tubular funnel or funnel shaped flowers.

You would need a microscope to see this, but, while the hair on "standard" rhododendrons will often branch, the hair on azaleas never does.

RHODODENDRON PROPAGATION

1. Cuttings - This is a vegetative method of propagation which produces plants that are identical to the mother plant. Cuttings (sometimes called scions) are taken off of semi-hard wood any time between less than a month after the new growth is made, to about six months after growth. In the northern hemisphere this would be somewhere between the months of May through November. Generally, softer wood roots more readily than harder wood, though the softer the wood, the more likely it is that problems will occur with fungus diseases. So sanitation is important. For planting use new bark, sawdust, clean (coarse if possible) peat, perlite, or coarse clean sand mixed in practically any combination. The main thing you want is a medium that has some humus (bark sawdust, peat) to hold moisture and an inert matter (perlite or sand) to provide air spaces and drainage.

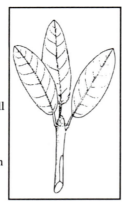

The cuttings should be made from the tip growth, cut from 1" to 4" long, depending on the growth size of the plant you are trying to propagate. The lower leaves should be removed and often the ends of the top leaves are shortened to provide more space between the cuttings, to allow air circulation and to lessen the amount of foliage the scion has to feed while it is rooting. Wound the cutting with a cut on each side, about 1/2" to 1", just deep enough to cut through the bark. Dipping the cutting in a rooting hormone containing indolebutyric acid will make rooting easier. The exact formula depends on the hardness of the cutting and the difficulty in rooting the cultivar you are trying to propagate. Experience is the only good teacher as to the strength needed, though most commercial rooting hormones will give some instructions.

Preferably the rooting bed you use for these cuttings has some form of heating to keep the soil temperature near 70°F (though many cuttings will root without heat) and some type of mist system that comes on and off to keep the foliage moist. You must be sure that the mist sytem does not put too much water in the soil, as soggy conditions will rapidly promote disease. A variation on this moisture supply is to build a frame over the cutting bed, cover it with plastic, and make sure it is not in direct sun. For summer propagation the simplest method may be a small wooden flat with a plastic cover set in a shaded location. To root one or two cuttings, even a glass jar filled half way with the above mentioned rooting soil, lightly watered, sealed with a lid and left in a north window may do the trick.

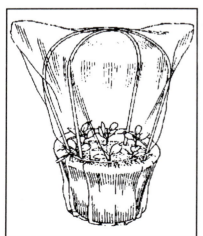

Remember, some rhododendron or azalea cuttings root easily, often within 6 weeks, while others may take 3, 6, 9, or 12 months to root, or may not root at all. Don't be discouraged by your first attempts. However, don't expect to cut a limb off of your plant, stick it into the ground next to your plant and have it root. It may stay green for several months, but has virtually no probability of forming roots.

An example of rooting cuttings in a pot in a plastic bag. A simple home method used to root a few plants.

2. Grafting - A different vegetative method of propagation, grafting, takes a difficult to root cutting and grafts it onto an already rooted plant. There are many methods of grafting and times of the year it can be done. Our brief discussion will tell of one method. In the spring just before growth starts, take a cutting and prepare it much as we mentioned in the section on cuttings, only this time cut the bottom end of the cutting into a long "V" shape. Then take the plant you are using as understock and cut a slit about the length of the "V" you cut on the cutting. This slit can either be at the tip of the limb of the understock (top grafting) or into the side of the limb (side grafting), but it should be in wood where the bark is still green. Be sure to match the cambium layers (the layer just under the bark) of the cutting and understock. Try to choose a cutting and an understock limb that are the same size so you can match the cambium layers on both sides, but if you can't, one side will be adequate.

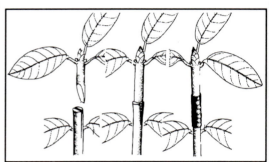

3. Layering - While not a commercial method of propagating rhododendrons, this can be a method for a gardener to grow an additional plant exactly like the parent plant. This is a another form of vegetative propagation. Simply pull a low limb of the plant down onto the ground, wound or notch the bottom side, cover it with loose soil mix and weight it down with a rock. It will take at least a year and possibly two before the limb is sufficiently rooted to be cut from the plant, though some evergreen azaleas root faster. The use of root hormone on the wound may speed the process, but is not absolutely necessary.

4. Seed - Raising rhododendrons from seed is a sexual rather than vegetative method of propagation, meaning that the resultant plant is not a clone (exact duplicate genetically) of its parent. When seed is grown from a species, the plant may look very similar to its seed parent, though when seed is grown from a hybrid the resulting plant could turn out looking very different. Of course controlled crosses between different parents and then raising the resulting seedlings is how new hybrids are introduced. Rhododendron seed is very tiny, almost like dust, so it requires a smooth fine surface in which to start growing. Peat moss or finely shredded sphagnum with about 1 part perlite mixed in, is a popular seed growing mix. Sow the seeds in a pot covered with a plastic bag or in a flat covered with glass or plastic. Generally no winter chilling is necessary to get the seeds to break dormancy. Keep the seed pots or flats in the 65°F to 75°F range. The seed will sprout in from 3 to 8 weeks (sometimes longer) and after they have formed their first set of true leaves, they can be transplanted into other flats or containers. Since they are so tiny, they will not stand frost until they are larger and some months old.

5. Tissue Culture - Tissue culture or micro propagation is becoming a very popular method of producing large numbers of rhododendrons for commercial use. Over simplified, it involves taking a piece of rhododendron wood and putting it in a test tube. Through the use of agars and auxins, absolute sanitation, proper temperatures and light, the piece of wood is induced to grow into multiple "seedling-like" growths with no roots. This tiny juvenile wood is then rooted. Needless to say this method is not for the general home gardener, though some "kitchen tissue culture" is being done.

WHAT RHODODENDRONS REQUIRE

Rhododendrons are forgiving plants, but there are some things they just won't tolerate. So, it is important to understand their basic requirements.

First: Rhododendrons must have a constant supply of moisture. You may occasionally see a rhododendron that will survive without being watered, but it does so only under protest.

Second: Rhododendrons must never sit in stagnant water. Roots submerged in poorly oxygenated water will likely die, though a plant may survive through better drained surface roots. Hot, wet conditions are more dangerous than cool, wet conditions. That is why a rhododendron will survive in a wet spot in the Northwest during heavy winter rains but would not survive in a wet spot in the Southeast's heavy summer rains.

Third: Rhododendrons must be grown in an acid medium (pH 5-6) that is coarse enough for the roots to have access to needed oxygen.

Understand and provide these three conditions and you will succeed wherever you live. These requirements aren't difficult to provide once you understand rhododendrons' needs relative to your specific soil and climatic conditions.

Next, logically, you will ask: "How can I provide these three basic needs?"

Consider the growing medium and include in your thinking the soil and drainage that is underneath the proposed planting. You must determine whether or not your soil has good drainage. If heavy clay is present you must overcome this barrier. Dig a small hole and run some water into it; if the water does not disappear in a very few minutes, you have poor drainage. This is not a sure test, but it will give you a good indication. Now, examine the soil texture: Is it sandy, or is it composed of fine clay particles? Sometimes the topmost soil layer will drain well, but there will be hardpan underneath it that will not drain. So, watch for this condition.

Now let's talk about the actual planting medium to use. We'll come back to natural soil later. There are a multitude of mediums available and almost any one of them, given the proper amounts of water and fertilizer, will produce healthy plants.

Something is needed that will provide adequate air spaces in the soil, and the slower this material decomposes the better. Second, something is needed that will hold a certain amount of water so that the plant does not dry out too rapidly. Barks are generally quite good, as they usually contain both fine and rough textured materials. However, the much heavier, coarser bark rock will not work well for this purpose although it will work as a mulch. Since they are on the outside of the tree, constantly exposed to the weather, nature has endowed barks with a sort of natural preservative which slows their break-down and inhibits many root-rot fungi. The breaking down process of organic material requires nitrogen; consequently, the faster it breaks down, the more nitrogen it uses.

Sawdust often breaks down very fast and, therefore, requires a lot of nitrogen. Some types tend to hold too much free water and can cause conditions that are too wet. This is particularly true in hot, wet summer areas and probably contributes to the myth that sawdust will kill a rhododendron. Leaves and needles of most kinds of trees are okay, although some kinds do break down rather fast and can be a hiding place for insects and diseases. Nut shells, spent hops, corn husks and a multitude of other things will work well as long as they are not alkaline and do not have toxic materials in them. If you do not know whether or not the material has been used with rhododendrons, try a small quantity for a time before going all out. While it is unlikely that anyone has ever used them, even ground-up rubber tires would provide air space in the soil and achieve the same purpose as many organic materials.

For the finer water-holding part of the growing medium, the choice is often peat moss. In some areas good local peat moss is available, but in recent years good peat moss has been difficult to obtain and often the powder that is sold as peat moss is worse than none at all. This is particularly true if you use only this very fine peat moss to mix with clay soil. The result will be a soppy soil that has no ability to hold air. Try to obtain the coarse nursery grind.

Now mix the actual medium (soil) in which you are going to plant your rhododendron. The old formula of one-third sawdust or bark, one-third peat moss, and one third garden loam is all right, providing the humus material (sawdust, etc.) is coarse enough to supply the necessary amount of air in the soil. Up to one-third of the soil volume should be air space, so use common sense to provide a mix that will give you this result. Almost any combination will work as long as it provides the necessary air. Remember: The slower the humus breaks down the better, because the longer those particles of humus are there, the longer the soil is going to contain a lot of needed oxygen. And, remember that organic material which breaks down too rapidly consumes lots of oxygen, which is going to have to be replaced.

We now have the planting medium figured out, so let's deal with the native soil. We have already determined how to tell if drainage is good or bad. If it is good, you can mix the planting medium into the top six to ten inches of soil and you are ready to plant. We are also assuming that the native soil is acid; if it is not, no matter how good the drainage, you are probably going to have to make a raised bed. If drainage is poor (and this true in many locations), you will need to plant nearly on top of the native soil. The illustrations will help show proper planting procedure.

Mulching is also important. The reasons for mulching are to keep the roots cool in the summer and protect them from sudden soil temperature changes in winter, to prevent drying out and to help keep the weeds down. In their natural environment rhododendrons have a mulch provided from their own leaves and those of the trees around them. The same is true of old

Mound mulch so water runs into root, not away from plant

Existing root ball

Humus soil mixture

Poorly drained or alkaline soil

Shows plant in simple raised bed (left side of drawing), or raised bed with retaining wall (right side of drawing).

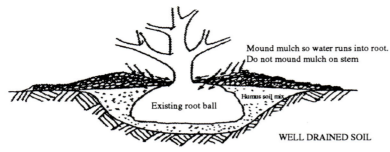

Mound mulch so water runs into root.
Do not mound mulch on stem

Existing root ball

Humus soil mix

WELL DRAINED SOIL

You may plant in a hole as this drawing shows if you have well drained soil. In poorly drained soil, if you dig a hole like this and fill it back with light soil, you may be creating a bucket which will hold stagnant water and kill your plant.

plants in the garden; they provide their own mulch from the leaves they drop each year, so don't be over anxious to rake out all of the fallen leaves. However, be aware that they are an excellent hiding place for pests and diseases. As to what to use as a mulch, just about any of those things which were stated earlier as good for providing air in the planting medium will also work as a mulch. Be inventive, almost every area has some kind of waste product that can used for this purpose. Note: Do not use fine peat moss alone as a mulch; it will dry out and shed water like a thatched roof. Similarly, the use of black plastic is a bad substitute for proper mulching.

We now have the rhododendron planted in a good soil mix; it is well drained and we have mulched the plant properly. The final thing that we must do to be sure that our plant grows well is to water it sufficiently. The method of watering makes little difference and depends on your geographic location and the amount of water available. Drip irrigation is fine and uses the least water. Overhead watering is also good and can be used to advantage to cool the plants and provide lost moisture on a hot day. Don't worry about the old tale that says you can't turn on sprinklers over a plant in the sun; it won't hurt, although once in a great while, you might get a small spot of burn on a leaf due to the magnifying glass effect of a bead of water. It will actually do much good providing moisture that the plant is not able to bring up fast enough through its own roots. Many commercial rhododendron growers now have watering systems that turn on and off automatically during hot weather for this very reason, enabling them to grow plants in full sun that would otherwise burn badly. However, it is true that during flowering, overhead watering may damage the flowers. Also, in wet climates (particularly hot areas), if the foliage never dries out during the day, you may have more trouble with fungus diseases.

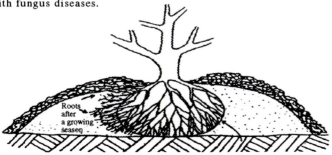

Roots after a growing season

When a rhododendron is newly planted, the roots are only in the existing ball and have not had time to grow out into the surrounding soil. If the ball gets dry, water will not easily be reasorbed into the ball from the moist ajoining soil. Since no roots have had time to grow into the new soil, the can be dry even though it is sitting in damp soil.

The main thing that we must make sure of is that the plant is getting wet. Quite often a plant will get completely dry and then no matter how much you apply water, the rootball will just keep shedding it. The top of the soil may seem wet, and the soil around the plant may even be very wet, but the actual root ball of the plant is bone dry. This is especially true for newly planted rhododendrons, and is a major reason for failure, or at least less than great success with that new plant. It is hard to believe that a plant can be within mere inches of a sprinkler that has been running for hours and still be dry, yet it can be SO TRUE!

FERTILIZATION

Rhododendrons do require adequate nutrients to grow and flower at their best, and these nutrients are usually provided from some form of fertilizer. Whether you use organic or "chemical" is your choice. Applied in proper amounts, either type will produce healthy plants. A properly fed plant is hardier and will withstand more cold than one that is under-fed. Research done by Dr. Robert Ticknor of Oregon State University indicates that more nitrogen is needed than was once thought. He is now recommends a 10-6-4 (nitrogen, phosphate, potash) formula. While phosphate does promote bud set, apparently the plant can only use a certain amount. Unlike nitrogen, phosphate and potash do not disappear from the soil, but build up little by little with successive fertilizing. Therefore, the old high phosphate formulas do not provide extra help to the plant. For the best growth and flowers on young plants in areas where the soil is not frozen all winter, apply fertilizer after the plant goes dormant sometime between late November and January, a second time in February/March, a third time in April/May and a final time in June/July. For most garden situations the old rule of "once before they bloom" and "once after blooming" is still a sensible approach. Actually the fertilizer timing has nothing to do with the time the plant flowers, it simply means once in the early spring, probably March/April and a second fertilization about June/July. This timing will vary, depending on your climate, and is not critical.

PESTS & DISEASES

This short section is intended to give a quick overview of the most common problems to be overcome in growing rhododendrons successfully. Controls listed are not the only ones, but they are the ones most commonly available and easiest for the home gardener. Be sure to check the pesticide label for instructions on the use of each pesticide. You must be sure the pesticide is labeled for use in your state or country, for control of the particular insect or disease you are seeing. We do not endorse or recommend any particular product.

1. Root Rot and Stem Dieback -

These diseases are caused by a number of fungi, most of which belong to the Genus Phytophthora. The most common of these to effect the root area is Phytophthora cinnamonia, with P. cactorum being a frequent cause of dieback of the stems. Many other fungi can be involved such as Pythlum, Botryosphaeria or Phomopsis and others, all of which produce similar symptoms.

These organisms are most active in poorly drained soil with much free water, i.e. soil in which you can pick up a hand full of soil and easily squeeze water out of it. Puddled surface water around the plant can also splash the infectious zoospores from infected plant debris to the plant above. This is particularly true in the case of stem dieback. So prevention is one of the most important ways of controlling these diseases. Plant high, in well drained soil. Don't forget that even if a plant was originally placed in a well drained site, the location may not always stay that way. As the humus material around the roots breaks down, the soil will become more dense and compact.

With the exception of Phytophthora syringae, most of these rot fungi seem to be more active in warm summer conditions. Good mulching, to keep the roots as cool as possible, may help limit the problem; and good sanitation in the removal of dead leaves and debris under the plant is probably helpful.

The use of new bark seems to have a limiting effect on the disease organisms, so the use of new bark in container mixes may be helpful. Container growing is always a problem with root rot diseases because high soil temperature and poor drainage frequently occurs. If you are planting in containers, be especially careful that the

container drains well and that the soil mix you are using is very porous.

The worst problem with these diseases is that even before symptoms occur it is often too late to save the plant. This is especially true of the root rot forms of the disease. However, on the limb dieback forms it may be possible to stop the disease by spraying with Subdue or other similar chemicals, and by cutting out the diseased limbs.

Symptoms of these diseases include wilting of one limb or the whole plant (see illustration at left), much as if you had cut the limb off. There may be yellowing or browning of some of the leaves as the plant can no longer supply nutrients to its top. Particularly in hot weather, this wilting can happen almost overnight and the plant can seemingly be growing well one day and dead the next. Of course in cooler weather the reaction time is slower. On the limb dieback forms, a browning of the stem, the leaf petiole and midrib of the leaf may occur. This generally happens on new foliage and growth as older foliage is more resistant. The cambium layer and part or all of the woody portion of the stem may turn a deep cinnamon brown. With the root rot forms this browning will occur just below the soil level and gradually move up the stem. The white feeder and larger supporting roots will also turn brown.

Above: Tip or limb die back

Above: Example of browning of stem due to root rot.

Right: Poor drainage in a field of rhododendrons. Note area in field where plants have never grown. All were planted at the same time and are the same variety.

Spraying with metalaxyl (Subdue) or other similar chemicals can be helpful. In hot, wet climates or other conditions conducive to these problems, preventative sprays may be necessary. **Most of all, be sure the plant is planted so that it has excellent drainage, is as cool as possible during hot weather, and has good air circulation.** Careful attention to sanitation in the removal of dead limbs, old leaves and the like may be helpful. If a plant has died, be sure to correct your conditions of poor drainage, etc., before replanting. It probably is a good idea to put new, clean soil in the immediate hole where the plant has died. Some cultivars are more resistant than others and in areas with greater problems it maybe necessary to select more resistant plants.

2. Powdery Mildew on Rhododendrons - Not too much is known about this disease. It seems to affect rhodoendrons in the coastal areas, such as the Pacific Northwest, the UK and New Zealand, but apparently has little affect in areas where the winter temperatures are quite cold. Some varieties are damaged much worse than others and can be defoliated by the disease. Can be controlled with Benlate or Bayleton.

3. Mildew (generally on deciduous azaleas) - A white powdery material appears on the leaves. This occurs most frequently in the late summer. Since these leaves will fall off anyway, it may not be necessary to treat. Good air circulation helps. Control is the use of Benomyl or similar spray.

4. Azalea Leaf Gall - This condition is most common on evergreen azaleas and occurs as a thickened gall on the leaf. It will infect a few rhododendrons causing the leaves to become an off-white or pinkish color and become slightly thickened. If the problem is limited, removing the thickened leaves and burning them may be sufficient. Good air circulation and sanitation is helpful. For best control, start spraying in the early spring with Ferban or Bordeaux.

5. Bud Blight - Flower buds turn brown and are covered with black bristles, which are spores from the fungus Briosia azaleae. Remove and destroy affected buds. Fungicide applications are not usually necessary. Factors such as freeze damage (including light freezing when the buds are not dormant), and other unknown factors, can cause the buds to brown and fall off. Certain cultivars such as one form of R. wardii will often lose most buds even without temperatures low enough to cause damage.

6. Flower Blight - Water-soaked spots appear on the flowers which become soft and brownish. It occurs more as the temperature warms and while there is much moisture. Especially in the southeastern United States, it is often caused by *Ovulinia azaleae* and is known as ovulinia petal blight. In the northwestern U. S., ovulinia is present, but similar symptoms can also be caused by *Botrytis cinerea* which is less damaging to the flowers and easier to control. Sanitation is important, so clean up spent flowers and litter around the plant. Spray with benomyl or triadimefon.

7. Rust - Orange-red pustules containing spores form on the lower surface of the leaf. Control by avoiding those hybrids and species which are very susceptible to rust. Good air circulation is helpful. Triadimefon seems to help, but may not be registered for use on rhododendrons.

8. Leaf Spotting - There are a number of leaf spots or burns caused by fungi such as *Botryis, Pestalotia, Phyllosticta, Septoria* and others. Many are secondary infections happening after mechanical damage or environmental stress, such as sunburn, drought, winter damage or windburn. They generally occur during wet weather and many times are self limiting with drier weather. Good sanitation is helpful, so remove brown and fallen leaves. Also provide good air circulation. Spraying with Benomyl or similar fungicide can be useful, but is frequently not necessary.

The vast majority of leaf spots that occur on many cultivars, including R. 'Blue Ensign' and 'Mrs. G. W. Leak', are physiological and not disease caused. These spots are generally purplish and are inherent in the cultivar. Environmental stress may increase their appearance. They do no harm to the plant.

Some leaf spots are caused by viruses, the most common ailment being called necrotic ring spot. The symptoms are reddish-brown rings or spots on the leaves. It generally occurs only on the two year leaves of a few rhododendron cultivars such as R. 'Unique', or on *Kalmia latifolia*. It also appears on the first year foliage of some R. 'Loderi' clones. Little is known about the disease and it does not seem to spread from one cultivar to another. No control is known or generally necessary.

Above: Virus (ring spot) Below: Chemical damage

Leaf spotting can also be caused by chemical injury, such as drift from cleaners, paints, or chemicals used to kill moss on roofs. Sometimes the results of such injury may not show up for weeks or months.

NON-DISEASE PROBLEMS

1. Sunburn - You will observe light yellow leaves, often with brownish burned areas, which will be on the sunny side of the plant. The under leaves, protected from the sun will be deeper green. Give the plant more shade or move it to a more protected site.

2. Windburn - There is often evidence of burn on the edges of leaves. The plant generally has a "blown" appearance. Provide a wind break.

3. Fertilizer burn - Burn is generally at the ends and edges of leaves and will be on any area of the whole plant, not just on the sunny side. Give as much water as possible to wash fertilizer out of roots.

4. Chlorosis - This condition is characterized by dark green leaf veins with yellow areas between them, often caused by lack of iron. However, it can also be shock-induced by damage to the roots from root rot, severe cutting of roots, root weevils or even root death due to an extreme amount of fertilizer.

5. Light yellow leaves - Light leaf color is often just the need for more nitrogen. This will be more noticeable in the full sun. Some less sun tolerant varieties will always be light green in full sun.

Same plant in July without nitrogen and six weeks later after applying nitrogen.

6. Frost burn on new growth - Even light freezing can damage cells as new growth is forming, causing the cells to develop improperly and make the leaf look deformed. Aphids will cause the same deformed appearance, as can high heat during critical cell development stage.

7. Freeze burn - Often there is a grayish appearance to burned areas in the leaf, or total browning, depending on the severity of the cold. (Photos below to left and center).

8. Bark Split - Damage due to subfreezing temperatures. This often happens in early fall freezes or late spring frosts, when the plant is not dormant.

9. Natural response to below freezing temperatures - When temperatures are below 32°F, it is difficult for the plant to move moisture from its roots to it top. To prevent desiccation, the leaves roll, exposing less surface to the cold. When temperatures warm to above freezing, the leaves return to normal.

10. Insufficient water - An adequate amount of water is necessary for plant growth and flower development. In spring when it is still raining, we assume that the plants are getting sufficient water. This may not be true. This is a time when the plants use large amounts of water to develop flowers and new growth, and rainfall falling off of the "umbrella-like" foliage may not reach the roots. Flowers on a dry plant will sometimes start to open and then fall off without opening, as shown in the photo below at left. Other times the new foliage may wilt during the heat of the day, and even after being watered will show burn on the soft leaves, shown in right photo.

INSECTS AND OTHER PESTS

1. Root Weevil -

Several different species of weevil are responsible for rhododendron plant damage and are a common problem. To understand their control it is necessary to understand their life cycle.

Adults - in the adult state they are small black beetles about 1/4" to 3/8" long, depending on the particular species. They are very mobile and can move great distances, though at times they will stay in one area and feed. Their cycle begins in late spring when they emerge as adults from the ground where they have overwintered as adults or matured from larva. Since they are nocturnal, they feed at night, and being cold blooded they do not feed until the night temperatures are sufficiently warm. After emerging they feed for two weeks to a month before beginning to lay eggs. At this time they almost become egg laying machines as they wander through your garden, and your neighbors' gardens, laying eggs in the leaves and mulch under the plants. All adults are female and parthenogenetic meaning that a male is not necessary for reproduction. The adults eat small notches in the edges of the leaves which may disfigure the plant, but will not kill it. They are a problem to control, since most control methods aim at putting a stomach poison on the leaves which the adults must eat. But before they eat they may lay eggs under the plant (or another plant that they didn't eat on), which eventually hatch and continue the life cycle of the insect.

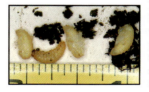

Larvae - The eggs that were laid under the plant hatch and become white larvae up to 1/4" long. This stage is where the most damage is done to the plant, and it is impossible to see that damage is happening until it is too late. The larvae eat the roots and often girdle the stem, eating the bark and essential cambium layer on the stem of the plant just at or below ground level, making it impossible for the plant to feed its top. These larvae eventually become pupae which are soft and white and look much like the adult. Before long these pupae become adults and the cycle is started again. Two or three generations a year are possible.

Control - For the home gardener the most often used control is Orthene which should be sprayed on the foliage at about three week intervals from about May to October, depending on the weather. This is done to control the adults, but is not fully effective because the weevil may lay eggs under the plant before they eat the foliage that has been sprayed. Better control was possible with long lived chemicals which could be placed in the soil under the plant, preventing the eggs from hatching, but these chemicals are no longer available for environmental reasons. There is a biological control in the form of a nematode which can be applied in the fall to control the larva. While this approach is promising, it has limitations in that the beneficial nematodes are very sensitive to temperature and moisture extremes and will not live over winter. If applied to soil that is too cold, too wet, too dry or too hot, they will die and provide no control. Best control is achieved by using both chemical and nematode methods with proper timing.

2. Aphids - These small sucking insects feed on the new growth as it begins to expand causing distorted leaf shapes. To control, use Orthene, Malathion or Diazinon.

3. Bark Scale - Small sucking insects feed on the bark and exude a sticky substance that turns the stems black. To Control, use Orthene.

4. Caterpillars, Leaf rollers, Sawflies (moth larvae) - The larvae of several species of insects are involved. Damage is the result of chewing on the new foliage. These pests hatch as the new growth is forming, and often eat out large areas of the soft growth. They may also roll the leaf with a white web. Damage only occurs on soft growth. To control, use Orthene, Malathion, or Diazinon.

Bark scale (above)

5. Leaf miner - This tiny caterpillar 'mines' through the leaf, and leaves a line wherever it goes. Leaf tissue below the line will often turn light green. There is an azalea leaf miner which creates larger, brown, blister-like mines in and skeletonization of the leaf. To control, use Orthene, although by the time you see the damage, the insect is often gone.

6. Spider mites - Very tiny reddish eight legged mites suck on the bottom of the leaf, causing the top of the leaf to turn to a mottled brown-green color. To control, use Malathion.

7. Lacebugs (Lacewing) - A small insect with transparent, lacy wings sucks on the bottom of the leaf, causing the top to take on a mottled grayish-brown appearance. The underside of the leaf will show a brownish residue exuded by the insect. To control, use Malathion or Orthene.

8. White Fly - A small white flying insect, that looks like an aphid with wings, sucks on the underside of foliage, leaving white spots where it has been. To Control use Malathion, Diazinon or Orthene.

9. Slugs and Snails - These pests feed on soft new growth and on flowers. To control, use Metaldehyde baits or sprays.

Lacewing damage

PRUNING RHODODENDRONS & AZALEAS
It's easy if you understand a little basic information!

1. Rhododendrons and azaleas flower on the prior year's wood. In other words, the buds for spring flowering form on the plants during the previous summer or fall. If you prune in the late summer, fall, or winter you may be trimming off your flowers for the following spring.

2. With the larger leaved rhododendrons (lepidotes), you must prune just above growth joints. Each year as the plant starts to grow there is a visible point where the plant started growth. We call this point a growth joint. Prune just above this point, because that is where the dormant growth buds are located. Don't prune between joints, because there are no dormant growth buds in that area. However, with azaleas and the small leafed rhododendrons (lepidotes), you may prune anywhere along the stem, though you may not be able to see them, these plants have dormant growth buds nearly everywhere.

An example of pruning between growth joints, an improper method

3. Generally prune right after the plant is through flowering. Light maintenance pruning will not affect flowering for the following year if done as directed. Cutting back a rhododendron heavily can stop the plant from flowering for a year or two. The pictures below show heavy pruning of a dense plant, cutting it back to a smaller size, but still leaving some prior year's foliage and maintaining an even shape. Note the plant flowered the following year, though not as heavily.

The above plant had grown too large for its location and had to be pruned. Here it is in May as it was flowering.

The same plant the following May with a few blooms.

Here it is in June just after heavy pruning.

4. Even very large plants can be cut back severely to stumps with no leaves. They will recover, though it will be a year before the plant has much foliage and two or more years before they flower.

5. As a plant grows some of the inside limbs will be shaded out and become weak and die. It is a good idea to remove these, plus other weak limbs that are on the ground or crossing over each other. This provides better air circulation and does not provide a place for insects and diseases to start.

6. Evergreen azaleas can be sheared for hedge or border. Unlike rhododendrons, evergreen azaleas can be sheared each year after flowering to create a dense rounded plant. Deciduous azaleas can be cut anywhere on the stem and they will branch from that point, though they should not be sheared as severely as evergreen azaleas.

DEADHEADING & PINCHING

Light pruning and shaping should be done every year at the time you deadhead (remove the spent flowers from the plant). This is an easy job if done on a yearly basis and will keep the plant compact and in good shape.

Deadheading is important so that the plant's energy goes to flower production for the coming year. Rhododendrons and deciduous azaleas benefit from deadheading, but it is not generally necessary for evergreen azaleas. Deadheading tidies the appearance of the plant, prevents seed production which wastes the plant's energy, and helps reduce disease and pest infestations.

Deadheading of spent flowers. This can be done simply by snapping off the old flower or by using pruners.

Same branch later in the season.

Pinching out single terminal growth buds just as they start to grow will cause the plant to immediately produce multiple growth buds, for a more bushy plant. This will not effect flowering for the following year.

Single growth terminal.

Pinching single terminal growth.

Multiple growth buds form a short time after single terminal bud has been removed.

Species ~
Native to Western North America

R. albiflorum
(Subgenus Candidastrum)

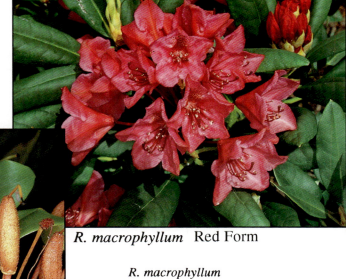

R. macrophyllum Red Form

R. macrophyllum
(Subgenus Hymenanthes
Section Hymenanthes
Subsect. Pontica)

R. macrophyllum
Seed Pods

R. camtschaticum (Subgenus Therorhodion)

R. occidentale Double Form

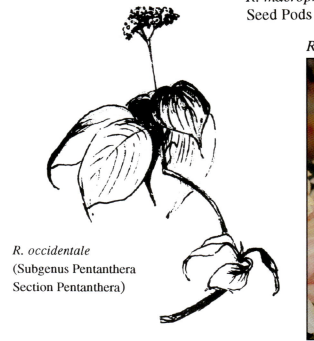

R. occidentale
(Subgenus Pentanthera
Section Pentanthera)

R. occidentale

canadense

R. vaseyi 'White Find'

R. canadense & vaseyi
(Subgenus Pentanthera Section Rhodora)

R. vaseyi

chapmanii (minus var. chapmanii)

R. catawbiense

R. maximum 'Rubrum'

Species ~ Native to Eastern North America

R. catawbiense & maximum (Subgenus Hymenanthes
Section Hymenanthes Subsect. Pontica)

R. carolinianum & chapmanii (Subgenus Rhododendron
Section Rhododendron Subsect. Carolina)

R. carolinianum (*minus* var. *minus* Carolinianum Group)

R. prunifolium

R. canescens

R. austrinum

R. periclymenoides

Species ~ Native to Eastern North America
Subgenus Pentanthera Section Pentanthera
(commonly referred to as deciduous azaleas)

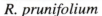

R. serrulatum

R. atlanticum

R. alabamense

R. arborescens

R. bake

R. viscosum 'Mary Dell'

R. flammeum

R. calendulaceum

RHODODENDRON SPECIES

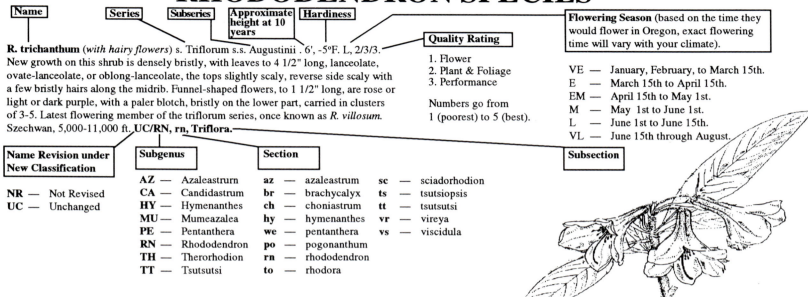

Name | **Series** | **Subseries** | **Approximate height at 10 years** | **Hardiness**

R. trichanthum (*with hairy flowers*) s. Triflorum s.s. Augustinii . 6', -5ºF. L, 2/3/3.
New growth on this shrub is densely bristly, with leaves to 4 1/2" long, lanceolate, ovate-lanceolate, or oblong-lanceolate, the tops slightly scaly, reverse side scaly with a few bristly hairs along the midrib. Funnel-shaped flowers, to 1 1/2" long, are rose or light or dark purple, with a paler blotch, bristly on the lower part, carried in clusters of 3-5. Latest flowering member of the triflorum series, once known as *R. villosum.* Szechwan, 5,000-11,000 ft. **UC/RN, rn, Triflora.**

Quality Rating

1. Flower
2. Plant & Foliage
3. Performance

Numbers go from
1 (poorest) to 5 (best).

Flowering Season (based on the time they would flower in Oregon, exact flowering time will vary with your climate).

VE — January, February, to March 15th.
E — March 15th to April 15th.
EM — April 15th to May 1st.
M — May 1st to June 1st.
L — June 1st to June 15th.
VL — June 15th through August.

Name Revision under New Classification

NR — Not Revised
UC — Unchanged

Subgenus

AZ — Azaleastrum
CA — Candidastrum
HY — Hymenanthes
MU — Mumeazalea
PE — Pentanthera
RN — Rhododendron
TH — Therorhodion
TT — Tsutsutsi

Section

az — azaleastrum
br — brachycalyx
ch — choniastrum
hy — hymenanthes
we — pentanthera
po — pogonanthum
rn — rhododendron
to — rhodora

Subsection

sc — sciadorhodion
ts — tsutsiopsis
tt — tsutsutsi
vr — vireya
vs — viscidula

R. aberconwayi (*after the second Lord Aberconway, 1879-1953, former President of the R.H.S.*) *s.* and *s.s.* Irroratum. 3', -5ºF, EM, 4/3/3. Habit is open and upright, rather loose. Oblong, deep green, lance shaped leaves, of medium size are hard, thick and heavily textured. Flowers, to 3" across, are saucer shaped, held in rounded trusses of 6-12. Color is white, or white tinged pink, either nearly unspotted, or heavily speckled crimson or red. Yunnan. **UC/HY, hy, Irrorata.**

R. achroanthum (*ill-colored*) *s.* Lapponicum. 3', -10ºF, EM-M, 3/3/2-3. Foliage is oblong-elliptic or elliptic, heavily scaled on both sides, and very small. Tiny flowers, only 1/2" long, widely funnel-shaped, are deep violet purple, with external scales on lobes, set in trusses of 3 to 5 flowers. Yunnan, N.E. Upper Burma 12,000-15,000 feet. **Syn. R. rupicola var. rupicola/RN, rn, lapponica.**

R. adenogynum (*with glandular ovary*) *s.* Taliense *s.s.* Adenogynum. 3', -15ºF, EM-M, 3/4/2-3. Foliage is large and rather narrow, lanceolate or oblong-lanceolate, dark green, smooth on top and thickly covered with light tan indumentum underneath. Funnel shaped flowers, to 2 1/2" long, are white, rose-tinged, occasionally reddish-blotched, with crimson spotting, carried in trusses up to 12. Yunnan, Szeehwan, S.E. Tibet, 11,000-12,000 ft. **UC/HY, hy, Taliensia.**

R. adenophorum (*bearing glands*) *s.* Taliense *s.s.* Adenogysum. 4' -10ºF, EM-M, 3/4/2-3. Foliage is medium large, oblong-lanceolate, smooth dark green on top, thickly indumented below. Funnel shaped flowers, to 2" long, are rose or rose tinged white, sparsely spotted light red, held in 10 flower trusses. Yunnan, 12,000 feet. Although differing from *R. adenogynum* in its glandular branches and petioles, it is now considered synonomous to this species. **R. adenogynum Adenophorum Group/HY, hy, Taliensia.**

R. adenopodum (*with glandular pedicels*) *s.* Ponticum *s.s.* Caucasicum. 5', -10ºF, EM-M, 3-4/4/3. Leaves are large, long and narrow, smoothly dark green above, with grayish fawn colored felt underneath. Flowers are funnel-campanulate, to 2 1/2" long, pale rose in color occasionally with purple spotting, carried in trusses of 6-10. Szechwan, Hupeh, 5,000-7,000 ft. **UC/HY, hy, Argyrophylla.**

R. afghanicum (*from Afghanistan*) *s.* Triflorum *s.s.* Hanceanum. 2'?, 5ºF, L, -/-/-. Growth habit is low and spreading Leaves, to 2 1/2" long, are lance shaped, smooth and light green on top, the reverse quite scaly. Bell shaped flowers, to 1/2" long, are greenish flushed white, held in trusses to 15. Afghanistan, 7,000-9,000 ft. **UC/RN, rn Afghanica.**

R. aganniphum (*snowy*) *s.* and *s.s.* Taliense. 3', 0ºF, ML, 3/4/-. Medium to large leaves are elliptic, oblong or oblong-oval. They are dull green, smooth at maturity, thinly layered with shiny white to yellowish indumentum. Bell shaped flowers, to 1 1/2" long, white or deep rose, with widely varying number of crimson spots, are held in trusses of 8-12. S.E. Tibet N.W. Yunnan, 14,000-15,000 ft. **R. aganniphum var. aganniphum/HY, hy, Taliensia.**

R. agapetum (*delightful*) *s.* Irroratum *s.s.* Parishii. 5', 5ºF, E-L, 4/3/3. Leaves are large, glossy smooth, green above, paler underneath. Scarlet flowers, to about 2" long, are tubular bell shaped, carried in trusses of about 10 flowers. Upper Burma, 6,000-7,000 ft. **Syn. R kyawii/HY, hy, Parishia.**

R. agastum (*charming*) *s.* and *s.s.* Irroratum. 5', 5ºF; VE E, 3/3/-. Foliage is large, oblong or obovate, smooth matte green, with a filmy layer of hairs underneath. Flowers are tubular-campanulate, to 2" long, set in trusses of 10 to 20. Color is pale or deep rose or white shaded pink, blotched crimson, occasionally spotted crimson. Yunnan, 6,000-9,000 ft. **UC/HY, hy, Irrorata.**

R. agglutinatum (*stuck-together, referring to indumentum on the lower surface of the leaves*) *s.* Lacteum. 4', -5ºF, EM, 2-3/2/3/-. Growth is tree-like and sturdy. Oval or oblong leaves, to about 3", smooth on top, have a sticky film of buff colored indumentum on the undersides. Saucer shaped flowers, to 1 1/2" long, range in color from ivory white to white or white flushed pink, are occasionally spotted crimson and are held in trusses to 15. Szechwan, Yunnan, Tibet, Bhutan, 11,000-16,000 ft. **R phaeochrysum var. agglutinatum/HY, hy, Taliensia**

R. alabamense (*from Alabama, U.S.A.*) s. Azalea s.s. Luteum. 4', -5ºF, M, 3/2-3/3. Leaves are on the small side, obovate or oblong, elliptic. The tops are slightly hairy, often waxy and much hairier underneath. Flowers, which open with the leaves, have a lemony fragrance, and are held in trusses of 6-10. Bloom is white, at times with yellow blotch, 1 1/2" across, tubular-funnel shaped. S.E. United States. **UC/PE, pe.**

R. albertsenianum (*after M. O. Albertson, Chinese Maritime Customs*) s. and s.s. Neriiflorum. 3', 5ºF, E-EM, 2-3/3/-. Mature foliage is medium size, oblong narrow, smooth topped, with a woolly, two layered indumentum. Bell shaped, fleshy flowers, to 1 1/2" long, are scarlet crimson, free of markings, carried in trusses of 5-6. Yunnan, 10,000 ft. **UC/HY, hy, Neriiflora.**

R. albiflorum (*with white flowers*) s. Albiflorum. 3', -25ºF, M-VL, 2/2/1. Growth habit is upright and open on this deciduous shrub. The leaves, to 3" long, are rather scattered, or in clusters at the ends of small branches. They are oblong in shape, smooth bright green above, paler undersides. 1" bell shaped flowers, white to pale lemony yellow, bloom either alone or in pairs at leaf axis, appearing after the leaves have emerged. A difficult plant to raise in the garden. Cascade and Rocky Mountains, North America. **UC/CA.**

R. albrechtii (*after Dr. M. Albrecht, Russian Naval Surgeon*) s. Azalea s.s. Canadense. 4', -15ºF, E, 4/3/3. Growth habit of this deciduous shrub is upright and open, with leaves, to about 4 1/2", obovate or oblong-obovate, in groups of 5 at branch ends. Tops are dark green with a few flat hairs, the undersides more or less downy grey. Flowers, which open before and with the leaves, are very openly bell shaped, to 2" wide. They are purplish rose or deep rose, spotted olive green, held in trusses of up to 5. Very beautiful. C. & N. Japan. **UC, br.**

R. alpicola (*dweller in high mountains*) s. Lapponicum. 2', -15ºF, EM, -/-/-. Elliptic leaves are quite small, to 1/4", densely scaly on both sides, with a yellowish cast above, darker below. Flowers bloom singly, to about 1/2" long, widely funnel shaped, rose or lilac colored. Szechwan, S.E. Tibet, 12,000-15,000 ft. **Syn. R. nivale ssp. boreale/RN, rn, Lapponica.**

R. alutaceum (*like soft leather*) s. Taliense s.s. Adenogynum. 5', -5ºF, EM, 3/4/2-3. Habit is compact, slow growing. Medium large, oblong leaves, have a leathery texture; the undersides have thick and woolly, light tan indumentum. Flowers, to 1 1/2", funnel-bell-shaped, rose color, are blotched and spotted crimson, set in trusses of up to 12. Yunnan, 12,000 ft. **R. alutaceum var. alutaceum/HY, hy, Taliensia.**

R. amagianum (*from Mount Amagi, Japan*) s. Azalea s.s. Schlippenbachii. 4-5', -5ºF, L-VL, 3/3/3. Growth habit is upright and open. Deciduous, medium sized leaves are distinctively diamond shaped. Shiny dark green, having undersides waxy grey or bluish green with a scattering of coarse hair, they are held in whorls of 3 at branch ends. Striking pinkish or orange-red funnel shaped flowers, blushed crimson, spotted darker, to 2" or more across, are set in trusses of 3-4. Japan. **UC/TT, br.**

R. ambiguum (*doubtful*) s. and s.s. Triflorum. 5', -5ºF, E-M, 3/3/3. Growth habit is compact and upright. Medium sized lance shaped leaves are dark green with a few scales, the undersides paler and densely scaly. The scales are brown, black or yellowish brown and rather large. Leaves are also aromatic. Flowers, to 1 1/2", are widely funnel shaped, pale or greenish yellow, spotted greenish, in trusses of 3-7. Szechwan, 7,500-14,700 ft. **UC/RN, rn, Triflora.**

R. amesiae (*after Mary S. Ames of North Easton, Massachusetts, U.S.A.*) s. Triflorum s.s. Yunnanense. 6', -5ºF, M, 2/2/-. Leaves are medium sized, ovate-elliptical, scaly topped, with heavy blackish scales underneath. Broadly funnel shaped flowers, 1 1/2" long, are purple or dark reddish purple, at times spotted darker, held in trusses of 2-5. Szechwan, 7,500-9,800 ft. **UC/RN, rn, Triflora.**

R. anhweiense (*from Anhwei, China*) s. Barbatum s.s. Maculiferum. 3', -10ºF, EM, 3/4/3-4. Appealing, somewhat twisted stiff foliage makes this plant attractive. Habit is spreading, with medium sized oblong or ovate leaves, bright, shiny, waxy green, paler undersides. Bell shaped flowers, to 1" long, open white blushed pink, turning snow white, with or without purplish red spotting, in trusses of 6-10. Anhwei, E. China, 5,000-6,000 ft. **R. maculiferum ssp. anhweiense/HY, hy, Maculifera.**

R. annae (*after a French lady*) s. and s.s. Irroratum. 5', 5ºF, ML-L, 2/2/3. Medium sized foliage is lanceolate or oblong-lanceolate, smooth textured brilliant matte green above, paler green and very slightly pitted underneath. Creamy white, cup shaped flowers are flushed rose or white with purple spotting, in trusses of 8-12. Kweichow, 4,500 ft. **UC/HY, hy, Irrorata.**

R. anthopogon (*with bearded flowers*) s. Anthopogon. 1', -5ºF, E-EM, 3/3/2. Foliage is small, obovate-elliptic or oval, aromatic, lightly scaled above, more heavily underneath. Narrow, tubular flowers, to 3/4" long, with flaring lobes, are pink or deep pink, set in a compact truss of 4-6. High Himalaya from Kashmir eastwards, 9,000-16,500 ft. **R. anthopogon ssp. anthopogon/RH, po.**

R. anthopogonoides (*resembling R. anthopogon*) s. Anthopogon. 1', 5ºF, EM, -/-/-. Aromatic leaves, to 1 1/2" long, are wide elliptic, with very scaly lower surfaces. Tubular shaped flowers, with spreading lobes, are quite small. Only 1/2", white, or pink flushed white, yellow or greenish yellow, they are carried in head-like compact trusses of up to 20. N.W. Kansu, 10,000-11,000 ft. **UC/RH, po.**

R. anthosphaerum (*with round flowers*) s. and s.s. Irroratum. 5', 5-10ºF, VE-E, 3/2-3/3. Leaves are medium large, oblanceolate or oblong-lanceolate, with glabrous tops, the undersides paler and scattered with shriveled hairs. 3" tubular-campanulate flowers, range in color from pink to purple to lilac to rose magenta, blotched crimson. They are carried in trusses of 10-15. S.E. Tibet, 10,000-11,000 ft. **UC/HY, hy, Irrorata.**

R. aperantum (*boundless*) s. Neriiflorum s.s. Sanguineum. 18", 0ºF, E, 3/4/3. Growth habit is compact, slow growing, usually dwarf, and extremely variable in both leaf shape and flower color. Leaves, oval to obovate or oblanceolate, are dark green above, the undersides a little knobby, glaucous white, with a few hairs. About 2" in length, they grow in whorls at branch ends. Tubular bell shaped flowers, to 2" long, may be white, orange, yellow, rose, or scarlet, held in trusses of 3-6. N.E. Upper Burma, Yunnan, 12,000-14,000 ft. **UC/HY, hy, Neriiflora.**

R. araiophyllum (*with slender leaves*) s. and s.s. Irroratum. 5', 10ºF, E-EM, -/-/-. Foliage is medium large and lanceolate, more or less smooth on both sides. Flowers, to 1 1/2" long, are cup shaped. White or white blushed rose, crimson blotched, with a widely varying number of crimson spots, they are held in trusses of 6-8. Yunnan, N.E. Upper Burma, 9,000-10,000 ft. **UC/HY, hy, Irrorata.**

R. arborescens (*becoming tree-like*) s. Azalea s.s. Luteum. 5', -10ºF, VL, 3/2-3/3. Plant is deciduous, with medium sized leaves, obovate, elliptic or oblong-lanceolate. Smooth shiny green on top, they are waxy smooth below. Tubular funnel shaped flowers, to 2 1/2" wide, open after the leaves into trusses of 3-6. White or white blushed pink or reddish, at times with a yellow blotch, the blooms have a pleasant fragrance. E. North America. **UC/PE, pe.**

R. arboreum (*tree-like*) s. and s.s. Arboreum. 6', 5ºF, E, 3/4/3. Name means "tree-like", and the growth habit is tree-like. Lance shaped foliage is hard and tough, dark and smooth shiny green, the underside with whitish indumentum of the plastered type. The flower, to 2", is cup shaped, typically blood red with dark nectar pouches, held in tight trusses of 15-20. Kashmir to Bhutan, Khasia Hills, 5,000-10,000 ft. **R. arboreum, ssp. arboreum/HY, hy, Arborea.**

    var. album-- Flowers are white, with purple spots. Hardier than the typical species. **R. arboreum ssp. cinnamomeum var. album.**

    var. roseum-- Flowers are rose or deep pink, with deeper colored spots. Hardier than the typical species. **R. arboreum ssp. cinnamomeum var. roseum.**

    var. wellesianum-- A variety with rosy pink flowers held in tight ball shaped trusses.

    ssp. campbelliae-- 5', 0ºF, E, 3/5/3. This subspecies has the most interesting foliage of the group, long and narrow, very similar in appearance to *R. makinoi*. This form also seems to be hardier than many of the other forms. An attractive plant worthy of the effort to grow it. Rose pink flowers. **R. arboreum ssp. cinnamomeum Campbelliae Group.**

    ssp. cinnamomeum-- 5', 5ºF, E, 3/5/3. The real beauty. A plant that is well known for its cinnamon indumentum. White flowers. **R. arboreum ssp. cinnamomeum var. cinnamomeum.**

R. argipeplum (*with a white covering*) s. and s.s. Barbatum. 5', 5ºF, VE-E, 3/3/2-3. Foliage is medium large, oval, oblong-oval or oblong-lanceolate in shape, with smooth top and dense indumentum underneath. Crimson flowers, to 1 1/2" long, are tubular-campanulate, set in trusses of 10-15. Bhutan, Tibet, 10,000-12,000 ft. **R. smithii Argipeplum Group/HY, hy, Barbata.**

R. argyrophyllum (*with silver leaves*) s. Arboreum s.s. Argyrophyllum. 5', 0ºF, E-EM, 3/5/3. Mature leaves are long and narrow, smooth dark green above with close, white scales underneath. Flowers, to 1 1/2" long, are bell shaped, white or white blushed rose or pink, with darker spots. Szechwan, 6,000-9,000 ft. **R. argyrophyllum ssp. argyrophyllum/HY, hy, Argyrophylla.**

    var. cupulare-- Has smaller, more cup shaped flowers. **R. argyrophyllum ssp. argyrophyllum Cupulare Group.**

    var. nankingense-- Has broader and longer shiny leaves and usually larger, deeper colored flowers. **R. argyrophyllum ssp. nankingense.**

    var. omeiense-- Has smaller leaves with deeper colored indumentum. **R. argyrophyllum ssp. omeiense.**

R. arizelum (*notable*) s. Falconeri. 5', 5ºF, E-EM, 3/4/2-3. Leaves are large, oval, obovate or oblanceolate, dark green and thickly indumented. Obliquely campanulate flowers, to 2" long, can range in color from creamy yellow, to deep yellow, to rose or pink, and occasionally white, with a dark reddish blotch. They are held in trusses of 15-25. Upper Burma, India, North East Frontier Agency, Yunnan, 9,000-12,000 ft. **R. rex ssp. arizelum/HY, hy, Falconera.**

    var. rubicosum-- Flowers are crimson. S.E. Tibet.

R. atlanticum (*from the Atlantic seaboard*) s. Azalea s.s. Luteum. 3-4', -15ºF, M, 3/3/3. This shrub is stoloniferous and deciduous, with smooth bright bluish green foliage on the small side, obovate, or oblong obovate. Fragrant flowers that open with the leaves are tubular-funnel-shaped, to 1 1/2" wide, carried in trusses of 4-10. Color is white, white blushed pink, or white blushed purple, occasionally pale yellow. Growth habit is open and upright. E. North America. **UC/PE, pe.**

R. augustinii (*after Augustine Henry, 1857-1930, medical officer in Chinese Customs, later Professor of Forestry, Dublin*) s. Triflorum s.s. Augustinii. 6', -5ºF, E-M, 4/3/3-4. Growth habit is compact, upright, with long, narrow, smooth dark green leaves, the undersides densely scaly. The leaf is not too big, but the plant is strong and will stand the sun. Bell shaped flowers, to 2" long, are held in clusters of 2-6. The fantastic color covers a wide spectrum, from white to white tinged pink, pale lavender-rose to a radiating deep violet blue, occasionally darker blotched, with yellow-green, olive green or brown spotting. Color can vary on the same plant from year to year. There are many named forms. Szechwan, Yunnan, S. Tibet, 4,500-13,000 ft. **R. augustinii ssp. augustinii/RN, rn, Triflora.**

    The following are selected forms:

        'Barto Blue'-- Clear, medium blue flowers.

        'Blue Cloud'-- Fluffy, blue flowers.

        var. chasmanthum-- Pale lavender flowers with a more backward curling corolla.

        'Green Eye'-- Dramatic green spotting within mauve-blue flowers.

        'Lackamus Blue'-- Periwinkle, flat faced blooms.

        'Marine'-- Deep lavender blue flowers with purple spotting.

        'Towercourt'-- Clear, lavender-blue flowers.

        'Whalley'-- Small, smokey blue flowers.

        Windsor form-- Royal lavender-blue flowers.

R. aureum (*golden*) s. Ponticum s.s. Caucasicum. 1', -15ºF, E-EM, 3/4/2-3. Mature foliage is medium size, obovate, oblong-obovate or elliptic. The leaves are smooth dark green on top, paler green or light tan below. Flowers, to 1 1/2" long, widely funnel shaped, are pale yellow or cream, greenish spotted, and are set in trusses of 5-8. Slow growing; good for rockery. Siberian-Mongolian mountains and Manchuria, south to Japan and Korea. **R. aureum var. aureum/HY, hy, Pontica.**

R. auriculatum (*eared or auriculate*) s. Auriculatum. 6', -5ºF, VL, 4/4/4. Growth habit is upright, spreading and tree like. The long and narrow lobed leaves are large, to 12". The tops of the leaves are dull dark green and slightly hairy; the undersides are paler green with whitish or brown hairs. Showy funnel shaped flowers, to 4", appearing as late as August, make this an exceptional plant. They are often scented and are white, sometimes rosy pink, with a greenish patch at base, held in loose trusses of 7-15. Hupeh, 5,000-7,000 ft. **R. auriculatum/HY, hy, Auriculata.**

R. auritum (*eared*) s. Boothii s.s. Tephropeplum. 3', 10ºF, E-EM, 3/3/3. Small foliage, lanceolate or elliptic, is scaly bright green on top, heavily scaled, golden to rusty brown below. Small tubular-campanulate flowers, to 1" long, are light yellow with slight pink blushing on the lobes, carried in trusses of 4-7. S.E. Tibet, 7,000-8,000 ft. **UC/RN, rn, Tephropepla.**

R. austrinum (*southern*) s. Azalea s.s. Luteum. 5', -15ºF, M, 3/3/3-4. This shrub is deciduous, with medium sized foliage, elliptic, oblong or oblong-obovate. The leaves are covered on both sides with short soft hairs, with denser hairs underneath. Flowers, opening either before or with the leaves, are tubular-funnel-shaped, creamy to golden yellow with shades of orange and red, held in trusses of 8-15. Growth habit is open and upright. **S.E. North America. UC/PE, pe.**

R. baileyi (*after Lt. Col. F. M. Bailey, 1882-1967, traveller in Tibet*) s. Lepidotum s.s. Baileyi. 3', 0ºF, ML, 3-4/2-3/2-3. The shrub is evergreen, with rather small, shiny dark green leaves, oblong-oval, elliptic or obovate. Flowers, shallowly saucer shaped, to 1 1/2" across, have external scales and red styles, short and sharply curved. They are set in trusses of 5-12 and more. Color is reddish purple or deep purple, sometimes with darker spots. Growth habit is upright and open. S.E. Tibet, Bhutan, 8,000-13,000 ft. **R. baileyi/RN, rn, Baileya.**

R. bainbridgeanum (*after Mr. Bainbridge, a friend of George Forrest*). s. Barbatum s.s. Crinigerum. 5', 5ºF, E-EM, 3/3/2-3. Foliage is medium sized, ovate, obovate or elliptic, somewhat smooth on top, with thin grey indumentum below. Bell shaped flowers, to 1 1/2" long, are white or creamy yellow, blushed pale rose, occasionally spotted, with a crimson blotch. S.E. Tibet, 10,000-13,000 ft. **UC/HY, hy, Selensia.**

R. bakeri (*after Dr. W. F. Baker, Amory University, U.S.A.*) s. Azalea s.s. Luteum. 4', -15ºF, VL, 3/3/3. This deciduous shrub has smallish obovate leaves, deep green on top and waxy below. Tubular-funnel-shaped flowers, to 1 3/4" wide, which open after the leaves, are held in trusses of 4-7. Color is usually orange to reddish orange, occasionally salmon, salmon-apricot or clear yellow. Growth habit is upright and spreading. S.E. North America. **UC/PE, pe.**

R. balfourianum (*after Sir Isaac Bayley Balfour, 1853-1922, former Regius Professor of Botany, Edinburgh*) s. Taliense s.s. Adenogynum. 5', 0ºF, E, 4/4/3. Mature foliage is medium sized and can be lanceolate, oblong-lanceolate, ovate-lanceolate or oblong. Nearly smooth, matte green on top, the leaves have a thin, finely textured layer of brown indumentum underneath. Flowers, to 2" long, are funnel-campanulate, light rose or white tinged rose, spotted crimson, held in trusses of 6-9. Yunnan, Szechwan, 11,000-12,000 ft. **UC/HY, hy, Taliensia.**

var. **aganniphoides**-- Has a thick, woolly indumentum and is more free-flowering; it is more common in cultivation. **No longer recognized.**

R. barbatum (*bearded*) s. and s.s. Barbatum. 4-5', 5ºF, VE-E, 4-5/3/2-3. In the very early spring when *barbatum* bursts into bloom, there are few flowers that can compare to the **bright** scarlet blooms that adorn this species. The leaf stalks have bristles from which *barbatum* gets its name. The leaves are medium sized elliptic-lanceolate and have an interesting bullate texture to them. An added bonus is the smooth reddish plum colored bark which develops as the plant gets older. An absolute must for the early garden. Nepal, Sikkim, Bhutan, 9,400-11,300 ft. **UC/HY, hy, Barbata.**

R. basilicum (*royal*) s. Falconeri. 6', 5ºF, E-EM, 3/3-4/2-3. Very large foliage is obovate or ovate-elliptic, smooth dark green above, with a dense reddish brown indumentum underneath. 2" long flowers, ventricose-campanulate and fleshy, are held in large trusses of 20-25. Color is pale yellow or ivory white tinged crimson, with a crimson blotch. Yunnan, N.E. Burma, 10,000-11,000 ft. **UC/HY, hy, Falconera.**

R. bathyphyllum (*densely leafy*) s. Taliense s.s. Roxieanum. 2', -5ºF, E-EM, 3/5/2-3. Matte green, oblong foliage is medium sized, nearly smooth on top, covered with a dense, rusty indumentum underneath. Bell shaped flowers, to 2" long, white or white tinged pink, liberally crimson spotted, are set in trusses of 10-15. S.E. Tibet, Yunnan, Szechwan, 11,000-14,000 ft. **UC/HY, hy, Taliensia.**

R. bauhiniiflorum (*with flowers like those of Bauhinia*) s. and s.s. Triflorum. 6', 0ºF, E-L, 2/2/2. Leaves are small, oblong-lanceolate or ovate-lanceolate, with unevenly spaced, uniformly colored scales underneath. Saucer shaped flowers, to 1 3/4" across, are held in trusses of 2-3. They are lemony yellow or nearly green, occasionally brown or green spotted. Assam, 8,000-9,500 ft. Differs from *R. triflorum* in its saucer-shaped flowers. **R. triflorum var. bauhiniiflorum/RN, rn, Triflora.**

R. beanianum (*after W. J. Bean, 1863-1947, former Curator, Royal Botanic Gardens, Kew*) s. Neriiflorum s.s. Haematodes. 3', 5ºF, E, 3/4/2-3. Habit is upright, with very interesting foliage. Medium sized dark shiny green leaves are oblong to oblong-elliptic, puckered and wrinkled, the undersides having a rusty indumentum. Tubular to tubular-bell-shaped flowers, to 1 1/2", with good substance, scarlet or crimson to pink with dark nectar pouches, are set in loose trusses of 6-10. Plant needs shade. E. North East Frontier Agency, N.E. Upper Burma, 9,000-11,000 ft. **UC/HY, hy, Neriiflora.**

R. beesianum (*after Messrs. Bees, nurserymen in Cheshire*) s. Lacteum. 4', -5ºF, E-EM, 2-3/3-4/2-3. Leaves, to 12" long, are oblong-lanceolate or oblanceolate, smooth dark green on top, thinly coated with whitish, fawn, or brown indumentum underneath. Bell shaped flowers, to 2 1/2" long, in trusses of 10-25, are rose colored or white, sometimes with crimson blotch and spotting. Good growth habit and fine foliage. Yunnan, Szechwan, Tibet, Burma, 11,000-12,000 ft. **UC/HY, hy, Taliensia.**

R. bergii (*after Mr. and Mrs. W. E. Berg, rhododendron growers in the U. S.*) s. Triflorum s.s. Augustinii. 6', 0ºF, E-EM, 3/3/2. Mature foliage is of medium size, oblong, oblong-lanceolate, or lanceolate in shape. The leaves can be either smooth or minutely scaly above, scaly and glabrous below. Widely funnel shaped flowers, to 1" long, set in trusses of 3-5, are red, spotted deeper. Formerly known as *R. augustinii var. rubrum*. Some taxonomists do not consider this to be an individual species. N. W. Yunnan, 13,000 ft. **R. augustinii ssp. rubrum/RN, rn, Triflora.**

R. bhutanense s.s. Taliensia. 5', -10ºF, EM, -/-/-. A rare, newly introduced species. Foliage has a orangey brown indumentum on the underside. Flowers are pale pink. **UC/HY, hy, Talensia.**

R. bodinieri. Wild material inadequate; cultivated plants possibly *R. rigidum* hybrids.

R. boothii (*after T. J. Booth, b. 1829, who first collected it in 1849*) s. and s.s. Boothii. 3', 15ºF, E-M, 2/2/2. Smooth, dark green foliage, sometimes hairy edged, is ovate or ovate-elliptic, a little larger than medium sized, heavy underneath scaling. Widely bell shaped flowers are bright lemony yellow color, to 1 1/4" long, set in trusses of 7-10. Growth habit is loose. N.E. Frontier Agency, 5,000-8,000 ft. **UC/RN, rn, Boothia.**

R. brachyanthum (*with short flowers*) s. and s.s. Glaucophyllum. 3', -5ºF, L, 2/2-3/2-3. Habit is spreading. Aromatic, smallish shiny dark green leaves, oblong-lanceolate or oblong, with a few scales, have waxy green or bluish green undersides, similarly scaly. Interesting thimble shaped flowers, to 3/4" long, are pale or greenish yellow fading to cream. Each has a large, leafy calyx, and is held in clusters of 3-10 on long nodding stems. **R. brachyanthum ssp. brachyanthum/RN, rn, Glauca.**

var. **hypolepidotum**-- Is a form where the undersurface of the leaf is more densely scaly. Yunnan, S.E. Tibet, 9,000-11,000 ft. **R. brachyanthum ssp. hypolepidotum.**

R. brachycarpum (*with short fruit*) s. Ponticum s.s. Caucasicum. 3', -10ºF, VL, 3/3-4/2-3. Creamy white, green spotted trusses have a slight pink flush. The medium sized leaves are oblong to oblong-obovate and have pale fawn indumentum below, although they often do not have indumentum until they are five or more years old. N. and C. Japan, Korea. **R. brachycarpum ssp. brachycarpum/HY, hy, Pontica.**

R. brachysiphon (*with a short tube*) s. and s.s. Maddenii. 4', 10ºF, L-VL, 3/3-4/3-4. The large pink flower is scented and lily-like. Foliage is rusty green on upper surface, covered below with rusty scales. Very attractive leaves are broad ovate to elliptical. Bhutan, 6,000-7,000 ft. Syn. **R. maddenii ssp. maddenii/RN, rn, Maddenia "Maddenii-Alliance".**

R. bracteatum (*with bracts*) s. Heliolepis. 5', 5ºF, L-VL, 2/2/-. Smallish dark green leaves, to 2" x 1", ovate-elliptic or oblong-oval, slightly scaly on top, and denser below have a spicy redolence. Bell shaped flowers are quite small, to 3/4" long, and are held in trusses of 3-6. Color is a pinkish purple or white tinged pink, blotched and spotted crimson. Szechwan, 7,000-10,000 ft. **UC/RN, rn, Heliolepida.**

R. breviperulatum (*with short bud scales*) s. Azalea s.s. Obtusum. 3', 5-10F?, ML-L?, -/-/-. New growth on this small evergreen shrub is glossy brown, with flat hairs. Oblong leaves, to little more than an inch long, are slightly hairy and rough textured above with paler undersides, densely covered with flattened grey or brown hairs. Reddish funnel shaped flowers, to 1" wide, are held in trusses of 3-6. Formosa, 4,900 ft. **UC/TT, tt.**

R. brevistylum (*with a short style*) s. Heliolepis. 5', 0ºF, L-VL, 3/2-3/3. Medium sized foliage is oblong or elliptic-lanceolate, dark green above, tannish green below, and lightly scaled on both sides. Pale to deep rose flowers with crimson markings, to 1 1/2" long, are funnel-campanulate, appearing in trusses of 4-8. Yunnan, S. E. Tibet, 11,000-12,000 ft. **R. heliolepis var. brevistylum/RN, rn, Heliolepida.**

R. bureavii (*after E. Bureau, 1830-1918, a French professor*) s. Taliense s.s. Adenogynum. 4', -10ºF, M, 3/5/3. This member of the Taliense Series has fabulous foliage with beautiful thick indumentum. The dark green leaves are lanceolate to oblong-lanceolate. White flowers have crimson markings. One of the finest foliage plants; certainly a must for your collection. There are a number of forms being sold and almost all are outstanding. Needs excellent drainage as it is prone to root rot, also requires shade. Yunnan, 11,000-13,000 ft. **UC/HY, hy, Taliensia.**

R. bureavioides (*resembling R. bureavii*) s. Taliense s.s. Adenogynum. 4', -10ºF, M, 3/5/3. This unique species is similar to *bureavii* except that it has larger more elongated leaves and a slightly larger flower. Flowers are white with a little rose coloration, crimson markings. Szechwan. **Syn. R. bureavii/HY, hy, Taliensia.**

R. burmanicum (*from Burma*) s. Maddenii s.s. Ciliicalyx. 4', 15ºF, E-EM, 4/3/4. Habit is open, upright and leggy. Medium sized lance shaped leaves are scaly on both sides, lending a lovely golden brown effect. Sweetly scented flowers, to 2 1/2", are tubular-bell-shaped, yellow to greenish yellow, held in trusses of 4-6. S.W. Burma, 9,000-10,000 ft. **UC/RN, rn, Maddenia "Ciliicalyx-Alliance".**

R. caesium (*bluish grey*) s. Trichocladum. 3', 5ºF, M-L, 2-3/4/2-3. Evergreen shrub, with smallish pleasantly aromatic foliage, elliptic, oblong-elliptic, or oblong-lanceolate. Leaves are smooth, green on top, distinctively waxy grey-blue below, with scattered scales. Flowers are only 3/4" long, widely funnel shaped, greenish yellow, spotted green, held in trusses of 3. Yunnan, 8,000-10,000 ft. **UC/RN, rn, Trichoclada.**

R. calendulaceum (*like a calendula*) s. Azalea s.s. Luteum. 5', -25ºF, ML-L, 4/3/3. This deciduous shrub has medium sized foliage. Leaves are broadly elliptic, elliptic-oblong, or oblong-ovate, both sides with fine short hairs. Funnel shaped flowers, which may open with or after the leaves, into trusses of 5-7, are yellow, orange to scarlet, occasionally partly salmon pink, blotched orange. Plant habit is upright to spreading. E. North America. **UC/PE, pe.**

R. callimorphum (*with a lovely shape*) s. Thomsonii s.s. Campylocarpum. 3', -5ºF, M, 3/4/3. Shiny dark green medium sized leaves are orbicular, broadly elliptic, or ovate, slightly hairy on top and waxy grey blue underneath, with vestiges of glands. Bell shaped flowers, to 2" long, opening from deep rose buds to deep rose or pink blooms, occasionally blotched crimson, are set into trusses of 5-8. Habit is upright and spreading. Whole plant is beautiful. Seems to be a variable species with several forms being sold. Yunnan, N. E. Burma, 9,000-11,000 ft. **R. callimorphum ssp. callimorphum/HY, hy, Campylocarpa.**

R. calophytum (*beautiful plant*) s. Fortunei s.s. Calophytum. 5', -15ºF, E, 4/4/3. Hardiest of the large leaved species, this plant eventually becomes a tree. The leaves are oblong-lanceolate or lanceolate. Beautiful pink flowers bloom early in the year. A grand rhododendron for both leaf and flower. An absolute must for the garden. Szechwan, 7,000-10,000 ft. **R. calophytum var. calophytum/HY, hy, Fortunea.**

R. calostrotum (*with a beautiful covering*) s. Saluenense. 2', -5ºF, M, 4/4/2-3. Saucer shaped flowers are rich purple crimson with crimson spots. The aromatic leaves are obovate-elliptic, oval or oblong, bluish green on the upper surface. The lower surface is densely covered with cinnamon colored scales. Upper Burma, Yunnan, S. E. Tibet, E. North East Frontier Agency, 10,000-15,000 ft. **R. calostrotum ssp. calostrotum/RN, rn, Saluenensia.**
>   var. **calciphilum**– Has leaves up to 1/2" long and pink flowers. Upper Burma, Yunnan.
>   **R. calostrotum ssp. riparium.**
>   'Gigha'– Named for an island west of Scotland; rosy red flowers.

R. caloxanthum (*of a beautiful yellow*) s. Thomsonii s.s. Campylocarpum. 3', -5ºF, EM, 3/3-4/2-3. Foliage is usually almost round, medium-sized, smooth dark green above, paler waxy green below, with scattered hairs and vestiges of glands. Bell shaped flowers, to 1 3/4" long, open from orange-scarlet buds to yellow blooms, sometimes tinged pink, into trusses of 4-6. Round, compact shrub. Burma, Tibet, Yunnan, 11,000-13,000 ft. Differs from *R. telopeum* in its larger leaves. **R. campylocarpum ssp. caloxanthum/HY, hy, Campylocarpa.**

R. calvescens (*becoming hairless*) s. Thomsonii s.s. Selense. 4'?, ?ºF, ?, -/-/-. Medium sized oblong foliage is smooth matte green above. The underside has a thin, reddish indumentum, which is eventually completely sloughed off, along with stalkless glands. Bell shaped rose colored flowers, to 1 1/2", are set in trusses of up to 8. S.E. Tibet. **R. calvescens var. calvescens/HY, hy, Selensia.**

R. camelliiflorum (*with flowers like a camellia*) s. Camelliiflorum. 6', 5ºF, M-L, 2-3/3/-. Medium sized foliage is oblong or oblong-lanceolate, glabrous dark green on top, densely scaly underneath. Flowers, to 2" wide, are white, white tinged pink or rose, campanulate or more or less shallowly saucer-shaped, held in trusses of up to 3. Sikkim, Bhutan, E. Nepal, 9,000-11,000 ft. **UC/RN, rn, Camelliiflora.**

R. campanulatum (*bell shaped*) s. Campanulatum. 4', -5ºF, EM, 3/5/3. Another of the fine rhododendrons known for its superior foliage. The leaves are elliptic, oblong-elliptic or obovate and are dark green above, coated below with the most beautiful cinnamon indumentum possible. The flowers are very light lilac to white, with slight spotting. Kashmir to Bhutan, 9,000-14,000 ft. **R. campanulatum ssp. campanulatum/HY, hy, Campanulata.**
>   var. **aeruginosum**– The Rolls Royce of foliage. This variety has that great indumentum mentioned above (a little more fawn colored on this one) combined with leaves that open as silver green deepening during the summer to a striking soft blue. Flower color is the same as campanulatum. Considered by Davidian to be a full species and not a ssp. of *R. campanulatum*. **R. campanulatum ssp. aeruginosum.**

R. campylocarpum (*with bent fruit*) s. Thomsonii s.s. Campylocarpum. 4', 0ºF, EM, 3-4/4/3. Round dark green leaves are pale glaucous green on the undersides. Pale yellow flowers make a beautiful sight in the spring. A good species that is the parent of many hybrids. Nepal, Sikkim, Bhutan, Assam, Tibet, 10,000-14,300 ft. **R. campylocarpum ssp. campylocarpum/HY, hy, Campylocarpa.**
>   var. **elatum**– Taller, with red-blotched flowers. **R. campylocarpum ssp. campylocarpum Elatum Group.**

R. campylogynum (*with bent ovary*) s. Campylogynum. 1', -10ºF, EM. 3-4/3-4/3. Small, smooth, bright dark green foliage, obovate to oblanceolate, is either pale green or slightly glabrous and glaucous underneath. Widely bell shaped flowers, barely 3/4" long, in trusses up to 3, nod on long stalks. Color ranges from creamy white to red, displaying shades of rosy purple, salmon pink, or almost black-purple. Compact, upright growth. Yunnan, S.E. Tibet, W. and N.E. Upper Burma, 9,000-14,000 ft. **UC/RN, rn, Campylogyna.**

> var. **celsum**-- 3', -10ºF, EM, 4/3-4/3. Growth habit erect. Yunnan. **R. campylogynum Celsum Group.**
>
> var. **charopoeum**-- 2', -10ºF, EM, 3-4/3-4/3. Has larger flowers, to 1". N.E. Upper Burma. **R. campylogynum Charopaeum Group.**
>
> var. **cremastum**-- 2 1/2', -10ºF, EM, 4/3-4/3. Has green on the underside of the leaf. The plant that was known as 'Bodnant Red' belongs here. **R. campylogynum Cremastum Group.**
>
> var. **myrtilloides**-- 1', -10ºF, M, 3/4/3. More dwarf in form and has smaller flowers, only 1/2" long. Burma, Tibet, Yunnan. **R. campylogynum Myrtilloides Group.**

R. camtschaticum (*from Kamtschatka*) s. Camtschaticum. 6", -25ºF, E, 3/3/2-3. This species is deciduous, and, for part of the winter, it looks dead, not showing even green growth tips. In the very early spring, it bursts forth with new leaves, which are obovate with hairy margins. It is interesting in that it flowers on the new growth instead of flowering from year old wood. Although the flowers are usually rosy plum colored, there is also a rare white form. While some botanists believe that this should be a separate genus, the latest information available includes it in subgenus Therorhodion. Alaska, Bering Strait, Shores of Okhotsk Sea to N. Japan. **NR/TH**

R. canadense (*from Canada*) s. Azalea s.s. Canadense. 2', -25ºF, E, 4/3/3. Growth habit of this hardy dwarf, native to Quebec and Maine, is compact, upright and bushy. Deciduous oblong leaves, to 2 1/4", are dull bluish green and sparsely hairy above, the undersides having filmy grey hairs. The lavender-pink flowers, to 1 1/2" wide, are so deeply cut to the base that each flower appears like five individual petals, making a truss that reminds one of a whirling ballerina. Trusses have 3-6 flowers. **UC/PE, ro.**

> var. **album**-- The rare pure white form.

R. canescens (*hoary*) s. Azalea s.s. Luteum. 6', -5ºF, E-M, 3/3/3. Deciduous shrub with medium-sized foliage that is oblong-obovate, oblanceolate or oblong in shape, either completely glabrous or very slightly pubescent on top, and normally densely pubescent underneath. Flowers are fragrant, tubular-funnel-shaped, to 2" wide, opening either before or with the leaves, into trusses of 6-15. Color ranges from pure white to white blushed pink to pink or purplish, with pink or reddish corolla tube. Compact to upright growth. E. North America. Very similar to *R. periclymenoides*, differing mainly in its glandular corolla tube. **UC/PE, pe.**

R. capitatum (*with flowers in a head*) s. Lapponicum. 5', 0ºF?, VE-M, 2-3/2-3/2. Rather small leaves are elliptic or oblong-elliptic, dull green and scaly on top, densely covered underneath with unequal pale and dark brown scales. Flowers, to 3/4" long, set in trusses of 3-5, are widely funnel shaped, ranging from lilac to bluish purple or deep purplish red, with no external scales. Kansu, S.E. Tibet, Szechwan, Shensi, 9,800-13,000 ft. **UC/RN, rn, Lapponica.**

R. cardiobasis (*with a heart shaped base*) s. Fortunei s.s. Orbiculare. 5', -5ºF, M-ML, 3/4/3. Foliage is medium large, ovate or elliptic, with heart shaped base. Flowers, to 2" long, are funnel-campanulate, white or rose, in trusses of 6-12. Differs from *R. orbiculare* in its glabrous pedicels and rachis. Kwangsi (S. China), 5,400 ft. **R. orbiculare ssp. cardiobasis/HY, hy, Fortunea.**

R. carneum (*flesh colored*) s. Maddenii s.s. Ciliicalyx. 4', 15ºF, E-M, 3/2-3/3. Leaves are medium large, elliptic or obovate, smoothly dark green on top, waxy bluish green with yellow scales underneath. Flesh pink flowers are fragrant, tubular campanulate to 2 1/2" long, and are held in trusses of 4-5. Upper Burma, 7,500 ft. **UC/RN, rn, Maddenii "Ciliicalyx-Alliance".**

R. carolinianum (*from Carolina, U.S.A.*) s. Carolinianum. 4', -25ºF, M-ML, 3/3/2-3. Leaves, smooth shiny green above, heavily scaly below, to almost 4" long, are obovate elliptic or elliptic. Flowers are funnel shaped, to 2", pale rosy purple or pink, occasionally faintly spotted, held in trusses of 4-10. Growth habit is rounded. This plant is hardy and sun tolerant, and often flowers heavily. E. United States. **R. minus var. minus Carolinianum Group/RN, rn, Caroliniana.**

R. catacosmum (*adorned*) s. Neriiflorum s.s. Haematodes. 4', -5ºF?, E-M, 3/3/2-3. Leaves to 4 1/2" long, are obovate or oval, smooth on top with tawny or dark brown indumentum underneath. Broadly bell shaped flowers of heavy substance, to 2" long, with nectar pouches and 1" long calyx, are carried in trusses of 5-9. Color is crimson rose, deep crimson or scarlet. S.E. Tibet, 13,000-14,000 ft. **UC/HY, hy, Neriiflora.**

R. catawbiense (*after the Catawba river, North Carolina, U.S.A.*) s. and s.s. Ponticum. 6', -25ºF, ML-L, 3/3/4. Growth habit varies from compact to loose and spreading. Medium large foliage is oval or oblong-oval, smooth and shiny dark green on top, paler green underside, possibly with vestigial early indumentum. Cup shaped flowers, to 2 1/2" long, set in large trusses of 15-20, are lilac-purple, rose-purple, pink or white, spotted yellow-green. Allegheny Mountains, U.S.A., 6,000 ft. **UC/HY, hy, Pontica.**

R. caucasicum (*from the Caucasus*) s. Ponticum s.s. Caucasicum. 3', -5ºF, E-M, 2/2-3/3. Plant habit is compact and upright. Oblong foliage, to 4" long, is smooth dull green above, with a thinnish layer of rust or fawn colored light felt below. Flowers, to 1" long, either widely funnel or campanulate shaped, held in full trusses of many blooms, are creamy white, yellowish tinted rose, or white tinged pink, spotted. Caucasus, N.E. Turkey, 6,000-9,000 ft. **UC/HY, hy, Pontica.**

R. cephalanthum (*with flowers in a head*) s. Anthopogon. 2', -5ºF, E-M, 4/3/1-2. Growth habit is low and spreading. Smallish aromatic leaves, elliptic or oblong-elliptic, are dark, smooth glossy green on top and densely scaly underneath. Flowers, to 3/4", are narrowly tubular with spreading lobes, held in compact trusses of up to 8 white, pink or yellow blooms. Yunnan, Szechwan, S.E. Tibet, Upper Burma, 9,000-16,000 ft. **R. cephalanthum ssp. cephalanthum/RN, rn, Pogonanthum.**

> var. **crebreflorum**-- A dwarf plant with pink flowers. Assam, North East Frontier Agency and Upper Burma. **R. cephalanthum ssp. cephalanthum Crebreflorum Group.**
>
> var. **nmaiense**-- Has yellow flowers. Upper Burma. **No longer recognized.**

R. cerasinum (*cherry colored*) s. Thomsonii s.s. Cerasinum. 3', -5ºF, EM, 3-4/4/3. Growth habit of this plant is compact and dense. Medium sized leaves are round to oblong or oval, with waxy bluish green undersides. Drooping flowers, to 2" long, are bell shaped, held in trusses of 5-7. They are brilliant scarlet or cherry red, sometimes creamy white with cherry a red band at the tip of each lobe, and dark purple nectar pouches. Very attractive. Burma, Tibet, Assam, 10,000-12,000 ft. **UC/HY, hy, Thomsonia.**

R. chaetomallum (*with woolly hair*) s. Neriiflorum s.s. Haematodes. 30", 5ºF, E- EM, 3/2-3/2. Growth habit is open and upright. Medium sized round to oval foliage is smooth dark green above with a rich dark brown indumentum below. Flowers, to 2" long, tubular-bell-shaped, with heavy substance, are held in trusses of 6-9. They are deep crimson, scarlet, or deep rose. It often seems difficult to grow. S.E. Tibet, Yunnan, N.E. Upper Burma, 10,000-15,000 ft. **R. haematodes ssp. chaetomallum/HY, hy, Neriiflora.**

  var. **chamaephytum**-- Is only 1-2 ft.; more or less prostrate; leaves are glabrous below. S.E. Tibet, 13,000 ft. May be a hybrid.

  var. **glaucescens**-- Leaves are rather glaucous above. N.E. Upper Burma, 13,000 ft. **R. haematodes ssp. chaetomallum Glaucescens Group.**

  var. **hemigymnum**-- Indumentum is thinner and less persistent. S.E. Tibet, Upper Burma, 12,000-14,000 ft. **R. x hemigymnum (R. eclecteum x pocophorum).**

  var. **xanthanthum**-- Creamy yellow flowers flushed rose pink, sometimes striped and margined pale rose. S.E. Tibet, 12,000-14,000 ft. **R. x xanthanthum (R. haematodes ssp. chaetomallum x stewartianum).**

R. chamaethomsonii (*dwarf R. thomsonii*) s. Neriiflorum s.s. Forrestii. 1', -5ºF, E, 3/4/3. This shrub grows open and upright. Small, rather roundish leaves are sometimes waxy blue-green above, usually smooth underneath. Tubular-bell-shaped flowers, with heavy substance, to about 2" long, range from crimson, rosy crimson or bright scarlet to rose-pink, and are sometimes even orangey crimson or white. They are held in trusses of up to 4. Differs from *R. forrestii* in its upright, not flat growing habit. Yunnan, Tibet, E. North East Frontier Agency, N.E. Upper Burma, 11,000-15,000 ft. **R. chamaethomsonii var. chamaethomsonii/HY, hy, Neriiflora.**

  var. **chamaedoron**-- Leaves are thinly hairy and glandular below. **R. chamaethomsonii var. chamaedoron.**

  var. **chamaethauma**-- 4 to 5 flowers in a truss; often has smaller leaves. **R. chamaethomsonii var. chamaethauma.**

R. chameunum (*sleeping on the ground*) s. Saluenense. 1', -5ºF, EM, 4/3/3-4. This small shrub has downward creeping branches and very bristly new growth. Leaves are small, to about 1/2", oval, smooth and glossy on top, scaly underneath. Flowers, to 1" long, are flat-faced, crimson-purple or rose-purple, spotted crimson. A superior plant. Yunnan, Burma, Tibet, Szechwan, 11,000-17,000 ft. **R. saluenense ssp. chameunum/RN, rn, Saluenensia.**

R. championiae (*after Mrs. Champion, the wife of its discoverer, J. G. Champion, 1815-1854*) s. Stamineum. 5', 10ºF?, E-M, 3-4/3-4/3. Leaves are large, lanceolate or oblong-lanceolate, dark green with pale bristles on top, bristly and frequently hairy underneath. 2 1/2" long flowers are axillary, widely funnel-shaped, held in trusses of 4-6. Tube is white, with lobes flushed heavily either pink or yellow, calyx deeply lobed. Hong Kong, Fukien. **UC/AZ, ch.**

R. chapmanii (*after A. W. Chapman, 1809-1899, American botanist*) s. Carolinianum. 4', -5ºF, EM, 3/3/2-3. Growth habit is rounded and rigid with light olive green oval leaves to 3" long, shiny on top, scaly on the reverse. Funnel-bell-shaped flowers, to 1 1/2" long, are pink or rose, with greenish brown spotting, sometimes with distinctive chocolate-purple anthers, held in compact trusses to 10. Should be a source of parentage for heat tolerant rhododendrons since it is native to Florida. **R. minus var. chapmanii/RN, rn, Caroliniana.**

R. charitopes (*with a graceful appearance*) s. and s.s. Glaucophyllum. 1', -5ºF, E-M, 3/2-3/3. Growth habit is upright and open. Smallish oval leaves are glabrous shiny dark green on top, paler and covered with shiny yellow unequal scales on the reverse. Flowers, either tubular-campanulate or broadly-campanulate, usually occurring in trusses of 3, are up to 1" long, with exserted stamens and leafy calyx. Often will flower in the fall. Upper Burma, Yunnan, 10,500-14,000 ft. **R. charitopes ssp. charitopes/RN, rn, Glauca.**

R. chionanthum (*with snowy flowers*) s. Neriiflorum s.s. Haematodes. 3', 0ºF, E-M, 2-3/3/3. Leaves are small, obovate to oblong-obovate, the undersides thickly covered with tawny indumentum, either patchy or continuous. White, fleshy, bell shaped flowers, to 1 1/2" long, with calyx to 1/2" long and large unequal lobes, are set in trusses of 4-6. Upper Burma, 13,000-14,000 ft. **UC/HY, hy, Neriiflora.**

R. chloranthum (*with greenish flowers*) s. Trichocladum. 3', 5ºF, ML, 2/2/3. Growth habit is upright and stiff. Plant is deciduous, with obovate or oblong-obovate leaves, to about 1" long, smooth on top and scaly underneath. Flowers, to 3/4" long, appear before the leaves, in trusses of about 4, broadly funnel-shaped, yellow tinged green at base. Yunnan, S.E. Tibet, 11,000-12,000 ft. **Syn. R. mekongense var. melinanthum/RN, rn, Trichoclada.**

R. chlorops (*with a green eye*) s. and s.s. Fortunei. 4', -5ºF, M, 3/4/3. The leaves on this dense plant are bluish olive green, oblong to 5". Charming saucer shaped flowers, in trusses of 6-8, sit on upright stems. They are cream to pale yellow, with a pale purple blotch and some reddish purple spotting, greenish inside at the base. Unknown in the wild. 'Lackamas Cream' is a well known plant which was selected from seed of this species. **Known only in cultivation; probably a hybrid between R. wardii and a member of subsect. Fortunea.**

R. chrysanthum-- see *aureum*.

R. chryseum-- see *rupicola* var. *chryseum*.

R. chrysodoron (*golden gift, referring to this yellow-flowered plant given to the Royal Botanic Garden, Edinburgh, by the Earl of Stair*) s. and s.s. Boothii. 3', 15ºF, 4/3-4/2-3. Medium sized foliage is elliptic or ovate-elliptic, smooth and bright green on top, waxy grey-bluish green and scaly on the reverse. Bell shaped flowers, to 1 1/2" long, are brilliant golden yellow, held in trusses of 3-6. Yunnan, N.E. Upper Burma, 6,500- 8,500 ft. Similar to *R. sulfureum*, but it has a smaller calyx and larger leaves and flowers. **UC/RN, rn, Boothia.**

R. chrysolepis (*with golden scales*) s. Boothii s.s. Tephropeplum. 1', 15ºF, E-M, -/-/-. This dwarf shrub has medium sized oblong-lanceolate foliage, smooth on top, glaucous purple with golden yellow scales underneath. Bell shaped flowers, to 1 1/4", are canary yellow, and are carried in 3-5 flower truss. Not in general cultivation. Upper Burma, 7,000-8,000 ft. **UC/RN, po.**

R. ciliatum (*fringed with hairs*) s. Maddenii s.s. Ciliicalyx. 3', 5ºF, EM, 4/4/3-4. Brownish red peeling bark and foliage covered with bristly hairs make this plant most attractive. Leaves are oblong and medium size, slightly scaly underneath. Flowers, to 2" long, are pink, white or white tinged pink, bell shaped or tubular-bell-shaped, carried in trusses of 2-4. One of the hardiest plants in the Maddenii series; well worth growing. Bhutan, S.E. Tibet, E. Nepal, 7,500-12,000 ft. **UC/RN, rn, Maddenia "Ciliicalyx-Alliance".**

R. ciliicalyx (*with a hair-fringed calyx*) s. Maddenii s.s. Ciliicalyx. 4', 15ºF, E-M, 3-4/3/3. A fast growing plant. Beautiful foliage is medium sized, elliptic, obovate-elliptic, or oblong-lanceolate. The leaves are shiny dark green on top, pale waxy blue-green underneath, with gold scales. Slightly fragrant funnel shaped flowers, to 3" long, are white or white tinged rose, held in trusses of up to 3. Yunnan, Szechwan, S.E. Tibet, N. Burma, 7,500-9,000 ft. **UC/RN, rn, Maddenia "Ciliicalyx-Alliance" Ciliicalyx agg.**

R. cinnabarinum (*cinnabar red*) s. Cinnabarinum. 5', 5ºF, EM-VL, 4/4/2-3. Foliage on this lovely plant is aromatic. Leaves to about 3 1/2" x 1 3/4" are elliptic or oblanceolate, smooth on top with a rather metallic grey-green cast, scaly bluish green to reddish brown beneath. Flowers, to 2" long, are tubular in shape, and typically cinnabar dark red, held in trusses of 3-5. Very variable. Nepal, Sikkim, Bhutan, S.E. Tibet, 9,400-13,000 ft.

    R. cinnabarinum ssp. cinnabarinum/RN, rn, Cinnabarina.

        var. aestivale-- Flowers unusually late (July) and has narrower leaves. **R. cinnabarinum ssp. cinnabarinum 'Astivale'.**

        var. blandfordiiflorum-- Has narrowly tubular flowers, red outside, yellow, apricot or greenish within. Nepal, Sikkim, 10,000-12,000 ft. **R. cinnabarinum ssp. cinnabarinum Blandfordiiflorum Group.**

        var. pallidum-- Has broadly funnel-campanulate flowers, pale pinkish purple. Nepal, Sikkim, Bhutan, 10,000-12,000 ft. **R. cinnabarinum ssp. xanthocodon Pallidum Group.**

        var. purpurellum-- Has shorter, campanulate flowers, rich plum purple or bright pinkish mauve. S.E. Tibet, 10,000 ft. **R. cinnabarinum ssp. xanthocodon Purpurellum Group.**

R. citriniflorum (*with lemon yellow flowers*) s. Neriiflorum *s.s.* Sanguineum. 3', 0ºF, EM-M, 3-4/3/2-3. Medium sized foliage, obovate to oblong, tends to be smooth on top and has a thick coating of fawn colored or grey-brown woolly indumentum underneath. Bell shaped yellow to yellow-crimson flowers, to 1 3/4" long, slightly fleshy, with glandular and tomentose ovary, are held in trusses of 4-8. Yunnan, S.E. Tibet, 13,000-16,000 ft. **R. citriniflorum var. citriniflorum/HY, hy, Neriiflora.**

    ssp. horaeum-- Has crimson flowers and a tomentose and eglandular ovary. S.E. Tibet, 13,000 ft. **R. citriniflorum var. horaeum.**

R. clementinae (*after Clementine, wife of George Forrest*) s. and *s.s.* Taliense. 3', -5ºF or colder, E-M, 3/4-5/2-3. This hardy plant has spectacular foliage. Large leaves are oblong-oval, smooth matte green with a thick coating of silky indumentum, white to pale fawn on the undersides. Flowers, to 1 3/4" long, are bell shaped, set in trusses of about 15. Color ranges from white or white tinged pink to creamy white, with deep crimson spotting. Yunnan, Szechwan, S.E. Tibet, 11,000-14,000 ft. **UC/HY, hy, Taliensia.**

R. coelicum (*heavenly*) s. Neriiflorum *s.s.* Haematodes. 4', -5ºF, EM-M, 3/3/-. Foliage is of medium size, obovate in shape, with a smooth top and heavy covering of dark brown indumentum underneath. Tubular-campanulate flowers of heavy substance, occurring in compact trusses of 6-15, are up to 1 1/2" long, bright scarlet or deep crimson, with nectar pouches. Yunnan, S.E. Tibet, Upper Burma, 12,000-14,000 ft. **UC/HY, hy, Neriiflora.**

R. collettianum (*after Gen. Sir Henry Collett, 1836-1901*) s. Anthopogon. 2', - 5ºF, M-ML, 2-3/2-3/1-2. This is a deciduous shrub with medium sized aromatic leaves, widely lanceolate or oblong-lanceolate. They are smooth bright green above and densely covered with hair-like scales underneath. 1" long flowers, held in capitate trusses of about 8-12, are white tinged rosy pink, with spreading lobes, narrowly tubular shaped. Afghanistan-Pakistan Frontier, 10,000-13,000 ft. **UC/RN, rn, Pogonanthum.**

R. columbianum (*of the Columbia*) Section Rhododendron, Subsection Ledum. 3', -15ºF, M, 2-3/3-4/4. This is the plant that has been known to belong to the *Genus Ledum*, but is now considered by some botanists to be a rhododendron. Sharp pointed leaves are about 2" long. The undersides are white-scurfy, glandular and distinctly veined. Flowers are white, and many to each truss; stamens generally 6 or 7 which is an unusual number for a rhododendron. California, Oregon and Washington, 0-1000 ft. **Not previously known as a rhododendron and has never been in a Series, or Subseries.**

R. compactum (*compact*) s. Lapponicum. 3', -5ºF, EM, 3/3/3. Leaves are covered with dense scales below and are bright green above. Flowers are in trusses of 5 or 6, broadly funnel shaped, violet to violet purplish mauve, about 1/2" long. N.W. Yunnan. **R. polycladum/RN, rn, Lapponica.**

R. complexum (*interwoven*) s. Lapponicum. 1', -10ºF, EM, 3/3/3. This dwarf grows very matted, with tiny ovate elliptic leaves to only 1/4" long, dark green with many semi-transparent scales on top, the undersides covered densely with reddish brown scales. Flowers, to 1/2" long, held in trusses of 3-4, are widely funnel shaped, and range in color from pale lilac to deep rose-purple. Yunnan, 11,000-15,000 ft. **UC/RN, rn, Lapponica.**

R. concatenans (*linking together*) s. Cinnabarinum. 3', 5ºF, EM, 3/4-5/2-3. This is one of the finest foliage plants. Deep bluish green leaves are oval to oblong, to 2 1/2" long, the tops glabrous, undersides tinged purple and densely scaly. Bell shaped flowers, to 2" long, with 5 half-spreading lobes, prominently veined, are apricot yellow, sometimes lightly tinged on the outside with pale purple or deeper yellow. S.E. Tibet, 10,000-12,000 ft. **R. cinnabarinum ssp. xanthocodon Concatenans Group/RN, rn, Cinnabarina.**

R. concinnum (*neat*) s. Triflorum *s.s.* Yunnanense. 5', -5ºF, M. 4/3/3-4. Growth is tree-like. Elliptic leaves, to 3 1/2" long, are dark bluish green, scaly on both sides. Widely funnel shaped flowers, to 1 1/2" long, range in color from white through all shades of purple to a beautiful wine red, occasionally spotted brownish or crimson, appearing in clusters of 3-6. Szechwan, 5,000-14,600 ft. **UC/RN, rn, Triflora.**

    var. pseudoyanthinum-- This variety is widely grown; two forms are well known. Szechwan, 9,500-12,000 ft.

        Exbury form-- More red.

        'Chief Paulina'-- More purple.

    var. benthamianum-- Has lavender-purple flowers. Szechwan.

R. cookeanum (*after R. B. Cooke, 1880-1973, rhododendron grower of Corbridge, Northumberland*) s. Irroratum *s.s.* Parishii. 5', 5ºF, ML-L, 3/2/-. Foliage is large, oblong-lanceolate or oblong-elliptic, and smooth on both sides. Bell shaped flowers, to 2" long, are white or pink, sometimes blotched crimson, held in trusses of 8-15. Szechwan, 12,000-13,500 ft. **UC/HY, hy, Maculifera.**

R. coriaceum (*leathery*) s. Falconeri. 5', 5ºF, E-EM, 3-4/4/3. Leaves are large, to 10", broadly obovate or ovate-elliptic. They are smooth and dark green on top with a heavy covering of greyish-fawn to pale brown indumentum below, sometimes patchy. Bell shaped flowers, to 1 1/2" long, held in lax trusses of 15-20, are white flushed rose, blotched crimson, sometimes with crimson spotting. Yunnan, S.E. Tibet, Upper Burma, 10,000-13,000 ft. **UC/HY, hy, Falconera.**

R. coryanum (*after R.R. Cory, 1871-1934*) s. Arboreum *s.s.* Argyrophyllum. 6', 0ºF, E-M, 3/3/-. Oblong-lanceolate leaves are medium large, smooth light green above, with sparse glands and a thin layer of greyish or fawn colored indumentum below. Funnel-campanulate flowers, to 1" long, set in lax trusses of 20-30, are creamy white with crimson spotting. Yunnan, S.E. Tibet, 12,000-14,000 ft. **UC/HY, hy, Argyrophylla.**

R. cowanianum (*after Dr. J. M. Cowan, 1892-1960, an authority on Rhododendron*) s. Trichocladum. 3', 0ºF, M-ML, 2/1-2/2-3. Small leaves, obovate or oblong-obovate, can be either smooth with hairy edges or densely scaly on top, yellow-green scales underneath. Flowers also are small, to 2/3" long, a short bell shape, held in trusses of 2-4, pink, pinkish magenta, or deep wine red in color. Nepal, 10,000-13,000 ft. **UC/RN, rn, Lepidota.**

Species ~
Native to Europe

R. luteum
(Subgenus Pentanthera
Section Pentanthera)

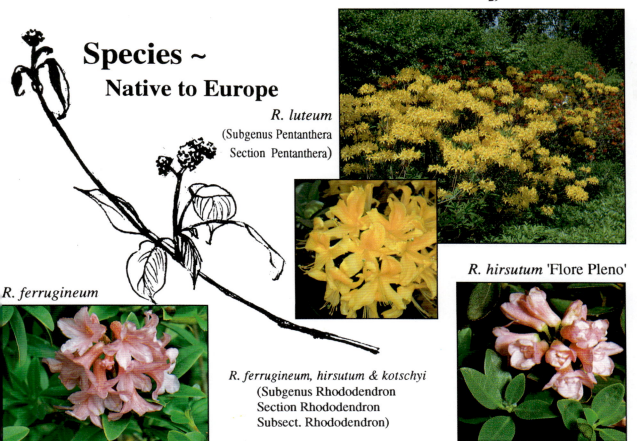

R. hirsutum 'Flore Pleno'

R. ferrugineum

R. ferrugineum, hirsutum & kotschyi
(Subgenus Rhododendron
Section Rhododendron
Subsect. Rhododendron)

R. kotschyi in wild in Eastern Europe
(photo by Norman Benton)

R. ponticum   (Subgenus Hymenanthes Sect. Hymenanthes Subsect. Pontica)   *R. ponticum* 'Variegatum'   *R. kotschyi*

Species ~
Native to Japan

Subgenus Tsutsutsi Section Tsutsutsi
(commonly referred to as evergreen azaleas)

R. kiusianum 'Komo Kulshan'

R. kiusianum 'Hanejiro'

R. kiusianum

R. sataense

R. macrosepalum 'Kochoh-zoroi'

R. yedoense var. *poukhanense*

R. indicum 'Balsaminiflora'

R. kaempferi 'Tachiene'

R. kaempferi 'Tubiflorum'

R. kaempferi 'Sempervirens'

Species ~ Native to Japan
Subgenus Pentanthera
(elepidote species commonly referred to as deciduous azaleas)

R. reticulatum (Subg. Tsustsutsi Sect. Brachycalyx)

R. quinquifolium (both Section Sciadorhodion)　*R. schlippenbachii*

R. schlippenbachii

R. amagianum (Subg. Tsustsutsi Sect. Brachycalyx)

Also Native to Japan

Subgenus Rhododendron
Section Rhododendron
Subsect. Rhodorastra
(lepidote rhododendron species)

R. albrechtii (Subg. Tsustsutsi Sect Brachycalyx)

R. japonicum (Section Pentanthera)

R. mucronulatum

R. dauricum

Species ~ Native to Japan
Subgenus Hymenanthes
Section Hymenanthes
Subsect. Pontica

R. metternichii var. *pentamerum*

R. metternichii var. *kyomaruense*
R. metternichii var. *kyomaruense*

R. metternichii var. *metternichii*
R. metternichii var. *metternichii*

R.yakushimanum 'Ken Janeck'

R. fauriei var. *nemotoanum*

R. makinoi

R. yakushimanum 'Phetteplace Tall Form'

R. yakushimanum 'Yaku Angel'

R. coxianum (*after E. H. M. Cox, 1893-1977*) s. Maddenii s.s. Ciliicalyx. 4', 15°F, E-EM, -/-/-. Medium sized leaves are oblanceolate, either smooth green on top or with a few scales or bristly hairs. The undersides are pale waxy grey or bluish green with scattered, unequal brown scales. Tubular-funnel-shaped flowers are white, to 3" long, set in 3 flower trusses. The cultivated plants do not run uniform and are not like the wild material, which is probably a form of *R. formosum*. North East Frontier Agency, 5,400 ft. **RN, rn, Maddenia, "Ciliicalyx-Alliance", but cultivated material does not match wild specimens which may belong to R. formosum.**

R. crassum (*fleshy*) s. and s.s. Maddenii. 5', 15°F, L-VL, 3/3-4/3-4. Foliage is medium large, lanceolate or obovate-lanceolate, thick, glossy dark green on top and densely covered with rusty scales underneath. Fragrant flowers, to 4" long, tubular-funnel-shaped, are set in trusses of 3-5. They are white, creamy white, or white blushed pink, blotched yellow. Similar to *R. maddenii*, but has hairy filaments and rough bark. Yunnan, S.E. Tibet, Upper Burma, 7,500-12,000 ft. **R. maddenii ssp. crassum/RN, rn, Maddenia "Maddenii-Alliance".**

R. crinigerum (*bearing hairs*) s. Barbatum s.s. Crinigerum. 4', 5°F, EM, 3/4/2-3. Growth habit is upright and loose, with hairy foliage. Leaves are lance shaped, to 7" long, dark shiny green above, felted with a dense whitish or deep buff indumentum underneath (not apparent on young plant). Bell shaped flowers, to about 1 1/2" long, are white or white flushed pink or rose, usually with an intense dark red blotch and occasionally spotted red, carried in trusses of up to 12. Yunnan, S.E. Tibet, 10,000-14,500 ft. **R. crinigerum var. crinigerum/HY, hy, Glischra.**

  var. euadenium-- Is more glandular, with a thinner indumentum. S.E. Tibet, Yunnan, 12,000-14,000 ft. **R. crinigerum var. euadenium.**

R. cubittii (*after G. E. S. Cubitt, c. 1875-1966, who collected in N. Burma*) s. Maddenii s.s. Ciliicalyx. 5', 20°F, E-EM, 4/2-3/3. Medium sized foliage is oblong-elliptic or oblong-lanceolate, with smooth tops, and scaly, pale glaucous green undersides. Flowers are broadly funnel shaped, to 4" long, and carried in trusses of 2-4. White or white blushed rose, they occasionally have an orange-yellow blotch and brownish spotting. N. Burma, 5,800 ft. **R. veitchianum Cubittii Group/RN, rn, Maddenia "Ciliicalyx-Alliance".**

R. cuffeanum (*after Lady Wheeler Cuffe, who discovered it*) s. Maddenii s.s. Ciliicalyx. 5', 20°F, E-M, 3/2/3. Leaves are oblanceolate or oblong-lanceolate, medium size, smooth and veined on top, densely covered with unequal brown scales on underside. Flowers, to 3" long, tubular-bell-shaped, held in 5-flower truss, are white, with a yellow blotch. S.W. Burma, 6,000 ft. **UC/RN, rn, Maddenia "Ciliicalyx-Allinace".**

R. cuneatum (*wedge-shaped*) s. Lapponicum. 3', -10°F, EM, 3-4/3/2-3. This open upright growing dwarf shrub is the largest member of the Lapponicum series, with elliptic leaves to about 2" long. The tops are dark shiny green and scaly; the undersides are duller and uniformly covered with rusty brownish yellow scales. Flowers, to 1 1/2" long, are open funnel shaped, ranging in color from pink through rose-lavender, deep rose, or deep rosy purple, and are set in clusters of 3-6. The species that was known as *R. ravum* is now included here. Yunnan, Szechwan, 9,000-13,000 ft.**UC/RN, rn, Lapponica.**

R. cyanocarpum (*with blue fruits*) s. and s.s. Thomsonii. 5', 0°F, E-EM, 3/3/2. Medium sized foliage is almost round. The leaves are smooth and dark matte green on top, waxy greyish or grey-blue green on the undersides, with tiny hairs and glands. Flowers, to 2 1/3" long, funnel-bell-shaped, carried in a lax truss of 8-10 are white, white tinged pink, pink, or rose. The cup-like calyx is about 1/2" long. Yunnan, 10,000-13,500 ft. **UC/HY, hy, Thomsonia.**

R. dalhaousiae (*after Christina, Countess of Dalhousie, 1786-1839*) s. Maddenii s.s. Magacalyx. 5', 15°F, ML, 3-4/3/3-4. Large foliage is obovate or oblanceolate, smooth dark green on top, pale glaucous green underneath, with a heavy covering of very small, unequal scales. Slightly fragrant, tubular-campanulate, flowers to 4" long, with large calyx, are pale yellow fading to creamy white with a golden center, often lightly flushed pink. They are held in trusses of up to 5. E. Nepal, Sikkim, Bhutan, S.E. Tibet, 6,000-8,000 ft. **R. dalhousiae var. dalhousiae/RN, rn, Maddenia "Dalhousiae-Alliance".**

R. dasycladum (*with hairy boughs*) s. Thomsonii s.s. Selense. 5', 0°F, E-M, 3/2/-. Medium sized leaves are oblong or oblong-elliptic, smooth dark green on top side, paler with tiny scattered glands and hairs underneath. Tubular bell shaped flowers, to 1 1/2" long, held in trusses of 5-8, are rose, purple or white, sometimes blotched and spotted purple. Yunnan, S.E. Tibet, 10,000-14,000 ft. **R. selense ssp. dasycladum/HY, hy, Selensia.**

R. dasypetalum (*with hairy petals*) s. Lapponicum. 2', -5°F, EM, 3/2-3/3. Tiny leaves, often crowded at the ends of the branches, are elliptic or oblong-elliptic. They are dark green with paler scales on top, densely covered with brown scales underneath. Bright purplish rose 3/4" flowers, in paired trusses of 1-4, with short, soft hairs on the outside, are broadly funnel shaped. Yunnan, 11,500 ft. **UC/RN, rn, Lapponica.**

R. dauricum (*from Dauria, S.E. Siberia*) s. Dauricum. 4', -25°F, VE, 4/3/3. Growth habit is compact and upright on this semi-deciduous or evergreen shrub. (Some years involve more leaf loss than others.) It is an extremely hardy plant, native to Siberia. Leaves, to 1 1/2" long, are elliptic, with slightly scaly, shiny dark green tops and paler, densely scaly undersides. Brilliant rosy purple flowers, to about 3/4" long, are widely funnel shaped, held either singly or in pairs along branches between leaf clusters. N.C. to N.E. Asia, Japan. **UC/RN, rn, Rhodorastra.**

  album-- Pure white flowers with no marking.
  'Arctic Pearl'-- Opalescent white flowers.
  'Madison Snow'-- Profuse blooming white form.
  'Mid-Winter'-- Bright rose purple flowers, before the leaves.
  var. sempervirens-- Evergreen. **R. dauricum Sempervirens Group.**

R. davidsonianum (*after Dr. W. H. Davidson, Friends Mission in China*) s. Triflorum s.s. Yunnanense. 6', 0°F, EM, 4/3/3. Growth habit is upright and open, occasionally leggy or straggly. Lance shaped leaves, to 2 1/2" long, are slightly scaly and shiny dark green on top, dense with scales on the undersides. Flowers occur in trusses of 2-6, either on the ends of branches or along the branch between leaf clusters. They are widely funnel shaped, to 2" across. The color ranges from white blushed pink, to pink, pale rose, or light purplish rose, and are sometimes spotted red. Szechwan, Yunnan, 6,500-11,500 ft. **UC/RN, rn, Triflora Yunnanense agg.**

  Exbury form-- A very good deep pink form.
  'Ruth Lyons'-- The most sought after form. Excellent clear deep pink. This form has no lavender in the flower. Interesting in that it becomes a more intense pink the longer it is in flower. May be a polyploid.
  'Seranade'-- A lighter pink form with smaller leaves.

R. decorum (*ornamental*) s. and s.s. Fortunei. 5', 0°F, EM, 4/3/4. Growth habit of this beautiful species is compact and upright, and the flowering is exceptionally abundant and fragrant, even on young plants. Oblong leaves, to about 6" long, often cupped upward, are medium green and smooth on top, bluish green with a few tiny hairs underneath. Open funnel shaped flowers, to 3" long, are white, white tinged pink or green, shell pink or pearl pink, with or without spots, and are carried in lax trusses of 8-14. Very lovely. Different from *R. diaparepes* because of its smaller flowers and leaves, and it flowers slightly earlier. Yunnan, Szechwan, 8,000-11,000 ft. **UC/HY, hy, Fortunea.**

R. degronianum (*after M. Degron, Director of French Posts in Yokohama in 1869*) s. Ponticum s.s. Caucasicum. 3', -5ºF, E-EM, 3-4/3-4/3-4. Growth habit is very tight, compact and rounded, with dense foliage almost to the base of plant. Leaves, to 6" long, are oblong-lanceolate, deep glossy green and smooth on top, thick fawn to reddish brown felt underneath. Flowers, to 2 1/2" across, are funnel-bell-shaped, normally 5-lobed, soft pale pink to reddish pink or rose, occasionally with deep pink lines through middle of corolla lobes. They are carried in trusses of 10-12. Japan. **R. degronianum ssp. degronianum/HY, hy, Pontica.**

R. delavayi (*after L'Abbe' J. M. Delavay, 1838-1895, an early collector in China*) s. and s.s. Arboreum. 6', 5ºF, VE-EM, 3/3/3. Mature foliage is large and smooth, shiny dark green on top, covered with greyish, white or fawn indumentum, sometimes spongy, underneath. Bell shaped flowers to 2" long, are usually blood red, set in compact trusses of 10-20. Not specifically different from *R. arboreum*, and, by the new classification, is considered a subspecies of *R. arboreum*. Yunnan, Burma, Indochina, 6,000-10,000 ft. **R. arboreum ssp. delavayi/HY, hy, Arborea.**

R. dendricola (*dweller on trees*) s. Maddenii s.s. Ciliicalyx. 5', 20ºF, E-M, 3-4/2-3/3. Medium sized dull green leaves are elliptic or oblong-elliptic, smooth on top with a dense layer of reddish brown scales on the undersides. Flowers, to 3" long, are funnel-bell-shaped, in trusses of 2-4, white or white tinged pink in color, occasionally with an orange or greenish blotch. Burma. **UC/RN, rn, Maddenia "Ciliicalyx-Alliance" Johnstoneanum agg.**

R. desquamatum (*without scales*) s. Heliolepis. 6', -5ºF, E-EM, 3/3/3-4. This upright shrub has lance shaped leaves to 4" long, dull dark green above, brownish green underneath, scaly on both sides. Flowers, widely funnel shaped, to 1 1/2" long, are pink, pinkish purple, or light to deep mauve, with crimson spotting, and are held in trusses of 4-8. In the new classification, this is now considered to be the same as *R. rubiginosum*. Yunnan, Szechwan, Burma, S.E. Tibet, 10,000-14,000 ft. **R. rubiginosum Desquamatum Group/RN, rn, Heliolepida.**

R. detersile (*clean*) s. Taliense s.s. Adenogynum. 3', 5ºF?, E-M, 3/3/2-3. Small leaves, elliptic or oblanceolate, are somewhat shiny and smooth on top, with woolly, loose, and somewhat patchy indumentum underneath. Red flowers, to 1 1/2", are funnel-bell-shaped, set in trusses of up to 8. Szechwan, 7,000-8,000 ft. **UC/HY, hy, Taliensia.**

R. detonsum (*shorn*) s. Taliense s.s. Adenogynum. 4', 0ºF, E-M, 2-3/4/2-3. Medium large leaves, oblong or oblong-lanceolate, are smooth matte green, thinly layered on the undersides with tawny indumentum. Bell shaped flowers, to 2" long, held in trusses of about 10, are rosy pink or white tinged pink, with crimson spotting. Yunnan, 9,000-11,000 ft. **Hybrid of R. adenogynum.**

R. diacritum (*distinguished*) s. Lapponicum. 18", -5ºF?, E-M, 2/2/-. Tiny leaves are widely-elliptic or oval. Tops of the leaves are grey-green with dense paler scales; the undersides also have overlapping dense pale scales, as well as a few darker ones. Tiny flowers, with scaly external lobes, broadly funnel shaped, occurring either alone or in pairs, are deep rosy purple with a white throat. Yunnan, 13,000-15,000 ft. **Syn. R. telmateium/RN, rn, Lapponica.**

R. diaprepes (*distinguished*) s. and s.s. Fortunei. 6', 5ºF, L-VL, 3/3/4-5. Quite large, oblong leaves, slightly shiny, are light green and smooth on top, pale glaucous green with sparse tiny hairs underneath. Fragrant flowers of heavy substance, to 4", are open funnel-bell-shaped, white or white, faintly flushed rose, held in loose trusses of 7-10. Yunnan, S.E. Tibet, 9,000-11,000 ft. **UC/HY, hy, Fortunea.**
    'Gargantua'-- Considered a triploid and is very large growing.

R. dichroanthum (*with flowers of two colors*) s. Neriiflorum s.s. Sanguineum. 4', -5ºF, M-L, 3/3/3. Growth habit is open and spreading. Smooth, dark green, medium sized leaves have a thin layer of whitish or fawn indumentum underneath. Tubular-bell-shaped flowers of heavy substance, to 1 1/2", carried in trusses of 4-8, have nectar pouches and a large, fleshy calyx similar in color to flower. Color is variable, either orange apricot or orange flushed salmon rose. Yunnan, 9,000-12,000 ft. **R. dichroanthum ssp. dichroanthum/HY, hy, Neriiflora.**
    ssp. **apodectum**-- Differs in appearance of leaves, which have rounded bases and leathery texture. Ovary is eglandular and tomentose. Yunnan, 10,000-12,000 ft. **UC.**
    ssp. **herpesticum**-- Usually a dwarf shrub, with leaves more like *R. sanguineum* and glandular-bristly new growth. Ovary is glandular and tomentose. E. Upper Burma and Burma-Yunnan border, 12,000-13,000 ft. **ssp. scyphocalyx Herpesticum Group.**
    ssp. **scyphocalyx**-- Rather like ssp. *herpesticum*, except with larger, thinner textured leaves, the plant usually taller, with non-bristly shoots. Flower color is extremely variable. Ovary glandular and tomentose. N.E. Upper Burma and Yunnan, 10,000-13,000 ft. **UC.**
    ssp. **septentrionale**-- Leaves are closely similar to ssp. *herpesticum*, but ovary differs in being eglandular and tomentose. Flowers are yellow to yellow blushed rose. N.E. Upper Burma and Yunnan. 12,000-14,000 ft. **UC.**

R. dictyotum (*with net-veins*) s. Lacteum. 4', 0ºF, M, 3-4/3/2. Medium large foliage is oblong, oblanceolate, or oblong elliptic, smooth on top, thinly layered with a rusty brownish indumentum underneath. Bell shaped flowers, to 2" long, held in trusses of 8-15, are white or white blushed rose, sometimes with a crimson blotch and spotting. Yunnan, Szechwan. S.E. Tibet, 11,000-14,000 ft. **R. traillianum var. dictyotum/HY, hy, Taliensia.**
    'Kathmandu'-- White flowers have striking red blotch and spotting.

R. dilatatum (*spread out, referring to the flowers*) s. Azalea s.s. Schlippenbachii. 6', -5ºF, M-L, 3/3/3. Small leaves, in clusters of 2 or 3 at the branch ends, are diamond shaped oval, dotted with glands, smooth and slightly hairy on top, smooth on the reverse. Purple or white flowers, to 2 1/2" wide, in trusses of 1-3, are broadly funnel shaped, opening ahead of the leaves. Japan. **NR/TT, br, syn. R. reticulatum.**

R. dimitrum (*with a double cap, alluding to the large calyx*) s. and s.s. Irroratum. 4', 5ºF, E-EM, 2/2/3. Medium sized leaves, oblong or oblong-lanceolate, are nearly smooth and pale matte green on top, smooth yellowish green on the reverse. Tubular bell shaped flowers, to 1 1/2" long, with a calyx of almost 1/2" (unusually large for the Series), are deep rose with crimson spotting, and are held in trusses of 10-12. Yunnan, 10,000 ft. **UC/Unplaced.**

R. diphrocalyx (*with a wide, flat calyx*) s. Barbatum s.s. Glischrum. 5', 5ºF, E-EM, 2/2-3/2-3. Foliage is large, oblong-oval or obovate, dark green on top, smooth except in midrib groove. The underside is pale, waxy grey or bluish green, either smooth or very slightly hairy. Widely tubular bell shaped flowers, about 1 1/2" long, have a large calyx colored as the corolla, and are set in trusses of 10-20. Flower color is crimson or rose crimson, blotched and spotted crimson. Yunnan, 10,000-11,000 ft. **UC/HY, hy, Neriiflora.**

R. discolor (*of various colors*) s. and s.s. Fortunei. 6', -5ºF, VL, 3/3/3-4. Growth habit is open and upright, with large oblong-lanceolate or lanceolate leaves, smooth dark green on top, smooth and pale on the reverse. Fragrant flowers, to 3 1/2" long, funnel shaped, held in trusses of 8-10, range from white to pink. Szechwan, Hupeh, 4,000-7,000 ft. **R. fortunei ssp. discolor/HY, hy, Fortunea.**

R. doshongense (*from the Doshong La, S.E. Tibet*) s. and s.s. Taliense. 3', -5ºF, E-M, 2/3/2-3. Medium sized leaves are obovate, oblong-lanceolate, or oblong-oval. The tops have a thin layer of white interrupted indumentum; the reverse sides have a thinnish covering of silvery or fawn colored indumentum, somewhat stuck together. Bell shaped flowers, to 1 1/2" long, set in trusses of 10-15, are white tinged pink or pink, spotted dark purple. S.E. Tibet, 12,000-13,000 ft. **Syn. R. aganniphum var. aganniphum/HY, hy, Taliensia.**

R. drumonium (*of woods*) s. Lapponicum. 12", -10°F, EM, 3/3-4/3. Oval leaves are tiny, only 1/3" x 1/10", both sides are very scaly, the underside a rich brown. Flowers, blooming either alone or in pairs, vibrant deep rosy purple, are wide funnel form, to about 1/2" long. Yunnan, 10,000-12,000 ft. **Syn. R. telmateium/RN, rn.**

R. dryophyllum (*with oak-like leaves*) s. Lacteum. 5', -5°F, E-M, 2/3/2. Medium large foliage is oblong, oblong-lanceolate, or lanceolate, shiny and nearly smooth on top, layered with a thin coating of brown or fawn indumentum underneath. Flowers, to 2" long, set in trusses of 8-16, are funnel bell shaped or bell shaped, and range from white to creamy white, white blushed rose, to pink or pinkish purple, occasionally with crimson spotting. Yunnan, Szechwan, S.E. Tibet, Bhutan, Burma, 11,000-14,000 ft. **R. phaeochrysum var. phaeochrysum/HY, hy, Taliensia.**

R. dumicola (*dweller in thickets*) s. Taliense s.s. Adenogynum. 2-3', 0°F?, E-M, 2/2/2-3. Medium sized foliage is oblong-elliptic, the underside thinly covered with a tan felt. Bell shaped flowers, to 1 1/2", white, blushed rosy pink, blotched faintly crimson, with a large, leafy calyx, are held in trusses of 5-7. Yunnan, 14,000 ft. **UC/HY, hy, Taliensia.**

R. dumosulum (*small and bushy*) s. Lacteum. 2-3', 0°F?, E-M, 2/2/2. Medium sized oblong or lanceolate foliage is dark green, thinly layered with rusty or brown indumentum underside. Flowers are bell shaped, sometimes tubular-bell-shaped, to 1 3/4" long, in trusses of 7-8, white, with faint rose flushing and spotted crimson. Yunnan, Szechwan, 13,000 ft. More dwarf, with smaller leaves than *R. dryophyllum.* **Syn. R. phaeochrysum var. agglutinatum/HY, hy, Taliensia.**

R. eclecteum (*picked out*) s. and s.s. Thomsonii. 3', 0°F, E, 2-3/3-4/2. Foliage on this plant is very interesting. Medium large, rounded or oblong-obovate leaves are glaucous, bright green under the waxy coating on the tops and pale green and smooth on the undersides. Flowers, to 2" long, of heavy substance, are tubular-bell-shaped, set in upright trusses of up to 12. Color varies widely from white through yellow, pink, rose or darker rose, sometimes with crimson spotting. Yunnan, Szechwan, S.E. Tibet, 10,000-14,000 ft. **R. eclecteum var. eclecteum/HY, hy, Thomsonia.**

R. edgarianum (*after Rev. J. H. Edgar, of the China Inland Mission*) s. Lapponicum. 3', -5°F, M-L, 3/3/3. Tiny leaves, broadly elliptic or oblong-elliptic, are beautiful. Topside of the foliage is covered with dense golden yellow shiny scales; underside is covered with dark reddish brown shiny scales. Funnel shaped flowers, equally tiny, to 1/2", in trusses of 1-3, are a superb bluish purple, with no outside scales. Now considered to be a natural hybrid of *R. nivale* subsp. *boreale.* Szechwan, Yunnan, S.E. Tibet, 12,000-15,000 ft. **Hybrid of R. nivale.**

R. edgeworthii (*after M. P. Edgeworth, 1812-1881, Bengal Civil Service*) s. Edgeworthii. 4', 15°F, E-EM, 4/4/3. Growth habit is open, with interesting foliage which has a swollen, puckered look. Medium large leaves can be elliptic, ovate-elliptic, or oblong-lanceolate, and are dark shiny green with heavily indumented undersides. Widely funnel shaped flowers, to 4 1/2" long, set in trusses of 2-3, are fragrant and vary in color from white through pale pink or pink, blushed deep red outside. Sikkim, Bhutan, S.E. Tibet, N.E. Upper Burma, Yunnan, 6,000-13,000 ft. **UC/RN, rn, Edgeworthia.**

R. elegantulum (*elegant*) s. Taliense s.s. Adenogynum. 4', 0°F, M, 3/5/3. Medium sized leaves, oblong-elliptic to oblong-lanceolate, are nearly smooth light green on top, with a somewhat woolly and dense covering of brownish red indumentum underneath. Flowers, to 1" long, funnel-bell-shaped, are pale purple pink, spotted darker, held in trusses of 10-20. This has the most attractive cinnamon indumentum in the genus. Szechwan, 12,000-13,000 ft. **UC/HY, hy, Taliensia.**

R. elliottii (*after Mr. Elliott, a friend of its discoverer, Sir George Watt*) s. Irroratum s.s. Parishii. 5', 15°F, ML, 4/2-3/3. Growth habit is upright and open. Rather large, oval leaves are elliptic-oblong or oblong, smooth shiny dark green on the tops, paler and usually glabrous underneath. Flowers, open funnel shaped or bellshaped, to about 2", held in trusses of 10, are scarlet or crimson, spotted darker. Manipur, 9,000 ft. **UC/HY, hy, Parishia.**

R. ellipticum (*elliptic*) s. Stamineum. 5', 5°F, E-EM, 3-4/2-3/3. Leaves, to almost 5" long, are oblong-lanceolate, with smooth dark glossy green tops, paler on the reverse. Flowers, to 2 1/2" long, funnel-bell-shaped, are pink to pale rose, appearing in trusses of 2-3 along branches between leaf clusters. Luikui to Fukien, including Formosa, 500-9,000 ft. **UC/AZ, ch.**

R. erosum (*eaten away*) s. Barbatum s.s. Glischrum. 5', 5°F, E-EM, 3/3-4/3. Medium large foliage can be oval, oblong-oval or obovate, somewhat glabrous olive green, with a covering of fawn-colored indumentum underneath, which tends to flake off. Flowers are funnel-bell-shaped, to 1 1/2" long, set in trusses of 12-15, deep rose pink or deep crimson. Similar to *R. barbatum*, but has more rounded leaves. S.E. Tibet, 10,000-12,000 ft. **UC/HY, hy, Barbata.**

R. erubescens (*blushing*) s. Fortunei s.s. Oreodoxa. 5', -5°F, E-EM, 3/3/3. Foliage is dark matte green, fairly large, either oblong-elliptic or oblong-lanceolate. Topside is glabrous, with paler green, very lightly hairy underside. Widely bell shaped flowers, to 2" long, pink to rose, are set in trusses of up to 8. Similar to *R. fargesii* but has larger leaves and hairy filaments. Szechwan, 12,000 ft. **Syn R. oreodoxa var. fargesii/HY, hy, Fortunea.**

R. erythrocalyx (*with a red calyx*) s. Thomsonii s.s. Selense. 4', -5°F, E-M, 2/2-3/2. Medium sized leaves are elliptic, oblong-elliptic, or ovate. The tops are matte olive green with traces of glands and hairs, the undersides paler green with tiny hairs. Flowers, to 2", are bell shaped and tubular, carried in trusses of 4-10, with a reddish calyx. Color ranges from white through white tinged pink and pink, sometimes spotted crimson, either with or without crimson blotch. Very similar to *R. selense*, but the leaves are generally larger. S.E. Tibet, Yunnan, 11,000-13,000 ft. **R. x erythrocalyx/HY, hy, Selensia.**

R. esetulosum (*hairless*) s. Thomsonii s.s. Selense. 3', 0°F, E-M, 2/3/2-3. Foliage is of medium size, oblong, elliptic, or oblong-elliptic, smooth dark green with a paler, thinly indumented underside. Bell shaped flowers, to 2", held in trusses of 8-10, can be creamy white, white blushed rose, or purplish, occasionally crimson spotted. Yunnan, S.E. Tibet, 10,000-14,000 ft. **UC/HY, hw, Selensia.**

R. eudoxum (*of good report*) s. Neriiflorum s.s. Sanguineum. 30", 0°F, E-ML, 3/3/3. Branches on this shrub are inclined to be rather thin and twiggy. Oval leaves, to 3" long, are smooth matte green on top, with a thin, grainy indumentum underneath. Bell shaped or tubular-bell-shaped flowers, to 1 1/2" long, sometimes partially hidden among the leaves, range in color from white tinged rose to rose to deep clear crimson-rose to pink or magenta-rose. The blooms are held in trusses of 3-6. Yunnan, S.E. Tibet, North East Frontier Agency, 11,000-14,000 ft. **R. eudoxum var. eudoxum/HY, hy, Neriiflora.**
    ssp. brunneifolium-- Has a non glandular ovary and usually more indumentum. 11,000-12,000 ft. **R. eudoxum var. brunneifolium.**

R. eurysiphon (*with a broad tube*) s. Thomsonii s.s. Selense. 4', 0°F?, M, 2/2-3/2-3. Growth habit is very attractive, whether blooming or not. Foliage is of medium size, oblong or oblong-elliptic, smooth dark green on the top, paler galucous green and minutely dotted with glands on the underside. Bell shaped blooms, to 1 3/4", held in 3-5 flower trusses, are white or creamy white, blushed wine red, liberally spotted with crimson, S.E. Tibet, 13,000 ft. **UC/HY, hy, Thomsonia.**

R. exasperatum (*rough*) s. and s.s. Barbatum. 5', 5ºF, E-M, 2/3-4/2-3. Large leaves are ovate or obovate, dark green on top, paler green and glandular-bristly on the reverse. Bell shaped flowers, to 1 3/4", are shades of scarlet and red, set in compact trusses of 10-12. Assam, S.E. Tibet, 9,500-12,000 ft. **UC/HY, hy, Barbata.**

R. eximium (*excellent*) s. Falconeri. 4', 5ºF, EM, 3/3/2-3. Growth habit is open and tree-like, with an eventual size of 30'. Very large leaves are oval, obovate or obovate elliptic. Leaf tops, at least for the first year, are covered with a fluffy brownished indumentum. The undersides are densely covered with rusty colored indumentum. Bell shaped flowers, to 2 1/2", held in huge trusses of 12-25, are fleshy, rose or pink, sometimes blotched. Similar to *R. falconeri* but has indumentum that tends to stay on the upper surface of the leaves. Bhutan, 10,000-11,000 ft. **R. falconeri ssp. eximium/HY, hy, Falconera.**

R. faberi (*after Rev. E. Faber, who collected in China, 1887-1891*) s. Taliense s.s. Adenogynum. 5', 5F?, M, 2/2-3/-. Oblong-oval leaves are medium large and nearly smooth on top, indumented buff to rusty brown underneath. 1 1/2" long bell shaped flowers, white, occasionally spotted crimson, are held in trusses of about 10. Szechwan. **R. faberi ssp. faberi/HY, hy, Taliensia.**

R. facetum (*elegant*) s. Irroratum s.s. Parishii. 5', 5ºF, L-VL, 3-4/3/3. Large leaves, oblong-elliptic, oblong-lanceolate, or elliptic-lanceolate, are glabrous matte green on top, glabrous and shiny underneath. Lovely scarlet or crimson flowers, with deep purple nectar pouches, are bell shaped or tubular-bell-shaped, to 2 1/2" long, and are set in trusses of 8-16. Yunnan, Burma, 8,000-11,000 ft. **UC/HY, hy, Parishia.**

R. falconeri (*after H. Falconer, 1808-1865, Supt., Saharanpur Gardens, India, in 1832*) s. Falconeri. 5', 10ºF, E-M, 3/3/2-3. This plant, with handsome red-brown flaking bark, can grow to 40-50'. Matte green wrinkled foliage is huge, sometimes to 12" x 10", layered with rusty brown indumentum on the underside. Large tight trusses hold 20-25 blooms, each to 2 1/2" long. Flowers are a swollen-bell shape, and range from white or creamy white to pale or deep yellow, occasionally to pink, with a purple blotch. Sikkim, Nepal to Bhutan, 8,000-11,000 ft. **R. falconeri ssp. falconeri/HY, hy, Falconera.**

R. fargesii (*after Pere Farges, 1844-1912, French Foreign Missions in N.W. Szechwan*) s. Fortunei s.s. Oreodoxa. 5', -10ºF, E, 3/3/3. Growth habit is open and upright on this hardy, early flowering, rarely seen species. Elliptic to oblong leaves, to 3" long, are dark green on top, paler with a waxy, blue-green cast underneath. Tubular bell shaped flowers, to 2" long, range in color from white or pink to rose or rosy lilac, sometimes purplish spotted. This is a heavy bloomer, and fairly easy to grow; however, old flowers should be removed, as a heavy seed crop could severely damage the plant. Similar to *R. oreodoxa* but has a densely glandular ovary. Hupeh, Szechwan, Yunnan, 7,000-13,000 ft. **R. oreodoxa, var. fargesii/HY, hy, Fortunea.**

R. farrerae (*after the wife of Capt. Farrer, East India Co., 1829*) s. Azalea s.s. Schlippenbachii. 2', 15ºF?, L, 2/2/2-3. Shrub is deciduous or semi-evergreen, with foliage usually set in clusters of 3 at branch ends. Ovate leaves are small, dark green on top with paler undersides, usually smooth on both sides. Flowers, occurring either singly or in pairs, open ahead of the leaves and are flat-funnel-shape, light to deep rose, spotted red-purple. E. China. **UC/TT, br.**

R. fastigiatum (*erect*) s. Lapponicum. 18", -15ºF, M, 4/4/3-4. The best forms of this species refute an upright growth habit, from which the species name is derived. They are dense, low growing plants that can be counted among the finest of all the scaly leaved rhododendrons. The leaves are elliptic or oblong. The flowers are a superb lilac purple on top of the shiny dark green foliage. This is one of the hardiest and most useful of the small alpine type rhododendrons. Yunnan, 11,000-16,000 ft. **UC/RN, rn, Lapponica.**

R. faucium (*of the gorges*) s. and s.s. Thomsonii. 5'?, 10ºF?, M, -/-/-. Medium sized leaves are oblanceolate, with smooth tops, stalkless glands on the reverse. Flowers with nectar pouches are bell shaped, to 1 3/4", held in trusses of 5-10, pale rose or white blushed rose, more rarely sulphur yellow with purple spots. S. Tibet (Tsangpo Gorge and neighboring area), 9,000 ft. **UC/HY, hy, Thomsonia.**

R. fauriei (*after Pere L. F. Faurie, French Foreign Missions, China*) s. Ponticum s.s. Caucasicum. 3', -10ºF, L-VL, 3/3/3. A dense plant of good substance with white, young shoots. Leaves, up to 5" long, are obovate or oblong-obovate, glabrous above and below. Funnel-campanulate flowers, in trusses up to 15, are yellowish or white flushed pink. Japan. **R. brachycarpum ssp. fauriei/HY, hy, Pontica.**

　　var. **nemotoanum**-- Ruffled lobed flowers of white with pink margins have protruding stamens.

R. ferrugineum (*rust-colored*) s. Ferrugineum. 2', -15ºF, M. 3/4/3. This species is known as the Alpine Rose of Switzerland. Foliage is unique and very attractive. Leaves, to 1 1/2" long, twist slightly. The tops are dark glossy green; the undersides have dense rusty brown scales. Flowers, only 3/4" long, are tubular with spreading lobes, dusty rose, rose-crimson, pink or white, held in trusses of 6-8. Will stand some sun, but needs perfect drainage. Alps of S. Europe from Pyrenees to Austrian Alps. **UC/RN, rn, Rhododendron.**

R. fictolacteum (*false R. lacteum*) s. Falconeri. 5', -5ºF, E-M, 3/4/3. Upright growing tree-like shrub with quite large leaves. Foliage is oblong-obovate or oblanceolate, smooth, dark shiny green on top, covered with a rich rusty or brown indumentum. Bell shaped flowers, to 2" long, in tight trusses of 12-20, range from cream to white to white tinged pink or rose, blotched dark crimson, sometimes heavily spotted. Yunnan, Szechwan, S.E. Tibet, 10,000-13,000 ft. **R. rex ssp. fictolacteum/HY, hy, Falconera.**

R. fimbriatum (*minutely fringed*) s. Lapponicum. 3', -15ºF, E-EM, 3/3/4. The new growth on this plant is yellow-green and somewhat scaly. Small lance shaped leaves are light green on top with shining silvery scales, paler and scaly with a waxy blue-green coating. Bell shaped funnel form flowers, to only 1/2" long, are a rich purple mauve, set in trusses of up to 8 blooms. **R. hippophaeoides var. hippophaeoides Fimbriatum Group/RN, rn, Lapponica.**

R. flammeum (*flame-colored*) s. Azalea s.s. Luteum. 3', -15ºF, ML-L, 3/3/3. Small leaves are ovate, elliptic or oblong, layered on top with stiff flat hairs closely set, on the undersides with short soft hairs. Tubular-funnel-shaped flowers, to 2" wide, open with the leaves, into trusses of 6-15. Color ranges from scarlet through bright red to orange or apricot, with an occasional orange blotch. E. North America. **UC/PE, pe.**

R. flavantherum (*yellow-flowered*) s. and s.s. Triflorum. 5', 5ºF?, ?, -/-/-. Small oblong-elliptic foliage is waxy grey or bluish, the underside unequally scaled. Clear yellow flowers, equally small, to 3/4", are tubular-campanulate, set in trusses of 3. May not be in cultivation. Tibet, 8,000-9,000 ft. **UC/RN, rn, Monantha.**

R. flavidum (*yellowish*) s. Lapponicum. 2', -10ºF, EM, 4/2/2-3. Growth habit of this small shrub is open and upright, with many branches. Leaves, to 1" long, are widely elliptic or oblong, bright dark green and rather scaly on top, paler grey-green to waxy blue-green below with brownish scales. Widely funnel shaped flowers, to about 1/2" long, are pale to bright yellow, held in trusses of 3-5. Great for the dwarf garden. Szechwan, 9,800-13,100 ft. **R. flavidum var. flavidum/RN, rn, Lapponica.**

　　var. **psilostylum**-- Has wider leaves; the scales are a mixture of dark and shining gold; also, the calyx is smaller. **R. flavidum var. psilostylum.**

R. flavorufum (*yellow-red*) *s.* and *s.s.* Taliense. 6', 0ºF?, E-M, -/-/-. Foliage is medium large, oblong-oval, elliptic, or oval, and is somewhat shiny and nearly smooth on top. The underside begins with a continuous light yellow indumentum which later becomes patchy and reddish. Flowers, to 1 1/2", are bell shaped, carried in trusses of 8 to 10, white or rose with sparse crimson spotting. Yunnan, 11,000-14,000 ft. **R. agapetum var. flavorufum/HY, hy, Taliensia.**

R. fletcheranum (*after H. R. Fletcher, 1907-1978, a former Regius Keeper, Royal Botanic Garden, Edinburgh*) *s.* Maddenii *s.s.* Ciliicalyx. 30", 5ºF, EM, 4/4/4. While this species is a member of the Maddenii Series, it is not tender like most of the other members. It may even deserve a hardier rating than 5ºF. The foliage is bristly and hairy, as are the branches. The leaves are 1 1/2" to 2" long and 1" broad, and turn deep attractive bronze in winter. The flowers are showy bright lemon yellow. Tibet, 13,000-14,000 ft. **UC/RN, rn, Maddenia "Ciliicalyx-Alliance".**

R. flinkii *s.s* Lanata. 5', -5ºF, EM, -/-/-. A relative of *R. lanatum*, this plant has recently been reinstated as a species. Foliage has orangy brown indumentum on both leaf surfaces, gradually becoming smooth above. Flowers are creamy yellow, tending toward light rose, on this tall growing plant. **UC/HY, hy, Lanta.**

R. floccigerum (*bearing flocks of wool*) *s.* and *s.s.* Neriiflorum. 3', 0ºF, E-M, 3/3-4/2. Growth habit is low and rounded, with medium large, smooth, dark dull green oblong-lanceolate leaves. The underleaf has uneven, brownish red indumentum which may flake off irregularly to reveal a waxy grey or bluish lower surface. Tubular-bell-shaped flowers, to 1 1/2", have good heavy substance, and are held in loose trusses of 4-8. Color is crimson, rose, or yellow edged crimson, with deep crimson nectar pouches. Yunnan, S.E. Tibet, 9,000-13,000 ft. **R. floccigerum ssp. floccigerum/HY, hy, Neriiflora.**
  var. **appropinquans**-- Lower surface of the leaves is glabrous. **R. floccigerum ssp. appropinquans.**

R. floribundum (*free-flowering*) *s.* Arboreum *s.s.* Argyrophyllum. 6', 5ºF?, E-M, 3/3/3. This shrub grows tall and well-branched, with lance shaped leaves to 8" long. The tops are dark dull green, rather puffy and wrinkled. The reverse carries a dense whitish indumentum. Widely bell shaped flowers, to 1 1/2" long, are rose, pink, or purplish lavender, blotched and spotted with dark crimson, are held in trusses of 8-12. Szechwan, 4,000-8,000 ft. **UC/HY, hy, Argyrophylla.**

R. formosanum (*from Formosa*) *s.* Arboreum *s.s.* Argyrophyllum. 5', 5ºF?, EM?, 3/3/3. Medium large and narrow leaves are smooth on top with a pale greyish or fawn colored indumentum underneath. Widely funnel shaped flowers, to 1 1/2", white or pink with purplish-brown spotting, are set in trusses of 10-20. Formosa, 4,000-6,000 ft. **UC/HY, hy, Argyrophylla.**

R. formosanum

R. formosum (*beautiful*) *s.* Maddenii *s.s.* Ciliicalyx. 4', 15ºF, ML, 4/3/4-5. Growth habit is rather loose and straggly, with very bristly and hairy young branches. Lance shaped leaves, to 3" long, are very hairy, shiny green on top, waxy bluish green and scaly underneath. Scented flowers, to 2 1/2" long, widely funnel shaped, are white, sometimes tinged rose or yellow in the throat, often with outside rose red stripes, and are held in trusses of 2-3. Assam, 5,000-5,500 ft. **R. formosum var. formosum/RN, rn, Maddenia "Ciliicalyx-Alliance".**

R. forrestii (*after George Forrest, 1873-1932*) *s.* Neriiflorum *s.s.* Forrestii. 6"-2', 0ºF, EM, 3/4/3. Growth habit is prostrate, spreading, very slow growing. Dark shiny green leaves are quite rounded in shape, with slightly puffy and wrinkled tops, purplish undersides. Tubular bell shaped flowers, rather fleshy, to 1 1/2" long, are bright scarlet or crimson, borne singly or in pairs. S.E. Tibet, Yunnan, Burma, 11,000-15,000 ft. **R. forrestii ssp. forrestii/HY, hy, Neriiflora.**
  var. **repens**-- Leaves are pale or glaucous green below. **R. forrestii ssp. forrestii Repens Group.**
    Exbury-- A selection from the Exbury Estate in England. Good form.
    KW 6832-- Collected by Kingdon Ward in 1926 in Burma and Assam. Bright red.
    Robbins free flowering form-- This is a very free-flowering form, given enough light exposure. One of the best forms.
    Rock form-- Grown by Dr. Carl Phetteplace out of seed collected by Dr. Rock's expedition 30 years ago. Foliage has slight tomentum, and its limbs are more stiff and upright than some forms. Still grows only about 6" tall and makes a tight, little bush. A very handsome foliage plant.
    'Scarlet Runner'-- The fastest growing form.
    Sunningdale form-- More tomentum than other forms.
  var. **tumescens**-- Differs in its dome-shaped habit and often in larger leaves and flowers. This variety has light tomentum on the upper surface of the leaves. Red flowers. **Close to R. forrestii ssp. papillatum.**

R. fortunei (*after R. Fortune, 1812-1880, collector in China*) *s.* and *s.s.* Fortunei. 6', -15ºF, M, 4/4/4-5. Growth habit is open, upright, and tree-like. Large leaves, to as much as 8" long, are oval to oblong-elliptic. The tops are dark matte green, undersides are paler. Hardiness <u>and</u> beauty all in one plant! The deliciously fragrant flowers, often more than 4" in diameter, are blush pink fading to white. This species must be included among the finest in the Genus Rhododendron. It has attractive form and foliage, is largely pest-free, and grows with great zest and vigor. The flowers are beautifully formed, falling and brimming over the entire plant, making a springtime display that is unequaled. *R. fortunei* is an exceptional plant, an aristocrat enjoying well earned popularity and a reputation for excellence, great beauty, and extreme hardiness. Chekiang (E. China), 3,000 ft. **R. fortunei ssp. fortunei/HY, hy, Fortunea.**

R. fragariiflorum (*with strawberry colored flowers*) *s.* Saluenense. 1', -5ºF, M-L, 3/3/3. Very small, aromatic foliage is elliptic-obovate. Leaves are shiny dark olive green with golden scales; scales are more scattered on the undersides. Slightly scented flowers, also small, to 3/4", either broadly-funnel or saucer shaped, carried in trusses of 2-6, are purplish crimson or pinkish strawberry. S.E. Tibet, Bhutan, N. North East Frontier Agency, 13,000-15,000 ft. **UC/RN, rn, Fragariiflora.**

R. fulgens (*shining*) *s.* Campanulatum. 4', 5ºF, E-EM, 3/4/2. Growth habit is very compact, spreading and mounding. Medium sized, oval to oblong leaves are smooth and dark shiny green on top, paler green with a heavy layer of reddish brown felt underneath. Beautiful! Tubular bell shaped flowers, to 2", held in tight trusses of 10-15, are scarlet-crimson with large, very dark nectar pouches. Nepal, Sikkim, Bhutan, Assam, Tibet, 11,000-15,000 ft. **UC/HY, hy, Fulgensia.**

R. fulvastrum (*somewhat tawny*) *s.* Neriiflorum *s.s.* Sanguineum. 3', 0ºF, M, 3/3/3. Small oblong or oblong-oval leaves are smooth on top with thin mesh-like indumentum underneath. Bell shaped flowers, to 1 1/2", with light substance, set in trusses of 3-6, are creamy yellow or pale lemon. S.E. Tibet, 12,000-14,000 ft. **Close to R. sanguineum ssp. himertum/HY, hy, Neriiflora.**
  Ssp. **trichomiscum**-- Distinguished because of its bristly stems. Flowers are pale rose pink. S.E. Tibet, Yunnan, 11,000-12,000 ft. **Syn. R. eudoxum var. eudoxum.**

R. fulvum (*tawny*) s. Fulvum. 4', 0ºF, EM, 3/5/2-3. Growth habit is open, upright, tree-like, with spectacular foliage. Leaves, up to 10" long, are obovate to oblanceolate and smooth shiny dark green on topside. Its fawn to bright cinnamon underside is the most fabulous indumentum of any rhododendron. Flowers, to 2" long, are open funnel shaped, white blushed rose to deep rose, occasionally blotched and spotted crimson and are held in great loose rounded trusses of up to 20. This is a special species, not seen in many gardens. Yunnan, Szechwan, Burma, Assam, S.E. Tibet, 8,000-14,500 ft. **UC/HY, hy, Fulva.**

R. fumidum (*smoke-colored*) s. Heliolepis. 4', 0ºF, L, 3/3/3. Foliage is medium sized, oblong or ovate oblong, dark green, the underside brownish and scaly. Bell shaped, lilac flowers, to 1", are held in trusses of 5-7. Yunnan, Szechwan, 10,000-12,000 ft. **Syn. R. heliolepis var. heliolepis/RN, rn, Heliolepida.**

R. galactinum (*milky*) s. Falconeri. 4', 5ºF, E-M, 2/3/-. Growth habit is open. Smooth, dark green leaves have dense, velvety pale grey or whitish indumentum on the undersides. Bell shaped flowers, 1 1/2" long, held in tight trusses of many flowers, are white to pale rose, blotched crimson. Szechwan, 9,000-10,000 ft. **UC/HY, hy, Falconera.**

R. genestieranum (*after Pere A. Genestier, b. 1858, of French Roman Catholic Tibetan Mission, friend of George Forrest*) s. Glaucophyllum s.s. Genestieranum. 3', 10ºF, E-M, 2/2/3. Foliage is medium sized, generally four times as long as wide, smooth bright green, very glaucous with scattered scales underneath. Tubular-bell-shaped flowers, only 1/2" long. in trusses of about 12, are brownish plum purple, covered with a glaucous bloom. Yunnan, S.E. Tibet, Upper Burma, 8,000-14,500 ft. **UC/RN, rn, Genestierana.**

R. giganteum (*gigantic*) s. Grande. 5', 15ºF, E-EM, 3-4/4/2-3. This plant eventually grows to an 80' tree in the wild. Spectacular! Leaves are enormous, to 16" x 8", elliptic or oblong-elliptic, glabrous dark matte green, with thin greyish fawn indumentum underneath. Tubular-campanulate flowers, to 2 3/4", carried in large trusses of 25 or more, are lovely rose crimson with crimson blotch and nectar pouches. Yunnan, 9,000-11,000 ft. **R. protistum var. giganteum/HY, hy, Grandia.**

R. glaucopeplum (*with a greyish covering*) s. and s.s.Taliense. 3', 0ºF?, E-M, - /-/-. Medium sized oblong-oval or oval leaves are smooth olive green with white to grey or fawn indumentum on the undersides. Bell shaped flowers, to 1 1/2" long, set in trusses of about 10, are bright rose, spotted crimson. Yunnan, 11,000 ft. **R. aganniphum var. aganniphum/HY, hy, Taliensia.**

R. glaucophyllum (*with a bluish grey leaf*) s. and s.s. Glaucophyllum. 3', 0ºF, EM, 3/2/3. This is a dwarf shrub with open upright habit. Aromatic leaves, to about 3" long, are lanceolate to elliptic-lanceolate, dark dullish green on top, white with a waxy bluish green cast and slightly scaly underneath. Bell shaped flowers, to 1" long, are white, pink or rose-pink to pinkish purple, and have a large leafy calyx. The blooms are carried in loose rounded trusses of up to 10. E. Nepal, Sikkim, Bhutan, S.E. Tibet, North East Frontier Agency, 9,000-12,000 ft. **R. glaucophyllum var. glaucophyllum/RN, rn, Glauca.**

   var. tubiforme-- Has a tubular flower. **R. glaucophyllum var. tubiforme.**

R. glischroides (*resembling R. glischrum*) s. Barbatum s.s. Glischrum. 4', -5ºF, EM-M, 2/3/2-3. Plant habit is open upright shrub. Large narrow leaves are dark green, glabrous and puckered, the reverse side densely hairy. Bell shaped flowers, to 2", held in loose trusses of up to 10, are white, creamy white or deep rose, blotched crimson. Quite similar to *R. glischrum*, but for the puffy and wrinkled upper leaf surface. N.E. Burma, 10,000-11,000 ft. **R. glischrum ssp. glischroides/HY, hy, Glischra.**

   var. arachnoideum-- The underside of the leaf is layered with a network of cobweb-like white hairs. **No longer recognized.**

R. glischrum (*sticky*) s. Barbatum s.s. Glischrum. 5', -5ºF, EM-M, 2-3/3-4/3. Growth habit tends to be open and leggy. Large, oblanceolate leaves are glabrous greyish green on top, paler and hairy on the reverse. Bell shaped flowers, to 1 1/2", set in trusses of 10-15, are pink, white or deep plum rose, blotched and spotted crimson. Yunnan, Upper Burma, S.E. Tibet, 13,000-14,000 ft. **R. glischrum ssp. glischrum/HY, hy, Glischra.**

R. globigerum (*bearing a globe*) s. Taliense s.s. Roxieanum. 2', -5ºF, E-M, 3/5/3. Habit is small, bushy and attractive, but plant tends to be slow to bloom. Medium sized leaves are obovate or oblong-lanceolate, nearly glabrous dark green, covered with dark brown indumentum on the undersides. Bell shaped flowers, to 1 1/2", set in tight trusses of 12-15, are white or white tinged pink, spotted crimson. Szechwan, 11,000-12,000 ft. **Syn. R. alutaceum var. alutaceum/HY, hy, Taliensia.**

R. glomerulatum (*with small clusters*) s. Lapponicum. 3', -15ºF, E-M, 4/4/3. Leaves on this little shrub are small, to only 3/4" long, ovate, ovate-elliptic, or oblong-elliptic, densely scaly on both sides. Pale lilac flowers also are very small, just a bit more than 1/2" long, wide funnel form, set in trusses of 4-6. Yunnan. **Syn. R. yungningense/RN, rn, Lapponica.**

R. grande (*large*) s. Grande. 5', 15ºF, VE-EM, 4/3/3. This plant can grow to a 30' tree in time. Very large foliage is oblong-elliptic, oblong-lanceolate, or oblanceolate, glabrous greyish green with silvery indumentum underneath. Three inch bell shaped flowers, appearing in rounded trusses of 20-30 blooms, are pale rose, creamy yellow or white, blotched purple in the nectar pouches. Nepal, Sikkim, Bhutan, 7,500-10,000 ft. **UC/HY, hy, Grandia.**

R. griersonianum (*after R. C. Grierson, Chinese Maritime Customs at Tengyueh, friend of George Forrest*) s. Griersonianum. 3', 10ºF, L, 3/3/4. This is the species that has produced so many great hybrids. Narrow, lance shaped leaves, to 8" long, are dull matte green on the tops with whitish loose woolly indumentum underneath. The flowers, to 3" long, tapered and conical, held in loose trusses of up to 12, are an unusual shade of geranium scarlet, quite unlike any other species. Plant seems to become hardier with age. Yunnan, N. Burma, 7,000-9,000 ft. **UC/HY, hy, Griersoniana.**

R. griffithianum (*after W. Griffith, 1810-1845, a former Supt., Calcutta Botanic Garden*) s. Fortunei s.s. Griffithianum. 6', 15ºF, M, 4/3/3. Growth habit is upright and open, with beautiful, peeling, reddish brown bark; this plant can grow to 20'. Light green foliage is large and oblong, and slightly glaucous and glabrous on the underside. Bell shaped, fragrant flowers, to 3", have 3/4" saucer shaped green or tinged pink calyx. White or white tinged pink, occasionally spotted green, they are held in trusses of 4-5. Sikkim, Bhutan, 7,000-9,000 ft. **UC/HY, hy, Fortunea.**

R. groenlandicum (*of Greenland*) s. Rhododendron, s.s. Ledum. 2', -30ºF, EM-ML, 3/3-4/4. This plant has always been in a genus of its own, the Genus Ledum. Some botanists are now including it in the Genus Rhododendron. Since it opens it seed backwards (from the stem end) and all other rhododendrons open their seed from tip end, I question its inclusion in the Genus Rhododendron. This is a very hardy plant with narrowly oblong or oval leaves up to 2" long and 1/2" wide. The leaf margins are much recurved and the underside of the leaf and the young stems are covered with thick, rust-colored indumentum. Leaves are very aromatic. Flowers are white in terminal trusses of up to 30 flowers. Each flower is about 1/2" across and is borne on a slender, downy pedicel up to 1" long. Northern North American and Greenland. **Not previously considered a rhododendron and has never been placed in a Series or Subseries.**

R. gymnocarpum (*with naked fruit*) s. Taliense s.s. Roxieanum. 3', -5ºF, EM, 3/3-4/3. This is a special plant, with superb foliage. Leaves, to 4 1/2" long, are oblong to oblong-elliptic, thick and rather leathery. The tops are smooth dark green, covered with brownish or fawn somewhat woolly indumentum on the undersides. Flowers, to 2" long, widely bell shaped, range from pale to deep crimson with darker spotting. S.E. Tibet, 12,000-14,000 ft. **R. microgynum Gymnocarpum Group/HY, hy, Neriiflora.**

R. habrotrichum (*with soft hairs*) s. Barbatum s.s. Glischrum. 4', 5ºF, E-M, 2/3/-. Growth habit is open and upright with very hairy stems, eventually forming a tree to 25'. Large dark green seaves are oval-.or oblong, with paler and somewhat glabrous undersides. Funnel shaped flowers, to 2" long, held in compact trusses of many blooms range from white through pink to pale rose, sometimes blotched. Yunnan, 10,000 ft. **UC/HY, hy, Glischra.**

R. haematodes (*blood-like*) s. Neriiflorum s.s. Haematodes. 3', -5ºF, EM, 3-4/4-5/4. This is a very compact small shrub that is excellent for both foliage and bloom, enjoyable to look at all year. Leaves, to 3" long, oblong to obovate, have smooth dark green tops and are densely covered with woolly brown to dark brown indumentum underneath. Flowers of heavy substance, to 2" long, tubular bell shaped, have a calyx up to 1/3" long that is normally red. They are glistening brilliant scarlet or deep crimson, and are carried in trusses to 10. Many forms of this species are grown with quite a wide variation. Yunnan, 11,000-14,000 ft. **R. haematodes ssp. haematodes/HY, hy, Neriiflora.**

R. hanceanum (*after H. F. Hance, 1827-1886, British Consul at Canton*) s. Triflorum s.s. Hanceanum. 1', 0ºF, EM, 3-4/4/4. Growth habit is upright and open. Leaves, to 4" long, are lanceolate or ovate-lanceolate, dark green and scaly on the tops and paler and less scaly on the undersides. Faintly scented, funnel shaped flowers, to 1" long, held in many-flowered trusses, are creamy white to pale yellow or yellow, with a large, deeply-lobed calyx. Szechwan, 5,000-13,000 ft. **UC/RN, rn, Tephropepla.**
  'Nanum'-- Covers several dwarf forms, commonly grown and are very nice. Most are cream colored, although there are deeper yellow forms. Plants are compact and attractive. **R. hanceanum Nanum Group.**

R. hardingii (*after H. I. Harding, H. M. Consul at Tengyueh, 1923-1925, who supplied the type flowering material to Forrest*) s. and s.s. Irroratum. 4', 5ºF, EM, 2-3/2-3/3. Medium size foliage is long, narrow, and sharply pointed, smooth matte green on top, paler green and glabrous underneath. Flowers, to 1 3/4" long, white or white blushed pink, spotted crimson, are held in lax trusses of 8-12. They are cup shaped or open-bell-shaped, to 1 3/4" long. Yunnan, 7,000 ft. **Syn. R. annae/HY, hy, Irrorata.**

R. hardyi (*after Maj. A. E. Hardy, of Sandling Park, Kent*) s. Triflorum s.s. Augustinii. 6', 0ºF, E-M, 3/2-3/3. Plant is deciduous or semi-deciduous. Medium sized foliage is lance shaped or oblong-lanceolate, with scales on both sides. Flowers, only 1 1/4", widely funnel shaped, set in trusses of 2-4, are white to greenish white tinged lilac, with yellowish or greenish spotting. E. Tibet, N.W. Yunnan, 11,000-12,000 ft. **R. augustinii ssp. hardyi/RN, rn, Triflora.**

R. headfortianum (*after the 4th Marquess of Headfort, 1878-1943*) s. Maddenii s.s. Megacalyx. 4', 15ºF, M, -/-/-. Medium large leaves are oblong to oblong-lanceolate, non-hairy and non-scaly on top, waxy grey or bluish with unequal scales beneath. Funnel shaped flowers, to 4" long, occurring either singly or in pairs, are cream, or cream tinged pink. S.E. Tibet, Assam, 8,000 ft. **Syn. R. taggianum/RN, rn, Maddenia "Dalhousiae-Alliance".**

R. heliolepis (*with shining scales*) s. Heliolepis. 4', -5ºF, L-VL, 2-3/2-3/2-3. Growth habit is upright and open, developing into a well rounded mound. Medium sized aromatic foliage is lance shaped, dark green on top, tannish green with a heavy covering of shiny scales underneath. 1" long, funnel-campanulate flowers range from white to pink, rose, or rosy red, blotched crimson, and are carried in trusses of 4-7. Yunnan, 10,000-11,000 ft. **R. heliolepis var. heliolepis/RN, rn, Heliolepida.**

R. hemidartum (*half-flayed*) s. Neriiflorum s.s. Haematodes. 3', 0ºF?, E-M, 3/3/2. Medium sized leaves are oblong to obovate, glabrous and glaucous, with spotty brown indumentum on the underside. Tubular-bell-shaped flowers of good substance, 2" long, crimson or scarlet, are set in trusses of 6-10. S.E. Tibet, 13,000-14,000 ft. **R. pocophorum var. hemidartum/HY, hy, Neriiflora.**

R. hemitrichotum (*half-hairy*) s. Scabrifolium. 3', -5ºF, E-EM, 3/2/3. Growth habit is upright and open growing. Leaves are rather small, narrow and oblong, dull green with soft hairs on the tops and waxy grey or bluish with dense scales on the undersides. Funnel shaped small flowers, to about 1/2" long, usually occurring in pairs, are white or white tinged pink. Szechwan, 8,000-13,000 ft. **UC/RN, rn, Scabrifolia.**

R. hemsleyanum (*after W. B. Hemsley, 1843-1924, English botanist*) s. and s.s. Fortunei. 6', -5ºF, ML-L, 3/3-4/3-4. Plant is open and upright, eventually forming a 20' tree. Foliage is fairly large, oval to oblong, dark, more-or-less shiny green on top, paler underside. Funnel shaped flowers, to a big 4" long, are white, and are held in upright loose trusses of up to 10. Szechwan (endemic to Mt. Omei). **UC/HY, hy, Fortunea.**

R. hippophaeoides (*resembling Hippophae, the sea buckthorn*) s. Lapponicum. 3', -25ºF, E, 4/2-3/4. Growth habit is spreading, upright and open. The best and hardiest of blues. Tolerant of sun and swampy conditions, this plant withstands frost even when in flower. Oblong or lanceolate leaves, to 1" long, are dullish dark green and scaly on the tops, grey and more densely scaly underneath. Flowers, to 1/2", broadly tubular, are a lovely lavender-blue to pale lilac or rose, or darker blue to purple, occurring in clusters of 6-8. Yunnan, Szechwan, 9,000-14,000 ft. **R. hippophaeoides var. hippophaeoides/RN, rn, Lapponica.**
  'Bei Ma Shan'-- Deep powder blue flowers and attractive foliage.
  fimbriatum form-- Species that was formally listed as *R. fimbriatum*. Flowers are more red-purple.
  'Haba Shan'-- Unique flowers with protruding stamens.

R. hirsutum (*hairy*) s. Ferrugineum. 1', -15ºF, L-VL, 2/3/3. Growth habit is twiggy, spreading, and open. Small leaves, oblanceolate or elliptic, with toothed and bristly edges, are darkish bright green with a few rusty scales on the undersides. 3/4" long flowers, tubular with flaring lobes, held in loose clusters of 5-8, are white, rosy pink, or nearly scarlet. Alps of South Central Europe. **UC/RN, rn, Rhododendron.**
  'Flore Pleno'-- A double-flowering form of garden origin.

R. hirtipes (*with a hairy foot*) s. Barbatum s.s. Glischrum. 5', 5ºF, E-EM, 2-3/3/2-3. Growth is tree like. Medium large leaves, widely-elliptic or oblong-oval, are smooth and shiny. The undersides are paler, and are sparsely covered with glandular hairs and heavily covered with bladder-like hairs. Bell shaped flowers, to 2", set in loose trusses of 3-5, are rosy pink or almost white, spotted carmine, with outside pink stripes. S.E. Tibet, 13,000 ft. **UC/HY, hy, Selensia.**

R. hodgsonii (*after B. H. Hodgson, a former East India Company Resident in Nepal*) s. Falconeri. 5', 10ºF, EM, 3-4/4/2-3. Shrub grows to a very handsome small tree with smooth, reddish brown peeling bark. Very large oblong leaves are smooth, dark shiny green with a smooth tawny indumentum underneath. Flowers are tubular-bell-shaped, to 2" long, in rosy or crimson shades of purple, set in large, compact, rounded trusses up to 20. Nepal, Sikkim to Bhutan, 10,000-12,500 ft. **UC/HY, hy, Falconera.**

R. hongkongense (*from Hong Kong*) s. Ovatum. 4', 10ºF?, E-EM, 3/4/3. Small foliage, ovate, oblong, sometimes diamond shaped, is smooth bright green on top and either waxy grey, bluish, or paler green and glabrous underneath. Slightly fragrant flowers, to 1 1/2" across, more or less saucer shaped, held in small trusses of 3-5, are white, spotted crimson purple. New growth is most a interesting shade of red purple. Hong Kong and adjacent mainland China. **UC/AZ, az.**

R. hookeri (*after Sir J. D. Hooker, 1817-1911, a former Director of Kew, botanist and traveler in the Himalaya*) s. and s.s. Thomsonii. 4', 15ºF, VE-E, 3/3/2-3. Growth habit is open and upright, eventually becoming a small tree, to 14'. Medium large oval or oblong oval leaves, smooth, dark matte green are glaucous green with veins and tufts of brownish hair on the undersides. Flowers may be pink, but are more often intense blood red, blotched deeper, with a 3/4" calyx. Tubular-campanulate, to 2" long, the blooms are carried in compact trusses up to 15. Different from *R. thomsonii* and *R. meddianum* in the hair tufts on the underside of the leaves. Bhutan, Assam, 10,000-12,000 ft. **UC/HY, hy, subsect. Thomsonia.**

R. horlickianum (*after Sir James Horlick, 1896-1972, of Gigha, Argyll*) s. Maddenii s.s. Ciliicalyx. 5', 15ºF, E-EM, 3/2-3/3. Medium sized foliage is lance shaped, glabrous dark green on top and pale waxy grey or bluish green with unequal brown scales underneath. Widely funnel shaped flowers, to 3" long, held in trusses of 2-3, are either white or ivory white with an internal yellow blotch, pink banded on the outside of the lobes. N. Burma, 4,000-7,000 ft. **UC/RN, rn, Maddenia "Ciliicalyx-Alliance".**

R. hormophorum (*bearing a necklace*) s. Triflorum s.s. Yunnanense. 4', 0ºF?, M, 3/3/3. Foliage of this deciduous shrub is of medium size, oblong or lance shaped, with distinctive fringed and hairy edges. The tops of the leaves are scaly; undersides have a scattering of pale yellowish scales. Widely funnel shaped flowers, to 1 1/2", held in trusses of 3-6 occurring both on the ends and along branches, range from white through white tinged pink, rose, lilac, or lavender, occasionally spotted brown. Yunnan, Szechwan, 8,000-12,000 ft. **R. yunnanense Hormophorum Group/RN, rn, Triflora Yunnanense agg.**

R. houlstonii (*after G. Houlston, Chinese Imperial Maritime Customs, friend of E. H. Wilson*) s. and s.s. Fortunei. 5', -5ºF, M, 2-3/3/3. Growth habit is upright and open, eventually growing to a 20' tree. Medium large foliage, oval or oblong, is smooth dark green on top and a great deal paler underside. Funnel-bell-shaped flowers, to 2 1/2" long, set in trusses of 6-10, are lavender-pink, pink, or white tinged pink. Hupeh, Szechwan, 4,500-7,000 ft. **R. fortunei ssp. discolor Houlstonii Group/HY, hy, Fortunea.**

R. hunnewellianum (*after a well known New England family*) s. Arboreum s.s. Argyrophyllum. 5', 5ºF, VE-EM, 2-3/3/3. This shrub becomes a small tree, with medium large, very narrow oblong glabrous leaves, covered with dense white or grey hairs beneath. Flowers, to 2" long, widely companulate, are white tinged pink, spotted pink inside, and are held in trusses of 5-8. W. Szechwan, 6,000-10,000 ft. **R. hunnewellianum ssp. hunnewellianum/HY, hy, Argyrophylla.**

R. hylaeum (*belonging to forests*) s. and s.s. Thomsonii. 5', 5ºF?, M, -/-/-. An open growing shrub, becoming tree-like in maturity. Large oblong or lance shaped leaves are smooth matte green with pale green, minutely pitted undersides. Flowers, caught in fairly good-sized trusses of up to 12, are tubular bell shaped, to 2" long, with a 1/3" calyx. They are pale rose with deeper spotting and nectar pouches. W. Burma, Yunnan, 7,000-12,000 ft. **UC/HY, hy, Thomsonia.**

R. hypenanthum (*with bearded flowers*) s. Anthopogon. 1', 0ºF, E-M, 4/3-4/2-3. This small shrub has aromatic foliage that appears on short, twiggy branches. The leaves are oval or obovate-elliptic, quite small and smooth, densely covered with scales underneath. Flowers, also small, to a mere 3/4" long, narrowly tubular with wider spreading lobes, cream-colored to yellow, are set in head-shaped clusters of 4-6. N. W. Himalaya, 11,000-18,000 ft. **R. anthopogon ssp. hypenanthum/RN, po.**

    'Annapaurna'-- A named clone that is delightful.

R. hyperythrum (*reddish below*) s. Ponticum s.s. Caucasicum. 3', -15ºF, EM, 3/4/3-4. Another of the hardy Ponticum Series, the foliage of which makes it of utmost interest. Leaves, up to 6", long, narrow, and curly, are smooth dark green on the tops, dotted with reddish pits on the undersides. Funnel shaped flowers, to 2" long, are white, occasionally with purple spotting, opening from pink buds into trusses to 10 or more. Formosa, 3,000-4,000 ft. **UC/HY, hy, Pontica.**

R. hypoglaucum (*blue-grey beneath*) s. Arboreum s.s. Argyrophyllum. 5', 5ºF, M, 2-3/3-4/4/3-4. Growth habit is tree-like, with good foliage. Leaves, to 5" long, are oblong to oblanceolate, bright glossy green on the tops with smooth, rather thin white indumentum underneath. Funnel bell shaped flowers, to about 1 1/2" long, are white to pale orchid pink, flushed rose, generously spotted deep rose, and are held in trusses to 8. Hupeh, E. China, 5,000-7,000 ft. **R. argyrophyllum ssp. hypoglaucum/HY, hy, Argyrophylla.**

R. idoneum (*suitable*) s. Lapponicum. 2', -5ºF, E-M, 2-3/2-3/3. Tiny leaves are widely elliptic or oval, scaly on the top, with the underside covered with over-lapping, very pale yellowish green scales of uniform size. Small funnel-shaped flowers, to 1/2" long, have scaly lobes (outside) and are held in pairs. Flower color is bluish purple with white throat. Yunnan, Szechwan, 11,000-14,000 ft. **Syn. R. telmateium/RN, rn, Lapponica.**

R. imberbe (*not bearded*) s. and s.s. Barbatum. 5', 5ºF, VE-E, 4/3/2-3. Oblong or lance-shaped foliage is medium large, glabrous dark green above and has paler green undersides. Flowers, to 2" long, are tubular-bell-shaped, scarlet or crimson scarlet, occasionally with inside darker spotting and blotched nectar pouches. They are carried in compact trusses of about 15. *R. imberbe* is different from *R. barbatum* in the absence of bristles and may be a form of it. W. C. Himalaya, 9,000 ft. **Hybrid or variant of R. barbatum.**

R. impeditum (*tangled*) s. Lapponicum. 1', -15ºF, EM, 4/4/3-4. Growth habit of this dwarf shrub is compact, tight and densely twiggy, with attractive silver-grey foliage. Leaves are small, to 1/2" long, and oblong-elliptic. Flowers, to about 2/3" long, are widely funnel-shaped, the color ranging from bluish-mauve to blue-purple or pinkish purple, contrasting nicely with the foliage and occurring either single or in pairs. This species is one of the best, most versatile of available dwarfs, considered to be ideal for rock gardens or bonsai, and making a distinctive bed edging as well. It is also extremely effective planted en masse, leaving 15" between plants. These will eventually grow together to make a dense ground cover of great beauty and hardiness, good to look at any time of the year, but especially lovely during the spring blooming cycle, when it becomes a virtual "blanket of blue". A very fine plant, though sometimes it is short lived in hotter climates. Yunnan, Szechwan, 9,000-16,000 ft. **UC/RN, rn, Lapponica.**

R. imperator (*emperor*) s. Uniflorum. 6", -5ºF, EM, 3-4/3/2. Growth habit is prostrate, spreading to perhaps 18" in 10 years. Small leaves are aromatic, lance-shaped or oblong, smooth and dark green, the underside waxy grey or bluish green with few dark scales. Flowers are small, funnel-shaped, appearing either alone or in pairs from each terminal growth, rose purple or pinkish purple. Burma, 10,000-11,000 ft. Splendid plant for the rock garden. **R. uniflorum var. imperator/RN, rn, Uniflora.**

R. inaequale (*of unequal size*) s. Maddenii s.s. Ciliicalyx. 4', 15ºF, VE-M, 3/2-3/3. Medium sized foliage is lanceolate or elliptic lanceolate and glabrous, the reverse side with somewhat unequal scales. Flowers, to 3 1/2" long and held in trusses of about 6, are widely funnel-shaped, fragrant, white, with an orange-yellow blotch. Assam, 4,000-6,000 ft. **R. formosum var. inaequale/RN, rn, Maddenia "Ciliicalyx-Alliance".**

Species ~ Subgenus Rhododendron

Section Rhododendron

Section Pogonanthum

R. trichostomum var. *ledoides*

Subsect. Boothia

R. chrysodoron

Subsect. Baileya

R. baileyi

Subsect. Campylogyna

R. campylogynum

R. campylogynum var. *myrtilloides*

R. sargentianum

R. megeratum

Subsect. Cinnabarina

R. cinnabarinum var. *blandfordiiflorum*

R. keysii

R. cephalanthum var. *crebreflorum*

R. leucaspis

R. cinnabarinum var. *roylei*

R. concatenans

Species ~ Subgenus Rhododendron
Section Rhododendron

Subsect. Edgeworthia

R. orthocladum
var. *microleucum*

R. flavidum

R. impeditum

R. edgeworthii

Subsect. Lapponica

R. fastigiatum

R. litangens

R. edgeworthii

R. pendulum

R. paludosum

R. pendulum

R. yungningense

R. rupicola var. *chryseum*

Subsect. Glauca

R. glaucophyllum var. *tubiforme*

R. luteiflorum

Subsect. Micrantha

R. micranthum

Subsect. Heliolepida

R.rubignosum 'Wakehurst'

R. desquamatum 'Finch'

Species ~
Subgenus Rhododendron
Section Rhododendron

Subsect. Moupinensia

R. moupinense

R. taggianum (Subsect. Maddenia)

Subsect. Maddenia

R. cubittii 'Ashcombe'

R. odoriferum

R. burmanicum

Species ~ Subgenus Rhododendron Section Rhododendron

Subsect. Saluenensia

R. calostrotum

R. prostratum

R. radicans

R. nitens

R. keleticum

Subsect. Scabrifolia

R. racemosum 'White Form'

R. racemosum 'Rock Rose'

R. spinuliferum

R. spiciferum

Subsect. Tephropepla

R. tephropeplum, auritum & hanceanum

R. hanceanum 'Nanum'

R. tephropeplum

R. auritum

R. indicum (*Indian*) s. Azalea *s.s.* Obtusum. 4', -5°F, ML, 3/3/4. Growth habit of this evergreen shrub is usually low and prostrate. Leaves, to 1 1/2" long, are narrow lance-shaped, dark glossy green on top, the reverse reddish brown, both sides somewhat hairy, and often changing color in the autumn to a lovely crimson or purple. Flowers to 2 1/2" across, and appearing either singly or in pairs, are wide funnel-form, the color red to scarlet or rose-red. The *Azalea indica* in the trade which is actually *R. simsii* or its allied forms, is often confused with this due to the similarity of the name. S. Japan.

> **'Balsaminiflora'**-- 2', -5°F, ML-L, 4-5/4-5/4-5. This little plant is a real treat. It has beautiful double salmon orange flowers that look like little roses. The plant has dense foliage and creeps right on the ground. It is a vigorous grower and makes an excellent ground cover or plant for the rock garden. The flower is unlike those of other rhododendrons. Very easy to grow. Formerly known as *var. balsaminaeflorum.* **UC/TT, tu.**

R. inopinum (*unexpected*) s. Taliense *s.s.* Wasonii. 5', 0°F, E-M, -/-/-. Foliage is medium size, oblong-oval, oblong, or oblong-lanceolate, dark green, the underside paler green with patchy brownish indumentum. Bell-shaped blooms, to 1 1/2" long, in trusses of up to 10, can be yellowish, white, pink or purple, sometimes blotched or spotted crimson. Unknown in the wild. **Hybrid of R. wasonii, known only in cultivation.**

R. insigne (*remarkable*) s. Arboreum *s.s.* Argyrophyllum. 3', 0°F, ML, 4/5/3. This is a slow-growing plant which fully lives up to its name: "remarkable." The leaves, to 5" long, oblong-lanceolate in shape, are dark glossy green above, the underside with a skin-like indumentum that is a tawny grey with a lovely coppery sheen. Leaves are extremely hard feeling. Flowers, to 2" long, in trusses to 8, are bell-shaped, the color pinkish white with crimson spotting and external rosy pink stripes. Beautiful! Szechwan, 7,000-10,000 ft. **UC/HY, hy, Argyrophylla.**

R. intricatum (*entangled*) s. Lapponicum. 2', -15°F, EM, 3-4/3/3. Profuse, early blooming and an attractive, intricate branch habit work together to make this plant an ideal choice for rock garden or bonsai use. Leaves are small, to only 1/2" long, somewhat rounded in shape, dark green above and paler below, both sides with dense covering of shiny greyish-green scales. Flowers, tubular-funnel-form, to 1/3" long, are mauve to rose-lilac or pale lavender-blue, carried in trusses of 5 or 6. Szechwan, Yunnan, 11,000-15,000 ft. **UC/RN, rn, Lapponica.**

R. iodes (*rust-colored*) s. Taliense *s.s.* Roxieanum. 3', -10°F, E-M, 3/4-5/3. Lance shaped leaves are of medium size, smooth, the underside with a reddish brown indumentum. Bell shaped flowers, to 1 1/2" long, are white or white tinged pink, spotted crimson, set in trusses of 8-12. S.E. Tibet, 12,000 ft. **R. alutaceum var. iodes/HY, hy, Taliensia.**

R. irroratum (*covered with dew, hence minutely spotted*) s. and *s.s.* Irroratum. 5', 0°F, E-EM, 3-4/3-4/3-4. Habit of this upright open-growing shrub is tree-like and inclined to be rather leggy. Leaves, to 5", are narrowly elliptic, the tops pale green and smooth, underside paler and equally hairless. Flowers, to 2" long, are tubular bell-shaped, the color white or creamy-yellow, pink or rose suffused, usually heavily spotted either crimson or greenish, and held in trusses of up to 15. Yunnan, Szechwan, 9,000-11,000 ft. **R. irroratum ssp. irroratum/HY, hy, Irrorata.**

> **'Polka Dot'**-- Creamy pink flowers have heavy spotting of red or green.

R. iteophyllum (*willow-leaved*) s. Maddenii *s.s.* Ciliicalyx. 4', 15°F, M-L, 3-4/3/3-4. Foliage is medium size, very narrow lance shaped, slightly scaly or slightly hairy on top, scaly beneath. Fragrant flowers, to 2 1/4" long, are funnel-shaped, white or white with a light kiss of pink, set in trusses of 2-3. Vigorous grower, similar in many ways to *R. formosum.* Assam, 2,000-6,000 ft. **R. formosum var. formosum Iteophyllum Group/RN, rn, Maddenia "Ciliicalyx-Alliance".**

R. japonicum

R. japonicum (*from Japan*) s. Azalea *s.s.* Luteum. 5', -25°F, M, 3/3/4-5. Growth habit of this deciduous shrub is compact and upright. Leaves to 4" long, are obovate to obovate-oblong, the tops a rather dull dark green with a few flattish stiff hairs, undersides paler green and with trusses to 12, are open funnel-form, the color yellow to bright orange or salmon or brick-red, with a large orange blotch. This is a very hardy species, and when planted in mass it will produce a show of color that is unmatched in intensity. C. & N. Japan. Often known as 'Azalea mollis' of which is supposed to be a parent. It is very close to *R. molle* and there is a possibility it may be considered a subspecies of *R. molle*. **UC/PE, pe.** Note: with the new classification it appeared that the name *japonicum* would be assigned to *R. metternichii*, fortunately this now does not appear necessary, thank goodness!

R. johnstoneanum (*after Mrs. Johnstone, wife of Political Agent, Manipur, 1882*) s. Maddenii *s.s.* Ciliicalyx. 4', 15°F, E-M, 4/3/3-4. Medium sized leaves are elliptic or obovate-elliptic, fringed with distinctive hairs along edge when young, glabrous, the underside with dense layer of scales. Fragrant flowers, to 3" long, are funnel-bell-shaped, with nice substance, in loose clusters of 4 blooms. They are creamy white to pale yellow, perhaps yellow blotched, occasionally red spotted. Assam, Manipur, 6,000-11,000 ft. **UC/RN, rn, Maddenia, "Ciliicalyx-Alliance" Johnstoneanum agg.**

R. juncundum (*pleasant*) s. Thomsonii *s.s.* Selense. 5', 0F?, M-L, -/-/-. Medium sized leaves are oblong or elliptic, nearly smooth dark green, the underside glaucous with vestigial glands and hairs. Flowers are funnel-campanulate, to 1 1/2", held in trusses of 5 to 8, and range in color from white to pink or rose, sometimes blotched crimson. Yunnan, S.E. Tibet, 9,000-12,000 ft. **R. selense ssp. jucundum/HY, hy, Selensia.**

R. kaempferi (*after E. Kaempfer, 1651-1716, who wrote about Japanese plants*) s. Azalea *s.s.* Obtusum. 4', -5°F, M-ML, 3/3/4. This semi-evergreen or deciduous plant grows upright and compact, with smallish leaves which can be ovate, lanceolate or elliptic. There will be a variation of leaf shapes and size from plant to plant within the species, and summer leaves will be smaller. All leaves are shiny green, with a few closely pressed stiff hairs on both sides. Widely funnel-shaped flowers, with frilled petals, to 2" wide, held in trusses of 2-4, are various shades of salmon-pink, salmon-orange, or red. Heavy bloomer. C. & N. Japan, Korea, sea-level-2,600 ft. **UC/TT, tu.**

R. kanehirae (*after R. Kanehira, 1882-1947, Japanese botanist*) s. Azalea *s.s.* Obtusum. 3', 10°F, E, 3/3/3-4. The evergreen or semi-evergreen shrub has two distinct leaf forms, spring and summer. Spring leaves are slightly smaller and wider. Summer leaves, to 2 1/4" x 1/4", are narrow-oblanceolate to narrowly obovate. Both types are dark green, with shiny, brown, stiff hairs on both sides. Funnel shaped flowers, to just 1" wide, are shades of pink or red, spotted scarlet, and are set in small trusses of 1 to 3. Formosa. **UC/TT, tt.**

R. kasoense (*from Kaso Peak, Delei Valley, Assam*) s. and *s.s.* Triflorum. 5', 0°F?, ?, -/-/-. Leaves are small, lance-shaped, with both sides sparsely scaly. Tiny flowers, to only 2/3" long, are tubular bell-shaped, yellow, in trusses of 2-3. Assam, 7,000-9,000 ft. **UC/RN, rn, Monantha.**

R. keiskei (*after Keisuke Ito, 1803-1901, the Japanese botanist who discovered it*) s. and *s.s.* Triflorum. 2', -5°F, EM, 4/3-4/4. Growth habit is usually low growing and compact, occasionally leggy and open. Long, pointed leaves, to 3", are lightly scaly on both sides and often a lovely bronzy-brown when young. Flowers, to 1 1/4" long, are wide funnel form, pale to lemon yellow, in color and held in clusters of 3-5. Japan, 2,000-6,000 ft. **UC/RN, rn, Triflora.**

  Dwarf form-- 1', -10°F, EM, 4/4/4. One of the most outstanding of all the dwarf species. It is the hardiest of yellow flowered species and is successful in the Northeast. The plant will grow into a tight mound about 1' tall, covered with small, olive green leaves which in winter change to wine red. In spring the plant transforms an outstandingly beautiful display of yellow.

  var. cordifolia-- 6", -10°F, E-EM, 4/5/4. The most dwarf form. This little creeper stays right on the ground. It is the form that was found on the island of Yakushima in Japan and is almost extinct in the wild. It buds very young and plants of just 3/4" will often flower. Like the other keiskei forms it is yellow flowered. 'Yaku Fairy' is a named clone of this variety.

R. keiskei

R. keleticum (*charming*) s. Saluenense. 1", -15°F, M, 4/4/4. Growth habit of this dwarf is tight, compact, semi-prostrate. Small leaves, to 1/2" long, are oblong to oblong-lanceolate. They are bright shiny green, with the tops just slightly scaly and the undersides having dense brown scales. Flowers to about 1 1/4" open flat and are set in trusses of 3 flowers each. The color is deep purple crimson, spotted red or deeper crimson, and the flowers bear a strong resemblance to pansies. One of the best in its series, and very good for bonsai use. S.E. Tibet, Yunnan, Upper Burma, 11,000-15,000 ft. **R. calostrotum ssp. keleticum/RN, rn, Saluenensia.**

R. kendrickii (*after Dr. G. Kendrick, 1771-1847, a friend of the botanist Dr. Nuttall*) s. and *s.s.* Irroratum. 5', 10°F, E-M, 3/3/3. Foliage is medium-large, oblong or lance-shaped, smooth and matte green, with the reverse paler green and more or less shiny and smooth. Flowers are bell-shaped-tubular, to 1 1/2". They have nectar pouches and are carried in trusses of over 15. Color ranges from pink through scarlet or crimson, spotted red or deeper crimson. Bhutan, S.E. Tibet, North East Frontier Agency, Assam, 7,000-9,000 ft. **UC/HY, hy, Irrorata.**

R. keysii (*after a Mr. Keys*) s. Cinnabarinum. 5', 5°F, L, 4/2-3/3. Leaves on this shrub are medium sized, oblong, and very scaly on both sides. Flowers are most unusual and distinctive, resembling firecrackers, tubular, to 1" long, brilliant red with yellow tips, or bright orange with deep red tips. They are held in trusses up to 20, terminal and lateral. S.E. Tibet, Bhutan, Assam, 9,000-16,000 ft. **R. keysii/RN, rn, Cinnabarina.**

  var. unicolor-- Has flowers that are almost a uniform red color. S.E. Tibet. **R. keysii 'Unicolor'.**

R. kiusianum (*from Kyushu, Japan*) s. Azalea *s.s.* Obtusum. 2', -10°F, M-ML, 5/5/4. This is one of the best of the native Japanese azalea series. It is evergreen or semi-evergreen, the habit spreading and densely branched, with two leaf forms: spring and summer. Spring leaves, to 1 1/2" long, are wide elliptic or obovate, bright green above, paler below, both sides with stiff, flat hairs; summer leaves are smaller. This plant buds young and heavily, making a solid mass of flowers. Blooms, to 1 1/2" wide, are funnel-form, pink to crimson or purple and very rarely white. They appear in trusses of 2-5. Terrific for use in bonsai. Japan, 4,000-5,600 ft. **UC/TT, tt.** Note: There are more than 40 named cultivars introduced from Japan. Following is a representative list.

  'Benichidori'-- One of the better known strong reddish orange forms. Excellent plant habit.

  'Benisuzume'-- Benisuzume means 'Red Sparrow' and is salmon orange. The plant is compact and has red foliage in the winter.

  'Hanekomachi'-- This one has exceedingly hairy foliage which is deep bronzy green. The flowers are a beautiful shade of pink touched with orchid.

  'Hinode'-- This is a deep rose red which is different from the normal pink colors of *R. kiusianum*. It seems to be more dwarf than many forms. The leaves are about 1/2" to 3/4" long and 1/4" wide. They are more pointed than other forms. 'Hinode' grows in flat layers creating an oriental look that is superb for bonsai. It flowers very young and heavily. Excellent for pot culture or the rock garden.

  'Komo Kulshan'-- Here is an American selection which is one of the best seen. It is a clear rose pink on the tips with a light pastel pink in the center. What a delightful two-toned appearance!

  'Mangetsu'-- A two-toned flower with a light pink center edged with lavender pink.

  White form-- It is pure snow white. Quite probably the finest plant in the Azalea series, it will never fail to attract attention. Like the other *R. kiusianum*, it flowers young and heavily. Also used for bonsai. There are also several named white forms.

R. kiyosumense (*from Mt. Kiyosumi, Japan*) s. Azalea *s.s.* Schlippenbachii. 5', - 10°F, E-EM, 3/3/3. Small, widely diamond shaped leaves occur in whorls of 3 at branch ends. They are smooth and green, the reverse side is paler and has hairy veins. Broadly funnel-shaped flowers, to 1 1/2", open with the leaves, either alone or in pairs. The blooms are lilac or lavender purple. Japan. **UC/TT, br.**

R. kongboense (*from Kongbo, S.E. Tibet*) s. Anthopogon. 2', -5°F, E-EM, 3-4/3/2. Aromatic leaves, quite small, to 1" x 1/2", are oblong or lance shaped, shiny-topped with sparse scales. The undersides have a dense covering of brown scales. Tubular flowers, only 1/2" long, have spreading lobes, are shades of pale to bright rose in color, and are set in compact trusses up to 7. S.E. Tibet, 11,000-15,000 ft. **UC/RN, po.**

R. kotschyi s. Ferrugineum.-- see *R. myrtifolium*.

R. kuluense (*from mountains of Kulu, Szechwan*) s. Barbatum *s.s.* Glischrum. 4', 5°F, E-M, 2-3/3/3. Shrub eventually grows to small tree. Medium-large foliage, ovate-lanceolate or lanceolate, has top side dark or olive green, paler underside, both sides somewhat bristly and hairy. Bell shaped flowers, to 2" long, held in trusses of 4-8, are white or white with a kiss of pink, perhaps with a crimson blotch and spotting. S.W. Szechwan, 11,000-11,600 ft. **R. adenosum/HY, hy, Glischra.**

R. kyawii (*after Maung Kyaw, a Burmese plant collector*) s. Irroratum *s.s.* Parishii. 5', 15°F, VL, 3/2/3. Habit is upright and open, with growth to a small tree of 20'. Bright green, quite large leaves are oblong or oblong-oval in shape. They are slightly puckery and glabrous, the reverse sides smooth and shiny. Funnel-shaped flowers, to 2 1/2", held in trusses up to 20 are bright, rich crimson, dark-blotched. Burma, Yunnan, 6,000-12,000 ft. **UC/HY, hy, Parishia.**

  var. prophantum-- 3/3/3. Superior growth habit and leaves. Flowers similar to *R. griersonianum*.

R. macabeanum (*after Mr. McCabe, a former Deputy Commissioner, Naga Hills, N.E. India*) *s.* Grande. 5', 10ºF, VE-EM, 4-5/4-5/3. This is a tree rhododendron which reaches 45' eventually. Foliage is enormous, to 18" x 8". It is broadly elliptic or oval, smooth dark green, and the undersides have a woolly indumentum of white or light tan. Large trusses of up to 20 flowers are usually compact, but are sometimes rather loose. Flowers, 2-3" long, are ventricose campanulate in shape. Color is light creamy yellow to deep yellow or greenish yellow, purple-blotched at the base. Outstanding! Manipur, 8,000-9,000 ft. **UC/HY, hy, Grandia.**

R. macrogemmum *s.* Azalea *s.s.* Obtusum. 3', -5ºF, M, 3/3/3. This is now considered to be synonymous with *R. kaempferi*. Japan. **UC/TT, tt.**

R. macrophyllum (*with big leaves*) *s.* and *s.s.* Ponticum. 5', -5ºF, M-L, 2-3/2-3/3. Medium large leaves are lance-shaped, smooth dark green, paler on the undersides. Flowers to 2" across, are widely bell shaped, held in dome-shaped trusses of 20 or more. Color ranges widely from rose purple through shades of pink to white, spotted reddish brown on upper lobes. The petal edges are crimped. British Columbia through Northern California, sea level to 6,000 ft. **UC/HY, hy, Pontica.**

R. macrosepalum (*with large sepals*) *s.* Azalea *s.s.* Obtustum. 3', 5ºF, M-L, 3-4/3-4/4. A semi-evergreen shrub with 2 distinct leaf forms, spring and summer. Spring leaves are small, about 2 1/2" x 1", ovate-elliptic or ovate-lanceolate, wrinkled dull green. They are slightly glandular, and hairy on both sides. Summer leaves are smaller and more lance-shaped. Lavender purple flowers, to 2" across, are widely funnel-shaped and are carried in trusses of 2-10. C. & S. Japan. **NR/TT, tu.**
    'Linearifolium'-- Is unknown in the wild and is now regarded as a cultivar. It previously was known as *R. linearifolium*, and *R. macrosepalum* was considered a variety of it. 'Linearifolium' has very narrow leaves about 1/8" wide and up to 2" long. The flowers are so deeply divided that they are also strap-like in the same manner as the leaves.

R. maculiferum (*spotted*) *s.* Barbatum *s.s.* Maculiferum. 5', 5ºF, E, 3-4/3-4/3. Foliage is medium large, oblong-oval, elliptic to obovate, smooth matte green. Paler waxy grey or bluish green and glabrous surfaces cover the underside. Flowers, to 1 1/2" long, are open-campanulate, white or white blushed rose. They are blotched very deep black-purple at the base and are set in lax trusses of up to 10. Szechwan, Hupeh, 8,000-10,000 ft. **R. maculiferum ssp. maculiferum/HY, hy, Maculifera.**

R. maddenii (*after Lt. Col. E. Madden, 1805-1856, traveller in India*) *s.* and *s.s.* Maddenii. 4', 15ºF, L-VL, 3/3/4. Growth habit is open and leggy, with distinctive papery bark. Medium-large leaves, lance-shaped or elliptic, are dull dark green and glabrous above. Undersides have a dense covering of overlapping rusty scales. Tubular-funnel-shaped flowers, to 4" long, have good substance and are fragrant. They are white or white blushed rose, occasionally pink, and are set in trusses of 2-4. Sikkim, Bhutan, 5,000-9,000 ft. **R. maddenii ssp. maddenii/RN, rn, Maddenia "Maddenii-Alliance".**

R. magnificum (*magnificent*) *s.* Grande. 5', 10ºF, VE-E, 4/4-5/3. The name of this species describes it well, for it is truly magnificent. Leaves are oblong to oblong obovate, extremely large, to 18" x 9", dark matte green. The reverse sides have a thin covering of whitish or light tan indumentum. Rose purple flowers, to 3" long, tubular-bell-shaped, are held in gigantic, compact trusses of up to 30 flowers. Very close to *R. protistum* and *R. giganteum*, differing from both in its leaf shape. Burma-Tibet frontier, 6,000-8,000 ft. **UC/HY, hy, Grandia.**

R. makinoi (*after T. Makino, a Japanese botanist*) *s.* Ponticum *s.s.* Caucasicum. 3', -10ºF, ML, 3-4/4/2-3. This unusual plant is most desirable for its superb foliage. It is notable that the new growth, covered with a lovely white to fawn indumentum, is produced very late, sometimes as late as August. Leaves are long and narrow, up to 7", curved downward and backward. The tops are bright green, slightly puffy and wrinkled; underneath is a thick tawny indumentum. Funnel bell-shaped flowers, to almost 2" long, are a delightful clear light pink, occasionally crimson spotted and carried in trusses to 10. Rounded habit, slow growing when young. Japan, 1,500-1,800 ft. At one time, the name was to be changed to *R. yakushimanum* ssp. *makinoi*, however, it remains **R. makinoi/HY, hy, Pontica.**

R. mallotum (*woolly*) *s.* Neriiflorum *s.s.* Haematodes. 3', 10ºF, E, 2-3/4/2. Growth habit is upright and open. Lovely, stiff, rounded leaves are medium large, dark green, with hair-free, wrinkled tops. The reverse sides have a very handsome, woolly indumentum of lively brownish red. Flowers, to 2", are tubular-bell-shaped, with good substance. They are dark crimson and are carried in compact trusses of up to 15. Yunnan, Upper Burma, 11,000-12,000 ft. **UC/HY, hy, Neriiflora.**

R. manipurense (*from Manipur, India*) *s.* and *s.s.* Maddenii. 4', 15ºF, M-L, 3/3/3-4. Foliage is fairly large, oval, elliptic or oblong-elliptic. It is shiny dark green on top surfaces with the undersides densely scaly. Flowers, scaly on the outside, are fragrant, pure white in color, tubular funnel shaped, to 4" long and are in trusses of 4-6. Assam, Burma-Tibet frontier, 7,000-10,000 ft. **Syn. R. maddenii ssp. crassum/RN, rn, Maddenia "Maddenii-Alliance".**

R. mariesii (*after C. Maries, c. 1851-1902, collector for Messrs Veitch*) *s.* Azalea *s.s.* Schlippenbachii. 4', -5ºF?, E, 2-3/2-3/3. Deciduous, with open and upright growth. Leaves are in groups of 2 or 3 at branch ends, and are medium sized, ovate or elliptic, and smooth dark green. The undersides are paler and also glabrous and heavily veined. Saucer-funnel-shaped flowers, to 2" wide, are rose purple, spotted purple red on upper lobes. S.E. & C. China, Formosa, 1,000-4,000 ft. **UC/TT, br.**

R. martinianum (*after J. Martin, gardener at Caerhays, Cornwall*) *s.* Thomsonii *s.s.* Selense. 4', 0ºF?, E-M, 3/3/2. Shrub has stiff, bristly branches, with small leaves, oblong or oblong-elliptic, often appearing in whorls. They are somewhat glabrous on upper surfaces and the undersides are pale waxy grey or bluish green with vestiges of glands. Bell-shaped flowers, to 1 1/2" long, are in loose clusters of up to 3. They are pale rose, white or creamy white, occasionally crimson spotted. S.E. Tibet, Burma, 10,000-13,500 ft. **UC/HY, hy, Selensia.**

R. maximum (*largest*) *s.* and *s.s.* Ponticum. 5', -25ºF, L-VL, 2/3/3-4. Shrub reaches 15' or more, with open and upright habit. Large leaves are ovate-lanceolate, obovate lanceolate or oblong lanceolate. They are glossy dark green above and have undersides which are sometimes thinly indumented. Bell-shaped or broadly-funnel-shaped flowers, to 1" long, are held in trusses of 15-20. They can be pink tipped in bud, and can range in color from white through shades of pink and rose, with yellow-green spots. E. North America. **UC/HY, hy, Pontica.**

R. meddianum (*after G. Medd, Agent I. F. Company, Bhamo, Upper Burma*) *s.* and *s.s.* Thomsonii. 5', 5ºF?, E, 3/3/2. Foliage is large, oval or oblong-oval, smooth, dark, dullish green, lighter green on the undersides. Flowers, of good substance, to 2 1/2" long, are tubular-bell-shaped. They are deep crimson or bright scarlet and are set in trusses of up to 12. Yunnan 10,000-11,000 ft. **UC/HY, hy, Thomsonia.**
    var. atrokermesinum-- Has much larger flowers and leaves, and the ovary is densely glandular. **UC.**

R. megacalyx (*with a large calyx*) s. Maddenii s.s. Megacalyx. 4', 15°F, EM-L, 3-4/3/3-4. Growth habit sometimes rather straggly and undisciplined, with medium large elliptic or obovate-elliptic leaves. Foliage is distinctively rounded at the apex and base, smooth on top; the undersides are a waxy grey or bluish green and heavily covered with small scales. Carried in trusses of about 5, flowers are deliciously fragrant, stark white or sometimes kissed with pink. There is also a light flush of pale yellow at the base of the tubular-bell-shape, which grows to 4" long. The lower petals are generally larger than the rest. The calyx is up to 1" long. Upper Burma, 7,000-9,000 ft. **UC/RN, rn, Maddenia "Megacalyx-Alliance".**

R. megeratum (*passing lovely*) s. Boothii s.s. Megeratum. 18", 5°F, EM, 3/3-4/2. Growth habit is compact, mound-like, with very hairy branchlets and purplish, scaling bark. Small leaves are oval or elliptic, and shiny. The leaf undersides are very glaucous and scaly, with bristly margins. Flowers, to 1 1/4" long, are bell-shaped, creamy or yellow, and are set in trusses of up to 3. Rare. Yunnan, Tibet, North East Frontier Agency, Burma, 8,000-13,000 ft. **UC/RN, rn, Boothia.**

R. mekongense (*from the Mekong river, China*) s. Trichocladum. 4', 0°F?, M, 2/2/3. This deciduous shrub has small leaves, of oblanceolate or oblong-oval shape, slightly hairy on the edges, the undersides scaly. Flowers usually open ahead of leaves, are widely funnel-shaped, to about 1" long, and are pale yellow. They are tinged with deeper yellow or green, and are in trusses of 3-4. Calyx is about 1/4" long, oblong lobes bristly. E. Tibet, Yunnan, 11,000 ft. **R. mekongense var. mekongense/RN, rn, Trichoclada.**

R. melinanthum (*with honey flowers*) s. Trichocladum. 3', -5°F, M-L, 2/2/3. Growth habit is open and upright, deciduous, with small oval or oblong-oval leaves, glabrous on top, the young leaves with hairy edges, underside glaucous and scaly. Flowers, open ahead of leaves, are widely funnel-shaped, to 1", yellow, held in clusters of up to 4. Upper Burma, 12,000-14,000 ft. **R. mekongense var. melinanthum/RN, rn, Trichoclada.**

R. metterianum-- see *metternichii* var. *kyomaruense*.

R. metternichii (*after Prince Metternich, 1773-1859, Austrian diplomat*) s. Ponticum s.s. Caucasicum. 3', -15°F, EM-M, 4/4/3. Growth habit is rounded and very compact, with beautiful foliage. Leaves are large, oblong or lance-shaped, smooth and shiny; the undersides are covered with handsome, smooth plastered type indumentum of an elegant cinnamon brown color. Flowers are light pink to rose or reddish, usually 7-lobed, spotted deeper rose inside, bell-shaped or funnel-shaped to 2" long, and set in rounded trusses of up to 15. **Note:** According to Peter Cox, it will not be necessary to change the name to *R. japonicum*, as has been done in some taxonomies (see name changes at paragraph end). In this case, the name change would be very confusing since *japonicum* has for many years been used for a popular azalea. S. Japan. **R. japonicum var. japonicum/HY, hy, Pontica.**
> var. **kyomaruense**-- 30", -15°F, M, 3-4/3-4/3-4. The name of this will change to
> *R. degronianum* ssp. *heptamerum* var. *kyomaruense*. Plastered tan indumentum and
> light pink to white flowers. A superior plant.
> var. **metternichii**-- 4', -15°F, M, 3-4/4/4. Medium clear pink flowers. Excellent foliage
> and form. Smooth tan indumentum.
> var. **micranthum**-- 3', -15°F, M, 4/3/3. One of the native Japanese geographical forms.
> Light pink flowers.
> var. **pentamerum**-- see *R. degronianum*.

R. micranthum (*small-flowered*) s. Micranthum. 4', -5°F, ML-L, 3/2-3/3. This is a very unusual rhododendron which, in its growth habit and appearance, strongly resembles a spirea or ledum. Leaves are small, less than an inch long and very narrow. They are glabrous on the topsides; the undersides are densely scaly and light brown. Bell shaped flowers are very tiny, to only 1/3" long, many in the truss, milky white. Hupeh, Szechwan, Kansu, 6,000-8,000 ft. **UC/RN, rn, Micrantha.**

R. microleucum (*small and white*) s. Lapponicum. 18", -5°F, EM-M, 3/3/2-3. Habit is compact and spreading, the new shoots densely scaly, dark rusty brown. Tiny leaves, to only 1/2" long, are very narrow. The tops are medium green with impressed, translucent, or glass-like scales. Undersides are paler green with a heavy covering of brown scales. Flowers, to about 1/2" long, are widely funnel-form, white, and appear in clusters of 2 or 3. Not known in the wild. **R. orthocladum var. microleucum/RN, rn, Lapponica.**

R. microphyton (*small plant*) s. Azalea s.s. Obtusum. 3', 5°F?, E-M, 3/3/3. This evergreen shrub has small leaves, elliptic to lance-shaped, dark green, paler on reverse side. Both sides have sparse, stiff hairs, set close, flat, red brown in color. Small flowers, to 3/4" across, are funnel-form, rose to nearly white, spotted carmine on upper lobes. They occur in trusess of 3-6, quite often with several trusses at branchlet ends. Yunnan, 6,000-10,000 ft. **NR/TT.**

R. mimetes (*imitative*) s. Taliense s.s. Adenogynum. 3', 0°F, M, 3/3-4/3. The shrub has short, thick branches, with medium sized leaves, elliptic or oblong-oval, nearly smooth on tops. The undersides have a pale or light tawny indumentum. Flowers are widely funnel shaped, to 1 1/2" long, white with faint blush and edge of rose. They are sparsely marked with crimson and are held in lax truss to 10. S. W. Szechwan, 11,000-12,000 ft. **UC/HY, hy, Taliensia.**
> var. **simulans**-- Has much wider leaves, and indumentum which splits. **R. simulans,**
> **UC/HY, hy, Taliensia.**

R. minus (*smaller*) s. Carolinianum. 4', -15°F, M-L, 2-3/2/2-3. Growth habit varies from rather dwarf to open and upright. The ovate-elliptic to elliptic, medium sized leaves have tops which are dark green and slightly scaly. Leaf underside is densely coated with rusty scales. Flowers are very scaly on the outside, funnel-bell-shaped, to 1 1/2" long, carried in trusses of 6-12. Color may be white, rose-pink or pale pinkish purple and spotted greenish or brown. S. E. United States, including Florida. **R. minus var. minus/RN, rn, Caroliniana.**

R. molle (*with soft hairs*) s. Azalea s.s. Luteum. 4', -15°F, M, 3/3/4. A deciduous, stoutly branched shrub with open, upright habit. Leaves are large, oblong or lance-shaped, with edges often hairy and downward rolling. The undersides are covered with short, soft, greyish colored hairs. Flowers occur in large, tight trusses of many blooms. Each flower is to 2 1/2" across, opens before the leaves, is wide funnel-form, orange or yellow in color, and has a large greenish blotch separated into dots. E. and C. China, in provinces of Chekiang, Hupeh and Hunan. **UC/PE, pe.**

R. mollicomum (*with soft hairs*) s. Scabrifolium. 4', -5°F, E-M, 2-3/2-3/3. Shrub habit is open and somewhat leggy. The small, narrow, lance-shaped leaves are dull green and have short, soft hairs. The reverse side is also softly hairy with a few scales. Flowers, to 2/3" long, are tubular shaped, narrow, and rose or crimson in color. They occur either singly or in pairs at the apex of leaf shoots. Yunnan, 8,000-11,000 ft. **UC/RN, rn, Scabrifolia.**
> var. **rockii**-- A more straggling form with larger flowers. **R. mollicomum Rockii Group.**

R. mollyanum-- see *R. montroseanum*.

R. monosematum (*with one blotch*) s. Barbatum s.s. Maculiferum. 5', 5°F, E, 2-3/3/3. Growth habit is rather compact, with large foliage which is oblong or oblong-lanceolate, smooth, and dark matte green. The undersides are paler and glossy. Flowers are tubular-bell-shaped, to 2" long, white or white blushed rose pink to pink or deep rose. They are blotched at the base and are carried in round trusses to 12. Szechwan. **Authentic wild material lacking; may be a hybrid.**

R. montroseanum (*after Molly, Duchess of Montrose*) s. Grande. 5', 10°F, E-M, 3-4/4/3. Grows to form a small tree. The large, oblong or lance shaped leaves are smooth, dark green with the reverse sides having a thin covering of silvery white indumentum. Flowers, to 2 1/2", are bell-shaped, intense pink, blotched crimson, sometimes white with pink edges, set in large trusses of 15-20. S.E. Tibet. **UC/HY, hy, Grandia.**

R. morii (*after U. Mori, collector in Formosa*) s. Barbatum s.s. Maculiferum. 4', -10ºF, EM, 3-4/4/3. Habit is upright and open, and the plant is most interesting in that the foliage maintains a symmetrical "collar" around the stem and truss. Leaves, to 6" long, are oblong lance-shaped, the tops glossy dark green, paler below. Flowers, to 2" long, bell-shaped, pure white or white blushed rose, erupt from soft pink buds. Accents of slight crimson speckling or heavy red blotching occur. Loose trusses of 12-15 are formed. Formosa, 6,000-10,000 ft. **UC/HY, hy, Maculifera.**

R. moulmainense (*from Moulmein, Burma*) s. Stamineum. 5', 10ºF?, E-EM, 3/3/3. Medium-sized foliage is elliptic-lanceolate, dark green, paler and glabrous underneath. Flowers, in clusters of up to 5, nestle among the leaves. The flowers are narrowly funnel-shaped, to 1 1/2" long, and may be white or rosy-red, blotched yellow. Burma, Siam, Malay Peninsula. **UC/AZ, ch.**

R. moupinense (*from Moupin, W. China*) s. Moupinense. 2', 0ºF, VE, 4/3/3. Habit is somewhat open and spreading on this finest of the early blooming species. When all else is dreary, the large, showy, snow white flowers with deep red-purple blotches begin their annual display. Leaves, to about 1 1/2", are elliptic or oval, shining and polished in appearance. Flowers are funnel-shaped to 1 1/2" long, in trusses to 3. An added bonus is the bright bronzy-red new growth, which gives a second display after flowers are gone. Szechwan, Kweichow, 6,500-10,000 ft. **UC/RN, rn, Moupinensia.**

R. mucronatum-- Now considered to be a hybrid of garden origin.

R. mucronulatum (*with a small point*) s. Dauricum. 5', -15ºF, VE, 3-4/3/3. This deciduous, open and upright-growing shrub is a real winter spirit-lifter, with flowers appearing well ahead of the leaves and long before any other hint of spring has shown. Lance shaped leaves, to 4" long, are scaly on both sides. Widely funnel-shaped flowers, to about 1 3/4", bloom singly along branches in between leaf clusters and are orchid pink to rose-purple. N.E. Asia, Japan, c. 1,000 ft. **UC/RN, rn, Rhodorastra.**
    var. **acuminatum**-- Has much longer, narrower leaves, and it flowers later in the season. **No longer recognized.**
    'Cornell Pink'-- This is a beautiful clear pink, selected cultivar.
    'Crater's Edge'-- A dwarf variety which has rich fuschia flowers.
    'Mahogany Red'-- Wide foliage is deep green, and flowers are muted crimson.
    'Pink Panther'-- Vibrant rose pink flowers on an open habit.
    var. **taguetti**-- A dwarf form collected in the wild in Korea. This form displays beautiful pink blossoms in the middle of winter. The prostrate, spreading plant is covered in eyecatching pink when all else is sleeping. Very interesting.

R. myiagrum (*the fly-catcher, alluding to the sticky pedicels*) s. Thomsonii s.s. Campylocarpum. 0ºF, EM, 2-3/2-3/2. Medium sized leaves are nearly round, although some are elliptic. They are smooth dark green, the reverse glaucous with a scattering of tiny hairs. Flowers, to 1 1/2" long, are white, bell-shaped, perhaps with a basal crimson blotch, spotted or unspotted, and set in trusses of 4 or 5. Yunnan, Burma, 10,000-13,000 ft. **R. callimorphym ssp. myiagrum/HY, hy, Campylocarpa.**

R. myrtifolium (*with leaves like Myrtus*) s. Ferrugineum. 2', -10ºF, M-L, 3/3/3. Leaves are quite small, oblong or lance-shaped with very tiny rounded teeth. They are shiny dark green, and glabrous on top, with sparse scales. The undersides are dense with reddish brown scales. Flowers are tubular-spreading to 1/2" long, rose pink or pinkish purple, or white (rarely), held in trusses of 8. This was previously known as *kotschyi*. Carpathians and mountains of Bulgaria and Yugoslav Macedonia. **UC/RN, rn, Rhododendron.**

R. nakaharae (*after G. Nakahara, Japanese collector*) s. Azalea s.s. Obtusum. 1', -5ºF, L-VL, 4/4/4. The habit of this little evergreen shrub is creeping, making it a very good choice for a border, rock garden, or ground cover. It is the late flowering, which misses all spring frosts. Leaves are tiny, to only 3/4" long, oblanceolate, with the tops a glossy dark green. The reverse sides are paler, and a sparse covering of flat stiff hairs occurs on both sides. Flowers, to 1" long, are funnel bell-shaped, rose red to dark brick red, in clusters of 2-3. Formosa. **NR/TT.**

R. nakotiltum (*having the wool plucked off*) s. Lacteum. 5', 0ºF, M, -/-/-. Foliage is medium-large and of oblong, elliptic or oval shape. Nearly smooth, dark, dull green leaves have reverse sides which are covered with thin greyish indumentum. Flowers, to 1 1/2", vary from funnel-bell shape to open bell-shaped. They are carried in trusses of 12-15, are pale rose or white blushed rose. Sometimes flowers are accented with a crimson-blotched base, and they occur either with or without crimson spotting. N. W. Yunnan, Mekong-Salwin Divide, 11,000-12,000 ft. **UC/HY, hy, Taliensia.**

R. nankotaisanense (*from Mt. Nankotaisan, Formosa*) s. Barbatum s.s. Maculiferum. 4', 5ºF?, M, -/-/-. Medium-sized leaves are ovate or oblong-lanceolate, smooth dark green; undersides are paler, with a few hairs near the middle. Flowers, to 1 1/4", are bell-shaped, pink to white, and sprout mostly from the tops of the stems. Formosa, 10,000 ft. **UC/HY, hy, poorly known; close to R. pseudochrysanthum.**

R. neriiflorum (*with flowers like Nerium [Oleander]*) s. and s.s. Neriiflorum. 18", 5ºF, EM, 3-4/3/3. Growth habit is variable, from compact to upright and spreading. Oblong leaves, to as much as 4" long, are dark green above, white with a waxy, blue-green cast beneath. Flowers are fleshy, to 2" long and tubular bell-shaped. The color is bright scarlet, rich crimson, or deep rose. The large calyx is usually the same color. Flowers are held in trusses to 12. Yunnan, S.E. Tibet, Burma-Tibet frontier, 7,000-12,000 ft. **UC/HY, hy, Neriiflora.**
    ssp. **agetum**-- Scarlet flowers, with small, very narrow leaves. Yunnan. UC.
    ssp. **euchaites**-- Grows taller, eventually may reach status of a small tree. Yunnan, North East Frontier Agency, Upper Burma, 9,000-11,000 ft. **ssp. neriiflorum Euchaites Group.**
    ssp. **phaedropum**-- Flower color ranges from straw yellow to scarlet. Leaves are generally larger. N.E. Upper Burma, North East Frontier Agency, Bhutan, 8,000-12,000 ft.
    ssp. **phoenicodum**-- Leaves, flowers, and calyx are all smaller. Upper Burma, 10,000 ft.
    ssp. **neriiflorum.**

R. nigroglandulosum (*with black glands*) s. Taliense s.s. Adenogynum. 4', 0ºF?, M, -/-/-. Oblong, lance-shaped leaves are large, shiny dark green, densely glandular on top. The reverse sides have light tan, thick indumentum. Flowers, about 1 3/4" long, are bell shaped, carmine red fading to yellowish pink and spotted carmine. They are set in trusses of about 10. Szechwan, 11,500 ft. **UC/HY, hy, Taliensia.**

R. nigropunctatum (*marked with black spots*) s. Lapponicum. 1', -10ºF, E-M, -/-/-. Quarter-inch long leaves are narrow-elliptic, with a dense coat of scales on both sides. Scales on the leaf undersides are a pale greenish-yellow and overlap each other slightly. Flowers are widely funnel shaped, only 1/3" long, with no external scales. They are pale pinkish purple, and occur either alone or in pairs. Szechwan, 10,000-15,000 ft. **Syn. R. nivale ssp. nivale/RN, rn, Lapponica.**

R. nipponicum (*from Japan*) s. Azalea s.s. Nipponicum. 4', -5ºF, ML-L, 3/3/3. A deciduous shrub with large leaves which are obovate or oblong-obovate. Both sides of leaves have a covering of close, flat bristles. Flowers, to 1" long, are bell-shaped tubular, white, and open either with the leaves or just after, held in trusses of 6-15. Rare in cultivation. C. Japan. **UC/PE, vs.**

R. nitens (*shining*) *s.* Saluenense. 1', -15ºF, L-VL, 3/3/3. Habit is dwarf, open and spreading. Foliage is small, oval to oblong-elliptic, shining with scales on top, the reverse dense with yellow-brown scales. Flowers, of 1-2", are widely funnel-shaped or saucer-like, and are held in trusses of 1-3. Crimson accent spotting occurs on base colors ranging from mauve blue or deep pink-magenta, to pinkish purple or deep rosy red. Burma, 12,000 ft. **Syn. R. calostrotum ssp. riparium/RN, rn, Saluenensia.**

R. nitidulum (*shining*) *s.* Lapponicum. 2', -10ºF?, E-M, 2-3/2-3/2. Foliage is quite small, a scant 1/2" x 1/4". Elliptic or ovate, dark green leaves are quite scaly on both sides. Funnel-shaped flowers, 1/2" long, are violet-purple to purple-blue, occurring either singly or in pairs. Szechwan, 10,000-16,400 ft. **R. nitidulum var. nitidulum/RN, rn, Lapponica.**

R. nivale (*snowy*) *s.* Lapponicum. 18", -10ºF, E-M, 3/3-4/3. Growth habit is upright but dwarf-like, with very small leaves to only 1/4" long. They are elliptic, grey-green and scaly on top, scaly and paler underneath, sometimes reddish. Flowers, to 1/2" long, are widely funnel shaped, with a few scales on outsides of lobes, and occur alone or in pairs. Color ranges from bright mauve to violet, purple or reddish purple. Nepal, Sikkim, Bhutan, S. Tibet, 10,000-19,000 ft. **R. nivale ssp. nivale/RN, rn, Lapponica.**

R. niveum (*snow-like*) *s.* and *s.s.* Arboreum. 5', 5ºF, EM-M, 3/3-4/3. Habit is open and upright, tree-like. Large, oblong-lanceolate leaves are smooth dark green. The undersides have a white to pale brown indumentum. Flowers, to 2" long, are tubular-bell-shaped and are held in tight rounded trusses of up to 25. The color is purplish-lilac or a rather dull smoky blue. Sikkim, Bhutan, 9,000-12,000 ft. **UC/HY, hy, Arborea.**

R. noriakianum (*after Noriak*) *s.* Azalea. 3', 5ºF?, M, -/-/-. Growth habit is low on a more or less evergreen shrub. The small foliage is ovate to ovate-oblong, smooth and green, with undersides having hairy veins. Flowers to 1" wide, are funnel shaped, red, in trusses of 3-4. N. Formosa, 6,500-10,000 ft. **UC/TT, tt.**

R. nudiflorum-- see *R. periclymenoides.*

R. nudipes (*with a naked foot, alluding to the glabrescent twigs*) *s.* Azalea *s.s.* Schlippenbachii. 4', 0ºF, M, 3/3/3. A deciduous, medium-sized shrub with diamond shaped leaves of medium size and nearly smooth texture. Flowers are large, to 3" across, deep rose, spotted purple. They occur either singly or in pairs. Japan, 660-3,300 ft. **UC/TT, br.**

R. nuttallii (*after T. Nuttall, 1786-1859, botanist and traveller*) *s.* Maddenii *s.s.* Megacalyx. 5', 15ºF, E-M, 4/2/3-4. This is one of the largest flowered of any rhododendron species in cultivation. Growth habit is rather loose and straggly, with very large leaves, to 12" x 5". The oblong or elliptic, dark green and very wrinkled or puffy foliage has a densely scaled underside. Beautiful flowers, to 5" or more, with calyx up to 1", are tubular-bell-shaped and fragrant. They are clear light yellow or creamy white, flushed yellow inside, with lobes sometimes tinged pink. Trusses are of 3-6 or more. India, North East Frontier Agency, Upper Burma, Tibet, 4,000-5,000 ft. **UC/RN, rn, Maddenia "Dalhousiae-Alliance".**

R. oblongifolium (*with oblong leaves*) *s.* Azalea *s.s.* Luteum. 3', -5ºF, L-VL, 2/2/3. Deciduous, spreading shrub with medium sized obovate, elliptic-obovate, or oblong-lanceolate foliage. The smooth dark green leaves have reverse sides paler with short soft hairs. Flowers, opening after the leaves, to 1 1/4" across are tubular funnel-shaped. The spicy scented blooms are carried in trusses of 7-12. Color is usually white, may be pale or medium pink. S.C. North America. **UC/PE, pe.**

R. obtusum (*blunt*) *s.* Azalea *s.s.* Obtusum. 3', -5ºF, M, 4/3/4. This is an evergreen or semi-evergreen shrub with 2 leaf forms, spring and summer. Spring leaves are oval, to 1 1/4" long, the tops bright green, paler underneath, with both sides slightly hairy. Summer leaves elongate and turn darker. Funnel shaped flowers, to about 1" across, are usually crimson, scarlet, or bright red, in clusters of 1-3. This is now regarded as one of the numerous intermediate forms between *R. kiusianum* and *R. kaempferi*, and thus should be known as *R. obtusum.* N.W. Japan. **UC/TT, tt.**

> **'Ramentaceum'** (Syn. *R. obtusum f. album* Schneid.)-- This is a form with white flowers instead of red.
> **'Amoenum'**-- This is very similar to *R. kiusianum*, a taller plant with attractive small leaves which turn red in winter, and a prolific flowering habit which seems to increase one year after the other. Flowers are hose-in-hose, the color bright wine red.
> **'Amoenum Coccineum'**-- This is an unstable branch sport of 'Amoenum', the flowers are also hose-in-hose, but a lighter carmine red in color.

R. occidentale (*western*) *s.* Azalea *s.s.* Luteum. 5', -5ºF, M, 4/3/3. Growth habit is compact and upright on this terrific shrub which is native to the Pacific Coast. Leaves are deciduous, to about 4" long, elliptic or oblong-lanceolate, the tops glossy green with a few hairs, undersides paler with a waxy blue green bloom. Color changes to yellow scarlet or crimson in the fall. Flowers, to 3" wide, with a delightful fragrance, usually open with the leaves, and are broad funnel-form. Flower color is creamy white or pale pink, often tinged pinkish outside, and blotched pale yellow or orange-yellow, many red in the bud, and held in trusses up to 12. There are many named forms, including 'Leonard Frisbee' (the best-known), 'Pistol Pete', 'Mini Skirts', 'Rogue River Bell', 'Stagecoach Cream', and others. W. North America. **UC/PE, pe.**

R. odoriferum (*fragrant*) *s.* and *s.s.* Maddenii. 5', 15ºF, ML, 3/3/4. This is a compact growing, heavy blooming, early flowering shrub, with very fine foliage. Leaves, to 4" long, are elliptic or lance-shaped, the tops smooth, dark, glossy green, underside with dense brown scales. Flowers, to 3" long, are tubular funnel-form and fragrant. Flower color is white, outside faintly blushed with rose, the tube tinged with green inside, carried in trusses of 6 or 7. S. Tibet, 8,000 ft. **Syn. R. maddenii ssp. crassum/RN, rn, Maddenia "Maddenii-Alliance".**

R. oldhamii (*after R. Oldham, 1837-1864, collector for Kew*) *s.* Azalea *s.s.* Obtusum. 4', 10ºF?, M, 3/3/3. This is an evergreen shrub, with 2 leaf types: spring and summer. Spring foliage is medium size, elliptic or oblong-elliptic, roughly hairy on top, underside with rusty colored, spreading, glandular hairs. Summer leaves are either oval or widely elliptic. Widely funnel-shaped flowers, to 2" across, are salmon red to brilliant brick red, set in trusses of 1-3. Formosa, sea-level to 8,000 ft. **UC/TT, tu.**

R. oleifolium (*with olive-like leaves*) *s.* Virgatum. 3', 10ºF, E-M, 3/2/3-4. Growth habit is upright and open, with small foliage, oblong to narrow lanceolate, glabrous, the reverse side dense with scales. Flowers, sprouting from leaf axils, alone or in pairs, are tubular-bell-shaped. The 1" long flowers are rose, pink or white in color. Yunnan, S.E. Tibet, 7,000-11,000 ft. B.M. 8802. **R. virgatum ssp. oleifolium/RN, rn, Virgata.**

R. orbiculare (*circular, alluding to the leaves*) *s.* Fortunei *s.s.* Orbiculare. 3', 5ºF, EM-M, 3/4/3. The well shaped plant habit is rounded and compact. Medium sized, bright green foliage is almost round, heart shaped and lobed at base, the underside very glaucous. 7-lobed flowers, to 2 1/2" long, are widely campanulate in shape, occuring in loose trusses of 7-10. Flower color is rose to rose-pink occasionally with a bluish cast. W. Szechwan, 8,000-10,000 ft. **R. orbiculare ssp. orbiculare/HY, hy, Fortunea.**

Species ~ Subgenus Rhododendron
Section Rhododendron
Subsect. Triflora

R. davidsonianum 'Ruth Lyons'

R. ambiguum

R. bodinieri

R. yunnanense

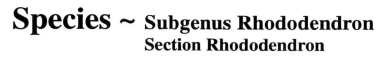

R. augustinii

R. trichanthum

R.lutescens

Subsect. Virgata

R. yunnanense
(R. chartophyllum)

R. virgatum

R. virgatum 'Album'

R. triflorum

R. oreotrephes

Species ~ Subgenus Hymenanthes
Section Hymenanthes

Subsect. Arborea

R. floribundum 'Swinhoe'

R. arboreum

R. argyrophyllum
var. *nankingense*

R. insigne

R. lanigerum

R. hunnewellianum

R. arboreum ssp. *campbelliae*

R. arboreum
var. *wellesianum*

R. lanigerum

R. niveum

Species ~ Subgenus Hymenanthes Section Hymenanthes

Subsect. Auriculata

R. auriculatum

R. souliei

Subsect. Campylocarpa

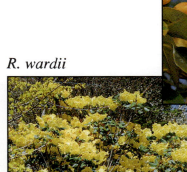

R. wardii

R. wardii

R. campylocarpum

R. erosum

Subsect. Barbata *(R. exasperatum, erosum, barbatum*

R. barbatum

R. exasperatum

Subsect. Campanulata

R. campanulatum var. *aeruginosum*

R. sutchuenense

R. fargesii 'Barto Rose'

R. diaprepes

R. fortunei 'Mrs. Charles Butler'

R. orbiculare

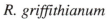

R. serotinum

Species ~
Subgenus Hymenanthes
Section Hymenanthes
Subsect. Fortunea

R. griffithianum

R. calophytum

R. decorum Hu & Yu

R. oreodoxa (*glory of the mountains*) s. Fortunei s.s. Oreodoxa. 5', -5°F, E-EM, 2-3/2-3/3. This plant has an open and upright growing habit. Medium sized, rather narrow foliage is smooth and dark green on top, lighter green and glaucous on the underside with scattering of minute hairs. Flowers, in trusses of 10 to 12, are 7-8 lobed, broadly bell shaped, to 2" long. Flower color is pale rose to pink in color, sometimes spotted purple. Very floriferous after a certain growth is reached. Needs a sheltered location because of early flowering, even though the buds themselves are very resistant to frost. W. Szechwan, Kansu, 7,000-10,000 ft. **R. oreodoxa var. oreodoxa/HY, hy, Fortunea.**

R. oreotrephes (*mountain bred*) s. Triflorum s.s. Yunnanense. 5', 0°F, EM, 3/4/4. Growth habit of this prolific-flowering species is upright and compact. A striking glaucous cast, occurs on the foliage, stems, and buds, making it quite distinct in the garden. Leaves to 3 1/2" long, are pendent, greyish-green and somewhat scaly held on red petioles. Flowers, to 1 1/2" long, are funnel-form or funnel-bell-shaped, and occur all along stems at stem tips. The blooms range in color from mauve to mauve-pink, rose, lavender-rose or purple, and are sometimes spotted crimson. Very variable. Yunnan, Szechwan, Tibet, Burma, 9,000-16,000 ft. **UC/RN, rn, Triflora.**

R. oresbium (*living on mountains*) s. Lapponicum. 30", -5°F, E-M, 3/3/3. This is a fairly small plant, with tiny (1/4" long) foliage, dark green and densely scaly on both sides. Funnel shaped flowers, which occur alone or in pairs, are 1/2" long, non-scaly externally, blue purple in color. Tibet-Yunnan frontier, 13,000-15,000 ft. **Syn. R. nivale ssp. boreale/RN, rn, Lapponica.**

R. orthocladum (*with straight twigs*) s. Lapponicum. 30", -5°F, EM, 3/3/3. This is a small, rather compact, spreading, densely branched shrub. Leaves, to no more than 3/4" long, are narrowly lance-shaped or oblong. Foliage is grey-green on top, with pale semi-transparent scales. The underside has golden scales, some even darker. Flowers, to about 1/2" long, are wide funnel-form, held in trusses of up to 4. The flower color is purple-blue, purple, pale mauve or deep lavender-blue. Yunnan, Szechwan, 11,000-14,000 ft. **R. orthocladum var. orthocladum/RN, rn, Lapponica.**

R. oulotrichum (*with curly hairs*) s. Trichocladum. 4', 5°F, E-M, 2/2-3/3. Shrub is deciduous, with flowers generally developing ahead of the leaves. Small, oval foliage is fringed with hair on the edges when young, glabrous both above and below. Yellow flowers, broadly funnel shaped, to 3/4" long, are held on long hairy pedicels to form trusses in groups of three. Yunnan, Tibet, Upper Burma, 9,000-10,500 ft. **Syn. trichocladum/RN, rn, Trichoclada.**

R. ovatum (*egg-shaped*) s. Ovatum. 3', 5°F, ML, 3/3/3. This is an unusual species, with distinctive pale bark and a dense twiggy habit. It is an elepidote, yet the leaves look more like a lepidote. They are small, to 2" long, and widely oval, coming to an abrupt long point, the texture more like a member of the azalea series. New growth is red or occasionally yellow. Flowers, to about 1 1/4" wide, are flatly saucer-shaped, appearing as singles coming from several buds at branch-ends. Flower color is white, light pink, or purplish, with purple spotting. Rare in cultivation. E. China. **UC/AZ, az.**

R. oxyphyllum (*with pointed leaves*) s. Stamineum. 6', 20°F, E, 3/3/3. This is a tree-like shrub with medium to large leaves, oblong and distinctively sharply pointed, smoothly non-hairy on both sides. Flowers to 2" long, are tubular funnel-shaped, white or white blushed rose, blotched yellow, and occur in axillary clusters of 3-5. S. Yunnan, Burma, N. Siam, Kwangsi, 4,000-5,000 ft. **UC/AZ, ch.**

R. pachypodum (*with a thick foot*) s. Maddenii s.s. Ciliicalyx. to 5', 15°F, E, 3/2-3/3. Rather narrow medium sized leaves are green and glabrous on the top side, glaucous with a dense covering of rusty scales on the reverse side. Flowers, either yellow or white, to 4" long and 4" wide, are tubular-funnel-shaped, held in trusses of 2 to 5. W. Yunnan, 7,000-11,000 ft. **UC/RN, rn, Maddenia "Ciliicalyx-Alliance" Ciliicalyx agg.**

R. pachysanthum (*with thick flowers*) s. Barbatum s.s. Maculiferum. 30", -5°F, EM-M, 3-4/5/3-4. This new species is a very beautiful foliage plant. The leaves, to 3 1/2" long, are oblong-lanceolate, generally becoming smooth on top; the undersides have a thick covering of whitish tan indumentum. Juvenile foliage of young plants, however, lacks this indumentum. Plant is similar to *R. pseudochrysanthum*, is probably of equal hardiness, and shows all indications of being the *R. yakushimanum* of the future, possessing the best features of both *R. pseudochrysanthum* and *R. yakushimanum*. It also retains the lovely silvery tomentum on leaf tops longer than *R. pseudochrysanthum*. Widely bell shaped flowers, to 1 1/2" long, are light pink to white, heavily spotted, and are set in trusses from 10-20 flowers. Also known as *R. venturi*. Formosa, c. 10,000 ft. **UC/HY, hy, Maculifera.**

R. pachytrichum (*with thick hairs*) s. Barbatum s.s. Maculiferum. 5', -5°F, E, 2/2/2-3. Growth habit is tree-like, open and upright. Long, narrow, fairly large foliage, is bright green above, paler shiny green on reverse side, glabrous on both sides. Bell shaped flowers, to 2" long, are white or rose to rose pink with a distinctive purple blotch, held in trusses of 7-10. W. Szechwan, 7,000-11,000 ft. **UC/HY, hy, Maculifera.**

R. x pallescens (*becoming paler in tint*) s. Triflorum s.s. Yunnanense. 4', -5°F, M, 4/3/4. This is now regarded to be a natural hybrid between *R. davidsonianum* and *R. racemosum*, raised from seed of Rock 59574 (*R. eritimum*) collected in W. China. Flowers are beautiful white, spotted carmine.

R. paludosum (*marsh-loving*) s. Lapponicum. 2', -15°F, EM-M, 2-3/3/3. Elliptic leaves are tiny, to only 1/2" long, heavily covered with impressed scales on top and densely scaly with both light and a few darker brown scales underneath. Flowers, to about 1/3" long, blooming singly, are pinkish purple, widely funnel-form. Yunnan, Tibet, 12,000-14,000 ft. **Syn. R. nivale ssp. nivale/RN, rn, Lapponica.**

R. panteumorphum (*altogether beautiful*) s. Thomsonii s.s. Campylocarpum. 5', 0°F, E-M, 2/3/2. Medium sized foliage is typically oblong-elliptic, hairless and dark green above, paler, with a scattering of tiny hairs below. Bell shaped flowers, to 2", are pale yellow, occurring in trusses of 4-8. S.E. Tibet, Yunnan, 11,000-14,000 ft. **R. x erythrocalyx Panteumorphum Group/HY, hy, Selensia.**

R. paradoxum (*paradoxical*) s. Taliense s.s. Wasonii. 3', -10°F, EM, 3-4/4-5/4. A beautiful, most interesting, rare species. White indumentum on the new foliage turns to a thin coat of brown. Oblong leaves, to 5" long, are dark green and more or less puffy-wrinkled on top, paler on the undersides. Tubular-bell-shaped flowers, to 2" long, are white, spotted and blotched deep crimson. Now considered to be a hybrid of *R. wiltonii* and known only in cultivation. **HY, hy, Hybrid of R. wiltonii, known only in cultivation.**

R. parishii (*after Rev. C. S. P. Parish, 1822-1897, chaplain at Moulmein*) s. Irroratum s.s. Parishii. 5', 15°F?, VE-E, 2-3/2-3/3. Habit is tree-like, with lovely tawny new growth, densely covered with short, cottony hairs. Medium to large older foliage is broadly elliptic to obovate, smooth, dark matte green on top, paler and eventually as smooth underneath. Flowers, to 2", tubular-bell-shaped, with nectar pouches, are red with deeper lines along lobes, and are held in trusses up to 12. Burma, 6,200 ft. **UC/HY, hy, Parishia.**

R. parmulatum (*with a small round shield*) s. Neriiflorum s.s. Sanguineum. 3', 5°F, E-EM, 2-3/3-4/2-3. Medium sized foliage is oblong-oval or obovate, glabrous and dark olive green above, glaucous below. Tubular-bell-shaped flowers, to 2" or more, range from creamy white or pale creamy yellow to pink or white tinged pink, spotted or veined crimson, and with deeper colored nectar pouches. The blooms are carried in trusses of up to 6. S.E. Tibet, 10,000-14,000 ft. **UC/HY, hy, Neriiflora.**

R. parryae (*after Mrs. A. D. Parry, wife of an officer in the Assam Civil Service*) s. Maddenii s.s. Ciliicalyx. 5', 20°F, M, 3-4/2-3/3-4. Growth habit is rather open and straggling, with distinctive smooth, thin pinkish purple bark. Large foliage is elliptic to oblong-elliptic, scaly dark green on top, glaucous green and somewhat scaly on the reverse. Nicely scented, widely funnel shaped flowers, to 4 1/2" across, held in lax trusses of up to 4, are white with conspicuous yellowish orange blotch. Assam, 6,000 ft. **R. johnstoneanum Parryae Group/RN, rn, Maddenia "Ciliicalyx-Alliance", Johnstoneanum agg.**

R. parvifolium (*with small leaves*) s. Lapponicum. 2', -15°F, VE, 2-3/2-3/2-3. This is a dwarf shrub with small oblong or lance shaped foliage that is dark green on the top, paler underneath, and scaly on both sides. Tiny funnel shaped flowers, to only 2/3" long, are pale magenta rose or reddish purple, occurring in trusses of 3-5. There is also an albino form known as *var. albiflorum*. E. Siberia to Russian Far East and south to N.E. China, N. Korea, Sakhalin and Hokkaido. **R. lapponicum Parvifolium Group/RN, rn, Lapponica.**

R. patulum (*spreading*) s. Uniflorum. 18", 5°F, EM, 3/3-4/3-4. Foliage on this dwarf or prostrate shrub is small, long and narrow. Scaly, dark green on top, the leaves are paler with small golden scales underneath. Flowers, occurring either alone or in pairs, to 1 1/4" long, either narrow or broadly funnel shaped are purple, spotted crimson on the upper lobe. E. North East Frontier Agency, 11,000-12,000 ft. **R. pemakoense Patulum Group/RN, rn, Uniflora.**

R. pemakoense (*from the province of Pemako, E. Tibet*) s. Uniflorum. 1', 0°F, VE-E, 3/4/4. Growth habit of this heavy-flowering dwarf is compact and semi-erect to erect or spreading. It is a cute little plant, easily grown, sometimes stoloniferous. Leaves, to 1 1/4" long, are rounded oblong with dark green, slightly scaly tops and paler, scaly undersides. Funnel-form flowers, to 1 1/4" long, appearing either singly or in pairs, are pinkish or pinkish purple. S.E. Tibet, 10,000 ft. **UC/RN, rn, Uniflora.**

R. pendulum (*hanging*) s. Edgeworthii. 2', 10°F, E-M, 3/5/2. This straggling, open growing shrub is sometimes epiphytic and has attractive, densely woolly new growth. Small leaves are oblong or oblong-elliptic, wrinkled on top and densely covered with fawn or brown cottony hairs underneath. Flat saucer shaped flowers, in clusters of 2-3, to 1 1/2" wide, are white tinged yellow inside, occasionally touched with pink. E. Nepal, Sikkim, Bhutan, Tibet, 7,500-12,000 ft. **UC/RN, rn, Edgeworthia.**

R. pentaphyllum (*with five leaves*) s. Azalea s.s. Canadense. 4', -5°F, E, 4/3-4/2-3. Growth habit is upright, open, sometimes spreading. Deciduous foliage grows in whorls on branch tips and turns orange or crimson in the fall. Smallish leaves are elliptic-lanceolate, medium green and glabrous above and below. Widely bell shaped flowers, to 2" wide, appearing ahead of the leaves, are clear, bright, rose pink, and occur either alone or in pairs. A beautiful plant. C. & S. Japan. **NR/PE, ro.**

R. peramabile (*very lovely*) s. Lapponicum. 2', -5°F, EM-M, 3/2/3. Growth habit of this lovely little plant is erect and sturdy. Tiny elliptic leaves are bright green with shining silvery scales above, paler and scaly underneath. Flowers, to 1/2" long, held in trusses of 7-10, widely funnel shaped, are lavender purple or deep violet-mauve. Closely allied to *R. intrictum*, and believed to be a more luxuriant form of this species. Probably Yunnan.
Syn. R. intricatum/RN, rn, Lapponica.

R. peramoenum (*very pleasing*) s. and s.s. Arboreum. 5', 10°F, E, 2-3/2-3/2-3. Leaves are long and very narrow, light green with impressed veins above, covered with white, grey, or fawn-colored indumentum underneath. Bell shaped flowers, to 2" long, are cherry red to deep rosy crimson, held in large tight trusses of up to 20. North East Frontier Agency, W. Yunnan, 8,000-11,000 ft. **R. arboreum ssp. delavayi var. peramoenum/HY, hy, Arborea.**

R. peregrinum (*foreign*) s. Grande. 5', 10°F, E, 3/3/2. Habit is tree-like. Mature foliage is large, broadly elliptic or oblong-elliptic, light matte green on top with buff or whitish indumentum underneath. Widely bell shaped flowers, to about 2" long, are delicate soft pink in the bud, opening to white, flushed rose, blotched bright red within. The blooms are carried in lax trusses of up to 20. Unknown in the wild, appeared as a rogue in *R. galactinum* Wilson 4254. **HY, hy, Known only in cultivation.**

R. periclymenoides (*like a honeysuckle*) s. Azalea s.s. Luteum. 5', -15°F, M, 3/3/3. Leaves on this deciduous shrub, to 3 1/2" long, are elliptic, obovate or oblong, bright green with a scattering of hairs on top and smooth underneath. Lightly scented clusters of intricately shaped and colored flowers enhance this azalea, native to the eastern United States. Opening to blends of pink and white, the tubular flowers allow the petal margins to curl backward and expose a long flower style and numerous stamens which extend beyond the flower tube. Blooms reach about 2" across, and open just ahead of the leaves, into trusses of 6-12. E. North America. **NR/PE, pe.**

R. phaeochrysum (*dark golden*) s. Lacteum. 5', 5°F, EM, 3/3/2-3. Foliage on this plant is very interesting and attractive. The young shoots are entirely covered with close woolly hair which sloughs away in tufts as they mature. Mature leaves are large, to 6" long, oblong or oblong-lanceolate, dark green and hairless above with a lovely, suede-like dark golden brown indumentum below. Flowers, to 2" long, are funnel-bell-shaped, and range in color from white to creamy white to white blushed rose, sometimes spotted crimson, held in trusses of up to 15. Yunnan, Szechwan, Tibet, 11,000-12,500 ft. **R. phaeochrysum var. phaeochrysum/HY, hy, Taliensia.**

R. pholidotum (*scaly*) s. Heliolepis. 4', -5°F, L-VL, 2/2/2-3. New growth on this species is purplish and scaly. Aromatic medium sized leaves, about 2 1/2" long, ovate-elliptic, are dark green with impressed veins above, scaly on the reverse. Flowers, to 1 1/4" long, are widely funnel-campanulate-shaped, rose to deep rose-purple, with darker spots, held in trusses of about 5. Yunnan, Tibet, Upper Burma, 10,000-12,000 ft. **Syn. R. heliolepis var. brevistylum/RN, rn, Heliolepida.**

R. piercei (*after Mr. and Mrs. L. J. Pierce, rhododendron growers in the United States*) s. Neriiflorum s.s. Haematodes. 3', 0°F, E-EM, 3/3-4/2-3. Young growth is covered with dense brown hairs. Older leaves are medium sized, about 4", oblong to oblong-oval or oblong-obovate, and are smooth and hairless on top with a thick brown indumentum below. Clear crimson flowers, to just over 1" long, tubular-bell-shaped, with nectar pouches, are carried in trusses of 6-8. Tibet. **UC/HY, hy, Neriiflora.**

R. pingianum (*after Professor C. Ping, former Director of Biological Laboratory, Science Society of China, Nanking*) s. Arboreum s.s. Argyrophyllum. 6', 15°F?, E?, -/-/-. Foliage on this shrub is large, to 6" long, narrow and lance shaped. The leaves are glabrous light green on top, covered with thick, whitish or grey indumentum underneath. Purple funnel- bell-shaped flowers, to 1 1/2", are held in trusses of 12-18. Szechwan, 6,500-9,000 ft. **UC/HY, hy, Argyrophylla.**

R. planetum (*wandering; appeared as a rogue in cultivation*) s. Fortunei s.s. Davidii. 5', -10°F, E, 2-3/2-3/3/3. New growth on this plant is covered with white indumentum. Leaves reaching 8" in length, oblong-lanceolate, are bright glossy green above, paler below. Funnel-campanulate flowers, to 2" long, are clear pink, most often without blotch or spots. Unknown in the wild. **HY, hy, Known only in cultivation; allied to, or hybrid of R. sutchuenense.**

R. pleistanthum (*with most flowers*) s. Triflorum s.s. Yunnanense. 6', 0°F?, M, 3/3/3. Growth habit is tree-like. Leaves are on the smallish side, to only 2 1/2" long, narrowly elliptic in shape. The tops are slightly scaly, the undersides pale green with uniformly spaced yellow or brown scales. Flowers, to 1 1/4" long, are pink, lilac, or rose-lavender, often with yellow or reddish sports. They are carried in loose trusses. Yunnan. **UC/RN, rn, Triflora Yunnanense agg.**

R. pocophorum (*wool-bearing*) s. Neriiflorum s.s. Haematodes. 4', 5°F, E-EM, 3/3-4/2. Foliage is fairly large, to 6" long, oblong to oblong-obovate, often waxy blue-green on top, covered with a thick, brown, woolly indumentum underneath. Fleshy tubular-bell-shaped flowers, to 2" long, are scarlet-crimson or deep crimson, and are held in compact trusses of up to 20. S.E. Tibet, 12,000-15,000 ft. **R. pocophorum var. pocophorum/HY, hy, Neriiflora.**

R. pogonostylum (*with a bearded style*) s. and s.s. Irroratum. 6', 10°F, EM-L, 2/2/3. The foliage on this small tree is sturdy, with great substance. Leaves are medium large, to 5" long, oblong-lanceolate or oblong-ovate, and are waxy blue green on top, pale and slightly pitted on the underside. Flowers, to 1 1/2" long, are tubular-bell-shaped, pink with dark red spotting, carried in trusses of up to 8. A form with much less spotting has been named *R. adenostemonum*. S.E. Yunnan, 7,000-10,000 ft. **R. irroratum ssp. pogonostylum/HY, hy, Irrorata.**

R. polyandrum (*with many stamens*) s. and s.s. Maddenii. 5', 15°F, ML, 3-4/3-4/3-4. Habit is open and upright but somewhat straggling. Lance shaped leaves, to 4" long, are glossy dark green, netted, and slightly scaly on top, densely covered with cinnamon brown scales underneath. Fragrant flowers, to over 2 1/2" long, tubular-funnel-form, are white blushed pink or white, deepening to yellow in the throat, held in trusses to 6. Bhutan, Assam, 7,000-8,000 ft. **R. maddenii ssp. maddenii/RN, rn, Maddenia "Maddenii-Alliance".**

R. polycladum (*with many small branches*) s. Lapponicum. 3', -5°F, EM, 3/3/3. Growth habit is upright and open, the branches stiffly erect. Rather small leaves, to only 1" x 1/2", are oblong-lanceolate, rusty brown and scaly on both sides. Funnel shaped flowers, about 1/2" long, are lavender-blue to violet or purplish mauve, held in trusses of 5-6. Probably N.W. Yunnan. **UC/RN, rn, Lapponica.**

R. polylepis (*with many scales*) s. Triflorum s.s. Yunnanense. 6', 5°F, EM-L, 2/2/3. Growth habit is rather open and thin on this shrub. Oblong-lanceolate medium sized leaves, to 4" long, are dull green and hairless on top, densely covered with dry, flaky, overlapping brown scales underneath. Flowers, to 1 1/2" long, are widely funnel shaped and range in color from pale to dark purple or violet-purple, sometimes spotted yellow, held in trusses of 3-5. S. W. Szechwan, 7,200-11,500 ft. **UC/RN, rn, Triflora.**

R. ponticum (*from the Pontus, Asia Minor*) s. and s.s. Ponticum. 4', -15°F, L, 2-4/4/4-5. Habit is upright and open with 9" long leaves, oblong or lance shaped, smooth, dark glossy green on the top, paler on the reverse. Widely funnel-shaped flowers, to 2" long, are deep reddish purple to white or purple tinged pink, and are held in trusses of 10-15. This species is naturalized in many parts of the British Isles. Asia Minor, Caucasus, Armenia, Balkans, S. Spain, Portugal. **UC/HY, hy, Pontica.**

'Cheiranthifolium'-- s. & s.s. Ponticum. This is a garden form, quite an unusual species. Leaves are very irregular in shape, with quite narrow, wavy margins. Light reddish purple flowers are displayed in fantastic trusses of 30 to 35 flowers!

'Variegatum'-- Also known as 'Cheiranthifolium' variegated form s. & s.s. Ponticum. This extremely different form has white variegation along the margins of the leaves.

R. poukhanense-- see *R. yedoense*.

R. praestans (*excellent*) s. Grande. 5', 10°F, EM, 3/4/3. This is a large-leaf plant with a tree-like growth habit. Mature leaves attaining a tremendous size of 18" x 8" are oblong-obovate or oblong-oval. The tops are glabrous dark green with impressed veining; the undersides are covered with thin, plastered grey-white, fawn, or pale brown indumentum. Leaf stalks are characteristically short, winged and flat. 8-lobed flowers, to nearly 2" long, obliquely bell shaped, range from pink, magenta, and magenta-rose, to deep purple-rose to white tinged pale yellow, blotched crimson, and occur 15-20 to truss. Yunnan, W. Burma, S.E. Tibet, 9,000-14,000 ft. **UC/HY, hy, Grandia.**

R. praeteritum (*passed over*) s. Fortunei s.s. Oreodoxa. 5', -5°F, E, 2-3/3/3. Young branches on this shrub are bright green, turning reddish brown with age. Medium sized leaves are oval-oblong or oblong elliptic, dull dark green on the tops, paler on the undersides, hairless on both sides. Pink flowers, to 1 1/2" long, are widely bell shaped, and are held in trusses of 7-10. Very similar to *R. oreodoxa*, but has a 5-lobed corolla instead of 7-lobed. W. Hupeh. **UC/HY, hy, Fortunea.**

R. praevernum (*before the spring*) s. Fortunei s.s. Davidii. 5', -5°F, VE-EM, 2/3/3. Habit is open and upright. Large lance shaped leaves are dark matte green on top, pale grey-green below, glabrous on both sides. Tubular-bell-shaped flowers, to 2 1/2" long, are white or white blushed rose to wine red, with a darker wine blotch at the base. The blooms are held in trusses of 8-10. This species has come to be generally thought of as just part of the regular variation in *R. sutchuenense*, differing in its smaller flowers and narrower leaves. Hupeh, 5,000-7,000 ft. **UC/HY, hy, Fortunea.**

R. prattii (*after A. E. Pratt, who first discovered it near Tatsienlu, E. Szechwan*) s. Taliense s.s. Adenogynum. 5', 0°F, M, 2-3/4/3. This beautiful, rare plant has lovely large elliptic leaves to about 8" long. They are smooth, glossy dark green with thin brown indumentum on the undersides. Widely bell shaped flowers, to 2" long, are white, spotted and blotched deep pink or crimson, with leafy calyx up to 1/2" long, and are held in trusses up to 20. Szechwan, 9,000-13,000 ft. **R. faberi ssp. prattii/HY, hy, Taliensia.**

R. preptum (*distinguished*) s. Falconeri. 5', 5°F, EM-M, 3/3/2-3. New growth on this shrub or small tree is densely hairy. Mature olive green leaves, to 8" x 4", lose the hairiness on the tops, while the undersides are still covered with pale buff, brown, or dark brown indumentum. Obliquely campanulate flowers, to 1 1/2" long, are creamy white, blotched crimson, held in trusses of up to 20. Upper Burma, Yunnan, 11,000-12,000 ft. **UC/HY, hy, Falconera.**

R. primuliflorum (*with flowers like a Primula*) s. Anthopogon. 3', 5°F, E-M, 3-4/3/2-3. This shrub has highly aromatic foliage, with very bristly and scaly new shoots and deciduous leaf bud scales. Leaves are rather small, to only 1 1/4" x 1/2", oblong or ovate-oblong, shiny and glabrous on top, densely scaly and white to brown underneath. Narrow tubular shaped flowers, with spreading lobes, to 3/4", are white, yellow or pale rose, and are carried in small, compact, bead-like trusses. Differs from *R. cephalanthum* because of its deciduous leaf bud scales. The two varieties, var. *cephalanthoides* and var. *lepidanthum* are different only in corolla indumentum. Yunnan, Szechwan, Kansu, 11,000-15,000 ft. **UC/RN, po.**

R. prinophyllum (*with leaves like Prinos*) s. Azalea s.s. Luteum. 5', -25°F, M, 3/2-3/3. This is a deciduous shrub, with clove scented flowers opening at the same time as the leaves. Small to medium sized foliage, is obovate or oblong-obovate, slightly hairy on the top and densely covered underneath with grey or bluish green hairs. Tubular funnel shaped flowers, to 1 1/2" wide are pale to deeper pink, most often with a dark brownish red blotch, and are held in trusses of 5-9. This is the plant that was known as *R. roseum*. E. North America. **UC/PE, pe.**

R. pronum (*prostrate*) s. Taliense s.s. Roxieanum. 1', -10ºF, EM-M, 3/4-5/2-3. This interesting dwarf shrub is slow growing and prostrate, with leaf-bud scales that persist for many years and distinctively gnarled, rooting branchlets. Leaves, to 2 3/4" x 1", oblong, oblong elliptic or oblanceolate, are bluish green on top when young, covered with thick dull grey or fawn indumentum underneath. Bell shaped flowers, to 1 1/2" long, held in trusses of 8-12, are creamy yellow, generously spotted deep crimson. Yunnan, Szechwan, S.E. Tibet, 12,000-15,000 ft. **UC/HY, hy, Taliensia.**

R. prostratum (*low-growing*) s. Saluenense. 1 1/2', -5ºF, EM, 3/3/3. Growth habit of this dwarf is low, prostrate, and spreading. Small leaves, to only 3/4" long, are elliptic or ovate-elliptic, glossy green with veins on top, dense brown scales underneath. Widely funnel shaped, flat and open flowers, to 3/4" long, are crimson or deep rosy purple, with crimson spotting, and occur in clusters of 1-3. Yunnan, Szechwan, Tibet, 12,000-16,000 ft. **R. saluenense ssp. chameunum Prostratum Group/RN, rn, Saluenensia.**

R. proteoides (*resembling a Protea*) s. Taliense s.s. Roxieanum. 1', -10ºF, EM, 3/5/3. This is a rare and unusual species, a slow growing, tightly compact and spreading shrub with typically outstanding Taliense foliage. Thick woolly, red-brown indumentum on the undersides of nicely shaped, rich green leaves contributes much to the appeal of this plant. Bell shaped flowers, to 1 1/2" long, are pink in the bud, opening to a creamy white or white blushed rose, generously spotted crimson. Difficult to propagate. The "connoisseur-collector's" ultimate goal. Yunnan, Szechwan, S.E. Tibet, 12,000-14,000 ft. **UC/HY, hy, Taliensia.**

R. protistum (*first of the first*) s. Grande. 6', 20ºF, VE, 3/3-4/3. "Grande" describes this plant well. It is a spectacular, large leaved, tree-like shrub, with foliage that reaches a size to 18" x 9". The young growth is densely covered with greyish yellow indumentum. Mature leaves are lanceolate to oblanceolate, dark, wrinkled and impressed with veins on top, indumented paler greyish green underneath. Trusses are beautiful and large, holding 20 to 30 flowers each. Flowers, to 2" long, are tubular-bell-shaped, creamy white, blushed rose. A truly fine species. Different from *R. giganteum* in its usually glabrous lower leaf surface. N.W. Yunnan, Upper Burma, 9,000-13,000 ft. **R. protistum var. protistum/HY, hy, Grandia.**

R. prunifolium (*with leaves like those of a plum*) s. Azalea s.s. Luteum. 4', -15ºF, VL, 4/3/3-4. This is one of the great Eastern native azaleas, considered especially valuable for its late flowering in July and August. Habit is upright and spreading, round topped when mature. Oval leaves, to 5" long, are smooth dark green on top, paler underneath. Tubular-funnel-form flowers, about 2" wide, open after the leaves are fully developed. They are apricot orange, scarlet, crimson, or orange-red, and are held in trusses of 4-5. S.E. North America. **UC/PE, pe.**

R. przewalskii (*after N. M. Przewalski, 1839-88, Russian traveller and geographer*) s. Lacteum. 5', 5ºF, EM, 2-3/2-3/2. New growth on this plant is lovely bright yellow. Medium sized mature foliage, is oblong-elliptic, dark green and glabrous on the top, indumented thin white to brown on the underside, sometimes with scattered hairs. Flowers, to 1 1/2" long, funnel-bell-shaped, are white or rosy pink, occasionally with rosy purple spotting, and are carried in trusses of 10-15. Kansu, Tibet, Szechwan, 10,000-14,000 ft. **UC/HY, hy, Taliensia.**

R. pseudochrysanthum (*false R. chrysanthum*) s. Barbatum s.s. Maculiferum. 1-3', -10ºF, EM, 3/4-5/4-5. Leaves seem to be crowded on this compact shrub. They are ovate, elliptic, or oblong-lanceolate, glossy dark green on top, paler on the undersides, both sides very slightly hairy. Bell shaped flowers, to 2" long, are dark pink in the bud, opening to pale pink or white, occasionally with rose lines outside, crimson spotted inside, held in trusses of 9-20. There are several forms of this variable species being grown. Formosa, 6,000-13,000 ft. **UC/HY, hy, Maculifera.**

    Ben Nelson's form-- Longer, larger leaves distinguish this form from the Exbury A.M. form. Indumentum occurs along the midvein on the leaf underside. Silvery tomentum dusts the leaves and stems of new growth for many weeks; glossy green leaf surfaces are exposed after the tomentum is worn away. *R. pseudochrysanthum's* unusual rigid leaves are recurved along the leaf margin. Pink buds open to white flowers.

    Dwarf form-- A dwarf in every sense of the word. Has a tight growth habit. Short stems bear small leaves which frequently are purple on the leaf underside.

    Exbury form-- The great silver foliage form. Won an award of Merit.

    'Komo Kulshan'-- Long foliage exhibits silvery tomentum when new.

    Sunningdale form-- An form interesting for its buff colored tomentum.

R. pseudoyanthinum-- see *concinnum*.

R. pubescens (*pubescent*) s. Scabrifolium. 4', -5ºF, EM, 3/3/4. Growth habit is compact and upright, with bristly and soft hairy new growth. Leaves, to about 3/4" long, quite narrow, are densely hairy on both sides, also somewhat scaly on the undersides. Funnel-form flowers, to 2/3" long, are rose or pinkish white, blooming along the branches between leaf clusters into trusses of 1-4. Szechwan, Yunnan, 10,000 ft. **UC/RN, rn, Scabrifolia.**

R. pudorosum (*very bashful*) s. Grande. 6', -5ºF, E, 3-4/3-4/3. Growth is tree-like, with densely hairy new growth, and young branches heavily coated with long lasting leaf bud scales. Adult leaves are large, to 9" long, oblong or oblanceolate, darker green on top with a rather thin silvery grey indumentum on the undersides. Thick tubular bell shaped flowers, to 1 1/2" long, are mauve-pink, with a magenta or purple blotch at the base, held in large trusses of up to 24. S. Tibet, 11,000-12,500 ft. **UC/HY, hy, Grandia.**

R. pumilum (*dwarf*) s. Uniflorum. To 8", -5ºF, ML, 3/3/2. Habit of this dwarf rhododendron is tight and compact, forming a low, spreading mound. Small elliptic leaves, to only 3/4" long, are smooth bluish green, scaly on the undersides. Bell shaped flowers, to 3/4" long, are pink or rose, and are in trusses of 1-3. This is an ideal rock garden plant, but needs very good drainage. Sikkim, Tibet, E. Nepal, N.E. Bhutan, 11,000-14,000 ft. **UC/RN, rn, Uniflora.**

R. puralbum (*pure white*) s. Thomsonii s.s. Souliei. 4', -5ºF, M, 3-4/3/2-3. Growth habit is upright and open to compact. Oblong leaves to 5" x 2", are dark green on top, bright blue-green underneath, hairless on both sides. Pure white flowers, to 1 1/2" long, with distinctive calyx up to 1/2" in depth, are saucer or open-cup shaped, and are held in trusses of up to 8. Differs botanically from *R. souliei* and *R. wardii* only in white flowers. Yunnan, 11,000-14,000 ft. **R. wardii var. puralbum/HY, hy, Campylocarpa.**

R. quinquefolium (*leaves in fives*) s. Azalea s.s. Schlippenbachii. 2 1/2', -5ºF, EM, 3/5/2-3. Growth habit is slow growing deciduous shrub is compact and tight, forming a finely shaped shilhouette, with many branches holding broadly elliptic or obovate leaves, to about 2" long. Delicate light green leaves unfold at stem tips in whorls of four or five leaves. Known for its beautifully shaded spring foliage, the plant often has leaf margins lightly edged with red. Wide bell shaped flowers, to 2" across, open with the leaves into pendulous trusses of 1-3. They are pure white, spotted green. C. **Japan. UC/TT, br.** Note: There is disagreement as to placement of this and some botanists have it in **PE, sc.**

R. racemosum (*flowers in racemes*) s. Scabrifolium. 2-5', -5ºF, E-EM, 4/3/4-5. Habit is upright and open on this pert plant. Find a sunny spot for it, and it will delight the eye at every season of the year with its glossy round leaves and many erect red stems. Leaves, to about 2" long, have scaly undersides with a waxy blue-green bloom. Funnel-form flowers, to about 1" long, white or white tinged pink open from deep rose pink buds, occuring along upper portions of the stems and in multiples at stem tips. Fairly early in the flowering season, this lovely shrub will appear as a bundle of clear pink plumes. Many forms are grown, some are dwarf and others are much taller growing. Yunnan, Szechwan, 6,000-14,000 ft. **UC/RN, rn, Scabrifolia.**
  'Rock Rose'-- A free-flowering selection with clear pink flowers.

R. radicans (*rooting*) s. Saluenense. To 3 to 6", -10ºF, EM, 3/4/3-4. Habit of this dwarf is prostrate and creeping, with rooting branches which weave a dense low mat against the earth. Leaves, quite small to only 1/2" long, narrowly lance shaped, are brilliant shiny green on top, densely covered with reddish brown scales underneath. Flowers, usually solitary, to 3/4" long, wide funnel form, are bright purple or deep purple-red. S.E. Tibet 14,000-15,000 ft. **R. calostrotum ssp. keleticum Radicans Group/RN, rn, Saluenensia.**

R. ramosissimum (*very branched*) s. Lapponicum. 2', -10ºF?, EM, 2/2/-. This semi-dwarf has very small foliage and tiny flowers. Broadly elliptic leaves, to only 1/4" long, have heavy scaling on both sides, with rusty brick red, uniform, overlapping scales on the underside. Flowers, to 1/3" long, widely funnel shaped, are deep purple, purplish red or dark purplish blue. Szechwan, 11,000-14,500 ft. **Syn. R. nivale ssp. boreale/RN, rn, Lapponica.**

R. ramsdenianum (*after Sir John Ramsden, who cultivated rhododendrons at Muncaster*) s. and s.s. Irroratum. 6', 10ºF, EM, 2-3/2-3/3. Growth habit is bushy and tree-like. Medium sized leaves are widely lanceolate to oblong-lanceolate, hairless on both sides, pale and shiny underneath. Fleshy flowers, to about 1 1/2" long, tubular bell shaped, are crimson, scarlet-crimson or deep rose, occasionally spotted or blotched dark crimson, with nectar pouches. The blooms are held in trusses of 12-15. S.E. Tibet, 8,000 ft. **UC/HY, hy, Irrorata.**

R. ravum (*grey*) s. Lapponicum. 18", -15ºF, EM-M, 3-4/3/2-3. New growth on this little evergreen shrub is densely scaly, whitish and brown. Mature leaves, to about 2 1/2" long, are oblong-elliptic with a heavy coating of scales on both sides. The tops are dark green with silvery scales, the undersides shining yellowish brown. Tiny funnel-form flowers, to only 3/4" long, in trusses of 3 to 5, are rosy purple or purple. Similar to *R. cuneatum*, except for its smaller flowers. Yunnan, 10,000-15,000 ft. **Syn. R. cuneatum/RN, rn, Lapponica.**

R. recurvoides (*resembling R. recurvum*) s. Taliense s.s. Roxieanum. 2', -10ºF, EM-M, 3/5/4. Habit is small and compact, and, if the Taliense series is the Rolls Royce of rhododendrons, *R. recurvoides* is a Silver Cloud. Foliage is long, narrow and pointed, to 3", heavily coated with a white indumentum which turns later to orangy brown. The Roxianum subseries includes numerous plants that are the best in the genus for foliage, and *R. recurvoides* is a star in this group. Funnel-bell-shaped flowers, to 2 1/2" wide, are white, or white blushed rose, spotted crimson, held in compact trusses of 4-7. Upper Burma, 11,000 ft. **UC/HY, hy, Glischra.**

R. repens-- see *forrestii* var. *repens*.

R. reticulatum (*netted, referring to the venation*) s. Azalea s.s. Schlippenbachii. 6', -10ºF, EM, 3-4/3/3. This famed "Three Leaf" Azalea from Japan is a deciduous, upright growing shrub. Leaves, to 2 1/2" long, are almost round, and occur in threes or pairs whorled at stem tips. However, juvenile growth shoots often occur with leaves all along the stem. Distinctively veined leaves are rather dull dark green on top, paler underneath. Fluorescent bright pinkish or rose purple flowers, occasionally spotted, which open before the leaves, to 2" wide, are rotate funnel-form, and occur either singly or in pairs. Japan. **UC/TT, br.**

R. rex (*king*) s. Falconeri. 6', 5ºF, EM, 3/4/3-4. Foliage on this large leaved plant reaches 18" x 6". Leaves, oblong-oval or oblong-elliptic, are shiny dark green above, indumented grey, buff or brown underneath. Flowers, to 2 1/2" long, tubular-bell-shaped, are pale pink, rose, or white, blotched and spotted crimson, and are held in large trusses of up to 30. A very fine, beautiful rhododendron. Is like *R. fictolacteum* but has longer, relatively broader leaves and stouter branchlets. Szechwan 10,000-11,000 ft. **R. rex ssp. rex/HY, hy, Falconera.**

R. rhabdotum (*striped*) s. Maddenii s.s. Megacalyx. 5', 25ºF, M-VL, 4/2/3. Growth habit is straggling and leggy, with very bristly, scaly, new foliage. Mature leaves, narrowly oblong in shape, to 6" long, are glabrous above, glaucous green and scaly underneath. Flowers, to 4" long, broadly tubular-bell-shaped, are creamy or ivory white, deeply flushed yellow inside, with conspicuous, external, very fine red stripes, and are carried in trusses of 4-6. S.E. Tibet, Bhutan, Assam, 5,000-8,000 ft. **R. dalhousiae var. rhabdotum/RN, rn, Maddenia "Dalhousiae-Alliance".**

R. rigidum (*stiff*) s. Triflorum s.s. Yunnanense. 6', -5ºF, EM, 4/3/4. This plant is a beautiful sight when in full flower, appearing as a cloud of smoky pink. Leaves, to 2 1/2" long, elliptic to oblanceolate, are pale bluish green and scaly. Widely funnel shaped flowers, to 1 1/4" long, are white to pink or intense rosy lavender, occasionally spotted red. Yunnan, Szechwan, 2,600-11,000 ft. **UC/RN, rn, Triflora Yunnanense agg.**
  'Album'-- A most beautiful white flower. It produces flowers in such profusion that the plant appears like a floating cloud of white.

R. ripense (*on the banks of rivers*) s. Azalea s.s. Obtusum. 4', 5ºF, EM, 3/3/3. This interesting semi-deciduous shrub is distinctive because of the nature of its foliage; there are 2 separate forms on the plant at the same time. Spring leaves, up to 2 1/4" x 1", lance shaped or oblanceolate, are grey or grey-brown, covered with stiff, flat hairs; summer leaves are smaller and more rounded at tip. Flowers, to 1 1/2" wide, sometimes, but rarely to 4 1/2", widely funnel shaped, are white to pale mauve and are held in trusses of 1-3. S. Japan. **UC/TT, tt.**

R. ririei (*after Rev. B. Ririe of the Chinese Inland Missions and friend of E. H. Wilson*) s. Arboreum s.s. Argyrophyllum. 5', -5ºF, VE, 3/3/3. This is an open, upright grower which might bloom as early as February if weather is mild. Oblong lance shaped leaves, up to 6" x 2", are glabrous bright matte green on top with a thin white or greyish indumentum on the undersides. Flowers, to 2" long, broadly bell shaped, range from light to dull purple or smokey blue, with distinctive dark purple nectar pouches, and are carried in trusses to 10. Szechwan (Mt. Omei), 4,000-6,000 ft. **UC/HY, hy, Argyrophylla.**

R. rockii (*after J. F. Rock, who was the first to collect it*) s. Arboreum s.s. Argyrophyllum. 5', 5ºF?, E-M?, 3/3/3. Foliage on this shrub is long and narrow, and on the large side. The top is deep green, and the underside is covered densely with thick, woolly greyish indumentum over a lower layer that is white and crusty. Funnel-bell-shaped flowers, to 1 3/4" long, are pale rose or pinkish purple, spotted darker reddish or magenta, held in trusses of 6-12. S. Kansu, N. Szechwan, 6,000-8,000 ft. **R. hunnewellianum ssp. rockii/HY, hy, Argyrophylla.**

R. rothschildii (*after L. de Rothschild, 1882-1942, of Exbury*) s. Falconeri. 5', 5ºF, EM, 3-4/4-5/2-3. Foliage is quite large on this species, to 14" x 5 1/2". Oblong-obovate, leaves are hairless and shiny green on the tops, covered on the undersides with a discontinuous, brownish indumentum atop a lower layer of very thin yellowish felt. Bell shaped flowers, to about 1 2/3" long, are pale creamy white to pale yellow, blotched crimson, and are carried in trusses of 12-17. Yunnan, Yunnan-Tibet border, 12,600 ft. **UC/HY, hy, Falconera.**

R. roxieanum (*after Mrs. Roxie Hanna of Tali-fu, China, friend of George Forrest*) s. Taliense *s.s.* Roxieanum. 3', -10ºF, EM, 3/5/4. Habit is compact and very slow growing. This plant is one of those rarities in the Taliense series that everyone wants. Oblong to lanceolate leaves, to 5" long, are deep green, heavily covered with cinnamon indumentum. New foliage has white tomentum which gradually turns into shades of tan. Bell shaped flowers, to 1 1/2" long, are creamy white or white faintly tinged rose, occasionally crimson spotted, held in trusses of up to to 20. Very variable. Yunnan, Szechwan, S.E. Tibet, 11,000-14,000 ft. **R. roxieanum var. roxieanum/HY, hy, Taliensia.**

> **var. oreonastes**-- The dwarf alpine form of this species. Flowers are white with pink. Should be considered as an investment which can only grow in value in the future. In fact, a specimen plant today would be "worth its weight in gold" as the old saying goes. **R. roxieanum var. roxieanum Oreonastes Group.**

R. roxieanum var. oreonastes

R. rubiginosum (*reddish brown*) s. Heliolepis. 6', 0ºF, EM, 3/2-3/3-4. Habit is open and upright, with distinctive, scaly, purplish new growth. Lance shaped leaves, to about 3 1/2", are smooth dull green on top, covered densely with reddish brown scales underneath. Funnel-bell-shaped flowers, to 1 1/4" long, are pink, rose, or rosy lilac, spotted brown, carried in trusses of 4-8. Very much like *R. desquamatum;* in fact, current revisions of the classification of rhododendron species list *R. desquamatum* as a synonym of *R. Rubiginosum.* Szechwan, Yunnan, S.E. Tibet, 7,500-14,000 ft. **UC/RN, rn, Heliolepida.**

> 'Rosey Ball'-- Form selected for superior flower and foliage.

R. rubrolineatum (*lined with red*) s. Trichocladum. 3', 0ºF, ML, 2/1-2/2. Habit is deciduous or semi-deciduous, with small leaves to only 1 1/3" x 3/4". Foliage is obovate-elliptic or oblong-oval with hairless dark olive green tops and yellow dense scales underneath. Wide funnel shaped flowers, to 3/4" long, are yellow, lined and flushed rose externally, held in trusses of 3-4. N.W. Yunnan, S.E. Tibet. 11,000-14,000 ft. **R. mekongense var. rubrolineatum/RN, rn, Trichoclada.**

R. rubropilosum (*with red hairs*) s. Azalea s.s. Obtusum. 4', 5FºF?, M, 2-3/3/3. This is an evergreen shrub, with interesting foliage which tends to crowd together at branch ends. Small leaves, to 1 3/4" x 3/4", are oblong-lanceolate or elliptic-lanceolate. The top sides are dark green with sparse, stiff flat hairs; the undersides are paler with a much denser covering of grey to brown appressed hairs. Funnel shaped flowers, to 1" wide, are pink spotted mauve, and are held in trusses of 2-4. Formosa. **UC/TT, tt.**

R. rude (*rough*) s. Barbatum s.s. Glischrum. 5', 5ºF, EM, 3/3/2-3. Foliage on this plant is large, to 8" x 3", oblanceolate, oblong-obovate, or lanceolate. The leaves are dark green and bristly with impressed main veins on the tops, paler and covered with long glandular bristles underneath. Bell shaped open flowers, to 1 1/2" long, are rose to purplish crimson. Blooms accented with darker lines and a calyx to at least 1/2" long are carried in trusses of up to 10. Like *R. glischrum* but has leaves that are hairy on both sides. Yunnan, S.E. Tibet, 11,000-12,000 ft. **R. glischrum ssp. rude/HY, hy, Glischra.**

R. rufum (*red*) s. Taliense s.s. Wasonii. 4', -5ºF, EM, 3/3-4/3. This shrub has medium large leaves, to 5" x 2", oblong, oblong-obovate or elliptic. The top sides are hairless, the reverse covered with a thick, tawny-to-dark brown indumentum. Funnel-bell-shaped flowers, to 1 1/2" long, are white or pinkish-purple, with crimson spots, held in trusses of 6-10. Foliage can be outstanding on this species. Szechwan, Kansu, 10,000-12,000 ft. **UC/HY, hy, Taliensia.**

R. rupicola (*dweller among rocks*) s. Lapponicum. 18", -10ºF, EM, 4/3/2. This small, upright, open growing shrub has densely scaly new growth. Attractive leaves, to only 3/4" long, are oblong-lance shape, with dark green and very scaly tops, yellowish grey and scaly underneath. Flowers, to 1/2" long, wide funnel-form, are rich royal purple or plum crimson with yellow stamens, held in trusses of 2-5. Must have good drainage and cool roots. Yunnan, Szechwan, 10,000-14,000 ft. **R. rupicola var. rupicola/RN, rn, Lapponica.**

> **var. chryseum** (*golden yellow*) Aromatic foliage surrounds trusses composed of up to 6 bright yellow flowers with scaley lobes on the outside.

R. russatum (*reddened*) s. Lapponicum. 3', -15ºF, EM, 4/3/4. Habit is upright and open, with scaly new growth. Oval leaves, to 1 3/4" long, are dark green, densely covered with rusty scales on the undersides. Wide funnel-form flowers, to 3/4" long, are royal purple, deep indigo blue, pink, or rose, and are carried in trusses from 4-10. A variable species; many forms are grown. Yunnan, Szechwan, 11,000-14,000 ft. **UC/RN, rn, Lapponica.**

> **F.C.C. form**-- From Exbury, widely grown in U.S.
> **white form**-- has brown-gold foliage.

R. russotinctum (*tinged with red*) s. Taliense s.s. Roxieanum. 3', -5ºF, EM, 2-3/3-4/3. Narrowly oblong leaves on this species, to 4" x 1", are matte green, almost hairless above, but indumented brownish or brick red underneath. Bell shaped flowers, to 1 1/2" long, are white or white blushed rose, with a few crimson spots, and are held in compact trusses of 8-12. S.E. Tibet, N.W. Yunnan, 9,000-14,000 ft. **R. alutaceum var. russotinctum/HY, hy, Taliensia.**

R. saluenense (*from the Salwin river, China*) s. Saluenense. 18", -5ºF, EM, 4/3-4/4. This appealing little shrub forms a small mound of many ascending stems which curve to form layers of horizontal branches. Small rounded leaves, to 1 1/2" long, are aromatic, glossy, and hairy along leaf margins, becoming shaded purple in winter. Open flat flowers, to 1 3/4" across, are rosy purple to deep purplish crimson or royal purple, spotted crimson, and are carried in trusses of 2-5. Very variable in growth habit. S.E. Tibet, Yunnan, Szechwan, 11,000-14,000 ft. **R. saluenense ssp. saluenense/RN, rn, Saluenensia.**

R. sanctum (*holy, found growing in the sacred area of the Great Shrine of Ise*) s. Azalea s. s. Schlippenbachii. 5', -5ºF, EM, 3-4/3-4/3. This is a deciduous or semi-evergreen shrub with interesting foliage grouped at the stem ends. Leaves, to 3" long, more or less diamond shaped, are somewhat shiny with rusty brown hairs on top, paler on the reverse. Open funnel-form flowers, to 1" long, are white or bright pinkish purple, held in trusses of 2-4. Japan. **UC/TT, br.**

R. sanguineum (*blood red*) s. Neriiflorum s.s. Sanguineum. 3', 0ºF, M, 3-4/3-4/3. Growth habit is compact, with medium sized leaves, obovate or narrowly oblong, hairless matte green on the top with a thin grey-white indumentum underneath. Tubular-bell-shaped flowers, to 1 1/2" long, with heavy substance, are a bright crimson to scarlet or carmine, with nectar pouches, and are held in trusses of 3-6. N.W. Yunnan, S.E. Tibet, 11,000-14,500 ft. **R. sanguineum ssp. sanguineum var. sanguineum/HY, hy,** Neriiflora.
   ssp. cloiophorum-- Leaf-bud scales are deciduous, with rose or rose slightly flushed yellow flowers. Ovary is eglandular and tomentose. N.W. Yunnan, S.E. Tibet, 11,000-14,000 ft. **R. sanguineum ssp. sanguineum var. cloiophorum.**
   ssp. consanguineum-- Different because of glandular and tomentose ovary. N.W. Yunnan, S.E. Tibet, 14,000 ft. **Syn. R. sanguineum ssp. sanguineum var. didymoides.**
   ssp. didymum-- Leaf-bud scales stay longer. Ovary is glandular and tomentose on black-crimson flowers. S.E. Tibet, 14,000-15,000 ft. **ssp. didymum.**
   ssp. haemaleum-- Leaf-bud scales are deciduous, with blackish crimson flowers, the ovary eglandular and tomentose. N.W. Yunnan, S.E. Tibet, 11,000-13,000 ft. **ssp. sanguineum var. haemaleum.**
   ssp. mesaeum-- Very nice plant for both foliage and flowers. Rounded leaves are waxy green with red stems. Flower color is dark black-crimson. The best of the *sanguineums*. S.E. Tibet, 12,000-15,000 ft. **Syn. R. sanguineum ssp. sanguineum var. haemaleum.**
   ssp. roseotinctum-- Similar to ssp. *cloiophorum*, except that flowers are usually creamy white, margined deep rose crimson. They also bloom in combinations of yellow and pink, glandular and tomentose ovary. N.W. Yunnan, S.E. Tibet, Upper Burma, 11,000-16,000 ft. **Syn. R. sanguineum ssp. sanguineum var. didymoides.**

R. sargentianum (*after C. S. Sargent, d. 1927, a former Director of the Arnold Arboretum, Mass.*) s. Anthopogon. 1', -5ºF, EM, 3/4/2. This is a very compact, dwarf shrub which spreads to 10" or 12" and is only 6"-12" high in 10 years. Small, oval, aromatic leaves, to 2/3" long, are bright shiny green with a network of veins on the top sides, densely scaly on the undersides. Tubular flowers with spreading lobes, to only 2/3" long, held in loose clusters of 2-5, are pale lemon yellow or white to creamy white. Szechwan, 9,000-11,000 ft. **UC/RN, po.**

R. sataense (*of Sata, Kyushu Island, Japan*) 4', -10ºF, M, 4/4/4. The location in which this plant grows will affect the mature size. Open areas will encourage a dense, shrubby habit between 3-6' in height, while specimens growing in woodland areas will have an open habit stretching to heights of 10'. Elliptic foliage is between 3/4 to 1 1/2". Flowers range from pink or red to purple. Mt. Takakuma, Kyushu, Japan. **UC/TT, tt.**

R. scabrifolium (*with rough leaves*) s. Scabrifolium. 4', 5ºF, E-M, 3/3/3-4. Not a neat shrub, the habit is often straggly and unkempt looking, with bristly and hairy new growth. Oblanceolate leaves, to about 3 1/2" long, have dark green tops with a rough textured, wrinkled appearance and paler undersides with soft hairs and scales. Tubular funnel-form flowers, to about 3/4" long, white to pink or deep rose, bloom in trusses of 2-3 between leaf clusters along the upper branches. Yunnan, 5,000-11,000 ft. **R. scabrifolium var. scabrifolium/RN, rn, Scabrifolia.**

R. scabrum (*rough*) s. Azalea s.s. Obtusum. 4', 15ºF, EM-M, 3/2-3/3. This evergreen shrub has dimorphic leaves. The first ones, to 4" x 1 1/2", elliptic-lanceolate to lanceolate, are dark green and hairless on top and paler with a layer of close, stiff, flat hairs underneath, the edges slightly toothed and slightly downward rolling. Later leaves are oblanceolate. Widely funnel shaped flowers, to 2 1/2" across, are rosy red to brilliant scarlet, spotted darkly on upper lobes, with a green calyx sometimes as large as 1/2". They are carried in trusses of 2-6. Liukiu Archipelago. **NR/TT, tu.**

R. schizopeplum (*with a split covering*) s. and s.s. Taliense. 3', -10ºF, EM-M, 3/3/-. Medium sized leaves, to 3 1/2" x 1 1/2", elliptic or oblong-elliptic to oblong, are matte green and almost hairless on the tops, covered underneath with a more or less sticky white to buff or brown indumentum which splits irregularly later on. Bell shaped flowers, to 1/2" long, are rose or white tinged pink, with darker crimson spots, held in trusses of 8-10. Yunnan, 12,000-14,000 ft. **Syn. R. aganniphum var. aganniphum/HY, hy, Taliensia.**

R. schlippenbachii (*after Baron von Schlippenbach, naval officer and traveller*) s. Azalea s. s. Schlippenbachii. 4', -25ºF, E-EM, 4/3-4/4. Growth habit of this deciduous shrub is upright and open with thinly textured leaves in whorls of five at each stem tip, and flowers which emerge either just before or along with the leaves. The light foliage will not tolerate excessive sun exposure, and the choice of a location protected from afternoon summer sun will result in a soft green well shaped plant. Obovate leaves, to 5", are dark green and smooth on top, paler beneath with a few hairs, turning to crimson, orange or yellow in autumn. Star-like delicate pink flowers, to almost 3 1/2" across, flat-saucer-shaped, may also be white tinged pink or white with reddish spots. They are held in trusses of 3-6. Korea, Manchuria and neighboring parts of Russia. **NR/TT, br.** Note: There is disagreement as to placement of this plant and some botanists place in **PE, sc.**
   'Sid's Royal Pink'-- Exceptional flowers of deeper pink.

R. scintillans (*sparkling*) s. Lapponicum. 2', -10ºF, Em-M, 3/2/3. Habit is low and sprawling. Small leaves, to only 1/2" x 1/16", oblanceolate, are dark green and densely covered with shiny yellowish scales on top. Undersides are greyish and heavily covered with shiny, uniform reddish brown scales. Flowers, to 2/3" long, broadly funnel-shaped, are purplish rose to lavender blue or almost royal blue, held in trusses of 3-6. Yunnan, 10,000-14,500 ft. **R. polycladum Scintillans Group/RN, rn, Lapponica.**

R. scopulorum (*of crags*) s. Maddenii s.s. Ciliicalyx. 5', 20ºF, EM-M, 3/2/3. Obovate-oblanceolate leaves, 2 1/2" x 1 1/4", crowded, are olive blue-green and hairless above with sparse tiny scales below. Fragrant flowers, to 2" long and 3" wide, funnel-bell-shaped, are white or white tinged pink, with a yellow blotch, and are held in trusses of 3-7. E. Tibet, 6,000 ft. **UC/RN, rn, Maddenia "Ciliicalyx-Alliance".**

R. scottianum (*after M. B. Scott, 1889-1917, a Kew botanist*) s. Maddenii s.s. Ciliicalyx. 6', 20ºF, M-L, 3/2/3. New growth on this species is covered heavily with scales. Mature leaves, to 4" x 1 1/2", are obovate or elliptic, hairless on the tops, densely covered with reddish brown scales underneath. Very fragrant flowers, to 4" long and nearly as much across, very wide funnel-shape, are white, sometimes tinged with rose, blotched yellow, and are held in trusses of 2-4. Yunnan, 6,000-8,000 ft. **Syn. R. pachypodum/RN, rn, Maddenia "Ciliicalyx-Alliance" Ciliicalyx agg.**

R. searsiae (*after Sarah C. Sears, an American artist*) s. Triflorum s.s. Yunnanense. 6', -5ºF, E-M, 3/3/3. Growth habit is open and upright. Medium sized lance shaped leaves are hairless and dark green on top, bluish green and densely scaly underneath. Flowers, to 1 1/2", are wide funnel shaped, ranging in color from white to pale rose or rose lavender, spotted pale green, held in trusses of 3-4. Szechwan, 7,500-9,800 ft. **UC/RN, rn, Triflora.**

R. seinghkuense (*from the Seinghku Valley, Upper Burma*) s. Edgeworthii. 2', 15ºF, E, 3-4/3/-. This plant may be epiphytic at times. New growth is very woolly. Leaves to 3" x 1 1/2", ovate to oblong-elliptic in shape, are almost hairless and quite wrinkled and puffy on top, scaly with dense reddish brown hairs underneath. Flowers, occurring either singly or in pairs, to 1" long, very open saucer shape, are bright sulphur yellow with reddish brown anthers. Burma, 6,000-10,000 ft. **UC/RN, rn, Edgeworthia.**

R. selense (*from Sie-La, W. Yunnan*) *s.* Thomsonii *s.s.* Selense. 4', -5°F, E-M, 3/3/3. Growth habit of this shrub is upright and open. The leaves, to 3 1/2" long, oblong to elliptic or obovate, are hairless and dark green on top, paler underside. Funnel-bell-shape flowers, to 1 1/2" long, range from white to pale pink or rose, sometimes crimson blotched or spotted, and are held in trusses of 3-8. Often blooms very slowly, with a tendency to hide flowers underneath the foliage. Tibet, Yunnan, Szechwan, 10,000-14,500 ft. **R. selense ssp. selense/HY, hy, Selensia.**

  var. duseimatum-- Leaves are oblong-lanceolate and ovary is tomentose. S.E. Tibet, 12,000 ft. **R. calvescens var. duseimatum.**

  var. pagophilum-- Leaves and flowers are smaller; with dark rose or crimson flower. Yunnan-Tibet border, 12,000-14,000 ft. **Syn. of R. selense ssp. selense.**

  var. probum-- Flowers are white, without spots. Yunnan, S.E. Tibet, 11,000-13,000 ft. **Syn. R. selense ssp. selense.**

R. semibarbatum (*partially bearded*) *s.* Semibarbatum. 4', -5°F, L-VL, 1/2-3/2-3. This is a rare, deciduous plant unlike any other rhododendron. Habit is upright and open. Elliptic or oblong leaves to 2" long, often red on the edges, are smooth dark green on top, paler on the reverse. Flowers, emerging after the leaves, are shy, their small size sometimes causing them to almost disappear in the foliage. They are flat-faced rotate-funnel-shaped, white or yellowish white with a touch of pink, spotted red, emerging from lateral buds crowded at branch ends. Japan. **UC/MU.**

R. semnoides (*resembling R. semnum*) *s.* Grande. 4', 5°F, E, 2-3/3/2-3. Growth habit is open and tree-like, the new foliage having a lovely greyish buff indumentum. Mature leaves are large, to 12" x 5", oblong-oval or obovate-elliptic. The top sides are hairless bright matte green, and the reverse sides have a thick covering of woolly light brown indumentum. Cup-bell-shaped flowers, to 2" long, carried in large trusses of 15-20 are white, blushed rose, with a heavy crimson blotch. S.E. Tibet, 12,000-13,000 ft. **UC/HY, hy, Falconera.**

R. serotinum (*late i.e. autumnal*) *s.* and *s.s.* Fortunei. 6', -5°F, VL, 3/3/3-4. Habit is often very lax and straggling. Large leaves, to 7" x 3", oblong-obovate, have hairless and dull green tops and pale bluish green undersides with a scattering of tiny hairs. Flowers, to 2" long, funnel-bell-shaped, are white inside, flushed rose on the outside, blotched deep crimson within, and are carried in trusses of 6-8. Note: Closely allied to *R. decorum*, but flowers later, in July or August, making it worthwhile to grow. It is said to flower as late as September in England, but always seems to bloom earlier in the U.S. Unknown in the wild. **Known only in cultivation; possibly a hybrid of R. decorum. HY, hy.**

R. serpyllifolium (*with leaves like Thymus serpyllum*) *s.* Azalea *s.s.* Obtusum. 30", -10°F, EM, 3/3/3. Growth habit of this deciduous shrub is low, but upright and many-branched. Tiny leaves, to only 3/4" long, usually smaller, crowded at branch tips, are elliptic or obovate, bright green above, paler below, both sides slightly hairy. Short funnel-form flowers, less than 1/2" across, are pale rose to rosy pink or almost white, and appear either singly or in pairs. C. & S. Japan. **UC/TT, tt.**

  'Albiflorum'-- Very branchy plant habit which is excellent for bonsai. Attractive, small white flowers.

R. serrulatum (*with small teeth*) *s.* Azalea *s.s.* Luteum. 5', -5°F, VL, 2-3/3/3. This deciduous shrub has a tall, upright growth habit, with reddish brown new growth with stiff, flat hairs. Leaves, to 3 1/2" x 1 1/2", lance shaped and distinctively toothed on the edges, are glabrous on both sides when mature. Flowers, which unfold after leaves have appeared, are funnel shaped, with a narrow tube to 1 1/2" long. They are white, occasionally flushed a pale violet red, opening into trusses holding 6-10 flowers. Close relative *R. viscosum* is more showy, but *R. serrulatum* is to be desired because of its late blooming habit. S.E. North America. **UC/PE, pe.**

R. setiferum (*bearing bristles*) *s.* Thomsonii *s.s.* Selense. 4', 0°F, EM-M, 3/3/2-3. Young growth on this shrub is very bristly and hairy. Medium sized leaves are oblong, almost hairless on the top, but have a thin indumentum of short hairs on the underside. Funnel-bell-shaped flowers, to 1 1/2" long, are ivory white, occasionally crimson-lined at the base, held in trusses of 8-10. Yunnan, 12,000-13,000 ft. **R. selense ssp. setiferum/HY, hy, Selensia.**

R. setosum (*bristly*) *s.* Lapponicum. 18", -10°F, M, 2/2/2. New growth is very bristly, with minute down. Tiny leaves, to 1/2" x 1/4", oblong elliptic, with densely scaly, tops and waxy bluish green, not quite so scaly undersides with bristly hairs on the edges. Broadly funnel-shaped flowers, to only 3/4" long, are reddish or pinkish purple to rose-purple, carried in trusses of 3-8. Nepal, Sikkim, Bhutan, S.E. Tibet, 9,000-16,500 ft. **UC/RN, rn.**

R. shepherdii (*after H. Shepherd, 1780-1854, a former Curator of Liverpool Botanic Garden*) *s.* and *s.s.* Irroratum. 5', 10°F, E, 3/2/3. Medium large foliage, to 4" x 1", oblong-lanceolate, is hairless and deep vibrant green on top, paler underneath. Tubular-bell-shaped flowers, to 2" long, are deep scarlet, sometimes spotted darker red, carried in trusses of 10-12. Bhutan. **Syn. R. kendrickii/HY, hy, Irrorata.**

R. sherriffi (*after Maj. G. Sherriff, 1898-1967, notable plant collector*) *s.* Campanulatum. 5', -5°F, E, 2-3/2-3/2-3. Medium sized leaves, oblong-elliptic to oblong-oval, are dark, dull green on top, covered with a soft, thick brownish indumentum on the reverse. Funnel-bell-shaped flowers, to 1 1/2" long, are a deep, rich carmine, the calyx crimson and glaucous, and are held in trusses of 3-6. S. Tibet, 11,500-12,500 ft. **UC/HY, hy, Fulgensia.**

R. shweliense (*from the Shweli River, China*) *s.* and *s.s.* Glaucophyllum. 3', -10°F, M-ML, 2/2/2. This small shrub has very aromatic foliage. Leaves, to 2" x 1", obovate to oblong-obovate, are hairless and pallid dull green on top, very scaly with a bluish green bloom underneath. Bell shaped flowers, to 3/4" long, densely scaly outside, are pink tinged yellow, spotted purple, and are held in trusses of 2-4. Yunnan, 10,000-11,000 ft. **UC/HY, hy, Glauca.**

R. sidereum (*excellent*) *s.* Grande. 6', 5°F, EM, 3-4/3-4/3. Long and narrow foliage on this shrub, to 10" x 2", is dark matte green and hairless on top, indumented thin silvery grey to fawn underneath. 8 lobed, bell shaped flowers, up to 2" long, held in spectacular trusses of up to 20, range from creamy white to clear yellow, blotched crimson. N.E. Upper Burma, Yunnan, 9,000-10,000 ft. **R. sidereum/HY, hy, Grandia.**

R. siderophyllum (*with rusty leaves*) *s.* Triflorum *s.s.* Yunnanense. 6', -5°F, M, 3-4/3/3. Medium sized foliage, oblong-lanceolate, elliptic, or lanceolate, is bright green and sparsely scaly on top, densely scaled yellowish to brown underneath. Widely funnel-shaped flowers, to 3/4" long, range in color from white to pink rose to purplish violet or lavender blue, occasionally with crimson or dark brown spotting, and are held in trusses to 8. Yunnan, Szechwan, Kweichow, 6,000-10,500 ft. **UC/RN, rn, Triflora, Yunnanense agg.**

R. simiarum (*of the monkeys*) *s.* Arboreum *s.s.* Argyrophyllum. 5', 10°F?, EM, 2-3/2-3/2-3. Leaves, to 4" x 1 1/2", oblanceolate to obovate with rounded tips, are nearly hairless above, with a greyish to fawn or buff indumentum underneath. Funnel-bell-shaped flowers, to 1 1/2" long, are pink, paler inside, with a few rosy pink spots, and are carried in trusses of 4-6. S.E. China, 3,200 ft. **R. simiarum ssp. simiarum/HY, hy, Argyrophylla.**

Species ~
Subgenus Hymenanthes
Section Hymenanthes

Large Leaves!

. *fictolacteum*

Subsect. Falconera
(R. fictolacteum, hodgsonii, arizelum & rex)

R. grande

R. montroseanum

Subsect. Grandia
(includes all other species on this page)

R. hodgsonii

R. arizelum
R. macabeanum

R. sinogrande

. *rex*

R. sinogrande

Species ~ Subgenus Hymenanthes Section Hymenanthes

Subsect. Fulva
(R. uvariifolium & fulvum)

Subsect. Gischra *(R. recurvoides, crinigerum & rude)*

Subsect. Fulgensia

R. uvariifolium

R. recurvoides

R. crinigerum

R. fulgens

R. fulvum

R. rude

Subsect. Irrorata
(R. irroratum & laxiflorum)

R. laxiflorum

Subsect. Griersoniana

R. griersonianum

R. irroratum 'Polka Dot'

R. pachysanthum

R. anhweiense

R. maculiferum

Subsect. Maculifera (pictured above)

Species ~ Subgenus Hymenanthes Section Hymenanthes

Subsect. Neriiflora (pictured below)

neriiflorum

R. beanianum

R. sanguineum ssp. haemaleum

R. pachytrichum
R. mallotum

neriiflorum 'Rosevalon'

R. sanguineum ssp. mesaeum

R. haematodes

Species ~ Subgenus Hymenanthes
Section Hymenanthes

R. balfourianum

R. alutaceum

R. roxieanum var. *oreonastes*

R. roxieanum

Subsect. Taliensia

R. adenogynum

R. roxieanum 'Branklin Fo

R. bathyphyllum

R. wiltonii

Subsect. Williamsia

R. williamsianum

R. lacteum

R. bureavii

R. elegantulum

R. elegantulum

R. simsii (*after J. Sims, 1749-1831, former editor of the Botanical Magazine*) s. Azalea s.s. Obtusum. 3', 15ºF, M, 3-4/3/3-4. Habit of this evergreen or semi-evergreen shrub is spreading and many-branched, with new growth distinctively covered with shiny brown, flatly pressed hairs. There are two separate leaf-forms, spring and summer. In spring, leaves, to 2" long, are elliptic to ovate or oblong-elliptic, with dull green, slightly hairy tops, paler and more hairy undersides. Summer leaves are shorter and wider. Flowers, to 2 1/2" in diameter, widely funnel-form, are bright to dark red or rosy red, with deeper spotting, and are held in clusters of 2-6. The term 'indicum' has been incorrectly used in the past to designate many of the 'Indian Azaleas' or 'R. indicum' of the trade. More correctly, they belong here under R. simsii, rather than under true R. indicum. China, Formosa, N.E. Upper Burma, 1,000-8,000 ft. UC/TT, ⚘.

    var. eriocarpum-- From the Kawanabe Islands. Flowers are rose, or white to pink, and summer leaves are wider.

    variegated form-- 3', 15ºF, M, 4/4-5/-. A fine variegated foliage azalea which, of course, is exceptionally interesting for its foliage. A vigorous grower. Bright rose red flowers make a showy contrast against the foliage. A most unusual and desirable plant.

R. sinogrande (*Chinese R. grande*) s. Grande. 5', 10ºF, E, 4/4/3. This is the largest leaved of all rhododendrons, a really spectacular, magnificent plant. Young growth is beautiful silvery grey. Mature leaves can grow to 30". They are glossy green on the tops with a thin layer of silver-white or fawn indumentum underneath. Bell shaped flowers with 8-10 lobes, to 3", generously proportioned, are creamy white to pale yellow, blotched crimson, held in ball trusses of up to 20 or more. Yunnan, Upper Burma, S.E. Tibet, 10,000-14,000 ft. **R. sinogrande/HY, hy, Grandia.**

    var. boreale-- Has shorter and narrower leaves. **No longer recognized.**

R. smirnowii (*after M. Smirnov, a friend of its discoverer, Baron Ungern-Sternberg*) s. Ponticum s.s. Caucasicum. 3', -15ºF, ML, 3/3-4/2-3. This is an upright open growing shrub, the new growth covered with a lovely white felt-like tomentum. Oblong or lance shaped leaves, to 6" long, are smooth dark green on top with a tawny, thick woolly indumentum underneath. Leaf edges bend downward. Frilled flowers, to almost 2" long, funnel-bell-shaped range from pale to deep rosy purple, and are carried in loose trusses of 10-12. Caucasus and N.E. Asia Minor. **UC/HY, hy, Pontica.**

R. smithii (*after Sir J. E. Smith, 1759-1828, English botanist and founder of the Linnean Society*) s. and s.s. Barbatum. 4', 5ºF, E, 4/4/3. Young growth on this plant with purplish bark is very bristly and sticky. Oblanceolate leaves, to 6" x 2", are glabrous and dark glossy green above, with a patchy, loose, greyish white, woolly indumentum and a few hairs underneath. Tubular-bell-shaped flowers, to 2" long, are scarlet or crimson to blood red, waxy, with darker blotched nectar pouches. They are held in compact trusses of 10-16. Very similar to R. barbatum, but has underleaf indumentum. E. Sikkim, Bhutan, 8,000-10,000 ft. **UC/HY, hy, Barbata.**

R. souliei (*after Pere J. A. Soulie, 1858-1905, French Foreign Missions, Tibet*) s. Thomsonii s.s. Souliei. 5', -5ºF, M, 4/3/3. This is an exceptional, superior member of the Thomsonii series, a compact and upright shrub with light waxy blue green or purple young growth. Leaves, to 3" long, are oblong to almost round, with a distinctive, somewhat metallic blue green hue on top, paler underneath. Flowers, to 2" or more in diameter, open saucer-shape, are creamy yellow, pink or rose, occasionally to almost white or soft, deeper rose, sometimes with spots. Szechwan, Tibet, 9,000-14,000 ft. **UC/HY, hy, Campylocarpa.**

R. sperabile (*to be hoped for*) s. and s.s. Neriiflorum. 3', 5ºF, M, 3/3/3. Growth habit is very tight and compact. Oblong or lanceolate leaves, to 4" x 1 1/2", dark green above, becoming eventually hairless, are covered with a thick brownish to pale cinnamon, woolly indumentum underneath. Tubular-bell-shaped flowers, of heavy substance, to 1 1/2" long, are clear scarlet or deep crimson, with black crimson blotches, held in loose trusses of up to 5. N.E. Upper Burma, N.W. Yunnan, 10,000-12,000 ft. **R. sperabile var. sperabile/HY, hy, Neriiflora.**

    var. weihsiense-- A taller plant; the slightly narrower leaves have a paler, thinner, indumentum below. Yunnan, S.E. Tibet, 9,000-13,000 ft. **UC.**

R. sperabiloides (*like R. sperabile*) s. and s.s. Neriiflorum. 3', 5ºF, E, 3/3/3. Growth habit of this species is neat and compact. Leaves to 3" x 1", oblong or lance shaped, are somewhat swollen and puckered on top, with patchy fawn or brownish indumentum underneath. Flowers of heavy substance, to 1" long, narrowly bell shaped, are light to dark shades of crimson or scarlet, and are held in trusses of 6-8. S.E. Tibet, 12,000-13,000 ft. **UC/HY, hy, Neriiflora.**

R. sphaeroblastum (*with rounded buds*) s. and s.s. Taliense. 4', -5ºF, EM, 3/4/3. Young growth on this plant is smooth and hairless, either greenish or purple. Leaves, to 6" x 3", oval or oblong-oval, are hairless olive green above, with a heavy, woolly, rusty indumentum below. Buds with a rosy blush open to funnel-bell-shaped flowers, to 1 1/2" long, that are white, spotted crimson, held in trusses up to 12. Szechwan, 11,000-14,000 ft. **UC/HY, hy, Taliensia.**

R. spiciferum (*bearing spikes*) s. Scabrifolium. 3', 5ºF, EM, 3/3/4. This shrub has a loose willowy habit with bristly, softly hairy stems and foliage. Light textured leaves, quite narrow, to about 1" long, are scaly underneath. Their appearance is made interesting by deep veins. Funnel-form flowers, to 1/2" long, are pinkish white to pale or deep rose, appearing along branches between leaf clusters, held in trusses of 1-4. Yunnan. **R. scabrifolium var. spiciferum/RN, rn, Scabrifolia.**

R. spilanthum (*with spotted flowers*) s. Lapponicum. 2', -10ºF, EM, 2/2/2. This plant has scaly, twiggy, new growth, and the bark is grey and splitting. Small lance shaped leaves, to 1/2" x 1/4", are green and scaly on top, densely covered with yellowish, overlapping scales underneath. Wide funnel shaped flowers, to 1/2" long, appearing alone, are mauve to purplish blue. Szechwan. **Syn. R. thymifolium/RN, rn, Lapponica.**

R. spilotum (*stained*) s. Barbatum s.s. Glischrum. 4', 5ºF, EM, 3/2/3. New growth on this shrub is very bristly. Leaves, to 5" x 1 1/2", oblong-lanceolate, are shining and veiny on top, paler and minutely pitted underneath. Flowers, to 1 1/2" long, funnel-bell-shaped, are pink or white flushed pink, blotched crimson, and are held in trusses of 6-8. N.E. Upper Burma. **UC/Unplaced.**

R. spinuliferum (*bearing spines*) s. Scabrifolium. 4', 5ºF, EM, 3-4/2/3-4. Growth habit, though upright, tends to be thin and leggy with bristly and softly hairy new growth. Leaves, to 3" x 1 1/2", look swollen and puckery on top, with sparse hairs on edges. The undersides have a net-like appearance, very slightly hairy, and scaly. Narrowly tubular flowers, to 1" long, appearing along the branches in a more or less upright manner in between leaf clusters are scarlet-crimson to brick red, with distinctive protruding stamens and anthers. Yunnan, 6,000-8,000 ft. **UC/RN, rn, Scabrifolia.**

R. stamineum (*with prominent stamens*) s. Stamineum. 6', 15ºF, EM, 3/3/3-4. Foliage on this plant is distinctively and attractively whorled. The leaves, to 4" x 1 1/2", are obovate to oblanceolate, with long, slender, sharp points, and are shiny dark green on top, paler underneath. Flowers, to 1 1/2", blooming in clusters of 1-3 along the branches, widely funnel shaped with narrow lobes, are white, blotched yellow. Yunnan, Szechwan, Hupeh, Kweichow. **UC/AZ, ch.**

R. stenaulum (*with a narrow groove*) s. Stamineum. 6', 15ºF, E, 3/3/3-4. Leaves, to 5" x 1 1/2", are long, narrow and sharply pointed; the tops are dark green, the undersides shiny, hairless on both sides. Long, slender funnel shaped flowers, to 2 1/2" long, blooming along the branches in loose trusses of 3-5, are pale lilac, paler inside, darker toward edges of lobes, with a yellow throat. Flower is fragrant. Yunnan, 9,000 ft. **UC/AZ, ch.**

R. stewartianum (*after L. B. Stewart, 1876-1934, a former Curator, Royal Botanic Garden, Edinburgh*) s. and s.s. Thomsonii. 5', 5ºF, VE-E, 2-3/2-3/2-3. Oval leaves, to 4 1/2" x 2 1/2", are grey-green above, paler with a thin, powdery indumentum on the undersides. Tubular-bell-shaped flowers, to 2" long, with calyx varying from very rudimentary to over 1/2" long, are held in trusses of 2-7. The color is extremely variable, ranging from pure white through all shades of primrose yellow, sometimes flushed with rose or deep crimson. S.E. Tibet, Upper Burma, Assam, 10,000-14,000 ft. **UC/HY, hy, Thomsonia.**

R. stictophyllum (*with spotted leaves*) s. Lapponicum. 2', -5ºF, E-EM, 2-3/2-3/3. Growth habit of this little shrub is very compact, with many small branches. Elliptic leaves, to only 1/3" x 1/10", are quite small, densely scaly on both surfaces. The tops are dark green, the underside scales reddish and yellowish. Widely funnel shaped flowers, to 1/3" long, are rose, deep rose, or purple to mauve, and are held in clusters of 1-4. W. Szechwan. **Syn. R. nivale ssp. boreale/RN, rn, Lapponica.**

R. strigillosum (*with short bristles*) s. Barbatum s.s. Maculiferum. 4', 5ºF, E, 5/4/3-4. Habit is upright and open, with very bristly red new growth which makes a lovely display all its own. Bright green leaves, long and quite narrow, to 7" x 2", are heavily coated with stiff bristles, the midrib on the underside densely covered with indumentum. Deep blood red flowers, to 2 1/2" long, tubular-bell-shaped, appear early in the spring in trusses of 8-12. Most beautiful. Szechwan, 7,000-10,000 ft. **UC/HY, hy, Maculifera.**

R. subansiriense (*from the Subansiri Division, N.E. India*) s. and s.s. Thomsonii. 5', 10ºF?, VE, -/-/-. Oblong leaves, to 4 1/4" x 1 1/2", are hairless above, glandular below. Tubular-bell-shaped flowers to 1 1/2" long, with nectar pouches, are crimson or scarlet with a few purple spots inside, and are held in trusses of about 15. North East Frontier Agency, 8,500-9,200 ft. **UC/HY, hy, Thomsonia.**

R. subsessile (*subsessile*) s. Azalea s.s. Obtusum. 4'?, 15ºF?, M, -/-/-. Evergreen elliptic or lance shaped leaves to 1 1/2" x 1", have tops covered densely with flat, white hairs. Lavender to purplish violet flowers, to 1" wide, are bell-shaped-funnel-form. Philippine Islands. **UC/TT, tt.**

R. succothii (*after Sir George I. Campbell of Succoth, rhododendron grower in W. Scotland*) s. Campanulatum. 5', 0ºF, E, 3/3/2-3. Growth habit is tree-like, with smooth, flaking bark. Oval leaves, to 5" x 2 1/2", are hairless and shiny dark green on top. Leaves are also hairless, but paler underneath. Flowers, to 1 1/2" long, tubular-bell-shaped, are scarlet or crimson, with nectar pouches, held in trusses of 10-15. Similar to *R. fulgens*, which differs in its heavily indumented leaves. Bhutan, 11,000-13,000 ft. **UC/HY, hy, Barbata.**

R. sulfureum (*sulphur-colored*) s. and s.s. Boothii. 30", 10ºF, E, 3/3/2-3. Leaves, to 3" x 1 1/2", oblanceolate to ovate, are dark green and glabrous on top and paler, glaucous and scaly below. Bell shaped flowers, to 1" long, are bright or deep sulphur yellow, rarely a greenish orange, and are held in trusses of 4-8. Yunnan, Burma, S.E. Tibet, 7,000-13,000 ft. **UC/RN, rn, Boothia.**

R. supranubium (*above the clouds*) s. Maddenii s.s. Ciliicalyx. 5', 15ºF, E, 3/2/3. Young branches on this shrub are dense with pale scales. Leaves, to 3 1/2" x 1 1/4", oblanceolate or obovate, are hairless and somewhat glossy on top, glaucous and scaly on the undersides. Fragrant flowers, to 2 1/2" long, widely funnel shaped, are white or white blushed rose, held in trusses of up to 3. Yunnan, 10,000-12,000 ft. **Syn. R. pachypodum/RN, rn, Maddenia "Ciliicalyx-Alliance" Ciliicalyx agg.**

R. sutchuenense (*from Szechwan*) s. Fortunei s.s. Davidii. 5', -10ºF, VE, 4/3/3-4. Habit is open, upright and tree-like. Large leaves, to 12" long, oblong or oblanceolate, are dark matte green on top, paler underneath. Widely bell shaped flowers, as much as 3" long, are pale lilac, rose pink or rose-lilac, sometimes white faintly tinged pink, sometimes spotted purple, and are carried in trusses of 8-12. Szechwan, Hupeh, 5,000-8,000 ft.
    R. sutchuenense/HY, hy, Fortunea.
        var. geraldii-- Light-textured flowers, clear pink with a prominent purple blotch.
            R. x geraldii (R. sutchuenense x praevernum).

R. taggianum (*after H. F. Tagg, 1874-1933, botanist at Royal Botanic Garden, Edinburgh*) s. Maddenii s.s. Megacalyx. 5', 25ºF, EM, 4/2/3. Growth habit is upright, but somewhat loose and leggy. Leaves are large, to 6" x 2 1/2", oblong-lanceolate or elliptic. The tops are smooth and hairless, undersides glaucous and darkly scaly. Broadly tubular shaped flowers, to 4" long and equally wide, are nicely scented. The flowers are white, blotched pale yellow, flowing in trusses of 3-4. Yunnan, Burma, Burma-Tibet frontier, 7,000-11,000 ft. **UC/RN, rn, Maddenia "Dalhousiae-Alliance".**

R. taiwanalpinum (*from the alpine regions of Taiwan (Formosa)*) s. Azalea. 3', 5ºF?, M, -/-/-. Leaves, to only 2/3", are ovate-oblong or oblong-lanceolate. The tops have a light covering of flat, stiff hairs, the undersides have a denser layer. Small flowers, to only 2/3" wide, are widely funnel-shaped. Flower color is clear pink accented with rosy spots. N. Formosa, 9,000-10,000 ft. **UC/TT, tt.**

R. taliense (*from Tali Range, Yunnan*) s. and s.s. Taliense. 5', -5ºF, EM, 3/3/3. Leaves on this shrub are medium large, to 4" x 1 1/2", and lance-shaped. The top surface is almost hairless and dark green, while the underside is buff-colored with felt-like indumentum. Flowers, to 1 1/2" long, are funnel-bell-shaped. The creamy yellow, or cream blushed rose, flowers have intense crimson markings. The flower stalks are very hairy, holding groups of up to 15 flowers into very tight trusses. Yunnan, 10,000-12,000 ft. **UC/HY, hy, Taliensia.**

R. tamaense (*from Tama Bum, N. Burma*) s. Cinnabarinum. 3', 0ºF?, M, 4/3-4/2-3. This is a deciduous or semi-deciduous shrub or small tree. Leaves, to 2 1/2" x 1", are elliptic, oblong, or oblong-oval. The top surface is medium green and hairless, while the underside is waxy blue-green or with brownish scales. Flowers, to almost 2" long, are tubular-bell-shaped, pale lavender to deep royal purple, in trusses of 2-5. N. Burma, 9,000-10,500 ft. **R. cinnabarinum ssp. tamaense/RN, rn, Cinnabarina.**

R. tanastylum (*with a long style*) s. and s.s. Irroratum. 6', 10ºF, EM, 2/2/-. Growth habit is often straggly or sprawling, with leaves to 5" x 2", widely lance-shaped with wavy edges. The top surface is dark, hairless, matte green, while the underside is paler, more or less shiny and with tiny shallow pits. Tubular bell-shaped flowers, to 2" long, are held in trusses of up to 8. The flowers range in color from scarlet to deep crimson or rose-purple, occasionally with deeper spots and with nectar pouches. S.E. Tibet, Upper Burma, W. Yunnan, 8,000-11,000 ft. **R. tanastylum var. tanastylum/HY, hy, Irrorata.**

R. tapetiforme (*carpet-like*) s. Lapponicum. 2', -5ºF, E, 2-3/2-3/3. Spreading low shrub with scaly new growth. Small leaves, to only about 1/2" are widely elliptic or oblong. The top side is dark green with semi-transparent scales, the reverse side is reddish-brown and scaly. Broadly funnel-shaped flowers to 1/2" long, range in color from pink to pale rose purple or deep purplish blue, carried in trusses of 2-4. Tibet, Burma, Yunnan, 11,500-15,000 ft. **UC/RN, rn, Lapponica.**

R. taronense (*from the Taron Gorge, Yunnan*) s. Maddenii s.s. Ciliicalyx. 5', 15ºF, EM, 3-4/2-3/3. Growth habit is somewhat ragged and straggling, with thin, brownish, peeling bark. Beautiful leaves are dark green, long and narrow, slightly scaly above and below. Widely funnel-shaped flowers, to 2 1/2" long, large and with a lovely fragrance, are white, blotched yellow, sometimes blushed pink, carried in trusses of up to 6. Upper Burma, Yunnan, 4,000-11,000 ft. **R. dendricola Taronense Group/RN, rn, Maddenia "Ciliicalyx-Alliance" Johnstoneanum agg.**

R. tashiroi (*after a Mr. Tashiro, Japanese botanist*) s. Azalea *s.s.* Obtusum. 5', 5ºF, M, 3/3/3. Leaves on this species are smallish, to about 2 1/2" x 1 1/3", obovate or oblong, sometimes rather diamond shaped. Foliage is bright, shiny green and hairless above, while the underside is paler and also glabrous. Flowers, to 1 1/2" wide, are funnel bell-shaped, pale rosy purple, with dark wine-purple spotting, in trusses of 2 or 3. Luikiu and Kawanabe Islands, S. Japan. **UC/TT, ts,** but will probably be move to **br.**

R. tatsienense (*from Tatsienlu, now Kang-ting, W. China*) s. Triflorum *s.s.* Yunnanense. 5', 5ºF, EM, 2/2/3. Small leaves, to 2" x 1", are ovate, elliptic, or oblanceolate. The top surface is dark green with a few scales, the reverse side has more scales. Flowers, to 1" long, are widely funnel-shaped, rose or purple, occasionally spotted red. Held in trusses of 1-6, the flowers bloom either on the branch ends or along the branches between the leaves. Szechwan, Yunnan, 7,000-12,000 ft. **UC/RN, rn, Triflora Yunnanense agg.**

R. telmateium (*of marches*) s. Lapponicum. 1 1/2', -5ºF, EM, 3/3/3. New growth on this little shrub is densely scaly, dark brown. Tiny leaves, to only 1/2" x 1/5", are oblanceolate. The tops are dull, darkish green with pale scales, the undersides are also scaly, and rusty brown. Funnel-shaped flowers, to 1/2" long, are deep rosy-purple, with a white throat, in trusses of 1-3. Yunnan, Szechwan, 9,500-14,000 ft. **UC/RN, rn, Lapponica.**

R. telopeum (*conspicuous*) s. Thomsonii *s.s.* Campylocarpum. 4', -5ºF, E-M, 2-3/2-3/2-3. Growth habit is compact, with oval or elliptic leaves, to 2" x 1", the top smooth and hairless, the underside a waxy bluish green with scattering of tiny hairs. Flowers, to 1 1/2" long, are bell-shaped, a bright clear yellow, sometimes blotched faintly crimson, and carried in trusses of 4-5. Different from *R. caloxanthum* in its smaller leaves. S.E. Tibet, Yunnan, 12,000-14,000 ft. **R. campylocarpum ssp. caloxanthum Telopeum Group/HY,** hy, **Campylocarpa.**

R. temenium (*from a sacred place near the Doker La, Tsarong, in E. Tibet*) s. Neriiflorum *s.s.* Sanguineum. 18", -5ºF, EM-M, 3/2-4/-. Growth habit is very compact in this highly variable species. Leaves, to 3" x 1", are oblong or oblong-oval, usually hairless on both sides. Flowers, to 1 1/2", are tubular-bell-shaped, and held in trusses of up to 6. The blooms, of great substance, range in color from red or scarlet to deep crimson or purplish crimson. S.E. Tibet, Yunnan, 13,000-15,000 ft. **R. temenium var. temenium/HY,** hy, **Neriiflora.**
  ssp. albipetalum-- This plant has white flowers. S.E. Tibet. **Syn. R. eudoxum var. eudoxum.**
  ssp. chrysanthemum-- Has eglandular, tomentose ovary and yellow flowers. S.E. Tibet, 13,000-14,000 ft. **R. temenium var. gilvum Chrysanthemum Group.**
  ssp. gilvum-- Has glandular, tomentose ovary and yellow flowers. S.E. Tibet, 13,000 ft.
  R. temenium var. gilvum. ssp. glaphyrum-- Ovary tomentose and eglandular, with either rose or cream-colored flowers or a blend of the two. S.E. Tibet, 13,000-15,000 ft. **Syn. R. temenium var. dealbatum.**
  ssp. pothinum-- Somewhat close to the type, but the ovary is eglandular and tomentose. S.E. Tibet, 13,000-14,000 ft. **Syn. R. temenium var. temenium.**

R. tephropeplum (*with an ash-grey covering*) s. Boothii *s.s.* Tephropeplum. 30", 5ºF, EM, 3/2/3. Habit of this plant tends to be open and sprawling, sometimes more upright. Leaves can vary in size from 1 1/2" long to 5", lance-shaped or oblong. The top surface is just a little scaly, while the underside is waxy blue-green with dense black scales. Tubular bell-shaped flowers, to 1 1/4" long, are held in trusses of 3-9. The slightly scented blooms range widely in color from pink to rose or carmine-rose to reddish purple, very rarely white. An extremely variable species, known for its vigor and dense foliage. Yunnan, S.E. Tibet, Assam, 8,000-14,000 ft. **UC/RN, rn, Tephropepla.**

R. thayeranum (*after a well known New England family, patrons of botany and horticulture*) s. Arboreum *s.s.* Argyrophyllum. 5', 0ºF, VL, 3/3-4/3. Compact upright growth habit, with leaves clustered closely around trusses. Large leaves, to 8" x 1 1/2", are lance-shaped or narrowly oblong, glabrous light green on top, the reverse with a very thin buff-colored indumentum. Flowers, to 1 1/2", are funnel bell-shaped, white tinged pink or pink, held in compact trusses from 10-20. A beautiful rhododendron, especially valued for its late flowering. W. Szechwan, 9,000 ft. **UC/HY, hy, Argyrophylla.**

R. thomsonii (*after Thomas Thomson, 1817-1878, a former Supt., Calcutta Botanic Garden*) s. and *s.s.* Thomsonii. 5', 5ºF, EM, 3/2-4/3-4. Growth habit is upright and open, with attractive peeling-red bark, the new growth a pale green with a short-lived waxy bloom. Leaves, to 4" long, are ovate or orbicular, the tops dark green, underside blue-white to pale green and glaucous. Flowers to 2 1/2" long, are bell-shaped, the color a deep blood red with cup-shaped calyx to 3/4" long, red or green. This is one of the finest of rhododendron species, often not flowering until a certain size has been achieved, but then blooming in great profusion, in loose trusses to 10 or 12. Sikkim, Nepal, Bhutan, Tibet 10,000-14,000 ft. **R. thomsonii ssp. thomsonii/HY,** hy, **Thomsonia.**
  var. candelabrum-- Flowers range in color from pale pink to rosy pink or even rose orange, occasionally blotched wine-red. Tibet, Sikkim, E. Himalaya, 10,000-13,000 ft. **R. x candelabrum.**

R. thymifolium (*with leaves like thyme*) s. Lapponicum. 2', -5ºF, EM, 2/2/2-3. Leaves on this shrub are quite small, to only 1/3" long, narrow oblanceolate, densely scaly on both sides, the underside a yellowish brown. Flowers, to a petite 1/3" long, are wide funnel shape, the color mauve to lavender-blue or purple, and occur either alone or in pairs. Szechwan, Kansu, 10,000-15,000 ft. **UC/RN, rn, Lapponica.**

R. tosaense (*from Tosa, Japan*) s. Azalea *s.s.* Obtusum. 3', 5ºF, EM, 2-3/2-3/3-4. This is an evergreen or semi-evergreen shrub with many branches, the leaves crowded at branch-tips. Leaves are small, to 1 1/2" long, lance-shaped or elliptic-lanceolate, with flat greyish hairs, changing to purplish crimson in the fall. Funnel-shaped flowers, to 1 1/2" wide, are lilac-purple, in trusses of 1-6. S. Japan. **UC/TT, tu.**

R. traillianum (*after G. W. Traill, 1836-1897, botanist and father-in-law of George Forrest*) s. Lacteum. 5', -5ºF, EM, 3/3-4/2-3. Mature leaves may reach 7" x 2", oblong-lanceolate or oblong. The top surface is hairless and dark green, while the reverse is covered with a fawn to rusty brown indumentum. Flowers, to 1 3/4" long, are bell-shaped or funnel-bell-shaped and are held in trusses of up to 15. The blooms range in color from white or white-blushed-rose, through pink or rose, sometimes spotted with crimson. Yunnan, Szechwan, 11,000-14,500 ft. **R. traillianum var. traillianum/HY,** hy, **Taliensia.**

R. trichanthum (*with hairy flowers*) s. Triflorum *s.s.* Augustinii. 6', -5ºF, L, 2/3/3. New growth on this shrub is densely bristly. Leaves, to 4 1/2" long, are lanceolate, ovate-lanceolate, or oblong-lanceolate. The top surface is slightly scaly, while the reverse side is scaly with a few bristly hairs along the midrib. Funnel-shaped flowers, to 1 1/2" long, have bristles on the lower surface and are carried in trusses of 3-5. The flowers range in color from rose to light or dark purple, and have a paler blotch. Latest flowering member of the triflorum series, once known as *R. villosum*. Szechwan, 5,000-11,000 ft. **UC/RN, rn, Triflora.**

R. trichocladum (*with hairy twigs*) s. Trichocladum. 2', -5ºF, EM, 2/2/2. This is a deciduous shrub with a loose, straggly growth habit. The oblong leaves, to 1 1/2" long, are fringed with hair. The top surface is dull, dark green, finely netted, the underside displaying minute scales. Flowers, to about 1" long, are widely funnel-shaped, pale yellow, greenish-yellow or ocher, with dark green spotting, in trusses of 3-5. N.W. Yunnan, westward through Upper Burma to the eastern Himalaya, 7,500-13,000 ft. **UC/RN, rn, Trichoclada.**
  var. longipilosum-- Upper surface of the leaves are covered with long hairs. **R. mekongense var. longipilosum.**

R. trichostomum (*with a hairy mouth*) s. Anthopogon. 30", -5ºF, M, 4/2-3/3-4. Growth habit is very twiggy, somewhat open and spreading. Leaves, to about 1" long, are quite narrow, sometimes ovate or oblanceolate. The aromatic foliage is hairless or scaly on the top surface, while the reverse is covered with loose flaky scales. Flowers, to 3/4" long, are narrowly tubular with spreading lobes, and are shaggy within the throat. The blooms are white, pink, or rose, and held in dense head-like trusses of up to 16 which last a month. They resemble the flowers of daphne more than rhododendron. Yunnan, Szechwan, 8,000-12,000 ft. **UC/RN, po.**

> var. **hedyosmum**-- Has a longer corolla tube. **No longer recognized.**
> var. **ledoides**-- The corolla is either non-scaly or only lightly so. **R. trichostomum Ledoides Group.**
> var. **radinum**-- The corolla is densely scaly on the outside. **R. trichostomum Radinum Group.**

R. triflorum (*with three flowers*) s. and s.s. Triflorum. 6', 5ºF, ML, 2/2/3. Growth habit of this shrub is open and upright, with beautiful, distinctive, smooth, peeling, dark red bark. Lance shaped leaves, to 3" long, are medium green and hairless on top, the reverse has a waxy, bluish green cast, and is densely covered with very small scales. Flowers, to 1 1/2" long, are widely funnel-shaped, pale lemony yellow, spotted green or yellow tinged pink, in trusses of 2-4. Flower color is so similar to foliage that they are often overlooked. E. Nepal, Assam, Tibet, Burma-Tibet frontier, 7,000-13,000 ft. **UC/RN, rn, Triflora.**

> var. **mahogoni**-- Flowers are yellow tinged pink, spotted and blotched mahogany. S.E. Tibet, 8,300-12,500 ft. **R. triflorum Mahogoni Group.**

R. triplonaevium (*with triple moles*) s. Taliense s.s. Roxieanum. 3', -10ºF, EM, 2/3-4/3. Mature leaves on this species are fairly large, to 6" long. The lance-shaped to oblanceolate foliage is hairless and matte green on the top, the underside has a thin fawn to rusty colored indumentum. Bell shaped flowers, to 1 1/2" long, are white or white blushed rose, with a distinctive, flaring crimson blotch, carried in tight trusses of up to 12. N.W. Yunnan, 11,000-12,000 ft. **Syn. R. alutaceum var. alutaceum/HY, hy, Taliensia.**

R. tritifolium (*with polished leaves*) s. Taliense s.s. Roxieanum. 3', -5ºF, EM, 2/3-4/3. Leaves, to 6" long, are lanceolate or oblanceolate, the tops olive green and nearly hairless, the undersides coated with cinnamon to rusty brown indumentum. Flowers, to 1 1/2" long, are funnel-bell-shaped, and carried in compact trusses of 12-15. The blooms open white blushed rose, with a few spots and a crimson blotch. N.W. Yunnan, 11,000-12,000 ft. **Syn. R. alutaceum var. alutaceum/HY, hy, Taliensia.**

R. tsangpoense (*from the Tsangpo River, China*) s. and s.s. Glaucophyllum. 3', 0ºF, M-ML, 2-3/2/3. Growth habit is upright and open, with oval, elliptic or oblong leaves. The foliage, to 2" long, has a hairless, dark matte green top surface, while the underside is very glaucous and scaly. Flowers, to 1" long, are widely tubular-bell-shaped, with a large calyx to 1/4" long. The blooms range from pink, pinkish purple to deep cerise or violet, and are held in clusters of 2-6. This is an extremely variable and free-flowering species. S.E. Tibet, Burma, 12,000-13,500 ft. **R. charitopes ssp. tsangpoense/RN, rn, Glauca.**

> var. **curvistylum**-- May be a natural hybrid. Flowers are smaller, narrowly tubular-bell-shaped, rich plum color. S.E. Tibet, 12,000- 13,500 ft. **R. charitopes ssp. tsangpoense Curvistylum Group.**
> var. **pruniflorum**-- Undersides of leaves are very densely scaly. S.E. Tibet, North East Frontier Agency, Burma, 8,000-13,000 ft. **R. pruniflorum.**

R. tsariense (*from Tsari, S.E. Tibet*) s. Campanulatum. 3', -5ºF, E-M, 3/5/3. Leaves, to 2 1/2" long, are obovate to elliptic-obovate, the tops green, the undersides with a covering of thick, woolly, dark brown indumentum. Bell-shaped flowers to 1 1/2" long, are cream or white flushed pink, often with sprinkling of red spots, held in loose trusses of 3-4. S.E. Tibet, Bhutan, 11,500-14,500 ft. Similar to *R. lanatum*, differing in its smaller leaves and color of the flowers. **UC/HY, hy, Lanata.**

R. tschonoskii (*after Tschonoski, a Japanese collector*) s. Azalea s.s. Obtusum. 3', -15ºF, M, 1-2/2-3/3. This deciduous shrub has a compact, upright growth habit. Small leaves, barely 1" long, are crowded at the ends of the branches. The lance-shaped foliage is covered on both sides with flat reddish brown hairs which change color in the fall to orange-red and crimson. Funnel shaped flowers, to only 1/3" wide, are white, in trusses of 3-6. Korea, Japan. **UC/TT, tt.**

R. ungernii (*after Baron F. von Ungern-Sternberg, 1800-1868, professor at Dorpat*) s. Ponticum s.s. Caucasicum. 3', -10ºF, VL, 2-3/3-4/3. Growth habit is open and upright. Leaves, to 8", are oblong to lanceolate, hairless and dark green above, with a dense, woolly fawn to grey indumentum below. Flowers, to 1 1/2" long, are funnel-bell-shaped, pinky-white or pale rose with faint greenish spotting, in trusses of 20-30. Outstanding foliage plant and quite hardy. Caucasus, N.E. Asia Minor, 2,500-7,000 ft. **UC/HY, hy, Pontica.**

R. uniflorum (*with one flower*) s. Uniflorum. 1', -5ºF, EM, 3/2/2. Growth habit of this dwarf is tight and compact, with lower branches lying on the ground. Leaves, to a scant 1" long, are obovate or oblong-obovate, dark green above, the undersides a waxy bluish green and scaly. Flowers, about 1" long, are widely funnel-shaped, pink-blue to purple, appearing either alone or in pairs. S.E. Tibet, 11,000-12,000 ft. **R. uniflorum var. uniflorum/RN, rn, Uniflora.**

R. uvariifolium (*with leaves like a Uvaria*) s. Fulvum. 4', 5ºF, E, 3/3-4/3. Growth habit is tree-like, with lovely, silvery young growth. Lance-shaped, oblong leaves, to 10" long, are hairless, dark green above, with an ash-grey to fawn colored indumentum below. Flowers, to 2" long, are either bell-shaped or tubular bell-shaped, from white to white-flushed-rose or pale rose, sometimes blotched crimson or spotted red, held in tight, rounded trusses of 6-18. Yunnan, Szechwan, S.E. Tibet, 7,000-14,000 ft. **UC/HY, hy, Fulva.**

> var. **griseum**-- Leaves are wider and thicker, oblong oval in shape, the underside covered with a whitish, silky, very thin felt. **No longer recognized.**

R. valentinianum (*after Pere S. P. Valentin, Tsedjong Mission, China*) s. Maddenii s.s. Ciliicalyx. 2', 15ºF, E, 3/3/3. Habit is neat and trim, with leaves growing in rosettes of 4-5 at the ends of shoots. Foliage, to about 1 1/2" long, is oval or oblong-elliptic, pale green and bristly above, the edges fringed with hair, the underside with dense tawny scales. Flowers, to 1 1/2" long, are tubular-bell-shaped, clear buttery yellow, in trusses from 2-6. N.W. Yunnan, 9,000-12,000 ft. **UC/RN, rn, Maddenia "Ciliicalyx-Alliance".**

R. vaseyi (*after G. S. Vasey, 1822-1893, who discovered it in North Carolina in 1878*) s. Azalea s.s. Canadense. 5', -15ºF, EM, 4/2/3-4. A deciduous species with an open and upright growth habit, displaying flowers which appear before the foliage. Leaves to 5" long, are elliptic or elliptic-oblong. The wavy edged foliage is dark green and hairless above with a paler underside. Flowers, to 2" wide, are widely funnel shaped, and held in clusters of 4-8. The 2-lipped flowers range in color from white, to rose-pink or deep pink, and are spotted red or orange-red. E. North America. **UC/PE, ro.**

R. veitchianum (*after the famous Veitch family of nurserymen*) s. Maddenii s.s. Ciliicalyx. 4', 20ºF, M-L, 4/3/3. This is a fine compact plant with outstanding foliage. Foliage, to 5" long, is elliptic or obovate-lanceolate, hairless and scaly on top, the underside paler, with a waxy blue-green bloom and scaly. Flowers to 3" long, are widely funnel-shaped, deeply 5-cleft, with crinkled petal edges. The fragrant flowers are white, tinged green externally, and held in trusses of 4 or 5. A precocious and prolific bloomer. Burma, Thailand and Laos, 3,000-6,000 ft. **UC/RN, rn, Maddenia "Ciliicalyx- Alliance".**

R. vellereum (*fleecy*) s. and s.s. Taliense. 5', -5ºF, E, 3-4/4/3-4. Very beautiful leaves, to 5" long, are very narrow lance-shaped, pale to dark green and hairless on top, covered thickly with silvery, creamy white or fawn indumentum underneath. Funnel-bell shaped flowers, to 1 1/2" long, are white or rosy colored, spotted carmine or purple, and are held in somewhat tight trusses of 15-20. Leaves have plastered, polished look despite indumentum. S.E. Tibet, 9,000-15,000 ft. **R. principis Vellereum Group/HY, hy, Taliensia.**

R. venator (*hunter, alluding to the scarlet color of the flowers*) s. Irroratum s.s. Parishii. 3', 5ºF, M, 3-4/3/3-4. A bushy plant which displays new growth covered with long white glandular hairs. Leaves, to 6" long, are oblanceolate or oblong-lanceolate. The top surfaces are hairless and bright medium green, with a finely wrinkled surface, the undersides are paler with a waxy blue-green hue. Flowers, to 1 1/2" long, with a spreading tubular-bell-shape, are scarlet to reddish-orange with black basal pouches, carried in trusses of 8-10. S.E. Tibet, 8,000-8,500 ft. **UC/HY, hy, Venatora.**

R. vernicosum (*varnished*) s. and s.s. Fortunei. 5', -15ºF, M, 2-3/2-3/3. Habit is upright and open, with leaves, to 5" long, oval or oblong-oval to oblong-elliptic, rounded at the apex. The tops are waxy matte green, becoming glossy when heated or rubbed, paler beneath. Flowers, to 1 1/2" long, are funnel-bell-shaped. 7-lobed flowers range in color from white to pink-rose-pink, bright rose or lavender-rose, sometimes with crimson markings. They are held in trusses up to 12. This is a very variable species. Yunnan, Szechwan, 9,000-14,000 ft. **UC/HY, hy, Fortunea.**
    var. rhantum-- A geographical form.

R. verruculosum (*with small warts*) s. Lapponicum. 2', -5ºF, M, 2-3/3/2-3. A very compact growth habit on this small shrub, supports densely scaled new growth. Leaves are small, to 1/2" long, elliptic or oblong. The top surface is slightly blue-green and waxy with a dense covering of thick, fleshy, shiny yellow scales. The underside has thinner scales, which are shiny yellow and dark brown. Flowers, usually produced alone, but sometimes held up to 3 per cluster, are about 1/2" long, widely funnel-shaped, pink or purple, with externally scaly lobes. W. Szechwan, 10,000 ft. **RN, rn, Hybrid of R. flavidum.**

R. vesiculiferum (*bearing vesicles*) s. Barbatum s.s. Glischrum. 5', 5ºF, EM, 3/3/2-3. Leaves, to 6" long, are oblanceolate, the tops dark green and somewhat wrinkled, the reverse paler and with hairs on the veins. Flowers, to 1 1/2" long, are bell-shaped, rosy-purple, purple or crimson blotched, in trusses of 10-15. Different from R. glischroides in the bladder-like hairs on the undersides of the leaves. Yunnan, Burma-Tibet frontier, 9,000- 11,000 ft. **UC/HY, hy, Glischra.**

R. vestitum (*clothed*) s. Thomsonii s.s. Selense. 3', -5ºF, L, 2/2-3/2-3. Leaves, to 2 1/2" long, are oval, elliptic, or oblong, smooth above, with a loose, patchy, buff-colored to brown indumentum underneath. Funnel-bell shaped flowers, to 1 1/2" long, are deep rose in the bud, opening white or white flushed rose, blotched crimson and with a few crimson markings, in trusses to 6. S.E. Tibet, 14,000 ft. **Syn. R. selense ssp. setiferum/HY, hy, Selensia.**

R. vialii (*after Pere Paul Vial, French Missions in Yunnan*) s. Ovatum. 4', 15ºF, EM, -/-/-. Leaves, to 4" long, are obovate or oblanceolate, smooth and non-hairy both above and below. Crimson flowers, up to 1 1/4" long, are bell-shaped. The flowers, blooming singly from each bud, appear along the branches between the leaves. Yunnan, 4,000-6,000 ft. **UC/AZ, az.**

R. vilmorinianum (*after the famous French seedsmen*) s. Triflorum s.s. Yunnanense. 5', 5ºF, M, 4/3/3-4. Small leaves, to 2 1/2" long, are oblong to lanceolate, dull, dark green on top, with the reverse scaly. Flowers, to 1 1/2" long, are funnel-shaped, white or white flushed pink, spotted ocher in clusters of 2-4. This species bears a close resemblance to R. augustinii, but with white flowers. Szechwan. **Syn. R. augustinii ssp. augustinii/RN, rn, Triflora.**

R. violaceum (*violet colored*) s. Lapponicum. 2', -10ºF, EM, 2/2/2-3. Leaves on this shrub are very small and narrow, to only 1/3" long. The tops are dark green and scaly, and the undersides are also densely covered with yellowish or pale brown scales. Flowers, barely 1/2" long, are open funnel-shaped, violet purple, in clusters of up to 3. Kansu, W. Szechwan, 10,000-14,000 ft. **Syn. R. nivale ssp. boreale/RN, rn, Lapponica.**

R. virgatum (*with willowy twigs*) s. Virgatum. 4', 10ºF, E-EM, 3-4/2-3/3-4. Growth habit of this plant is open, spreading, rather leggy. Oblong or broadly lanceolate leaves, to about 3", are slightly scaly above, the reverse densely scaly. Flowers, either alone or in pairs, bloom between leaf clusters along the branches and reach a size to 1" long. The tubular bell-shaped flowers range from white to pink or various shades of rose and purple. Sikkim, Bhutan, 9,000 ft. **R. virgatum ssp. virgatum/RN, rn, Virgata.**

R. viridescens (*becoming green*) s. Trichocladum. 3', -5ºF, ML-L, 2/2-3/3. Growth habit is low and spreading, with very bristly new growth. Leaves, to about 1 3/4", are oblong-oval or oblong elliptic. The top surface is pale sea green and without hair, the underside is paler, waxy blue green, and scaly. Widely funnel-shaped flowers, to 3/4" long, are pale yellowish green, spotted green, held in trusses of 4-5. S.E. Tibet, 10,000-11,000 ft. **R. mekongense var. mekongense Viridescens Group/RN, rn, Trichoclada.**

R. viscidifolium (*with sticky leaves*) s. and s.s. Thomsonii. 4', 10ºF, EM, 2-3/2-3/2-3. Oval or orbicular leaves, up to 4" long, are smooth and non-hairy on top, the reverse white, sticky, and glandular. Tubular-bell-shaped flowers, of great substance, to 1 1/2" long, are bright copper red, crimson spotted, and with crimson nectar pouches. S.E. Tibet, 9,000-11,000 ft. **UC/HY, hy, Thomsonia.**

R. viscosum (*sticky*) s. Azalea s.s. Luteum. 5', -15ºF, VL, 3/3/3-4. Growth habit is upright and spreading, with many branches. Plant is deciduous, the young growth hairy. Leaves, to 2" long, are lance shaped, ovate, or elliptic to obovate, the top dark green and hairless, the reverse usually with a waxy blue green cast. Flowers, to 1 1/2" wide, are narrowly tubular-funnel-shape, and open after the foliage to form trusses in groups of 12. Scented blooms are white or creamy white, sometimes tinged pink. Known as "Swamp Honeysuckle." E. North America. **UC/PE, pe.**
    'Betty Cummins'-- A fragrant selection with pretty pink flowers.
    'Lemon Drop'-- Late blooming selection which has pink buds opening to expose scented yellow flowers.

R. wadanum (*after K. Wada, of Japan*) s. Azalea s.s. Schlippenbachii. 5', -5ºF, EM, 3/3/3. Growth habit of this deciduous shrub is rather tree-like, with leaves in groups of 3 at branch ends. Foliage is almost as wide as long, more or less oval-diamond-shape, to 2 1/3" long. Widely funnel-shaped flowers, to 1 1/2" across, appearing either alone or in pairs, are deep purple, spotted darker. Probably closely allied with R. reticulatum. Japan. **UC/TT, br.**

R. wallichii (*after N. Wallich, 1786-1854, a former Superintendent, Calcutta Botanic Garden*) s. Campanulatum. 4', -10ºF, EM, 2-3/3/3. This shrub has dark brown bark and interesting foliage. Leaves to 5" long, are elliptic, oblong or obovate, the tops dark green and hairless, the reverse paler and with a covering of sparse tufts of powdery rusty brown hairs. Flowers, to 2" long, are bell-shaped, and held in trusses of up to 10. The blooms range in color from lilac to rose, pink or white, occasionally spotted rose. Very closely allied to R. campanulatum, with only minute differences of indumentum. Nepal, Sikkim, Bhutan, Assam, 10,000-17,000 ft. **UC/HY, hy, Campanulata.**

R. walongense (*after an Indian outpost in Lohit Valley, near Rima*) s. Maddenii s.s. Ciliicalyx. 5', 20ºF, EM, 3/2-3/3. Leaves, to 5" long, are elliptic in shape, the underside scaly. Funnel-shaped flowers, to almost 3" long, are white, scented, carried in trusses of 3-4. S.E. Tibet, 5,000-7,000 ft. **UC/RN, rn, Maddenia "Ciliicalyx-Alliance" Johnstoneanum agg.**

R. wardii (*after F. Kingdon Ward, 1885-1958, collector and explorer*) s. Thomsonii s.s. Souliei. 4', 0ºF, M, 4/3-4/3-4. Growth habit is open and upright. The leaves to about 4" long, are rounded oval, the tops dark green and non-hairy, underside paler and glaucous. Flowers to 2 1/2" long, are bowl or cup shaped, clear lemon to bright yellow, occasionally flushed with green or with a crimson basal blotch, in loose trusses from 7-14. Is different from R. litiense in that it has more rounded leaves. Yunnan, Szechwan, S.E. Tibet, 10,000-14,000 ft. **R. wardii var. wardii/HY, hy, Campylocarpa.**

R. wasonii (*after Rear-Adm. C. R. Wason, 1874-1941, friend of E. H. Wilson*) s. Taliense s.s. Wasonii. 4', -5ºF, EM, 3/3-4/3. Young foliage buds on this shrub are densely clothed on top with a pale greyish-buff tomentum. Leaves, to 4" long, are oval or widely lanceolate, dark shiny green on top, almost hairless, the underside with a thick layer of dark brown or rust-colored indumentum. Bell-shaped flowers, to 1 1/2" long, ranging in color from white to creamy white, pink, rose, or yellow, sometimes spotted crimson, are carried in loose trusses of 6-10. **UC/HY, hy, Taliensia.**
> **var. rhododactylum**-- White flowers, lined with pink, with a large crimson blotch. W. Szechwan, 9,000-11,000 ft. **R. wasonii 'Rhododactylum'.**

R. watsonii (*after W. C. Haines-Watson, Chinese Customs*) s. Grande. 6', 5ºF, E, 3/3/2-3. This is one of the large-leaved species, which makes it a handsome foliage plant. Leaves, to as much as 9" long, have virtually no stem. The oblanceolate, elliptic or obovate foliage is dark glossy green on top, with a scant covering of silvery to fawn indumentum underneath. The leaf stalk is thick, winged, and rather yellowish. Flowers, to 1 1/2" long, are widely campanulate, white or white flushed pink, blotched crimson, in loose trusses of up to 15. W. Szechwan, 9,000-11,000 ft. **UC/HY, hy, Grandia.**

R. websteranum (*after F. G. Webster of Boston, U.S.A.*) s. Lapponicum. 3', -5ºF, EM, 2/2/2-3. A small shrub with densely scaly new growth. Small leaves, to only 3/4" long, are lance shaped or narrowly elliptic. The tops are dull, dark grey-green with pale luminous scales, with densely scaled, straw colored undersides. Flowers, to about 3/4" long, are open funnel-shape, rose-purple, sometimes slightly hairy, usually appearing alone. W. Szechwan, 10,000-14,000 ft. **R. websteranum var. websteranum/RN, rn, Lapponica.**

R. weldianum (*after General S. M. Weld, a former President of the Massachusetts Horticultural Society*) s. Taliense s.s. Wasonii. 4', -5ºF, EM, 2-3/3-4/3. Leaves, to 5", are oblong-elliptic, oval, or oblong-oval, glossy and non-hairy on top, the underside thickly indumented fawn to brown. Flowers, to 1" long, are funnel-bell-shaped, white or pinky-purple, spotted crimson, and held in somewhat loose trusses up to 12. W. Szechwan, 9,000-10,000 ft. **Syn. R. rufum/HY, hy, Taliensia.**

R. westlandii (*after A. B. Westland, who discovered it*) s. Stamineum. 6', 25ºF, EM, 3/3/3. Habit is tree-like, and flowers have a lovely scent. Leaves, to 5" long, are oblong-lance shape to elliptic-lanceolate. Non-hairy, dark glossy green leaf surfaces have pale undersides. Flowers, blooming along branches in between leaf clusters in trusses to 8, are 2 1/2" long, narrow funnel shape, lilac in color. Kwangtung, Lantas Island, Kowloon and Swatow, 2,500 ft. **UC/AZ, ch.**

R. weyrichii (*after Dr. Weyrich, 1828-1863, Russian naval surgeon*) s. Azalea s.s. Schlippenbachii. 5', -10ºF, EM, 3/3/3. This deciduous shrub grows open and upright, the new growth a yellowish brown color with darker brown indumentum. Leaves, occurring in groups of 2 or 3 at branch ends, are broad-ovate or almost orbicular. The foliage, to 3" long, is non-hairy, pale green above, with a grey-green underside. Flowers, blooming either before or with the leaves, to 2 1/2" across, are rotate-funnel-shaped, salmon or bright brick-red, blotched purple, in trusses of 2-4. Japan and Quelpaert (Korea). **UC/TT, br.**

R. wightii (*after R. Wight, 1796-1872, a former Supt., Madras Botanic Garden*) s. Lacteum. 5', 5ºF, EM, 3/2-3/2-3. Growth habit is quite open and tree-like, with sparse foliage. Leaves, to a generous 8" long, are oblong lance-shaped, hairless bright green above, the undersides covered with a fawn or reddish-brown felt-like indumentum. Bell-shaped flowers, to 2" long, are pale to lemon yellow or tannish yellow, very occasionally white, with crimson spotting, sometimes blotched crimson. They are carried in lop-sided, lax trusses of up to 20. Nepal, Sikkim, Bhutan, Tibet, N.E. Upper Burma, 11,000-14,000 ft. **UC/HY, hy, Taliensia.**

R. williamsianum (*after J. C. Williams, 1861-1939, of Caerhays, Cornwall*) s. Thomsonii s.s. Williamsianum. 18", -5ºF, EM, 3/4/4. Growth habit is tight, compact, low-spreading and dwarf, not usual in the Thomsonii series. New growth has glandular bristles and is a lively bronze. Leaves, varying from 1/2" to 2" in length, the shape orbicular or ovate, are brilliant green on top. The undersides have a waxy bluish green cast and a scattering of tiny glands and hairs. Bell-shaped flowers, to 2" long, bloom in loose trusses of 2 or 3 flowers, the color various shades of pink. This plant, because of its many pleasing features, is used extensively in hybridization. One of the loveliest and most highly regarded in the genus, *R. williamsianum* grows in a perfectly rounded, evergreen shape, with the delicate, dainty little bells hanging like fairy lanterns amidst the dense foliage. Szechwan, 8,000-10,000 ft. **UC/HY, hy, Williamsia.**

R. wilsoniae (*after Mrs. Wilson, d. 1931, wife of E. H. Wilson*) s. Stamineum. 3', -10ºF, EM-L, 3/3/3. Growth habit is compact and spreading, with oval-shaped leaves in whorls. Leaves are about 4" long, glossy on top, paler and non-hairy underneath. Fragrant flowers, blooming usually alone at branch tips and along the branches between leaf clusters, are about 1 1/2" long, widely funnel shaped, flesh pink to pale lilac, spotted brownish. W. Hupeh, 5,000-6,000 ft. **UC/AZ, ch.**

R. wiltonii (*after Sir Colville E. Wilton, b. 1870, Chinese Consular Service, Ichang*) s. Taliense s.s. Wasonii. 3', -5ºF, EM, 3/4/3-4. Young growth on this shrub is clothed with greenish-white felt. Leaves, to 5" long, are oblong-lance-shaped or oblong-obovate, the tops shiny and wrinkled, non- hairy, the underside with a fawn or brown indumentum. Flowers, to 1 1/2" long, are bell-shaped or funnel bell-shaped, white or white blushed pink, spotted and blotched crimson, and are held in trusses of up to 10. W. Szechwan, 7,000-9,000 ft. **UC/HY, hy, Taliensia.**

R. wrayi (*after L. Wray 1853-1942, who first collected it, in 1905*) s. and s.s. Irroratum. 6', 25ºF, VE, 2-3/2-3/2-3. Leaves on this small tree-like shrub are oblong to elliptic. They are 6" long, growing in whorls of 4 or 5. The tops are almost hairless, the reverse more densely hairy or woolly, the color rusty or grey. Flowers, to slightly more than 1" long, are white, sometimes flushed pink, or with red spots, in trusses of 8-12. Malay Peninsula, 3,000-7,000 ft. **UC/HY, hy, Irrorata.**

R. xanthocodon (*yellow bell*) s. Cinnabarinum. 5', 5ºF, ML, 3/3/2-3. Growth habit is upright, but quite compact, with lovely golden, scaly new growth. Oval leaves, to 3" long, are slightly scaly grey-green above, with a waxy blue green bloom and scaly underside. Aromatic flowers, to 1 1/2", are tubular bell-shaped, of heavy substance, yellow or a rich cream yellow, either spotted or free of spots, and carried in trusses to 10. Bhutan, S.E. Tibet, 11,000-12,000 ft. **R. cinnabarinum ssp. xanthocodon/RN, rn, Cinnabarina.**

R. xanthostephanum (*yellow garland*) s. Boothii s.s. Tephropeplum. 4', 15ºF, EM, 3/2-3/3. This shrub has a straggly, leggy growth habit. Leaves, to 4" long, are lance-shaped to oblanceolate, smooth, dark, shiny green above, the reverse greyish, with a waxy blue green cast and dense scales. Flowers, to 1" long, are tubular bell-shaped, scaly outside, in shades of yellow, sometimes tinged green, with erect calyx lobes, in trusses of 3-8. Somewhat like *R. auritum*, except that the lobes of the calyx are not reflexed. Yunnan, Tibet, Burma, 7,000-13,000 ft. **UC/RN, rn, Tephropepla.**

R. yakuinsulare (*from the island of Yakushima*) s. Azalea. 18", 15ºF, L, 3/3-4/3. Leaves, 1" x 2 1/2", are ovate-oblong to elliptic. Flowers, to about 1 1/2" long, are funnel-shaped, the color rose-red, held in trusses of 1-3. Apparently only a few plants of this are in cultivation in Japan, but another plant which is actually a Satsuki azalea named 'Otakumi' was widely distributed under this name. 'Otakumi' has very narrow leaves, while the true *R. yakuinsulare* has much wider leaves. **UC/TT, tt.**

R. yakushimanum 'Ken Janeck'

R. yakushimanum (*from Yakushima Island, Japan*) s. Ponticum *s.s.* Caucasicum. 1-4', -25°F, EM, 5/5/4. Growth habit is rounded, compact, mound-like, with white-felted new growth. Mature leaves, to 3 1/2" long, are linear-oblanceolate to lanceolate, the tops smooth, glossy, dark green, the undersides thick with woolly brown indumentum. Bell-shaped flowers, to 1 1/2" long, are a rich rose color in the bud, change to dainty pink and then white when fully open, and are set in trusses to 10 flowers. This is a hardy plant, with excellent foliage and fabulous indumentum. Height varies from 1' to 4' depending on form. Yakushima Island, Japan. **R. yakushimanum ssp. yakushimanum/HY, hy, Pontica.** The following are some of the most well-known forms:

Exbury form-- This variety has smaller convex leaves. Very much in demand.

'Ken Janeck'-- Named selection from the Seattle area. Larger leaf and plant size than most. Excellent representation of the larger size of the "yaks". A very fine plant, it is the deepest pink of the "yaks", and it won the coveted Award of Excellence. Considered by some to be a hybrid.

'Koichiro Wada'-- The new name of the F.C.C. form. It is certainly one of the best forms and one that should be in your collection. It makes an extremely good plant that puts on a real display. Buds are a deep pink opening to white.

'Mist Maiden'-- One of the larger forms which was selected by the well known rhododendron authority, David Leach. The large flowers are apple blossom pink turning white. Beautiful! Considered by some to be a hybrid.

Phetteplace tall form-- Probably the tallest form. Dr. Phetteplace's original plant, though old is about 6' high. Flowers are large though typical color and shape of *yakushimanum.*

'Pink Parasol'-- Larger leaves, slightly deeper pink. Considered by some to be a hybrid.

'White Velvet'-- A form with medium to large leaves.

'Yak-ity-Yak'-- This is a large leaved selection somewhat like 'Ken Janeck'. The foliage is larger and the flowers are more satiny white. Considered by some to be a hybrid.

'Yaku Angel'-- This has longer, narrower, more convex leaves than most. It buds younger and more heavily, and grows more easily. Even when not in flower, it is the most attractive plant in the garden. The flowers show a bit of pink in bud and then open to the purest white of the *R. yakushimanum* clones.

R. yedoense (*from Yedo, now Tokyo, Japan*) s. Azalea *s.s.* Obtusum. 4', -5°F, M, 3/3/4. This is a form of double-flowered azalea, cultivated in Japan and Korea, growing wild in the latter country. This plant, with its rose-purple double flowers, has come to be accepted as the cultivated form of what frequently is called *R. yedoense* var. *poukhanense*, and has been given the clonal name 'Yodogawa'. Flowers are rose to mauve or purple, with darker spots. **UC/TT, tt.**

R. yedoense var. poukhanense (*from Mt. Poukhan, Korea*) s. Azalea *s.s.* Obtusum. 4', -15°F, E, 3/3/4. This is an open, spreading, deciduous shrub, having 2 distinct leaf forms: spring and summer. First leaves, to 3 1/2" x 1", are oblanceolate to ovate-lanceolate, the tops dark green, underside paler, and both sides with sparse covering of flatly pressed stiff grey or brown hairs. Summer leaves are the same length, but only about half as wide. Flowers, to about 2" wide, are widely funnel-shaped, from rose to pale lilac, and are in clusters of 2-4. Korea. **UC/TT, tt.**

R. yungningense (*after Yungning, Szechwan*) s. Lapponicum. 2', -15°F, EM, 3/3/4. A dwarf shrub with an open upright habit, displaying densely scaled new growth. Leaves are tiny, to only 1/4" long, oblong-lanceolate, both sides very scaly, the underside rust-colored. Flowers, only 1/3" long, are wide funnel-shape, ranging in color from pale rose purple to deep purple or dark purplish blue, appearing either alone or in pairs. Szechwan, Yunnan, 11,000-14,000 ft. **UC/RN, rn, Lapponica.**

R. yunnanense (*from Yunnan*) s. Triflorum *s.s.* Yunnanense. 6', 0°F, EM-M, 4/2-3/3-4. This is an extremely variable species. It is very free-flowering, with an open upright habit, evergreen, but sometimes semi-deciduous. Leaves, to 4" long, are oblanceolate or lanceolate, bright green and scaly on both sides, with marginal bristles. Flowers appear in trusses of 3-5, both on the ends and along the branches in between leaf clusters. Flowers, about 1 1/2" long, are open funnel shape. They range in color from white to pink, or rosy lavender, sometimes spotted or blotched crimson. Yunnan, Szechwan, Burma, S.E. Tibet, Kweichow, 6,500-14,000 ft. **UC/RN, rn, Triflora Yunnanense agg.**

R. zaleucum (*very white*) s. Triflorum *s.s.* Yunnanense. 6', 5°F, E, 3/3/3. Leaves, to 3 1/2" long, are lanceolate, obovate, or elliptic, the tops dark green and slightly scaly, the undersides whitish glaucous and scaly. Flowers appear in clusters of 3-5, either at the ends or along the upper part of branches between the leaves. The 1 1/2" long blooms are widely funnel-shaped, pale purple, rose, yellow or white, occasionally spotted crimson. Burma, Yunnan, 6,000-13,000 ft. **UC/RN, rn, Triflora.**

R. zeylanicum (*from Ceylon*) s. and *s.s.* Arboreum. 5', 10°F, EM, 3/3/3. Growth habit is open and tree-like, with lovely foliage. Leaves, to 5" long, are oval, elliptic or oblong-elliptic, glossy dark green, wrinkled and convex above, the reverse with a dense covering of yellowish to rusty or copper-colored woolly indumentum. Flowers, to 2" long, are bell shaped, red to scarlet-red and sometimes pink, held in dense, compact trusses up to 20. Ceylon, 3,000-8,000 ft. **R. arboreum ssp. zeylanicum/HY, hy, Arborea.**

FREQUENTLY USED SYNONYMS

Previous Name	Current Name
adenosum	kuluense
aechmophyllum	yunnanense
aeruginosum	campanulatum var. aeruginosum
agetum	neriiflorum ssp. agetum
aiolosalpinx	stewartianum var. aiolosalpinx
apodectum	dichroanthum ssp. apodectum
artosquameum	oreotrephes
astrocalyx	wardii
aucklandii	griffithianum
augustinii var. rubrum	bergii
aureum Franch. (non Georgi)	xanthostephanum
baeticum	ponticum L.
beanianum compactum	piercei
benthamianum	concinnum var. benthamianum
blandfordiiflorum	cinnabarinum var. blandfordiiflorum
brunneifolium	eudoxum ssp. brunneifolium
bullatum	edgeworthii
caeruleum	rigidum
calciphilum	calostrotum var. calciphilum
californicum	macrophyllum
campbelliae	arboreum ssp. campbelliae
candelabrum	thomsonii var. candelabrum
cantabile	russatum
cephalanthoides	primuliflorum var. cephalanthoides
charopoeum	campylogynum var. charopoeum
chartophyllum	yunnanense
chartophyllum f. praecox	hormophorum
chasmanthum	augustinii var. chasmanthum
chengshienlanum	ambiguum
chrysanthum	aureum
cinnamomeum	arboreum ssp. cinnamomeum
cloiphorum	sanguineum ssp. cloiophorum
coryphaeum	praestans
cosmetum	chameunum
crebreflorum	cephalanthum var. crebreflorum
cremastum	campylogynum var. cremastum
croseum	wardii
cumberlandense	bakeri
cyclium	callimorphum
decandrum	reticulatum
decipiens	probably hodgsonii and falconeri hybrid
decumbens	indicum
didymum	sanguineum ssp. didymum
dilatatum	reticulatum
elaeagnoides	lepiotum
eriocarpum	simsii var. eriocarpum
eriogynum	facetum
eriphyllum	cyanocarpum var. eriphyllum
euchaites	neriiflorum ssp. euchaites
exquisitum	oreotrephes
fittianum	natural hybrid of racemosum
flavum	luteum
flinckii	lanatum
fulvoides	fulvum
glaucum	glaucophyllum
glischrum var. adenosum	kuluense
haemaleum	sanguineum ssp. haemaleum
hedyosmum	trichostomum var. hedyosmum
horaeum	citriniflorum ssp. horaeum
hypolepidotum	brachyanthum var. hypolepidotum
impeditum hort. p.p. (*non Balf. f.*)	fastigiatum
kingianum	probably an arboreum hybrid
kotschyi	myrtifolium
lagopus	reticulatum
ledoides	trichostomum var. ledoides
lepidotum var. chloranthum	lepidotum
linearifolium	macrosepalum 'Linearfolium'
lochmium	natural hybrid; possibly davidsonianum x trichanthum
luciferum	lanatum var. luciferum
maddenii var. obtusifolium	manipurense
mesaeum	sanguineum ssp. mesaeum
metternichii var. pentamerum	degronianum
mollyanum	montroseanum
mucronatum	'Mucronatum', hybrid of uncertain parentage
muliense	chryseum
myrtilloides	campylogynum var. myrtilloides
nikoense	pentaphyllum
nikomontanum	hybrid of uncertain parentage
niphargum	uvariifolium
nmaiense	cephalanthum var. nmaiense
notatum	dendricola
nudiflorum	periclymenoides
obtusum f. japonicum	kiusianum
oporinum	heliolepis
pallescens	natural hybrid of racemosum and davidsoniaum
pankimense	kendrickii
phaedropum	neriiflorum ssp. phaedropum
phoenicodum	neriiflorum ssp. phoenicodum
pontica (Azalea)	luteum
poukhanense	yedoense var. poukhanense
probum	selense var. probum
pruniflorum	tsangpoense var. pruniflorum
pseudoyanthinum	concinnum var. pseudoyanthinum
radinum	trichostomum var. radinum
repens	forrestii var. repens
repens var. chamaedoron	chamaethomsonii var. chamaedoron
repens var. chamaethauma	chamaethomsonii var. chamaethauma
repens var. chamaedoxa	chamaethomsonii var. chamaethauma
repens v. chamaethomsonii	chamaethomsonii v. chamaethomsonii
rhantum	vernicosum
rhodora	canadense
riparium	calostrotum
roseotinctum	sanguineum ssp. roseotinctum
roseum	prinophyllum
rosaflora	indicum 'Balsaminiflora'
roylei	cinnabarinum var. roylei
rubroluteum	mekongense
scyphocalyx	dichroanthum ssp. scyphocalyx
semilunatum	melinanthum
sheltoniae	vernicosum
silvaticum	lanigerum
sinense	molle
sinensis	molle
sinonuttallii	nuttallii
speciosum	flammeum
suberosum	yunnanense
tanakae	Tsusiophyllum tanakae = R. tsusiophyllum
thomsonii var. cyanocarpum	cyanocarpum
thomsonii var. pallidum	thomsonii var. candelabrum
timeteum	oreotrephes
villosum	trichanthum

Current Name	Previous Name
ambiguum	chengshienianum
arboreum ssp. campbelliae	campbelliae
arboreum ssp. cinnamomeum	cinnamomeum
augustinii var. chasmanthum	chasmanthum
aureum	chrysanthum
bakeri	cumberlandense
bergii	augustinii var. rubrum
brachyanthum var. hypolepidotum	hypolepidotum
callimorphum	cyclium
calostrotum var. calciphilum	calciphilum
calostrotum	riparium
campanulatum var. aeruginosum	aeruginosum
campylogynum var. charopoeum	charopoeum
campylogynum var. cremastum	cremastum
campylogynum var. myrtilloides	myrtilloides
canadense	rhodora
cephalanthum var. crebreflorum	crebreflorum
cephalanthum var. nmaiense	nmaiense
chamaethomsonii var. chamaedoron	repens var. chamaedoron
chamaethomsonii var. chamaethauma	repens var. chamaethauma
chamaethomsonii var. chamaethauma	repens var. chamaedoxa
chamaethomsonii v. chamaethomsonii	repens v. chamaethomsonii
chameunum	cosmetum
chryseum	muliense
cinnabarinum var. blandfordiiflorum	blandfordiiflorum
cinnabarinum var. roylei	roylei

The Balfourian Classification

1. Albiflorum Series
R. albiflorum

2. Anthopogon Series
R. anthopogon
R. anthopogonoides
R. cephalanthum
R. collettianum
R. hypenanthum
R. kongboense
R. laudandum
R. primuliflorum
R. sargentianum
R. trichostomum

3. Arboreum Series
Subseries Arboreum
R. arboreum
  ssp. arboreum
  ssp. campbelliae
  ssp. cinnamomeum
  ssp. nilagiricum
R. delavayi
R. lanigerum
R. niveum
R. peramoenum
R. zeylanicum
Subseries Argyrophyllum
R. argyrophyllum
R. chienianum
R. coryanum
R. floribundum
R. formosanum
R. hunnewellianum
R. hypoglaucum
R. insigne
R. pingianum
R. ririei
R. rockii
R. simiarum
R. thayeranum

4. Auriculatum Series
R. auriculatum

5. Azalea Series
Unplaced in Subseries
R. noriakianum
R. taiwanalpinum
R. yakuinsulare
Subseries Canadense
R. albrechtii
R. canadense
R. pentaphyllum
R. vaseyi
Subseries Luteum
R. alabamense
R. arborescens
R. atlanticum

R. austrinum
R. bakeri
R. calendulaceum
R. canescens
R. flammeum
R. japonicum
R. luteum
R. molle
R. oblongifolium
R. occidentale
R. periclymenoides
R. prinophyllum
R. prunifolium
R. serrulatum
R. viscosum
Subseries Nipponicum
R. nipponicum
Subseries Obtusum
R. breviperulatum
R. indicum
R. kaempferi
R. kanehirae
R. kiusianum
R. macrogemmum
R. macrosepalum
R. microphyton
R. minutiflorum
R. nakaharae
R. obtusum
R. oldhamii
R. pulchrum
R. ripense
R. rubropilosum
R. scabrum
R. serpyllifolium
R. simsii
R. subsessile
R. tashiroi
R. tosaense
R. tschonoskii
R. yedoense
Subseries Schlippenbachii
R. amagianum
R. dilatatum
R. farrerae
R. kiyosumense
R. mariesii
R. nudipes
R. quinquefolium
R. reticulatum
R. sanctum
R. schlippenbachii
R. wadanum
R. weyrichii

6. Barbatum Series
Subseries Barbatum
R. argipeplum
R. barbatum

R. exasperatum
R. imberbe
R. smithii
Subseries Crinigerum
R. bainbridgeanum
R. crinigerum
Subseries Glischrum
R. diphrocalyx
R. erosum
R. glischroides
R. glischrum
R. habrotrichum
R. hirtipes
R. kuluense
R. rude
R. spilotum
R. vesiculiferum
Subseries Maculiferum
R. anhweiense
R. longesquamatum
R. maculiferum
R. morii
R. nankotaisanense
R. pachysanthum
R. pachytrichum
R. pseudochrysanthum
R. strigillosum

7. Boothii Series
Subseries Boothii
R. boothii
R. chrysodoron
R. sulfureum
Subseries Megeratum
R. leucaspis
R. megeratum
Subseries Tephropeplum
R. auritum
R. chrysolepis
R. tephropeplum
R. xanthostephanum

8. Camelliiflorum Series
R. camelliiflorum

9. Campanulatum Series
R. campanulatum
R. fulgens
R. lanatum
R. sherriffii
R. succothii
R. tsariense
R. wallichii

10. Campylogynum Series
R. campylogynum

11. Camtschaticum Series
R. camtschaticum

12. Carolinianum Series
R. carolinianum
R. chapmanii
R. minus

13. Cinnabarinum Series
R. cinnabarinum
R. concatenans
R. keysii
R. tamaense
R. xanthocodon

14. Dauricum Series
R. dauricum
R. mucronulatum

15. Edgeworthii Series
R. edgeworthii
R. pendulum
R. seinghkuense

16. Falconeri Series
R. arizelum
R. basilicum
R. coriaceum
R. eximium
R. falconeri
R. fictolacteum
R. galactinum
R. hodgsonii
R. preptum
R. rex
R. rothschildii

17. Ferrugineum Series
R. ferrugineum
R. hirsutum
R. myrtifolium

18. Fortunei Series
Subseries Calophytum
R. calophytum
Subseries Davidii
R. planetum
R. praevernum
R. sutchuenense
Subseries Fortunei
R. chlorops
R. decorum
R. diaprepes
R. discolor
R. fortunei
R. hemsleyanum
R. houlstonii
R. serotinum
R. vernicosum
Subseries Griffithianum
R. griffithianum

Subseries Orbiculare
R. cardiobasis
R. orbiculare
Subseries Oreodoxa
R. erubescens
R. fargesii
R. oreodoxa
R. praeteritum

19. Fulvum Series
R. fulvum
R. uvariifolium

20. Glaucophyllum Series
Subseries Genestieranum
R. genestieranum
R. micromeres
Subseries Glaucophyllum
R. brachyanthum
R. charitopes
R. glaucophyllum
R. luteiflorum
R. shweliense
R. tsangpoense

21. Grande Series
R. giganteum
R. grande
R. macabeanum
R. magnificum
R. montroseanum
R. peregrinum
R. praestans
R. protistum
R. pudorosum
R. semnoides
R. sidereum
R. sinogrande
R. watsonii

22. Griersonianum Series
R. griersonianum

23. Heliolepis Series
R. bracteatum
R. brevistylum
R. desquamatum
R. fumidum
R. heliolepis
R. pholidotum
R. rubiginosum

24. Irroratum Series
Subseries Irroratum
R. aberconwayi
R. agastum
R. annae
R. anthosphaerum
R. araiophyllum

R. dimitrum
R. hardingii
R. irroratum
R. kendrickii
R. laxiflorum
R. lukiangense
  ssp. adroserum
  ssp. ceraceum
  ssp. gymnanthum
  ssp. lukiangense
R. pogonostylum
R. ramsdenianum
R. shepherdii
R. tanastylum
R. wrayi
Subseries Parishii
R. agapetum
R. cookeanum
R. elliottii
R. facetum
R. kyawii
R. parishii
R. venator

25. Lacteum Series
R. agglutinatum
R. beesianum
R. dictyotum
R. dryophyllum
R. dumosulum
R. lacteum
R. nakotiltum
R. phaeochrysum
R. przewalskii
R. traillianum
R. wightii

26. Lapponicum Series
R. achroanthum
R. alpicola
R. capitatum
R. chryseum
R. compactum
R. complexum
R. cuneatum
R. dasypetalum
R. diacritum
R. drumonium
R. edgarianum
R. fastigiatum
R. fimbriatum
R. flavidum
R. glomerulatum
R. hippophaeoides
R. idoneum
R. impeditum
R. intricatum
R. lapponicum
R. litangense

R. lysolepis
R. microleucum
R. nigropunctatum
R. nitidulum
R. nivale
R. oresbium
R. orthocladum
R. paludosum
R. parvifolium
R. peramabile
R. ramosissimum
R. ravum
R. rupicola
R. russatum
R. scintillans
R. setosum
R. spilanthum
R. stictophyllum
R. tapetiforme
R. telmateium
R. thymifolium
R. verruculosum
R. violaceum
R. websteranum
R. yungningense

27. Lepidotum Series
Subseries Baileyi
R. baileyi
Subseries Lepidotum
R. lepidotum
R. lowndesii

28. Maddenii Series
Subseries Ciliicalyx
R. burmanicum
R. carneum
R. ciliatum
R. ciliicalyx
R. coxianum
R. cubittii
R. cuffeanum
R. dendricola
R. fletcheranum
R. formosum
R. horlickianum
R. inaequale
R. iteophyllum
R. johnstoneanum
R. lasiopodum
R. ludwigianum
R. lyi
R. pachypodum
R. parryae
R. pilicalyx
R. scopulorum
R. scottianum
R. supranubium
R. taronense
R. valentinianum
R. veitchianum
R. walongense

Subseries Maddenii
R. brachysiphon
R. crassum
R. maddenii
R. manipurense
R. odoriferum
R. polyandrum
Subseries Megacalyx
R. dalhousiae
R. headfortianum
R. kiangsiense
R. lindleyi
R. megacalyx
R. nuttalii
R. rhabdotum
R. taggianum

29. Micranthum Series
R. micranthum

30. Moupinense Series
R. moupinense

31. Neriiflorum Series
Subseries Forrestii
R. chamaethomsonii
R. forrestii
Subseries Haematodes
R. beanianum
R. catacosmum
R. chaetomallum
R. chionanthum
R. coelicum
R. haematodes
R. hemidartum
R. mallotum
R. piercei
R. pocophorum
Subseries Neriiflorum
R. albertsenianum
R. floccigerum
R. neriiflorum
    ssp. agetum
    ssp. euchaites
    ssp. neriiflorum
    ssp. phaedropum
    ssp. phoenicodum
R. sperabile
R. sperabiloides
Subseries Sanguineum
R. aperantum
R. citriniflorum
    ssp. citriniflorum
    ssp. horaeum
R. dichroanthum
    ssp. apodectum
    ssp. dichroanthum
    ssp. herpesticum
    ssp. scyphocalyx
    ssp. septentrionale

R. eudoxum
    ssp. brunneifolium
    ssp. eudoxum
R. fulvastrum
    ssp. fulvastrum
    ssp. trichomiscum
R. parmulatum
R. sanguineum
    ssp. cloiophorum
    ssp. consanguineum
    ssp. didymum
    ssp. haemaleum
    ssp. mesaeum
    ssp. roseotinctum
    ssp. sanguineum
R. temenium
    ssp. albipetalum
    ssp. chrysanthemum
    ssp. gilvum
    ssp. glaphyrum
    ssp. pothinum
    ssp. temenium

32. Ovatum Series
R. hongkongense
R. leptothrium
R. ovatum
R. vialii

33. Ponticum Series
Subseries Caucasicum
R. adenopodum
R. aureum
R. brachycarpum
R. caucasicum
R. degronianum
R. fauriei
R. hyperythrum
R. makinoi
R. metternichii
R. smirnowii
R. ungernii
R. yakushimanum
Subseries Ponticum
R. catawbiense
R. macrophyllum
R. maximum
R. ponticum

34. Saluenense Series
R. calostrotum
R. chameunum
R. fragariiflorum
R. keleticum
R. nitens
R. prostratum
R. radicans
R. saluenense

35. Scabrifolium Series
R. hemitrichotum
R. mollicomum
R. pubescens
R. racemosum
R. scabrifolium
R. spiciferum
R. spinuliferum

36. Semibarbatum Series
R. semibarbatum

37. Stamineum Series
R. championiae
R. ellipticum
R. moulmainense
R. oxyphyllum
R. stamineum
R. stenaulum
R. westlandii
R. wilsoniae

38. Taliense Series
Subseries Adenogynum
R. adenogynum
R. adenophorum
R. alutaceum
R. balfourianum
R. bureavii
R. bureavioides
R. detonsum
R. dumicola
R. elegantulum
R. faberi
R. mimtes
R. nigroglandulosum
R. prattii
Subseries Roxieanum
R. bathyphyllum
R. globigerum
R. gymnocarpum
R. iodes
R. pronum
R. proteoides
R. recurvoides
R. roxieanum
R. russotinctum
R. triplonaevium
R. tritifolium
Subseries Taliense
R. aganniphum
R. clementinae
R. doshongense
R. flavorufum
R. glaucopeplum
R. schizopeplum
R. sphaeroblastum
R. taliense
R. vellereum

Subseries Wasonii
R. inopinum
R. paradoxum
R. rufum
R. wasonii
R. weldianum
R. wiltonii

39. Thomsonii Series
Subseries Campylocarpum
R. callimorphum
R. caloxanthum
R. campylocarpum
R. myiagrum
R. panteumorphum
R. telopeum
Subseries Cerasinum
R. cerasinum
Subseries Selense
R. calvescens
R. dasycladum
R. erythrocalyx
R. esetulosum
R. eurysiphon
R. jucundum
R. martinianum
R. selense
R. setiferum
R. vestitum
Subseries Souliei
R. litiense
R. puralbum
R. souliei
R. wardii
Subseries Thomsonii
R. cyanocarpum
R. eclecteum
R. faucium
R. hookeri
R. hylaeum
R. lopsangianum
R. meddianum
R. stewartianum
R. subansiriense
R. thomsonii
R. viscidifolium
Subseries Williamsianum
R. williamsianum

40. Trichocladum Series
R. caesium
R. chloranthum
R. cowanianum
R. lepidostylum
R. lophogynum
R. mekongense
R. melinanthum
R. oulotrichum
R. rubrolineatum
R. trichocladum
R. viridescens

41. Triflorum Series
Subseries Augustinii
R. augustinii
R. bergii
R. hardyi
R. trichanthum
Subseries Hanceanum
R. afghanicum
R. hanceanum
Subseries Triflorum
R. ambiguum
R. bauhiniiflorum
R. flavantherum
R. kasoense
R. keiskei
R. lutescens
R. triflorum
Subseries Yunnanense
R. amesiae
R. bodinieri
R. concinnoides
R. concinnum
R. davidsonianum
R. hormophorum
R. longistylum
R. oreotrephes
R. pleistanthum
R. polylepis
R. rigidum
R. searsiae
R. siderophyllum
R. tatsienense
R. vilmorinianum
R. yunnanense
R. zaleucum

42. Uniflorum Series
R. imperator
R. ludlowii
R. patulum
R. pemakoense
R. pumilum
R. uniflorum

43. Virgatum Series
R. oleifolium
R. virgatum

GENUS	SUBGENUS	SECTION	SUBSECTION

RHODODENDRON - RN
LEPIDOTES

RHODODENDRON - rn
MOST LEPIDOTES

POGONANTHUM - po
ANTHOPOGON

VIREYA - vr

Alboivireya
Euvireya
Malayovireya
Phaeovireya
Pseudovireya
Siphonovireya
Solenovireya

ALL ABOVE THIS LINE
ARE LEPIDOTES

ALL BELOW THIS LINE
ARE ELEPIDOTES

**GENUS
RHODODENDRON**

HYMENANTHES - HY
ELEPIDOTES

HYMENANTHES - hy
"MOST TYPICAL RHODODENDRONS"

PENTANTHERA - PE
AZALEAS (DECIDUOUS)
(PSEUDOANTHODENDRON -
Sleumer Classification)

PENTANTHERA - pe
LUTEUM

RHODORA - ro
CANADENSE

VISCIDULA - vs
NIPPONTICUM

SCIADORHODION - sc
(Philipson Classification Only)

TSUTSUTSI - TT
AZALEAS (MOSTLY
EVERGREEN)
(ANTHODENDRON -
Sleumer Classification)

TSUTSUTSI - tt
OBTUSUM

TSUSIOPSIS - ts

BRACHYCALYX - br
MOSTLY DECIDUOUS

AZALEASTRUM - AZ

AZALEASTRUM - az
OVATUM

CHONIASTRUM - ch
STAMINEUM

CANDIDASTRUM - CA
ALBIFLORUM

MUMEAZALEA - MU
SEMIBARBATUM

THERORHODION - TH
CAMTSCHATICUM

SUBSECTION list (Lepidotes):
Afghanica
Baileya
Boothia
Camelliiflora
Campylogyna
Caroliniana
Cinnabarina
Edgeworthia
Fragariiflora
Genestierana
Glauca
Heliopida
Lapponica
Lepidota
Maddenia
Micrantha
Monantha
Moupinensia
Rhododendron
Rhodorastra
Saluenensis
Scabrifolia
Tephropepla
Trichoclada
Triflora
Uniflora
Virgata

Maddenia branch:
Ciliicalyx Alliance — Cillicalyx Aggregate
Dalhousiae Alliance — Johnstoneanum Aggreg...
Maddenii Alliance
Megacalyx Alliance

SUBSECTION list (Elepidotes - Hymenanthes):
Arborea
Argyrophylla
Auriculata
Barbata
Campylocarpa
Campanulata
Falconera
Fortunea
Fulgensia
Fulva
Glischra
Grandia
Griersoniana
Irrorata
Lanata
Maculifera
Neriiflora
Parishia
Pontica
Selensia
Taliensia
Thomsonia
Venatora
Williamsia

The Genus Rhododendron Revised

SUBGENUS RHODODENDRON
SECTION POGONANTHUM
anthopogon   ssp. anthopogon
           ssp. hypenanthum
anthopogonoides
cephalanthum   ssp. cephalanthum
           ssp. platyphyllum
colletianum
kongboense
laudandum   var. laudandum
         var. temoense
primuliflorum
sargentianum
trichostomum

SECTION RHODODENDRON
subsect. Afghanica
afghanicum
subsect. Baileya
baileyi
subsect. Boothia
boothii
chrysodoron
leucaspis
megeratum
micromeres
sulfureum
subsect. Camelliiflora
camelliiflorum
subsect. Campylogyna
campylogynum
subsect. Caroliniana
minus   var. chapmanii
minus   var. minus
subsect. Cinnabarina
cinnabarinum   ssp. cinnabarinum
           ssp. tamaense
           ssp. xanthocodon
keysii
subsect. Edgeworthia
edgeworthii
pendulum
seinghkuense
subsect. Fragariiflora
fragariiflorum
subsect. Genestierana
genestieranum
subsect. Glauca
brachyanthum   ssp. brachyanthum
           ssp. hypolepidotum
charitopes   ssp. charitopes
        ssp. tsangpoense
glaucophyllum   var. glaucophyllum
           var. tubiforme
luteiflorum
pruniflorum
shweliense
subsect. Heliolepida

bracteatum
heliolepis   var. brevistylum
         var. heliolepis
rubiginosum
subsect. Lapponica
capitatum
complexum
cuneatum
dasypetalum
fastigiatum
flavidum   var. flavidum
        var. psilostylum
hippophaeoides   var. hippophaeoides
           var. occidentale
impeditum
intricatum
lapponicum
nitidulum   var. nitidulum
        var. omeiense
nivale   ssp. austral
      ssp. boreale
      ssp. nivale
orthocladum   var. longistylum
        var. microleucum
        var. orthocladum
polycladum
rupicola   var. chryseum
      var. muliense
      var. rupicola
russatum
tapetiforme
telmateium
thymifolium
websterianum   var. websterianum
        var. yulongense
yungningense
subsect. Ledum
columbianum
groelandicum
other species yet to be agreed upon
subsect. Lepidota
cowanianum
lepidotum
lowndesii
subsect. Maddenia
    Ciliicalyx -- Alliance
        burmanicum
        ciliatum
        cuffeanum
        fletcheranum
        formosum   var. formosum
                var. inaequale
        scopulorum
        valentinianum
           Ciliicalyx Aggregate
              carneum
              ciliicalyx
              horlickianum
              ludwigianum

        lyi
        pachypodum
        veitchianum
    Johnstoneanum Aggregate
        dendricola
        johnstoneanum
        walongense
    Dalhousiae -- Alliance
        dalhousiae   var. dalhousiae
                var. rhabdotum
        kiangsiense
        lindleyi
        nuttallii
        taggianum
    Maddenii -- Alliance
        maddenii   ssp. crassum
                ssp. maddenii
    Megacalyx -- Alliance
        megacalyx
subsect. Micrantha
micranthum
subsect. Monantha
concinnoides
flavantherum
kasoense
monanthum
subsect. Moupinensia
moupinense
subsect. Rhododendron
ferrugineum
hirsutum
myrtifolium
subsect. Rhodorastra
dauricum
mucronulatum
subsect. Saluenensia
calostrotum   ssp. calostrotum
        ssp. keleticum
        ssp. riparioides
        ssp. riparium
saluenense   ssp. chameunum
        ssp. saluenense
subsect. Scabrifolia
hemitrichotum
mollicomum
pubescens
racemosum
scabrifolium   var. pauciflorum
        var. scabrifolium
        var. spiciferum
spinuliferum
subsect. Tephropepla
auritum
hanceanum
longistylum
tephropeplum
xanthostephanum

subsect. Trichoclada
caesium
lepidostylum
mekongense   var. longipilosum
              var. mekongense
              var. melinanthum
              var. rubrolineatum
trichocladum
subsect. Triflora
ambiguum
amesiae
augustinii   ssp. augustinii
         ssp. chasmanthum
         ssp. hardyi
         ssp. rubrum
concinnum
davidsonianum
keiskei
lutescens
oreotrephes
pleistanthum
polylepis
rigidum
searsiae
siderophyllum
tatsienense
trichanthum
triflorum   var. bauhiniiflorum
        var. triflorum
yunnanense
zaleucum
subsect. Uniflora
ludlowii
pemakoense
pumilum
uniflorum   var. imperator
        var. uniflorum
subsect. Virgata
virgatum   ssp. oleifolium
       ssp. virgatum

SUBGENUS HYMENANTHES
SECTION HYMENANTHES
subsection Arborea
arboreum   ssp. arboreum
       ssp. cinnamomeum var. cinnamomeum
       ssp. cinnamomeum var. roseum
       ssp. delavayi var. delavayi
       ssp. delavayi var. peramoenum
       ssp. lanigerum
       ssp. niveum
subsection Argyrophylla
adenopodum
argyrophyllum   ssp. argyrophyllum
           ssp. hypoglaucum
           ssp. omeiense
           ssp. nankingense
coryanum
floribundum
formosanum
hunnewellianum   ssp. hunnewellianum

       ssp. rockii
insigne
pingianum
ririei
simiarum ssp. simiarum
thayerianum
subsection Auriculata
auriculatum
subsection Barbata
barbatum
erosum
exasperatum
smithii
succothii
subsection Campanulata
campanulatum   ssp. aeruginosum
            ssp. campanulatum
wallichii
subsection Campylocarpa
callimorphum   ssp. callimorphum
          ssp. myiagrum
campylocarpum   ssp. caloxanthum
           ssp. campylocarpum
souliei
wardii   var. puralbum
      var. wardii
subsection Falconera
basilicum
coriaceum
falconeri   ssp. eximium
        ssp. falconeri
galactinum
hodgsonii
preptum
rex   ssp. arizelum
     ssp. fictolacteum
     ssp. rex
rothschildii
semnoides
subsection Fortunea
calophytum var. calophytum
decorum
diaprepes
fortunei   ssp. discolor
       ssp. fortunei
griffithianum
hemsleyanum
orbiculare   ssp. cardiobasis
         ssp. orbiculare
oreodoxa   var. fargesii
       var. oreodoxa
praeteritum
praevernum
sutchuenense
vernicosum
subsection Fulgensia
fulgens
sherriffii
subsection Fulva
fulvum
uvarifolium
subsection Glischra

crinigerum   var. crinigerum
        var. euadenium
glischrum   ssp. glischroides
       ssp. glischrum
       ssp. rude
habrotrichum
kuluense
recurvoides
vesiculiferum
subsection Grandia
grande
macabeanum
magnificum
montroseanum
praestans
protistum   var. giganteum
       var. protistum
pudorosum
sidereum
sinogrande
watsonii
subsect. Griersoniana
griersonianum
subsect. Irrorata
aberconwayi
agastum
annae
anthosphaerum
araiophyllum
dimitrum
irroratum   ssp. irroratum
       ssp. pogonostylum
kendrickii
lukiangense
ramsdenianum
tanastylum var. tanastylum
subsect. Lanata
lanatum
tsariense
subsect. Maculifera
cookeanum
longesquamatum
maculiferum   ssp. anhweiense
        ssp. maculiferum
morii
pachysanthum
pachytrichum
pseudochrysanthum
strigillosum
subsect. Neriiflora
albertsenianum
aperantum
beanianum
catacosmum
chamaethomsonii   var. chamaedoron
           var. chamaethauma
           var. chamaethomsonii
chionanthum
citriniflorum   var. citriniflorum
        var. horaeum
coelicum

dichroanthum   ssp. apodectum
               ssp. dichroanthum
               ssp. scyphocalyx
               ssp. septentrionale
diphrocalyx
eudoxum   var. brunneifolium
           var. eudoxum
floccigerum   ssp. appropinquans
             ssp. floccigerum
forrestii   ssp. forrestii
         ssp. papillatum
haematodes ssp. chaetomallum
            ssp. haematodes
x hemigymnum
mallotum
microgynum
neriiflorum   ssp. agetum
           ssp. neriiflorum
           ssp. phaedropum
parmulatum
piercei
pocophorum var. hemidartum
            var. pocophorum
sanguineum ssp. sanguineum var. cloiophorum
                         var. didymoides
                         var. didymum
                         var. haemaleum
                         var. sanguineum
sperabile   var. sperabile
         var. weihsiense
sperabiloides
temenium var. dealbatum
          var. gilvum
          var. temenium
x xanthanthum
subsect. Parishia
elliottii
facetum
kyawai
parishii
subsect. Pontica
aureum var. aureum
         var. hypopitys
brachycarpum ssp. brachycarpum
                ssp. fauriei
catawbiense
caucasicum
hyperythrum
japonicum var. japonicum
          var. pentamerum
macrophyllum
maximum
ponticum
smirnowii
ungernii
yakushimanum ssp. makinoi
                ssp. yakushimanum
subsect. Selensia
bainbridgeanum
calvescens var. calvescens
           var. duseimatum
x erythrocalyx

esetulosum
hirtipes
martinianum
selense ssp. dasycladum
       ssp. jucundum
       ssp. selense
       ssp. setiferum
subsect. Taliensia
adenogynum
aganniphum var. aganniphum
             var. flavorufum
alutaceum var. alutaceum
          var. iodes
          var. russotinctum
balfourianum
bathyphyllum
beesianum
bureavii
clementinae
comisteum
dignabile
dumicola
elegantulum
faberi   ssp. faberi
       ssp. prattii
lacteum
mimetes
nakotiltum
nigroglandulosum
phaeochrysum var. agglutinatum
              var. levistratum
              var. phaeochrysum
pomense
principis
pronum
proteioides
przewalskii
roxieanumum var. cucullatum
             var. roxieanum
rufum
simulans
sphaeroblastum
taliense
traillianum   var. dictyotum
              var. traillianum
wasonii
wightii
wiltonii
subsect. Thomsonia
x candelabrum
cerasinum
cyanocarpum
eclecteum   var. bellatulum
           var. eclecteum
eurysiphon
faucium
hookeri
hylaeum
meddianum var. atrokermesinum
            var. meddianum
stewartianum
subansiriense

thomsonii   ssp. lopsangianum
           ssp. thomsonii
viscidifolium
subsect. Venatora
venator
subsect. Williamsia
williamsianum

SUBGENUS PENTANTHERA

Deciduous Azaleas
(pseudoanthodendron -- Sleumer classification)
   Sect. Pentanthera
   Sect. Rhodora
   Sect. Sciadorhodian
   (Philipson Classification)
   Sect. Viscidula

SUBGENUS TSUTSUTSI

Evergreen Azaleas
(Anthodendron -- Sleumer classification)
   Sect. Brachycalyx
   Sect. Tsusiopsis
   Sect. Tsutsutsi
   Sect. Tashiroi
   (Philipson Classification)

SUBGENUS AZALEASTRUM

   Sect. Azaleastrum
      ovatum
   Sect. Choniastrum
      stamineum

SUBGENUS CANDIDASTRUM

   albiflorum

SUBGENUS MUMEAZALEA

   semibarbatum

SUBGENUS THERORHODION

camtschaticum

RHODODENDRON HYBRIDS

Name | **Parentage** | **Approximate height at 10 years** | **Hardiness**

Quality Rating

Flowering Season (based on the time they would flower in Oregon, exact flowering time will vary with your climate).

'Hallelujah' ('Kimberly' x 'Jean Marie de Montague'). 4', -15°F, M, 4-5/5/4-5. For foliage and plant, there are few rhododendrons that can come near its beauty. The leaves are deep woodland green, extremely heavy-textured, and have a downward bend in the middle of the leaf that creates a most attractive effect. For foliage it will be the plant in your garden that draws the most attention as your friends inspect your garden "beauties". The flowers are rose red and form a large, tight truss. This is an adaptable rhododendron that you will admire every time you see it. (Greer 1976) A.E. 1982 Northwest. — **Plant Awards** - See page 227

Hybridizer or introducer & year

1. Flower
2. Plant & Foliage
3. Performance

Numbers go from 1 (poorest) to 5 (best).

VE — January, February, to March 15th.
E — March 15th to April 15th.
EM — April 15th to May 1st.
M — May 1st to June 1st.
L — June 1st to June 15th.
VL — June 15th through August.

'Abe Arnott' ('Marchioness of Lansdowne' x 'Lee's Dark Purple'). 5', -5°F, M-ML, 3-4/3-4/3. Plant habit is upright and moderately open. Flowers are two-tone purple, the light purple base color is accented with a large very dark flare. Large ball shaped trusses. (Weber 1974).

'A. Bedford' (mauve seedling x *ponticum*). 6', -5°F, ML, 4/3/5. Growth habit is large, upright, and vigorous, with a tolerance for full sun exposure. Foliage to 6 1/2" long, is dark glossy green. Open funnel-form flowers, to 3 1/4" across are pale mauve to lavender blue with a distinctive dark blotch, held in compact dome-shaped trusses with up to 16 flowers. Petal edges are slightly ruffled. This is a beautiful plant to use in background planting. Also registered as 'Arthur Bedford'. Frequently listed as 'Anne Bedford', which is incorrect. (Lowinsky before 1936) A.M. 1936, F.C.C 1958.

'Abigail' ('Loder's White' x *calophytum*). 5', -5°F, E, 3-4/3/3. These soft pink flowers have good substance form ball shaped trusses. The upright plant has large and sturdy leaves. (Dr. Carl Phetteplace 1979).

'Abendsonne' ('John Walter' x *dichroanthum* var. *syphocalx*). 4', -5°F, M, 4/3/3. Orange-red flowers form ball shaped trusses which give the plant its appropriate name, 'Evening Sun'. Plant habit is low, rounded and compact. Foliage is dense, dark green and held for three years on the plant. (Hobbie 1952).

'Abraham Lincoln' (*catawbiense* x unknown). 5', -25°F, M, 3/3/3. A plant of great hardiness and lovely flowers. Trusses begin as strong red and gradually fade to pink. An old hybrid well worth a spot in your garden. (S. B. Parsons before 1875).

'Acclaim' (['Pygmalion x *haematodes* x 'Wellfleet'] exact combination unknown) 5', -5°F, M, 3/3/3-4. Purplish red flowers in a ball shaped truss. Vigorous grower with light green leaves. (Dexter, Scott Hort. Foundation 1980).

'Accomac' ('Pygmalion' x *haematodes* x 'Wellfleet'] exact combination unknown). 4', -5°F, M, 3/3/3-4. Similar to 'Acclaim' but a little smaller. (Dexter, Scott Hort. Foundation 1980).

'Accomplishment' (['Pygmalion' x *haematodes* x 'Wellfleet'] exact combination unknown). 5', -15°F, M, 3-4/3-4/3. From the Dexter Collection. It has bright rose flowers highlighted by a warm, golden brown blotch on the upper petal. This blotch fans out into an array of spots extending around the rest of the petals. (Dexter before 1943, registered 1985).

'Agate Pass Jewel' (*dichroanthum* x unknown). 3', 5°F, L. 3/3-413- This plant has medium-sized foliage. The light orange flowers, to 1 1/2" wide, lightly striped green, are carried in lax trusses of 5 flowers. (Lancaster, Putney 1974).

'Aglo' (*minus* var. *minus* Carolinianum Group x *minus* var. *minus*). 3', -25°F, EM, 3-4/3-4/3-4. A sister seedling of the very beautiful 'Olga Mezitt', this upright growing plant exhibits all of the same super qualities, such as sun tolerance and early flowering. It is slightly lighter pink with a reddish eye. (Mezitt not registered).

'Airy Fairy' (*lutescens* x *mucronulatum* 'Cornell Pink'). 4', 0°F, E, 3-4/3/3-4. Leaves on this hybrid are on the small side, to about 2 3/4" long. Bright, clear pink flowers, to 1 3/4" wide, are spotted a dull red in the throat. There are usually 3 flowers to the truss. (Maloney, Granston 1977).

'Aksel Olsen' ('Essex Scarlet' x *forrestii* ssp. *forrestii* Repens Group). 2', -15°F, M, 3/4/3-4. This is related to the 'Elizabeth Hobbie', 'Scarlet Wonder' and 'Bad Eilsen' hybrids. It has blood red flowers and distinctive green foliage. The plant is interesting in that the upper branches are strong and upright white the lower branches are prostrate creeping along the ground. (Hobbie).

'Aladdin' (*griersonianum* x *auriculatum*). 6', 0°F, L, 3/3/4. Growth habit is open and stiffly upright on this rhododendron, which flowers when most are finished. Leaves are large, to 7", with narrow, sharply pointed shape and with a dense covering of short hairs. Large trumpet shaped flowers are pastel pink, deeper in the throats, in an open truss of up to 10. (Crosfield 1930) A.M. 1935.

'Albatross' ('Loderi' g. x *fortunei* ssp. *discolor*). 6', 0°F, L, 4/3/3. Growth habit is tall and open on this vigorous growing plant which has leaves to 6" long. The white flowers are very large, fleshy, and sweetly scented, a lovely pink when still in the bud, set in tall, open trusses. (Rothschild 1930) AM 1934, AM 1953.

'Albert' ('Viola' x 'Everestianum'). 4', -5°F, EM, 3/3/3. The flowers are a delicate lilac blue with a lighter center and a greenish-yellow eye. The plant habit is rounded and spreading with dull green leaves. It buds as a young plant. (Seidel 1899).

'Albert Close' (*maximum* x *macrophyllum*). 5', -10°F, L, 3/2/3. Growth habit is open and somewhat ragged on this hybrid, but foliage is an attractive blue-green, which effectively shows off the medium-sized, bright rose-pink flowers. The flowers have throats generously spotted chocolate-red, and they are held in tight cone-shaped trusses. This is a great plant for tolerance of sun and heat. (Fraser, Gable 1951).

'Albert Schweitzer' (unknown, *catawbiense* type). 5', -15°F, M, 3/3/3. Rose colored flowers have a deep striking red blotch and are held in large pyramidal trusses of up to 15 flowers. (van Nes).

'Albion Ridge' (selected white clone *macrophyllum*). 6', 15°F, M, 3/3/3. Foliage is large, to 6 1/2" long. White flowers, sporting small green blotches, and are held in trusses of up to 15 blooms. Flowers are 2 1/2" wide and are attractively ruffled. (Drewry, Gerrnan 1976).

Rhododendron Hybrids

Superior Plant Awards

'Trude Webster' (Greer) S.P.A. 1971 N.W.

R. 'Lem's Cameo' (Lem) S.P.A. 1971 N.W.

R. 'Patty Bee' (Berg)
S.P.A. 1985 N.W.

R. 'Ginny Gee'
(Berg) S.P.A.
1985 N.W.

R. 'Taurus' (Mossman) S.P.A. 1990 N.W.

'Party Pink' (Leach) S.P.A. 1983 G.L.

R. 'Scintillation' (Dexter) S.P.A. 1991 N.E.

Hybrids ~

With double flowers

R. 'Queen Anne's'

R. 'Betty Sears'

R. 'April Snow'

R. 'Weston's Pink Diamond'

R. 'Double Date'

R. 'Creamy Chiffon'

R. 'April White'

Hybrids ~ Foliage can be beautiful too!

R. 'Snow Lady'

R. 'Pioneer'

R. 'Noyo Brave'

R. 'Elizabeth Red Foliage'

R. 'Goldflimmer'

Hybrids ~ Fragrant

R. 'Loderi Game Chick'

R. 'Perfume'

R. 'Sue'

R. 'Mi Amour'

R. 'Dexter's Spice'

R. 'Loderi Pink Diamond'

R. 'Heavenly Scent'

'Album Elegans' (*catawbiense* hybrid). 6', -20ºF, L, 2/2-3/4. Habit is rather open, with good foliage and strong growth. Lovely, mauve-tinged, white flowers have greenish yellow throats, spotted dark on upper petal and set in rounded trusses. (H. Waterer before 1876).

'Album Novum' (*catawbiense* hybrid). 5', -20ºF, ML, 3/3/3. As with many of the *catawbiense* hybrids the flowers are white tinged with rose lilac, having greenish yellow spots. (L. van Houtte).

'Alena' ('Cunningham's White' x *decorum*). 5', -10ºF, EM, 4/4/4. A newer introduction from The Czech Republic, this one boasts fragrance and sun tolerance. The flowers are white with yellow spotting in the throat. Foliage is dark and glossy, covering a broad mounding plant. (Kyndl 1992).

'Alfred' ('Everestianum' selfed). 6', -15ºF, M-ML, 3-4/3-4/4. Flowers abundantly produced are frilled, brilliant lilac with faint green markings. Though a hybrid that is nearly 100 years old, it is still considered one of the best of the color. (T. J. R. Seidel 1899).

'Alfreda Wiaczek' (*minus* var. *minus* Carolinianum Group dark pink form x *dauricum*). 3', -25ºF, E, 3/3/3. An early blooming plant which has lavender pink flowers, lighter in the center. (Lewis).

'Alice' (*griffithianum* hybrid). 6', -5ºF, M, 4/3-4/4-5. Habit of this hybrid is upright and healthy. An easy to grow plant, it is tough and sun-tolerant. 'Alice' is an old favorite, having received the Royal Horticultural Society Award of Merit in 1910. This longevity indicates the admiration felt by rhododendron fanciers over 3 generations. Leaves are large, to 6", and plentiful. Flowers are pink, opening two-toned with darker edges and later developing into a clear solid pink. They are carried in large upright trusses. It propagates easily but is a bit slow to bud when young. (J. Waterer) A.M. 1910.

'Alice Franklin' ('Ole Olson' x 'Loderi King George'). 6', 0ºF, ML, 3/3/2-3. Plant habit is strong, with medium-green leaves to 5" long. Funnel-shaped flowers, to 4" wide, are light yellow, greenish in the throat. Slightly fragrant blooms are held in large rounded trusses of up to 10 flowers. Seldom grown now, but its hybrid 'Sunspray' has become a popular newer plant. (Lem, H. L. Larson 1959) P.A. 1959.

'Alice in Wonderland' (probably a subsect. Fortunea hybrid). 5', -10ºF, M, 3/3/3-4. Clear purplish pink flowers adorn this sturdy growing plant. Leaves are slender light green. (Dexter, Tyler Arboretum 1980).

'Alice Martineau' (*fortunei* ssp. *discolor* x unknown). 5', -15ºF, L, 3/3/3. Rosy crimson flowers have a dark blotch and throat. Fantastic for its very late blooming season. (W. C. Slocock).

'Alice Street' ('Diane' x *wardii*). 4', -5ºF, M, 3/4/2-3. This plant grows into a symmetrical mound of glossy, round, emerald foliage. Flowers, to about 2 1/2", are soft lemon-yellow in a medium-sized, nicely shaped truss. Synonym, 'Miss Street' (M. Koster & Son 1953).

'Alice Swift' ([*racemosum* x *mucronulatum*] x *minus* var. *minus* Carolinianum Group). 3', -15ºF, E, 3/3/3. Terminal clusters of bright, clear pink flowers form on an upright plant. Winter foliage is a bright green. (Leon Yavorsky).

'Alison Johnstone' (*yunnanense* x *concatenans*). 5', 5ºF, EM, 4/4/3. This plant has a narrow upright growth habit and foliage similar to *concatenans* in shape and size. The leaves are similar in color as well, a lovely blue at various times of the year. Flowers are golden amber, blushed pink with no marks or spots. (G.H. Johnstone) A.M. 1945.

'Alix' (*barbatum* x *hookeri*). 6', 10ºF, E, -/-/-. Very strong red flowers appear almost out of place on this tall, open tree-like plant from Exbury. (Rothschild 1930) A.M. 1935.

'Aloha' ('Vulcan' x *yakushimanum* Exbury form). 3', -15ºF, M, 3-4/4-5/4. Vivid red buds open to deep pink flowers with a slight red spotting in the throat. Blooms fade to a pale purplish pink giving the truss a two-toned appearance. Leaves are wrinkled and display white indumentum when young. The plant is rounded, dense and branches well, an attractive plant in every aspect. The flower is beautiful, though it will never win best truss in the show as it will show brown imperfections before it is fully open. But never mind that, it is still a beautiful flower on a plant you will enjoy ALL year. (Phetteplace hyb. 1973, grown by Don Paden of Urbana, IL, Briggs intro. 1983, D.W. Paden reg. 1988).

'Alpine Gem' (*brachyanthum* x *ferrugineum*). 6", 0ºF, M-ML, -/-/-. Almost a ground cover, this stays low and has a vigorous spreading habit. Leaves are very small, delicately pointed. Flowers are abundant, deep pink. (Thacker intro., sold by Cox in Scotland).

'Alpine Glow' ('Loderi' g. x *calophytum*). 6', 0ºF, VE, 5/4/3. This is the pink form of 'Avalanche'. Possibly one of the finest of the early rhododendrons, this plant, with a tree-like habit, is absolutely superb. It isn't fast, but will grow to great stature. A light fragrance also adds to its desirability. (Rothschild) A.M. 1938.

'Alpine Meadow' (selection of *leucaspis*). 18", VE-E, -/-/-. Flowers are yellowish white, and profusely cover the dwarf plant. Habit is tidy and compact, with attractive foliage. (Balch, Dunedin Rhododendron Group, N.Z., sold by Riverview Gardens).

'Always Admired' ('Scintillation' x *haematodes*). 4', -15ºF, M, 4/4/3. Capturing the beautiful foliage of its parent, 'Scintillation', this delightful hybrid displays peachy pink and yellow flowers. Different. (John Wister 1965).

'Amaretto' (*dichroanthum* ssp. *scyphocalyx* x 'Hachmann's Marina'). 4', -5ºF, M-ML, -/-/-. Masses of shining orange flowers in broad, open trusses carpet the neatly rounded shape of this plant. Color tones are rosy-caramel and bright creamy orange, with 12-16 flowers to the truss. Foliage is handsome, dark green. (Hachmann 1987).

'Amazement' (*fortunei* ssp. *fortunei* x *wardii*). 6', -5ºF, ML, -/-/-. Foliage is medium-sized to 5" long. Seven-lobed flowers, to 3" across, are yellow and very fragrant set in trusses up to 13 blooms. (Hardgrove, Royce 1979).

'Amazing Grace' ('Mrs. C. S. Sargent' x 'Swansdown'). 3', -30ºF, ML, 3/3/4. Leaves on this very hardy little plant reach a size to about 4 1/2" long. Flowers, to 3 1/2" across, are pink, spotted yellowish green below, held in trusses up to 12. (Pride 1979).

'Amber Lantern' (*keiskei* hybrid). 2', -10ºF, EM, -/-/-. A densely foliated, compact, dwarf lepidote with small, narrow leaves. Flowers are yellow and of large size for the type. (Arsen).

'Ambie' (*minus* var. *minus* x 'Pioneer'). 4', -20ºF, M, -/-/-. Flowers are held in trusses of 5-18. The blooms are variegated creamy white with a single lobe of each flower solid pink. The broad funnel shape flowers open from deep blue-red buds. A plant from the lepidote group. (Fetterhoff 1979).

'Ambrose Light' ('Rochester Pink' open pollinated). 4', -10°F, L, -/-/-. The trusses are lavender-pink and comprised of some of the largest flowers to be found on lepidote rhododendrons. The compact, upright plant has small leaves. (Arsen 1989).

'America' ('Parson's Grandiflorum' x dark red hybrid of unknown parentage). 5', -20°F, ML, 3/2-3/3-4. The hardiness of this hybrid makes it very popular in many areas of the country which have adverse weather conditions. The plant habit is low-growing and rather straggly, but will be improved if placed in more sun. Medium sized foliage, to 4" long, is matte green and heavily veined. Small flowers, bright blue-toned red, appear in tightly compact, ball-shaped trusses. (M. Koster & Sons about 1920).

'Amethyst' (*fortunei* ssp. *fortunei* x unknown). 4', -5°F, M, 3/3-4/4. A Dexter selection from Howard Phipps. This is a vigorous grower with large, frilled light purple flowers having a dark eye. (Dexter, introduced by Westbury Rose Co. 1959).

'Amethyst' (parentage unknown). Another plant with the same name. Bright rose purple. (Noble before 1850) A.M. 1931.

'Amigo' (*aberconwayi* x 'Witch Doctor'). 3', 5°F, M, 4/3-4/3-4. Leaves are narrow, to 5" long by 1 1/2" wide. Flowers are open and flat, like a saucer, to 3" across, yellow in the center, blushing outward to a deep pink margin, generously spotted with red, in trusses up to 15. (Goheen 1974).

'Amity' (['Grosclaude' x 'Britannia'] x *yakushimanum* 'Koichiro Wada'). 3', -10°F, M, 4/4/3. A well manicured plant having very nice silvery pubescence on the foliage in the early spring. The flowers are a delicate rose pink and each has red speckles and a very large calyx. (Elliott 1983).

'Amor' (*griersonianum* x *thayerianum*). 3', 5°F, L, 3/3/3. The white flowers have a hint of pink on the outside of the petals. It has very attractive foliage, derived from both of its parents. (J. B. Stevenson 1927) A.M. 1951.

'Amy' (*griffithianum* hybrid). 5', -5°F, M, 3/3/3-4. Plant habit is vigorous, with medium green foliage to 6" long, which does well in full sun. Flowers are large, rosy-pink, held in upright, very compact trusses. (J. Waterer, Sons & Crisp).

'Anah Kruschke' (*ponticum* seedling). 6', -15°F, ML-L, 3-4/4/5. This attractive hybrid has a compact habit and grows well in full sun. Foliage is dense and lush, with dark green leaves to 5". Flowers, from pale lavender-blue to reddish purple, are carried in tight, conical-shaped, medium-sized trusses. (Kruschke, Wright, Sr. & Jr. 1973).

'Ananouri' ('Britannia' x *fortunei* ssp. *discolor*). 3', -5°F, ML, 4/3-4/4. This small plant has large foliage, to 7" long, with medium-tone red flowers, their blotches rather ill-defined and faint. Flowers are carried in trusses of 10-12 blooms. (Phipps 1971) C.A. 1973.

'Andrew Patton' ('Scintillation' x *calophytum*). 5', -5°F, E, -/-/-. Glossy green foliage of large size is the backdrop for bi-color flowers of white with rosy-red markings. The flowers are large and form tight trusses. (Furman hyb., Dorothy Swift introduced 1988).

'Angelo' (*griffithianum* x *fortunei* ssp. *discolor*). 6', -5°F, L, 4/3-4/3-4. The plant is very vigorous, and has large, dark green leaves, to 8" long. The fragrant flowers are huge, to 5 or 6" across. They are pale blush pink outside, and the inside is white with faint green spots. Enormous, tall trusses are formed of up to 13 flowers. More than one form is being grown. (Rothschild 1930) A.M. 1935.

'Angel Powder' (*minus* var. *minus* Carolinianum Group 'Epoch' x white *mucronulatum*). 3', -15°F, M-ML, -/-/-. Light yellow green buds open to white, wavy edged flowers with yellow green spotting. Foliage is scaly. (Delp 1992).

'Angel's Dream' ('Whitney's Orange' x *fortunei* ssp. *discolor*). 4', 5°F, ML, 4/3/-. Fragrant, double, pink flowers are speckled with reddish pink. Matte green leaves cover a well branched plant. (unknown).

'Anica Bricogne' (unknown, contains *ponticum*). 5', -10°F, M-ML, 3-4/3-4/4-5. Growth habit is dense and strong-stemmed. Light green, slightly glossy foliage is dense and quite tolerant to sun and heat. Generously sized flowers, pale mauve to orchid, the upper petal strikingly marked with a small green-golden blotch, are held in large, billowy trusses. (unknown).

'Anilin' ('Sammetglut' x *yakushimanum* 'Koichiro Wada'). 3'. -15°F, ML, -/-/-. Flowers have rosy red petal edges which fade to soft pink, then white along the vein. Thick trusses hold 14-18 flowers. Leaves curl slightly and are dark forest green. Plant is low growing and has a width twice the height. (Hachmann 1983).

'Anita Dunstan' ('Crest' x 'Hotei'). 4', 0°F, M, 4/3-4/-. Brilliant yellow, funnel-shaped flowers are tipped in orange. The growth habit has stiff, upright branches that form a perfect compact mound, as broad as tall. It is easier to grow than either parent. (W. Hill hyb., B. Briggs reg. 1986).

'Anita Gehnrich' ('Jean Marie de Montague' x *yakushimanum*). 4', -15°F, L, 3-4/4-5/4. Deep, frilly pink flowers are held in tight trusses on a round, compact plant. Foliage is typical of the *yakushimanum* parent: slender and dark green. (Waldman).

'Anka Heinje' (*yakushimanum* 'Koichiro Wada' x 'America'). 3', -15°F, ML, -/-/-. Beige indumentum coats the leaf undersides of this broad, compact plant. Splendid red buds open to rosy-pink flowers which are sprinkled with golden markings. (Heinje).

'Anna' ('Norman Gill' x 'Jean Marie de Montague'). 6', 0°F, M, 5/3/4. New growth is bronze, slowly changing to deep green, the narrow leaves reaching to 7" x 2 1/2". Ruffled flowers, to 4" across, open deep rose pink, gradually lightening to pastel pink, each one marked in the center with a rich deep-red eye, and appearing in very large trusses up to 12 blossoms. While this plant is not seen too often in gardens today, it is an excellent parent which has produced some outstanding hybrids. (Rose, Lem 1952) P.A. 1952.

'Anna Baldsiefen' ('Pioneer' selfed). 3', 0°F, E, 3/3/4. Habit is small, compact and mound-like with oval, fleshy leaves to 1" x 1/2". Star shaped flowers, to 1 1/4" across, are a vibrant light pink, darker on the edges, blooming along the branches and in groups on the branch ends. Prone to rust disease and for this reason is not seen as much as it was in previous years. (Baldsiefen 1964).

'Annabella' (*campanulatum* x 'Loderi'). 4', 0°F, M, 4/3/3. Attractive downturned leaves have a slight indumentum. Flowers are white with blushed accents of mauve. (Rothschild 1933).

'Anna Delp' (['America' x 'Blaze'] x 'Red Brave'). 4', -15ºF, L, -/-/-. Deep red flowers with deeper red spots, held in trusses of 18, open from deep red buds. This hybrid grows as wide as tall. (Fetterhoff hyb., Delp 1992).

'Anna H. Hall' ('Catalgla' x yakushimanum). 3', -25ºF, M, 3/3/4. This is a hardy little semi-dwarf with medium-sized leaves, to 3 1/2" x 1 1/2". Flowers to 2 1/4" across are intense pink in the bud, opening white, in trusses to 15 flowers. (Leach 1962).

'Anna Rose Whitney' (griersonianum x 'Countess of Derby'). 6', -5ºF, ML, 4/3/5. Growth habit is vigorous and it quickly grows to form a very large, tall, upright, well-shaped plant. Leaves are dense, large, to 8" long, and matte olive green. Funnel-form flowers, to as much as 4" wide, are deep rose-pink, held in large, somewhat open trusses of 10-12 blossoms. (Van Veen, Sr., Whitney 1954) P.A. 1954, A.M. 1987.

'Anna's Riplet' (forrestii ssp. forrestii Repens Group x 'Letty Edwards'). 3', 0ºF, EM, 4/3/3. At first it appears as though this flower will be a lovely rose-pink, however, as it matures the color changes to a soft yellow! The plant has a rounded habit and it buds well. (Lem not registered).

'Anna Vojtec' (keiskei 'Yaku Fairy' open pollinated). 12", -15ºF, EM, -/-/-. A tight and mounded dwarf, this plant is covered with clusters of creamy white flowers. Ideal for the rock garden as it reaches only 6-8" height by 2' width. (Millstream).

'Ann Carey' (keiskei x spinuliferum). 5', 5ºF, E-EM, 3-4/3/3-4. A most unusual flower which opens chartreuse and gradually changes to coral pink. There is more than one form of this plant being grown. The form with petaloid stamens is one of the most desirable. (Lem, Anderson 1966) P.A. 1966.

'Anne George' ('Day Dream' x 'Ice Cream'). 5', 5ºF, M, -/-/-. Salmon pink buds open pale pink with deeper markings. Foliage is slender and soft green. (George, Hydon 1966).

'Anne Hardgrove' ('C. P. Raffill' x 'Moser's Maroon'). 6', 0ºF, L, 3/3/3. Leaves are large, and red flowers, up to 11 per truss, are 3 1/2" wide. (Hardgrove, Burns 1978).

'Anne's Delight' (unknown). 3', 0ºF, EM, 4/3-4/3-4. Wavy, glossy, dark green leaves accompany lovely, yellow flowers which have red spotting in the throat. (Whitney, Sather 1985).

'Annie Dalton' ([decorum x griersonianum] x 'America'). 5', -15ºF, ML, 3/2/3. Very large foliage provides a handsome backdrop for the 4" wide, apricot pink flowers which have darker throats. A lax truss is formed. Synonym, 'Degram'. (Gable 1960) A.E. 1960.

'Annie Dring' ('Loderi King George' x 'Corona'). 5', -10ºF, M, 4/4/-. The flowers are reddish-purple with a darker basal blotch of purple. They are held in trusses of 14. (W. V. Joslin hyb., Mrs. Lillian Hodgson reg. 1977).

'Annie E. Endtz' ('Pink Pearl' hybrid). 5-6', 0ºF, ML, 3/3/3. A hybrid similar to 'Antoon van Welie' in both plant habit and flower. This is a lighter shade of pink with frilled margins. A dependable, vigorous plant. (L. J. Endtz & Co. 1939).

'Ann Lindsay' ('Blinklicht' x ['Mars' x yakushimanum 'Koichiro Wada']). 3', -15ºF, ML, 5/4/4. Strong red, frilled flowers are held on reddish-brown pedicels in groups of 14-17. The inner throat has a white glow, which adds an air of flamboyance. Synonym, 'Flamerose'. (Hachmann, Stuck 1988).

'Antigua' ('Mary Belle' x 'Dexter's Apricot'). 5', -5ºF, M, 3/3/3. Leaves are large. Flowers, also a generous size, are red, suffusing to a yellow throat, blotched and spotted red, and held in lax trusses up to 10 blooms. (Becales, Herbert 1978).

'Anton Rupert' ('Sir Frederick Moore' x 'Kilimanjaro'). 5', 0ºF, M, 4/3/2-3. These pink flowers have throats of deeper pink. (Rothschild 1972).

'Antoon van Welie' ('Pink Pearl' hybrid). 6', -5ºF, ML, 4/3-4/4. The large flowers are deep, pure pink and make big trusses. The broad leaves are waxy and deep green. It is a vigorous, sturdy and handsome plant. (L. J. Endtz & Co.).

'Anuschka' ('Sammetglut' x yakushimanum 'Koichiro Wada'). 4', -5ºF, ML, 4/4/4. Deep pink buds open to ball shaped trusses of rose fading to soft pink in the centers of each flower. Flowers are lightly sprinkled with red spots in the throat. The plant is compact and spreading. Leathery forest green leaves are coated beneath with thick indumentum. (Hachmann 1982).

'Applause' ('Catalgla' x ['Adrian Koster' x williamsianum]). 5', -20ºF, M, 3/3/4. Foliage is medium-sized. Flowers, to 2 1/4" across, are white blending to ivory, held in rounded trusses to 11 flowers. (Leach 1972).

'Apple Brandy' (yakushimanum x unknown hybrid). 3', -5ºF, EM, 4/4/4. The plant has a compact habit and bears foliage with a silver tomentum. Silvery pink flowers complete the shimmering affect. (unknown).

'Apricot Fantasy' ('Hotei' x 'Tropicana'). 4', -5ºF, M, 4-5/-/-. Red freckles and a double calyx add the final touches to these bi-color flowers of soft orange melding with golden yellow. Buds are deep orange. Foliage is dusky green and densely covers the spreading plant. (Brockenbrough 1987).

'Apricot Nectar' ([{dichroanthum x neriiflorum} x 'Fabia'] x 'Jalisco'). 3', -5ºF, ML, 4/4/3. Orange flowers, accentuated by scarlet edges, are held in a striking ball-shaped truss. The plant habit is neat and compact with large leaves. (Lyons 1971).

'Apricot Sherbet' ('Comstock' x 'Dido'). 4', 5ºF, M, 4/4/4. These unique colors are not found in many other rhododendrons. The flower is a buffy-apricot color enhanced by a prominent calyx of the same color. The plant is mounding and leaves are long, oval, and lime-green. Benefits from being planted in some shade. (Greer 1982).

'April Blush' (minus var. minus Carolinianum Group album x mucronulatum). 2', -25ºF, E, 3/3/3. Foliage is small, and almost entirely deciduous. Small flowers are a soft blush pink. (Nearing 1968).

'April Chimes' (hippophaeoides x mollicomum). 3', 0ºF, E-EM, 4/3/4. Small flowers are showy, rosy mauve, in lax trusses. The small foliage is sharply pointed, perky and attractive. (Messrs. Hillier & Sons 1969).

'April Dawn' (minus var. minus Carolinianum Group x dauricum). 4', -25ºF, E, -/-/-. Flowers are white with a hint of pink, accented by a darker pink petal margin. Foliage provides a color display as the small, glossy, dark green leaves become burnished in fall. The plant is compact and densely covered with foliage. (Mehlquist).

'April Dream' (parentage unknown). 6', -5ºF, E, -/-/-. This hybrid, originally known as 'April Showers', has medium sized leaves. The flowers are pink with a large red blotch, held in trusses to 12. (Whitney, Sather 1976).

'April Fire' (['Elizabeth' x 'Little Gem'] x 'Gipsy King'). 3', 5°F, E, -/-/-. The mounding plant becomes fully covered with campanulate blossoms of true red. Leaves are rich dark green. (Walt Elliott before 1990).

'April Gem' ([minus var. minus Carolinianum Group album x mucronulatum 'Cornell Pink'] x [dauricum album x dauricum]). 3', -25°F, VE-E, 4/4/4. The small leaves are elliptic, smooth and olive green. The plant has a rounded shape and compact habit. Small, white, double flowers profusely cover the plant. (Mehlquist about 1992).

'April Glow' (williamsianum x 'Wilgens Ruby'). 3', -10°F, E-EM, 3-4/4/3-4. Originated in Holland. 'April Glow' forms an evenly shaped mound reaching 4-5' in time. Trusses contain 7-10, beautiful, rosy pink blossoms. Leaves are green with copper red new growth. This plant has been sold as 'April Showers', but there is an azalea registered by that name, so the rhododendron name was changed to 'April Glow'. (van Wilgens Nurseries 1975) A.M. Boskoop 1965, G.M. Boskoop 1966, H.C. 1975.

'April Love' ([{'PJM' group, dbl flw form x mucronulatum pink} x dauricum white] x ['Gable's Pioneer' x 'PJM' group]). 5', -25°F, E-EM, -/-/-. The small leaves are typical of the lepidote group. Semi-deciduous in nature, the autumn foliage is bronze. The plant is wide-growing and it displays frilly, double flowers of light pink with yellow-toned inner petals. (Mezitt 1987).

'April Mist' ([minus var. minus Carolinianum Group x mucronulatum 'Cornell Pink'] x [dauricum album x dauricum]). 3', -25°F, E, -/-/-. This plant stays low although the growth habit is fairly upright. Leaves are sage-green and densely cover the plant. Double flowers of soft pink are prolific. (Mehlquist).

'April Reign' (minus var. minus Carolinianum Group x dauricum). 3', -20°F, EM, -/-/-. Double, funnel-shaped, lavender flowers are slightly scented and held in lax trusses above small, elliptical foliage. (Mehlquist 1988).

'April Rose' ([minus var. minus Carolinianum Group x mucronulatum 'Cornell Pink'] x [dauricum album x dauricum]). 3', -25°F, VE-E, 4/4/4. Small leaves are held for 2 to 3 years on this broad, upright lepidote. Foliage has burnished red tones during fall and winter. Double rose flowers are wide, lightly fragrant, and abundant. (Mehlquist 1989).

'April Snow' ([{'PJM' x mucronulatum} x dauricum] x [minus var. minus Carolinianum Group x 'PJM']). 3', -20°F, EM, 4/3-4/-. Double white flowers form small snowball trusses which are held above the small leaves. The foliage takes on a burnished glow for fall and winter. A compact plant with distinctive yellow limbs. (Mezitt 1987).

'April Song' ([{'PJM' group, dbl flw form x mucronulatum pink} x dauricum white] x ['Gable's Pioneer' x 'PJM' group]). 5', -25°F, E-EM, -/-/-. Double flowers have an unusual bi-color petal combination. The outer petals are soft pink, while the inner petals are blush white. Flowers are very ruffled and of large size. This semi-deciduous lepidote has a wide, upright habit. Foliage is dark green, reddening in fall and winter. (Mezitt 1987).

'April White' ([{minus var. minus Carolinianum Group x mucronulatum 'Cornell Pink'} x dauricum F2 white] x [dauricum album x dauricum]). 3', -25°F, E-EM, 4/4/4. Semi-double flowers of pure white have a slight fragrance and are profusely produced. Small leaves remain on plant for 2-3 years, maintaining a dense appearance on a compact plant. Foliage changes in fall to bright yellow. (Mehlquist).

'Arabella' (yakushimanum x 'Kluis Sensation'). 2', -5°F, ML, -/-/-. Pink flowers have a darker center and dark pink fringe. Foliage is dark green. Plant form is of average compactness. (Heinje, Germany).

'Arctic Dawn' (Behring) (maximum x brachycarpum ssp. tigerstedtii). 2.5', -35°F, L, -/-/-. Funnel-shaped flowers of snowy white are accented with red margins and a yellowish-green dorsal spot. Narrow foliage is glossy green on top with a thick covering of indumentum below. (Behring 1984).

'Arctic Dawn' (Lewis) (minus var. minus Carolinianum Group album x dauricum album 'Arctic Pearl'). 3', -15°F, E, 3-4/3/3. The white flowers have just a hint of lavender that seems to float among the white. Foliage is slightly aromatic and recurved. (Lewis not registered).

'Arctic Glow' (minus var. minus Carolinianum Group album x dauricum album 'Arctic Pearl'). 3' -15°F, E, 3-4/3/3. A sister of 'Arctic Dawn' with very similar characteristics. The lavender blush is a little stronger and more concentrated along the petal edges. (Lewis).

'Arctic Gold' (cross of two unknown white hybrids). 3', -20°F, M-ML, -/-/-. A dusting of powdery tomentose, like arctic frost, covers the new foliage which later forms long, deep green leaves. Large trusses are comprised of ivory flowers with a rich yellow glow in the throat. (Mezitt 1988).

'Arctic Pearl' (selected seedling of dauricum album). 4', -25°F, E, 3-4/3- 4/2-3. Leaves on this plant are typical of the species, small and somewhat glossy. Flowers, to 2" across, are white, carried in trusses to 5 flowers. (Baldsiefen 1971).

'Arctic Snow' (maximum white selection x brachycarpum ssp. tigerstedtii). 4', -20°F, ML-L, -/-/-. White, fragrant flowers emerge from light pink buds to form dome trusses. Each blossom is lightly marked with yellow flecks. Plant habit is dense and upright. (Behring).

'Arctic Tern' (trichostomum x Ledium species?). 2', 0°F, M, 3/3/3. A miniature that has trusses which resemble full, larger, more typical rhododendron trusses. Tight, white globes cover each terminal and are surrounded by one inch long leaves. For good plant shape it needs lots of pruning. It is also a plant that is susceptible to rust. Note: The Genus Ledium is now considered by some botanists to belong to the Genus Rhododendron. (Larson, Caperci intro. as trichostomum var. ledoides white, later intro. by Cox as 'Arctic Tern').

'Argentina' ([catawbiense var. album 'Glass' x yakushimanum] x ['Fanfare' x 'Gertrud Schale']). 4', -25°F, ML, -/-/-. A hardy plant with good growth habit and dense foliage. Freely produced, deep rose red flowers of rounded shape, are held in groups of up to 25 to the truss. (Leach 1991).

'Argosy' (fortunei ssp. discolor x auriculatum). 6', -5°F, VL, 3/3/3. Very late blooming trusses of huge white flowers grace this fast growing, upright plant. The leaves are quite long, resembling those of its parent, R. auriculatum. (Rothschild 1933).

'Arkle' ('Carmen' x 'Moonshine Supreme'). 2', -5°F, M, 3-4/4/3. Very large waxy red bells form on a compact grower. Habit is more spreading than upright. (Hydon Nurseries 1972).

'Arnold Piper' ('Anna' x 'Marinus Koster'). 6', -5°F, M, 4/4/4. Out of the same group of plants that made up the 'Wallopers'. This plant has red buds opening to expose deep pink flowers with a darker blotch. Very large trusses sit above shiny green mature leaves, which develop from bronzy new growth. (Lem hyb., raised by Piper, Lofthouse intro. 1971, registered 1981).

'Aronimink' (['Pygmalion' x *haematodes* x 'Wellfleet'] exact combination unknown). 6', -5ºF, M, 4/3/-. Large, purplish-red flowers have a slight browinish spotting on the upper lobe. The 4" blooms are held in a gigantic truss of up to 20. A vigorous plant as wide as it is tall. (Dexter hyb. 1940, Swarthmore College reg. 1980).

'Arsen's Pink' (*keiskei* x *racemosum* forest form). 2', -15ºF, E, 3-4/3-4/4. Clouds of small pink flowers cover this compact dwarf. Very floriferous and easy to grow. (Arsen not registered).

'Arthur J. Ivens' (*williamsianum* x *houlstonii*). 3', -10ºF, EM-M, 3/3/3-4. Sun tolerant foliage is medium size and rounded. Although slow to bud, the bell shaped persian rose flowers, held in a lax truss, are well worth the wait. (Hillier & Son) A.M. 1944.

'Arthur Osborn' (*sanguineum* ssp. *didymum* x *griersonianum*). 3', 5ºF, VL, 3/3- 4/3. This hybrid is especially desirable for its very black red flower and exceptionally late flowering time. The foliage is deep green and is somewhat hairy. Plant where it receives the orange rays of the setting sun and the effect is superb. (Kew Gardens 1929) A.M. 1933.

'Arthur Pride' (natural hybrid of *maximum* and *catawbiense*, collected wild). 5', -30ºF, L, 3/3/3-4. Leaves are medium-large. Flowers are white with orchid colored edges and a spotty chartreuse blotch. The 2" wide blooms are held in a ball truss to 29 blooms. (Pride 1979).

'Ascot Brilliant' (*thomsonii* x 'Blandyanum'). 5', 5ºF, EM, 3/2-3/3. A very old hybrid that should be grown more. Deep crimson flowers are borne on a free flowering plant with lax, open habit. (Standish 1861).

'Ashes of Roses' (*fortunei* ssp. *fortunei* hybrid). 4', -15ºF, M, 3/3/3-4. Lavender flowers, nice foliage. Quite similar to 'Anna Rose Whitney'. (Dexter hyb., named by DuPont, Gladsgay Gardens intro., reg, 1958).

'Astrid' ('Fantastica' x 'Hachmann's Feuerschein'). 3', -15ºF, M-ML, -/-/-. A first class red *yakushimanum* hybrid with flowers opening from deep red buds to form very full, round ball trusses, each holding 19-21 flowers. The red flowers show only a muted streak of white along the vein and this is sprinkled with deep red markings. The flowers are of heavy substance and resist damage by rain and sun. Lush, slightly glossy, dark green foliage is long and densely covers the plant as do the trusses, which are very profuse. A superior hybrid with a compact habit. (Hachmann 1991).

'Atlantis' (*catawbiense album* x [{*dichroanthum* x *griffithianum*} x *auriculatum*]). 5', -20ºF, L, -/-/-. Abundant buds of orange transform into large bi-color flowers of coral with a yellow throat. This plant is also known as 'Asia'. It has dense growth and a spreading habit. (Leach).

'Atrier' ('Atrosanguineum' x *griersonianum*). 5', -10ºF, M, 3/1/3. Habit is open and lax, with thin-textured foliage. The flowers are clear red, held in large trusses. A later plant, Atrier #10, eventually known as 'Redhead', is claimed to be superior to other forms. Grex. (Gable 1945).

'Atroflo' ('Atrosanguineum' x *floccigerum*). 5', -5ºF, M, 3/3-4/4. Crepe textured, bright rose flowers gaily color this medium growing rhododendron. Its lance shaped leaves are flocked with a fawn indumentum. 'Atroflo' will grow to 6' in time. Grex. (Gable 1940) A.E. 1960.

'Atrosanguineum' (*catawbiense* hybrid). 6', -20ºF, ML, 2/3/3. This is a well-shaped plant with good foliage, the flowers a rich dark red. (H. Waterer before 1851).

'Attar' (selected seedling of *decorum*, Hu Yu Expedition). 6', 5ºF, E, 3-4/3/3- 4. Foliage is medium-sized, and typical of *decorum*. Flowers are light blush rose, blending to a pale green in the throat and set in large trusses. (Barto, Henny 1963).

'Augfast' (*augustinii* x *fastigiatum*). 3', 0ºF, EM, 4/4/4. Plant habit is dome- shaped. It displays dense, creamy yellow, new growth of very small leaves. Outward facing, prolific flowers are violet blue, held in a small truss. (Magor 1921).

'August Lamken' ('Dr. V. H. Rutgers' x *williamsianum*). 3', -5ºF, M, 3/4/-. Flowers are ruffled dark rose, accented by red freckles in the throat. The truss is low and broad, to 7" across with 9-11 flowers. The plant has a broad habit and is densely clothed. The foliage is deep olive green after the new leaves put on a spring show of red tones. (Hobbie 1971).

'Aunt Martha' (*ponticum* hybrid). 5', -10ºF, M-ML, 4/3-4/4. Full of attributes, it is hardy, vigorous, densely foliated and heavy blooming. Plenty of leathery leaves enable the plant to grow well in full sun and moderate heat. Bright red-purple flowers are speckled with gold in the center. (Clark 1958).

'Aunt Mildred' ('Mrs. Davies Evans' x 'Virginia Delp'). 3', -10ºF?, L, -/-/-. This hybrid has vivid, deep reddish purple buds which open to light purple. The flowers are edged with strong red purple and have a white flare with medium olive green spotting. The plant grows to equal width and height. (Smith, Delp 1992).

'Aurora' ('Kewense' x *thomsonii*). 5', 0ºF, M, 4/4/2-3. Beautiful soft pink flowers appear on this rare and unusual rhododendron. It is the parent of the tremendous hybrid 'Naomi'. (Rothschild) A.M. 1922.

'Austin H.' ('Fabia Tangerine' x *yakushimanum*). 3', -5ºF, M, 4/4/-. An interesting tricolor flower shows cream, orange and pink, while the attractive green leaves display tan indumentum. (unknown, sold by Kelleygreen).

'Autumn Gold' (*fortunei* ssp. *discolor* x 'Fabia'). 5', -5ºF, ML, 3-4/3-4/4. Salmon orange trusses invite attention to this late season bloomer. A deep orange eye glows at the center of the flower. This large growing hybrid has dense, medium toned green foliage and tolerates heat well. It out performs most of the newer oranges in less than perfect growing conditions. (Van Veen, Sr. 1956).

'Avalanche' ('Loderi' g. x *calophytum*). 6', 0ºF, VE, 5/4/3. Leaves are quite large, held only one season. Fragrant flowers are white with a ruby-wine colored blotch. The blooms of good substance are held in a many-flowered flat truss. The pink form is known as 'Alpine Glow'. (Rothschild) A.M. 1934, F.C.C. 1938.

'Avocet' (*fortunei* ssp. *discolor* x *fortunei* ssp. *fortunei*). 6', -15ºF, L, 3/3/3-4. Sweetly scented, large white flowers appear in June. With these two outstanding parents the result could only be good. (Rothschild 1933).

'Avondale' (['Pygmalion' x *haematodes* x 'Wellfleet'] exact combination unknown). 4', -5ºF, M, 3/3-4/3-4. A strong red flower with black spotting on the upper lobes. Narrow, foliage is olive green. (Dexter, Scott Hort. Foundation 1980).

'Award' ('Anna' x Margaret Dunn). 5', 0ºF, ML, 4/2-3/3. A unique tricolor of primarily white, pink and yellow with a touch of green. A most unusual flower which has heavy substance and is unlike other rhododendrons. The leaves are long and narrow, somewhat cup shaped, and medium matte green. (James, Ward 1973) C.A. 1974.

'Axel Olsen' see 'Aksel Olsen'.

'Ayah' (*fortunei* ssp. *discolor* x *eriogynum*). 6', -10ºF, L, 3/3-4/3. A beautiful pastel pink with light yellow in the throat. Worthwhile for late flowering. There are at least two forms of this being grown. (Rothschild 1933).

'Azma' (*griersonianum* x *fortunei* ssp. *fortunei*). 6', 10ºF, ML, 3/2/3. Leaves are long and narrow on a round, somewhat open plant. Flowers, up to 4" wide, are light salmon pink held in a lax truss. (Stevenson 1933).

'Azor' (*griersonianum* x *fortunei* ssp. *discolor*). 5', 5ºF, L, 3/3/3. Habit is upright, slightly open and spreading, with large, medium-green leaves. Mid-sized flowers are soft apricot or salmon-pink, carried in loose trusses. Several forms are being grown. (Stevenson 1927) A.M. 1933.

'Aztec Gold' ('Indiana' x 'Inca Gold'). 4', 0ºF, EM, 3/3/3. Clear primrose yellow flowers are a full 4" across. New growth is an attractive bronze maturing into a glossy green 8" long. (Lancaster 1965).

'Azurika' (*russatum* x *impeditum*). 1.5', 0ºF, E-EM, 3/3/3. Abundant dark violet blue flowers blanket the small very dark green foliage on this petite rhododendron with tight round shape. Easy to grow! (Hachmann 1979).

'Azurro' ('Danamar' x 'Purple Splendour'). 4', -15ºF, L, 3-4/3-4/3-4. An appealing plant with dark, glossy green foliage covering its tight, compact shape. Flowers are rich purple, both inside and out, and each flower has a prominent red blotch. (Hachmann, Stuck 1988).

'Azurwolke' (*russatum* x 'Blue Diamond') 3', -5ºF, EM, 3/3/3. This lepidote has an open shape when young but matures to a broadly round and compact plant. The flowers are dark lilac blue, 1" across, and form small trusses of 5-8 blooms. It flowers profusely. (Hachmann 1977).

'Babette' (*wardii* x *yakushimanum* 'Koichiro Wada'). 3', -5ºF, M, 3/4/-. Bright yellow flowers, shaped like round bells, are discreetly speckled with reddish brown points. (Hachmann hyb., reg. Stuck 1988).

'Baby Bear' (*tsariense* x *yakushimanum*). 18", -10ºF, EM-M, 3/5/4. Tiny, oval leaves with thick, light brown indumentum make this a very special foliage plant. Small trusses of barely pink flowers turn to white. (Sold by Riverwood Gardens, New Zealand).

'Babylon' (*calophytum* x *praevernum*). 5-6', -10ºF, E, 5/4/3. Huge, satiny white flowers with a chocolate blotch appear at a time when spring is just beginning. This plant has large, lustrous leaves with deep red petioles. It forms a dense rounded mound. There are few *calophytum* hybrids and all are outstanding, but this one is the best. Sometimes buds quite young. (Reuthe 1955).

'Bacher's Gold' ('Unknown Warrior' x 'Fabia'). 5', 5ºF, ML, 3-4/3/3. Growth habit is rather dense, the leaves light green, long and narrow. Large flowers are broadly funnel-shaped. Salmon pink transforms to yellow, then to crimson at the flower center. Uneven, cream-colored stamens with brown anthers provide an accent feature. (Bacher 1955) P.A. 1955.

'Bad Eilsen' ('Essex Scarlet' x *forrestii* ssp. *forrestii* Repens Group). 2', -15ºF, M, 3/4/3-4. 'Bad Eilsen' is from the same cross pollination as 'Elisabeth Hobbie'. Cheery bright red flowers splash color to this deep green mound of foliage. (Hobbie) A.M. 1969.

'Baden Baden' ('Essex Scarlet' x *forrestii* ssp. *forrestii* Repens Group). 2', -15ºF, M, 3-4/4/3-4. This low growing plant is laden with bright forest green foliage. The flowers are clear, glowing red with darker centers. (Hobbie 1945). H.C. 1972.

'Bad Zwischenahn' (['Doncaster' x *yakushimanum*] x 'Catharine van Tol'). 3', 0ºF, ML, -/-/-. Shapely trusses of rosy-pink with a greenish-yellow eye are borne above long, glossy, oval leaves generously presented on a compact and spreading plant. This is a semi-dwarf that prefers either sun or partial shade. (Bruns hyb. 1964, reg. 1985).

'Balalaika' ('Omega' x *dichroanthum* ssp. *scyphocalyx* hybrid). 3', -15ºF, M, 4/4/3-4. Eye-catching tricolor flowers, pink with salmon spotted edges and yellow throats, augment the attractive foliage to provide additional ornamental value for this dense, nicely compact plant. It is thought to be one of the hardiest of the orange rhododendrons. (Hachmann hyb. 1987, reg. Stuck 1988).

'Bali' (*catawbiense* var. *album* x 'Buff Lady'). 4', -20ºF, ML, 4/4/3. Luminescent pink flowers with creamy yellow throats sit atop a plant that is hardy for most climates. Plant habit is neat and growth is slightly more wide than tall. (Leach hyb. 1952, reg. 1983).

'Ballad' ('Dexter L-1' x 'America'). 5', -15ºF, ML, 3/3/3-4. Foliage is of a medium size. It has good-sized, pink flowers which are blotched dark red, and are held in trusses to 15. (Leach 1972).

'Bally Cotton' (*yakushimanum* 'Koichiro Wada' x *aureum*). 30", -5ºF, EM, 3-4/4/3. Leaves are small on this little semi-dwarf. Flowers are 2" wide and white, blotched and spotted yellowish green. They are set in ball-shaped trusses of about 7 flowers. (Reese hyb. 1971, reg. 1980).

'Balta' (*minus* var. *minus* Carolinianum group x 'PJM'). 3', -25ºF, E, 4/4/3. Looking like a lighter colored form of 'PJM' this plant can fade to almost white. It blooms slightly later than 'PJM' and has attractive, convex leaves of dark green. (Mezitt, Weston Nurseries).

'Bambi' (*yakushimanum* x 'Fabia Tangerine'). 3', 5ºF, M, 3/4/3-4. Red buds open to bright salmon pink flower clusters which are flushed with yellow. Dark green foliage is long and oily. Plant requires partial shade. (Wiseman 1951, Waterer reg. 1986).

'Bambino' (['Britannia' x *yakushimanum*] x 'Lem's Cameo'). 3', -5ºF, M, 4/4/4. Showy peach flowers are warmed with an infusion of soft yellow. It is lightly dotted with red on the upper petals and touched with red in the center. It has a huge calyx giving the flower a double appearance. The forest green foliage is lightly textured and densely clothes the compact, sturdy plant. It buds young and grows with vigor. (Brockenbrough 1988).

'Bambola' ('Bad Eilsen' x *yakushimanum* 'Koichiro Wada'). 3', -10ºF, ML, -/-/-. Same origin as 'Lampion'. Delicate bell-shaped flowers of luminous red have a hint of orange in their frilled edges. Plant is round and compact, densely covered with narrow, convex foliage. (Hachmann 1988).

'Banana Boat' (*keiskei* x *dauricum* 'Arctic Pearl'). 2', -10ºF, E, 3/3/3. A super little plant with bright yellow flowers and aromatic foliage. (Lewis).

'Bananaflip' (*fauriei* var. *rufescens* x 'Goldsworth Orange'). 3', 0ºF, M, -/-/-. Deep green, glossy foliage is the backdrop for lax trusses of golden yellow bells touched with pink striping. The plant is well shaped and compact. (Hachmann 1987).

'Bandoola' ('Matador' x 'Redlamp'). 3', 0ºF, EM, 3-4/3/3-4. Glowing scarlet red flowers are enhanced by long, slender leaves. (Reuthe).

'Bangkok' (*catawbiense* var. *album* x [*dichroanthum* x {*griffithianum* x *auriculatum*}]). 3', -15ºF, M, 3-4/3-4/3. Foliage is medium size. Large pink flowers, suffusing to orange yellow at center with reddish orange spotting below, are held in trusses to 13. (Leach 1973).

'Barbara Behring' ('Sappho' x ['Catalgla' x 'Sappho']). 4', -25ºF, M, 3/3/-. White flowers, each with a deep burgundy blotch, are held in small, ball trusses. (Behring 1986).

'Barbara Houston' ('Virginia Scott' x 'Belvedere'). 5', 10ºF, L, 4/3-4/3. Leaves are medium size. 3" flowers are buff with orange tone. They have pink margins, large red spots on the 3 lower lobes, and are carried in trusses of about 9. (Larson 1979).

'Barbara Reuthe' ('Jalisco' hybrid). 4', 5ºF, ML, 4/4/-. Flowers are a deep, rich yellow. The plant is very difficult to propagate. (Reuthe 1985).

'Bariton' ('A. Bedford' x 'Purple Splendour'). 4', -10ºF, ML, 3-4/3-4/3-4. Deep violet-purple flowers, each with a deep red splotch, are held in large ball shaped trusses which enhance the dark green foliage of this nicely rounded plant. (Hachmann 1979, reg. Stuck 1988).

'Barmstedt' ('Sammetglut' x *yakushimanum* 'Koichiro Wada'). 3', -15ºF, M, -/-/-. Very floriferous, this hybrid has rose-red flowers, a bit darker red inside, fading to lighter pink towards the center. The new growth is silvery, changing to dark, recurved leaves on a compact plant. (Hachmann 1982).

'Barnaby Sunset' (formally sold as *flavidum* x 'Lady Rosebery' biscuit form). 5', 0ºF, EM, 3/3/2-3. This hybrid has flowers that are pale yellow inside and strawberry pink on the outside. Small, glossy foliage dresses a plant with an upright habit. This is out of the same cross as 'Strawberry Cream'. (Brandt).

'Barnstable' (probably a subsect. Fortunea hybrid). 5', -5ºF, M, 3/3-4/3-4. Fragrant flowers are pale purplish-pink with greenish-yellow spotting on the dorsal lobe. Olive green leaves. (Dexter, Wister, Tyler Arboretum 1980).

'Baroness Schroeder' (*catawbiense* x unknown). 5', -10ºF, ML, -/-/-. Dark, glossy green foliage is crowned with white flowers which have a pale magenta flush and dark spotted flare. Trusses of 20 flowers are formed. The plant has a spreading habit. (J. Waterer before 1900).

'Barry Rodgers' (*yakushimanum* x 'Pink Petticoats'). 3', 0ºF, M, -/-/-. Large trusses of 24 pale pink, frilled blooms with darker edges appear on this wide, low growing plant. Attractive foliage lasts one year. (F. Peste, S.P. Johnston 1986).

'Barto Alpine' (Lapponicum Series hybrid). 3', -10ºF, EM, 3/4/4. A very hardy, rugged plant that dances in the sun. Orchid rose flowers open all along the stems. Warm sunshine upon the bark and leaves brings out a sweet spicy scent similar to freshly ground nutmeg. Its dense, upright growth habit provides a form well suited for planting as a short hedge or screen reaching 5'. (Barto, Greer 1964).

'Barto Ivory' (*fortunei* ssp. *fortunei* hybrid or a selection of *fortunei* ssp. *fortunei*). 6', -10ºF, EM-M, 4/3/3. This plant strongly resembles R. *fortunei* ssp. *fortunei*, except for its rich ivory flowers. It is graced with thick-textured heavy foliage, and covers itself with delightfully fragrant blooms. Difficult to propagate. (Barto, Steinmetz, Greer 1962).

'Barto Lavender' (probably *fortunei* ssp. *fortunei* and *ponticum*). 6', -10ºF, M, 3/3-4/5. Growth habit is vigorous and sturdy, and leaves are large and wavy. Large, tall, trusses of orchid pink flowers are quite fragrant. This is a strong grower and would make an excellent hedge. (Barto, Steinmetz, Greer 1962).

'Bashful' (*yakushimanum* x 'Doncaster'). 3', -15ºF, E, 3/3/3. One of the 'Seven Dwarfs' from Waterer. This hybrid has compact growth and great foliage. Each rose pink flowers has a reddish brown blotch on the upper lobes. (Waterer 1971).

'Bashful Betty' ('Halcyone' x 'Carmen'). 3', 0ºF, EM, 4/3/3. Glossy, dark green foliage hides behind masses of wonderful, dark rosy red flowers which are not shy at all! (Elliott hyb., Fisher intro.).

'Bass River' (*fortunei* subseries hybrid). 3', 0ºF, M, 3/3-4/3-4. A very easy flowering plant with a mounding habit. Large, frilled flowers are purplish pink with slight spotting. (Dexter, Scott Arboretum, Tyler Arboretum reg. 1983).

'Beatrice Keir' ('Logan Damaris' x *lacteum*). 5', 0ºF, EM, 4/3/2-3. A tall growing plant with beautiful, large trusses of lemon yellow. Needs some protection, but is well worth the extra effort. (Crown Estate, Windsor) A.M. 1974.

'Beau Brummell' ('Essex Scarlet' x *eriogynum*). 5', -5ºF, L, 3/3/3. Very waxy, dark blood red flowers with darker speckling are held in a compact ball-shaped truss. The foliage is an attractive dark, matte green. Especially good, desirable for its late flowering. (Rothschild) A.M. 1938.

'Beaufort' ('Boule de Neige' x *fortunei* ssp. *fortunei*). 5', -20ºF, M, 2-3/3-4/3. Habit is compact, with large leaves, and a tendency to be a shy bloomer. Lovely, fragrant flowers are white, lightly kissed with mauve, in trusses to 14. (Gable).

'Beautiful Day' ('Hotei' x 'Crest'). 4', -5ºF, L, 4/3/3. Foliage is medium sized. Flowers, to 3 1/2" wide, are strong yellow. A narrow stripe of tangerine orange graces the outer petal surface as the flower starts to open. This flower blooms in trusses of 12. (Whitney, Sather 1976).

'Beautiful Dreamer' (parentage unknown). 6', -5ºF, E, 4/3/3. Foliage is medium sized. Flowers are yellow, lightly tinged with orange on each lobe, fading to a pure yellow. The 2 1/2" blooms are set in trusses up to 12. (Whitney, Sather 1976).

'Beauty of Littleworth' (*griffithianum* x unknown). 6', -5ºF, M, 4/3/4-5. Although the other parent is uncertain, it is believed to be R. *campanulatum*. Habit is large-growing, upright, very vigorous and somewhat spreading. Leaves are smooth-textured, large, somewhat glossy, dark green above and bronze underneath. Flowers are huge, to 5" across, white, spotted dark reddish purple on top petal, opening a mauve pink and held in enormous, tall trusses of up to 19 flowers. (Miss Mangles about 1900) F.C.C. 1904, F.C.C. 1953.

'Beckyann' (*fortunei* ssp. *discolor* x *campylocarpum* selfed). 4', -10ºF, ML, -/-/-. Leaves are medium in size. Flowers, to 2 3/4" across, are light yellow, with brownish dorsal spotting, the color growing more intense with age. The blooms are carried in ball shaped trusses to 12. (M. Yates 1977).

'Beechwood Pink' ('Atrosanguineum' x *fortunei* ssp. *fortunei*). 6', -15ºF, M, 4/3/-. Leaves are quite large. Flowers are also good-sized, to 3 1/2" across, the color a vibrant fuchsia pink, held in large trusses. (Gable, Herbert 1960) A.E. 1960.

'Beefeater' (elliottii x 'Fusilier'). 5', 10ºF, M, 4/3-4/3-4. Large flat topped trusses hold up to 26 flowers of geranium red. (R.H.S. Wisley 1962) A.M. 1958, F.C.C. 1959.

'Beer Sheba' (cerasinum seedling). 3', -5ºF, EM, -/-/-. White flowers with a hint of rose are held in small trusses of about 5. Foliage is medium sized. (Rothschild 1964).

'Belkanto' ('Mrs. J. G. Millais' x 'Golddekor'). 3', -15ºF, ML, -/-/-. Trusses are composed of 14-17 pale yellow funnel shaped flowers. Each bloom has a pink tinge with greenish yellow spotting on the dorsal lobe and a bright chartreuse base. The smooth foliage on this compact plant is medium green. (Hachmann, Stuck 1988).

'Bellefontaine' (fortunei ssp. fortunei x smirnowii). 6', -15ºF, L, 3-4/4/3-4. Leaves are large. Flowers are 7-lobed, to 3 1/2" across, are set in trusses to 10. The color a lovely rose fading to lighter rose in the throat, the upper lobe speckled olive brown. (Pike, Craig 1978).

'Belle Heller' ('Catawbiense Album' x white catawbiense seedling). 5', -10ºF, M, 4/3/3. Here is hardiness, sun tolerance, lush foliage, and a lovely flower all in one. The large flower is pure white with a striking gold blotch, set in a large, globular truss. This is a vigorous grower with an attractive habit. (Shammarello 1958).

'Belle of Tremeer' (rigidum var. album x augustinii). 4', 5ºF, EM, 3-4/3/3-4. A natural hybrid with lovely pale mauve flowers in dainty clusters on a tall, slender shrub. (Gen. Harrison 1957).

'Bellringer' (unknown). 3', 0ºF, M, -/-/-. A well formed plant with soft, creamy white flowers. (Consolini).

'Bellrose' (smirnowii x 'Mrs. C. S. Sargent'). 5', -15ºF, M, -/-/-. Olive green leaves have a kiss of light indumentum. Flowers are in a tall, upright truss of rose-pink with a dark flare. (unknown).

'Bell Song' ('Bow Bells' x 'Day Dream' [red form]). 3', 0ºF, M, -/-/-. A delightful spreading plant, more wide than tall, with enticing two-toned pink flowers each having ruffled edges. (The Bovees Nursery).

'Bellvale' (minus var. minus Carolinianum Group x dauricum album). 4', -25ºF, M, -/-/-. Foliage is small. Flowers, to 2" across, are a clear light pink, with a mauve blush. (Baldsiefen 1976).

'Belva's Joy' ('Noyo Brave' x 'Elizabeth') 3', 5ºF, EM, 4/5/4. A tight, compact growing plant with attractive foliage. True red buds open to expose long lasting bright red blooms, a real joy to behold. (Cecil Smith hyb. 1982, Merle Sanders 1993).

'Ben Briggs' ('Bowbells' x 'Loderi King George'). 3', 0ºF, VE, -/-/-. A broad growing, heavy flowering plant. It produces funnel-shaped white flowers with a slight tinge of pink held in a lax truss. The wavy edges are accented as the bloom color fades to a greenish white in the center. (B. Briggs, W. Elliott 1988).

'Ben Foster' (racemosum x keiskei 'Yaku Fairy'). 2', -20ºF, EM, -/-/-. Small leaves are held by reddish stems providing an excellent contrast for the deep pink flowers. Forms a compact mound and is a good plant for rock gardens. (L. Foster).

'Bengal' ('Essex Scarlet' x forrestii ssp. forrestii Repens Group). 3', -5ºF, EM, 3/3-4/3-4. Scarlet red flowers hang like little bells on this very low growing hybrid from Germany. (Hobbie 1960).

'Ben Moseley' (A subsect. Fortunea hybrid). 5', -15ºF, EM, 3/3-4/4. Light purplish pink flowers have deeper coloring along the edging. Medium size leaves are olive green. (Dexter, Moseley, Vossberg, Wister 1980).

'Bergie Larson' (wardii x 'Jasper'). 3', 10ºF, L, 3-4/4-5/4. A nicely rounded plant that is a delight to grow. It branches easily by itself to maintain a great shape. The beautiful, yellow-orange trusses arrive late in the year. (Larson 1978).

'Berg's Yellow' ('Mrs. Betty Robertson' x 'Fred Rose'). 4', 0ºF, M, 4/3/3-4. Typifying the Warren Berg hybrid, this little beauty has great form and superior flowers. Very bright trusses of yellow green are enhanced by perfect foliage. (Berg).

'Bernard Shaw' (calophytum x 'Pink Pearl'). 5', 0ºF, EM, 4/3/3. A very large sugar pink truss on a plant with big, deep green leaves. (Reuthe 1955).

'Bernstein' ('Goldsworth Orange' x 'Mrs. J. G. Millais'). 5', -10ºF, ML, -/-/-. Soft yellow-orange flowers have a pronounced bright orange-red blotch, achieving an overall amber appearance as the German name indicates. The plant is well-covered with long, dark green leaves that have a slightly hairy covering. (Hachmann, Stuck 1983).

'Berryrose' ('Doncaster' x dichroanthum). 3', 0ºF, ML, 4/2/2. Here is a rounded plant with an open habit. Spotted leaves are held for one year. Flowers are bright, apricot orange in color with a delicate yellow center. (Rothschild) A.M. 1934.

'Bert Larson' ('Diva' x strigillosum). 5', 10ºF, EM, 3/3/3. Foliage is medium to large and narrow. Flowers, to 3" wide, are red with darker reddish brown dorsal spotting, and held in trusses to 14. (Larson 1979).

'Besse Howells' (red catawbiense hybrid x 'Boule de Neige'). 3', -15ºF, EM, 3-4/3-4/4. Leaves are medium in size on this compact growing plant. Frilled flowers, to 2 1/2" across, are rosy red, blotched darker, in globe-shaped, plentiful trusses. (Shammarello 1964).

'Betsie Balcom' ('Princess Elizabeth' x 'Elizabeth'). 4', 0ºF, ML, 3-4/3-4/3. Well-branched with a rounded shape, this plant attractively displays its foliage. The new growth is tinged red. Medium sized leaves have an attractive rough texture. Flowers are red, to 2 3/4" wide, and unlike most reds, which tend to have flat-topped trusses, this plant sports rather large conical-shaped trusses with flowers up to 13 per truss. (McGuire 1977).

'Betsy Kruson' (['Catalgla' x wardii] x 'Mars'). 4', -10ºF, ML, 3/3/3. Dark rose flowers fade to white in the throat, which shows a small yellowish flare. The blooms, to 2 3/4" wide are held in trusses up to 10. Leaves are large. (Yates, M. Yates 1977).

'Better Half' (probably an 'Elizabeth' hybrid). 3', 0ºF, EM, 3/4/3. This is the "better half" of two seedlings growing together as one plant in the famous Whitney Gardens. The other half is called 'Half and Half'. What appropriate names! It is a neat compact plant, with dense foliage and attractive red trusses. Buds heavily. (Whitney, Sather).

'Betty Arrington' (Dexter hybrid of unknown parentage). 5', -15ºF, L, 4/3-4/4. Leaves are large on this showy hybrid. Plant habit is quite good. Seven-lobed, fragrant flowers, to 3 3/4" across, are rosy-pink with a conspicuous rich red flare, set in trusses up to 17. (Dexter, Arrington 1970).

'Betty Hume' (probably a fortunei ssp. fortunei hybrid). 6', -10ºF, ML, 4/3/3. Flowers, to 4" wide, are pink in color, frilled on the edges, and nicely scented. Leaves are large. (Dexter, Baldsiefen and Effinger 1963).

R. 'America'

R. 'Abraham Lincoln'

R. 'Hudson Bay'

R. 'Manitau'

Hybrids ~ Cold Hardy

R. 'English Roseum'

R. 'PJM'

R. 'Thunder'

R. 'President Lincoln'

R. 'Album Novum'

R. 'Peter Alan'

R. 'Valley Sunrise'

R. 'Torlonianum'

R. 'Fragrans Affinity'

Hybrids~ With Blotches

R. 'Blue Crown'

R. 'Windsor Lad'

R. 'Edwin O. Weber'

R. 'Frank Gaulsworthy'

R. 'Sappho'

R. 'Sugar & Spice'

R. Mrs. G. W. Leak

R. 'Mrs. Furnival'

Hybrids ~ With Picotee

. 'Rainbow'

. 'Princess Mary of Cambridge'

R. 'President Roosevelt'

R. 'Marley Hedges'

R. 'Forever Yours'

R. 'Topsvoort Pearl'

R. 'Crimson Pippin'

R. 'Noble Mountain'

R. 'Yaku Frills'

R. 'Lavender Haze'

R. 'Shrimp Girl'

R. 'Tanyosho'

R. 'Queen Alice'

Hybrids ~
Yakushimanum Parentage

R. 'Centennial Celebration'

R. 'Yaku Queen'

R. 'Bob Bovee'

R. 'Yaku Prince'

'**Betty's Bells**' (*campylogynum* x *racemosum*). 4', -5°F, E-EM, 4/4/4. Bright, vivid shining pink flowers cover this easy to grow plant by the thousands. Like its parent *racemosum*, it produces buds along the stem, giving each limb a large number of buds which burst forth in a mass of glowing color. From its other parent *campylogynum* it gets its interesting down-curved style that makes the flower unusual. Small leaves of attractive olive green with reddish stems make a well clothed plant. (Betty Shedy, Thurston Skei).

'**Betty Sears**' (*yakushimanum* x 'Corona'). 3', 0°F, EM, 4/4/4. Tight trusses of frilly pink flowers with partially double blooms. The rounded truss is dusted with red freckles for added interest. A most unusual flower. Delightful foliage and excellent plant habit are derived from it parent *R. yakushimanum*. (Whitney, Sather).

'**Betty Wormald**' ('George Hardy' x red hybrid). 6', -5°F, M, 3-4/3/3. This is a fast grower with an upright, spreading habit and medium-large leaves. Flowers are very large, opening almost flat, and carried in huge, showy, dome-shaped trusses. Color is pastel pink, paler in the center, and heavily spotted light purple on upper petal. (M. Koster & Sons before 1922) A.M. 1935.

'**Bewitched**' ('Racil' x *mucronulatum* 'Cornell Pink'). 3', 0°F, E, 3/3/3-4. Foliage is quite small on this little hybrid, and lavender-pink flowers are set in nice ball shaped trusses up to 5. (Guttormsen 1969).

'**Bibiani**' ('Moser's Maroon' x *arboreum*). 6', 5°F, E, 4/4/4. Growth habit is full-foliaged and upright, with large, glossy, heavy-textured, deep green leaves. Bell shaped flowers, to 2 1/4" wide, are a bright, waxy red, held in cone-shaped trusses to 15. A very vigorous, easily grown plant. (Rothschild) A.M. 1934.

'**Big Deal**' (white hybrid x yellow hybrid). 2', -20°F, ML, -/-/-. Large ball trusses are composed of pale ivory blooms with a dark greenish-yellow blotch. Large, rounded foliage has a dusty-green appearance when young, that matures to a smooth texture. The leaves densely cover this low, spreading plant. (E. Mezitt, Weston Nurseries 1988).

'**Big Mama**' (unknown). 5', 0°F, M, -/-/-. Very large flowers have a pink background with multi-colored accents. Foliage is large and medium green. (Whitney not registered).

'**Big Red**' ('Anna' x 'Loderi Pink Diamond'). 5', 5°F, M, 4-5/4/3-4. An upright growth habit has large, waxy, deep green leaves which surround large, conical trusses of currant red. As an added bonus the new foliage is a bronze-red. (Nielson, Sinclair 1984).

'**Big Savage Red**' ('Mars' selfed). 6', -20°F, ML, 3/3/3-4. Leaves are medium to large. Flowers, to 2 1/2" across, are clear pink in color, with a sparsely-green-spotted white flare, in trusses to 16. (Yates, M. Yates 1978).

'**Big Willy**' ('LaBar's White' x *williamsianum*). 5', -10°F, M, 3/3-4/3-4. The beautiful rounded leaves of *R. williamsianum* and the exceptional large white flowers of 'LaBar's White' are both found in this lovely new hybrid. (Knippenberg).

'**Bikini**' (unknown). 4'?, -15°F?, -/-/-. Hopefully this is the missing link for hybrid collectors. The long awaited hardy, red rhododendron. Scarlet red blooms are shown off against flat, smooth foliage. (Leach).

'**Bill Massey**' (*ciliatum* var. *bergii* x *nuttallii*). 6', 20°F, M, 4-5/3-4/4. Foliage is medium sized. 3 1/2" flowers are pink in the center, fading paler pink toward the edges, with stripes on the reverse side. The fragrant blooms are carried in trusses to 6. Synonym, 'Nutberger'. (Druecker, Trillium Lane Nursery 1978).

'**Billy Budd**' ('May Day' x *elliottii*). 3', 10°F, M, 3/4/3-4. Fantastic waxy red, flat-topped trusses of 10-12 flowers show up on this very free flowering plant. Foliage maintains a slight indumentum beneath. (Francis Hanger, RHS Garden, Wisley 1958) A.M. 1957.

'**Binfield**' ('China' x 'Crest'). 5', -10°F, EM, 4/3-4/3. Large, beautiful, primrose yellow flowers, with just a hint of red in the throat, adorn this great looking plant. The foliage is a combination of its parents - large and sturdy. (Crown Estate, Windsor) A.M. 1964.

'**Birthday Greeting**' ('Naomi' x *fortunei* ssp. *fortunei*). 5', -5°F, M, 4/3-4/3-4. Yellow orange flowers diffuse to red purple. (Rothschild 1979) A.M. 1979.

'**Bishopsgate**' ('Jalisco Elect' x 'Crest'). 5', -10°F, L, -/-/-. A very tall, open growing plant, much like 'Crest'. Flowers are yellow with a crimson blotch in the upper throat. Great for a slightly later yellow. (Crown Estate Commissioners) P.C. 1974.

'**Biskra**' (*cinnabarinum* var. *roylei* x *ambiguum*). 5', 5°F, M, 4/3-4/2-3. Leaves are medium-sized on this upright-growing hybrid, which is hardier than most *cinnabarinum* varieties. Bell shaped flowers to 2 1/2" long, are a rich vermilion, set in lax trusses of 4-6 flowers. (Rothschild 1934) A.M. 1940.

'**Black Eye**' ('Anah Kruschke' x 'Purple Splendour'). 5', -10°F, ML, 3-4/3-4/3-4. An ideal plant for that sunny location. This plant has great, shiny leaves and flowers of red-purple with a deep black eye in the upper lobe. (Greer intro. 1982).

'**Black Magic**' ('Jean Marie de Montague' x 'Leo'). 4', 5°F, ML, 4/4/3. Black-red flowers cover this plant in the late spring. They are exceptionally dark and show off their beauty best if planted in a location where the setting sun will shine through the flowers, causing them to glow magically. The medium foliage is matte, forest green and covers the plant well. A beautiful rhododendron in an unusual color not seen in many other plants. (Greer 1988).

'**Black Prince**' (*thomsonii* x 'Romany Chal'). 5', 0°F, ML, 4/2/3. Plant habit is not as fine as others, but this hybrid has most interesting flowers. Very large blooms are the deepest black-red possible. (Brandt 1962).

'**Black Prince's Ruby**' (*sanguineum* ssp. *haemaleum* x *thomsonii*). 3', 10°F, E, 4/3/3. Foliage is of a medium size. Flowers, to 2 1/2" across, are a vibrant, waxy red, with black veins and nectar glands, carried in lax trusses up to 5 flowers. (Nelson, Short 1977).

'**Black Satin**' ('PJM' cross). 3', -20°F, M, -/-/-. Strong, reddish-purple funnel shaped flowers are borne in trusses of 5. The small foliage is aromatic and takes on a dark mahogany color after blooming. (Mezitt, Weston Nurseries 1988).

'**Black Sport**' (unknown). 5', -5°F, ML-L, 3/3/3. This interesting new hybrid from Ben Nelson, registered by Bruce Briggs, most certainly contains some *R. ponticum* in its background. Habit is stiffly upright, often showing the underside of the deep green leaves, giving an unusual and different appearance from other rhododendrons. Flower color is also quite unique, a rich purple-red with a deep black-red blotch on the upper lobe. (Nelson, Briggs 1982).

'**Blanc-Mange**' ('Godesberg' x *auriculatum*). 6', -5°F, L-VL, -/-/-. A statuesque shrub, capable of reaching a height and width of 15'. Large, matte foliage is accented by pure white ruffled flowers held in upright trusses of 18 blooms each. (Rothschild 1934).

'Blaney's Blue' (*augustinii* 'Towercourt' x 'Blue Diamond'). 4-5', -5ºF, EM, 4/4/4. This hybrid, produced by Dr. L. T. Blaney of Oregon State University and introduced after extensive testing by Dr. Robert Ticknor of the North Willamette Experiment Station, is a vigorous growing, prolific-flowering plant. It propagates well and buds young, with attractive dense foliage. Leaves are forest green in summer, changing to a bronze tone in winter. Flowers are misty blue, covering plant with masses of blooms, which at their peak glow and sparkle with an almost electric quality. (Ticknor 1978).

'Blanka' ('Babette' x ['Hachmann's Ornament' x 'Furnivall's Daughter']). 2.5', -15ºF, M, -/-/-. Trusses are formed by white flowers which are tinged with a purplish-red hue. (Hachmann, Stuck 1988).

'Blaze' ('Mars' x *catawbiense* var. *rubrum*). 4', -25ºF, M, 2/3/3-4. Leaves are medium to large. Flowers are a strong red, the edges deeper red, blotched pale pink with faint yellowish orange spotting, and held in firm triangular trusses to 18. (D. G. Leach 1959).

'Blewbury' (*roxieanum* x *anhweiense*). 2', 0ºF, M, 3/4/3. A delightful little hybrid from Windsor. Flowers are pure white with red spotting on the upper throat. Leaves are similar in shape to *roxieanum* with slight pale brown indumentum covering them. (Crown Estate, Windsor 1968) A.M. 1968.

'Blind Date' (parentage unknown). 6', 0ºF, ML, -/-/-. Foliage is large. Flowers are a generous 4 1/2" wide, 6-lobed, with a lovely fragrance. The blooms are medium pink shading to a yellow center with a small rusty brown eye, held in trusses to 12. (Whitney, Sather 1975).

'Blinklicht' ('Nova Zembla' x 'Mars'). 5', -20ºF, ML, -/-/-. Huge trusses of bright red flowers have darker red markings. Foliage is elliptical with a slightly hairy exterior. (Hachmann, Stuck 1983).

'Blitz' (*haematodes* x 'G. A. Sims'). 3', 5ºF, M, 3/4/4. Growth habit is mound-like on this sun and heat tolerant variety. It is beautiful all year, with dense deep-green leaves that hide all but the lowest lines and trunk. Flowers are very dark red, a degree of darkness not often seen in sun tolerant rhododendrons. (Clarke 1945).

'Blood Ruby' (*forrestii* ssp. *forrestii* Repens Group x 'Mandalay'). 2', 0ºF, M, 3/3/3. Foliage is small. Rich red flowers, to 1 1/2", are held in trusses to 5. (Brandt 1954).

'Blue Admiral' (parentage unknown). 3', -5ºF, EM, 4/4. Blue flowers sit above attractive, dark green foliage. (unknown).

'Blue Bird' (*intricatum* x *augustinii*). 3', 0ºF, EM, 4/4/3. The dense small leaves of 'Blue Bird' create a finely textured plant in the garden. The plant will eventually reach 4' in height and measure 5' or 6' in diameter. Numerous electric blue flowers. (Aberconway 1930).

'Blue Boy' ('Blue Ensign' x 'Purple Splendour'). 5', -10ºF, ML-L, 4/3/3-4. This is a heavy blooming, upright and open-growing, well-shaped plant. Leaves are rather long and narrow, dark green. Funnel-form flowers, to 2 1/2" wide, are of good substance. The vibrant violet blooms, with wavy edges, and an almost black blotch, are held in a tight rounded truss of up to 20 flowers. (Watson 1981).

'Blue Chip' (*russatum* x 'Blue Diamond'). 2', 5ºF, EM, 3-4/3-4/3-4. Purple violet flowers on a compact plant with small, scaly leaves. (George, Hydon 1978) AM 1978.

'Blue Cloud' (selected seedling of *augustinii*). 6', 0ºF, EM, 4/4/3. Leaves are typical of species. Plant blooms very profusely, with 2 1/2" wide, powder blue flowers. (Hansen 1958).

'Blue Crown' ('Blue Peter' x 'Purple Splendour'). 4', -5ºF, M, 4/3-4/3-4. Showy blue-purple flowers with a lighter center are accentuated by a large, striking purple flare. The glossy foliage shows the influence of 'Purple Splendour' (K. Van de Ven reg. 1981)

'Blue Diamond' ('Intrifast' x *augustinii*). 3', -5ºF, EM, 4/4/4. A favorite of many gardeners, 'Blue Diamond' has small flowers all along the stems. Dense, finely branched stems grow vertically. A sunny location is best for this well shaped plant. Many times it is used as a border. At least two forms are being grown. (Crosfield) A.M. 1935, F.C.C. 1939.

'Blue Ensign' (probably a *ponticum* hybrid). 4', -15ºF, M, 4/3/4. Very hardy, sun tolerant, lilac blue flowers have a striking purple blotch. Its truss is similar to 'Blue Peter', and while they both become huge plants, 'Blue Ensign' is more compact. Foliage tends to spot, especially if plant is low in nitrogen. (W.C. Slocock 1934) A.M. 1959.

'Blue Frost' (*ponticum hybrid*). 6', -10ºF, ML, 2/3/4. Leaves are medium to large. Flowers, to 2 3/4" across, are light purple with white throats that are spotted with shades of orange, in trusses to 20. (Whitney, Sather 1976).

'Blue Gown' (parentage unknown). 3', -10ºF, EM, 4/4. Blue-green foliage is dressed in a mass of delicate, bright blue blooms. (sold by Hammond).

'Blue Hawaii' ('Blue Ensign' x 'Purple Splendour'). 4 1/2', 0ºF, ML-L, 3-4/3/3-4. Growth habit is broader and more open than 'Blue Boy' with glossy leaves similar in length, but not as narrow or dark. Flowers are also larger, to 3 1/2" wide. The frilled blooms are darker violet, fading very pale lavender in the throats. They have a greenish blotch and bronze spotting, and are set in a rounded truss to 16 flowers. Floriferous. (Watson 1981).

'Blue Jay' (selected seedling *ponticum*). 5', -10ºF, ML-L, 3/4/5. A vigorous plant covered by bright green foliage. Profuse lavender blue flowers have a distinctive brown dorsal blotch. (Larson 1965).

'Blue Lagoon' ('Purple Splendour' x 'A. Bedford') 5', -10ºF, ML, 3/4/4. Blue purple flowers are enhanced by a striking large deep purple eye. Excellent shiny green foliage is held on a strong and vigorous growing plant. (Greer hyb. 1963, raised by G. Baxter, W. Thompson).

'Bluenose' (*augustinii* hybrid). 4'?, -10ºF?, EM-M, -/-/-. An extremely floriferous plant. The blooms are a beautiful, bright blue. (Brueckner).

'Blue Pacific' ('Purple Splendour' x 'Susan'). 5', -5ºF, ML, 4/3/3-4. This blue-purple flower has a deep black-purple blotch. The hybrid came from the hand of the late Bill Whitney, and has become legendary for its outstanding truss. The attractive foliage becomes darker green if given shade. There is another *ponticum* hybrid improperly introduced under the same name. The true 'Blue Pacific' has light, dull green leaves, while the imposter has darker, shiny leaves. (Whitney 1976).

'Blue Peter' (probably a *ponticum* hybrid). 4-5', -10ºF, M, 4/2-3/3. Its frilled trusses are light lavender blue with a prominent purple flare and the lush leaves are glossy green. It's vigorous growing, cold hardy, and heat and sun resistant. One of the most popular hybrids in the eastern United States. Weevils like the plant, too. (Waterer, Sons & Crisp) A.M. 1933, F.C.C. 1958.

'Blue Rhapsody' ('A. Bedford' x 'Purple Splendour'). 5', -5ºF, ML, 4-5/3/3. Exceptional trusses are large, blue-purple. Each flower has a blotch of black purple on the upper petal and throat. The white stamens contrast nicely with the purple flower. The foliage is long and narrow, somewhat cup shaped. A good hybrid. (Whitney, Sather 1976).

'Blue Ridge' ('Russautinii' x *augustinii*). 4', -15ºF, M, 4/3-4/4. Iridescent blue flowers are borne freely on this well rounded, compact plant. Fragrant foliage and very faint flower fragrance are an added attraction to this wonderful little plant. (Haag hyb. 1966, T. Richardson intro. 1975, reg. by Haag 1981).

'Blue River' ('Van Nes Sensation' x 'Emperor de Maroc'). 5', -5ºF, M, 3/2-3/3. Unusual violet blue flowers cover this plant. Foliage is glossy green, and trusses hold up to 17 flowers. (Lyons 1961).

'Blueshine Girl' ('Soulkew' x *wardii*). 5', 0ºF?, EM-M, -/-/-. A unique hybrid regarded for its blue foliage and silky stems. The flowers, held in large trusses, are a delicate creamy white with red blotching. (Hobbie).

'Blue Silver' (*hippophaeoides* hybrid). 3', -25ºF, E, 3/3/3. A hardy plant with numerous reddish-purple flowers held against blue-gray foliage. Holds a strong resemblance to *R. yungningense*. (sold by Cox).

'Blue Star' ('Saint Tudy' x *impeditum*). 2', 0ºF, EM-M, -/-/-. Small leaves, similar to the *impeditum* parent cover this small, compact plant. Richly colored mauve-blue flowers are small and funnel-shaped. (Gen. Harrison 1971).

'Blue Thunder' ('Blue Diamond' x unknown). 2', -5ºF, EM, -/-/-. New growth appears light green rimmed with red, in contrast to the winter color of reddish brown. Wide, funnel-shaped flowers are violet with a strong red-purple throat. (Newcomb 1987).

'Blue Tit' (*impeditum* x *augustinii*). 3', -5ºF, EM, 3/4/4. A very compact plant habit displays bright yellow new growth. Profusely produces grey-blue blooms. (J. C. Williams 1933).

'Bluette' (*augustinii* x *impeditum*). 3', -5ºF, ML, 3-4/4/4. A myriad of fine stems interweave, shaping a plant 4' tall and quite broad. The foliage is dense and glossy olive green. Flowers are light blue, in trusses to 8. (Lancaster 1958).

'Blue Wonder' (*russatum* x *augustinii*). 4', -10ºF, EM, 4/3. A surprisingly erect growing plant considering the lepidote parentage. Foliage is small, nearly covered by profuse blooms of slate blue with a darker eye. (Hobbie 1967).

'Blunique' ('Blue Peter' x 'Unique'). 4', -5ºF, M, 3/3/3. Light yellow-cream flowers have blue speckling that forms a darker blotch. Glossy green foliage is medium sized and elliptic in shape. (S. Hall 1990).

'Blurettia' ('Blue Peter' x *yakushimanum* 'Koichiro Wada'). 3', -10ºF, M, -/-/-. Flowers have a rich purple wavy margin, paling to a much lighter center. Oval shaped foliage has a slightly hairy coating. (Hachmann, Stuck 1983).

'Blutopia' ('Catawbiense Grandiflorum' x 'A. Bedford'). 5', -15ºF, L, -/-/-. Trusses are composed of 12-15 wavy, vibrant purple blooms. Each flower has pronounced greenish-yellow spotting on the dorsal lobe. (Hachmann, Stuck 1988).

'Bob Bovee' (*yakushimanum* 'Koichiro Wada' x *wardii*). 3', -5ºF, M, 3/4/4. Foliage is medium to large. Yellow flowers, up to 3" wide, have red and green spotting in the throat, and are held in trusses to 12. (Bovee, Sorenson & Watson 1976).

'Bob's Blue' ('Ilam Violet' x 'Blue Diamond'). 3', 0ºF, M, 4/4/4. Electric blue flowers on a compact plant. This flowers extremely well and is an easy and enjoyable plant for the garden. The small leaves are deep green in summer, turning rich maroon in winter. (Robert C. Rhodes 1979).

'Boddaertianum' (*campanulatum* x *arboreum* ssp. *cinnamomeum* var. *album*). 6', 0ºF, E-EM, 3/3/3-4. According to Bean, the parentage may actually be *arboreum* x *ponticum* white form (or a hybid of *ponticum*). A very large, handsome tree with tight trusses of white with radiating magenta spotting. Because of its early blooming time the plant retains its trusses for an extended period. This plant is not seen much in the U.S., but is magnificent in many older European gardens. (Van Houtte 1863).

'Bold Adventure' ('Ruby F. Bowman' x 'Skipper'). 3', 10ºF, M, -/-/-. Strong red buds open to expose fragrant, pale purplish-pink flowers. Two red dorsal flares, and a darker red throat serve as an effective accent. (Dr. L. W. Bulgin 1988).

'Bombay' ([[*scyphocalyx* x *kyawii*] x 'Catalgla'] x ['Catalgla' x *wardii*]). 3', -10ºF, EM, 3/2/3. Leaves are medium sized. Flowers, 1 3/4", are greenish yellow, spotted and blotched darker. They show darker color on the outer petal sufaces as well, and they are set in trusses to 14. (Leach 1972).

'Bonfire' ([*fortunei* ssp. *discolor* x 'Mrs. R. T. Shaw'] x *griersonianum*). 5', - 5ºF, ML, 3/3/4. Long, narrow leaves are dull green in color. Flowers are a brilliant orange-red and held in a large, loose truss. The young plant is open in growth, becoming very compact later, especially if planted in a sunny location. (Waterer, Sons and Crisp 1928) A.M. 1933.

'Bonito' (*fortunei* ssp. *discolor* x 'Luscombei'). 6', -5ºF, ML, 4/3/3. The plant habit is upright and vigorous, with large dark green leaves. Flowers are very large, up to 5" across, the color light blush pink, fading to white, with heavy chocolate spotting and blotch. The slightly fragrant blooms are held in a rounded truss. (Rothschild 1934) A.M. 1934.

'Bonnie Babe' ('Inca Gold' x dwarf orange hybrid). 3', 0ºF, ML, 3-4/3-4/3-4. Small yellow flowers are highlighted by a super calyx that almost doubles the size. Not only that, both the flowers and the calyx are spotted with bright red. Named in honor of the late Margaret Thompson of Waldport, Oregon, whose late husband, Willard, affectionately called 'Babe'. (James A. Elliott 1983).

'Bonnie Brae' ('Scintillation' x 'Gable's Red Head'). 6', -5ºF, ML, -/-/-. Foliage is quite large. 4" wide flowers are fragrant, with 7 lobes, orchid pink in color, darker edges, and a yellowish green blotch, 17 per truss. (Herbert 1978).

'Bo-peep' (*lutescens* x *moupinense*). 4', 5ºF, VE-E, 3/3/3. Habit is open-growing and low, with small, scaly, light green leaves. Yellow early flowers make a real show. (Rothschild 1934) A.M. 1937.

'Born Winner' ([*maximum* x *yakushimanum*] x 'Adele's Yellow'). 5', -10ºF?, L, -/-/-. Strong purplish red flowers with paler edge. (Delp 1990).

'Boskoop' (unnamed hybrid x 'Max Sye'). 5', -5ºF?, M?, -/-/-. Dark green leaves surround rounded trusses of rosy red flowers having a dark brown blotch. (van Nes 1961).

'Boskoop Concorde' ('Antoon van Welie' x 'Max Sye'). 5', -15ºF, M, 3-4/3-4/3. This plant is often called 'Concorde' and has another synonymous name of 'Georges Royer'. Dark rose flowers with a prominent darker blotch appear in profusion. The foliage is medium-large, dark green, somewhat twisted and has a rough surface. (A. van Nes 1965, intro. G. C. Stolwijk & Co. 1970).

'Boule de Neige' (*caucasicum* x hardy *catawbiense* hybrid). 5', -25ºF, M, 3/3/3. Bright green leathery leaves, and flowers which look like snowballs, abound on this medium size rounded plant. It is known for its heat, sun, and cold tolerance. (Oudieu 1878).

'Boule de Rose' (red *catawbiense* hybrid x 'Boule de Neige'). 6', -20ºF, EM, 2/4/3. Growth habit, closely resembling 'Boule de Neige', is dense and compact. The flowers are a bright rose pink and they have a slight brownish flare on upper lobe. (Shammarello, D. G. Leach 1957).

'Boulodes' ('Boule de Neige' x 'Loderi' seedling). 6', 0ºF, ML, -/-/-. Leaves are large. The 3 1/2" flowers are pink which ages to white. The petal edges are ruffled, and the flowers are sweetly scented. (Nearing 1973).

'Bow Bells' ('Corona' x *williamsianum*). 3', -5ºF, EM, 3/4/3. In blossom 'Bow Bells' is a perfect mound of light pink flowers appearing first as deep pink buds, and contrast with the opened flowers to give a two-toned effect. The flowers are followed by shiny, copper, new leaves appearing at every stem tip, a display in itself. As the season changes, the plant becomes a superb jade green, with rose red bud scales. Another superb contrast of colors! In ten years it is 3' tall, but it will become a larger plant. A site with filtered light exposure is best for 'Bow Bells'. A final note: fertilize lightly, an excess of fertilizer will cause foliage burn. (Rothschild 1934) A.M. 1935.

'Bowie' (*chapmanii* x *minus* var. *minus*). 6', 0ºF, L, 3/3/3. Foliage is medium in size. 1 1/2" flowers are pink, blotched brownish, growing at branch tips in up to 3 buds of 14 flowers each. (Skinner, U.S. National Arboretum 1979).

'Bow Street' ('Bow Bells' x ['Socrianum' x 'Rima']). 3', 0ºF?, ?, -/-/-. Yellow flowers are blushed with pale pink. (George, Hydon Nursery 1976).

'Brandt Red' ('Grosclaude' x 'Britannia'). 4', 0ºF, ML, 3-4/3-4/3. An alluring shade of ruby red surrounded by a soft blanket of indumented leaves. It's as pretty as it sounds. (Brandt).

'Brandt's Tropicana' ('Britannia' x 'Goldsworth Orange'). 3', 0ºF, L, 5/3/3. A sister seedling of 'Kubla Khan', this is a unique orange salmon color not seen in most flowers. The foliage is light green and requires some shade for optimum performance. (Brandt not registered).

'Brandywine' (*pubescens* x *keiskei*). 3', -10ºF, EM, 4/2/3. Leaves are medium sized. The small cream-colored flowers are edged with rose and they are held in 2", ball shaped trusses. (Nearing 1950).

'Brasilia' (['Omega' x *wardii*] x [*wardii* x 'Alice Street']). 3', -5ºF, EM, -/-/-. Deep green foliage densely covers this rounded plant. The flowers have a tri-color appearance as they open creamy apricot, slightly blushed with red and have a golden-yellow throat to finish the effect. (Hachmann 1982).

'Bravo!' (*catawbiense* var. *album* x [*fortunei* ssp. *fortunei* x {*arboreum* x *griffithianum*}]). 5', -15ºF, ML, 4/4/4. Flowers are a light purplish pink, shading lighter in the center, with sparse dorsal brown spotting. (Leach 1974).

'Break of Day' ('Dawn's Delight' x *dichroanthum*). 4', -5ºF, M, 3/3/3. Again *R. dichroanthum* has imparted some of its unusual colors on one of its hybrids. Loose trusses hold 14 flowers which are deep orange at the base and flare to orange pink on the edges. The plant is more broad than tall. (Rothschild 1934) A.M. 1936.

'Bremen' (garden hybrid x *williamsianum*). 3', -10ºF, EM, 3-4/3-4/4. This is one of the few *williamsianum* hybrids with a more upright truss, and it is quite desirable for that reason. It covers itself with masses of deep rose pink flowers. It is an easy to grow hybrid with delightful foliage. You will note, there are two plants from Germany with the same name. (Hobbie hyb. about 1944).

'Bremen' (*haematodes* x unnamed red *catawbiense* hybrid). 2', -5ºF, E, 4/4/4. A dwarf, compact shrub with scarlet flowers and a small calyx. (Arends, Bohlje 1964).

'Brenda Lee' (*catawbiense* var. *compactum* x 'Purple Splendour'). 4', -20ºF, ML, -/-/-. Foliage is medium sized. 2 1/4" flowers are violet with a lighter maroon-spotted blotch, and held in ball trusses to 11. (Yates, M. Yates 1977).

'Bric-a-Brac' (*leucaspis* x *moupinense*). 30", 5ºF, VE, 3/3/3. A woodsy, low growing graceful plant. Fine stems and round leaves are fuzzy and pretty. Earlier than expected, flowers open pink and white. (Rothschild 1934) A.M. 1945.

'Brickdust' (*williamsianum* x 'Dido'). 30", -5ºF, M, 4/4-5/4. Terrific all around, this low growing hybrid has dense, cheery, round, green leaves and a plenitude of dusty orange rose flowers tumbling over the foliage. (R. Henny 1959).

'Bridal Bouquet' (unknown *yakushimanum* hybrid). 3', 0ºF, M, -/-/-. A wonderfully different plant which has yellow flowers with peachy edging. Compact habit is typical of "yak" hybrids, but the leaves have no indumentum. (Whitney, Sather not registered).

'Bridge North' ('Henry R. Yates' x 'Boule de Neige'). 4', -5ºF, ML, -/-/-. Leaves are medium sized. Flowers, 3 1/2" wide, are rose, fading lighter in throat with gold spotting, in ball shaped trusses to 14. (Herbert, Reese 1977).

'Brigadoon' (unknown x *yakushimanum*). 3', 0ºF, M, 4/4/4. A dense-growing, medium sized plant that produces lots of vivid red, double, funnel shaped flowers. (H. Larson, F. & J. Minch 1989).

'Brigitte' (*insigne* x 'Mrs. J. G. Millais'). 3', -10ºF, ML, -/-/-. Large trusses hold many blooms of rosy purple with an olive green blotch. Glossy, pointed foliage covers this dense and compact plant. (Hachmann, Stuck 1983).

'Brilliant' ('Elizabeth' x *Ledium columbianum*). 2', 0ºF, M, 3/3/3. This plant has small, bright red, funnel shaped flowers that are held above smooth green leaves. Following flowering, it has bronzy-red new growth. The open growth habit does make an enjoyable plant and it is said to be tolerant of both heat and lime, but will be happiest if given some shade. Now, if you want to be confused, here is your chance! Originally, so the story went, the hybridizer of this plant believed he was crossing 'Elizabeth' with a rhododendron native to the Northwest. It was later thought that the plant he knew as a rhododendron was probably *Ledium columbianum* (also native to the N.W.), and for about 25 years 'Brilliant' was considered to be the single member of the new Genus Ledudendron. However, recently all Genus Ledium species have been reclassified and now belong to Genus Rhododendron. So it would seem that 'Brilliant' actually is a cross of a rhododendron ('Elizabeth') with a rhododendron (*R. columbianum*). There are, however, those us who do not agree that Genus Ledium should be included in the Genus Rhododendron. For one thing, all of the Genus Ledium open their seed pods in reverse (from back to front, instead of front to back), reason enough to not include Ledium in Rhododendron. To confuse you even more, there are leading experts, including my very much respected friends, the Coxes in Scotland, who feel that 'Brilliant' is actually a cross between 'Elizabeth' and an evergreen azalea. This is an idea with which I could easily agree, so maybe the given parentage was wrong all along. You should be confused by now, and at this point I suggest you write all of the possibilities on slips of paper, draw a small circle on the floor and then toss the slips of paper in the air. The one that lands in the circle must be the truth, or probably as much truth as "we experts" have given you! (Leonard Brooks & Son Nursery, grown by Halfdan Lem and recorded as being introduced by Greer Gardens).

'Brinny' (['Day Dream' x 'Margaret Dunn'] x unnamed seedling). 4', -5ºF, M, 3/3/3. An impressive and unusual flower with bronze flower buds which open as straw yellow with a bronze center. (Graves, Janeck 1964).

'Britalier' ('Britannia' x 'Fusilier'). 4', -5ºF, L, 4/4/4. A great late blooming red. Sturdy and rigid, this plant is the best of its parents. (Davis).

'Britannia' ('Queen Wilhelmina' x 'Stanley Davies'). 4', -5ºF, ML, 3/2-3/3. Bright scarlet trusses and large pendulous leaves enhance the strong limbs of this sturdy plant. Foliage tends to be light green. (C. B van Nes & Sons 1921) A.M. 1921, F.C.C. 1937.

'Brittany' ('Bowie' x keiskei 'Mt. Kuromi'). 4', -20ºF, ML, -/-/-. A perfect example of a lepidote, 'Brittany' has small, rounded leaves and forms a dense, compact mound. Flowers, pale yellow maturing to shades of pink, provide prolonged interest and beauty. (Leach).

'Britton Hill' ('Jean Marie de Montague' x 'Red Loderi'). 5', -5ºF, M, 4-5/4/4. Large waxy, deep forest green foliage provides a backdrop for large perfect, bright red trusses. This has one of the most magnificent, large red trusses you will find on a rhododendron. As for hardiness, probably -5ºF is its limit, however after the '91 freeze when we went to 0ºF after 70ºF the week before, and even 'Nova Zembla' did not bloom well, this plant produced magnificent trusses of "show quality". I wish it were a little more compact in growth habit, but otherwise, it is one of the finest foliage plants you could grow. I'm not partial to many rhododendrons, but, I'll have to say I like this one! (Britt Smith about 1990).

'Britton Hill Bugle' ('Karkov' x 'Red Loderi'). 5', 5ºF, M-ML, 4/4/4. Large, red trusses are composed of blooms having a dark eye and a pronounced bugle shape. It buds very heavily and covers itself with magnificent flowers. Matte green foliage always densely covers the plant. (Britt Smith 1995).

'Brocade' ('Vervaeniana' [an Indian azalea] x williamsianum). 3', 0ºF, M, 3/3/-. A plant of the above parentage would be an azaleodendron. The plant grown in our gardens is a R. williamsianum hybrid, but without doubt the plant we are growing is not an azaleodendron. So someone got their records mixed up! Peachy pink bells start as vivid carmine buds. The plant is open in habit but attractive and rounded. (Rothschild 1934).

'Bronze Wing' (unknown [something like 'Elizabeth' x a williamsianum hybrid]). 3', 0ºF, M, 3/4-5/4. Pink buds fade to a creamy white while retaining a nice rosy edge. New foliage is a very deep bronze red color, to about 3" long. The plant is nice and compact. This plant is absolutely superb for its red bud bracts in winter. (Teese, Australia 1981).

'Brookside' ('Jalisco Goshawk' x griersonianum). 4', -10ºF, EM, -/-/-. A beautiful hybrid from Windsor. Buds are a very vibrant red, opening to yellow ocher with just a hint of rose. Flowers are in a lax truss. Different and attractive. (Crown Estate, Windsor) A.M. 1962.

'Brookville' ('Westbury' x 'Meadowbrook'). 5', -10ºF, ML, 3/3/-. Pastel pink with a gold throat. A sister seedling of 'Wheatley', known also as Phipps #1. (H. Phipps).

'Broughtonii' (arboreum x unknown). 5', -10ºF, M, 3/3/4. Rosy crimson flowers with darker spotting are held on a dense, easily grown plant. Both flower and shrub habit resemble 'Cynthia' and many rhododendron "experts" have mis-identified this as such. Also, don't confuse this with 'Broughtonii Aureum', which is an azaleodendron. (Broughton before 1853).

'Broughtonii Aureum' ([maximum x ponticum] x molle). 4', -5ºF, ML, 3-4/2/4. A bright yellow azaleodendron, which means it is a cross between an azalea and a rhododendron. There are very few of these crosses around! Full sun exposure is best and it will tolerate heat. It is semi-deciduous. (Smith of Norbiton) F.C.C. 1935.

'Brown Eyes' (fortunei ssp. fortunei hybrid). 5', -15ºF, M, 3-4/3-4/4. An excellent plant for that hot spot in the garden. The showy trusses are made of melon pink flowers with distinctive golden brown flares. The substantial foliage is fir green. (Dexter, Bosley).

'Bruce Brechtbill' (bud sport of 'Unique'). 4', 0ºF, EM, 3-4/5/4. This hybrid looks identical to 'Unique' until it flowers. It has the same top rated, oblong foliage and excellent mounded plant habit. For shape of bloom and time of flowering it is also identical. Then comes the difference: it's pink! There is a touch of yellow in the throat, too. (Bruce Brechtbill 1974, intro. by Greer Gardens at the request of Mrs. Brechtbill after his death around 1980).

'Buchanan Simpson' (possibly erubescens hybrid). 5', -5ºF, EM, 4/3-4/3-4. This thick, bushy rhododendron has interesting, heavily veined leaves which roll under at the leaf margin. Phlox pink trusses are accented with a small double blotch of maroon deep in the throat of each flower. The flowers open wide to display their markings. (Grieg 1963).

'Bud Flanagan' (unknown x ponticum). 6', -5ºF, ML, -/-/-. Very large conical trusses hold mauve flowers with chestnut in the throat. (Rothschild 1967).

'Buff Lady' ('Nereid' x fortunei ssp. discolor). 4', -5ºF, L, 3/3/3. Leaves are long and narrow. Flowers, to 3 1/2" wide, are 6-lobed, buff colored, shading to coral pink, and held in a rounded truss to 12. (Rose, Lancaster 1958).

'Buketta' ('Spitfire' x 'Fruhlingszauber'). 3', -10ºF, M, -/-/-. Deep, clear red flowers have faint markings of darker red. Foliage is thin and elliptic in shape with a slight hairy covering. (Hachmann, Stuck 1983).

'Bulstrode Park' (griffithianum hybrid x 'Sefton'). 6', -5ºF, M, 3/3/3. No matter what the records show, this is probably out of the same cross as 'Langley Park', but who knows? Dark green leaves are very long, narrow and pointed. Waxy flowers are bright scarlet. Truss is quite large, loose, and high. All this on a healthy, strong growing, upright plant. (C. B. van Nes & Sons).

'Bumble Bee' ('Purple Splendour' x 'Blue Peter'). 5', -10ºF, ML, -/-/-. Huge trusses of 25 or more flowers are produced on this large growing shrub, reaching up to 8-9' in height. The blooms are purple with a large eye, and spotting of maroon and black on the dorsal lobe. (H.W. King 1984).

'Burgundy' ('Britannia' x 'Purple Splendour'). 5', -15ºF, ML, 4/3/3. Distinctive burgundy red flowers are held in dome-shaped trusses of up to 15. An attractive plant with large leaves. (Rose, Lem 1958).

'Burgundy Cherry' (parentage unknown). 5', -10ºF, ML, -/-/-. Foliage is medium to large. 2 1/4" flowers are carmine red, with purple spotting and blotch, in trusses to 12. Synonym, 'Dexter #105 Black Cherry'. (Dexter, Knippenberg 1978).

'Burgundy Rose' ([ungernii x auriculatum] x 'Romany Chal'). 6', -0ºF, L, 3/3/4. Most interesting for its deep red new growth which stays red for up to 2 months. It has very vigorous upright growth habit, which, when growing well can produce up to 18" of growth at a time, and far surpasss the 6' at 10 yrs. mark. I would imagine it is the fastest, and tallest (at a young age) growing rhododendron I grow. Flowers are a light pink with small, deeper pink markings. Bloom often occurs at the same time or after the new growth. (Lem not registered).

'Burma' ('Mars' x 'Fanfare'). 5', -20ºF, ML, 4/4/4. A very exciting hybrid for those in colder climates. Bright red flowers are speckled with heavy black spots. This plant grows wider than tall. (Leach 1958, intro. 1982, reg. 1984).

'Burning Love' ('Essex Scarlet' x *forrestii* ssp. *forrestii* Repens Group). 3', -15ºF, M, 3/3/3. Foliage is smooth and twisted on this compact, mounding plant. Red winter buds open to small scarlet flowers held in an upright truss. (Hobbie).

'Butter Brickle' ('Hotei' x 'Lem's Cameo' hybrid). 5', 5ºF, M, -/-/-. Beautiful flowers are buttery gold, marked with a maroon star in the center of the flower which radiates onto the upper petal and calyx. The outside of the flower is flushed with rose. The large calyx creates a double effect. The new growth is bronze, turning fir green at maturity. Compact plant habit. (Lofthouse 1982).

'Buttered Popcorn' ('Mrs. Lammot Copeland' x 'Mary Drennen'). 4', -5ºF, L, 4/3/4. The wonderfully different yellow flowers have two rays of brown converging on a dark eye. The trusses are surrounded by light green foliage held on an upright plant. (Larson hyb., Clint Smith intro.).

'Butterfly' (*campylocarpum* x 'Mrs. Milner'). 5', 0ºF, M, 3/3/3. The plant is rounded and compact, with medium sized leaves. Flowers are pale yellow, faintly spotted darker, in round, tight trusses. (W. C. Slocock) A.M. 1940.

'Buttermint' ('Unique' x ['Fabia' x *dichroanthum* ssp. *apodectum*]). 3', -5ºF, M, 4/3-4/3. These thick leathery leaves are pleasing in appearance and are extremely dense on a plant of compact habit. The plump flower buds mature early in the season, so that the plant seems to anxiously await its blooming time. It has yellow flowers which are large and handsome. (Mauritsen 1979).

'Buttersteep' ('Jalisco' x 'Crest'). 6', -10ºF, ML-L, -/-/-. Although 'Crest' is one of the parents, this hybrid does not grow open like many of 'Crest's hybrids. Flowers are very strong yellow with a small blotch of currant red deep in the throat. (Crown Estate Commissioners) A.M. 1971.

'Butter Yellow' ('Crest' x 'Golden Yellow'). 5', 0ºF, M, -/-/-. A delightful, compact plant with yellow flowers. (Hill).

'Cabaret' (unknown). 4', 5ºF, M, -/-/-. Different! To quote the Whitney Gardens catalog..."The bright cerise bud color opens to a cerise-edged flower with a light pink throat with a lime-green eye. Each flower has a cerise stripe running from the throat to the margin, creating a star effect." (Whitney, Sather 1986).

'Cadis' ('Caroline' x *fortunei* ssp. *discolor*). 5', -15ºF, ML, 3/4/5. The pretty, long, narrow leaves and fragrant, light pink trusses of 'Cadis' deserve the recognition afforded this cold hardy hybrid from the eastern United States. A sun tolerant selection. (Gable 1958) A.E. 1959.

'Cairo' (['Catalgla' x *fortunei* ssp. *fortunei*] x ['Eidam' x *williamsianum*]). 5', -20ºF, ML, 3/3/4. Foliage is medium sized. 3 1/4" flowers are white, conspicuously blotched and spotted greenish yellow, and are held in trusses to 16. (Leach 1973).

'Calcutta' ([*dichroanthum* ssp. *scyphocalyx* x *kyawii*] x 'Catalgla'). 3', -15ºF, L, -/-/-. 1 1/2" flowers are yellow with orange edges, and are held in trusses to 13. Medium sized foliage. (Leach 1972).

'California Blue' (*augustinii* x unknown). 4', -5ºF, EM, 4/4. Masses of electric blue blooms are produced above smooth, fir green foliage. (Intro. by Greer).

'California Gold' ('Else Frye' x 'Eldorado'). 3', 15ºF, E, 4/3/3-4. Beautifully fragrant flowers, to a generous 3 1/4" across, are primrose yellow, beautifully fragrant, held in trusses to 6 on a background of medium sized foliage. (Bowman 1976).

'Calsap' ('Catalgla' x 'Sappho'). 4', -25ºF, ML, 4/3/4. Lavender buds open to form conical trusses of white blooms with a striking burgundy blotch. Smooth, oblong shaped, emerald green foliage densely covers this plant which is more wide than tall at maturity. (M. Michener 1986).

'Calstocker' see 'Exbury Calstocker'.

'Cameo' see 'Lem's Cameo'.

'Campirr' (*campylocarpum* x *irroratum*). 4', 0ºF, EM, -/-/-. Pale yellow flowers are brightened by crimson spotting. (Magor 1919, intro. 1926).

'Canada' (unknown [probably a *campylogynum* hybrid]). 2', -5ºF, M, 3-4/3/3. Small, tubular, deep rose pink flowers and cute rounded leaves cover this compact plant. Grown well, this is an exceptionally delightful dwarf. Red stems contrast with the green foliage. The plant sometimes gets rust, but if planted in an area with good air circulation the condition is easily controlled. (Grieg, Caperci 1977).

'Canadian Beauty' ('Mrs. Horace Fogg' x 'Walloper'). 6', 0ºF?, ML, 4-5/4/4. Foliage is large. The 4 1/2" flowers are light pink with the centers shading darker to the edges. They are held in large trusses of 16. This is a large growing, showy plant. (Lofthouse 1971).

'Canadian Gold' ('Hotei' x *wardii* hybrid). 4', 5ºF, EM, 4/4/3. The flower buds appear as gold nuggets and open to deep yellow flowers with a large calyx. It is a compact plant with dark green, glossy foliage. (Lofthouse 1979).

'Canadian Lilac' ('Rocket' x ['Catalgla' x 'Lady Bessborough']). 1', -25ºF, ML, -/-/-. This tiny plant has a spreading growth habit. The creeping branches are covered with yellow-green foliage and many flowers. The blooms are comprised of triangular, light purple petals spotted with tan. (Behring 1983).

'Canadian Magenta' ('Rocket' x ['Catalgla' x 'Lady Bessborough']). 2', -25ºF, ML, -/-/-. Growing as wide as tall, this plant has a dense habit. Triangular shaped petals of pale pinkish purple form blooms with darker spotting. (R. Behring 1983).

'Canadian Sunset' (*yakushimanum* x 'Gipsy King'). 3', 0ºF, M, 4/4/4. Quite different! The buds begin as a good solid red and open to flowers of an almost salmon-orange color which fades to creamy yellow toward the center. Add to this the beauty of a compact, rounded bush with indumented leaves and it's almost too good to be true. (R. Henny, Liningston, Lofthouse 1974).

'Canary' (*campylocarpum* x *caucasicum* f. *luteum*). 3', -10ºF, EM, 3/3/3. One of the hardiest of the deep yellow rhododendrons. Deeply veined, rounded leaves draw attention to this compact growing plant. 'Canary' is as yellow as 'Crest', although not colored as brightly. It is an excellent subject for future hybridizing of hardy yellows. (M. Koster & Sons 1920).

'**Creeping Jenny**' (*griersonianum* x *forrestii* ssp. *forrestii* Repens Group). 2', 5ºF, EM, 3/4/3. This hybrid, a sister of 'Elizabeth', is compact, low growing, and small leaved. Bell shaped flowers are vibrant bright red, held in lax trusses of up to 6. (Aberconway).

'**Creole Belle**' ('Vulcan' x 'Harvest Moon'). 4-5', -5ºF or colder, ML, 3-4/4-5/4-5. This plant has attractive, deep forest green foliage. It is a tough plant that branches well and grows vigorously. The flower is bright, showy deep pink with a slight touch of blue to give it a special radiance and glow. (Thompson 1982).

'**Crest**' (*wardii* x 'Lady Bessborough'). 6', -5ºF, M, 4-5/3/3. Bright, sunny yellow trusses are quite large. It grows to be wide, and taller than 8' as it continues to age. The heavy limbs of the plant become exposed as the plant gains height. Some gardeners enjoy the appearance of the strong open boughs, and others prefer growing lower foliage plants in front of 'Crest' to add fullness. 'Crest' is slow to set flower buds as a young plant, but once it becomes established, it will bud heavily. (Rothschild 1958) F.C.C. 1953.

'**Crete**' (*smirnowii* x *yakushimanum*). 4', -15ºF, M, 4/4-5/4. Magenta-rose buds open to very light purple with just a few light spots. With age, the flowers gradually fade to white. The blooms are held in a very tight dome shaped truss. Leaves are a blend of the two parents, displaying a soft beige indumentum. (B. Lancaster hyb., Leach intro., reg. 1982).

'**Cricket**' ('Britannia' x *yakushimanum* 'Koichiro Wada'). 3', -5ºF, M, 4/4/4. Rosy pink buds open to lighter pink encircled by silvery new leaves which mature to dark green with a hint of indumentum. (Elliott).

'**Crimson Glory**' (parentage unknown). 5', -10ºF, ML, 3/3/3. A hybrid that originated at Cottage Gardens in Eureka, California, probably in 1950 or earlier. The crimson red flowers are long lasting and are produced in great quantities on top of the dark fir green leaves. A good dependable rhododendron that is hardy for the more adverse areas. At one time this was known as #113. (Cottage Gardens not registered).

'**Crimson Pippin**' (*yakushimanum* x *sanguineum* ssp. *haemaleum*). 2', -10ºF, M, 5/4/3. Silver indumentum is but one beautiful aspect of this plant. Flowers of bright currant red are held in trusses of 10. (Larson 1983).

'**Crossbill**' (*spinuliferum* x *lutescens*). 3', 5ºF, E, -/-/-. "Different" is the word to describe this plant. Flowers display soft combinations of yellow and apricot with hints of peach. The new foliage is red. Plant habit is much like *lutescens*. (J. C. Williams 1933).

'**Crossroads**' (*strigillosum* hybrid). 5', 0ºF, EM, 4/3-4/3-4. The cardinal red flowers are shaped from intricate folds of moisture-rich tissue. Midveins of the narrow leaves are woolly with thick, coarse hair bristles, as are the plant stems. Under the leaves there is a light coating of indumentum. A beautiful flower and plant. (Larson).

'**Cunningham's Blush**' (probably *caucasicum* x *ponticum* var. *album*). 4', -15ºF, ML, 2/3/4. Although not given a high rating for the flower, this old hybrid is consistently a good grower and bloomer. The habit is tight and rounded. Very light pink flowers are kissed with a yellow-pink blotch on the upper lobe. (Cunningham in the mid 1800's).

'**Cunningham's Sulphur**' (parentage uncertain, probably *caucasicum*). 3', -5ºF, VE-E, 2/3/3. Growth habit is compact, full and cylindrical. Foliage is glossy and medium sized. Small, pale yellow blossoms form spherical trusses of up to 15. (Cunningham in the 1800's).

'**Cunningham's White**' (*caucasium* x *ponticum* var. *album*). 4', -15ºF, ML, 2/3/4. An attractive compact plant with small white flowers enhanced by a greenish yellow blotch. These lovely and numerous flowers open from buds which are flushed with pink. The plant will tolerate sunny locations. Very often it flowers in the autumn. More tolerant of alkaline conditions than most rhododendrons, it is frequently used as a root stock for other rhododendrons in Europe. (Cunningham 1850).

'**Cupcake**' (*yakushimanum* x 'Medusa'). 3', -5ºF, ML, 4/4/3. Orange-apricot blended flowers cover this wonderful hybrid. Small, dark green leaves with thick brown indumentum completely hide its stems. Dense growing and heavy flowering, it is a joy in the garden. It will frequently flower in the autumn, but has enough buds to still flower heavily in spring. (Thompson 1990).

'**Cupday**' ('Albatross' x 'Fusilier'). Fragrant, rosy flowers are heavily spotted on all lobes. Foliage is slender and dark green. (K. Van de Ven, Australia, reg. 1965).

'**Cupie**' (parentage unknown). 1', -5ºF, EM-M, -/-/-. A low-growing, evergreen dwarf that is well suited as a groundcover. Large, open, lavender flowers provide spring interest, and the foliage takes on a burgundy-wine color in fall. (Winkler).

'**Curlew**' (*ludlowii* x *fletcheranum*). 18", -5ºF, EM, 4-5/4-5/3-4. Large, beautiful, bright yellow flowers bounce amid tiny shamrock green leaves. A growing note for 'Curlew's care: fertilize sparingly and provide excellent drainage. (Cox 1969) F.C.C. 1969.

'**Cutie**' (*calostrotum* hybrid). 3', -15ºF, M, 3/3/4. Growth habit is upright and rounded, usually more tall than wide. Leaves are quite small, 1" x 1/2", and have a slight coating of tan indumentum on the undersides. Large numbers of small, pink flowers with a lilac tint are produced. Gets rust easily. Synonym, 'Calostrotum Rose'. (Grieg, Larson 1961) P.A. 1959, A.E. 1962.

'**Cynosure**' ('Essex Scarlet' x *fortunei* ssp. *fortunei*). 6', 0ºF, M, -/-/-. A strong growing plant. The purplish buds open to sizable pink flowers that have a dark eye and a center that pales to white. (Shapiro reg. 1993).

'**Cynthia**' (*catawbiense* x *griffithianum*). 6', -15ºF, M, 4/3/4. An old favorite which is still one of the best for a strong growing background plant. It produces a bounty of large, conical, rosy crimson trusses. Sun and heat tolerant. (Standish & Noble before 1870).

'**Cyprus**' ('Mrs. Furnivall' x *catawbiense* var. *album*). 3', -20ºF, ML, 4/3-4/4. Flowers are white with a conspicuous, light bronze blotch inside. They form large, ball shaped trusses. Plant configuration is excellent as it stays a nice mounded shape, slightly more wide than tall. Synonym, 'Capri'. (Leach intro. 1973, reg. 1983.) C.A. 1982, A.E. 1983.

'**Dad's Indian Summer**' ('Ring of Fire' x 'Pink Petticoats'). 5', 0ºF, M, 4-5/4/4. Warm orange flowers with reddish orange edges and yellow centers are gathered into many-flowered trusses which suggest the warmth of a long "Indian summer". 'Pink Petticoats' gives it abundant flowers in each truss, and 'Ring of Fire' gives it dynamic flower color. Medium sized, smooth green foliage creates this plant an attractive appearance all year. This valuable plant has excellent growth habit, strong stems and good roots - a winning combination! (Willard Thompson hyb. about 1985, Thompson Nursery intro. 1996).

'**Dagmar**' (*decorum* x 'Pink Pearl'). 5', -15ºF, M, -/-/-. This Czechoslovakian introduction bears ruffled flowers that are light, purplish pink with green and yellow spotting inside, accented by a gleaming gold throat. (Kavka).

'**Dainty Jean**' (*williamsianum* x 'Helene Schiffner'). 1', 0ºF, ML, -/-/-. Leaves are on the small side. Flowers are flat and ruffled, about 3" across, white flushed pink on the back, held in a loose truss of about 6 flowers. (Bovee 1972).

'**Dainty Maiden**' (*yakushimanum* x 'Dainty'). 2', -5ºF?, M, -/-/-. A compact plant with dark green foliage having the indumentum characteristic of *yakushimanum* crosses. The large, bright pink trusses fare well in both sun and shade. (Riverwood Gardens 1995).

'**Dairymaid**' (*campylocarpum* x unknown). 3', -10ºF, EM, 3/4/3. Light yellow flowers have red spotting in the throat. This plant will perform best in a shaded location. (Slocock 1930) A.M. 1934.

'**Daisy Mae**' ('Mrs. Horace Fogg' x 'Argosy'). 4', 5ºF, ML, -/-/-. Fragrant, bright pink flowers give summer highlight to the attractive matte green leaves. (Unknown).

'**Dalkeith**' (chance seedling, possible natural hybrid from *pemakoense* or similar species). 30", 0ºF, E-EM, 4/4/-. This low growing hybrid from New Zealand is covered with small, deep green leaves and masses of lilac-rose flowers. (McLaughlin 1966, Warren reg. 1977).

'**Damaris**' ('Dr. Stocker' x *campylocarpum*). 4', 5ºF, M, 4/3/3. Springtime brings sunny yellow flowers and shiny new leaves. (Magor 1926).

'**Dame Nellie Melba**' ('Standishii' x *arboreum*). 6', 0ºF, E-EM, 3-4/4/4. The growth habit is upright and vigorous, with medium to large, shiny dark green leaves. Generous sized flowers are bright pink, speckled crimson-pink, and are held in large, rounded, upright trusses. (Loder) A.M. 1926.

'**Damozel**' (A. W. (bright rose?) x *griersonianum*). 6', 5ºF, ML, 4/2/4-5. Long and narrow dark green leaves decorate an open, spreading plant. Flowers, about 2 1/2" wide, are brilliant red with darker spotting, held in an upright truss. Vigorous, easy to grow plant that is easily rooted. (Rothschild 1936) A.M. 1948.

'**Daniela**' ('Nachtglut' x ['Mars' x *yakushimanum* 'Koichiro Wada']). 3', -15º, M, -/-/-. The *yakushimanum* influence is evident in this compact plant's silvery new growth and dark green foliage clothed in indumentum. The salmon rose flowers are accented with a white blotch and appear in large, rounded trusses on this plant which obtains a form nearly twice as wide as tall. (Hachmann 1969, Stuck reg. 1988).

'**Dan Laxdall**' ('Elizabeth' x 'Mrs. G. W. Leak'). 3', 0ºF, ML, -/-/-. Foliage is medium sized. Flowers, up to 10 per truss, are rose colored, with deeper tint in throat, running up center of lobes in narrow stripes. (Laxdall 1976).

'**Dan's Early Purple**' (*ponticum* hybrid). 5', 0ºF, E-EM, 3/3/4. The earliest large leaved purple, this plant looks much like many of the later flowering R. *ponticum* hybrids but blooms much earlier than the rest. Like the other R. *ponticum* hybrids, it has good foliage and is vigorous. (Dan Bones).

'**Daphne Jewiss**' (*oreotrephes* x *davidsonianum*). 5', -10ºF, M, -/-/-. Soft pink blooms in tight trusses on an upright plant. A prolific producer of fantastic flowers. (Reuthe).

'**Daphnoides**' (*ponticum* selection or cross). 4', -15ºF, ML, 2-3/4/4. Foliage unlike any other rhododendron. Rolled, glossy leaves are tightly spaced on the stems of this dense mound. This great looking plant enhances any garden with its unusual, deep green leaves. Small, pom-pom trusses are deep purple. The plant under this name in the RHS registry is a said to be a R. *virgatum* hybrid, which this plant is NOT. There is little question that' the plant described here is variant of R. *ponticum*. (T. Methven 1868).

'**Darigold**' ([*wardii* x 'Medusa']) x 'Autumn Gold'). 4', 0ºF, M, -/-/-. This unregistered Whitney hybrid has orange-cream flowers. (Whitney).

'**Darren Mckay**' ('Dexter's Giant Red' x 'Vulcan's Flame'). 5', -15ºF, M, -/-/-. First to appear on this dense plant is the red tinged new growth. Dark buds soon follow, opening to deep pink flowers with an orange flare. (Betty Hager hyb., selected by Jane Mckay).

'**David**' ('Hugh Koster' x *neriiflorum*). 6', 5ºF, EM, 4/3/4. A very upright, somewhat compact plant with medium sized dark green leaves. Bell shaped flowers are rich blood red, held in tall trusses. (Swaythling 1930's) F.C.C. 1939, A.M. 1957.

'**David Forsythe**' (*catawbiense* var. *compactum* x 'Mars'). 4', -20ºF, ML, 4/3/3-4. Very deep scarlet flowers are abundant on this cold hardy red. Nice, slender dark green leaves. (Baldanza reg. 1972).

'**David Gable**' ('Atrosanguineum' x *fortunei* ssp. *fortunei*). 5', -15ºF, EM-M, 4/4/3-4. Long and narrow, medium green foliage on a fairly dense growing plant. Large flowers, pink with a red throat compose well-set, dome shaped trusses. Prolific bloomer. Synonym, 'Gable's Pink No. 1'. (Gable 1962) A.E. 1960.

'**Dawn's Delight**' (*griffithianum* hybrid). 5', 5ºF, ML, 3/3/3-4. Darkish green leaves support flowers of pale pink, flushed with rose pink. A brilliant crimson base and light red spotting in the upper corolla accent the blooms which are carried in tall, open, mid-sized trusses. (Mangles early 1900's) A.M. 1911.

'**Day Dream, Biscuit form**' ('Lady Bessborough' x *griersonianum*). 5', 5ºF, ML, 3/3/3. A wide, open growth habit is covered with light green, medium to large sized narrow leaves. Flowers are vibrant orange-pink, orange red in the throat, and are held in rounded, loose, mid-sized trusses. Outer part of the corolla fades to biscuit color. There is also a red form. (Rothschild) A.M. 1940.

'**Dazzler**' (contains *dichroanthum*, *griersonianum* and probably other species). 4', 5ºF, EM, -/-/-. Growth habit is upright when young, spreading with maturity, supporting dark olive green leaves and truly dazzling flowers. The plentiful blooms are salmon orange and have a wide funnel shape. (J. Elliott).

'**Debbie**' ('May Day' x 'Carmen'). 2', 0ºF, EM, 3/4/4. One of the most attractive plants, this hybrid is round and compact growing and dense with dark fir green foliage. Flower buds completely cover this plant during the winter and appear to be impatiently anticipating spring. When spring finally arrives, 'Debbie' bursts into a solid mass of bright blood red. (J. Henny & Wennekap 1963).

'**Debijo**' (*minus* var. *minus* Carolinianum Group x *saluenense*). 2', -15ºF, EM, 3/3/3. A cute little plant with lavender-purple flowers held in trusses of up to eight blooms. An upright grower. (Caperci 1965).

'**Delaware**' (*pubescens* x *keiskei*). 3', -10ºF, EM, 3/2/-. Leaves and flowers are small. The blossoms are apricot, fading to white. (Nearing 1958).

'**Delicatissimum**' (*catawbiense* hybrid). 6', -10ºF?, ML, -/-/-. A vigorous growing hybrid with a full and bushy habit. White flowers have a prominent yellow flare. (J. Waterer before 1851).

'**Delitissimo**' ('Vulcan' x 'Autumn Gold'). 3', -5ºF, EM, -/-/-. Attractive foliage densely covers this pleasing, compact plant. Pink flowers open from darker buds to expose intriguing spotting on the dorsal lobe. (Lansing Bulgin).

'Delp's Cindy Lou' see 'Cindy Lou'.

'Delp's Dream' ('Si Si' x 'Serendipity'). 3', -10ºF?, L, -/-/-. Trusses hold 8 pale greenish yellow flowers above foliage with tan, woolly indumentum. (Delp 1992).

'Delp's Quest' ([{brachycarpum x 'Crest'} x 'Stokes Bronze Wings'] x 'Goldsworth Yellow'). 3', -10ºF?, L, -/-/-. Delicate yellow flowers with bright orange spots are held in trusses of 12. Foliage is medium green. (Delp 1992).

'Delta' (A selection of *catawbiense*). 6', -15ºF, ML-L, -/-/-. A vigorous growing plant which produces many large blue-mauve flowers, similar to the 'Catawbiense Grandiflorum'. Attractive dark green foliage. (Fa. Boot & Co., Boskoop).

'Deming Brook' (*keiskei* 'Yaku Fairy' open pollinated). 1', -20ºF, EM, 4/4/4. White flowers with a slight pink accent are borne in clusters on this dense, mounding, very compact plant. An excellent rock garden accent plant. (Linc Foster).

'Denali' ('Vanessa Pastel' x 'Pink Walloper'). 6', -5ºF, M, 4/4/4. Gigantic trusses of rose pink flowers bloom on this dense, deep green plant. Strong growing and somewhat sun tolerant, it makes an attractive, desirable plant all year. (Jim Elliott 1984).

'Deserie' (unknown parentage). 3-4', 5ºF, EM, -/-/-. Foliage is rounded and glossy, creating a lovely background for the delicate lavender pink flowers in spring. (sold by Hammond Nursery).

'Desert Gold' ('Darigold' x 'Idealist'). 5', 0ºF, M, 4-5/4/4. Huge, beautiful, deep golden flowers cover this delightful plant. Each luscious yellow is accented with a small amount of red in the throat. The medium sized, heavy textured foliage is lovely olive green. This well shaped, strong branched plant is vigorous and upright. (Thompson 1988).

'Desmit' (*ferrugineum* x *minus* var. *minus* Carolinianum Group). 2', -15ºF, M, 4/4/-. Little pink balls of the *carolinianum* flowers, and deep green foliage grace this nice, hardy plant. (Ticknor).

'Devonshire Cream' (*campylocarpum* hybrid). 3', 0ºF, EM, 3/4/3. Compact, mounding, and very slow growing, this pretty plant has cream yellow flowers held in tight, ball shaped trusses. It will grow to be 3-4' high, having an equal width. (W.C. Slocock about 1924) A.M. 1940.

'Devonshire Tea' ('Bowbells' hybrid). 3', 5?ºF, ML, -/-/-. An upright growth habit, with shiny rounded foliage, supports large cream colored trusses of long lasting blooms that have a strawberry pink eye. (Riverwood Gardens 1995).

'Dexter's Appleblossom' (unknown, probably contains *fortunei* ssp. *fortunei*). 6', 0ºF, ML, 3/3/4. Foliage is large. Fragrant 6-lobed, 3" flowers are white with pink edge, blotched and spotted yellowish green, and are held in flat trusses of about 15. Synonym, DE #631. (Dexter, Cowles, Heritage Plantation 1978).

'Dexter's Apricot' (parentage unknown). 6', 0ºF, ML, 4/3-4/3-4. Fragrant 6-lobed flowers, 4" across, are pink with darker edges and a yellow green central blotch, and are carried in flat trusses of about 15. Large foliage. Synonym, DE #225. (Dexter, Cowles, Heritage Plantation 1978).

'Dexter's Brandy-Green' (parentage unknown). 6', 0ºF, ML, -/-/-.Fragrant flowers are 4" wide, 6-lobed, and pink, heavily spotted with green on top lobes, and are held in flat trusses of up to 8. Large leaves complement the lovely flowers. Synonym, DE #491. (Dexter, Cowles, Heritage Plantation 1978).

'Dexter's Brick Red' (parentage unknown). 3', 0ºF, ML, -/-/-. Leaves are medium sized. Flowers, about 3 1/2" across, 7-lobed, are pink with red blotch on the top 3 lobes, in lax trusses of up to 12. Synonym, DE #427. (Dexter, Cowles, Heritage Plantation 1978).

'Dexter's Champagne' (parentage unknown). 4', -15ºF, M, 4/3/3. Flowers are pastel hues of buff mixed with pink and apricot on a white background. Somewhat glossy foliage is an unusual bronze-green. (Dexter, N.Y. Botanical Garden, Westbury Rose Co. 1958).

'Dexter's Count Vitetti' (believed to be a *fortunei* ssp. *fortunei* hybrid). 5', -15ºF, M, -/-/-. This plant has a spreading habit and full trusses of lavender flowers. Prefers shade. (Dexter).

'Dexter's Cream' (parentage unknown). 3', 0ºF, ML, -/-/-. Foliage is medium sized. Fragrant 6-lobed flowers, 3 1/2" wide, are cream colored, shaded pink with a pale yellow blotch and stripes, and are carried in lax trusses of about 8. Synonym, DE #437. (Dexter, Cowles, Heritage Plantation 1978).

'Dexter's Crown Pink' (parentage unknown). 6', 0ºF, L, -/-/-. Large leaves provide the background for 6-lobed flowers, in a medium sized truss of up to 10 flowers, that are pink with an olive green blotch. Synonym, DE #600. (Dexter, Cowles, Heritage Plantation 1977).

'Dexter's Giant Red' (parentage unknown). 6', 0ºF, L, 4/3-4/4. Foliage is large. Flowers, 4" wide, are pink with a blotch of dark red in the throat, spotted red over the whole corolla, and are held in large trusses of up to 15. Synonym, DE #431, 'Dexter's Big Red'. (Dexter, Cowles, Heritage Plantation 1978).

'Dexter's Glow' (parentage unknown). 6', 0ºF, L, -/-/-. Somewhat fragrant flowers, 3 1/2" wide, are vibrant pink shading lighter in throat, with a dark red ring around the corolla base, and are carried in a lax truss of up to 10. Medium leaves provide the perfect contrast. Synonym, DE #317. (Dexter, Cowles, Heritage Plantation 1978).

'Dexter's Harlequin' ('Pygmalion' x [*haematodes* x 'Wellfleet'] exact combination of parentage is unknown). 5', -5ºF, M, 4/3/-. A good plant habit, covered with glossy, olive green foliage. Rounded trusses hold bicolor flowers, deep pink along the wavy margins, paling to a nearly white center. The funnel shape is accented by dorsal rays of dark, purplish red. (Dexter, Vossberg, Tyler Arboretum, 1983).

'Dexter's Horizon' (parentage unknown). 5', 0ºF, L, -/-/-. Foliage is large. Two-toned 6-lobed flowers, are white in the center, with yellowish green blotch, edged deep pink. The blooms, up to 3 1/2" across, are held in a ball shaped truss of up to 12. Synonym, DE #480. (Dexter, Cowles, Heritage Plantation 1977).

'Dexter's Orange' (parentage unknown, may be *haematodes* hybrid). 3', -5ºF, M, -/-/-. A low and spreading plant blooming profusely with lax trusses of 8. The flowers are deep pink and orange with a brownish orange blotch. The plant is densely covered with small, glossy foliage. (Heritage Plantation 1977).

'Dexter's Orchid' (parentage unknown). 4', -15ºF, M, -/-/-. A compact plant with beautiful orchid colored blossoms. (Dexter).

'Dexter's Peppermint' (parentage unknown, possibly a *decorum* hybrid). 5', -5ºF, ML, -/-/-. Superbly fragrant light purplish pink flowers have a blotch of light yellowish green. (Heritage Plantation 1977).

'Dexter's Pink Glory' (parentage unknown). 6', 0ºF, L, -/-/-. Leaves are large. Fragrant, 6-lobed flowers, also large, up to 4 1/2" wide, are intense pink with yellow, green, and red blended spotting over the center, and are carried in a flat truss of up to 8. Synonym, DE #219. (Dexter, Cowles, Heritage Plantation 1977).

'Dexter's Spice' (parentage unknown). 6', 0ºF, L, -/-/-. Foliage is medium to large. Fragrant flowers, 7-lobed, are white, pale yellowish green spotting in the throat. The 5" blooms are held in group of 7 to form a lax truss. Synonym, DE #968. (Dexter, Cowles, Heritage Plantation 1977).

'Dexter's Springtime' (parentage unknown). 3', 0ºF, L, -/-/-. Fragrant, bicolor flowers with 6 lobes, are cream edged deep pink, with red-brown rays of spots in the throat. The blooms, to 3 1/2" wide, form flat trusses in groups of 10. Leaves are medium to large. Synonym, DE #314. (Dexter, Cowles, Heritage Plantation 1977).

'Dexter's Vanilla' (parentage unknown). 3', 0ºF, ML, -/-/-. Foliage is medium large. Scented, 7-lobed flowers are creamy white with deep pink edges and veins, and a smallish red-brown blotch. The 3 1/2" blooms are held in 8-flower lax trusses. Synonym, DE #997. (Dexter, Cowles, Heritage Plantation 1977).

'Dexter's Victoria' (catawbiense x smirnowii). 6', 0ºF, L, -/-/-. 3" flowers, deep pink with large greenish brown patch, carried in a 15 flower truss, complement the medium sized foliage. Synonym, DE #441. (Dexter, Cowles, Heritage Plantation 1977).

'Diana' ('Goldsworth Orange' x 'Prof. J. H. Zaayer'). 4', -5ºF, ML, -/-/-. This plant forms a lush mound of dense, dark green foliage. Lovely blooms of salmon-orange are accented with a yellow eye. (Bruns).

'Diane' ('Mrs. Lindsay Smith' x campylocarpum hybrid). 4', -5ºF, EM, 3/2/2-3. Planted in humus rich soil, with sunshine filtering through a tree canopy, 'Diane' has rich emerald green leaves and trusses of cream flowers. (M. Koster & Sons 1920) A.M. 1948.

'Diane Titcomb' ('Marinus Koster' x 'Snow Queen'). 5', -5ºF, M, 4-5/3-4/3-4. Absolutely huge white flowers with pink edging form trusses so perfect that it is hard to resist picking them. Large foliage adds to the desirability of this variety. (Larson 1958) P.A. 1958.

'Dido' (dichroanthum x decorum). 3', 5ºF, ML, 3/4/3. 'Dido' has a compact habit shaped by sturdy stems with bright, colorful, stiff rounded leaves. Orange flowers with yellow at the centers complete the picture.(Wilding 1934).

'Diny Dee' ('Mrs. Lammot Copeland' x deep yellow hybrid). 3', 0ºF, M, 4/4/4. Lemon yellow flowers appear from bright orange-red buds in mid-season. Very compact and neat in appearance. (Larson 1969, Davis intro. 1982, reg. 1986).

'Disca' (fortunei ssp. discolor x 'Caroline'). 6', -10ºF, ML, 3/3/4. This hybrid is probably better than its rating, because it is a vigorous grower with a good plant habit. Scented flowers are white with a tinge of pink and have frilled edges, appearing in large domed trusses. The foliage has better green coloration if it is grown in light shade. (Gable 1958).

'Diva g.' ('Ladybird' x griersonianum). 6', 0ºF, ML, 3/2/3. Long narrow leaves are medium, dull green. Vivid orange-pink flowers are carried in a medium sized, cylindrical, open truss. Growth is fairly open and leggy. Note: The "g." behind the name stands for grex which means all the seedlings out of the cross are named 'Diva'. (Rothschild 1937) A.M. 1937.

'Dixy Lee Ray' ('Zuiderzee' x 'Naomi Pink Beauty'). 6', 10ºF, EM, 3-4/3-4/3-4. Foliage is medium to large. 7-lobed flowers, quite large, to 4 1/2" wide, are orchid pink with slight red spotting and a white, star shaped throat. Trusses have up to 17 flowers. (Larson 1979).

'Doc' (yakushimanum x 'Corona'). 3', -15ºF, M, 4/4/4. Another of the dwarf series, this hybrid has rose pink flowers with deeper shading on the margins. A medium sized plant with compact growth habit. (Waterer, Sons & Crisp 1972).

'Doctor Richard Anderson' ('Else Frye' x johnstoneanum). 3', 15ºF, E, 4-5/3/3-4. Medium sized leaves provide the basis for large, scented flowers, to 4 1/4" across, white with blushed pink edges and an orange blotch, carried in 6-flowered trusses. (Anderson, Braafladt 1979).

'Doctor Tom Ring' ('Fireman Jeff' x 'Anna Delp'). 4', -5ºF?, L, -/-/-. Strong red buds open to vivid red hose-in-hose flowers. (Ring, Delp 1993).

'Dolly Madison' (catawbiense var. album x [fortunei ssp. fortunei x {arboreum x griffithianum}]). 5', -20ºF, M, 4/4/4. Large foliage and white flowers, to 3 1/4" across, distinguish this plant. Flowers are held in trusses of up to 13 flowers. (Leach 1972).

'Doncaster' (arboreum hybrid). 3', -5ºF, M-ML, 2/3/3. The flowers on this old stand-by are crimson scarlet setting off the dark green leaves. Of medium vigor, this plant is, however, easy to grow. Stands heat. (A. Waterer before 1900).

'Donna Hardgrove' (fortunei ssp. fortunei x [wardii x dichroanthum]). 3', -5ºF, ML, -/-/-. Flowers, 2 1/2" wide, are apricot pink, flushed yellow, held in trusses of up to 8 flowers. (Hardgrove, Burns 1978).

'Donna's Day' (unknown). 6', -15ºF, L, -/-/-. A hardy plant with red flowers that are brighter than the blue-red of 'Nova Zembla'. (Moniz, Richardson about 1990).

'Donna Totten' (probably a racemosum hybrid). 4', -5ºF, EM, 3-4/3-4/3-4. Very pretty, pink flowers, tinged with cream. The attractive foliage is about the same size as racemosum. This plant originated in the Eastern United States; therefore, it may be hardier than rated. (Nearing).

'Dopey' ([eriogynum hybrid x 'Fabia'] x [yakushimanum x 'Fabia Tangerine']). 3', 5ºF, M, 4-5/4/4. An upright, compact plant that is very free flowering. Glossy red flowers fade toward the margins. (Waterer, Sons & Crisp 1971) A.M. 1977.

'Dora Amateis' (minus var. minus Carolinianum Group x ciliatum). 3', -15ºF, EM, 4/4/4. Pure white flowers cling to this low growing bushy plant, which is becoming a favorite of many people. Its deep green, dense foliage is highlighted with bronze tones and is prettiest when grown in full sun. This spicy scented hybrid is planted as a low border and as a small mass planting to bring attention to its pretty foliage. (Amateis 1958) A.E., A.M. 1976.

'Doris Bigler' (advanced generation hybrid including catawbiense and maximum). 6', -15ºF, M, -/-/-. Foliage is medium sized. Smallish flowers, 2" across, are light purple, edged darker reddish purple, with a yellow blotch and are carried in 17-flowered ball shaped trusses. (W. Smith 1979).

'Doris Caroline' ('Loderi' x 'Lady Bligh'). 5', -5ºF, M, -/-/-. A large growing plant with extremely large leaves and a very upright habit. Flowers are rose colored. (R. Henny reg. 1961) P.A. 1960.

'Dormouse' ('Dawn's Delight' x williamsianum). 3', 0ºF, EM, 3/4/3-4. Looking like a 4' ball of cheerful round leaves, 'Dormouse' is always pretty. Light pink, bell shaped flowers are cheerful. (Rothschild 1936).

'Glory of Littleworth'

R. 'Martha Issacson'

R. 'Fragrans'

R. 'Odoratum'

R. 'Martine'

Hybrids ~ Azaleodendrons
& Other unusual rhododendron hybrids

'Oregon Queen'

Ledudendrons   Note: The Genus Ledium is now merged with the Genus Rhododendron

R. 'Arctic Tern'

R. 'Brilliant'   (This has also been known as Ledudendron 'Brilliant')

R. 'Pioneer'

Hybrids ~

Early Blooming

R. 'Tessa Bianca'

R. 'Praecox'

R. 'Lee's Scarlet'

R. 'Olive'

R. 'Christmas Chee

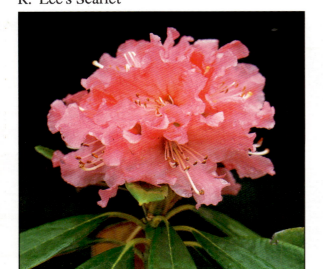

'Lodauric Iceburg'

R. 'Midsummer'

R. 'Aladdin'

Hybrids ~ Late Blooming

'Goldsworth Orange'   R. 'Polar Bear'   R. 'Madame Jules Porges'

R. 'Good News'

R. 'Betty Arrington'

R. 'Tiffany'

R. 'Madame Guillemont'

R. 'Bruce Brechtbill'

Hybrids ~ Pink Flowering

R. 'Sausalito'

R. 'Cotton Candy'

R. 'Countess of Derby'

R. 'Queen Mary'

R. 'Pioneer Silvery Pink'
(lepidote hybrid)

'Dorothy Amateis' ('America' x 'Purple Splendour'). 5', -15ºF, ML, 4/2-3/3. A new purple that is hardy to all but the most severe climates. The large trusses are deep purple with a deeper purple eye. This plant shows the influence of 'Purple Splendour', but it gained its hardiness from 'America'. The leaves are matte olive green and are held in an upright position, making a vigorous looking plant. If you are love purple, you'll like this one. (Amateis, Baldsiefen 1971).

'Dorothy Ella' (*nuttallii* hybrid). 4', 20ºF, ML, 5/4/3. Large, fragrant flowers are held in trusses displaying colors of light pink, cream and white. The heavily veined leaves cover a very upright growing plant that takes well to pruning. (sold by Riverwood Gardens, New Zealand).

'Dorothy Peste Anderson' ('Vincent van Gogh' x 'Loderi King George'). 4', 5ºF, ML, -/-/-. Jade green leaves, 8" in length, cover this plant which grows as wide as tall. Fragrant, cone shaped blooms are held in tight trusses of 24. The light pink of the flower is accented with a darker edge. (Peste hyb. 1975, Sather reg. 1985).

'Dorothy Robbins' (*campylocarpum* x 'Margaret Dunn'). 3', 0ºF, M, 4/4/3. This nice round plant has beautiful pink buds that gradually open to yellow flowers, edged light pink, with a deep red center in the throat. (Brandt 1970).

'Dorothy Russell' ('Pygmalion' x *haematodes* x 'Wellfleet'). 5', -5ºF, M, 3/3/4. A rounded plant with glossy foliage. Large flowers are rose red with darker spotting inside. (Dexter, Schwoebel Nursery, Briarwood Gardens reg. 1989).

'Dorothy Swift' (*smirnowii* x *yakushimanum*). 2', -20ºF, M-ML, 4-5/5/4. Both parents exhibit positive influence over little 'Dorothy'. A compact plant displaying silvery new growth which rises above leaves that are dark green above and sueded with beige indumentum below. This plant is covered with free flowering pink buds that open to expose large white flowers. (Mehlquist 1994).

'Dot' ('Mrs. Lindsay Smith' x *fortunei* ssp. *fortunei*). 5', -5ºF, M, 4/3/3-4. One of the better large growing white rhododendrons, this one received an award of merit. Habit is upright and open, with impressive looking large trusses composed of large flowers with an unusual satiny texture. (Swaythling 1945) A.M. 1945.

'Double Date' (parentage unknown). 5-6', -5ºF, M, 4/3/4. Double rose pink flowers grace this heavily foliated, medium sized plant. This Whitney hybrid was formerly known as 'Whitney Pink Double'. (Whitney, Sather, Griswold 1975).

'Double Dip' ('Catalgla' x *yakushimanum* 'Koichiro Wada'). 4', -25ºF, M, 4/4/-. Pink buds open to reveal white flowers. A compact plant with thinly indumented foliage. (J. Gable before 1960).

'Double Winner' (*strigillosum* hybrid). 5' 0ºF, EM, 4/4/4. A long blooming variety that opens a few buds at a time. Long foliage with a light indumentum, and bright red flowers in tight trusses distinguish this hybrid. (Larson).

'Doubloons' ('Moonstone' x 'Carolyn Grace'). 4', -5ºF, EM, 3/4/3. This is a nicely shaped, mid-sized plant with oval leaves up to 3" long. Bell shaped flowers are light creamy yellow, and are held in numerous trusses of 7-8 flowers. (Wright Sr. & Jr. 1963).

'Douglas McEwan' (*griffithianum* hybrid x 'Monsieur Thiers'). 6', 0ºF, M, 3/3/3. Large, open trusses of rosy pink flowers decorate this large plant. (van Nes & Sons before 1938).

'Douglas R. Stephens' ('Jean Marie de Montague' x unnamed white hybrid). 4', -10ºF, EM-M, 4/4/4. Strong rose red flowers with even deeper coloring in the throat and scattered spotting on the upper lobes complement large, glossy, deep green foliage. (Stephens 1973).

'Dover Rose' ('Dido' x 'Chlorops'). 5', 0ºF, ML, -/-/-. Peachy pink flowers are composed of 5 lobes with ruffled edges, and are borne in lax trusses of 10 on this statuesque and beautiful plant. (M. Stewart 1987).

'Dr. A. Blok' ('Pink Pearl' x *catawbiense* hybrid). 6', -5ºF, M, 3/3/3-4. There are numerous pink rhododendrons, but this is still the favorite of many. Large flowers are pink, lighter in the center, with a pale yellow marking on the upper petal. The very large leaves are matte palm green. This is frequently known as 'Dr. O. Blok'. (L. Endtz & Co. 1930's) A.M. 1937.

'Dragonfly' (*auriculatum* x *facetum*). 4', 0ºF, VL, -/-/-. This should be grown more often. In essence, it's a red R. *auriculatum*! Large leaves and large flowers cover this dense growing tree-like plant. (Rothschild 1936).

'Dreamland' (['Fabia' x *fortunei* ssp. *discolor* x *griersonianum* x *facetum* x *yakushimanum* x 'Jalisco'] exact combination of parentage is unknown). 4', -10ºF, M, -/-/-. A prolific bloomer with pale pink flowers bordered with deeper pink edges. Low and compact growing with attractive foliage. (Waterer, Sons & Crisp).

'Dr. Dresselhuys' ('Atrosanguineum' x 'Doncaster'). 6', -15ºF, ML, 2/3/3. An upright growing selection that produces many long lasting red blooms. (H. den Ouden 1920).

'Dr. Ernst Schale' ('Prometheus' x *forrestii* ssp. *forrestii* Repens Group). 2', -10ºF, M, 3/3-4/3. This low growing, compact plant is densely covered with dark, slightly twisted foliage. The light scarlet blooms are quite beautiful. (Hobbie 1966).

'Dr. Masters' ('Prince Camille de Rohan' x *japonicum*). 5', -15ºF, ML, 4/3/3. This is an azaleodendron which has a splendid salmon pink flower displaying a yellow tinge. One of the best of the azaleodendrons in flower. Foliage is best when grown in shade (G. Vander Meulen 1892).

'Dr. Stocker' (*caucasicum* x *griffithianum*). 5', 5ºF, EM, 3/2/3. Medium green large leaves are elliptical in shape. Open bell shaped, waxy flowers, 3" wide, are milky ivory-white, spotted lemon brown, and are held in well rounded 12-flower trusses. Growth habit upright and open. Easily rooted. (North before 1900) A.M. 1900.

'Dr. V. H. Rutgers' ('Charles Dickens' x 'Lord Roberts'). 5', -15ºF, ML, 3/3/3. The flowers of this hybrid are a bright aniline or crimson red, fringed and frilled. A wide growing plant that is densely covered with dark green leaves. (H. Den Ouden & Sons 1925).

'Duchess of York' (*fortunei* ssp. *fortunei* x 'Scipio'). 5', 5ºF, M, 3/3/3. Nicely fragrant, very large salmon pink flowers have a slight greenish spotting in the throat. Plant shape and foliage is similar to R. *fortunei*. (G. Paul) A.M. 1894.

'Duet' (*catawbiense* var. *album* x [{*dichroanthum* x *griffithianum*} x *auriculatum*]). 5', -25ºF, ML, 4/3/3. Great for that really cold climate, this hybrid has wonderful pale yellow flowers with pink edging, a green blotch, and spotting in the throat. (Leach 1960).

'Duke of York' (*fortunei* ssp. *fortunei* x 'Scipio'). 5', 5ºF, M, 3/3/3. Large, rosy pink, fragrant flowers have cream spotting in the throat. (G. Paul) A.M. 1894.

'Dupont's Apricot' ([catawbiense var. album x fortunei ssp. fortunei] x campylocarpum). 5', -5ºF, ML, -/-/-. Pink flowers have a lovely apricot blush. (Gable before 1960).

'Dusky Wood' (['Cavalcade' x 'Mary Swaythling'] x 'Hawk Crest'). 5', 5ºF, M, -/-/-. Rose pink flowers, flushed with red grow on this medium sized plant. (Waterer, Sons & Crisp 1975).

'Dusty Miller' (yakushimanum x unnamed hybrid). 3', 0ºF, M, -/-/-. Fairly dense plant habit has pale pink and cream flowers. (Waterer, Sons & Crisp 1975).

'Earlene' ('Shaazam' x yakushimanum 'Koichiro Wada'). 3', -15ºF, ML, -/-/-. Foliage is of medium size. Flowers, 2" wide, are salmon colored, claret rose on back, and are carried in ball shaped trusses of up to 14 flowers. (Yates, M. Yates 1977).

'Earl Murray' ('Kubla Khan' x 'Lem's Cameo'). 5', 0ºF, M, -/-/-. A vigorous growing plant with an upright and well branched growth habit. Foliage is matte green. Flowers, held in spherical trusses, are salmon-orange with wavy margins, paling toward the center. Has also been known as 'Cathy Harper'. (Murray).

'Earl of Athlone' ('Queen Wilhelmina' x 'Stanley Davies'). 5', 0ºF, EM, 5/2/2-3. This is an open growing plant with medium large dark green leaves. Bell shaped flowers are brilliant blood red, held in very fine, tight, dome shaped trusses. One of the very best red trusses. (C. B. van Nes & Son early 1900's) F.C.C. 1933.

'Earl of Donoughmore' (griersonianum x [hardy hybrid x 'Mrs. L. A. Dunnett']). 5', 5ºF, M, 3/3/3-4. Extremely vibrant red-orange flowers bloom profusely on this great plant. (M. Koster & Sons 1953).

'Early Accent' ([fortunei ssp. fortunei x griersonianum x 'Pygmalion'] exact combination unknown). 5', -5ºF, M, -/-/-. Large, rosy red blooms with deep purplish red spotting are held in lax trusses of 15. A vigorous and slightly open growth habit holds large, olive green leaves. (A. Consolini hyb., Tyler Arboretum reg. 1985).

'Earlybird' (williamsianum x oreodoxa var. fargesii). 3', -15ºF, E, -/-/-. Clusters of funnel shaped rose flowers fade to white in the throat. Small, rounded leaves are bright green and heavily textured. (Rudolph Henny 1960).

'Early Brilliant' ('Ascot Brilliant' x barbatum). 4', 0ºF, E, -/-/-. This plant flowers profusely early in the year with bright scarlet red trusses. Synonym, 'Fireball'. (W. C. Slocock).

'Easter Bells' (williamsianum x 'China'). 4', EM, 3/4/3. The flowers are very light pink, becoming white, and are held in somewhat lax, loose trusses. Foliage is medium sized. (Lancaster 1967).

'Easter Dawn' (minus var. minus x mucronulatum 'Pink Panther'). 7', -15ºF, E, -/-/-. A semi-deciduous variety that has brilliant red fall foliage, this plant boasts heat resistant flowers. Ball shaped trusses hold blooms that are strong reddish purple at the edges, fading to light purplish pink at the centers. (G. D. Lewis 1988).

'Easter Parade' ('Unique' x 'Crest'). 4', -5ºF, M, 4/4/3-4. Large, creamy yellow flowers and wonderful, rounded foliage make a very nice plant. (Fawcett).

'Ebony' (minus var. minus Carolinianum Group album x 'PJM'). 1', -10ºF, EM, 4/4/4. Smallish leaves turn to a glossy, rich maroon in winter on this little dwarf. Lilac to light purple flowers are set in trusses of up to 10. (Mezitt, Weston Nurseries 1979).

'Edeltraud' ('Hachmann's Ornament' x 'Furnivall's Daughter'). 4', 0ºF, ML, 4/4/-. Flowers of deep to moderate purplish pink with a conspicuous blotch of very deep red are held in dense trusses of 13-16. (Hachmann hyb. 1969, Stuck reg. 1988).

'Edith Bosley' ('Dexter's Bosley #1035' x 'Lee's Dark Purple'). 4', -25ºF, M, 4/3/3-4. A plant very similar to 'Purple Splendour' but hardier with larger blooms. The flowers, held in rounded trusses, are dark purple, accented by a darker eye. The growth habit is upright and well-branched with a generous amount of deep green leaves. (Bosley 1994).

'Edith Boulter' ('Marion' x 'Unique'). 4', -5ºF, E, 4/4/4. Frilled, dark margins surround lavender pink flowers. (Boulter 1962).

'Edith Pride' ('English Roseum' x maximum). 6', -25ºF, VL, 3/3/4. Leaves are medium to large. Flowers, 2" wide, are pink, spotted yellow, with a small white blotch, and are held in a large truss of up to 22. (Pride 1979).

'Edmond Amateis' (catawbiense var. album x Dexter seedling). 6', -15ºF, M, 4/4/4. Flowers, to 3 1/4", are white, with a strong dual-rayed red dorsal blotch, and are held in trusses of 13 flowers. (Amateis, Leach 1969).

'Edmondi' (arboreum x barbatum). 5', -5ºF, EM, 4/3/3. This very old hybrid has beautiful, elongated foliage and large blood red trusses. Quite a combination! (R. Gill 1876).

'Edmund de Rothschild' ('Fusilier' x 'Kilimanjaro'). 5', 10ºF?, ML, -/-/-. Deep maroon red flowers are held in trusses of 22 on this upright, vigorous plant. I have not had the opportunity to see this plant, but the man whose name it bears is an outstanding person with a dedication to an exceptional garden. The plant must be exceptional! I just wish 'Edmund de Rothschild's' parents were more cold hardy (I mean the plant, that is!), so it could be grown in a larger area of the world. (Rothschild 1969) A.M. 1968.

'Edna McCarty' ('Alice' x auriculatum). 6', -5ºF, L, 3/2-3/2-3. Foliage is large, with very large, fragrant white flowers. This is a sterile hybrid having no stamens. Synonym, 'Lily #3'. (Ostbo 1962) P.A. 1959.

'Edward Dunn' ([neriiflorum x dichroanthum] x fortunei ssp. discolor). 5', -5ºF, L-VL, 4/3/2-3. Attractive moss green leaves adorn this wide spreading rhododendron. Among the orange-yellow blooming rhododendrons, this is one of the best. Great because it flowers so late. (Ostbo 1958) P.A. 1958.

'Edward S. Rand' (catawbiense hybrid). 6', -15ºF, ML, 2/3/2-3. Plant habit is compact with yellowish green foliage. Flowers are crimson red, with a distinctive bronze-yellow eye. Not easily rooted. (A. Waterer 1870).

'Edwin O. Weber' ('Purpureum Elegans' x 'Madame Albert Moser'). 6', -5ºF, ML, 3-4/4/4. Flowers, to 3 1/2" wide, are royal purple, with a large uranium green blotch, and are held in large trusses of up to 28 flowers. Large foliage. (Weber 1974).

'Edwin Parker' ('Day Dream' x 'Albatross'). 6', 5ºF, L, -/-/-. Flat, 4 1/2" wide flowers, peach-pink with cream center, are carried in 16-flower trusses. Leaves are medium to large. (R. Henny, L. Henny 1968).

'Egret' (campylogynum white x racemosum 'White Lace'). 2', -5ºF, E-EM, 4/4/4. You have to look twice to see that this is a rhododendron. Each terminal is covered with dainty little dangling white bells. Very appealing. (Cox 1982) A.M. 1982, H.C. (Wisley Trials) 1983.

'**Ehrengold'** ([astrocalyx] *wardii* var. *wardii* hybrid). 4', -10ºF, ML, -/-/-. Rose buds open to rounded trusses of pale, creamy yellow long-lasting flowers. The upright habit is clothed in glossy, recurved foliage. (Hobbie 1950-53).

'**Eider'** (*minus* var. *minus* Carolinianum Group *album* x *leucaspis*). 18", -5ºF, E-EM, 4/4/4. Flowers are compact little balls of snow highlighted by dark anthers on a great, tight plant with spreading habit. (Cox) H.C. 1979, A.M. 1981.

'**Eileen'** (unknown, possibly 'Duchess of Teck' x *griffithianum*). 5', 0ºF?, L, -/-/-. A combination of pale and deep pink flowers make this beautiful. It is not well known; while it originated in England, it may be better known in New Zealand. It has good foliage and buds young. (Waterer, Sons & Crisp before 1958).

'**Eileen Byrnes'** ('Pioneer' seedling). 2', -15ºF, E-EM, -/-/-. A very free flowering plant with raspberry blossoms early in the year. Leaves are small and semi-deciduous. Good for a sunny location. (Waterer).

'**El Alamein'** (*griffithianum* hybrid). 5', -10ºF, EM-M, -/-/-. This is a beautiful plant. Flowers are deep, dark blood red, with conspicuous dark brown blotches, held in nearly ideal trusses. (Kluis 1946).

'**Elam'** ('Chesapeake' seedling). 2', -20ºF, M, -/-/-. Leaves are quite small. Deep rose flowers are 1 1/2" wide, held in clusters of 3-4. (Nearing 1972).

'**El Camino'** (unknown, but the parentage is probably close to that of 'Walloper'). 5', -5ºF, M, 4/4/4. An introduction from Whitney that many think is a cross that was made by Lem. Its foliage is huge and thick and certainly reminds one of the 'Walloper' group. The plant has heavy stems. The terrific flowers are dark pink with darker blotch and spotting. One word describes this hybrid, "magnificent". (Lem?, Whitney, Sather 1976).

'**Eldorado'** (*valentinianum* x *johnstoneanum*). 4', 15ºF, E, 3/3/3. Small leaves are dark yellow-green, and scaly. Bright yellow flowers are funnel shaped with brown scales on the outside. Open growth habit. Easily propagated. (Rothschild 1937).

'**Eleanore'** (*desquamatum* x *augustinii*). 6', 10ºF, EM, 3/3/3. This upright plant has small dark green foliage. Prolific flowers are lavender-blue. Plant does very well in full sun. (Rothschild 1937) A.M. 1943.

'**Electra's Son'** (seedling of 'Electra'). 6', 10ºF, ML, -/-/-. Medium foliage is accompanied by 3" flowers that are lavender, reddish lavender on back, with a yellowish green blotch. The blooms occur in trusses of 4 on branch ends. (Parker 1977).

'**Elena'** (*cinnabarinum* var. *blandfordiiflorum* x *yunnanense*). 4', -5ºF, M, 4/3-4/3. Soft pink tubular flowers hang in delicate clusters on this upright plant, which is similar in appearance to 'Lady Chamberlain'. (Lionel de Rothschild).

'**Elie'** (pink *catawbiense* seedling x pink *catawbiense* seedling). 5', -10ºF, EM, 3/3/3-4. This is a plant that will do well in difficult areas where other varieties may fail. Glossy green leaves are medium sized. Cerise pink flowers, with a deeper colored blotch, are set in rounded trusses of about 10. (Shammarello 1958).

'**Elisabeth Hobbie'** ('Essex Scarlet' x *forrestii* ssp. *forrestii* Repens Group). 30", -5ºF, EM, 4/4-5/3. Lax trusses of up to 9 bell shaped lipstick red flowers nod over leathery, elongated, rounded deep green foliage. Tolerates full sun. (Hobbie 1945) H.C. 1974.

'**Elite'** see 'PJM'.

'**Elizabeth'** (*forrestii* ssp. *forrestii* Repens Group x *griersonianum*). 3', 0ºF, EM, 3-4/4/5. Among low growing red rhododendrons, 'Elizabeth' has been the chosen one. Lovely foliage and plant habit characterize this vigorous and floriferous plant. Large red trumpet flowers celebrate spring. (Aberconway 1939) A.M. 1939, F.C.C. 1943.

'**Elizabeth de Rothschild'** ('Lionel's Triumph' x 'Naomi' seedling). 5', -5ºF, M, 4/3/3. Primrose yellow flowers have maroon spotting. A nice, upright growing plant with medium foliage. (Rothschild 1966) A.M. 1966.

'**Elizabeth Lockhart'** (Sport of 'Humming Bird'). 30", 0ºF, EM, 3/3/3-4. Deep green leaves are overlaid with dark, reddish chocolate brown. Young foliage is very red. Flowers are deep red. (Lockhart 1965) H.C. 1972.

'**Elizabeth of Glamis'** (['Tidbit' x *caucasicum*] x [*wardii* x {*yakushimanum* x 'Crest'}]). 5', -5ºF, M, 4/4/4. A compact plant that produces large rounded trusses of pale yellow flowers. The flowers mature to deeper greenish yellow with a very small, vivid reddish orange eye in the throat. Named with permission of H. M. Queen Elizabeth and the Queen Mother. (Cox 1987).

'**Elizabeth Red Foliage'** ('Elizabeth' hybrid or sport). 3', 0ºF, EM, 3/3-4/3. New growth on this interesting plant is red. The new leaves stay red through the seasons, although color tones brighten, then become muted as winter closes. Little is known about the origin of this plant except that it came from Ostbo some years ago and, for some mysterious reason, was not propagated. No one knows for sure whether it is a hybrid or a sport of 'Elizabeth'. Also known as 'Ostbo's Red Elizabeth'. (Ostbo before 1960, though it was not distributed until the 1980's).

'**Elizabeth Titcomb'** ('Marinus Koster' x 'Snow Queen'). 5', -5ºF, M, 4/4/3-4. Good strong growth habit with medium large, dark green foliage. Flowers, pale pink in the bud, open pure white. They are very large, of heavy substance, and are set in large, rather tall conical trusses. (Larson 1958) P.A. 1958.

'**Ella'** (*dichroanthum* x *wardii*). 4', 5ºF, ML, 4/3/2-3. This plant is a prolific bloomer which roots easily. Buds of apricot-copper open to flat, 3" flowers, orange shaded to yellow, and are held in trusses of 7 or 8 flowers. Medium sized foliage completes the picture. (R. Henny 1958).

'**Else Frye'** (*ciliicalyx* hybrid). 4', 15ºF, E, 5/3/4. This splendid fragrant hybrid is white, kissed with a flush of pink, becoming sunburst yellow in the throat. Leathery, glossy foliage is deeply veined. (Bowman 1963).

'**Elsie Straver'** (*campylocarpum* x unknown). 5', -5ºF, M, 3/3/2-3. Creamy yellow flowers have a dark red blotch in the throat. Leaves have an interesting crinkly edging. (Straver reg. 1968) Gold Medal (Boskoop) 1966.

'**Elsmere'** ('Chesapeake' seedling). 4', -25ºF, M, -/-/-. Leaves are rather small. Small, 1" wide flowers, scattered all over plant, are well defined yellow. (Nearing 1972).

'**Elspeth'** (*campylocarpum* x hardy hybrid). 4', 0ºF, EM-M, 3/4/2-3. A compact, upright plant with medium sized, light green foliage. The unique flowers are bright scarlet in bud, opening deep pink apricot, fading to cream, and are held in a small rounded truss. There is another plant by the same name which is white flowering and which is apparently not well known (if known at all) today. (Slocock before 1937) A.M. 1937.

'Elviira' (*brachycarpum* ssp. *tigerstedii* x *forrestii* ssp. *forrestii* Repens Group). 2', -25ºF, ML, -/-/-. A very low growing, densely branched plant, this hybrid produces bright red flowers from equally vibrant buds that are guaranteed hardy. (Marjatta Uosukainen, Univ. of Helsinki, Finland, pending registration).

'Elya' (['Fabia' x *bureavii*] x *yakushimanum*). 3', -5ºF, E, 4/5/4. Great indumented foliage and rose colored flowers compose this hybrid. With these parents, only superior foliage could be attained. (Larson 1982).

'Emanuela' ('Mars' x *yakushimanum* 'Koichiro Wada'). 2', -10ºF, ML, -/-/-. A compact bush growing as wide as tall. Showy red buds open to expose white, funnelshaped flowers with rosy rims and exteriors. The hardy blooms have a light pink throat for added interest. (Hachmann hyb. 1968, Stuck reg. 1988).

'Emasculum' (*ciliatum* x *dauricum*). 5', -10ºF, VE, 4/3/3. Twiggy ascending branches become full of light pink blossoms early in the spring. Pert small leaves provide added interest on this columnar plant. (Waterer).

'Empire Day' ('Moser's Maroon' x *griersonianum*). 5', 0ºF, ML, 3/2/3. A rather open growing plant with nice deep green foliage and blood red flowers. (Rothschild, shown by Knap Hill) A.M. 1932.

'EMS' (*forrestii* ssp. *forrestii* Repens Group x 'Purple Splendour'). 2.5', -5ºF, EM, -/-/-. A free flowering, compact mound, this plant produces loose trusses of deep crimson-purple funnel shaped blooms very early in the season. (D. Hobbie 1951).

'Enborne' (*aberconwayi* x *anhweiense*). 3', -5ºF, M, 3-4/3/3. White flowers with a flush of pink and spotting in the upper throat. Interesting recurved leaves are an added attraction. (Windsor) A.M. 1966.

'Enchanted Evening' (unknown). 4', 5ºF, ML, 3-4/3-4/3. An improvement over the great 'King of Shrubs'. Dark buds open to soft salmon flowers with a peachy orange stripe beginning in the throat and running to the edge of the petals. Add to this dark lime green spotting on the upper lobe and it's great. Very difficult to tell from 'Golden Belle'; probably is either a sister seedling or maybe the same plant. (Whitney, Sather 1976).

'Endre Ostbo' (*souliei* x *fortunei* ssp. *discolor*). 6', 0ºF, ML, 3-4/3/2. An upright plant with medium sized, medium green foliage. Flowers are pale pink, fringed deeper pink, with red spotting in the upper part of corolla. 4" saucer shaped blooms are held in rounded trusses of up to 8 flowers. (E. Ostbo 1958) P.A. 1954.

'English Roseum' (probably a sport of 'Roseum Elegance'). 6', -25ºF, ML, 2-3/3/3-4. This vigorous hybrid is tolerant of extremes in cold, heat and humidity. Plentiful, smooth glossy leaves roll slightly at the leaf margin. Flowers are soft rosy lavender. (A. Waterer 1900's).

'Enticement' ('Sunup Sundown' x 'Lem's Cameo'). 3', 0ºF, M, -/-/-. A plant with low growing, bushy habit that is tolerant of both sun and shade. Vivid red buds open to soft pink blooms with lighter pink rays. A delicate orange-red spotting is apparent in the throat. (Lofthouse reg. 1986).

'Epoch' (grown from colchicine treated seed of *minus* var. *minus* Carolinianum Group *album*). 3', -10ºF, M, 3/2/3. Saucer shaped flowers, with strong substance, are bent sharply down. The white blooms, to 2 1/2", are white shading to blush, and are held in a ball shaped trusses of up to 12. (Kehr 1972).

'Erato' ('Oratorium' x 'Hachmann's Feuerschein'). 5', -15ºF, ML, -/-/-. Dark red buds open to uniformly deep red flowers with darker speckles. Trusses are compact on this bushy plant. (Hachmann hyb. 1976, Stuck reg. 1988).

'Erchless' ('C.O.D.' x 'Mrs. Furnivall'). 5', -10ºF, ML, -/-/-. A vigorous growing plant, with an open and spreading habit. Flowers of pale purplish pink have frilled edges and a bold red eye. (Howard Phipps 1972).

'Ermine' ('Britannia' x 'Mrs. A. T. de la Mare'). 6', 0ºF, ML, 3/3/3. Growth habit is stiff, upright, and well clothed in large medium green leaves. Pure white flowers, to 3 1/2", with strong character, are held in compact conical trusses. (R. Henny 1959).

'Ernest Inman' (*yakushimanum* x 'Purple Splendour'). 4', -10ºF, EM, 4/4/4. Lavender purple flowers fade to white in the center. Dense, deep green foliage on a most compact plant. (George, Hydon Nurseries Ltd. 1979) A.M. 1979.

'Ernie Dee' (*dauricum* x *racemosum*). 1', 0ºF, EM, 3-4/4/3. This Caperci hybrid is quite new and very appealing. It appears the dwarf won't grow taller than 2', but it will readily grow in width to a low cushion. Purple, lightly frilled flowers are long lasting and plentiful. This hybrid was raised by Ernest Dzurick, hence, its name. (Caperci 1977.)

'Eskimo' (unknown). 5', -20ºF, ML, -/-/-. Beautiful white flowers with a small orange flare appear in abundance on this Hachmann hybrid from Germany. Medium to large leaves cover the plant. (Hachmann 1990).

'Esquire' (*griersonianum* hybrid). 4', 5ºF, M, 4/3/3. Elongated buds open to huge, soft watermelon pink 4" flowers. The open, upright habit is enhanced by the very dark red leaf petioles. This was known in Oregon a few years ago, but, as beautiful as it is, it seems to be disappearing from cultivation. (Barto, James intro. before 1958).

'Estacada' (*yakushimanum* x *arboreum*). 4', 5ºF, VE, -/-/-. Cardinal red buds open to flowers ranging from crimson to carmine to carmine rose, 2 1/2" wide, held in dome shaped trusses of 18-20. This well branched plant is furnished with elliptic, slightly convex, dark green leaves displaying a greyed white indumentum. The juvenile foliage has a white tomentum. Synonym, 'Vivid-O'. (Goheen hyb. 1967, reg. 1983).

'Ethel' ('F. C. Puddle' x *forrestii* ssp. *forrestii* Repens Group). 18", 5ºF, EM, 3-4/3-4/2-3. Fresh, deep green leaves twist and trail upon creeping yellow stems. Bright red bell shaped flowers ornament this dwarf. Excellent planted among large rocks or as a low border. (Aberconway 1934) F.C.C. 1940.

'Ethel-Mae' (*chapmanii* x *mucronulatum*) 4', -10ºF, E, -/-/-. Leaves, on the small side, provide the backdrop for lavender-pink bell shaped flowers, to 1 1/2" across, occurring at branch ends in groups of 4 trusses. Each truss holds up to 10 flowers. (Herbert 1965).

'Etta Burrows' ('Fusilier' x *strigillosum*). 5-6', 5ºF, E, 4/4/3-4. Bright blood red flowers and sensational foliage distinguish this plant. The best from both parents, it is a sight long remembered when it is in bloom. The rugged fir green, indumented foliage shows much of the appearance of *R. strigillosum*. (Larson 1965).

'Euan Cox' (*hanceanum* 'Nanum' x *ludlowii*). 1', -5ºF, EM, 4/3/3. Delicate yellow blooms, each spotted red on the upper lobes, are held on a tiny plant that grows much wider than tall. Scales are very prominent and visible on both the leaves and flower stems. Another excellent dwarf yellow from Cox. (E. H. M. Cox hyb. 1965, Glendoick Gardens reg. 1980) A.M. 1981.

'Euclid' (unknown, probably contains *catawbiense*). 5', -25ºF, M, 2/3/3. "Hardiness" is the key word in the description of this fine old hybrid. It was developed by Noble in 1850 and is still used today; therefore, you know it has withstood the test of time. It is compact growing, has delightful foliage and is covered with tight trusses of rosy violet. (Noble 1850).

'Eugene' ('Unique' x 'Jean Marie de Montague'). 4', -5ºF, M, 3-4/3/1-2. One of the most unusual features of this hybrid is its pine-cone-like flower buds. Early in the fall, the buds develop to an exceptionally large size with interesting bracts. The flowers are medium to deep coral red, held in a tight rounded truss. Foliage is deep green and very dense, covering the compact plant completely. Difficult to propagate and slow to grow. This is unfortunate, because it is an unusual plant but will probably not stay in cultivation. (Greer not registered).

'Eunie' ('Diny Dee' x 'Sierra del Oro'). 5', 5ºF?, EM, -/-/-. An upright growing plant that achieves a height greater than it's width. Sturdy flowers are held in dome shaped trusses. The blooms are light yellow showing a dark red blotch. (Joe Davis 1991).

'Evelyn' ('Loderi Venus' x 'Britannia'). 6', 0ºF, L, -/-/-. Pale pink flowers gradually change to white; however, the pink is retained as darker veining in each petal. Very large, good textured foliage. (Henny 1956).

'Evening Glow' (*fortunei* ssp. *discolor* x 'Fabia'). 5', -5ºF, L, 4/3/4. The compact growth habit supports narrow, shamrock green leaves that stay bright and attractive all year. The late blooming time is an asset. Flowers are lovely yellow on a very lax truss. A deep yellow which is still one of the best for heat. (Van Veen Sr. 1958).

'Everestianum' (*catawbiense* hybrid). 6', -15ºF, ML, 3/3/4. This versatile plant flowers heavily in either sun or light shade. Vigorous growing, it achieves a full, rounded form. Medium large, dark green leaves are oval-oblong. Frilled flowers, to 2" wide, are rosy lilac, spotted in the throat, and are held in full rounded trusses of about 15. (A. Waterer before 1850).

'Everything Nice' ('Comstock' x 'Unique'). 4', 5ºF, E-EM, 4/4/3-4. Delightful clear pink flowers are rayed lighter pink, lending a glowing radiance. Then, as a bonus, the flowers have a calyx which rolls back its lobes as they age, resulting in a star shaped appearance down in the center of the truss. Most interesting! It flowers at a time of the year when there are not many other hybrids like this in bloom, which adds to its value. There is a need for an early, compact pink, and this hybrid fills that spot. The foliage is medium sized, an attractive matte green on a compact, good looking plant. Unfortunately, it is neither extremely sun tolerant nor cold hardy. (Greer 1982).

'Exbury Calstocker' (*calophytum* x 'Dr. Stocker'). 6', -5ºF, E, 5/4/3-4. With grand blossom, foliage and stature, this hybrid knows no other way to grow. Perfectly huge trusses are creamy light pink with a rich red flare at each flower center. Large, thick leaves cloak this tree-like rhododendron. (Rothschild) A.M. 1948.

'Exbury Naomi' ('Aurora' x *fortunei* ssp. *fortunei*). 5', -5ºF, M, 4/3/3. Here is real beauty. Richly textured flowers are pink with shading of yellow and apricot. (Rothschild).

'Excelsior' (*yakushimanum* hybrid). 3', -15ºF?, M, -/-/-. A compact plant offering lovely, large pink flowers with red rims. Dark green foliage is attractive as well as cold hardy. (Distributed in France).

'Exotic' ('Loderi King George' x 'Ostbo Y3'). 6', 5ºF, M, 4-5/3/3-4. Leaves on this hybrid are large and attractive, although, like those of its 'Loderi' parentage, they can develop brown spots, especially on the edges. The flowers are warm orange blended with yellow and pink, and are carried in trusses of up to 11 florets. If you see this flowering in its peak, you will never forget it. (Bovee 1962) PA 1961.

'Extraordinaire' ('Gold Medal' x 'Olin O. Dobbs'). 5', -5ºF, M, -/-/-. An unusual hybrid. Rose pink buds open to flowers with pink-edged petals. A huge dark garnet red flare graces the upper petals, and the lower petals have a soft yellow center. Little by little, the whole flower becomes a creamy pink, causing the dark textured flare to stand out even more. Many large 5" individual flowers make large trusses. The foliage is a matte fir green. An interesting cross between a yellow and a purple. (Greer intro. 1994).

'Fabia' (*dichroanthum* x *griersonianum*). 3', 5ºF, M, 3/4/3-4. The flowers are interesting orange colors and the plants grow compactly. Fabia is actually a grex, or large group of sister seedlings, and there is great variation in color. Many forms have been named; one of the best known of these is 'Fabia Tangerine'. (Aberconway 1934) A.M. 1934.

'Fabia Tangerine' (*dichroanthum* x *griersonianum*). 3', 5ºF, M, 3/4/3-4. The tangerine form of 'Fabia' is always popular. Its flower is a slightly lighter orange than 'Fabia'. This is a well known orange rhododendron that is worthy of its reputation. (Aberconway 1940) A.M. 1940.

'Fabulous' (parentage unknown). 3', 0ºF, E-EM, -/-/-. Various shades of pink emerge from nice dark pink buds. Round foliage covers this broad, dense plant. A good addition to early blooming pinks. (Whitney, Sather 1985).

'Faggetter's Favourite' (*fortunei* ssp. *fortunei* hybrid). 6', -5ºF, M, 5/4/3. White, pink and cream melt together in the flower of this outstanding plant. Certainly one of the best for plant and flower. (Slocock) A.M. 1933, A.M. 1955.

'Fair Lady' (*arboreum* var. *roseum* x 'Loderi Venus'). 6', 0ºF, M, 4/3/2-3. The large leaves are greeted each spring with magnificent trusses of rosy pink with darker shading. It is a hybrid that is not often seen and it is worth growing. (R. Henny 1959) P.A. 1959.

'Fair Sky' (selected seedling of *augustinii*). 6', -5ºF, M, 3-4/3/3. Foliage is typical of the species. Flowers are rather flat and square shaped, purple blue, spotted yellowish green, often blooming from 2 terminal buds. (Barto, Phetteplace 1976).

'Fairweather' (['Fabia' x *yakushimanum*] x 'Hello Dolly'). 3', -10ºF, EM, 4/4-5/4. This hybrid is both vigorous and easy to grow, with outstanding foliage, heavily indumented. Flowers are a delightful warm yellow tone. Synonym, 'Seafoam'. (E.C. Brockenbrough, M.D. 1971).

'Fairy Mary' (*keiskei* 'Yaku Fairy' x 'Mary Fleming'). 3', -15ºF, EM, -/-/-. This densely mounding plant is a vigorous grower. White flowers have a light yellowish tinge and are accented with shades of pink and apricot. A selection that is both hardy and beautiful. (Berg).

'Faisa' (*minus* var. *minus* Carolinianum Group x *polycladum* Scintillans Group). 4', -20ºF, EM, -/-/-. Striking buds of dark reddish purple open to reveal delicate flowers of light purplish pink. Small, narrow leaves accent the star-shaped flowers on this tight, upright growing plant. (W. Delp).

'Falling Snow' (*yakushimanum* hybrid). 3', -15ºF, ML, -/-/-. Pure white flowers with small yellow markings in the throat make this a beautiful hybrid. Trusses contain about 18 flowers and are 3-4" tall. Of dense, rounded plant habit, it makes a plant that is wider than tall. Leaves are glossy green. (O. Pride 1980).

'Fancy' ('Mrs. Lindsay Smith' x 'Mrs. Helen Koster'). 5', 0ºF, M, 4/3/3. Pale mauve flowers encircle a large, deep red blotch which fades to speckles on the upper lobe. Light green, large leaves. Requires some sun protection. (Koster) A.M. 1955.

'Fandango' ('Britannia' x *haematodes*). 4', 0ºF, M, 4/4/3. Deep crimson flowers of good substance dance on a plant with dense, compact growth. (Rothschild 1938).

'Fanfare' ('America' x 'Kettledrum'). 5', -20ºF, ML, 3/2/3. Growth habit is rather spreading and open. Medium green, medium to large foliage is wavy on the edges and oblong in shape. Flowers are an unfading bright red, in a dome-shaped truss. (Leach 1958).

'Fantastica' ('Mars' x *yakushimanum* 'Koichiro Wada'). 3', -5ºF, ML, 4-5/4. Long, elliptic leaves are blanketed underneath with woolly indumentum. The flowers are a strong rose color, fading to white in the throat and accentuated by a light citron green spotting inside. (Hachmann, G. Stuck 1985).

'Farewell Party' (parentage unknown). 5', -5ºF, L, -/-/-. Leaves are medium to large; flowers are scented, white with throat spotting of yellowish green, to 4 1/2" across, carried in a flat truss of up to 12 flowers. (Kersey, Frederick Jr. 1976).

'Fascinator' (*forrestii repens* x 'Hiraethlyn'). 18", 5ºF, EM, 3/4/3. Cherry red, bell flowers open all over this low mound. Leaves are small. (Aberconway 1950) A.M. 1950.

'Fastuosum Flore Pleno' (*catawbiense* x *ponticum*). 6', -15ºF, ML, 3/3/3. Growth habit is somewhat open but rounded on this hardy, sun-tolerant hybrid. The flowers are double, lavender blue, with a large golden flare on the upper dorsal lobe of the large outer petals. The small inner petals roll and curl around the short stamen cluster. The foliage is dense and dark green. (Geber Francoisi, Ghent before 1846) A.G.M. 1928.

'Fawn' (*fortunei* ssp. *fortunei* x 'Fabia'). 6', 5ºF, M, 4/3/3. The plant has upright growth habit, with medium green, medium-sized leaves. Flowers of up to 5" across are salmon pink shading to orange yellow in center, with a very flat corolla, held in open-topped cylindrical trusses up to 9 flowers. (James 1958) P.A. 1959.

'F. C. Puddle' g. (*neriiflorum* x *griersonianum*). 5', 5ºF, EM, 3/3/2-3. This upright plant has medium sized, dull, dark green leaves. The flowers are brilliant, orangey scarlet. They are carried in a lax truss of medium size. (Aberconway 1932) A.M. 1932.

'Felicitas' ('Goldkrone' x 'Perlina'). 4', -10ºF, M, -/-/-. Warm peach flowers have a flare of red-brown spotting on the upper petal. Edges of the flower are more peach pink, the center a showy yellow. Deep green foliage is somewhat glossy and covers the plant from top to bottom. An attractive plant. (Hachmann hyb. 1977, Herbst intro. 1988).

'Festivo' ('Hachmann's Polaris' x *wardii*). 2', -5ºF, ML, -/-/-. This slow-growing shrub will become nearly twice as wide as it is tall. Flowers are borne in loose trusses composed of 12-14 flowers. The bloom color is a pale yellow with red markings. (Hachmann, Stuck 1988).

'Fiery Orange' ('Ginny Mae' x 'Dead Ringer'). 4', -5ºF?, L, -/-/-. Medium red flowers with light yellow throats and flare are held in trusses of 10. (Delp 1992).

'Fiesta' ('Eros' x 'F.C. Puddle'). 5', 15ºF, ML, -/-/-. This hybrid whose parentage is over half *R. griersonianum*, certainly shows its relationship to the species. Masses of red flowers top the narrow leaves. (Lord Aberconway 1950).

'Fiji' ('Russell Harmon' x 'Goldsworth Orange'). 5', -20ºF, L, 4/3/3. Dark red buds open a dusty rose with spotting in the throat. Leaves are light green and plant habit is more broad than tall. (Leach 1976, reg. 1982).

'Fine Feathers' ('Cilpinense' x *lutescens*). 3', 5ºF, E, 3/3/3. This hybrid has a good name because the white-with-yellow flowers are kissed with pink and are so delicate they look like fine feathers. (Aberconway 1946).

'Finlandia' ('Catalgla' x ['Adrian Koster' x *williamsianum*]). 3', -15ºF, E, 4/5/4. Leaves are medium-sized. Flowers are pink in the bud, opening white, to 3" wide, and are held in a 12-flowered truss. (Leach 1974).

'Fiona' ('Bow Bells' x 'Loderi Pink Diamond'). 3', 0ºF, E, 3/3/3. Large, soft pink, 7-lobed flowers are almost too big for the plant. Foliage is sensitive to excessive sun, so it needs protection. (Brandt 1962).

'Fire Bird' ('Norman Shaw' x *griersonianum*). 6', 5ºF, ML, 3/3/3. Bright yellow anthers offer a beautiful contrast to the salmon red flowers of this tall hybrid. Leaves are light green, slightly upturned on the edges to give a two-toned effect. (Rothschild 1938).

'Firedance' (probably a hybrid containing *forrestii* var. *repens* and *williamsianum* and other species). 3', -5ºF, M, 3/3-4/3. Pointed green leaves are plentiful on this low plant. Superb red flower buds stand upright on many stems to adorn the plant all winter, and later create a profusion of scarlet red flowers. Interestingly, if the plant sets buds in early summer, the bud scales are not as red through the winter as are the buds which are set in fall. (Whitney, Greer, Boltman unregistered).

'Firedrake' ('Sardis' x *kyawii*). 5', 5ºF, VL, -/-/-. This tall, but compact, plant has great red flowers very late in the season. (Rothschild 1938).

'Fireman Jeff' ('Jean Marie de Montague' x 'Grosclaude'). 3', 0ºF, M, 4/4/4. This is one of the brightest blood reds you will find. It is not a blue-red or an orange-red but a hot red. It has a huge calyx nearly as large as the flower and is also bright red. The foliage is a medium green and has a slight amount of tomentum when it is new. (Brandt, Eichelser 1977).

'Firestorm' ('Vulcan' x 'Chocolate Soldier'). 3', -25ºF, M, 3/3/3. A plant of mounded habit, it obtains a width twice the height. The plant is densely foliated with matte, olive green leaves. Huge numbers of red buds open to red flowers. (Mehlquist 1991).

'Firewine' ('Firebird' x 'Purple Splendour'). 4', 0ºF, ML, 4-5/3/4. Here is an unusual color for a rhododendron. It's hot red wine purple, it's really bright! Each individual flower is ruffled and frilled in a most attractive manner. Buds heavily. Grass green leaves are narrow. (Greer 1979).

'First Love' (*oreotrephes* x 'Royal Flush'). 5', 5ºF, M, 4/4/3. Leaves are on the small side; flowers are pink with a burgundy colored eye, in trusses of up to 8 flowers. (R. Henny, L. Henny 1976).

'Flair' ('Catalgla' x ['Adrian Koster' x *williamsianum*]). 4', -15ºF, E, -/-/-. These flowers are white with creamy ivory shading on the dorsal lobe. They grow to 2 3/4" across, and are held in a 12 flowered truss. Leaves are medium sized. (Leach 1974).

'Flaming Snow' (parentage unknown). 4', -5ºF, M, 4/3/4. An apropos name, as large, snowy white flowers have blazing red speckling in the upper lobes. Trusses are quite large and last for an extended period. Easy to grow. (Dexter).

'Flaming Star' ('Ring of Fire' x 'Lem's Cameo'). 5', 0ºF, M, 4-5/4/4. This has a vibrant flower that will light up the garden! Its yellow center has a hot red-orange edge and it forms large trusses of many flowers. The foliage is deep fir green, lightly shiny. The plant is handsome during all the months it is not in flower. (Roy Thompson hyb. about 1985, intro. Thompson Nursery 1996).

'Flatterer' ('Corona' x 'Day Dream'). 5', -5ºF, M, 3/3/3. An enjoyable plant with watermelon red flowers. Narrow, pointed foliage make for an interesting plant. (R. Henny 1957).

'Flautando' (*brachycarpum* ssp. *fauriei* x 'Goldsworth Orange'). 3', -10ºF, ML, -/-/-. Glossy, elliptical leaves provide a subtle background for the very showy, funnel-shaped flowers. The blooms are composed of light yellow, wavy petals ringed on the edges with pink. A reddish-brown marking draws attention to the dorsal lobe. (Hachmann, Stuck 1988).

'Flava' (*yakushimanum* x *wardii*). 3', -10ºF, ML, 3-4/4/4. Flowers appear in cone-shaped clusters of 11. Each pale to creamy yellow blossom is highlighted by a showy red eye. The dark green leaves are amply produced on this charming, mound-like shrub. (Hobbie hyb., Slocock exhibitor) H.C. Wisley Trials 1987.

'Flava Lackblatt' (selection of *yakushimanum* x *wardii*). 3', -10ºF, M, -/-/-. Similar to 'Flava', however derived from a cross of a special selection of *yakushimanum*. The pale yellow flowers vary, some have red freckling and others are without. The rounded plant attains a greater size than 'Flava'. (unknown).

'Flawless' ('Rocky Road' x 'Rougemont'). 2.5', ?ºF, L, -/-/-. Wavy edged flowers are strong purplish red with a white flare and dark olive spotting. (Delp 1995).

'Flip' (*flavidum* x 'Lady Rosebery'). 5', 0ºF, EM, 3/3/3. Flowers are a beautiful combination of cream and pink. Flower shape is typical of the *cinnabarinum* group and they hang in clusters of about 4 or 5. Foliage is small, dark green and scaled. The plant is upright in habit. (Brandt, Greer). This plant was registered in the early '90's by my friends the Coxes from Scotland under the name of 'Strawberry Cream', but I wish the name 'Flip' would have stayed with it. The word flip in American slang means "falling head over heals for something", and you could easily "flip" over this plant, however, the name 'Flip' for this plant actually came from abbreviating *flavidum* x Lady Rosebery in pink (incidentally, there was also a "Fliy", f L i yellow out of the same cross).

'Flirt' ('Britannia' x *yakushimanum* 'Koichiro Wada'). 3', -10ºF, M, 4/4/4. Like so many 'yak' hybrids this little beauty is a compact, low growing plant that buds well. Deep red buds open to a strong pink fading as it approaches the throat. Slight indumentum. (Elliott, 1980).

'Floda' (*keiskei* x selected pink *mucronulatum*). 3', -20ºF, E, -/-/-. At a distance one might think this plant is shrimp pink, however, upon closer inspection it is actually a rainbow of colors. Flowers are almost white with pink stripes radiating through each petal, the whole bloom being suffused with yellow. The foliage is very showy in the fall. (Waldman, Roslyn Nursery).

'Floralies' (*yakushimanum* hybrid). 3', -10ºF, M, -/-/-. Growth habit is very low and wide, covered with elliptical, dark green foliage. The trusses have an orange glow as the exterior of the blooms are lightly colored orange, offset by the creamy interiors. (Grown in France).

'Flora Markeeta' (*thomsonii* x ['Unique' x 'Luscombei var. Leonardslee']). 4', -5ºF, M, 4/4-5/3. Round, glossy leaves shape a full, deep green knoll in your garden. Creamy flowers are trimmed in bright pink. (Markeeta Nursery 1967) P.A. 1967.

'Flora's Boy' (*forrestii* var. *repens* x 'Jean Marie de Montague'). 2', 5ºF, EM-M, 3-4/3-4/3. A *R. repens* hybrid that holds its flowers upright. Each flower is extremely large and is a bright, waxy red. One cannot over-emphasize the difference between this hybrid and other repens hybrids. For those of you interested in hybridizing, this may be the link needed to produce small reds with big upright trusses. The foliage is glossy green and the plant habit is also upright instead of spreading. (Not registered, Markeeta Nursery).

'Florence Archer' (*wardii* x 'Marcia'). 3', 10ºF, L, 4/3-4/4. Foliage is medium sized. Flowers are yellow flushed red, with red edges and dorsal spotting of yellow green, to 3 3/4" across, in truss of up to 8 flowers. (Larson 1979).

'Floriade' ('Britannia' hybrid). 5', -5ºF, ML, 3/2/3. Lush, deep green foliage adorns this outstanding Dutch hybrid. Flowers are extremely vibrant red. (Adr. van Nes 1962) G.M. 1960.

'Flower Girl' ('Moonstone' x 'Crest'). 3', -5ºF, EM, 3/3/-. Dark yellow buds open to strong yellow flowers in a large, lax truss almost too big for the plant. Foliage is glossy green and rounded. A hybrid of two good parents, this is a special plant when in bloom. (Probably a hybrid from Seattle, Washington).

'Fluff' (*yakushimanum* 'Koichiro Wada' x 'Vanessa' FCC). 3', -10ºF, ML, -/-/-. Pink buds open to delicate soft-pink rounded trusses, abundantly borne. A mound like and dense plant which exhibits polished rich green leaves, held for 3 years. (Bovee).

'Forever Amber' (['Cavalcade' x 'Mary Swaythling'] x 'Hawk Crest'). 5', 5ºF, M, -/-/-. A most interesting color, as the name implies. It is amber, a smoky orange, on a taller, open-growing plant. (John Waterer Sons & Crisp 1975).

'Forever Yours' ('Creamy Chiffon' x 'Vulcan'). 3', -5ºF, EM, -/-/-. This compact, mounding plant consistently produces many buds, starting at a young age. The buds are vivid red and open to expose frilled, white blooms with accents of red inner speckling and a red margin. Elliptical foliage is an attractive deep, glossy green. (McCulloch, Briggs 1991).

'For Pete's Sake' (unknown). 5', -15ºF, M, -/-/-. A dense growing, compact plant with long, narrow foliage. It produces a large number of red buds which open to form upright, dome shaped trusses of salmon-pink flowers. A unique color for such a hardy plant. (Hardgrove, Sheuchenko 1991).

'Forsterianum' (*veitchianum* x *edgeworthii*). 5', 20ºF, EM-M, 4/4/4. This lightly fragrant plant has upright, compact growth habit. Flowers are huge, white, funnel shaped, with a distinctive yellow flare, in a lax truss of 3 to 4. Leaves are lance-shaped, medium size and narrow. (Forster before 1889).

'Fortune's Child' ('Essex Scarlet' x hardy *fortunei*). 5', -15ºF, LM, -/-/-. Bright red buds open to reveal large trusses of pink, flat blooms. A floriferous plant with an attractive growth habit. (Shapiro).

'Fortwilliam' (*fortunei* ssp. *fortunei* x *williamsianum*). 3', -5ºF, ML, 3-4/4/4. These leaves are of medium size. The flowers are light pink with darker pink stripes and yellow throats. They grow to 4" across, are scented, and are held in trusses of 12. (Herbert 1967).

'Fox Hunter' ('Matador' x 'Gaul'). 4', 10ºF, M, -/-/-. Large, bright red flowers are in trusses of 12. Upright plant habit. (Gen. Harrison 1967).

'Fragrans' (*catawbiense* x *viscosum*). 4', -10ºF, L, 2-2/2/3. This hybrid has been around for more than 150 years and is still grown in many gardens. It is one of the first rhododendron hybrids ever produced. Actually, it is what is called an azaleodendron, because it is a cross of a rhododendron species and a rhododendron in the Azalea Series (Section Pentanthera). The flowers are a light lavender with centers that lighten to white. It is fragrant, hence its name. Foliage is small and is held on the plant a year or less. (Cross made about 1815; Paxton, of Chandler & Sons, intro 1843).

'Fragrans Affinity' (parentage unknown). 5', -10ºF, L, 3/3/4. The plant listed here is not 'Fragrans'. It is possibly out of the same cross but is far superior. It is, of course, an azaleodendron. It has showy orchid blue flowers on a hardy plant with good foliage. A strong grower, it makes a very dense plant and holds its foliage better than most azaleodendrons. (Greer not registered).

'Fragrantissimum' (*edgeworthii* x *formosum*). 3', 15ºF, EM, 4/2-3/4. This is a rather tender, leggy, but easily trained plant with medium-sized leaves. It enjoys the distinction of being one of the most fragrant of shrubs. Flowers, to 4" across, are blushed carmine in the bud, and open white with a tinge of pink. They are carried about 4 to a lax trusses. (Rollison) F.C.C. 1868.

'Francesca' ('Britannia' x 'Dexter #202'). 6', -10ºF, ML, 4-5/3-4/3-4. This rhododendron is patented with the U. S. Patent office. Leaves are large on a wide, open plant. Flowers are black red in the bud, opening bright carmine red, in large trusses. (Consolini 1972).

'Frango' (*yakushimanum* 'Koichiro Wada' x 'Noyo Chief'). 3', 0ºF, EM, 4/4/4. Slightly fragrant flowers, empire rose with orange spotting, are carried in trusses over 5" wide, holding 14-18 flowers. The plant has rounded a silhouette and is clothed with lustrous dark green leaves held for 4 years. (David Goheen 1982).

'Frank Baum' ('Mars' x 'Jasper'). 5', -5ºF, L, 4/3-4/4. The flowers of this hybrid are such a unique color that they are hard to describe. The round, full, coral watermelon trusses are made of numerous wide, cupped flowers. A "pot-of-gold" rests at the center of each flower cup. The deep fir green leaves have a rich, somewhat rough, texture and the red petiole adds interest and an attractive appearance. (Seabrook 1969).

'Frank Galsworthy' (*ponticum* x unknown). 4', -15ºF, L, 4/3/3. A unique and very showy combination of deep maroon-purple flowers with yellow-gold flares. Trusses are not extremely large, but the striking colors are traffic stoppers. Is also known as 'Purple and Gold'. (Raised by A. Waterer, shown by W. C. Slocock) A.M. 1960.

'Frank Heuston' ('Golden Bell' x 'Autumn Gold'). 4', 0ºF, ML, -/-/-. An earthy blend of salmon-orange margins blending to a golden buff-colored throat, with brick-red spotting on the upper flower lobes, presented in abundant globular flat-topped trusses. It buds consistently. This is an upright, multi-branching plant that has deep olive green leaves held for 2 years. (Elliott, Maranville, Heuston 1983).

'Frank Maranville' ('Britannia' x 'Van Nes Sensation'). 4', 0ºF, EM, -/-/-. A rounded, well-branched plant covered with smooth, elliptical, medium green leaves. Dome-shaped trusses are comprised of vivid, reddish purple funnel-shaped flowers. Each bloom is edged in paler red with a darker throat. (Briggs hyb. 1963, Heuston reg. 1985).

'Fran Labera' ('Helen Everitt' x 'Dexter's Honeydew'). 6', -15ºF, ML, -/-/-. Foliage is medium to large; flowers are 7-lobed and large, to 4" across, white to cream color, with chartreuse throat, held in a truss of up to 11 flowers. Fragrant. (Fuller 1978).

'Freckles' ('Jacksonii' x [*catawbiense* x *haematodes*]). 6', -10ºF, M, 3/3/3. Pink flowers have interesting brown spotting. Foliage is dark green. (Gable).

'Fred Hamilton' ([*neriiflorum* x *griersonianum*] x *dichroanthum*). 3', -5ºF, ML, 3-4/3-4/3. Lively yellow trusses are accented by bands of pink radiating between the petal lobes. Elliptical leaves are dense on this low growing, wide spreading rhododendron. (Lem, Van Veen 1972).

'Fred Peste' (*yakushimanum* x 'Corona') x *haematodes*. 3', 0ºF, ML, 4/4/4. Lovely, non-fading, cardinal-red flowers have deep maroon-red throats. Deep red spotting occurs heavily on the dorsal lobes, and flowers are gathered in flat trusses of 14. Leathery, narrowly elliptic, 3-4" long leaves of dark olive green are coated beneath with moderate orange-yellow indumentum. (Peste 1986).

'Fred Robbins' ('Carmen' x 'Choremia'). 18", 0ºF, M, 4/4/3. A tight little mound of dark green leaves with silvery indumentum below. Flowers are bright crimson with an obvious little calyx of the same color. Sister seedling to 'Honore Hacanson' and 'Little Nemo'. (Brandt 1965).

'Fred Rose' ('Mary Swaythling' x *lacteum*). 5', -10ºF, M, 4/3/3. Plant habit and trusses are round. Flowers are lemon yellow with slight red spotting. Very compact and free flowering. (Raised by Fred Rose, Sunningdale Nurseries, reg. 1962) H.C. 1973.

'Fred Wynniatt' (*fortunei* ssp. *fortunei* x 'Jalisco'). 4', -5ºF, M, 4/4/4. Golden yellow flowers are surrounded by a halo of rose edging. Light green leaves are held on an upright growing plant. (Rothschild) A.M. 1963, F.C.C. 1980.

'Freeman R. Stephens' ('Jean Marie de Montague' x unnamed large white). 5', -10ºF, EM, 4/4/4. The plant has large, dark green foliage similar to the 'Wallopers'. The blossoms are very large and cherry red. (Stephens 1973).

'French Creek' (parentage unknown). 6', -15ºF, ML, -/-/-. Ruffled, 3 1/2" flowers are pink fading to white, with green spotting in throat, and are carried in a truss of up to 20. (Herbert 1970).

'Friday' ('Purple Splendour' x unknown). 5', -5ºF, ML, 4/3/3. A black velvet blotch is surrounded by a field of satiny purple. The flower is curved back so as to expose the dark blotch even more. With 'Friday' looking this good, I can't wait for 'Saturday'. (Landauer).

'Frilled Petticoats' ('Hotei' x ['Pink Petticoats' x *wardii*]). 3', 0ºF, M, 4/3-4/3-4. Frilly chartreuse yellow flowers are darker on the reverse side. A good, strong, solid color. The rounded plant grows more wide than tall. (Lofthouse 1981).

'Frilled Yak' (*yakushimanum* hybrid). 3', -5ºF, M, -/-/-. A multitude of frilly light pink flowers bloom against foliage which is longer and more pointed than most "yak" hybrids. (unknown).

'Frontier' ('Letty Edwards' x 'Crest'). 6', 10ºF, ML, 4/4/4. An upright growing, rounded plant whose frame, stretching to be as wide as it is tall, is covered with medium sized foliage. Flowers are 7-lobed, to 4" wide, rose colored shading to yellow center, borne in a ball-shaped truss in groups of up to 14. (J. Elliot 1978).

'Frosty Pink' (*carolinianum* 'Achiever' x 'Gable's Pioneer'). 4', -15ºF, M, -/-/-. A blend of mauve and light purplish pink is displayed by the flowers of this hybrid that has been reported to be as hardy as -25ºF. (Delp 1992).

'Full Moon' ('Hawk' x 'Adrian Koster'). 4', -5ºF, M, 4-5/4/2-3. Sunburst yellow "moon-like" flowers rise above the lively, shiny and interestingly textured leaves of 'Full Moon'. This is the same deep yellow as the famous 'Crest', only more compact in growth habit. (J. Henny 1958).

'Fundy' (*fortunei* ssp. *fortunei* x *smirnowii*). 6', -15ºF, L, 4/4/4. Foliage is large. Pleasantly scented, 7-lobed flowers are rose colored on edges, fading lighter to centers, with olive brown blotch, to 3 1/2" across, held in 10 flowered truss. Synonym, 'Evangeline'. (Hancock, Swain, Canada Dept. of Agric. Research).

Hybrids ~
Orange Flowering

R. 'Ooh Gina'

. 'Wizard'

. 'Circus'

R. 'Whitney Orange'

R. 'Exotic'

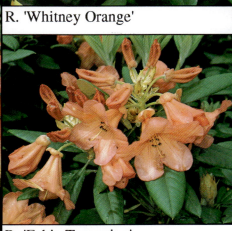

R. 'Fabia Tangerine'

R. 'Dido'

Hybrids ~ Purple Flowering

R. 'Purple Lace'

R. 'Midnight'

R. 'Anah Kruschk

R. 'Purple Splendour'

R. 'Top Gun'

R. 'Dorothy Amateis'

Hybrids ~
Yellow Flowering

R. 'Hotei'

R. 'Hotei'

R. 'Top Banana'

R. 'Sunspray'

R. 'Morning Sunshine'

R. 'Yellow Pages'

R. 'Odee Wright'

R. 'Markeeta's Prize'

R. 'Jean Marie de Montague'

Hybrids ~
Red Flowering

R. 'Elizabeth'

R. 'Britton Hill'

R. 'Vulcan's Flame'

R. 'Johnny Bender'

R. 'Francesca'

R. 'Grace Seabrook'

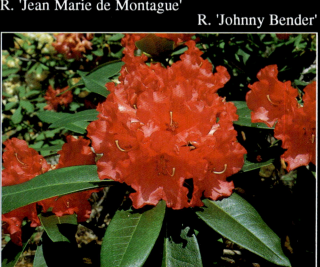

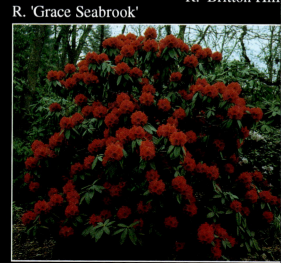

'**Furnivall's Daughter'** (probably a 'Mrs. Furnivall' selfed). 5', -5°F, M, 4-5/4/4. Beautifully shaped, tall trusses are a fresh, bright pink. A cherry pink blotch in each flower gaily accents the plant. Lively large leaves and a pretty growth habit show the vigor of this hybrid. (Knap Hill Nurseries 1957) H.C. 1957.

'**Fusilier'** (*elliottii* x *griersonianum*). 5', 10°F, ML, 3-4/3/4. The plant has an upright growth habit and large, dark green foliage. Flowers are bright orange red in a lax, medium size truss. Several forms of this plant are grown. (Rothschild) A.M. 1938, F.C.C. 1942.

'**Gabriel'** ('Dr. H. C. Dresselhuys' x *smirnowii*). 5', -15°F, L, -/-/-. Leaves are medium to large. Flowers, 2 3/4" wide, are pink, with olive brown spotting, held in truss of up to 18. (Swain, Craig, Canada Dept. of Ag. 1977).

'**Gala'** ('Big Sam' x 'Lem's Cameo'). 4', 0°F, M,-/-/-. Loose, ball shaped trusses of ruffled, rose-colored flowers lighten to soft pink in the throats. Speckles of red accent the upper lobes. Abundant, medium green leaves dress the nicely rounded, well branched, upright plant (J. Elliott 1987).

'**Gandy Dancer'** (['Crest' x 'Lionel's Triumph'] x 'Diane'). 5', -5°F, E, 4/4/4. Note the ratings! This would be an excellent addition to your yellow collection. Very large trusses of golden yellow cover a tidy, easy-to- grow plant. (Larson hyb., Clint Smith intro.).

'**Gartendirektor Glocker'** ('Doncaster' x *williamsianum*). 3', -5°F, M, 3-4/5/4. This low growing plant is ideally suited for the sun. It's pink flowers have deeper pink edging. (Hobbie 1952).

'**Gartendirektor Rieger'** ('Adriaan Koster' x *williamsianum*). 4', -10°F, E, 4/4/4. Rounded leaves cover plant taller than *R. williamsianum*. The abundant cream flowers have dark red spotting. (Hobbie hyb. about 1947, intro. 1971).

'**Gary Herbert'** (parentage uncertain, possibly a selfed seedling of *vernicosum aff.*, R. 18139, or F2 seedling of *vernicosum* #1 and #2). 6', -5°F, M, -/-/-. Foliage is medium to large. Scented flowers are 7-lobed, to 3" across, scented and ruffled, of shaded salmon tones, and carried in a flat truss of 7. (Gable, Herbert 1976).

'**Gaul'** ('Shilsonii' x *elliottii*). 5', 0°F, ML, 4/3/3. 'Gaul's' waxy, deep red trusses are shaped like globes. An extremely showy red, the color glows like a bright torch. It is upright growing, so pinch it each year if you want it to grow wider. Foliage is deep green. (Rothschild) A.M. 1939.

'**Gay Hostess'** (parentage unknown). 5', -5°F, ML, -/-/-. Leaves are large. Flowers, 3" wide, rosy pink with light green spotting, are held in 14 to the trusses. (Kersey, Frederick 1976).

'**Gay Princess'** ('Atroflo' open pollinated). 5', -5°F, ML, -/-/-. Leaves are long and narrow. 3" wide flowers are pink, with lighter pink on the petal edges, outer surfaces and in the throat. Trusses hold up to 18 flowers. Synonym, 'Pink Princess'. (Herbert 1979).

'**Gene'** (*spiciferum* x *ciliatum*). 3', 5°F, E, 4/2/3. Foliage is small. Flowers, to 1 1/4" across, rosy purple in color, are held in a rounded truss. The plant is susceptible to rust. (Mulligan 1962).

'**General Anthony Wayne'** ('Scintillation' x 'Atrier'). 6', -5°F, ML, 3-4/4/4. Leaves are quite large. Fragrant flowers, to 4" across, are pink in color, with faint spotting in the light green throats. They are carried in a truss of up to 17. (Herbert 1976).

'**General Eisenhower'** (*griffithianum* hybrid). 6', -10°F, M, 3-4/3/4-5. Large, carmine red trusses sit atop big waxy leaves on this strong growing hybrid. (Anthony Kluis 1946).

'**General Eric Harrison'** (*yakushimanum* x 'Shilsonii'). 3', 0°F, ML, -/-/-. Trusses are ball shaped and comprised of long lasting, bright crimson flowers with darker red freckling in the throat. The plant has a rounded frame. Dark green, matte leaves are held for 3 years. (Hydon Nurseries reg. 1972).

'**Genevieve Schmidt'** ('America' x *yakushimanum*). 3', -20°F, L, -/-/-. Here is a tricolor blend of strong red, medium pink, and mauve, with strong red dorsal spots. Flowers are held in trusses of 12. (Delp 1992).

'**Genghis Khan'** ('Britannia' x 'Felis'). 4', -5°F, M, 4/4/3. From the collection of the late Lester Brandt, this compact plant has rich, dense foliage and bright red flowers which are encircled by an enlarged calyx. (Brandt, 1969).

'**Genoveva'** (*catawbiense* x unknown). 5', -20°F, ML, -/-/-. Flowers of pale lilac to white display a yellow-green blotch. A parent of 'Moerheim's Pink'. (Seidel 1918).

'**George Ritter'** (*griersonianum* x unknown). 4', 15°F, L, -/-/-. Leaves are quite large. Flowers are pink with crimson throats, a generous 4 1/4" wide, and are carried in lax trusses of up to 6. (Frye, Druecker 1976).

'**George's Delight'** ('Whitney 6002' x 'Crest'). 3', 0°F, M, -/-/-. These flowers do delight as the dark pink borders fade to soft creamy yellow and become darker yellow in the throat. The plant has good form blooms readily. (Whitney 1967, reg. Sather 1985).

'**George Sweesy'** ('Vera Elliott' x 'Dr. A. Blok'). 4', 5°F, EM, -/-/-. Growth habit is rounded and upright, with branching of greater spread at maturity. The plant is free-flowering and it has medium sized, dark green leaves. Flowers, to 3 1/4" wide, are open funnel-form with wavy margins. They are soft pink, rayed and spotted golden brown, and form a rounded truss of 12 flowers. (Elliott 1981).

'**Georgette'** (*yakushimanum* x 'Exbury Cornish Cross'). 3', 0°F, EM, -/-/-. A neat, compact plant with deep, glossy foliage. Flowers are white, and flushed pink when young. (George, Hydon Nurseries Ltd. 1972) H.C. 1977.

'**George Watling'** (*wardii* or *campylocarpum* hybrid). 4-5', 0°F, M, 3-4/3-4/3. The flowers are a glowing pale primrose yellow with a delightful touch of green. Foliage is glossy, with leaves that are rounded on the ends. (Grieg, Cook not registered).

'**Germania'** ('Antoon van Welie' x *williamsianum*). 4', -15°F, ML, 4/4/4. The plant is compact, and Cox while reports that no sign of *williamsianum* is evident, the dark green, oblong leaves do not mimic those of their other parent either. They are a very handsome blend, showing hybridizing at its best! Flowers of rose pink are paler in the center, lightly freckled with burgundy, and have ruffled rims of deeper pink. The 5-lobed corollas open widely to create very full, frilly, rounded trusses. (D. Hobbie) Gold Medal, IGA, Munich, 1983.

'**Gertrude Bovee'** ('Loderi King George' x 'Ostbo Y3'). 5', -5°F, ML, 4/3-4/3-4. Foliage is very large, handsomely textured. Flowers are large, soft creamy ivory with a blush of pink as they first open. Deep in the throat there is a small accent of maroon spotting. Flowers held in 12-flowered trusses. (Bovee 1972).

'**Gertrude Saxe'** (*carolinianum* x *mucronulatum* 'Paul's Pink'). 5', -25°F, EM, -/-/-. Electric pink flowers appear on an upright plant which has small leaves. (Murcott 1987).

'Gertrude Schale' (*forrestii* ssp. *forrestii* Repens Group x 'Prometheus'). 3', -5ºF, M, 4/3-4/3-4. The plant is similar to 'Scarlet Wonder' but has slightly more elongated leaves. Flowers are scarlet red bells which hang in clusters of 4 or 5. (Hobbie 1951).

'Ghost' ([*maximum* x *yakushimanum*] x *maximum*). 3', -20ºF, VL, -/-/-. Broad foliage with woolly, tan indumentum forms a bush more wide than tall. Yellowish white buds open to white flowers with bright yellow green spots. (Delp 1993).

'Giganteum' (*catawbiense* hybrid). 6', -15ºF, EM-M, 2-3/3/4. This plant should not be confused with the much larger species of the same name. Medium sized leaves are dark green. Light crimson flowers are held in a nicely shaped medium size truss. (Waterer before 1851).

'Gigi' (parentage unknown). 5', -5ºF, ML, 4/3/-. Leaves are medium-sized. Flowers, 3 1/4" wide, are rose red with deeper red spots sprinkled all over the petals. They are held in trusses of up to 18. (Dexter, Burns 1973) A.E. 1973, C.A. 1972.

'Gill's Crimson' (*griffithianum* hybrid). 6', 5ºF, E, 4/3-4/3-4. This plant has a dense, upright, and sturdy habit, with medium to large light green leaves. It is somewhat slow to flower, but once it reaches flowering age it rewards us with blooms that last a long time. Flowers are the brightest blood red, and are held in rounded, tight trusses. (R. Gill & Son).

'Gill's Triumph' (*arboreum* x *griffithianum*). 5', 0ºF, M, 3/3/3. Flowers of strawberry red fade to pink after opening from deep strawberry buds. (R. Gill & Son before 1906) A.M. 1906.

'Ginny Beale' (*metternichii* x *adenopodum*). 30", -10ºF, M, -/-/-. Foliage is medium-sized and quite narrow. Flowers are rose colored with faint pink stripes on the back sides. They are 2" across, have no blotching, and are held 16 to the truss. (Gable, Davis 1978).

'Ginny Gee' (*keiskei* prostrate form x *racemosum*). 2', 0ºF, EM, 5/5/4. Leaves are quite small. Flowers, only 1" across, are pink, dappled white both inside and outside. They bloom at branch ends from groups of up to 11 buds which hold 4 or 5 flowers each. (Berg 1979) S.P.A. (Northwest 1985).

'Gipsy King' ('King George' x *haematodes*). 3', 5ºF, M, 4/3/3. The plant habit is compact and attractive on this little hybrid. Flowers of heavy waxy substance are a rich, deep red. They are held in rather lax trusses. Also spelled 'Gypsy King'. (Rothschild 1939).

'Gipsy Queen' ('Bow Bells' x 'Barclayi Robert Fox'). 3', 0ºF, EM, 3/3/4. Deep red flower bud scales contrast beautifully against deep green, rounded foliage. Flowers open to medium blue-toned pink bells which are more deeply colored on outer petal surfaces. The nodding flowers are held by bright red pedicels which are counterfoil to the bright yellow stamens. Could also be spelled 'Gypsy Queen'. (Roy Clark? Has been grown in Northwestern America since the 1970's).

'Girard's Lucky Stars' (*yakushimanum* hybrid). 4', -25ºF, ML, -/-/-. White flowers with a yellow flare, held in rounded trusses, bloom against small, excellent foliage. This is a very compact, hardy plant. (Girard).

'Girard's Remarkable Pink' (*yakushimanum* x 'Girard's Ruffled Red'). 5', -25ºF, M, -/-/-. Deep pink flowers shaded to silver white centers are held in attractive trusses. Upright and spreading in habit, this plant has glossy leaves that turn slightly at the ends. (Girard).

'Glad Tidings' ('China' x *williamsianum*). 4', 0ºF, E, 3/3/-. Leaves are large. Flowers are also large, to 4" wide, a blended pink and cream color, with a reddish flare. They are held in trusses up to 12. (Lancaster 1965).

'Gladys Johnson' (Diva x *fortunei* ssp. *fortunei*). 5', 0ºF?, ML, -/-/-. Scented flowers are large, to 4" across, rose pink fading lighter, held in 15-flowered truss. The leaves are large. (Johnson 1958) P.A. 1958.

'Glamour Girl' ('Essex Scarlet x *fortunei* ssp. *fortunei*). 5', -15ºF, ML, -/-/-. Each rich pink flower has a dark eye, adding glamour to truss. The vigorous plant has a broad habit. (Shapiro 1959).

'Gleam' (*cinnabarinum* ssp. *cinnabarinum* Roylei Group x 'Royal Flush'). 6', 5ºF, ML, 4/3/2-3. Long tubular flowers are apricot yellow inside the corolla while outer petal surfaces are salmon pink. The flowers hang pendulously in groups of 6-7. Shiny round leaves are gray-blue when new, and as they mature the color changes to deep green with a glaucous cast. Small, upright branches form a columnar plant in keeping with the *cinnabarinum* parentage. (Rothschild).

'Glenda Farrell' (probably a *fortunei* ssp. *fortunei* hybrid). 4', -10ºF, M, 4/4/4. Pure, clean, vibrant rosy red flowers make a very showy display. Foliage is deep green with a slight wave. Note the ratings, this is an attractive plant with a striking flower color. (Dexter hyb. 1943, Efinger intro. 1959, Tyler Arboretum reg. 1983).

'Glenfalloch Blue' (*intricatum* hybrid). 2', EM, 0ºF, -/-/-. This low growing plant has a tight growth habit, and is very floriferous. The vivid blue flowers are showy. (Dunedin, New Zealand).

'Glenn's Orange' see 'Fred Hamilton'

'Gletschernacht' (*russatum* x 'Blue Diamond'). 3' -5ºF, EM, 4/4/3-4. Very deep violet flowers are especially showy on this fine hybrid. Small, scaly leaves are somewhat bronzy green and have an attractive twist. It is sold in the U.S. as 'Starry Night'. (H. Hachmann, G. Stuck reg. 1983).

'Glory of Littleworth' (parentage unknown). 5', -5ºF, M, 5/3/3. Huge orange blotches radiate from the flowers of each snowy white truss. It puts on a stunning display, one that is not forgotten. The plant does well in a sunny location. It has attractive gray-blue foliage during the summer. (Mangles) A.M. 1911.

'Glowing Embers' ('Romany Chal' x *griersonianum*). 4', 5ºF, ML-L, 3-4/3/3. This interesting flower has no stamens. 'Glowing Embers' is a good name because the warm orange-red flowers of waxy texture really do appear to glow. The deep fir green foliage is long and narrow. (Henny 1958).

'Glowing Star' (*fortunei* ssp. *fortunei* x 'C. P. Raffill'). 5', -5ºF, EM, -/-/-. The flowers are coral rose with a red throat. They form tight trusses which are held against light green foliage. (Hardgrove reg. 1958).

'Glowlight' ('Fabia' x *fortunei* ssp. *fortunei*). 5', -5ºF, M, -/-/-. A unique combination of parentage. Flowers are yellow in a semi-lax truss. (Hardgrove).

'Gloxineum' (*fortunei* ssp. *fortunei* hybrid). 5', -15ºF, M, 3-4/3-4/4. The *fortunei* ssp. *fortunei* parentage gives this hybrid an attractive and vigorous growth habit. Foliage of medium size is dark green, narrowly elliptic and has distinctive veining and recurved margins. Slightly ruffled, mid-size flowers are gloxinia pink with a dramatic golden flare on the upper lobes. They are subtly fragrant. (Dexter, deWilde 1958).

'Goldbukett' ('Scintillation' x *wardii*). 3', -10ºF, EM-M, -/-/-. A yellow 'Scintillation'! The foliage has the same size, substance, texture and appeal as 'Scintillation'. The flowers are yellow and have a ruby red blotch. (Hachmann, Stuck reg. 1983) Gold Medal, IV International Garden Exhibition (Munich) 1983.

'Goldbug' (*wardii* [*croceum*] x 'Fabia'). 3', 5ºF, M, 3/3/3. 'Goldbug' is fun because its flower is so unusual. When the truss opens, brick red flowers speckled with lots of maroon dots tumble out. The flowers lighten, becoming yellow. The plant is compact and will become very wide. Its deep green leaves have an interesting twist to them. (R. Henny 1958).

'Golden Anniversary' (*chlorops* x ['Golden West' x 'Mariloo']). 4', 0ºF, M, 4/4/4. A bright reddish flare surrounds the primrose yellow of these bell shaped flowers. (Lancaster 1970).

'Golden Bee' (*keiskei* 'Yaku Fairy' x *melinanthum*). 2', -10ºF, EM, 4-5/4-5/4-5. Flowers are very bright yellow and occur in lax trusses of about 5-6. The plant is more broad than tall. (Berg 1982) C.A. 1983, A.E. 1984.

'Golden Belle' (*fortunei* ssp. *discolor* x 'Fabia'). 4', -5ºF, ML, 3-4/3-4/3. Flowers of warm orange and yellow tones are bright upon this well shaped, broad hybrid. (R. Henny 1958).

'Golden Coach' ('Elizabeth de Rothschild' x 'Jalisco Elect'). 4', 0ºF, M-ML, -/-/-. Yellow flowers have shadings of rose pink and orange. (Drayson 1990).

'Golden Cockerel' ('May Day' x 'Lascaux'). 3', 5ºF, M, -/-/-. A large calyx enhances each of the soft yellow flowers. Buds are scarlet and trusses are lax. (George, Hydon Nurseries Ltd. 1968).

'Goldendale' ([{Loderi x *wardii*} x *campylocarpum*] x 'Skipper'). 6', -5ºF, ML, 3-4/3-4/3-4. Leaves are medium sized. Buttery-yellow flowers, to 3" wide, have dark red centers, and are held in trusses of up to 14. (McNew 1974).

'Golden Dream' ('Naomi' x *campylocarpum*). 5', 5ºF, EM, 4/3/3. The growth habit of this plant is open and tall. Oval leaves are medium green and of average size. Flowers are creamy yellow, shaded pink, in beautiful trusses. A sister plant to 'Carita'. Has been known as 'Carita Golden Dream'. (Rothschild).

'Golden Falcon' (['Socrianum' x 'Rima'] x 'Hawk Crest'). 5', 5ºF?, M, -/-/-. Very pale yellow flowers bloom on this open plant. (George, Hydon Nurseries Ltd. 1976).

'Golden Fantasy' (parentage unknown). 6', 0ºF, ML, -/-/-. Large flowers, up to 5" across, are 7-lobed, cream colored with yellow centers and a have a greenish blotch. They are held in a fragrant, 8-flowered truss. Leaves are large. (Kersey hyb. 1963, Frederick reg. 1979).

'Golden Fleece' see 'Princess Anne'.

'Golden Fleece' ('Goldsworth Orange' x 'Yvonne'). 4', -5ºF, M, -/-/-. These very large, frilly, golden yellow flowers create large trusses. Leaves are big and rounded. This is the true 'Golden Fleece', not 'Princess Anne', which is mistakenly called 'Golden Fleece'. (Slocock 1966).

'Golden Flute' (*burmanicum* hybrid). 2', 15ºF, M, -/-/-. A compact, bushy plant, it has good, bright yellow-gold flowers and handsome foliage. (Sold by Riverwood Gardens, New Zealand).

'Golden Gala' ('Great Lakes' x 'Good Hope'). 3', -20ºF, ML, 4/4/3. Soft yellow- ivory blossoms cover a free flowering shrub. Dorsal lobes have sparse greenish spotting. (Leach reg. 1983).

'Golden Gate' (seedling from *dichroanthum* ssp. *scyphocalyx*). 3', -5ºF, M, 3/4/4. The current consensus is that this is a hybrid. It is an interesting, easy-to-grow plant that has a compact growth habit. The flower color is attractive, one of those good orange colors that Uncle Theodore used to say was "just larapon." (Everything he liked was "just larapon" and that word is not in the dictionary, so don't try to look it up!) The plant is not registered. (unknown introducer).

'Golden Genie' ('Lem's Cameo' x 'Crest'). 4', 0ºF, M, -/-/-. Large yellow trusses bloom heavily and from a young age. They are displayed against dense, glossy green foliage. The new growth foliage continues the color display as it emerges in mahogany tones. The plant has a mounding habit. (Gene Brady, Briggs Nursery 1991).

'Golden Incense' ('Lemon Custard' x 'Crest'). 5', 0ºF, M, 4/4/3. This hybrid is much like 'Crest' except for darker yellow flowers and more compact plant habit. (Elliott).

'Golden Moments' ('Hotei' x ['Pink Petticoats' x *wardii* selfed]). 4'. 5ºF, M, -/-/-. Attractive, golden yellow flowers are heavily produced. This medium sized plant is round growing and has glossy green leaves. Note: This parentage is different from the parentage recorded when the plant was registered. It is based on later information from Lofthouse. (Lofthouse 1981).

'Golden Orfe' (*concatenans* x 'Lady Chamberlain'). 4', 5ºF, M, 4-5/3/3. The small foliage has scales below the leaves. The yellow flowers have a hint of orange. (Harrison 1964) A.M. 1964.

'Golden Pheasant' ('Day Dream' x 'Margaret Dunn'). 4', 5ºF, ML, 3-4/3/3. Opening buds reveal golden yellow flowers which are enriched with brilliant crimson at the flower center. (Brandt 1965).

'Golden Princess' (*keiskei* 'Yaku Fairy' x *mekongense* var. *melinanthum*). 2', -5ºF, EM, 4/4/4. A compact, tidy plant which is covered with small, pointed leaves and lax trusses of yellow flowers. A sister of 'Golden Bee'. (Berg 1982).

'Golden Salmon' (['Atrier' grex x 'Atrier' grex] probably crossed with a sibling from the same cross, not a self). 5', -15ºF, ML, -/-/-. Leaves are medium large. Blooms of strong substance have 7 lobes and measure to 3 1/2" across. The color is salmon, with a darker blotch of radiating stripes. Flowers are fragrant and are held in a lax trusses of up to 10. (Gable, Nearing 1973).

'Golden Spur' ('May Day' x 'Lascaux'). 4', -10ºF, ML, -/-/-. Golden yellow flowers begin as vibrant red buds and form into a lax truss. The plant is neat and compact. (George, Hydon Nurseries 1975).

'Golden Star' (*fortunei* ssp. *fortunei* x *wardii* Croceum Group). 5', 0ºF, ML, 4/3-4/3-4. Each flower has wavy petals of solid mimosa yellow that shimmers in the sunlight. The foliage is rounded and of medium size. (Hardgrove, Burns 1978).

'Golden Torch' ('Bambi' x ['Grosclaude' x *griersonianum*]). 4', 5ºF, ML, 4/4/4. Warm pink buds open to a delightful soft yellow flower. The foliage is deep green with a light kiss of brown indumentum on the underside. A feast for the eye to behold, and sorry to say it is also a feast for the weevils who consider its foliage a delicacy. So, keep it sprayed! There is some question about its correct parentage. (John Waterer, Sons & Crisp 1971) H.C. 1977.

'Golden Wedding' (*yakushimanum* x 'Mrs. Lammot Copeland'). 3', 0°F, M, 4/4/4. Very dark red buds open yellow. Each flower has seven lobes, creating a full truss. The plant is as broad as tall and it has dark green foliage. (Larson hyb. 1969, Davis intro. 1980, reg. 1986).

'Golden Wit' (*dichroanthum* ssp. *scyphocalyx* seedling [possibly a hybrid] x ['Moonstone' x 'Adrastia']). 3', 0°F, M, 4/4/3. When this was first shown in Seattle, it was acclaimed as one of the finest yellows yet to be introduced. The plant is low, with fine foliage. The flowers are an exquisite primrose yellow, blotched red, held in trusses to 9. Like most of the yellow elepidote rhododendrons, it easily gets root rot in hot, wet conditions. (Witt, Michand 1966).

'Goldfee' ([*wardii* x 'Alice Street'] x ['Omega' x *wardii*]). 3', -10°F, M, -/-/-. Coppery buds open to funnel-campanulate flowers which are pale greenish yellow tinged with light orient pink and which have oxblood red dorsal spots. Dark, rich green foliage densely covers the compact, mounding plant. Synonym, 'Goldstar'. (Hachmann hyb. 1969, Stuck reg. 1988).

'Goldfinch' (*wardii* x 'Mrs. P. D. Williams'). 4', -15°F, ML, -/-/-. If you like predominant blotches, here's a plant to consider! The pink flowers are highlighted by a beautiful golden eye. Very attractive. (Collyer hyb., exh. by Collingwood Ingram 1945).

'Goldflimmer' (sport of *catawbiense* or *ponticum*?). 5', -10°F, L, 3/4-5/4. This neat, compact plant has interesting variegated foliage of emerald green with touches of primrose yellow. The ponticum-like, mauve, ruffled flowers are carried in fairly small trusses. It is a good plant, not weak rooted and brittle as is often the case with other varigated foliage hybrids. (Hobbie, Hachmann 1983).

'Goldfort' ('Goldsworth Yellow' x *fortunei* ssp. *fortunei*). 5', -15°F, M, 3-4/3/4. Here is a light yellow that shows far more hardiness and adaptability than most of the yellows. For this reason it is extremely popular. The foliage is a gold-toned green. (Slocock 1937).

'Goldika' (*wardii* x 'Adriaan Koster'). 3', -10°F, M, -/-/-. Flat faced, bright yellow flowers have carmine spotting. The compact plant has rounded foliage that resembles that of *R. wardii*. (Hobbie 1955).

'Goldilocks' (*xanthostephanum* x *chryseum*). 2', 0°F, M, 4/3/3. While there is a registered British hybrid by the same name, this is the hybrid most often grown in the United States. Very dark foliage covers a small plant with small, bright yellow flowers. (Plant patent No. 5149, by Howard Kerrigan, Hayward, CA, about 1980?).

'Goldkrone' ([*wardii* x 'Alice Street'] x 'Hachmann's Marina'). 4', -15°F, M, -/-/-. Golden yellow flowers have ruby red freckles on the upper petals, and are held in trusses of 16-18. The compact, rounded plant has rich, green foliage. (H. Hachmann hyb. 1969, G. Stuck reg. 1983).

'Gold Medal' ('Cream Glory' x 'Seattle Gold'). 5', -5°F, M, 4-5/4/4. Huge, golden, sunny yellow flowers are among the largest of any rhododendron. The upper petals are lightly spotted with a kiss of red and they arch broadly backwards to fully display their size. The vigorous growing plant has matte forest green leaves of medium-large size, about three times as long as wide. (Greer 1988).

'Gold Mohur' ('Day Dream' x 'Margaret Dunn'). 5', 0°F, ML, 4/3/3. Golden yellow flowers have bands of rainbow pink on the outside to mark the division of each petal lobe. The flower throat is tinted deep gold. Myrtle green leaves are more long than wide and have a gentle downward roll. Also registered as 'Mohur'. (Brandt 1955) P.A. 1955.

'Gold Moon' ('Goldfort' x 'Full Moon'). 3', -10°F, EM, -/-/-. Leaves are large. 7-lobed flowers, 4" wide, are white with throats tinged yellowish green. They are held in trusses of up to 11 fragrant flowers. (Bagoly, Tietjens 1976).

'Goldrausch' ('Hachmann's Marina' x [*wardii* x 'Alice Street']). 3', -10°F, M, -/-/-. Orange buds open to reveal golden yellow flowers which retain an orange tint on outer petal surfaces. Trusses are loose, with 9-11 slightly pendulous flowers. The plant grows round and compact. (Hachmann hyb. 1983, Stuck reg. 1984).

'Goldstrike' (*oreotrephes* x 'Royal Flush'). 4', 0°F, M, 4/4/3. An outstanding, unusual plant. Fleshy, tubular flowers have sunny yellow exteriors and the inner petal color is buttercup yellow. The foliage is glossy, olive green. (R. Henny 1961).

'Goldsworth Crimson' (*griffithianum* x hardy hybrid). 5', 0°F, EM-M, 2/3/3. This is a vigorous plant, spreading but compact, with dark green, glossy, long, narrow leaves. It exhibits a prolific bloom of bright crimson, rounded trusses. Flowers have black spotting on the upper lobes. (Slocock 1926).

'Goldsworth Orange' (*dichroanthum* x *fortunei* ssp. *discolor*). 5', -5°F, L, 3-4/3-4/3. Tropical orange flowers are bright in the early summer sun. Each truss holds many widely flared, funnel form blooms. Felt green leaves are held by red petioles. The plant is shapely and heat tolerant. (Iocock 1938).

'Goldsworth Pink' (*griffithianum* x unknown). 6', -10°F, M, 3-4/3-4/3-4. Trusses are lax, yet tall. Large, shell pink flowers fade to almost white. The plant grows large. (Slocock 1933) A.M. 1958.

'Goldsworth Yellow' (*caucasicum* x *campylocarpum*). 5', -15°F, ML, 2-3/3/3. This hybrid has dense growth habit and medium sized yellowish leaves. Apricot colored buds open to buff yellow flowers which have bronze dots on the upper lobe. The flower deepens in color as it ages. Trusses are medium size and compact. Hardy, but difficult to root. (Slocock 1925) A.M. 1925.

'Golfer' (*yakushimanum* x *pseudochrysanthum*). 18", -15°F, EM, 3-4/5/4. This plant is a foliage lover's dream. The leaves are shaped much like the "yak"s but these carry the upper coating of tomentum for almost the entire year. The undersides are blanketed with pale gray indumentum. Flowers are clear pink and are held in tight ball-shaped trusses of up to 13. (Berg hyb. 1966, Caperci intro. & reg. 1983) C.A. 1985.

'Gomer Waterer' (*catawbiense* hybrid). 6', -15°F, ML, 3/4-5/4-5. This old standby is one of the best whites ever hybridized. Flower buds are a delicate pink which open white, but retain just a hint of pink until fully mature. The upper lobe is accented with a handsome golden green flare. Large, deep green leaves are sun tolerant. (J. Waterer before 1900) A.M. 1906.

'Good News' ('Britannia' x 'Romany Chal'). 4', -5°F, VL, 3/3-4/3. A beautiful, free-flowering, compact plant favored for its late blooming season. Red buds open to translucent crimson red flowers which have slightly wavy lobes. Foliage has pale green new growth that is thinly covered with fawn tomentum. Mature leaves maintain a slight tan indumentum on the undersides. (J. Henny 1973).

'Goosander' (*ludlowii* x *lutescens*). 18", -5°F, EM, 3-4/3-4/3. Considering the miniscule size of the foliage, these little 1 1/2" flowers are large! They are a good, strong yellow speckled with red on the upper lobes. Scales are noticeable on both sides of the leaves, making them appear even darker green. (Cox 1981) A.M. 1981.

'Gordon Jones' ('Sappho' x *yakushimanum* Exbury form). 3', -5°F, M, -/-/-. Strong purplish pink buds open very pale purple then fade to white. They have prominent dark red spotting and form domed trusses. This compact *yakushimanum* hybrid has silvery new growth and glossy oblong foliage. (R. Murcott hyb. 1975, W. Brack reg. 1989).

'Gosh Darn!' (['Catalgla' x 'Mrs. H. R. Yates'] selfed). 3', -15°F, L, -/-/-. The 'Gosh Darn!' buds are yellowish orange and pinkish yellow and the colors blend to variations of the same as the flowers open. (Delp 1992).

'Hobbie Salute' ('Essex Scarlet' x *forrestii* ssp. *forrestii* Repens Group). 3', -15°F, E, -/-/-. Abundant bell shaped flowers of dark red make a lovely show against slightly turned, deep green leaves. This semi-dwarf has a mounding growth habit. (Hobbie?, sold by Roslyn Nursery 1994).

'Hockessin' (*pubescens* x *keiskei*). 3', -25°F, E, 3/2/3. Flowers are apricot fading to white. All terminals bud. Leaves are smallish. It is the same as 'Chesapeake', but larger. (Nearing 1958).

'Holden' (red *catawbiense* seedling x 'Cunningham's White'). 4', -15°F, EM-M, 3/3-4/4. Another "hardy" rhododendron, with lustrous dark green foliage and compact growth habit. It bears rose red flowers which are each marked with a small red spot. (Shammarello 1958).

'Hollandia' ('Pink Pearl' x 'Charles Dickens'). 6', 0°F, ML, 3/3/3-4. This plant has good foliage and vibrant red flowers. Synonym, 'G. Streseman'. (L. J. Endtz & Co.)

'Holstein' ('Humboldt' x 'Catawbiense Grandiflorum'). 5', -15°F, ML, -/-/-. Lilac purple, 5-lobed flowers, shading to paler, have a dark red blotch and bloom in trusses of 15-16. The oval leaves are sparsely hairy. (Hachmann hyb. 1959, Stuck reg. 1983).

'Holy Moses' (*smirnowii* x 'King of Shrubs') or ('Souvenir of Anthony Waterer' ['Anton Waterer'?] x 'King of Shrubs') or a (reverse cross of either). 4', -5°F, ML, 4/4/3-4. If you are confused about the above parentage, so am I. One year I listed it with unknown parentage. Then I received a number of letters quoting the parentage Mr. Lem had given. Shown above is the result. Many of the letters I received were written in Mr. Lem's own handwriting, so it appears he was not positive of the parentage himself. I feel from observing the plant that it is probably *smirnowii* x 'King of Shrubs' (or reverse cross). In fact, in one letter, Mr. Lem states he sent a leaf to David G. Leach, and Mr. Leach felt it was a *smirnowii* cross. Anyway, it is a sensational orange and yellow bicolor and a choice garden variety. The foliage and plant are exceptional. It sets gigantic flower buds in the early fall that sit on the plant as if they just can't wait for spring. (Lem before 1965, not registered).

'Homer' ('Kaiser Wilhelm' x 'Agnes'). 4', -5°F, M, -/-/-. Pure pink flowers have markings of red brown, faintly detected on the upper petals. (Seidel hyb. 1906, intro. 1916).

'Honey' ('Hawk' x 'China'). 5', 5°F, M, -/-/-. A vigorous plant, growing as wide as tall, this hybrid has flowers of clear yellow, opening with a pink flush, held in large trusses. (Slocock) H.C. 1975.

'Honey' (*wardii* x 'Bow Bells'). 3', 5°F, M, -/-/-. This plant, growing to 3' wide, has broad, orbicular leaves and flowers of Egyptian buff, fading paler. (Rudolph Henny 1960, reg. 1962).

'Honey Bee' (*hanceanum* x *ludlowii*). 1', 0°F, E-EM, 4-5/4-5/3-4. Creamy yellow bells almost hide the plant, as it blooms so profusely. Dark green, small foliage is preceded by striking bronze juvenile growth. Like all of Warren Berg's crosses, it is an outstanding plant. (Berg before 1990).

'Honeydew' ('Carolyn Grace' x 'Moonstone'). 4', 5°F, M, 3-4/4/3-4. Plant habit is compact and rounded. Flowers are sunny yellow, similar to 'Moonstone' except smaller. (Wright Sr. & Jr. 1962).

'Honeymoon' ([*wardii* {Barto form} x 'Devonshire Cream'] x *wardii* {former var. *croceum*}). 4', 5°F, M, 3/3-4/3. The plant is compact, with heavy, dark green foliage. Yellow flowers, accented with a small orange blotch in the greenish throat, are set in flat trusses of up to 15. (Whitney, Sather 1976).

'Hong Kong' ('Catalgla' x 'Crest'). 5', -20°F, ML, 3/3/3. A welcome addition to the garden not only because of its primrose yellow flowers but also because of its super hardiness. Not many yellows can take such winter abuse. Leaves are glossy green. (Leach intro. 1974, reg. 1983).

'Honore Hacanson' ('Carmen' x 'Choremia'). 18", 0°F, M, 4/3/3. Silvery indumentum on deep green foliage encircles cardinal red flowers with a large calyx. Sister seedling to 'Fred Robbins' and 'Little Nemo'. (Brandt 1965).

'Honsu's Baby' (*keiskei* 'Yaku Fairy' x *spiciferum*). 1', 5°F, E, 4/4/4. Masses of white flowers with margins of pale purplish pink emerge from strong pink buds to cover this spreading plant. The leaves are convex and scaly. It is a beautiful, low growing plant. When flowering, it blooms so profusely, you can't tell that it has leaves. (Dr. H. Spady reg. 1987).

'Hope Braafladt' (*lindleyi* x 'Countess of Haddington'). 3', 20°F, E, 4/3/4. Leaves are of medium size. Fragrant, white flowers, to 3 1/4 inches, have a dull lavender blotch and faint stripes, and are held in lax trusses of up to 5. (Braafladt 1979).

'Hope Findlay' (['Loderi' x 'Earl of Athlone'] x 'Creeping Jenny'). 5', -10°F, EM, -/-/-. Large, globular lax trusses of currant red cover this super, vigorous plant. Dark green, glossy leaves frame each truss. (Windsor Great Park) P.C. 1974, A.M. 1979.

'Hoppy' (*yakushimanum* x 'Doncaster' selfed). 3', -10°F, M, 4/4/4. Ball shaped trusses of white flowers with yellow spots adorn this tight growing dense shrub. (John Waterer, Sons & Crisp 1972) A.M. 1977.

'Horizon Dawn' (['Hotei' x 'Tropicana'] x [*yakushimanum* x {'Alice Franklin' x 'Virginia Scott'}]). 4', 5°F, EM, -/-/-. This plant has abundant pale, clear yellow flowers, shading to vivid yellow throats. Attractive jade green leaves cover the compact, rounded plant. (Brockenbrough 1991).

'Horizon Lakeside' ('Nancy Evans' x 'Lem's Cameo'). 3', 0°F, -/-/-. Budding young, this compact plant bears ball shaped trusses of 15 or more delicately fragrant, large flowers, that are pale yellow with a bright carmine throat, spotted above. (Brockenbrough 1992).

'Horizon Monarch' ('Nancy Evans' x 'Point Defiance') 6', 10°F, M, 4-5/4/4. Very heavy, gigantic trusses of 15 pale greenish yellow flowers, with a small, vivid red flare, open from red scarlet buds. Large, leathery deep green leaves form an upright, spreading, yet well manicured plant. (Brockenbrough 1989).

'Horizon Snowbird' (['Britannia' x *yakushimanum*] x ['Mrs. Lindsay Smith' x *yakushimanum*]). 3', 0°F, ML, -/-/-. A rounded, compact bush with narrow medium green foliage. This hybrid bears creamy white flowers, with pink filaments, which turn snowy white. The flowers open from strong purplish pink buds. Formerly called 'Peony'. (Brockenbrough 1989).

'Hotei' ('Goldsworth Orange' x [*souliei* x *wardii*]). 3', 5°F, M, 5/4/3. Growth habit is compact and pleasing, holding are medium sized leaves. The flowers, to 2 1/2" wide, with a well defined calyx, are terrific canary yellow, and are set in ball shaped trusses of up to 12 flowers. Must be planted in well drained, cool soil as it is prone to root rot. (Sifferman, Nelson 1968).

'Hot Stuff' ('Carmen' x 'Leo'). 2', 5°F, M, 3-4/4/3. Deep red flowers, that look as if they were made of wax, light up this luscious little plant. The small foliage is super dark green and looks as if it were just polished by a leprechaun to an exceptional gloss. Strong branches make a good plant habit. (Greer 1988).

'Hudson Bay' (*minus* var. *minus* Carolinianum Group white form x *dauricum* white form). 3', -20ºF, E, -/-/-. Terminal 3-flower clusters of wide, white, wavy lobed flowers bloom against glossy yellow-green leaves which have rusty brown scales on the undersides. The foliage, which is held for 2 years, becomes bronze in the fall. (Leach reg. 1983).

'Hugh Koster' ('George Hardy' x a 'Doncaster' hybrid). 6', 5ºF, ML, 2/3/3. Growth is upright and spreading, with grooved leaves of medium large size. Medium sized, crimson flowers with lighter center are held in an upright cylindrical truss. (M. Koster & Sons 1915) A.M. 1933.

'Hugtight' (*forrestii* ssp. *forrestii* Repens Group x *aureum*). 2', 0ºF, EM, 4/4/4. Great name and flower! The dark rose flower is actually a double peony type not found in many rhododendrons. The plant is very compact and has dark green, small foliage. (Larson hyb., Fisher intro.).

'Humboldt' (*catawbiense* hybrid). 5', -5ºF, M, 3-4/3/3-4. The plant has an upright habit clothed with dark green leaves. Flowers of pale mauve with a dark eye are held in a ball shaped truss. (Seidel 1926).

'Humboldt Sunrise' ('Else Frye' x *johnstoneanum*). 3', 15ºF, EM, 4/3/3-4. Foliage is medium sized. Flowers are scented, yellow with a darker blotch, to 3 1/4" across and are set in trusses to 6. (Anderson 1967, Braafladt 1979).

'Humming Bird' (*haematodes* x *williamsianum*). 30", 0ºF, EM, 3/4/3-4. Deep pink to red flowers cover this plant. The Exbury form has flowers which are more red than other forms. The rounded foliage has a light coating of indumentum, and densely covers the compact habit. (J. C. William 1933).

'Hunting Hill' (possibly a Fortunea subsection hybrid). 4', -5ºF, M, -/-/-. This upright plant is nicely trimmed with strong pink flowers. (Dexter before 1943, Ross, Wister 1980).

'Hurricane' ('Mrs. Furnivall' x 'Anna Rose Whitney'). 5', 5ºF, M, 3-4/4/3-4. These flowers are a beautiful shade of pink with markings of deep pink. It is a vigorous growing plant, yet compact. (Whitney, Sather 1976).

'Hussar' ([*eriogynum* x 'Fabia'] x 'May Day'). 4', 5ºF, M, -/-/-. Blood red flowers have brown speckling. The plant has compact habit. (John Waterer, Sons & Crisp 1971).

'H. W. Sargent' (*catawbiense* hybrid). 5', -25ºF, ML, 2-3/2-3/3. Extra cold tolerance has helped this plant stand the test of time. The flowers are a magenta rose. (A. Waterer 1865) F.C.C. 1865.

'Hydon Ball' (*yakushimanum* x 'Springbok'). 3', 0ºF, M, 4/4/4. Dull green, elongated foliage surrounds the flowers, which are pink with cream tones. Flowers have light brown spotting. The plant is compact. (George, Hydon Nurseries 1969) A.M. 1977.

'Hydon Dawn' (*yakushimanum* x 'Springbok'). 3', 5ºF, M, 4/4/4. Glossy green foliage coats a vigorous, compact plant. Pink flowers fade to a paler tone at the frilled edges and the neyron rose throats are accented with reddish brown spots. Large, compact trusses of 16 are formed. (George, Hydon Nurseries 1969) F.C.C. Wisely Trials 1986.

'Hydon Glow' (*yakushimanum* x 'Springbok'). 3', 0ºF, M, 4/4/4. Large, compact, rounded trusses are composed of 14, widely funnel-shaped, rosy pink, lightly freckled blooms. (George, Hydon Nurseries 1968).

'Hydon Harrier' ('May Day' x 'Jervis Bay'). 4', 5ºF, M, -/-/-. The open plant is set ablaze with orange scarlet flowers. (George, Hydon Nurseries 1975).

'Hydon Hunter' (*yakushimanum* x 'Springbok'). 3', 5ºF, M, 4/4/4. This vigorous, compact plant has dark green leaves and dome-shaped trusses of 14 white flowers, blushed light orchid pink. (George, Hydon Nurseries 1972) A.M. 1976, F.C.C. Wisley Trials 1979.

'Hydon Mist' (*russatum* x 'Blue Diamond'). 2', -5ºF, EM, 3-4/3-4/3-4. Light violet flowers are held in trusses of 6-7 on this dwarf, compact plant. (George, Hydon Nurseries 1976).

'Hydon Pink' ('Moser's Maroon' x 'Ice Cream'). 4', 0ºF, ML, -/-/-. A large compact truss formed from pinkish lavender flowers which open to expose a crimson throat. Foliage is glossy. (George, Hydon Nurseries 1968).

'Hydon Rodney' (*augustinii* x 'Azamia'). 4', -5ºF, EM, -/-/-. Vibrant violet flowers with darker spotting bloom on this taller growing, twiggy plant. (George, Hydon Nurseries 1972).

'Hydon Salmon' (*fortunei* ssp. *discolor* hybrid x *griersonianum*). 5', 0ºF, M, -/-/-. Foliage is dull green. Funnel-shaped, glowing salmon pink flowers are more deeply colored in the throat and gather to form full, rounded trusses of 12-14. (George, Hydon Nurseries 1970) A.M. 1976.

'Hydon Snowflake' (*orthocladum* var. *microleucum* x 'Chikor'). 2', 0ºF, EM, -/-/-. White flowers in trusses of 3 decorate this small, open plant. (George, Hydon Nurseries 1978).

'Hyperion' (unknown hybrid from Waterer). 5', -5ºF, ML, 3/3/3. The plant habit is rather open and somewhat spreading. Large, dark green leaves are long and narrow. Flowers are white with a blue tinge, blotched deep chocolate purple. (A. Waterer before 1925).

'Ibex' (*griersonianum* x *pocophorum*). 5', 5ºF, EM, 4/3-4/4. Bright, fiery red describes these flowers. The foliage is frosted on the underside with a layer of cinnamon indumentum. An attractive plant. (Rothschild 1941) A.M. 1948.

'Iceberg' see 'Lodauric Iceberg'.

'Ice Cream' ('Dido' x *fortunei* ssp. *discolor*). 5', -10ºF, L, -/-/-. Very large flowers of yellowish pink fade to yellow and then to white in the throat. There is faint olive green spotting on the upper petal. (Slocock 1962). A.M. 1960.

'Ice Cube' ('Catalgla' x 'Belle Heller'). 4-5', -20ºF, ML, 4/3/4. This is a favorite hardy rhododendron. Flowers are a delightful ivory white with a kiss of lemon at the base of the upper petal. They are held in cone shaped trusses. The leaves are colored towards the olive tones and have a slight white tomentum on the undersides. (Shammarello 1973).

'Ida Bradour' ('Mary Belle' x *vernicosum* aff., R. 18139, #2). 5', -10ºF, ML, 3-4/3-4/3-4. Leaves are medium to large, and very narrow. 3 1/2" flowers are shades of pink with yellow green throat, held in a ball-shaped truss up to 14. (Gable 1959, Yates 1978).

'Idealist' (*wardii* x 'Naomi'). 5', 5ºF, M, 4/3/3. The growth habit is upright and vigorous, with long, flat, rounded leaves that are a colorful frog green. Pale yellow, widely bell-shaped flowers also have a faint tinge of green. (Rothschild) A.M. 1945.

'Idol' ('Loderi King George' x 'Britannia'). 5', -5ºF, M, 4/4/4. As the very large, nicely formed, rose red flowers fade to lighter centers, they create a striking two-toned effect. The plant is upright and vigorous. (Henny) P.A. 1957.

'Ignatius Sargent' (*catawbiense* hybrid). 5', -25ºF, ML, 2/2/4. This hardy plant has an open growth habit. Leaves are large and flowers are deep rose in color. (A. Waterer before 1900).

'Igtham Gold' (*wardii* hybrid). 4', -10ºF, L, -/-/-. A great season extender for yellow flowers! Each flower has a crimson blotch on a good, strong yellow background. Originally named 'Soleil d'Or'. (Reuthe 1952).

'Igtham Peach' (*dichroanthum* hybrid). 3', -10ºF, M, -/-/-. A very prolific bloomer with many truly peach colored flowers. It blooms reliably. (Reuthe).

'Igtham Purple' (*ponticum* hybrid). 5', -10ºF, M, -/-/-. Flowers are very dark purple and conspicuous white stamens add a nice accent. (Reuthe).

'Igtham Yellow' (*wardii* x *decorum*). 5', -10ºF, EM, 4/3-4/3-4. Very large creamy yellow trusses form on an appealing, bushy plant. (Reuthe).

'Ilam Cream' ('Loderi' x unknown). 5', 5ºF, M, 4-5/3. Huge, fragrant flowers form huge trusses. The heavy petals are rich satiny cream touched with soft pink. The leaves are strong and leathery. Often incorrectly called 'Loderi Ilam Cream'. (Edgar Stead hyb. 1950, L. Roland Stead reg. 1981) A.M. 1985.

'Ilam Violet' ('Electra' x *russatum*). 4', 5ºF, M, 4/3/3. The flowers are deep violet blue, and additional color is provided by bronze winter foliage. The plants needs good drainage. (Stead 1947).

'Illahee' ('Mrs. Furnivall' x 'Evening Glow'). 3', -5ºF, ML, 4/3-4/3-4. Leaves are large. Flowers are lavender pink with a yellowish pink throat and an orange-yellow flare. The calyx is striped with orchid pink. Blooms of about 3" across are held in a flat truss of up to 12. (A. Van Veen 1977).

'Imperial' ('Purple Splendour' x 'A. Bedford'). 4', -5ºF, ML, 4/2-3/3. Here is a plant that buds at an extremely young age, sometimes even on a rooted cutting. Very showy flowers are blue purple with a prominent black purple flare coming from the throat. The leaves are glossy, wax green and have red petioles. (Greer 1988).

'Impi' (*sanguineum* ssp. *didymum* x 'Moser's Maroon'). 4-5', 5ºF, ML-L, 3-4/3/3. Interesting black-red flowers are held in a loose truss. This flower color is not seen often. It's most striking when planted to allow the later afternoon sun to shine through the flower. The foliage is deep ruddy green, and both petioles and stems are red. (Rothschild) A.M. 1945.

'Inca Chief' ('Mars' x ['Mars' x *catawbiense* var. *rubrum*]). 5', -20ºF, ML, -/-/-. Foliage is medium to large. 3" wide flowers are purple red, shading lighter to the center. They have a darker blotch and are carried in globular trusses to 18. (Leach 1972).

'Inca Gold' (*chlorops* x unknown). 3', -5ºF, EM, 4/4/3. Leaves are of medium size. Barium yellow flowers are about 3" across, somewhat rayed with mahogany color, and are in a 12-flower truss. (Lancaster 1962) P.A. 1961.

'Independence Day' (unknown, possibly *maximum* cross). 5', -15ºF, L, -/-/-. So named because it can actually still be in bloom on July 4. This rounded, well-formed, mounding plant has light green leaves, held for 3 years. Small, rounded, red flowers fade to lighter red with a dark eye. (Waterer 1915).

'Indiana' (*dichroanthum* ssp. *scyphocalyx* x *kyawii*). 3', 5ºF, L, 3/5/3. Orange flowers play against some of the best foliage you will find on a rhododendron. Very shiny, deep green leaves look as if they were just polished. The foliage on this hybrid is hard to beat. (Rothschild 1941).

'Ingrid Mehlquist' (*yakushimanum* x 'Besse Howells'). 3', -25ºF, ML, 4/4/4. Grayish green leaves have slight bronze indumentum underneath. This semi-dwarf, compact, dense plant is floriferous. The ruffled, soft pink blooms fade to blush pink. (Mehlquist 1994).

'Inheritance' ('Jock' x 'Antoon van Welie'). 4', -5ºF, M, 3-4/3/3. Bright pink flowers in tight trusses accompany very attractive, deep green foliage. (Farwell about 1985).

'Intrifast' (*intricatum* x *fastigiatum*). 2', -15ºF, E, 3/3/3. There is plenty of blue in this plant with electric violet blue flowers and delicate, small foliage which, when new, has an almost metallic blue cast. (Lowinsky 1958).

'Invicta' ([*yakushimanum* x 'Britannia'] x ['Loderi' x 'Britannia']). 4', 0ºF, ML, -/-/-. This plant with upright growth habit has flowers of pale purple. (J. Waterer, Sons & Crisp 1975).

'Irene Bain' (*yakushimanum* x 'May Day'). 3', 0ºF, EM, -/-/-. Pale pink flowers fade to cream while retaining deeper pink, frilled margins. The handsome foliage is slightly coated with indumentum underneath, characteristic of "yak" hybrids. (Dr. Yeates hyb., Mrs. Irene Bain reg. 1979).

'Irene Stead' ('Loderi' selfed). 6', 0ºF, M, 4/3-4/3. Quite similar in growth habit and flower to the 'Loderis' but displaying very strong, deep lilac pink flowers. They provide the unmistakable Loderi fragrance. The plant has long, deep green foliage and it eventually grows into large shrub. (Stead, NZ, reg. 1958) A.M. 1987.

'Irresistible Impulse' ('Mars' x 'Purple Splendour'). 5', -15ºF, ML, 4/3-4/3. Large trusses of deep red purple completely cover this attractive plant. Each flower has a large, deep purple blotch on the upper lobe. It flowers very young, often on a one year old plant. Propagates quite easily. Deep green leaves have a leathery texture. (Dobbs, Greer 1988).

'Isabella Mangles' (*griffithianum* hybrid). 5', -10ºF, EM, -/-/-. This is an old hybrid that has been re-introduced by Littleworth. Large, trumpet-shaped, pink flowers appear on a plant of very vigorous, upright growth. Leave are large. (Mangles before 1880).

'Isabel Pierce' ('Anna' x 'Lem's Goal'). 6', 5ºF, M, 4/3-4/3-4. Rich pink flowers have a creamy appearance that gives them depth and exquisite beauty. The long, narrow leaves are deep glossy green and are made even more rich looking by their bright, straw yellow midvein. (Lem before 1960, Pierce 1975).

'Istar' (*dichroanthum* x 'Naomi'). 3', 0ºF, M, 4/4/3. The yellow flowers have pink markings. This plant is low growing and dense. (Rothschild 1941).

'Ivan D. Wood' (['King of Shrubs' x 'Fawn'] x 'Dido'). 3', 5ºF, ML, 4/3-4/4. Deep cream flowers diminish in pigment at petal edges. The vigorous plant grows with loose, sometimes sprawling branches. (Coker 1979).

'Ivanhoe' ('Chanticleer' x *griersonianum*). 6', 5ºF, M, 3/3/3. Brilliant red trusses have flowers with deeper red spattering on the upper lobes. The plant grows rather tall with an open, loose habit. (Rothschild 1941) A.M. 1945.

'Ivery's Scarlet' (parentage unknown). 6', 10ºF, EM, 3/3/3. This hybrid has upright growth which tends to be willowy. It roots easily. The light green leaves are medium large and narrow. Brilliant red flowers are held in a small, round truss. Synonym, 'Ivorianum'. (RHS reg 1958).

'Ivory Bells' ('Chlorops' x *williamsianum*). 3', -5ºF, EM, 4/4/3. Dainty trusses of 10 light yellow flowers are held on a compact, dense plant which has oval leaves. (Lancaster 1966).

'Ivory Coast' (*keiskei* x *dauricum* 'Arctic Pearl'). 4', -20ºF, VE, 3-4/3-4/3. Small, elliptic, scaly, chartreuse leaves are retained year round. The wide, 5-lobed, pale greenish ivory flowers age to white. This hybrid blooms very early, bringing spring to the winter garden. (Leach reg. 1985).

'Ivory Queen' ('Diane' x 'Phryne'). 4', 5ºF, EM, -/-/-. Glossy green foliage provides the background for the large, creamy white flowers which each have a red eye. (Waterer, Sons & Crisp 1965).

'Ivory Tower' (*catawbiense* var. *album* x [*wardii* x *fortunei* ssp. *fortunei*]). 5', -25ºF, EM, -/-/-. Leaves are medium size and narrow. Blooms of 3" across are held in a globular truss of up to 13 flowers. They are ivory-colored with dorsal blushing and 2 disconnected greenish yellow stripes. (Leach 1964).

'Jabberwocky' (*cubittii* x *moupinense*). 2', 15ºF, E, -/-/-. These light violet pink flowers have deeper red pink spotting on the upper petals. (George, Hydon Nurseries 1976) P.C. 1976.

'Jackie Ann' (*macrophyllum* hybrid). 5', -10ºF, ML, 4/3/3. A very appealing, perfect cone shaped truss is composed of pink blossoms which each have an eye of pure yellow. Attractive deep green foliage. (unknown, from Washington state).

'Jack Owen Yates' ('Cataldi' x 'Mars'). 3', -10ºF, ML, -/-/-. Leaves are large. 2 1/2" wide flowers are a light burgundy color, fading to a white center with 2 yellow flares, carried in a 13-flower truss. (Yates 1960, M. Yates 1977).

'Jack Skelton' (*lacteum* x 'Mrs. Lindsay Smith'). 5', -10ºF, M, -/-/-. The plant exhibits strong growth habit and creamy white flowers with red spotting. (unknown).

'Jacksonii' (*caucasicum* x 'Nobleanum'). 4', -15ºF, E, 3/3/3. A medium-sized bush with medium green foliage, this plant is rounded and slow growing. The flowers are bright rose pink with maroon markings and paler spots. The widely funnel shaped flowers bloom profusely and early. This hybrid tolerates industrial pollution. (Herbert 1835).

'Jackwill' (*williamsianum* hybrid). 4', -10ºF, EM, -/-/-. Round leaves accent light rose pink flowers in a lax truss. (Hobbie before 1960).

'Jade' ('Fabia' x 'Corona'). 3', 5ºF, EM, 3/3/3. Leaves are medium size. Flowers are very colorful, orange and pink combined, changing later to greenish yellow. The 2" wide blooms are held in a tight truss. (R. Henny 1958).

'Jaipur' (*forrestii* ssp. *forrestii* Repens Group x *meddianum*). 3', 5ºF, E, 4/2/3. Flowers of heavy substance and rich crimson color droop and nod on this open, low-growing plant. Rather difficult to grow, but blooms young. (Rothschild 1942).

'Jalipeno' ([{'Fabia' x *haematodes*} x 'Earl of Athlone'] x 'Jean Marie de Montague'). 30", 5ºF, EM, 4/3-4/3-4. Attractive, deep green foliage is rough textured and medium sized. Flowers are bright red, sparsely spotted brown, and have dark brown nectaries. The blooms, to 2" wide, are displayed in a truss of up to 18. (Goheen 1976).

'Jalisco' ('Lady Bessborough' x 'Dido'). 4', 5ºF, ML, 4/3/3. A good yellow orange that is a must for hybridizing. Some of the best have come from this. Leaves are medium large in size and medium green in color. Flowers are shades of yellowish orange, with some reddish spotting. They are held in open, floppy trusses of 8-10. (Rothschild 1942).

'Jalisco Eclipse' ('Lady Bessborough' x 'Dido'). 4', 5ºF, ML, 4/4/3. The primrose yellow flowers have a crimson blotch and spotting. Trusses are loose and lax. (Rothschild 1942) A.M. 1948.

'Jalisco Elect' ('Lady Bessborough' x 'Dido'). 4', 5ºF, ML, 4/3-4/3. This is the primrose yellow form of 'Jalisco'. (Rothschild 1942) A.M. 1948.

'Jalisco Goshawk' ('Lady Bessborough' x 'Dido'). 4', 5ºF, ML, 4/3/3. Deep yellow flowers, each having a rich, red eye. This hybrid is considered by some to be the best of the group. (Rothschild 1948).

'Jalisco Jubilant' ('Lady Bessborough' x 'Dido'). 4', 5ºF, ML, 4/3/3. Sulphur yellow flowers, with faint greenish spotting in the throat, are highlighted by a beautiful yellow calyx. Very nice. (Rothschild) A.M. 1966.

'James Barto' (probably *williamsianum* x *orbiculare*). 5', -5ºF, EM, 3/4/3. A rather compact plant which has tough textured, medium sized leaves. Flowers are slightly fragrant, and held in a somewhat loose truss of 3-5. The funnel shaped blooms are fuchsine pink. (Barto, Prentice 1958) P.A. 1953.

'James Burchett' (*fortunei* ssp. *discolor* x unnamed hybrid). 5', -5ºF, M-ML, -/-/-. The large growing plant achieves a size twice as wide as high. Each flower of the large truss is white with a very faint pink edge and slight yellow in the throat. (Slocock reg 1962) A.M. 1960.

'James MacIntosh' (parentage unknown). 5', 0ºF, M, 3/3/3. Deep pink-red flowers bloom on this hybrid which has an upright habit. (Waterer 1870).

'Jan Bee' (Captain Jack' x *kingianum*). 3', 5ºF, M, 4/5/4. Tubular funnel-shaped flowers of heavy substance are deep blood red, spotted with even darker maroon. Tall, ball-shaped trusses hold 18-20 blooms against a background of narrow leaves. It is a broad, upright plant. (W. E. Berg reg. 1981) C.A. 1982.

'Jan Dekens' (unknown, probably similar parentage to 'Antoon van Welie'). 5', - 5ºF, ML, 3-4/3-4/3. This is a strong, vigorous plant with large, boldly curled leaves. Frilled flowers are vibrant bright pink, deeper on the edges, fading to pale pink shortly after they open. The large blooms are set in compact, upstanding trusses. (Blaauw 1940).

'Jane Grant' (*yakushimanum* x *smirnowii*). 4', -20ºF, M, 4/4/4. Dark green foliage covers a well-shaped, attractive plant. Deep pink buds open to very pale pink, ruffled flowers which are shaded darker at the edges. The leaves are characteristic of *yakushimanum*; the growth habit is more similar to *smirnowii*. (White Flower Farm before 1994).

'Jane Henny' ('Lady Bligh' x 'Loderi Venus'). 6', 0ºF, ML, -/-/-. Foliage is large. White flowers are 4" wide, with pink shading and speckling, held in a truss up to 13 flowers. Synonym, 'Rosebud'. (R. Henny 1978).

'Jane Mamot' (*griffithianum* hybrid). 6', -5ºF, M, 4/4/-. This is supposedly a sister seedling to 'Jean Marie de Montague', having a taller habit but similar bright red flowers. Does well in full sun. (possibly C. B. van Nes & Sons before 1940).

'Jane Rogers' ('Mrs. Donald Graham' x 'Mrs. R. S. Holford'). 5', -5ºF, ML, 4/3/3. One of the most distinctive pinks, splashed with a dark vibrant flare. Petals are strong medium pink and the burgundy flare originates deep in the throat. (Ostbo 1957).

'Janet Blair' (Dexter hybrid?). 6', -15ºF, ML, 4/3/4. David Leach selected this variety for naming. Frilled, light pink flowers have a distinctive green flare on the upper petal. It is a vigorous, good-looking plant. This is the proper name of the plant which was called 'John Wister'. (Leach 1962).

'Janet Scroggs' ('Virginia Scott' x 'Jasper'). 6', 5oF, ML, 4/4/3-4. Leaves are fairly large. Yellow, 2 3/4" flowers have dorsal spotting of dull orange, and are carried in a 9 flower truss. (Larson 1978).

'Janet Warrilow' (probably *campanulatum* cross). 4', -5oF, M, -/-/-. A pale center deepens to lavender blue toward the petal edges. Dark green foliage is outstanding. (D. Waterer, Knaphill Nursery 1975).

'Java' ('Mars' x ['Mars' x red *catawbiense*]). 5', -10oF, ML, 4/2/3. Compact, full trusses of red show accents of rose pink in the throats of each flower. (Leach 1958, reg. 1983).

'Jay Murray' (*minus* var. *minus* Carolinianum Group x *mucronulatum* 'Pink Panther'). 5', -15oF, EM, -/-/-. Moderate purplish red buds open to reveal frilled, light purplish pink flowers with brownish orange spotting. The 5-lobed blooms are held in ball shaped trusses of 4-6. The leaves have a scaly coating. (Dr. David Lewis reg. 1987).

'Jean' (*griersonianum* x *decorum*). 5', 10oF, L, 3/3/3. Grown first in Scotland, and now in New Zealand, this hybrid has dark green pointed leaves and glowing pink flowers. (Stirling-Maxwell 1936).

'Jean Marie de Montague' see 'The Honorable Jean Marie de Montague'.

'Jeanne Church' (*macabeanum* x 'Unique'). 4', 5oF, EM, 4/4/-. Rough textured, thick, round leaves resemble *macabeanum*. Primrose yellow flowers have a pink blush and 3 red flares inside the throat. Attractive trusses hold up to 21 flowers. (New Zealand Rhododendron Association raiser, Mrs. Wynne Rayner reg. 1982).

'Jean Rhodes' ('Naomi' x 'Mrs. Horace Fogg'). 5', -5oF, M, 4/4/3. Bright rose flowers, darker dull crimson in the throat, which are held in trusses of 14, distinguish this hybrid. (R. Rhodes hyb., Mrs. L. Hodgson raiser, reg. 1979).

'Jennie Dosser' ('Britannia' x 'Trilby'). 6', -5oF, L, 4/3/3. Violet-purple flowers with a large, deep purple eye are borne in tall, full trusses. Leaves are held at right angles to the stem making a nice, rounded collar on which the truss is set. (Dosser 1964).

'Jennifer Marshall' ('Jasper' x 'Alice Franklin'). 5', -5oF, M, 4/4/3. This plant has lovely yellow flowers with a hint of bronze, which are speckled with poppy orange spots on the upper lobes. (Larson 1983).

'Jerico' (*keiskei* Mt. Kuromi form x *minus* var. *minus* Carolinianum Group 'Epoch'). 3', -20oF, M, 3/3/3. This hybrid is more wide than tall and is extremely floriferous. There are six, 5-lobed, flowers per truss. Pale yellow green flowers with pale yellow dorsal spots open from light yellow-green buds. Low and spreading in habit and dome shaped, it can make a good foundation plant. (D. Leach hyb., reg. 1986).

'Jezabel' ('Fabia' hybrid). 4', -5oF, M, 3/3/3. Elongated leaves surround blood red flowers on a plant that is more wide than tall. (Clark before 1958).

'J. G. Millais' ('Ascot Brilliant' x 'Pink Pearl'). 6', 0oF, EM-M, 3/2/3. Growth is strong and open, with medium green leaves of medium to large size. Heavily spotted flowers, in medium sized round trusses, are deep blood red. (J. Waterer about 1915).

'J. H. van Nes' ('Monsieur Thiers' x *griffithianum* hybrid). 5', -5oF, M, 3/3/3-4. Plant habit is rather compact, with medium-large pale green leaves. Flowers are a glowing soft red, paler in the center, held in a tall, compact truss. (C. B. van Nes before 1940).

'Jim Dandy' ('Mrs. Horace Fogg' hybrid). 5', 0oF, M, 4/3-4/3-4. Fragrance, gracefulness and beauty are all here. Flowers are sweetly scented, white-blushed-pink with slight yellow spotting, and held in tall, erect trusses. Dark green leaves and good branching habit add to its appeal. (Elliott before 1988, not reg.).

'Jim Dandy' (*fortunei* ssp. *fortunei* yellow form x 'Marcat') 5', -10oF?, ML, -/-/-. Rosy peach flowers cover this hybrid developed in the eastern U.S. As you will note, there are two plants with the same name, neither of which are registered. (Haag hyb., Cardinal Nurseries intro. before 1994).

'Jim Drewry' ('Ruby F. Bowman' x *elliottii*). 5', 10oF, M, 4/3-4/4. This plant is listed in the registry records as 'Betty Wormald' x *elliottii*. However, it has always been my understanding that 'Ruby F. Bowman' was the correct parentage. Growth habit is upright and slightly open, and it has mid-sized leaves. Flowers are funnel-form, bright burgundy red, spotted darker, in large trusses to 27. (Druecker 1971).

'Jingle Bells' ('Lem's Goal' x 'Fabia'). 3', 5oF, M, 4/4/4. Busy, colorful flowers are scarlet when they unfold, then as if by trickery, many bright colors pass and the flowers change to yellow. 'Jingle Bells' is low growing and densely foliated. (Lem, Elliott 1974).

'Joan Leslie Hammond' (['Holy Moses' x 'Albatross'] x 'Abe Arnott'). 4', -5oF, ML, -/-/-. Olive green foliage covers an upright, spreading, moderately dense plant. Funnel shaped flowers have wavy lilac edges which shade paler purple at the center, ending in a deep carmine throat. The flower has a prominent dark red flare, and heavy freckling on the upper petal. Petals are marked with a strong fuchsia purple ray along the midvein. Domed shaped trusses are formed. (Newcomb 1993).

'Jo Ann Newsome' ('Jasper' x 'Dido'). 5', -5oF, L, 4/4/3. Bright orange red flowers are lightly spotted with darker color and long stamens stretch out from the throat. This is a plant of strong growth. (Larson 1983).

'Jock' (*williamsianum* x *griersonianum*). 3', -5oF, EM, 2-3/3-4/4. Rosy pink flowers are everywhere upon this rolling mound of green. The plant gives best results in full sun, and is easily rooted. (Maxwell 1939).

'Jodi' (*racemosum* x *moupinense*). 2', 0oF, E, 4/3-4/3-4. Vigorous growth and small leaves make this a desirable plant. Flowers are pink, with a light spotting, held in trusses at branch tips. They open from clusters of up to 6 buds, each with 4 flowers. (Lem before 1966, Granston 1977).

'Jodie King' (*yakushimanum* x unknown). 3', -5oF?, M?, -/-/-. Attractive dark, rounded foliage is held on a plant with *yakushimanum* habit. Deep pink flowers, fading with age, are grouped together in compact, rounded trusses. (M. King reg. 1984).

'Joe Brooks' (parentage unknown). 5', -10oF, ML, 3/3/3. This hybrid has attractive foliage and rose pink flowers. (Dexter before 1945).

'Joe Gable' ('Catalgla' x *wardii*). 5', -10oF, M, 3/3/3. Habit is wide, compact and dense. Funnel bell-shaped flowers, to 3 1/2" across, are pale ivory, set in somewhat loose trusses of 13-15 flowers each. (Gable 1972).

'Joe Paterno' ('Catawbiense Album' x 'Swansdown'). 5', -20oF, ML, 3-4/4/4. Ball shaped trusses are composed of white flowers with a splash of bronze yellow. Glossy, dark green leaves cover this well manicured, rounded plant. (Orlando Pride hyb., micro-propagated 1987-88).

'John Barr Stevenson' (*lacteum* x 'Logan Damaris'). 5', 0oF, EM, -/-/-. Lemon yellow trusses, and rounded foliage are carried on a tall, vigorous shrub. (Stevenson 1962) A.M. 1971.

'John Caller' ('Idealist' (selfed) x 'Jalisco Orange'). 5', 5ºF, M, -/-/-. An open plant of strong growth habit with chartreuse flowers. (J. Waterer, Sons & Crisp 1975).

'John Coutts' (['Grand Arab' x *griffithianum*] x *griersonianum*). 4', 0ºF, L, 4/3/3-4. Here is an uncommon flower color for rhododendrons: it is deep salmon pink with a warm, glowing aura. The foliage is long and pointed and completely covers the plant, making it dense and full. It flowers late, escaping spring frosts. (R. B. G. Kew 1946).

'Johnny Bender' ('Jean Marie de Montague' x 'Indiana'). 4-5', -5ºF, M, 3-4/5/4. This is an outstanding rhododendron in every respect, and it is beautiful in all seasons. The foliage is elliptical, about 5-7" long and 2 to 2 1/2" wide, dark, glossy green and of a heavy texture reminiscent of a polyploid. You'll swear these leaves were just polished! The flowers are also of a heavy texture and are a bright, but deep, blood red. Round, tight trusses are formed. (Seabrook about 1960, Eichelser 1980).

'John Walter' (*catawbiense* x *arboreum*). 5', -10ºF, ML, 2/3/3. Ruffled flowers of crimson red cover this compact growing plant. It buds easily and is a good grower. This originated in England before 1860, so you know it is a tough hybrid to still be grown today. The leaves are slightly rough textured, matte olive green. (Waterer before 1860).

'John Waterer' (*catawbiense* hybrid). 4', -15ºF, M, 2/3/4. A very old hybrid still in cultivation. Blooms are purple-red on a sun tolerant plant. (Waterer before 1860).

'John Wister' see 'Janet Blair'.

'Jonathan Shaw' ('Melanie Shaw' x 'Brenda Lee'). 3.5', -10ºF, L, -/-/-. Large, vivid violet purple flowers have a strong purplish red center and prominent black flare. The wavy edged blooms are held in ball trusses of 19. Matte green foliage with undulating margins densely covers this compact bush. (J. Leonard hyb. 1981, reg. 1988).

'Joseph Dunn' (*minus* var. *minus* x *racemosum*). 4', -15ºF, ML, -/-/-. Small pink clusters on each branch terminal are complimented by rich, dark green leaves. Slightly more tall than broad. (Lewis hyb. 1974, reg. 1994).

'Josephine Everitt' (probably a *fortunei* ssp. *fortunei* hybrid). 4', L, -10ºF, -/-/-. Frilled, fragrant flowers of white have pink edges. (Dexter).

'Joshua' (['America' x 'Nova Zembla'] x ['Mars' x 'America']). 5', -25ºF, ML, -/-/-. Large, deep red flowers form large trusses on this hardy compact hybrid which has slightly twisted dark green foliage. (sold by Roslyn Nursery about 1994).

'Joshua Huddy' (*rupicola* x *mucronulatum* 'Pink Panther'). 3', -15ºF, E, -/-/-. Red-purple flowers abound on this upright plant with small leaves. (Lewis hyb. 1974, reg. 1988).

'Joy Ride' (parentage unknown). 6', 10ºF, EM, 3-4/3-4/3-4. Foliage is medium to large. Pale pink flowers sport an orange blotch in the upper throat. The 2" blooms are held in a truss up to 15. (Whitney, Sather 1976).

'Juan De Fuca' ('Blue Ensign' x *ponticum*). 6', 10ºF, L, 3/3/3. Flowers are up to 3" wide. The lilac blooms have a dark red blotch and spotting, and are held in a 12 flower truss. Foliage is large. (Larson 1964, Northwest Ornamental Society 1977).

'Judy Spillane' (*maximum* x 'John Wister'). 4', -5ºF, L, -/-/-. A late blooming light purplish pink with a prominent yellow green blotch. (Wister, The Tyler Arboretum 1980).

'Julia Grothaus' ('Albatross' x 'Golden Belle'). 6', 0ºF, L, -/-/-. Leaves are large. Ruffled, 7-lobed flowers are rosy peach with a white edging that increases the longer the flower is out. The scented flowers display a smallish light brown blotch and are carried in a flat truss up to 12. (Grothaus 1975) A.E. 1988 Northwest.

'Julie Titcomb' ('Marinus Koster' x 'Snow Queen'). 6', 0ºF, M, 3-4/3/3-4. Flowers, to 4 1/2" wide, are carmine colored outside, with the upper petals blushed pink inside. Delicate crimson spotting accents the blooms, which are held in 16 flower trusses above large foliage. (Larson before 1958) P.A. 1958.

'Julischka' ('Thunderstorm' x *yakushimanum* 'Koichiro Wada'). 3', -15ºF, M, 4/4/4. An exceptional hybrid with bright red buds that open to electric rose with a darker accent, the colors softening toward the center. Smooth, deep green leaves cover a well-shaped, mounding plant. (Hachmann 1968, reg. Stuck 1983).

'July Fragrance' ('Isabella' x *diaprepes*). 5', 0ºF, ML, -/-/-. New foliage is brushed with bronze hues. Flowers are funnel-shaped, rather frilled, white with crimson at base and display a pale rose glow toward the outside. It has a narrow calyx, and strong fragrance. (Hillier & Sons 1967).

'June Fire' see 'Junifeuer'.

'June Pink' (parentage unknown). 5', -15ºF, L, -/-/-. Rich, bright pink flowers touched with gold in the throat, attractive foliage, and tidy plant habit are the endearing features of this hybrid. (Stan Hall before 1990).

'Junifeuer' ('Mary Waterer' x 'Moser's Maroon'). 3', -10ºF, ML-L, 4/3-4/3-4. Bright red flowers sport a glowing yellow flare sprinkled with red "cinders", and the ashy white throat provides the final contrast. The blooms occur in compact trusses of 11-15 flowers. The plant is more broad than wide. Dark green mature foliage provides a rich backdrop for the red tinged new growth. This plant is synonymous with 'Hachmann's Junifeuer' and is sometimes sold as 'Junifire' or 'June Fire', a translation of the German. (Hachmann 1983).

'Junifreude' ('Omega', selfed). 2', -15ºF, ML, -/-/-. Flowers of 5 wavy-edged lobes are strong purplish red, shade to strong purplish pink in the throat, and have olive green dorsal markings. The trusses of 13-16 flowers contrast nicely against the dark, glossy leaves. The plant has a very compact habit, more broad than high. (Hachmann hyb., Stuck reg. 1988).

'Juniperle' ('Mary Waterer' x 'Moser's Maroon'). 3', -10ºF, ML, -/-/-. Trusses hold 14-19 blooms. Flowers, colored with a band of bright carmine red along the outer petal edge, fade to a white center accented with golden brown markings. Broad, compact plant habit. (Hachmann hyb. 1968, Stuck reg. 1984) BUGA 1991 silver.

'Jutland' g. ('Bellerophon' x *elliottii*). 6', 5ºF, L, 4/2/3. Dull dark green leaves are long and narrow. Bright red flowers are set in a ball shaped truss. (Rothschild) A.M. 1947.

'Kalimna' ('Edith Boulter' x 'Unknown Warrior'). 5', 0ºF, EM, 3/3/3. Dense, round trusses are formed by medium rose to paler rose flowers with light yellowish brown on the upper lobe. Good foliage also characterizes this hybrid. (V. J. Boulter 1971).

'Kalinka' ('Morgenrot' x ['Mars' x *yakushimanum* 'Koichiro Wada']). 3', -10ºF, ML, -/-/-. Glossy foliage with brown indumentum on a dense, mounding plant provide a background for bright red buds. These open to flowers of medium rose, pale pink at the center, with darker rims. The flowers are marked with moderate yellow-green and are held in trusses of 12-18. (Hachmann hyb., Stuck reg. 1984).

'Kaponga' (*arboreum* x 'Ivery's Scarlet'). 6', 10ºF, EM, -/-/-. A large, tree-like habit and long, soft green foliage distinguish this plant. Bright red flowers are held in attractive trusses. Vigorous, and sun tolerant. (Holland 1979).

'Kapunatiki' ('Pacific Queen' x *wardii*). 6', 5oF, M, -/-/-. Funnel shaped flowers in huge trusses of 11 are pale greenish yellow with the throat half green and half red. Blooms in November in New Zealand where it is sold as 'Grant's Gold'. (Grant 1988).

'Karalee' ('Hotei' x 'Whitney Late Yellow #1'). 4', 5oF, M-ML, -/-/-. Abundant creamy yellow flowers bloom on this hybrid. Not yet widely known. (Thompson Nursery grower).

'Karen Triplett' ('Seattle Gold' x late-flowering yellow) 4', 5oF, ML, 4/4/4. The 4" x 4" trusses are formed of 10-12 flowers which are aureolin yellow in color and surrounded by a calyx. This is a well branched plant with medium-sized, jade green leaves which are held for 3 years. (Larson 1982).

'Karin' ('Britannia' x *williamsianum*). 3', -15oF, EM, 4/4/4. Broad, egg shaped leaves cover this compact plant. Large, ruffled, pink flowers are held in a full trusses which are unusual for *williamsianum* hybrids. (Experimental Station Boskoop Holland 1968) G.M. 1966, A.M. 1968.

'Karin Seleger' (*impeditum* x *dauricum*). 2.5', -25oF, M, -/-/-. Flowers are medium purple-violet and have 5 wavy-edged lobes. The are held in groups of 5-7 to form many ball shaped trusses. The plant is densely foliated with small, scaly leaves on a more wide than tall growth habit. (Brueckner hyb. 1971, reg. 1989).

'Karkov' (*griersonianum* x 'Red Admiral'). 5', 15oF, EM, 3/3/3. Lightly spotted, large, round trusses are formed from carmine rose flowers with frilled margins. (Rothschild 1943) A.M. 1947.

'Kate Waterer' (*catawbiense* hybrid). 5', -10oF, ML, 2/3/3. Growth habit is fairly compact and upright. Flowers are pink, with a stunning golden yellow eye. (J. Waterer before 1890).

'Katherine Dalton' (*smirnowii* x *fortunei* ssp. *fortunei*). 5', -15oF, M, 3/4/3. Foliage is somewhat indumented. Very light pink flowers open from brighter buds. (Gable 1937).

'Kathie Jo' (['Purple Splendour' x 'Britannia'] x *ponticum* hybrid). 5', -5oF, ML, 4/3/3-4. A deep wine purple flower. Each of the lobes fold back, making the flower appear to have a very flat face. (Disney not registered).

'Kathryna' (advanced generation hybrid of *catawbiense* and *maximum*). 6', -15oF, ML, -/-/-. Foliage is medium sized and narrow. Flowers are pink with a small yellow blotch, up to 2 1/2" wide, carried in a 17 flower truss. (Smith hyb. 1967, W. Smith reg. 1978).

'Kathryn Reboul' (*spinuliferum* x *racemosum*). 3', -5oF, EM, -/-/-. Leaves are small. Tiny, 1" flowers are pale yellow with salmon pink blushing, held in truss of up to 14. (Hardgrove hyb. about 1960, Reboul reg. 1975).

'Kathy Van Veen' (sport of 'Jean Marie de Montague'). 3', 0oF, M, 4/4/4. Strong red buds open to 5-lobed flowers of heavy substance. The wavy edged petals are vivid red outside and variable colors inside, ranging from dark pink to clear red. 15 flowers form the domed truss. Attractive deep green leaves are held for 3 years. (W. Rhein selection, Van Veen Nursery reg. 1990).

'Katja' ([*catawbiense* var. *album* x *fortunei* ssp. *discolor*] x 'Madame de Bruin'). 4', -10oF, ML, -/-/-. Leaves are large. Flowers have strong substance, to 2" across, vibrant pink in color, shading paler pink in throat, held in a ball truss of up to 16 flowers. (Raustein 1976).

'Katrina' ('Anna' x 'Purple Splendour'). 5', 0oF, ML, 4/4/3-4. Magenta rose flowers with a prominent black blotch make this a showy flower. Large green elliptical leaves are glossy. It's an upright growing plant that branches moderately. (Elsie Watson 1982).

'Kay Kirsten' ('Jasper' x 'Belvedere'). 4', -5oF, M, 4/3/3. Glimmering satin amber ball shaped trusses are most attractive with the very smooth foliage. (Larson 1982).

'KECA' (*keleticum* x *carolinianum*). 1.5', -15oF, M-ML, -/-/-. This low growing, compact plant is very floriferous, blooming with lavender, flat faced flowers in clusters against thick, leathery foliage. (Nearing hyb. before 1970, not reg.)

'Kelley' (['Pygmalion' x *haematodes* x 'Wellfleet'] x ['Pygmalion' x *haematodes* x 'Wellfleet']). 6', 0oF, M, -/-/-. Round trusses of deep purple red with some spotting. Light olive green leaves are an interesting contrast. (Dexter hyb. before 1943, Wister reg. 1983).

'Ken Janeck' (selected form of *yakushimanum*). 3', -15oF, M, 5/5/4. There is a long list of selected forms of the species. 'Ken Janeck' is one of the best forms for its appealing, heavily indumented foliage and its richly colored pink flowers. This is the only *yakushimanum* selection to receive an Award of Excellence. There is continuing debate as to whether the large type 'yaks' are varieties of the species or perhaps are hybrids with *R. smirnowii* or other species. (Janeck 1964) A.E. 1969.

'Kentucky Cardinal' (*brachycarpum* x 'Essex Scarlet'). 4', -15oF, ML, 2/2/3. Growth habit is open, with dark green leaves and small flowers of very dark red. Synonym, 'The Cardinal'. (Gable 1946).

'Kettledrum' (*catawbiense* x unknown). 5', -20oF, ML -/-/-. This hybrid is very hardy, but the habit and foliage is inferior. The flowers are purplish crimson. It is used as a parent for hardiness. (A. Waterer 1877).

'Kevin' (*yakushimanum* 'Koichiro Wada' x 'Jade'). 4', 0oF, M, 4/4/4. Foliage is medium to large, indumented, and curves downward. Intensely pink flowers shade to a yellowish pink, with the outside and edges maintaining the darker tones. Flowers, up to 2 1/4" across, are carried 14 to the truss. (Bovee, Sorenson & Watson 1976).

'Kickoff' (*carolinianum* 'Achiever' x *mucronulatum*). 3', -15oF, EM, -/-/-. Wavy margined, light purple flowers with vivid reddish purple spots are held in trusses of 12. Foliage is olive green, glossy and scaly above, scaly below. (Delp, Anderson 1989).

'Kilimanjaro' (*elliottii* x 'Dusky Maid'). 5', 0oF, ML-L, 5/2-3/2-3. A rare hybrid from Rothschild that is pictured in <u>Rothschild Rhododendrons</u> and consequently has become well known. It is a terrific rhododendron, but still very uncommon as it is difficult to propagate and has so few limbs to use for propagation. While not a compact plant (it does not branch readily), the formal, currant red trusses make up for any lack of plant form. Deep green attractive leaves. It buds young and the flowers are huge. (Rothschild) F.C.C. 1947.

'Kim' (*campylogynum* x *campylogynum* var. *cremastum*). 1', -5oF, M, 4/4/3. This Caperci selection of *campylogynum* is an interesting yellow shade. Its delightful flowers are like little, nodding lanterns. It is a rare dwarf, a plant of real interest. (Caperci 1966) A.E. 1973.

'Kimberly' (*williamsianum* x *fortunei* ssp. *fortunei*). 3', -10oF, EM, 3-4/4/4-5. A very beautiful, heavy-flowering pastel pink. The slightly fragrant flowers blanket the plant in such profusion that all the foliage is covered. The foliage is moss green with bright purple bud scales which make the plant attractive all winter long. (Greer 1963) P.A. 1963.

'Kimberton' (unknown x 'Crest'). 5', -5oF, ML, -/-/-. Foliage is medium to large. The fragrant, pink flowers, blotched yellow green, are 3 1/2" across and held in a truss of up to 12. (Bagoly hyb. 1969, Herbert reg. 1979).

'**Kimbeth**' ('Kimberly' x 'Elizabeth'). 3', -5ºF, EM, 4/4-5/4-5. A perfect semi-dwarf for landscaping. Rouge pink buds provide color through the winter. Rosy flowers appear on every stem of the plant, making a solid mass of color. (Greer 1979).

'**King Bee**' (*yakushimanum* x *tsariense*). 2.5', 5ºF, EM, 3/5/3-4. Flowers with 5 wavy lobes, opening pale rose, fading to white, with scarlet spots and stripes of lighter scarlet, bloom on this upright hybrid. The foliage has heavy indumentum. (Berg 1983) C.A. 1984.

'**Kinglet**' (*racemosum* Forrest 19404 x *desquamatum* 'Finch'). 5', 0ºF, E, -/-/-. This wonderful plant exhibits the beautiful little pink trusses of *R. racemosum* but has the longer leaves of *R. desquamatum*. Very nice. (Henny 1963).

'**King of Shrubs**' (*fortunei* ssp. *discolor* x 'Fabia'). 4', 0ºF, ML, 4/2-3/3. One of the nicest of the oranges. It has yellow stripes originating deep in the throat, which flare and merge with the orange as they reach the end of the petals. The foliage is narrow and pointed in a most attractive way. (Ostbo 1958) P.A. 1950.

'**King's Destiny**' (unknown x 'Purple Splendour'). 3', -10ºF, ML, -/-/-. Leaves are large. Flowers are deep lavender, with deeper purple blotch and spots, held in a truss of up to 11. (Frederick Jr. 1977).

'**King's Favor**' ('Purple Splendour' x 'A. Bedford'). 5', -10ºF, ML, -/-/-. Leaves are quite large. Flowers to 3 1/4" wide are orchid in color, with a mottled blotch of sunny golden yellow. The ball shaped truss is made of 12 flowers. (Frederick Jr. 1977).

'**King's Ride**' (*insigne* x *yakushimanum*). 3', 0ºF, M, 4/4-5/4. Long, smooth, dull dark green leaves with silver-beige indumentum clothe a vigorous, compact, spreading plant. White flowers, flushed phlox pink and speckled brown, are held in trusses of 17. (Crown Estate Commissioners 1972) H.C. 1975.

'**Kingston**' ('Lem's Cameo' x 'Polynesian Sunset'). 6', 5ºF, M, 4/3-4/3-4. Upright and rounded plant habit, as wide as high. This hybrid has glossy, dark green foliage held for 3 years, with new leaves terracotta brown. The flowers have 7 wavy lobes, are carrot red and fade to orange-buff with rhodonite red edges. They are held in lax trusses of 8-10. (Holmeide & Smith 1983).

'**King Tut**' ([*smirnowii* x 'America'] x red *catawbiense* seeding). 5', -20ºF, ML, 3/3-4/3. For hardiness this plant is super. The flowers are rose pink with yellowish hues in the center and brown spotting on the upper lobes. Yew green leaves have yellow green leaf stems. (Shammarello 1958).

'**Kiss of Lemon**' (parentage unknown). 4', 0ºF, M, 5/3/3. The clear yellow flowers have very heavy substance, allowing the flowers to last longer than most yellows. Leaves are deeply veined and are dark green. (Sifferman before 1975).

'**Kitsap King**' ('Grenadier' x *yakushimanum*). 4', -5ºF, ML, -/-/-. Mauve buds decorate the matte green leaves which have tan indumentum. Large, ball shaped trusses are formed from greenish white flowers, showing strong pink margins on the inside and outside of the lobes. (Alice Smith hyb. 1972, reg. 1992).

'**Kiwi Magic**' ([*yakushimanum* x 'Dido'] x 'Lem's Cameo'). 4', 5ºF, M, -/-/-. Flowers on this hybrid open from deep pink buds, and, at first, are soft pink with a brilliant yellow center, slowly transforming to pale yellow at the petal margins. Each truss holds 13-14 flowers. (J. Elliott 1988).

'**Klassy's Pride**' ([*neriiflorum* x *strigillosum*] x ['Loderi' x *thomsonii*]). 5', -10ºF, EM, -/-/-. Foliage is medium to large and narrow. 2" wide, red flowers are spotted black in a 14 flower truss. (Nelson 1966, Heller 1979).

'**Kluis Sensation**' ('Britannia' hybrid). 5', -5ºF, ML, 3-4/3-4/3-4. This rather compact plant has deep green leaves that curve slightly upward at the edges, giving the plant a robust and vigorous look. Flowers are dark red in a tight truss. (A. Kluis 1946).

'**Kluis Triumph**' (*griffithianum* hybrid). 6', 0ºF, ML, 2/3/4. Growth habit is erect, somewhat compact. Leaves are 6" long, with good appearance. Flowers are deep terracotta red, held in neat trusses. (Kluis).

'**Knight's Beauty**' ('Old Copper' x 'Van Nes Sensation'). 4', 10ºF, ML, -/-/-. Buds are a strong purplish red, opening to a strong purplish pink flower which has spotting on the upper lobes, and is capped with a small calyx. Light green foliage appears on the compact shrub. (Elliott 1966, Knight 1980).

'**Kokardia**' ('Humboldt' x 'Direktor E. Hjelm'). 5', -10ºF, ML, 3-4/3/4. Trusses of 12-17 are formed by strong mauve pink flowers flecked ruby red, with a striking dark red-brown blotch. (Hachmann hyb., Stuck reg. 1983).

'**Kristin**' (*yakushimanum* 'Koichiro Wada' x 'Bow Bells'). 4', 0ºF, M, 4/4/4. Leaves are medium size. 2 1/2" flowers are pale pink with slight reddish spotting, held in a truss of up to 14. (Bovee, Sorenson & Watson 1975).

'**Kristin Marie**' ('Chionoides' x 'Graf Zeppelin'). 4', 0ºF, ML, -/-/-. Wider than tall, this plant has deep green, dense foliage on a plant of rounded habit. White flowers, deeply incised and with a vivid yellow spotted flare, open from white buds tipped strong purplish red. (B. & M. Shapiro 1989).

'**KSW**' ('King of Shrubs' x 'Walloper'). see 'Victor Frederick'.

'**Kubla Khan**' ('Britannia' x 'Goldsworth Orange'). 5', -5ºF, ML, 4-5/2-3/2-3. This fine hybrid from the late Lester Brandt is really super. The flower color is a salmon, pink, orange, and red combination with a creamy cast to the centers of the petals. It has a huge red flare that is duplicated on the gigantic calyx. It makes the calyx and the whole flower really different! The color is so unusual that it is difficult to capture in pictures. The foliage is fairly large and a moss green. It is best planted in a cool location. (Brandt 1961).

'**Kulu**' (natural hybrid of *vernicosum* aff., Rock 18139). 6', -10ºF, M, -/-/-. Foliage is of medium size and narrow. Fragrant, 7-lobed flowers are up to 4" wide, pink blushing to deeper pink in the throat, with a dim blotch, held in 10 flowered truss. (Gable, C. Gable 1979).

'**Kunming**' (*rupicola* var. *chryseum* x *minus* var. *minus* Carolinianum Group *album*). 3', -15ºF, M, -/-/-. The plant has twiggy habit and yellow flowers that turn matte orange at the edges as they mature. (Leach 1981).

'**LaBar's White**' (clone or natural hybrid of *catawbiense*). 5', -20ºF, M-L, 3/3/4. Very similar to *catawbiense*, with white flowers, marked yellowish in the throat. (LaBar 1959).

'**Lachsgold**' (*astrocalyx* hybrid). 4', -15ºF, M, -/-/-. Salmon gold ... the word combination doesn't work quite so well in English, but it certainly describes the rich color play of these soft orange buds nestling among the mature butter yellow to cream flowers. 10-13 flowers form each truss. The broad, round plant has slightly rounded, bright green foliage. (Hobbie 1985).

Hybrids ~ White Flowering

'Faggetter's Favourite'

R. 'Dora Amateis'

R. 'Travis L.'

R. 'Loder's White'

R. 'Pawhuska'

R. 'White Swan

Hybrids ~ by Hachmann

R. 'Sonatine'

R. 'Felicitas'

R. 'Balalaika'

R. 'Edeltraud'

R. 'Hachmann's Charmant'

R. 'Junifeuer'

R. 'Goldkrone'

R. 'Gletschernacht'

R. 'Bariton'

R. 'Schneebukett'

R. 'Blutopia'

R. 'Hachmann's Rosita'

R. 'Hachmann's Diadem'

R. 'Lilofee'

R. 'Kalinka'

R. 'Hachmann's
Feuerschein'

Hybrids ~ by Thompson

R. 'Tiddly Winks'

R. 'Cupcake'

R. 'Sunspot'

R. 'Sweet Mystery'

R. 'Flaming Star'

R. 'Tweedy Bird'

R. 'Ring of Fire'

R. 'Pom Pom'

'**Lackamas Blue**' (selected seedling of *augustinii* from Kerr Estate). 6', -5ºF, EM, 3-4/4/3-4. Leaves are large, typical of the species. Lavender-blue blooms are flat, to 3 1/4" wide, in a truss of up to 4. (Lancaster 1964) P.A. 1963.

'**Lackamas Cream**' (form of *chlorops*). 3.5', -5ºF, M, 3/3/3. 7-lobed flowers are primrose yellow to rich cream, rayed with mahogany, and held in trusses of 11. Foliage is an attractive bluish green on this easily rooted plant. (Benjamin Lancaster reg. 1962) P.A. 1962.

'**Lackamas Firebrand**' ('Essex Scarlet' x *griersonianum*). 4', -5ºF, VL, 3/3/3. Spherical trusses hold 18 campanulate currant red flowers. An upright, bushy plant clothed with dark green leaves. (B. Lancaster reg. 1966).

'**Lackamas Gold**' (*chlorops* x *wardii*). 3', -5ºF, M, 3/3/3. Habit is compact and neat. Medium sized leaves are unusual blue-green and quite narrow. Bell shaped, primrose yellow flowers, to 3" wide, are held 12-15 to the truss. (Lancaster 1962) P.A. 1962.

'**Lackamas Spice**' (*chlorops* x *diaprepes*). 6', 0ºF, M, 3/3/3. Leaves are large. Flowers also are large, to 4" across, light yellow to ivory or cream, in a 12 flower truss with delightful spicy fragrance. (Lancaster 1963) P.A. 1962.

'**Ladies' Choice**' ('Moonstone' x 'Hawk'). 3', 0ºF, M, 4/4/3. Red spotting on the field of primrose yellow petals forms the palette for this lax truss. The plant has rounded shrub habit and glossy green leaves. (Elliott 1983).

'**Lady Adam Gordon**' ([*yakushimanum* x *dichroanthum*] x [*wardii* x *decorum*]). 3', 0ºF, M, -/-/-. Pale shell pink flowers. (George, Hydon Nurseries 1975).

'**Lady Alice Fitzwilliam**' (parentage unknown). 5', 20ºF, EM, 3-4/3/4. Growth habit is similar to 'Fragrantissimum', but bushier and more erect. Roots easily. Medium sized foliage is rather narrow with inward curving margins. Fragrant flowers are very wide funnel shaped, pink in the bud opening into white, held in a lax truss of 2 to 4 flowers. (RHS reg. 1958) F.C.C. 1881.

'**Lady Annette de Trafford**' (*maximum* hybrid). 5', -15ºF, L, -/-/-. Very soft hues of pink radiate outward from this gorgeous flower which has a dark brown blotch. Synonym, 'Black Eyed Susan'. (Waterer 1874).

'**Lady Armstrong**' (*catawbiense* hybrid). 6', -20ºF, ML, 4/3/-. This is a hardy plant with a good habit. Flowers are showy carmine rose pink with white throats. (A. Waterer before 1867).

'**Lady Berry**' ('Rosy Bell' x 'Royal Flush'). 5', 5ºF, EM, 5/3-4/4/2-3. Growth habit is open and upright. Foliage is noted for blue green color and aromatic quality. Drooping trusses carry funnel-form flowers up to 8 per truss, rosy opal inside and rich red outside. (Rothschild) A.M. 1937, F.C.C. 1949.

'**Lady Bessborough**' (*fortunei* ssp. *discolor* x *campylocarpum* var. *elatum*). 6', -5ºF, ML, 3-4/3/3. Growth habit is open and upright, with large, medium green foliage. Flowers are pale yellow to ivory white, yellow at base of throat. Blooms are very showy, but tend to be delicate. (Rothschild) F.C.C. 1933.

'**Ladybird**' (*fortunei* ssp. *discolor* x 'Corona'). 5', -10ºF, VL, 5/3-4/3. Exceptional, very late flowering pink flowers are held in large trusses. This is one of the most difficult plants to propagate. (Rothschild) A.M. 1933.

'**Lady Bligh**' (*griffithianum* hybrid). 5', -5ºF, ML, 4/3/4. Strawberry-like buds open dark pink and turn to pastel pink, creating a two-toned effect of the utmost beauty. Leaves are large, medium green, held for 2 years. (C.B. van Nes & Sons) A.M. 1934.

'**Lady Bowes Lyon**' ('Pilgrim' x *yakushimanum*). 4', -15ºF, M, -/-/-. Nicely rounded trusses of white suffused pink with even stronger phlox pink highlights. (Hanger, RHS Garden, Wisley) A.M. 1962.

'**Lady Chamberlain**' (*cinnabarinum* var. *roylei* x 'Royal Flush'). 5', 10ºF, ML, 4/3/2-3. This is an upright growing plant with slender, graceful branches and interesting blue-green new foliage which ages gradually to mid-green with reddish stems. Bright salmon orange-pink flowers of great substance are tubular-trumpet shaped, held in very droopy, lax trusses of 3-6. (Rothschild 1930) F.C.C. 1931.

'**Lady Clementine Mitford**' (*maximum* hybrid). 5', -5ºF, ML, 3/3/4. A hardy plant with distinctive gray-green leaves. The flowers are beautiful soft peach pink. A distinguished plant whose foliage looks like it was sprinkled with silver creating a most unusual effect. Can withstand both sun and heat. Also known as 'Lady Clementina Mitford'. (A. Waterer 1870).

'**Lady de Rothschild**' (*griffithianum* x 'Sappho'). 5', -5ºF, M, 4/2-3/4. This is the plant that is commonly known as 'Mrs. Lionel de Rothschild'. It is white with a flush of pink and has a big crimson blotch. A very beautiful and showy flower. Actually the true 'Mrs. Lionel de Rothschild' is pink and, as far as is known, is not grown in this country. (A. Waterer) A.M. 1952.

'**Lady Eleanor Cathcart**' (*maximum* x *arboreum*). 4', -10ºF, M, -/-/-. An interesting cross done over a century ago. This plant has clear pale pink flowers with a reddish purple blotch. (Waterer before 1850).

'**Lady Grey Egerton**' (*catawbiense* hybrid). 5', -15ºF, ML, 3/2/3. Pale lilac flowers held in a tight truss and a plant habit that is somewhat open and loose distinguish this hybrid. (Waterer before 1888).

'**Lady Longman**' ('Cynthia' x 'Lady Eleanor Cathcart'). 5', -15ºF, ML, -/-/-. Plant is heat resistant, with distinctively veined leaves. Flowers are clear pale pink, with a conspicuous chocolate eye, held in large trusses. (H. White before 1958).

'**Lady Luck**' ('Purple Splendour' x 'Loderi Superlative'). 5', 0ºF, ML, 3/3/3. Large flowers of magnificent orchid pink profusely cover this fragrant plant. The large foliage is quite attractive. (J. Elliott before 1990).

'**Lady of Spain**' ('Mrs. Horace Fogg' x 'Point Defiance'). 6', 0ºF, M, 4/4/4. Frosted rose red flowers on a plant with medium green, quite long, heavy textured foliage. Vigorous growth on a large plant. (Lofthouse 1981).

'**Lady Primrose**' (*campylocarpum* hybrid). 4', 0ºF, EM-M, 3/3/3. Habit is dense and compact, clothed with medium sized, light green, rounded leaves which hold well. Flat buds are yellow, tinged with pink which open to clear primrose yellow flowers, dotted red, in a compact ball shaped truss. Plant is slow growing, needs shade, and is difficult to root. (Slocock) A.M. 1933.

'**Lady Rosebery**' (*cinnabarinum* var. *roylei* x 'Royal Flush'). 5', 5ºF, M, 4/3/2-3. Habit is tall and willowy. Much like 'Lady Chamberlain', in foliage as well as flower, but it is softer shell pink, shading to rose. (Rothschild) A.M. 1930, F.C.C. 1932.

'**Lady Stuart of Wortley**' (parentage unknown, possibly a 'Coombe Royal' or *griffithianum* hybrid). 5', 0ºF, ML, 3/2/3. Growth habit is upright and open, with large foliage. Glowing pink flowers also are large, and are held in a big, somewhat drooping truss. (M. Koster & Sons 1909) A.M. 1933.

'**Lajka**' (*smirnowii* x 'C. S. Sargent'). 5', -15ºF, ML, -/-/-. Purplish violet buds open as bright violet purple flowers with a striking blotch of yellow-green. (Scholz intro. 1966).

'**Lake Labish**' ('Lady Bligh' x 'Loderi Venus'). 5', 5ºF, ML, 4/3/3-4. Growth habit is open and wide spreading, with medium large, medium green foliage. Strawberry red flowers, 3 1/2" wide, are bowl shaped, with stamens somewhat rudimentary. Attractive, tall trusses hold up to 17 flowers. (R. Henny) P.A. 1955.

'**Lalique**' (parentage uncertain, possibly a seedling of 'Loderi' or *griffithianum*). 6', 0ºF, M, -/-/-. This vigorous, open and upright plant has trusses of 14-15 flowers, white tinged pink and lilac. (Mrs. A. G. Holmes 1979).

'**Lamellen**' (*campanulatum* x *griffithianum*). 4', -10ºF, EM, -/-/-. A lovely combination, the best of both parents! This hybrid creates a large pale mauve truss on a plant with tree-like habits. Striking. (Magor, Lamellen 1943).

'**Lampion**' ('Bad Eilsen' x *yakushimanum* 'Koichiro Wada'). 3', -10ºF, ML, -/-/-. A dense, compact plant, this one has ovate-elliptic leaves which are thinly covered with brown indumentum. Campanulate flowers on long pedicels open bright rose red to rose pink, then fade to a paler pink. (Hachmann hyb., Stuck 1988).

'**Lamplighter**' ('Britannia' x 'Madame Fr. J. Chauvin'). 5', -5ºF, M, 4/3/4. Plant habit is compact and rounded, with large, rather narrow leaves. Tall, 12-flower trusses of brilliant light red have a luminous salmon-pink glow. (M. Koster & Sons 1955) F.C.C. 1955.

'**Langley Park**' ('Queen Wilhelmina' x 'Stanley Davies'). 5', -5ºF, M, 3/2/3. Growth habit is wide spreading and bushy. Long, narrow, dark green foliage is distinctively folded upward at mid-rib. Deep, rich red flowers of fragile texture, need protection from full sun. Trusses are large and rounded, holding 12 to 15 flowers. (C.B. van Nes & Sons before 1922).

'**Langworth**' (*fortunei* ssp. *fortunei* x 'Sappho'). 5', -15ºF, M, -/-/-. A tall grower with large white flowers, each with streaks of brown in the throat. Trusses are large and conical yet somewhat lax. (W. C. Slocock Ltd. 1932) H.C. (Wisley Trials) 1960, A.M. 1962.

'**Lartag**' (probably *taggianum* hybrid). 6', 15ºF, VE, 4/4/4. Leaves are long and narrow. Fragrant, 3" wide, funnel-form flowers are white, and are held in a loose truss of up to 4 flowers. (Bowman 1965).

'**Last Chance**' ('Mars' x *eriogynum*). 6', -5ºF, ML, 3/3/3-4. Leaves are long, emerald green, and curly. Rosy light wine flowers, 3 1/2" across, shade to rich rose at center, and are held 14 to the truss. (R. Henny 1958) P.A. 1957.

'**Last Hurrah**' ('Belle Heller' x *aureum*). 2', -10ºF, EM, 4/5/3-4. This plant could have been named "Wrigley", as it brings double the pleasure with fall blooms nearly as profuse as in spring! This is characteristic of the *aureum* parentage. Near-white flowers are tinged faint yellow-green, with some dorsal spotting of grayed chartreuse. They are 5 lobed, of flat saucer-shape, and are held in trusses of 13. This well-branched plant bears dark, olive green leaves of heavy texture that are held for 3 years. At maturity, the plant will be 3 times wider than tall. Synonym, 'Athens'. (Leach intro. 1974, reg. 1981).

'**Laurago**' ('Moser's Maroon' x *yakushimanum*). 4', 5ºF, M, 4/4/4. Fragrant flowers of neyron rose with dark olive green dorsal spotting are held in conical trusses of 16-18. This hybrid is as wide as tall, and has dark green leaves richly covered with golden buff indumentum. (Lancaster 1962, Goheen 1983).

'**Laurel Pink**' ('Boule de Neige' x [*catawbiense* x 'F. C. Puddle']). 4', -20ºF, EM, 4/4/4. Leaves are small, as are the flowers, to 1 1/4" across. The blooms are reddish rose, composing globular trusses of 12 flowers. (Knippenberg hyb. 1955, reg. 1966).

'**Laurie**' (*minus* var. *minus* Carolinianum Group *album* x 'PJM'). 3', -20ºF, E-EM, 4/4/3. Aromatic foliage has bronze winter coloration. Flowers are white with a hint of pink in the early stages and a dorsal spotting of gold. Very attractive. (Mezitt 1983).

'**Lava Flow**' (*griersonianum* x [KW 13225 x *griersonianum*]). 2', -10ºF, L, -/-/-. KW 13225 may be *forrestii* ssp. *forrestii* Repens Group. This very low, spreading plant has vibrant scarlet red flowers. A good name! (Sunningdale Nurseries 1955).

'**Lavender Charm**' ([*decorum* x *griffithianum*] x 'Purpureum Elegans'). 6', -5ºF, ML, -/-/-. Foliage is large. The 4 1/2" flowers are pale pink, shadowed with lavender, bearing a small blotch. The outer petal color is much darker. Trusses hold up to 14 flowers. (Gable 1954, Herbert 1976).

'**Lavender Girl**' (*fortunei* ssp. *fortunei* x 'Lady Grey Egerton'). 5', -5ºF, M, 3/4/4. A good looking plant, which has an attractive growth habit. The foliage is glossy, tending toward light green. The flower is light orchid, appearing almost white if viewed from a distance. (Slocock 1950) A.M. 1950, F.C.C. 1967.

'**Lavender Haze**' (*yakushimanum* x 'Purple Splendour'). 3', -15ºF, M, 4/4/4. This plant will cover itself with masses of lovely lavender flowers, a reminder of the lavender haze of twilight. It is a superior, round growing plant that stays compact. Very attractive. (Everett Hall 1992).

'**Lavender Princess**' (probably *fortunei* ssp. *fortunei* and/or *catawbiense* or *ponticum* or both). 4', -10ºF, ML, 3/4/5. Light lavender pink flowers on a compact, dense plant holding great dark green leaves. A vigorous grower that makes an excellent plant in the garden. (Dexter-Bosley before 1950).

'**Lavender Queen**' (red *catawbiense* seedling x 'Boule de Neige'). 5', -10ºF, EM-M, 3/4/4. Excellent growth habit, sturdy and bushy, with glossy, dark green foliage. Small, slightly frilled flowers are light bluish lavender touched with a dim brown blotch. (Shammarello).

'**Lavendula**' ([*russatum* x *saluenense*] x *rubiginosum*). 3', -15ºF, M, 3-4/3-4/3-4. Large, intensely lavender flowers, disproportionate to the size of the plant, cover the upright, compact shrub. Very showy! (Hobbie).

'**Lawton's Chinese Red**' (parentage unknown). 3', -5ºF, ML, -/-/-. Leaves are narrow and medium sized. Flowers are clear red with no markings, up to 2 3/4" across, held in a truss up to 15. (Lawton, Hoogendoorn Nurseries 1979).

'**Leah Yates**' ('Mars' selfed). 4', -15ºF, ML, -/-/-. Leaves are large. Flowers are cerise with a white dorsal flare with 2 rays of tan spots. The blooms are carried in a tall truss. (Yates 1956, M. Yates 1977).

'**Leeann**' (['Carmen' x 'Choremia'] x 'Gill's Crimson'). 3', 10ºF, E, -/-/-. Ruby red flowers with a light blotch of maroon spots are widely funnel-campanulate, and are held in lax trusses of 8. This rounded plant is well branched and has dark green leaves held for 3 years. (Carl G. Heller hyb., Shirley Lent raiser, reg. 1979).

'**Lee's Best Purple**' (*catawbiense* hybrid). 6', -20ºF, L, 2-3/3-4/4. This hybrid is noted for its excellent smooth, dark and glossy foliage. Flowers are deep purple. (Lee before 1851, RHS reg. 1958).

'**Lee's Dark Purple**' (*catawbiense* hybrid). 6', -15ºF, ML, 2-3/3-4/4. Reliable and popular for many years! Foliage is handsome, dark and wavy. The flowers are a deep, dark purple. (Lee before 1851).

'Lee's Scarlet' (*caucasicum* hybrid). 4', -5ºF, VE, 3/3/3. The extremely early flowering period is the most valuable quality of this hybrid. Rosy crimson trusses tell you spring is on its way long before most other rhododendrons are even thinking of blooming. Thin plastered indumentum on the leaf undersides makes us believe that its unknown parent is probably *arboreum*. (Lee).

'Legal Johnny' ('Bow Bells' x ['Socrianum' x 'Rima']). 3', 0ºF, M, -/-/-. Strawberry flowers with creamy yellow centers. (George, Hydon Nurseries 1976).

'Lemonade' ('Damaris' x 'Crest'). 5-6', -5F?, M, 4/4/3. Bright yellow, beautifully textured trusses radiate color through the garden. Glossy green, rounded leaves and good plant habit characterize this regal yellow hybrid. (Eichelser before 1980).

'Lemon Custard' ('Crest' x ['Mrs. Betty Robertson' x *wardii*]). 5', 10ºF, EM, 4/4/3-4. Habit is rounded, well-branched, growing broader than tall. The leaves are dull dark green, the flowers slightly fragrant. Flowers are open funnel-bell-shaped, to 4" wide, with wavy edges. The buff-yellow color has no markings. Rounded, lax trusses of 8-12 flowers are abundantly borne. (Elliott 1981).

'Lemon Float' ('Hotei' x ['White Wedding' x *lacteum*]). 4', 0ºF, EM, 4/4/3-4. Strong lemon yellow flowers on a compact plant with attractive foliage. (Lofthouse 1979).

'Lemon Girl' (*minus* var. *minus* Carolinianum Group yellow form x *lutescens*). 3', -10ºF, EM, -/-/-. Terminal flower clusters are comprised of 1-3 trusses of 7-14 flowers each. Blooms are light mimosa yellow with lemon yellow dorsal spotting. The upright plant, nearly as broad as high, has stiff branches. (Mraw hyb. 1967, Louis B. Mraw reg. 1983).

'Lemon Ice' (*ponticum* x unknown). 3', -10ºF, ML, 3/4/4. A good plant for exposed locations. White flowers on this broad, dense shrub have just a tint of yellow. This hybrid is very similar to 'Chionoides' and may, in fact, be the same plant. (Bosley before 1958).

'Lemon Lodge' ('Prelude' selfed). 4', -5ºF, M, -/-/-. Huge, primrose yellow flowers with a few tiny spots deep in the throat abound on a somewhat compact plant which has blue-green foliage. (Pukeiti Rhododendron Trust, NZ 1972).

'Lemon Marmalade' ('Mrs. Lammot Copeland' x 'Mary Drennen'). 4', -10ºF, L, 4/4/3. This flower looks good enough to put on toast. Clear yellow trusses appear late in the season, extending the yellow year. A great looking plant, this is a sister seedling of 'Buttered Popcorn'. (Larson hyb., Clint Smith intro.).

'Lemon Mist' (*xanthostephanum* x *leucaspis*). 3', 10ºF, EM, 3-4/3-4/4. Bright green-yellow flowers cover this plant each spring. An attractive plant with narrow cinnamon-green leaves. (Scott 1968) A.E. 1969.

'Lemon Tea' ('Mary Fleming' x *keiskei*). 2.5', -5ºF, M, -/-/-. The flowers are bisque yellow, streaked and blotched salmon; similar to 'Mary Fleming' but larger. (Ben Shapiro 1995).

'Lem's 121' ('Anna' x 'Lem's Goal'). 5', 5ºF, M, 4-5/2-3/3. Rich, luminescent violet-pink petal edges fade to cream, becoming yellow toward the center and finally maroon red in the throat. New foliage is bronze with crinkly waves which flatten as the leaves mature. The parentage of this plant has been in question for years, and, I'm sorry to say, the second edition of this book confused things more by accidentally adding 'Tally Ho' to the parentage. ('Tally Ho' was evidently picked up from 'Lem's Aurora', which is the next listing). 'Lem's 121' has all appearances of being a sister seedling of 'Isabel Pierce', which would give it the parentage shown above. It is not, as was once thought, out of the same cross as 'Lem's Cameo'. The name 'Lem's 121' is not a registerable name but it seems to have stuck with this plant. (Lem before 1965).

'Lem's Aurora' ([*catawbiense* x 'Fabia' x 'Tally Ho'] exact combination uncertain). 3', -10ºF, M, -/-/-. Another superior Lem cross. Compact and low, this lovely plant sports a rainbow of color. The flowers are a blend of yellow, red and pink. (Lem).

'Lem's Cameo' ('Dido' x 'Anna'). 5', 5ºF, M, 5/3/3. A sensational apricot cream and pink, with a real glow. Super foliage is deep shiny green in summer and bright bronzy red when new, a show in itself! When you see this plant in flower, you will know why, it, along with 'Trude Webster', was the first of all the rhododendrons to be given the coveted Superior Plant Award. Extremely difficult to propagate. Still being sold under the name 'Cameo', which is actually the name of a different plant. (Lem hyb. 1975, Pierce reg. 1976) S.P.A. 1971 Northwest.

'Lem's Fluorescent Pink' ('C. P. Raffill' x 'Loderi King George'). 5', 5ºF, ML, -/-/-. Glowing, pastel pink flowers with rosy pink edges emerge from bright, rose pink buds to form fragrant, ball shaped trusses. The attractive foliage is rich green. (Lem before 1965).

'Lem's Goal' ('Lady Bessborough' x 'Azor'). 5', 0ºF, ML, 3-4/3/3-4. Upright and not too open growing, the plant is covered with narrow, pointed, rather dull light green leaves. Flowers are soft creamy apricot, shading darker in the throat, and are held in neat trusses of 6-7 flowers. (Lem 1958) P.A. 1952.

'Lem's Monarch' ('Anna' x 'Marinus Koster'). 6', -5ºF, M, 4-5/4-5/4-5. Here is a plant from the famed Lem collection that is really terrific. It is a member of the great 'Walloper' group. The huge showy trusses are pink and are of utmost perfection. The foliage is large and attractive. The plant known as 'Pink Walloper' is now considered to be a synonym of 'Lem's Monarch' and the plants are often sold interchangeably. 'Lem's Monarch' will grow into a strong stemmed full plant of kingly proportions. Plant it in a special location where you can enjoy it all year. (Lem) C.A. 1971.

'Lem's Stormcloud' ('Burgundy' x 'Mars'). 5', -15ºF, ML, 4/3-4/4. Very large, glossy red flowers are quite flat, showing off a faint white glow at the base of the throat, from which the stamens protrude dramatically. (Lem about 1962, B. Smith 1980).

'Lem's Tangerine' ('Margaret Dunn' x ['Anna' x 'King of Shrubs']). 4', -5ºF, M, 5/3/3. The color of this flower was as close to orange as any rhododendron had gotten for many years. With the number of recent introductions, this color is not now as unique as it once was; however, it remains a very fine plant and flower. The truss nicely ball shaped, complimenting the light green foliage. (Lem hyb. 1967, Newcomb reg. 1987).

'Lenape' (*pubescens* x *keiskei*). 3', -10ºF, E, 3/4/-. Leaves are a little under medium size and narrow. Flowers are light yellow and rather small, carried in trusses the size of a large walnut. (Nearing 1950, reg. 1958).

'Leo' ('Britannia' x *elliottii*). 5', -5ºF, ML-L, 5/3/3-4. Excellent late deep red flowers. Dark green foliage with good shrub habit. The very best tight truss, composed of heavy, waxy flowers. (Rothschild 1948) A.M. 1948.

'Leona' ('Corona' x 'Dondis'). 5', 0ºF, ML, 3/3/3. Medium green leaves are medium large sized, on an open growing plant. Very open flowers are intense pink, slightly spotted with darker rose. The 3" wide blooms are set in a domed truss. Easily rooted. (R. Henny 1958).

'Leona Maud' (*yakushimanum* x 'Thomaleum'). 3', 0ºF, M 4/4/3. Bright red buds open to vivid, mauve pink flowers with deep red spotting. The blooms are held in ball shaped trusses of 18. A well-branched, rounded, compact bush with elliptic leaves, which display greenish indumentum underneath. (A. P. Johnson hyb. 1968, Johnson reg. 1986).

'Leonardslee Giles' ('Standishii' x *griffithianum*). 6', 0ºF, M, 4/3/4. First to appear are buds of cameo pink which open to huge upright trusses of very pale pink, soon becoming pure snowy white. Wide, handsome leaves give this sturdy plant. Part shade gives the best flowers and allows them to develop their full splendor. (Sir E. Loder) A.M. 1948.

'Leonore' (*auriculatum* x *kyawii*). 5', 5ºF, VL, -/-/-. Gigantic flowers and plant. Trusses are composed of about 12 flowers, raspberry red with darker shading on the outer edges. Leaves are narrow and hairy and occur in giant rosettes. (Rothschild 1947) A.M. 1948.

'Letty Edwards' g. (*campylocarpum* var. *elatum* x *fortunei* ssp. *fortunei*). 5', 0ºF, M, 3/3/3. Plant grows rounded, somewhat compact, with medium to large leaves. Pale yellow flowers are held in rounded trusses of up to 11 flowers. (Clarke) A.M. 1946, F.C.C. 1948.

'Leverett Richards' ([*wardii* x 'F. C. Puddle'] x 'Mrs. Betty Robertson'). 4', 0ºF, M, 3-4/3-4/3. Sister seedling of 'Virginia Richards' has flowers that are slightly more yellow, while still exhibiting the wonderful blending of pink and apricot. (Whitney).

'Libretto' ('Lee's Best Purple' x 'Purple Splendour'). 3.5', -5ºF, ML, -/-/-. Dramatic funnel shaped blooms of deep reddish purple are accented with dorsal markings of bright yellow green. The slightly ruffled edged flowers are held in groups of 11-14 to form a rounded truss. The dark green foliage is lightly covered with pale beige hairs. (Hachmann hyb. 1979, Stuck reg. 1991).

'Lightly Lavender' (*yakushimanum* x 'Purple Splendour'). 4', -15ºF, M, 3-4/4/4. Delicate lavender flowers blanket this pretty, compact growing plant. In fall, it will often reward you with another display of blossoms. It is well clothed with deep green leaves which are about 3 to 4" long. The foliage has very light indumentum beneath. This plant has also been sold under the unofficial name of 'Lenore' in the Seattle, Washington area. (Greer 1988).

'Light Touch' ('Vulcan' x 'Sun Devil'). 3', 5ºF, EM, -/-/-. Characteristic of this hybrid are the coral flowers, which have a deep red throat, and the deep green foliage, which has pronounced veining. (Lansing Bulgin before 1990).

'Like Fluff' (*yakushimanum* x 'Vanessa'). 3', -5ºF, M, 3/4/4. A plant of almost flawless habit. Light pink flowers fade to almost white. (Bovee before 1960).

'Lila Pedigo' ('Odee Wright' x 'Crest'). 4', 5ºF, M, 4-5/4-5/4. Shiny, deep green leaves accent the ruffly edged, chartreuse yellow flowers which have very light red spotting in the throat. Very free flowering. (Pedigo before 1990).

'Lillian Peste' (*yakushimanum* 'Koichiro Wada' x unnamed Whitney hybrid). 2', 0ºF, M, 4/4/4. A medium growing plant of dense habit with very attractive flowers of pink, yellow and orange combinations. (Peste 1981).

'Lilofee' (['Nova Zembla' x 'Purple Splendour'] x 'Purple Splendour'). 3', -15ºF, M-ML, -/-/-. Each lacy looking truss is formed from 14-16 ruffled, funnel shaped flowers. The flowers are composed of purple petals which act as a backdrop for the conspicuous white stamens which frill from under the darker tatting on the upper lobes. Foliage is glossy dark green, brown hairs beneath. Plant habit is erect but compact. (Hachmann hyb. 1990, Stuck reg. 1991).

'Limelight' ('Catalgla' x [*fortunei* ssp. *fortunei* x *wardii*]). 4', -25ºF, ML, -/-/-. Foliage is medium to large. Seven lobed, pale yellow flowers, to 3 1/2" wide, with heavy yellowish green dorsal blotch, are carried in a rounded truss of up to 15 flowers. (Leach 1962).

'Linda' ('Britannia' x *williamsianum*). 3', -15ºF, M, 3-4/3-4. This beautiful compact plant bears 7 to 8 rosy red flowers in each truss. Oval leaf shape reflects some of its parent *williamsianum*. (Experimental Station Boskoop, Holland) A.M. 1968.

'Lionel's Triumph' (*lacteum* x 'Naomi'). 5-6', -5ºF, M, 5/4/3. One of the most superb hybrids from Lionel de Rothschild. There are very few *lacteum* hybrids and this is probably the best. Difficult to propagate and has few stems; therefore, not many cuttings are available. Huge trusses of dresden yellow have crimson spotting. (Rothschild). A.M. 1954.

'Lisa' ('Catalgla' x 'Madonna'). 6', -15ºF, ML, 3/3/-. Leaves are quite large and wide. Large flowers are white, with light green blotch, held in a good-sized truss up to 18. (Gable 1963) P.A. 1962.

'Lissabon' ('Nova Zembla' x *williamsianum*). 3', -10ºF, M, -/-/-. This compact hybrid has flowers of deep rhodonite red with cardinal red margins, which are held in groups of 8 to form lax trusses. (V. von Martin, Bruns 1971).

'Little Augie' (*augustinii* hybrid). 3', 5ºF, EM, 3/3/3. A hybrid developed in California. Bright blue flowers illustrate the influence of its parentage. Good foliage and compact plant habit. (Barber before 1980).

'Little Ben' g. (*neriiflorum* x *forrestii* ssp. *forrestii* Repens Group). 2', 10ºF, EM, 3/3/3. Foliage is small, stiff, and dark green on a low growing, dense plant. Bell shaped, deep scarlet flowers bloom in clusters. (C.R. Scrase-Dickins) F.C.C. 1937.

'Little Bert' (*forrestii* ssp. *forrestii* Repens Group x *euchaites*). 2', 10ºF, EM, 3/3/3. Ideal for rock gardens, this plant requires good drainage. Elliptic-ovate leaves, rather long for plant size, are rounded at each end. Bell shaped flowers, with spreading lobes, are 2" wide. The bright scarlet-crimson blooms hang in clusters of 4 or 5, forming a rather loose truss. (C. R. Scrase-Dickins) A.M. 1939.

'Little Dragon' ('Fabia' x *venator*). 3', 5ºF, M, 3/3/3. Red stemmed leaves complement fiery red flowers. (Lancaster 1958).

'Little Gem' ('Carmen' x *elliottii* KW 7725). 18", 0ºF, M, 4/4/3-4. Blood red flowers on a prostrate plant with glossy deep green leaves. A superb variety for both foliage and flower. (Whitney hyb. before 1956, Sather reg. 1976) P.A. 1962.

'Little Imp' (*impeditum* hybrid). 3', 0ºF, EM, 3/3/3. Grown in California, this is a more vigorous *impeditum*. Blue-purple flowers profusely cover the plant. Foliage shows the silver-blue that is so good in some forms of *impeditum*. A compact grower. (Barber before 1980).

'Little Joe' (*forrestii* ssp. *forrestii* Repens Group x 'May Day'). 1', 5ºF, EM, 3/3/3. Plant habit is compact and wide spreading, with small, dark green leaves. Very waxy, bright currant red flowers, 2" wide, are held up to 4 per lax truss. (Brandt 1951).

'Little Lou' ('Lucy Lou' x *valentinianum*). 18", 5ºF, E, -/-/-. Growth habit is low and spreading, with small leaves. Flowers are yellow in the bud, opening greenish yellow tinged with apricot. (Sumner 1963) P.A. 1963.

'Little Miss Muffett' (*yakushimanum* x unknown). 2.5', -5ºF, M, -/-/-. Twice as wide as tall, this low growing, dense plant bears flowers of heavy substance. Strong red buds open to deep pink flowers, forming ball trusses of 11-12. The elliptic leaves are leathery with felt-like hairs below. (Whitney hyb. about 1967, Watters reg. 1989).

'Little Nemo' ('Carmen' x 'Choremia'). 1', -5ºF, M, 3/3/3. Small, shiny dark leaves on an almost prostrate plant. Flowers are scarlet red with a very large calyx of the same color. (Brandt 1964).

'**Little Red Riding Hood**' (parentage unknown). 3', -5°F, M, -/-/-. A compact, mounding plant, this hybrid has a good red flower and attractive foliage. (sold by Hammond's Acres of Rhodys and Kelleygreen Rhododendron Nursery 1994).

'**Little Sheba**' (['Earl of Athlone' x 'Fabia'] x *forrestii* ssp. *forrestii* Repens Group). 1', 5°F, M, 3/4/3. Growth habit is very low, prostrate, and quite vigorous once established. Foliage is small, darker green on top side. 2" flowers are blood red, up to 3 in a terminal cluster. (R. Henny 1958) P.A. 1954.

'**Little White Dove**' (*fortunei* ssp. *fortunei* x *yakushimanum*). 3', 5°F, M, 4/4/3. Leaves are small. White flowers, to 2 1/4" across, are held in rounded trusses of up to 12 flowers. (Lancaster, Elliott 1974).

'**Livonia Lindsley**' ('Loderi King George' x 'Mars'). 4', -5°F, M, 4/3-4/3-4. Flowers, up to 3" across, are lavender pink, fading somewhat, carried in large 24 flower trusses. Leaves are medium large. (Wright grower, Lindsley, Sr. reg. 1968).

'**Liz Ann**' (selected seedling of *sargentianum*). 18", -5°F, M, 4/3/2. This is a selected pink form of the hybrid 'Maricee'. It is an excellent dwarf with little Daphne-like flowers that open pastel pink and gradually lighten. Needs especially good drainage. (Caperci unregistered).

'**Llenroc**' (*minus* var. *minus* Carolinianum Group *album* x *mucronulatum* 'Cornell Pink'). 3', -20°F, E, 4/3-4/3-4. 'Cornell' reversed. The neat thing about this plant is the vibrant orange foliage in the fall. Blossoms are bright, light pink with a faint yellow eye. (Mezitt).

'**Loch Rannoch**' (['Tidbit' x *caucasicum*] x [*wardii* x {*yakushimanum* x 'Crest'}]). 4',-5°F, M, 4/4/4. Precocious and floriferous, this hybrid displays flowers of yellow with a red throat. Foliage is attractive. (Cox hyb. 1976, Glendoick Gardens reg. 1990).

'**Loch Tay**' ('Hotei' x *caucasicum*). 4', -5°F?, M, 4-5/4-5/-. Deep golden amber flowers are dotted on the upper lobes with maroon red. Behind this is a large golden calyx, also spotted with red. The trusses are full and rounded with just enough opening to expose the showy calyx. Deep green, rounded, leathery foliage makes an excellent contrast to the bright golden flowers. It forms a sturdy plant which branches well. (Cox hyb. 1971, reg. 1987).

'**Lodauric**' ('Loderi' x *auriculatum*). 6', 0°F, L, 4/3/4. Trumpet shaped white flowers glow with a sunny yellow throat. The classic flowers are fragrant and crinkly in texture. Vigorous grower. (G. Taylor for Sir J. Ramsden, Crosfield 1939).

'**Lodauric Iceberg**' ('Loderi' x *auriculatum*). 6', 0°F, L, 4/3/4. Late, fragrant, pure white flowers make this outstanding. Place this plant where it receives afternoon shade, and it will reward you with beautiful lily-like flowers. The warmth of the spring day releases the sweet fragrance, which is often even more noticeable in the evening. Nice, abundant light grass green foliage. (Slocock 1946).

'**Loderi**' (*fortunei* ssp. *fortunei* x *griffithianum*). 6', 5°F, M, 4/3-4/4. This is the "grex" or group of sister seedlings from which the named clones that follow have been derived. 'Loderi' will form a large tree-like shrub of strong stature. Large flowers are sweetly scented and range from pastel pinks to pure white. (Sir E. Loder 1901).

'**Loderi Fairyland**' (*fortunei* ssp. *fortunei* x *griffithianum*). 6', 5°F, M, 4/3/4. Pink buds open to expose a fragrant white flower. It is very similar to the other white 'Loderi' types. (Loder 1901).

'**Loderi Game Chick**' (*fortunei* ssp. *fortunei* x *griffithianum*). 6', 5°F, M, 4/3-4/4. Pale pink flowers with a faint blotch. Fragrant. (Loder 1901).

'**Loderi Irene Stead**' (*fortunei* ssp. *fortunei* x *griffithianum* exact combination unknown). 6', 5°F, M, 4/3-4/4. The plant is similar to others of the 'Loderi' group, but these flowers show a stronger pink coloration. (Stead before 1960).

'**Loderi Julie**' (*fortunei* ssp. *fortunei* x *griffithianum*). 6', 5°F, M, 4/3-4/4. The flowers are cream, suffused with sulphur yellow. They are the closest to a "yellow" 'Loderi'. (reg. 1958) A.M. 1944.

'**Loderi King George**' (*fortunei* ssp. *fortunei* x *griffithianum*). 6', 5°F, M, 4/3-4/4. Known as the best white form of the 'Loderi' group. The huge flowers open pale pink and then become white. Deliciously fragrant. A magnificent plant that will some day approach proportions and size of a tree. Allow plenty of room and give wind and sun protection. It is not unusual for this plant to get purplish spots on the foliage during the summer which are probably caused by a virus. They do not hurt the plant and can occur on any 'Loderi' as well as on several other rhododendrons. (Loder 1901).

'**Loderi Patience**' (*fortunei* ssp. *fortunei* x *griffithianum*). 6', 5°F, M, 4/3-4/4. White flowers with a crimson throat. Nice foliage and fragrant. (Loder 1901).

'**Loderi Pink Diamond**' (*fortunei* ssp. *fortunei* x *griffithianum*). 6', 5°F, M, 4/3-4/4. This is one of the pinkest of the 'Loderi' group, but it is still a pastel shell pink. Like 'King George' in other respects. (Loder 1901) F.C.C. 1914.

'**Loderi Pink Topaz**' (*fortunei* ssp. *fortunei* x *griffithianum*). 6', 5°F, M, 4/3-4/4. Fragrant pink flowers with a faint green throat. (Loder 1901).

'**Loderi Pretty Polly**' (*fortunei* ssp. *fortunei* x *griffithianum*). 6', 5°F, M, 4/3-4/4. Pink flowers. (Loder 1901).

'**Loderi Princess Marina**' ('Loderi King George' x 'Loderi Sir Edmund'). 6', 5°F, M, 4/3-4/4. Pale pink flowers turning white. (Loder 1901) A.M. 1948.

'**Loderi Sir Edmund**' (*fortunei* ssp. *fortunei* x *griffithianum*). 6', 5°F, M, 4/3- 4/4. Also fragrant, very large, pale pink flowers. (Loder 1901) A.M. 1930.

'**Loderi Sir Joseph Hooker**' (*fortunei* ssp. *fortunei* x *griffithianum*). 6', 5°F, M, 4/3-4/4. Deeper shell pink flowers are fragrant. (Loder 1901) A.M. 1973.

'**Loderi Superlative**' (*fortunei* ssp. *fortunei* x *griffithianum*). 6', 5°F, M, 4/3/4. Fragrant white flowers with slight pink flush. (Loder 1901).

'**Loderi Titan**' (*fortunei* ssp. *fortunei* x *griffithianum*). 6', 5°F, M, 4/4/4. Delicately scented, very pale blush flowers and good foliage distinguish this beautiful hybrid. (Reuthe Ltd. intro before 1958).

'**Loderi Venus**' (*fortunei* ssp. *fortunei* x *griffithianum*). 6', 5°F, M, 4/3-4/4. Deepest pink of the 'Loderi' group and one of the most desired. Extremely fragrant. In flower, the sight and fragrance is something you will not soon forget. (Loder 1901).

'**Loderi White Diamond**' (*fortunei* ssp. *fortunei* x *griffithianum*). 6', 5°F, M, 4/3-4/4. Ivory white flowers with blotch. (Loder 1901).

'Loder's White' (['Album Elegans' x *griffithianum*] x 'White Pearl') 5', 0ºF, M, 4/3-4/3-4. This hybrid is often thought to be a member of the 'Loderi' group because of the word "Loder" in its name. While it does have *R. griffithianum* in its parentage as does 'Loderi', that is the only relationship. 'Loder's White' has a large upright truss opening from a tall candelabrum bud. It opens white with slight yellow in the throat and pink picotee edges. In many books its parentage is recorded as probably *arboreum album* x *griffithianum*. This appears to be incorrectly recorded, or, at one time, there was another plant named 'Loder's White' which has been lost from cultivation. (Mangles) A.M. 1911, A.G.M. 1931.

'Lodestar' (*catawbiense* var. *album* x 'Belle Heller'). 5', -20ºF, ML, 3-4/3-4/4. Leaves are medium large. Flowers, to 3 1/4" across, will vary from the more usual white to extremely pale lilac, with a strongly spotted dorsal blotch of dark greenish yellow. There are 15 flowers to the truss. (Leach 1964).

'Loeb's Moonlight' (parentage unknown, may contain *ponticum*). 5', -10ºF, ML, 3/3/3. This plant displays glossy foliage and rosy orchid flowers with a yellow green blotch. (Loeb 1965).

'Lois' (*pemakoense* x *racemosum*). 18", -5ºF, E, 3/4/3. Pink flowers are extremely heavily borne. 'Lois' has delicately small leaves and a dwarf stature which lend well to use in a border or rock garden. (Greer hyb. 1955, reg. 1980).

'Longwood' ('Vernus' x 'Olympic Lady'). 4', 0ºF, M, 3/3/-. Foliage is small. 2 1/2" flowers are lilac pink, spotted dark red in the throat, held in a truss of up to 7. (Leach hyb. 1972, Longwood Gardens 1976).

'Looking Glass' (*yakushimanum* x 'China'). 5', -15ºF, M, 3-4/3-4/3. Deep red buds open to deep pink flowers with frilled edges. This is a well-branched, moderate sized plant, canopied with matte fern green leaves above, pale indumentum below. (Gordner, Briggs 1988).

'Lord Roberts' (parentage unknown, probably contains *catawbiense*). 5', -15ºF, ML, 2-3/3/4. A vigorous rounded, upright plant. The foliage is glossy green and crinkled. The flowers are deep red with a black blotch and are held in tight ball shaped trusses. (Fromow & Chiswick before 1900, Mason reg. 1958).

'Lord Swaythling' (*griffithianum* x unknown). 6', -5ºF, EM, -/-/-. Coral red buds open creamy pink with dark maroon spots in the throat. A tall growing plant. (Schulz 1890, C. B. van Nes and Sons intro. 1896).

'Lori Eichelser' (*forrestii* ssp. *forrestii* Repens Group (pink form) x 'Bow Bells'). 2', -5ºF, EM, 4/4/4. A most outstanding hybrid. 'Lori Eichelser' has a tight, dense growth habit, with deep jade green leaves that are most attractively round. Unlike many hybrids, 'Lori Eichelser' excels in both flower and overall plant appearance. The flowers are proportionately large and cover the little plant with cherry pink bells. As a very old plant, it will measure less than 3' tall, twice that in width. (Brandt, Janeck 1966).

'Loreley' ([*yakushimanum* 'Koichiro Wada' x 'Doncaster'] x *dichroanthum scyphocalyx* hybrid). 2', -10ºF, M, -/-/-. Large reddish orange buds open and mature to creamy yellow, very luminous flowers. Lax trusses are comprised of 11-12 flowers. Medium dark green foliage rolls under slightly to add distinction to this plant. A compact plant, growing twice as wide as tall. (Bruns 1987).

'Louis Pasteur' ('Mrs. Tritton' x 'Viscount Powerscourt'). 5', -5ºF, ML, 3/1-2/3-4. This plant, with a spreading growth habit, is difficult to propagate. Two-toned red and white flowers are held in dense, rounded trusses. (L. J. Endtz & Co. 1923).

'Lovely William' (*euchaites* x *williamsianum*). 2', -10ºF, EM, -/-/-. A nice, low growing, spreading plant with deep rose pink flowers. (Horlick 1940).

'Love Story' (parentage unknown). 4', -5ºF, M, -/-/-. Foliage is medium sized and rather narrow. Light peach flowers, shading to pale yellow, have a darker yellow blotch and orangey red throat spotting. The 3 1/2" blooms, edged with deep peach, are held in trusses of up to 10. (Whitney 1965, Sather 1976).

'Lucky Strike' (*griersonianum* x 'Countess of Derby'). 4', 10ºF, ML, 3/3/4. Large dull green leaves are held on a plant which does best in partial shade. Waxy, 3" wide flowers are deep salmon pink, funnel shaped, and are carried 9 to the conical truss. This is a sister seedling of 'Anna Rose Whitney'. (Van Veen, Sr. 1958).

'Lucy' (cross of two rhododendrons similar to the parents of 'PJM'). 4', -25ºF, EM, -/-/-. Compact, mounding, and slow growing, this plant achieves a habit wider than tall. This low growing plant has small green foliage, turning to dark mahogany in winter, and lilac pink flowers that cover the foliage. One of the earliest plants to bloom in the spring. (Mezitt hyb. 1972, Weston Nurseries intro. about 1990).

'Lucy Lou' (*leucaspis* x [*ciliatum* x *leucaspis*]). 3', 5ºF, E, 3-4/4-5/3-4. Freely produced flowers are pure snow white. Charming, rounded, fuzzy leaves are soft green. (Larson 1956).

'Lucy's Good Pink' ('Ruby F. Bowman' x *griersonianum*). 6', -15ºF, L, -/-/-. Leaves are large. Flowers, to a generous 4 1/2" wide, are rose with red calyx. The 7-lobed blooms are carried in lax trusses of up to 7. (Druecker 1976).

'Lugano' ('Fantastica' x ['Hachmann's Ornament' x 'Furnivall's Daughter']). 3', -15ºF, ML, -/-/-. Flowers are light lavender pink with a very prominent dark violet blotch, well displayed in the flat, open flower. The striking trusses are large, formed by 17 flowers. The glossy medium green foliage densely covers this broad, compact growing plant. (Hachmann 1990).

'Luise Verey' (*yakushimanum* x 'Glamour'). 3', 0ºF, M, -/-/-. Flat pink flowers have crimson in the throat. (George, Hydon Nurseries 1978).

'Lumina' ('Kokardia' x ['Mars' x *yakushimanum* 'Koichiro Wada']). 3', -15ºF, M, -/-/-. The flowers are soft rose with some lilac flecks. The large foliage, heavily covered with indumentum, curves slightly to the inside. Blooms when young and matures to a broad plant. (Hachmann 1982).

'Lunar Queen' (*griffithianum* x 'Hawk'). 4', -5ºF, EM, -/-/-. A handsome shrub with pale yellow trusses composed of flowers 4" across. (Gen. Harrison 1966).

'Luscombei' (*fortunei* ssp. *fortunei* x *thomsonii*). 6', 0ºF, EM, 3/4/3. Medium green, softly glossy leaves, medium sized, on a sturdy, upright, rounded plant. Deep pink flowers shade to mauve, in a loose, open-topped truss. Rather slow to set buds. See also 'Pride of Leonardslee'. (Luscombe 1880, Loder).

'Luxor' (*catawbiense* var. *album* x 'Goldfort'). 6', -25ºF, M, 4/3/3. Formerly called 'Morocco'. Rounded trusses of 14-15 flowers emerge as light rose pink, then fade to light yellow with dark spotting on the upper lobe. Foliage is smooth and attractive on this super hardy plant. (Leach hyb. 1952, intro. 1973, reg. 1983).

'Lydia' ('Antoon van Welie' x 'Day Dream'). 6', 0ºF, ML, 4/3-4/4. This brilliant, waxy, fluorescent pink flower literally sparkles and shines. A most unusual color! An exceptional plant, with large glossy leaves, which also buds heavily. (Greer 1963) C.A. 1972.

'Lynne Robbins Steinman' (parentage from the 'PJM' group and possibly *mucronulatum*). 4', -25ºF, E, -/-/-. Abundant, ruffled, double pink flowers with yellow throats cover this hybrid very early in the season. (Mezitt, Weston Nurseries before 1990).

'Macopin' (chance seedling of *racemosum*, probably *racemosum* x 'Wyanokie'). 3', -20ºF, M, -/-/-. Leaves are round and shiny, with pale lavender flowers held in globular clusters. (Nearing 1972).

'Madah Jean' ('Marinus Koster' selfed). 6', 0ºF, ML, 4/4/4. Very large trusses have ruffled edges. Flowers of cameo pink, fading to cream in the center, have spotting on the upper petal. Large leaves are deep green. (Newberry, Philp 1986).

'Madame Carvalho' (*catawbiense* hybrid). 5', -15ºF, L, 2/3/4. A hardy plant that does well wherever it is grown. The flowers are a delightful white with green spots. (J. Waterer 1866).

'Madame Cochet' (unknown parentage). 4', -10ºF, L, 4/3/3. Medium purple, open faced flowers, shade to white centers with a light golden yellow blotch. They are held in large trusses surrounded by forest green leaves. (Bertin before 1888).

'Madame de Bruin' ('Prometheus' x 'Doncaster'). 4', -10ºF, ML, 3/2/4. The ball shaped trusses are bright cerise red. This is a vigorous growing plant. (M. Koster 1904).

'Madame Fr. J. Chauvin' (*fortunei* ssp. *fortunei* x unknown). 5', -10ºF, ML, 4/3/4. This is a sturdy grower, with an upright habit and long, narrow, light green leaves. Flowers are rich rose-pink, blushing paler in the throat. A diminutive red blotch accents flowers held in a rounded truss. (M. Koster 1916) A.M. 1933.

'Madame Guillemot' see 'Monsieur Guillemot'.

'Madame Jules Porges' (unknown parentage, probably contains *ponticum* and *catawbiense*). 6', -10ºF, L, 4/2-3/4. The growth habit tends to be rather open, sprawling, and leggy. Medium-sized leaves provide the backdrop for mauve to pale orchid flowers, which have a huge golden blotch. (Moser & Fils before 1900).

'Madame Masson' (*catawbiense* x *ponticum*). 5', -15ºF, M, 3/3/4. This hybrid, also known as 'Madame Mason', is large-growing, with a well-shaped, rounded, fairly dense habit. The foliage is shiny dark green, and the snow-white flowers have a golden-yellow blotch. (Bertin 1849).

'Madame Wagner' (*caucasicum* hybrid). 5', -25ºF, ML, 3/3/-. Light rose pink edging encircles the white center of the flower. The plant that is most often known as 'Madame Wagner' in the U.S. is actually 'Princess Mary of Cambridge'. The true 'Madame Wagner' is seldom grown and may not actually exist in the United States. (J. Macoy before 1900).

'Madras' ('Mars' x 'Fanfare'). 4', -15ºF, M, 3/3/3. Bright cardinal red flowers have dorsal spotting. They are very bright and showy, and bloom readily. This was originally named 'Bengal'. (Leach intro. 1973, reg. 1983).

'Madrid' ('Dexter #L-1' x 'America'). 5', -20ºF, ML, 3/3/3. Bright rosy pink flowers with white stamens have a ruby red blotch in the throat and faint spotting on the upper lobes. This was originally named 'Seville'. (Leach intro. 1973, reg. 1983).

'Maestro' ('Barclayi' x *williamsianum*). 3', -5ºF, EM, -/-/-. This plant has neat, compact growth and deep rosy red flowers. (Gen. Harrison 1961) P.C. 1969, A.M. 1975.

'Maggie Stoeffel' (parentage unknown). 5', 0ºF, ML, 4/4/-. Leaves are narrow and of medium size. Double flowers are light rose with brownish crimson marks, to 3 1/2" wide, held in a 19 flower truss. (Whitney, Rutherford 1968).

'Magic Moments' (*aberconwayi* x *yakushimanum*). 4', -10ºF, M, 4/4/3. Bright white flowers have a maroon blotch. Tough, shiny green foliage is on a compact plant that looks good all year. (Lofthouse 1979).

'Magnagloss' ([*wardii* x *fortunei* ssp. *discolor*] x unknown). 6', -15ºF, L, -/-/-. Leaves are small to medium size. Lilac orchid flowers, to 2 1/2" wide, have a showy blotch and are carried in a truss of up to 12. (Nearing 1973).

'Magnificat' ('Disca' x 'Graf Zeppelin'). 7', 0ºF, ML, -/-/-. Domed trusses of 12-13 fragrant, wavy edged flowers open from red buds. The white flowers have rims of deeper pink and a brilliant yellow dorsal spot. There is a calyx of tiny pink straps. The foliage is elliptical and flat. (M. & B. Shapiro hyb. 1966, reg. 1989).

'Maharani' ('Harvest Moon' x 'Letty Edwards'). 6', -10ºF, M, -/-/-. Large trusses of 16 flowers are grayish white tinged with orchid pink, shaded to ruby red toward the center. The 5-lobed flowers are blotched with red. Elliptic-oval, smooth foliage covers this German hybrid. (Hachmann hyb. 1964, G. Stuck reg. 1983) G.M. 1987.

'Mah Jong' ('Chink' x *valentinianum*). 2', -5ºF, E, -/-/-. Chartreuse flowers appear on this attractive, small plant. (Crown Estate Commissioners 1971) P.C. 1971.

'Mahmoud' (unknown, probably contains *ponticum* and *catawbiense*). 5', 0ºF, ML, 3-4/3/3. The unusually striking coloration of the flower always attracts attention when 'Mahmoud' is in bloom. The blossom is lavender pink with a large golden yellow eye. Matte green foliage is long, narrow and slightly concave. (Unknown origin, reg. RHS 1958).

'Malahat' ('Gill's Triumph' x *strigillosum*). 5', 5ºF, M, 4/3/4. This hybrid has brilliant red flowers showing a darker red blotch. Long, narrow, forest green leaves have undersides of sparse reddish indumentum. I have seen this plant described as being late flowering, but I have also seen it in full flower in British Columbia in late April! (Larson hyb. 1949, reg. 1983).

'Malemute' ('Loderi King George' x unnamed orange Lem hybrid). 5', 10ºF, EM, -/-/-. Foliage is large. Huge, fragrant flowers, to 5" across, are a lovely pink color with darker blotch and edging, and form a lax truss of up to 11 blooms. (Elliott hyb. 1966, reg. 1977).

'Maletta' ([*auriculatum* x *fortunei* ssp. *discolor*] x *ungernii* hybrid). 5', 5ºF, ML, -/-/-. The 15-flower truss is formed of 3 1/4" flowers. They are ivory colored in the center and edged with antique gold. Leaves are large. (Yates 1971).

'Malta' ('Gable's Pioneer' [selfed]). 4', -25ºF, EM, 3-4/4/4. This hardy rhododendron has small, dark green leaves that turn maroon in winter. It is a heavy flowering plant with very light orchid flowers kissed in areas with slightly deeper orchid pink. The green stamens are very short, giving the appearance of a light green spot at the base of the flower. (Leach 1981).

'Mandalay' (*haematodes* x *venator*). 4', -10ºF, EM, 3-4/3-4/3. Showy, waxy scarlet red flowers are held in loose trusses on a compact bush. (Rothschild 1947).

'Manda Sue' ('Vulcan' x 'Elspeth'). 3', 0ºF, M, 4/3-4/3-4. This is a beautiful hybrid with shell pink flowers which have a picotee edge of red and a yellow throat. The plant has a compact habit and deep green leaves that it gets from its parent 'Vulcan'. (Baker 1969).

'Manderley' ('Scandinavia' x 'Fabia'). 4', -5ºF, M-ML, 3/4/4. A hybrid from Boskoop, Holland. It is cardinal red, spotted darker inside the flower. New foliage is reddish. Good compact plant habit. (Slootjes 1968) A.M. 1965.

'Manitou' ('Conestoga' x unknown). 3', -25ºF, EM, 4/3/-. Similar to 'Windbeam' but more compact, this sun resistant hybrid has dense, medium green, small foliage. The prolific light pink flowers open almost white and darken to a deeper pink with age. The heavy production of golden orange buds makes the plant attractive in winter. (Nearing hyb., intro. D. Knippenberg, Laurelwood Gardens before 1990).

'Mannheim' ('Essex Scarlet' x *forrestii* ssp. *forrestii* Repens Group). 3', -15ºF, ML, 3/3/3. Taller and later blooming than other hybrids in this group, this compact plant has loose trusses of 3-7 dark glowing red flowers. It is upright, broad and floriferous. (Hobbie intro. 1976).

'Mannie Weber' ('Catawbiense Boursault' x 'Madame Albert Moser'). 4', -5ºF, ML, 3/3/3. Flat faced flowers are royal purple with slight greenish spotting on the dorsal lobe. Plant habit is erect with very dark green leaves. (Weber 1974).

'Manon' (*tephropeplum* x *ciliatum*). 3', 5ºF, EM, 3/3/3-4. Flowers are very light pastel pink, fading to almost white. Leaves are long and narrow and the plant is free flowering. Nice. (Adams-Acton 1942).

'Manuela' ('Blinklicht' x ['Mars' x *yakushimanum*]). 3', -10ºF, ML, -/-/-. Strong mallow purple flowers, paling in the throat, have vivid magenta midveins· The dorsal lobe is marked lettuce green on a white background. The broad, ovate leaves have thin, pale indumentum. (Hachmann hyb. 1969, Stuck reg. 1974).

'Marchioness of Lansdowne' (*maximum* hybrid). 5', -15ºF, L, 3/2-3/3. Flowers are violet rose with an almost black blotch. Plant grows in a spreading, open manner. A good hardy plant with an unusual flower. (A. Waterer before 1915).

'Marcia' (*campylocarpum* x 'Gladys'). 4', 0ºF, M, 4/3/2. Foliage is of medium size and medium green, on an upright, slow growing plant. Bright primrose yellow flowers are in rounded trusses up to 10 flowers per truss. It's a super yellow that likes some shade. (Swaythling) F.C.C. 1944.

'Mardi Gras' (*yakushimanum* 'Koichiro Wada' x 'Vanessa'). 30", 0ºF, M, 4/4/4. Leaves are large. Flowers, 3" wide, pink blushed white, have no spotting. They are held in a 12-flower truss. (Bovee hyb. 1976, Sorenson & Watson reg. 1976).

'Mareike' ('Omega' x *wardii*, G Sherriff 5679). 4', -15ºF, M, -/-/-. The broad, compact plant has medium green, slightly glossy foliage. Flowers are funnel shaped, 10-11 to the truss, pale greenish yellow with sparse bright purplish red markings on the upper lobe. (H. Hachmann 1990).

'Margaret Dunn' (*fortunei* ssp. *discolor* x 'Fabia'). 4', 0ºF, ML, 4/3/-. Openly funnel shaped flowers are apricot pink, flushed shell pink. They are held in loose trusses of 8-9 on this floriferous bush. Slim elliptic leaves. (Lord Swaythling) A.M. 1946.

'Margaret Falmouth' (*griffithianum* x *auriculatum*). 5', -10ºF, L, -/-/-. Frilly white flowers have intense cardinal red markings in the throat. (Col. G. H. Loder, Boscawen reg. 1968) A.M. 1968.

'Margaret Mack' ('Annie E. Endtz' x 'Marion'). 5', 0ºF, M, 3-4/3-4/3-4. Rosy red, frilled flowers play against large, deep green, twisted leaves. (Boulter 1964).

'Marge Danik' ('Achiever' x 'PJM' group). 5', -25ºF, M, -/-/-. Open, funnel shaped, reddish purple flowers bloom in trusses of 6 to distinguish this plant. (W. Delp hyb. 1977, Delp reg. 1992).

'Marianne' see 'Hachmann's Marianne'.

'Maricee' (selected form of *sargentianum*). 2', -5ºF, M, 4/3/2. A dwarf, twiggy plant with small, shiny leaves. Creamy-white flowers are very small and form a delicate miniature truss. Compared to the species *sargentianum*, this form is easier, faster growing and more floriferous. (Caperci 1962) A.E. 1961.

'Marie Forte' (*catawbiense* hybrid). 4', -15ºF, M-ML, -/-/-. Rich dark green foliage in an open, spreading habit provide a base for huge trusses of lustrous purple-red blooms with a dark eye. (Waterer 1881?).

'Marie Starks' ([*yakushimanum* Exbury form x 'Fabia' red form] x 'Odee Wright'). 4', -10ºF, EM, -/-/-. 7 lobed flowers, light yellow-green to brilliant yellow-green, with a dark red dorsal blotch, open into trusses of 14-18. Dark green leaves are held for 2 years on this somewhat spreading plant. Blooms at 4 years. (Murray hyb. 1974, M. Starks reg. 1985).

'Marie Tietjens' ('Mount Siga' x 'Full Moon'). 3', -10ºF, ML, -/-/-. Foliage is large. The 7-lobed flowers are pink, shaded darker at the edges. They are free of any marks, measure to 3 1/2" across, and are carried in trusses of up to 7 blooms. (Bagoly, Tietjens 1976).

'Marietta' ('Tosca' x *yakushimanum* 'Koichiro Wada'). 3', -15ºF, ML, -/-/-. Wavy edged, campanulate flowers appear from deep pink buds. Flowers are pale greenish yellow with a pink tinge, and have chestnut red dorsal spots. Ovate, shiny leaves have scant indumentum underneath. (Hachmann hyb. 1968, Stuck reg. 1988).

'Mariloo' ('Dr. Stocker' x *lacteum*). 6', 10ºF, EM, 4/2-3/2. Growth habit is a little slow, not too vigorous. Leaves are medium green, curve slightly downward, are fairly large and are heavily textured. Flowers are creamy yellow, rather pale, with some crimson spotting, and are held in a large rounded truss. (Rothschild 1941).

'Marilyn Horne' ('Bonita' x a hardy *fortunei* ssp. *fortunei*). 5', -15ºF, L, -/-/-. Trusses display striking white flowers with a bright cerise margin and pronounced brown throat. This plant has a mounding habit. Also known as 'Late Brown Throat.' (Nat Hess before 1990).

'Marine' (selection of *augustinii*). 6', 0ºF, EM, 4/3/3-4. Growth habit is typical of species, slender until quite mature. Leaves are small, medium green. Deep lavender blue flowers are flat, held in a three flowered truss. (Bovee) P.A. 1960.

'Mariner' ('Daydream' x ['Hawk' x 'China']). 4', -10ºF, L, -/-/-. Large trusses hold up to 20 flowers of deep primrose yellow with a greenish yellow blotch. (A. F. George, Hydon Nurseries 1965).

'Marinus Koster' (*griffithianum* hybrid). 6', -5ºF, M, 4/3/4. Deep pink flowers with lighter shading form large dome-shaped trusses. This grows to be a large sized shrub with an upright habit and shiny dark green leaves. (M. Koster 1937) A.M. 1937, F.C.C. 1948.

'Marion Street' ('Alice' x *yakushimanum*). 3', -15ºF, M, -/-/-. Deep pink buds open to a softer pink flower with a white throat and greenish spotting. Foliage is indumented and the plant is very compact. (Street reg. 1964) A.M. 1978.

'Markeeta's Flame' ('Loderi Venus' x 'Anna'). 5', -5ºF, M, 4/4/4. This plant, was formerly known as 'Markeeta's Prize #2'. Being the same cross as 'Markeeta's Prize', it is equally as good in many ways. This vigorous grower makes a beautiful plant even when not in flower, showing off deep fir green leaves and red leaf stems. It flowers in magnificent rose red trusses. Introduced by Flora Markeeta Nursery. (Beck, Korth 1977).

'Markeeta's Prize' ('Loderi Venus' x 'Anna'). 5', -5ºF, M, 5/4/4. Watching this plant grow is a joy because it is so strong stemmed and vigorous, and each new leaf seems even more lush and leathery than the last. The flowers are bright red, absolutely huge and are set on top of a swirl of deep green, thick, waxy leaves. The weight of the giant trusses is held high by the heavy stems. (Markeeta Nursery 1967).

'Marlene Peste' ([yakushimanum x 'Corona'] x haematodes). 3', 0ºF, M, 3-4/4/3-4. Medium sized, ball shaped trusses are made of 13 flowers. They are non-fading red with light to deep red spotting. The multitude of glossy, olive green leaves are moderately coated beneath with amber indumentum and they are on a rounded, well manicured plant. (Peste 1986).

'Marley Hedges' ('Anna' x 'Purple Splendour'). 5', 0ºF, M-ML, -/-/-. Showy purple flowers have white centers, along with a red-purple flare which stretches from the throat to the upper petals. Glossy, deep green leaves add to the attractiveness of this plant. (Elsie Watson hyb. 1970, intro. 1987).

'Mars' (griffithianum hybrid). 4', -15ºF, ML, 4/3/3. A deep true red with flat waxy flowers and contrasting white stamens. Deep green leaves are ribbed to create an interesting texture. It is the truest red that can be grown in colder climate areas. Prefers some protection from afternoon sun. (Waterer, before 1875 [According to W. J. Bean, this 'Mars' is not identical to an older hybrid under the same name by Waterer in 1875, but it is actually a hybrid raised by Lee about 1928]) A.M. 1928, F.C.C. 1935.

'Martha Isaacson' (occidentale x Ostbo seedling #70). 5', -5ºF, L, 3/3-4/4-5. This fragrant azaleodendron is an outstanding foliage plant that does well in the sun. The leaves are a deep maroon color and contrast nicely with the white, pink-striped flowers. (Ostbo 1958) P.A. 1956.

'Martha Peste' ('Lillian Peste' selfed). 2.5', 0ºF, ML, -/-/-. Very floriferous, this hybrid has trusses of 13 pale yellowish-pink flowers, tinged and streaked with strong pink. The throat of the flower is coral. Deep green foliage is heavily indumented in saffron yellow. (Peste hyb., S.P. Johnston reg. 1986).

'Martha Phipps' (parentage unknown). 6', -10ºF, ML, -/-/-. Leaves are large and narrow. Pale yellow flowers are flushed pink, and have mandarin orange inside edges. They measure to 4" across and are held in a compact truss of up to 10. (Phipps 1973).

'Martha Robbins' (forrestii ssp. forrestii Repens Group x sperabile). 18", 0ºF, EM, 4/4/3-4. This delightful, bright red dwarf makes an outstanding show. It has forrestii ssp. forrestii Repens Group foliage and habit, however it is slightly larger and more vigorous. It reaches 3 ft. high and twice as wide in 20 years. (Brandt 1970).

'Martian King' ('Gipsy King' x 'Mars'). 3', 0ºF, M, 4/4/4. Dark green foliage and deep, dark black-red flowers show the lineage of its parents. Planted where the early evening sun beams through the flowers, they appear to glow like fire. (Winston Hanke before 1990).

'Martine' (racemosum x evergreen azalea). 30", -5ºF, EM, 4/3-4/4. Here is an azaleodendron which is similar to the famous 'Ria Hardijzer' and 'Hardijzer's Beauty'. It is extremely free flowering. Multiple buds appear up and down the stems, erupting each spring into flowers of beautiful clear pink. Shiny foliage adds interest the remainder of the year. (Hardijzer 1965).

'Mary Belle' ('Atrier' x 'Dechaem'). 5', -15ºF, M, 3-4/3-4/4. Leaves are medium-size. Generous 4" flowers open light salmon pink from a darker bud, then fade to a golden peach, spotted red all around the inside of the flower. Flowers have much substance, and edges are charmingly ruffled. (Gable 1963) P.A. 1962.

'Mary Briggs' (haematodes x 'Elizabeth'). 2', 0ºF, M, 3/3/3. Funnel-campanulate, blood red flowers are in compact trusses of 8-10. Dark green elliptic foliage covers the low growing, compact plant which grows twice as wide as tall. (Vernon Wyatt reg. 1967).

'Mary Drennen' ('Angelo' x wardii). 5', -5ºF, L, 4/4/4. Also known as 'Whitney's Late Yellow', this beauty is a welcome addition to the yellow family because of its season extension. The trusses are dome shaped and held high on olive green foliage. (Larson 1983).

'Mary Fleming' ([racemosum x keiskei] x keiskei). 3', -15ºF, EM, 4/3/4. A most interesting plant and flower. The flowers are bisque yellow with streaks of salmon pink throughout. Foliage is attractive with good winter color, shading bronze. (Nearing 1972) A.E. 1973.

'Mary Guthlein' (['Scintillation' x 'Inamorata'] x [{fortunei ssp. fortunei x wardii} x dichroanthum]). 4', -5ºF, EM, -/-/-. Attractive, dense, glossy, deep green foliage covers this plant of mounding habit. Rich yellow flowers form conical trusses. (Murcott before 1990).

'Maryke' (fortunei ssp. discolor x 'Fabia'). 5', -5ºF, ML, 4/3/3. 'Maryke' is a blend of pink and yellow that merges in a kaleidoscope of color. Leaves are matte green and stems are very heavy on this plant. Upright growth habit. (Van Veen intro 1955, reg. 1974).

'Mary Kittel' (unknown dwarf white x 'Mrs. P. den Ouden'). 3', -10ºF, M, -/-/-. This mounding plant has glossy green leaves which are held all year. Pink flowers are abundantly produced. (Mezitt hyb. 1963, not registered).

'Mary Mayo' ('Loderi King George' x 'Ostbo Y3'). 4', -5ºF, M, 4-5/3-4/3-4. Large, frilled flowers, up to 4 1/2" wide, are many shades of pink with a very bright yellow throat. (The Bovees 1961) P.A. 1960.

'Master Mariner' ('Daydream' x 'Honey'). 4', -10ºF, L, -/-/-. Large trusses of lovely apricot blends are enhanced by bronze new foliage. (Hydon Nurseries, not registered).

'Matador' (griersonianum x strigillosum). 4', 0ºF, EM, 3-4/3-4/3-4. Attractive, hairy, elongated leaves and orange-scarlet tubular flowers are a great combination. (Lord Aberconway) A.M. 1945, F.C.C. 1946.

'Matilda' ('Wachtung' hybrid x minus var. minus Carolinianum Group album). 3', -15ºF, EM, -/-/-. This good blue flowered dwarf has typically small lepidote leaves covering the entire plant. At first, the growth is upright, but as it matures, it fills in and becomes dense and compact. (Yavorsky).

'Maureen' (williamsianum x 'Lem's Goal'). 3', 0ºF, M, 3/3/3. Light orchid pink flowers with a yellow cast at the base abound on this delightful little plant. The flowers are usually 7-lobed and appear very full and large. (Lem reg. 1973).

'Mavis Davis' ('Orange Marmalade' x 'Lem's Cameo'). 4', 0ºF, M, -/-/-. An upright and spreading plant with flat, elliptic dull green leaves. This hybrid has abundant pale yellow flowers of heavy substance. The wavy lobes are edged with moderate reddish orange. (J. A. Davis reg. 1987).

'Maxecat' (maximum x catawbiense). 6', -25ºF, L, 4/3/4. This very hardy hybrid, upright and spreading, has pink flowers and dark green leaves. (J. Gable before 1960)

'Maxhaem Salmon' (maximum x haematodes). 4', -5ºF, ML, 3/3/3. Flowers appear in full trusses of salmon pink with lighter color toward the center of each flower. Leaves are medium in size with sparse, tan indumentum. (Gable 1935, Gable Study Group reg. 1991).

'Maxhaem Yellow' (*maximum* x *haematodes*). 4', -5°F, L, 3/3/-. Small pale yellow flowers appear on a low growing plant. Bronzy new growth. (Gable 1935, not registered).

'Maxine Childers' (*strigillosum* x 'Elizabeth'). 3', -5°F, E, 3-4/4/3-4. Flowers of heavy wax-like substance are bright, fiery blood red. The textured olive green leaves have a light, orange brown indumentum on the undersides, heavy along the mid rib. New growth is reddish bronze and the whole plant shows the influence of its parent *strigillosum*. (Childers, Phetteplace 1977).

'Max Sye' ('Chevalier Felix de Sauvage' hybrid). 4', 0°F, ML, 2/3/3. Large, medium dark green leaves are narrow, and somewhat grooved. The plant habit is rather open and spreading. The red flowers with dark blotch are carried in rounded trusses. (C. Frets & Son about 1935).

'May Day' (*haematodes* x *griersonianum*). 3', 5°F, EM, 3/3-4/4. Habit is vigorous, and rapid-growing, becoming more wide than tall with age. Leaves are an attractive dark green, covered with tan indumentum beneath. This plant is a heavy bloomer. The flower are brilliant orange scarlet and are held in lax trusses. Several forms are in the trade. (Williams 1932) A.M. 1932.

'May Morn' ('May Day' x *beanianum* pink form). 3', 5°F, EM, -/-/-. Funnel shaped, azalea pink flowers, flushed on the edges with porcelain rose are held in trusses of 8-10. (Lord Aberconway 1946) A.M. 1946.

'May Schwartz' ('Candi' x *tephropeplum*). 2', 5°F, E, -/-/-. Foliage is rather small. Flowers are 1 1/4" across, pink with darker pink outsides, and show dark pink streaks. They form trusses of up to 6 flowers per truss. (Scott 1977).

'May Song' ('Bow Bells' x 'Day Dream'). 3', 0°F, M, -/-/-. Pink flowers, blushing deeper pink are 3 1/2" across, carried 11 to a truss. Leaves are small. (Grace, Bovee 1972).

'May Time' (*catawbiense* var. *album* x *yakushimanum* 'Koichiro Wada'). 3', -15°F, M, 3-4/4/3-4. Foliage is medium sized and narrow. Flowers are white with faint orchid pink flushing on the outside ribs. They are held in a 14 flower truss. (Leach 1973).

'Meadowbrook' ('Mrs. C. S. Sargent' x 'Everestianum'). 5', -15°F, ML, 3/3/3. Plant growth habit is good and foliage is medium large. Ruffled flowers are up to 2 1/4" wide, bright vibrant pink and have with a white blotch that is spotted green. A large, 22 flower truss is formed. (Vossberg 1928).

'Meadowgold' (*burmanicum* x 'Lemon Mist'). 30", 15°F, E, 4/3/3-4. Small foliage. Flowers measuring to 1 1/2" across are sulphur yellow, with halo-like spotting on the dorsal lobe. Flowers occur at branch tips from groups of up to 3 buds, with each bud containing 6 flowers. (Scott 1976).

'Meath' ('Boule de Neige' x *yakushimanum* 'Koichiro Wada'). 3', -5°F, ML, -/-/-. Leaves are slightly larger than medium size. Flowers are scented, with 7 lobes, shaded pink with yellowish green dorsal patch and spots, held in 9 flower truss. (Reese 1979).

'Medusa' (*scyphocalyx* x *griersonianum*). 3', -5°F, M, 3/3/3. A most beautiful shade of orange. Cascading flowers are borne on long pedicels. The leaves are mid sized and greyish green with a very light woolly tomentum on the undersides. (Aberconway 1936).

'Melidioso' ('Herme' x *dichroanthum* ssp. *scyphocalyx*). 3', 0°F?, ML, -/-/-. Flowers of purplish pink have a greenish yellow accent on the 3 upper lobes. These wavy edged, funnel shaped blooms are held 15 to a truss above elliptical, glossy green foliage that exhibits a thin brownish indumentum on the under side. (Hachmann hyb. 1977, Stuck reg. 1988).

'Melody' (*yakushimanum* x 'Leo'). 4', 0°F, M-ML, -/-/-. This broad and spreading plant, of mounding habit, has dark green foliage with leaf margins that show a slight curve. Trusses are of rose red flowers with radiating light pink stripes. (Whitney, Sather before 1990).

'Melrose Pink' (*fortunei* ssp. *fortunei* hybrid). 5', -20°F, M, 3-4/3/4. Extremely hardy, this plant has delicately fragrant, pink flowers in large trusses. Leaves are large and forest-green. (Eichelser before 1972).

'Merganser' (*campylogynum* x *luteiflorum*). 2', -5°F, EM, 4/4/3-4. A super little introduction from Cox. Flowers are in trusses of up to 5 bells, each held by a very long petiole, which makes them stand out even more. Color is strong primrose yellow and is a vibrant contrast to the surrounding dull, dark green foliage. (Cox reg. 1981) H.C. (Wisely Trials) 1981.

'Merley Cream' (Dexter #62). 4', -5°F, M, -/-/-. This delightful plant has creamy, funnel-shaped flowers, each with a yellow blotch. They are held in dome shaped trusses of 12-13. Dense foliage is slightly yellowish green. (Dexter hyb., Well Nursery intro. 1961, Briarwood Gardens reg. 1994).

'Merry May White' (parentage unknown). 30", -10°F, ML, -/-/-. Leaves are medium size. Six lobed blooms are white, with 2 smallish purple rays, carried in a truss of up to 11. (Hardgrove, Royce 1978).

'Mi Amor' (*lindleyi* x *nuttallii*). 6', 15°F, M, 5/3/4. The growth habit is open. The leaves are dark green on top, grey-green beneath. Fragrant flowers are huge, up to 6" wide, bell shaped, white with yellow throat, and set in trusses of about 5 flowers each. (Sumner 1961) C.A. 1969, A.M. 1975.

'Michael Rice' (advanced generation hybrid including *catawbiense* and *maximum*). 6', -15°F, M, -/-/-. Foliage is medium sized and narrow. Flowers, to 3 1/2" across, are pink, with deeper pink edges and spots, in a rounded truss up to 15. (W. Smith 1979).

'Michael's Pride' (*burmanicum* x *dalhousiae*). 3', 15°F, M, -/-/-. This hybrid has attractive bronze new foliage and lime green buds opening to fragrant flowers. They are creamy yellow with long, waxy, lily shaped petals. It requires a cool greenhouse in most locations. (Charles Michael reg. 1963).

'Michael Waterer' (*ponticum* hybrid). 6', -15°F, L, 2/3/4. Very good, compact growth habit. Narrow leaves are of medium length and medium green color. Flowers are small, magenta red, and form a rounded truss. Easily rooted. (J. Waterer before 1894).

'Midnight' ('Cup Day' x 'Purple Splendour'). 5', -5°F, M, 4/4/4. Deep red- purple flowers are heavily spotted with red on the upper lobe. Foliage is glossy green. (Van de Ven 1978).

'Midnight Mistique' ('Midnight' x 'One Thousand Butterflies'). 4-5', 0°F, M, -/-/-. This is a very showy hybrid with an outstanding flower. The unusual silver-gray flower centers are surrounded on the edges with a picotee of dark purple, and then spotted brown and gold. The dome-shaped trusses are very full with many flowers in each truss. The plant grows with an attractive, loose structure and is covered with excellent foliage. Frank Fujioka does not release new plants until he is satisified that they are superb. (Frank Fujioka hyb. 1986, reg. 1995).

'Midsummer' (*maximum* x unknown). 5', -15°F, VL, 4/2/3. Rosy pink flowers with a golden flare on the upper lobe are held in compact trusses of about 13. The foliage is deep green on this open, spreading plant (Waterer & Crisp before 1958).

'Midsummer Snow' ('Isabella' x *diaprepes*). 5', 5°F, L, -/-/-. The flowers are white with a green tinge in the throat. Very large plant. (Hillier & Sons 1967).

'Midway' (probably contains 'Coronation Day' and 'Purple Splendour'). 4', -5ºF, ML, 4/4/4. Matte green, elliptic leaves and large flowers of deep red purple with a darker flare comprise this plant. Tight, mounded plant habit. (Van de Ven in Australia before 1982).

'Mike Davis' (unnamed *yakushimanum* hybrid x 'Lem's Cameo'). 3', 0ºF, M, -/-/-. The deep forest green foliage creates a handsome backdrop for the prolific, frilly edged flowers, which are pale mauve and speckled copper. Habit is mounding and well-branched. (Davis 1990).

'Mildred Amateis' (*minus* var. *minus* Carolinianum Group x *edgeworthii*). 3', -5ºF, M?, -/-/-. White flowers are softly flushed pink. (Amateis 1958).

'Mildred Fawcett' ('Faggetter's Favourite' x 'Mrs. Donald Graham'). 6', 5ºF, M, -/-/-. Leaves are large. Blooms are soft pink in color, with an orangey-pink blotch, to 3" across, in a large truss. (Fawcett 1961) P.A. 1960.

'Milestone' (*minus* var. *minus* x *dauricum* var. *sempervirens*). 3', -15ºF, EM, 3-4/3/3. Small, frilled flowers of vivid purplish red grow 3-10 per truss. The small lepidote leaves are rusty green and clothe a plant of dense growth habit. (Mezitt hyb., Weston reg. 1987).

'Millard Kepner' ('Decatros' x *yakushimanum*). 4', -5ºF, EM, -/-/-. Foliage is long and narrow. Dark pink flowers, to 3 1/2" across, fade to lighter pink with lilac undertone. Flowers have an indistinct blotch, and are held in a ball-shaped truss up to 15. (Schumacher, Byrkit 1975).

'Millicent Scott' ([*racemosum* x 'Saffron Queen'] x [*racemosum* x 'Saffron Queen']). 30", 5ºF?, E, -/-/-. Leaves are small. Buff colored flowers are also rather small, to 1" across, and have light red markings. They bloom along branches and at branch tips from buds which produce up to 3 flowers each. (Scott 1977).

'Mill Reef' (*insigne* x *griersonianum*). 4', 5ºF, ML, -/-/-. Medium size plant which has elongated foliage. The flower is red-purple with darker red dorsal spotting. (Hydon Nurseries Ltd. 1972).

'Minas Maid' ('Nova Zembla' x *yakushimanum*). 3', -15ºF, L, -/-/-. Leaves are of medium size, elliptical, glossy olive green above and with light indumentum below. Flowers are pink, to 2 1/4" wide, have rubescent dorsal flecks, and are carried in a rounded, 15 flower truss. (Swain hyb., Craig reg. 1979).

'Minas Peace' (*catawbiense album* 'Glass' x [*degronianum* x *yakushimanum*]). 3', -15ºF, ML-L, -/-/-. Attractively shaped and widely branched, this hybrid has narrow forest green leaves with very thick bronze indumentum and small, delicate pink flowers, veined darker on outside. (Craig 1983).

'Minas Rose' (['Nova Zembla' x *yakushimanum*] x [*catawbiense album* 'Glass' x 'Elizabeth']). 3', -15ºF, ML-L, -/-/-. Deep red buds open to iridescent claret flowers with round shape and wavy edges. These are further accented by very deep claret colored speckles on the upper lobes. The foliage is dark green with reddish brown indumentum. The low growing plant has an open habit. (Craig 1983).

'Minas Snow' ('Cunningham's White' x *yakushimanum* 'Nakai'). 3', -15ºF, M, -/-/-. Prolific in bloom and foliage, this hybrid has pure white flowers which open from pink tinged white buds. The forest green leaves have tan indumentum underneath. (Swain, Craig 1981).

'Ming Toy' ('Medusa' x 'Crest'). 3', -10ºF, EM, -/-/-. A most attractive hybrid. Deep yellow flowers have a slight shading of orange. Plant is as broad as tall. (Childers 1977).

'Mini Brite' (*racemosum* apricot form x *keiskei*). 2.5', -15ºF, E, -/-/-. Bicolor yellow-pink flowers with red spotting bloom on this low growing hybrid. (Delp before 1990).

'Minnetonka' (*ponticum* x unknown). 4', -25ºF, M, 3/4/4. This compact hybrid grows a bit wider than tall. The reddish purple flowers shade to light purple and are spotted vivid, yellow green on the upper petal. They are held in small dome shaped trusses of 15. (H. Motzkau hyb., Van Veen reg. 1990).

'Minterne Cinnkeys' (*cinnabarinum* x *keysii*). 4', 5ºF, L, 4/3/3. A tall slender shrub, this has masses of orange-red trusses, each having as many as 30 flowers per truss. Sister of 'Cinnkeys'. (Lord Digby 1931) A.M. 1951, F.C.C. 1952.

'Minus' see 'Myrtifolium'.

'Mission Bells' (*williamsianum* x *orbiculare*). 4', -5ºF, EM-M, 3/4/3-4. This is a sun-tolerant, compact grower. Leaves are shiny and medium sized. Pale pink campanulate flowers, slightly fragrant, to 2 1/2" across, are in a lax truss of 6-8 flowers. (Lancaster before 1958).

'Miss Kitty' see 'Oh! Kitty'.

'Miss Prim' (*decorum* x *irroratum*). 4', -5ºF, E, 3/3/-. Foliage is medium sized. White blooms, up to 4" across, sport an almost fluorescent yellowish green blaze, and are in a 15 flower truss. (Bovee 1961).

'Misty Moonlight' ('Kimberly' selfed). 4', -5ºF, EM, 3-4/4/4. Flowers open a delightful orchid color and heavily cover the plant. They have a heavenly fragrance! The foliage is glossy green with a deep red purple petioles and deeply colored stems and buds. This hybrid has vigorous growth habit on a compact plant. (Greer 1988).

'Moerheim' (*impeditum* hybrid). 1', -15ºF, EM, 3/4/3. This little import from Holland is most attractive. The flowers are an intriguing shade of violet. The plant habit is low and tight, with alluring little green leaves that turn maroon in winter. Like *impeditum* it makes a distinctive bonsai. Buds young. (Ruys, Moerheim Nursery 1965).

'Moerheim's Pink' (*williamsianum* x 'Genoveva'). 3', -10ºF, M, 4/4/4. Clear, pale pink bells with darker edges are borne in profusion on this compact shrub. Growth is more wide than tall, and this plant is heavily clothed with many dull, dark green leaves. (Hobbie, shown by Royal Moerheim Nurseries reg. 1973) A.M. 1972.

'Mohamet' (*dichroanthum* x 'Tally Ho'). 4', 5ºF, ML, -/-/-. Large, bell shaped, bright scarlet flowers with frilled margins are surrounded by large petaloid calyces of the same color. Loose trusses of 5-6 flowers form on this medium sized, rather open plant. The light green leaves have fawn indumentum beneath. Clones grown in N.W. United States are deep salmon pink and orange-red, often blooming in autumn. (Rothschild before 1958) A.M. 1945.

'Mollie Coker' ('Loderi' x unknown). 6', 0ºF, M, 4/3/3. Rosy pink flowers which have a purplish blotch distinguish this hybrid. (Mrs. R. J. Coker, NZ, reg. 1979).

'Molly Ann' ('Elizabeth' x garden hybrid). 3', -10ºF, EM, 4/4-5/4. 'Molly Ann' has cute round leaves that make for a dense, compact plant. The flowers are a beautiful shade of rose, of heavy substance, and last well. They form a lovely truss which is more upright than those of other dwarfs of this type. It has well survived winters with temperatures dipping to -12ºF. An attractive plant that buds heavily. (Freimann 1974).

'Molly Fordham' ('Balta' x *minus* var. *minus* Carolinianum Group). 4', -20°F, EM, 4/4/4. The masses of nearly white, small, beautiful trusses are resistant to rain damage! The darkish green, glossy foliage contrasts with the reddish and maroon leaves of the others in this group. It forms an upright and somewhat compact plant. (Weston Nurseries before 1985).

'Molly Miller' (*yakushimanum* x 'Fabia Tangerine'). 3', 5°F, M, -/-/-. Flowers are yellow with a tinge of rose on the edge. Foliage has some tomentum and is medium sized. (J. Waterer, Sons & Crisp Ltd. 1971).

'Molly Smith' (*yakushimanum* 'Koichiro Wada' x 'Mrs. Furnivall'). 4', 0°F, M, 4/4/4. White flowers with a prominent blotch of marigold orange, openly funnel shaped, 5 lobed, are held in conical trusses of 12 on this floriferous plant. As wide as tall, it has heavy, dark green leaves with gray-brown indumentum beneath. Leaves are held for 3 to 4 years. (Cecil C. Smith reg. 1984).

'Monaco' (*catawbiense* var. *album* x [*dichroanthum* x {*griffithianum* x *auriculatum*}]). 6', -20°F, VL, -/-/-. Crinkly, light orange-pink flowers, with cream to yellow throat, emerge from red buds. Plant is rounded, as broad as tall, and has narrow leaves. (Leach 1952, reg. 1984).

'Monica Wellington' (*cinnabarinum* hybrid). 4', -5°F, ML, -/-/-. These rosy lilac flowers are a very different color for this group of plants. Like most *cinnabarinum* hybrids, the habit is upright and slender. 2" oval leaves are glossy above and scaly below. (Stevenson, raised by Hydon Nurseries, reg. 1981) A.M. 1980.

'Monique Behring' ('Rocket' x *yakushimanum* 'Pink Parasol'). 5', -25°F, M, -/-/-. Deep rose flowers and attractive foliage comprise this plant. (R. Behring 1983).

'Monsieur Guillemot' (parentage unknown). 6', -10°F, L, 2/3/3-4. Medium to large, dark green, glossy, downward-curving leaves are on an upright, fairly compact plant. Dark rose flowers form a compact truss. Lavish bloomer. Synonym, 'Madame Guillemot'. (Moser before 1930).

'Montchanin' (*pubescens* x *keiskei*). 3', -25°F, EM, 2-3/2-3/3. Plant habit is elegant. Foliage is small, as are the pretty white flowers which bloom prolifically. (Nearing before 1950).

'Montego' ('Sefton' x 'Purple Splendour'). 5', -15°F, M, -/-/-. Funnel shaped flowers, violet purple with a green blotch, are held in ball trusses of 18. This plant is much wider than tall, and the current year's growth is near pink in color. (D. G. Leach hyb. 1957, reg. 1983).

'Monterey' ([*catawbiense* var. *album* x {*decorum* x *griffithianum*}] x red *catawbiense* hybrid). 6', -25°F, L, 4/4/3. A sibling of 'Pink Flourish', this hybrid has bright pink flowers shading to lighter pink centers. It is a vigorous, broad, compact, floriferous plant. (David Leach before 1990 not registered).

'Mood Indigo' (*augustinii* x unknown). 5', 0°F, EM, 4/3/4. This hybrid is distinguished by deep indigo blue flowers which appear in a loose truss. The dark aromatic foliage turns bronze in winter. (L. Brandt before 1960 not registered).

'Moonbeam' ('Naomi' x *griffithianum*). 4', -5°F, M, -/-/-. A tall plant with pale yellow flowers held in a nice, rounded truss. (Rothschild 1947).

'Moonshine Bright' ('Adriaan Koster' x *wardii* Litiense Group). 5', 0°F, M, -/-/-. Rich yellow flowers, in trusses of 20-22, bloom on a background of thin, glossy foliage. (RHS Gardens, Wisley 1952).

'Moonshine Crescent' ('Jervis Bay' x *litiense*). 4', 0°F, M, 4/4/3. Here is an upright growing plant with primrose yellow, compact trusses. (RHS Gardens, Wisley 1961) A.M. 1960.

'Moonshine Supreme' ('Adriaan Koster' x *litiense*). 3', 0°F, M, 4/4/3. On this hybrid, primrose yellow flowers have darker upper petals. (RHS Gardens, Wisley 1953) A.M. 1953.

'Moonstone' (*campylocarpum* x *williamsianum*). 3', -5°F, EM, 3-4/4/3. This plant forms a compact mound covered with smooth, oval, green leaves. The flowers are cream yellow and are borne in profusion. One of the best yellow flowered semi-dwarfs. (Williams 1933).

'Moontide' (*wardii* x 'Loder's White'). 4', 0°F, EM, 3/2/-. Growth habit is somewhat open, but rounded and upright. Medium green foliage is flat and of medium to large size. White, funnel shaped flowers are over 3" wide and are carried in a full rounded truss of up to 16 flowers. (R. Henny 1958) P.A. 1955.

'Moonwax' ('Holy Moses' x 'Albatross'). 5', 0°F, M, 4/4/3. Large, fragrant, 7-lobed flowers with warm yellow center and light mauve edges, are held in large trusses of 12. Narrow, elliptic leaves form a plant that is broader than tall, with stiff, upright branches. (Lem hyb., L. L. Newcomb reg. 1981) C.A. 1983.

'Morgenrot' (*yakushimanum* 'Koichiro Wada' x 'Spitfire'). 3', -10°F, M, 3-4/4/3-4. Dark red buds open to lighter red then fade to lighter rose color. The plant is rounded and compact and has light indumentum on the leaf undersides. (Hachmann hyb. 1963, Stuck reg. 1983).

'Morning Cloud' (*yakushimanum* x 'Springbok'). 3', -5°F, M, -/-/-. Compact plant. Flowers are white, flushed very light lavender. (Hydon Nurseries 1971) AM 1971.

'Morning Frost' ('Fabia' x unnamed hybrid). 3', 5°F, M, -/-/-. Flowers are white, tinged red-purple and have greenish yellow spotting on the upper lobes. It is a compact plant with dense habit. (John Waterer Sons & Crisp Ltd. 1972).

'Morning Magic' (*yakushimanum* x 'Springbok'). 3', -5°F, M, -/-/-. This densely foliaged plant has light red flowers which are flushed white and have pronounced spotting. (Hydon Nurseries 1971) A.M. 1976.

'Morning Sunshine' (parentage unknown). 5', 5°F, EM, 4/3/3-4. Foliage is medium sized. Primrose yellow flowers are 7-lobed, to 4" across, and held in a rounded truss of 14 flowers. (Whitney hyb. 1967, Sather reg. 1977).

'Morocco' see 'Luxor'.

'Mortimer' ('Gladys' x 'Yvonne Pearl'). 5', -5°F, M, -/-/-. Big trusses are made of 12 white flowers, each suffused with yellow and accented with a crimson blotch. (Crown Estate, Windsor 1964) A.M. 1964.

'Moser's Maroon' (parentage unknown). 5', -10°F, ML, 2/3/4. Growth habit is vigorous and sprawling. New leaves are rosy red, retaining some red to maturity. Foliage is slightly waved, blunt-tipped and heavily ribbed. Tight, smallish trusses are formed from very small, dark-wine red flowers. (Moser and Fils before 1932) A.M. 1932.

'Moth' (*megeratum* x *boothii* Mishmiense Group). 2', 15°F, M, -/-/-. This hybrid has lemon yellow flowers, heavily spotted reddish brown. Foliage is deep green. (Lord Aberconway 1950) A.M. 1955.

'Mother Bear' (*yakushimanum* x *bureavii* x 'Fabia'). 3', -10ºF, M, -/-/-. Very attractive dark, shiny green foliage supplies a backdrop for deep salmon flowers which open from vermilion buds. (Unknown).

'Mother Greer' (*hippophaeoides* x Triflorum series). 18", -15ºF, M-ML, 3-4/4/4. This hybrid is a cross made by my mother some years ago and it is named in her honor. The flowers are reminiscent of *hippophaeoides* in shape, although they are much larger. A very nice feature is provided by the brilliant blue flowers which appear after all of the other blues are done. The foliage and plant also resemble *hippophaeoides*, but this plant is much more compact. It does not go through the distressed appearance during winter which is often typical of *hippophaeoides*. (Greer 1988).

'Mother of Pearl' (sport of 'Pink Pearl'). 6', -5ºF, M, 4/3/3-4. Pearl white flowers mature from pink buds. This is a beautiful plant with rapid growth habit and good foliage. (J. Waterer 1925) A.M. 1930.

'Mountain Aura' ('Dorothea' x red hybrid). 4', -15ºF, ML, 4/4/-. Leaves are large. White-centered, 4" flowers are flaxen blue in color, held in a rounded truss. (Nearing 1968).

'Mountain Dew' ('Idealist' x 'Jalisco'). 5', 5ºF, M, -/-/-. Sweetly scented, primrose yellow flowers have brown throats and appear on an attractive bush. (J. Waterer, Sons & Crisp 1971).

'Mountain Flare' ('Boule de Neige' x 'Loderi King George'). 6', -15ºF, ML, -/-/-. Foliage is large. Flowers are also large, to 4 1/2" across, light pink with darker red spotting, and held in a fragrant 15-flower truss. (Nearing 1973).

'Mountain Glow' ('Dorothea' x red hybrid). 3', -15ºF, ML, 4/4/-. Large, oval shaped foliage forms a dense background for the purple-red flowers which are up to 4" across, and are carried in a ball-type truss. (Nearing 1968).

'Mountain Queen' ('Dorothea' x red hybrid). under 4', -15ºF, ML, 4/4/-. Slightly scented flowers, to 4" across, are rose colored, paler in the center, held in a ball-shaped truss. Leaves are large. (Nearing 1969).

'Mount Clearview' ('Van Nes Sensation' x 'Purple Splendour'). 5', -5ºF, M, 4/4/4. Rich, royal purple flowers are accented with purple spots which bleed together to become red in the throat. The trusses are large, crowning a plant that is rounded and sturdy. (Newcomb 1981).

'Mount Everest' (possibly contains *campanulatum*, *griffithianum* and *catawbiense*). 5', -10ºF, E, 3-4/3-4/4. A large, prolific bloomer with fragrant white flowers which have a speckling of red brown in the throat. (Slocock 1930) A.M. 1953, F.C.C. 1958, A.G.M. 1969.

'Mount Mazama' ('Britannia' x 'Loderi' or reverse). 5', 0ºF, M, 4/4/4. Mount Mazama is the mountain in Oregon that contains Crater Lake. This is a good hybrid to name after such a beautiful place. The flowers are fuchsia red with brighter red spotting on the upper petal. At the base of the flower are five prominent dark red nectar pouches and on the outside of the flower are dark red candy stripes. A most unusual flower. The large leaves are ponderosa pine green. (Grace hyb., Grothaus reg. 1980).

'Mount Mitchell' (selected seedling of red *maximum*). 6', -25ºF, M, 3/3/4. Foliage is large. Red buds open to bright pink flowers, red on the outside, with yellow-green dorsal blotch. They are held in a ball-shaped truss of up to 15. (Leach 1964).

'Mount Siga' (natural hybrid of *vernicosum aff.*, Rock 18139). 5',-5ºF, EM, -/-/-. Leaves are medium sized and narrow. The 8-lobed flowers are large, to 4" across. They are pink in color, shade to a deeper pink throat, and are accented with a dull red dorsal blotch and spots. They are held in a 12 flower truss. (Gable, C. Gable 1979).

'Mr. Dee' (open pollinated 'Marinus Koster'). 5', -10ºF, M, -/-/-. Deep forest green leaves are combined with white flowers which have pink margins. (Lem?, Pauline Newberry?).

'Mrs. A. F. McEwan' (selected seedling of 'Loderi'), 6', -5ºF, EM, 3/3/3. Growth habit is compact and roundish. Foliage is shiny green, waxy and quite large. Flowers are white-throated, fuchsine pink to persian rose, 5" wide and in a lax dome shaped truss. (Ihrig, Univ. of Washington 1958) A.E. 1956.

'Mrs. A. J. Holden' ('Polar Bear' x 'Evening Glow'). 5', -5ºF, L, -/-/-. Leaves are long and rather narrow. Nicely scented, 7-lobed flowers, are a huge 5 1/4" across. They are sunny yellow with a pink edge and are spotted light green. 10 flowers form the truss. (Holden 1979).

'Mrs. A. T. de la Mare' ('Sir Charles Butler' x 'Halopeanum'). 5', -15ºF, M, 3/3-4/4. Slightly fragrant white flowers with a greenish spot form a large dome-shaped truss. Plant takes full exposure in most climates. (C. B. van Nes & Sons before 1930) A.M. 1958.

'Mrs. Bernice Baker' ('Dawn's Delight' x *fortunei* ssp. *fortunei*). 5', -5ºF, M, 4/3/3. This pink hybrid with large trusses makes a real display. It has a two-toned appearance as the flowers emerging deep pink are mixed in the truss with the blossoms which have lightened with age. (Larson 1958).

'Mrs. Betty Hager' ([*decorum* x *fortunei* ssp. *discolor*] x 'Madame de Bruin'). 5', 0ºF, EM, -/-/-. Leaves are medium to large. Blooms are dark pink, have a red blotch with spots, and are held in a ball-shaped truss of 15. (Raustein 1974).

'Mrs. Betty Robertson' ('Mrs. Lindsay Smith' x *campylocarpum* hybrid). 4', -5ºF, M, 3/3/3. Creamy yellow flowers have a red blotch. Compact growth. Interesting rough textured foliage has pointed, slightly twisting tips. (M. Koster & Sons 1920).

'Mrs. C. B. van Nes' ('Princess Juliana' x 'Florence Sarah Smith'). 5', 0ºF, M, 3-4/3/3-4. A hybrid of good growth habit and foliage. Very tight, perfect trusses have a two toned appearance as rosy red changes to pink. (C. B. van Nes & Sons before 1930).

'Mrs. Charles E. Pearson' ('Coombe Royal' x 'Catawbiense Grandiflorum'). 6', -5ºF, M, 4/4/4-5. Flowers are light pink with brown spots. This hybrid is another "oldie but goody" that has stayed around and kept winning awards through the years. It was developed in 1909, received an Award of Merit in 1933 and then a First Class Certificate as late as 1955. Most hybrids win something only when they are new, never to be heard from again. Super vigorous with lush, large, deep green foliage. Sun and heat tolerant. (M. Koster & Sons 1909) A.M. 1933, F.C.C. 1955.

'Mrs. Charles S. Sargent' (*catawbiense* hybrid). 6', -25ºF, ML, 3/3/4. Growth habit is rounded and fairly compact on this dependable plant from the "ironclad" *catawbiense* group. Wavy edged flowers are rosy pink or dark carmine rose, with yellow spotted throat and carried in tight rounded truss. (A. Waterer 1888).

'Mrs. Davies Evans' (parentage unknown). 4', -10ºF, L, -/-/-. A free-flowering plant which has large, blue-purple flowers that are accented by very conspicuous white anthers. It has compact habit and rounded shape. (Waterer before 1915) H.C. 1957, A.M. 1958.

'**Mrs. Donald Graham**' (['Corona' x *griersonianum*] x Loderi group). 6', 5ºF, L, 3/3/3. Growth habit is open and upright, with large medium green leaves. Flowers are intense salmon pink, carried in a flat-topped, open truss of up to 9 flowers. (Rose, Ostbo before 1954) P.A. 1954, A.E. 1958.

'**Mrs. E. C. Stirling**' (*griffithianum* hybrid). 6', -5ºF, M, 4/3-4/4. Habit is upright in young plants, later spreading and rather open. Leaves are large and light green. Flowers are somewhat ruffled, silvery pink, and form a perfect upright truss. (J. Waterer before 1900) A.M. 1906.

'**Mrs. Furnivall**' (*griffithianum* hybrid x *caucasicum* hybrid). 4', -15ºF, 5/3-4/3-4. Light pink flowers have a striking crimson blotch. This is an excellent plant. It is reported to perform reliably in gardens of the East. (A. Waterer 1920) A.M. 1933, F.C.C. 1948.

'**Mrs. G. W. Leak**' ('Coombe Royal' x 'Chevalier Felix de Sauvage'). 6', 0ºF, EM, 4/3/4. This tall, vigorous plant has olive green leaves. The dramatic light pink flowers each have a burgundy blotch and are held in upright, compact trusses. Grows in sun or shade. Foliage frequently develops brownish-purple spots which do not harm the plant. (M. Koster & Sons 1916) F.C.C. 1934.

'**Mrs. Helen Jackson**' (*yakushimanum* 'Koichiro Wada' x 'Chlorops'). 4', 0ºF, EM, -/-/-. From yellowish pink buds, 7-lobed, yellowish white flowers open to display bright olive green flared markings which bear strong greenish yellow spots. This plant is multi-branched, rounded and compact. It has polished dark green leaves with light tan indumentum underneath. Leaves are held for 3 years. (F. Bump hyb., G. Kesterson reg. 1986).

'**Mrs. Helen Koster**' ('Mrs. J. J. Crosfield' x 'Catawbiense Grandiflorum'). 5', -5ºF, ML, -/-/-. There are two plants currently being grown under the name 'Mrs. Helen Koster'. The true plant, with the above parentage, has light orchid flowers with a purplish red blotch. At least in the Northwest, this plant is seldom grown. There is, however, another plant that has been distributed fairly widely under the name of 'Mrs. Helen Koster' which opens orchid, gradually turning white with a prominent yellow eye. At one time it was also known under the name of 'Helen Koster', but no 'Helen Koster' is listed as a rhododendron. The yellow-eyed form has been grown for at least 30 years under the name of 'Mrs. Helen Koster' and is a hybrid of *catawbiense album*. The descriptive codes for this plant are as follows: (5', -10ºF, ML, 3/3/3-4). (M. Koster & Sons intro., reg. 1958).

'**Mrs. Horace Fogg**' (*griersonianum* x 'Loderi Venus'). 5', 0ºF, ML, 4/2-3/3-4. This plant has a pretty, compact habit, and grows in full sun. Flowers are very large, silvery-pinkish-rose, darker in the throat, and are carried in big upright trusses. (Larson hyb., Ridgeway intro., reg. 1958).

'**Mrs. Howard Phipps**' (Phipps 45 x 'Naomi'). 5', -10ºF?, M, -/-/-. Medium orchid pink flowers, in compact trusses of 13, are surrounded by matte green leaves. The plant is wide and compact plant. (Howard Phipps intro. 1958, reg. 1971).

'**Mrs. J. A. Withington III**' (['PJM' x *minus* var. *minus* Carolinianum Group *album*] x *dauricum album*). 4', -25ºF, E, -/-/-. A compact, rounded plant, with upright and wide growth. This very prolific hybrid is covered with lavender, double flowers whose frilly petals create a rose-like appearance. The foliage is reddish brown in winter, becoming bronze in early spring, turning green in summer. (Mezitt hyb. 1977, Bob Carlson named before 1993).

'**Mrs. J. Comber**' (*diaprepes* x *decorum*). 6', 5ºF, ML, -/-/-. White flowers are tinged yellow at the base. Long, narrow leaves, bronze when new, also grace this hybrid. (Messell before 1932) A.M. 1932.

'**Mrs. J. C. Williams**' (parentage unknown). 6', -15ºF, L, 4/3/3-4. Foliage is long, narrow and rough textured on a dense, upright and spreading, twiggy plant. Ruffled white flowers have a small blotch of reddish dots and form compact, ball-shaped trusses. (A. Waterer, Knap Hill Nursery before 1960) A.M. 1960.

'**Mrs. J. G. Millais**' (unknown). 6', -5ºF, ML, 5/2-3/3-4. The plant buds heavily even when young. The white flower with a huge gold blotch is one of the most magnificent flowers you will find. As it first opens it has a slight orchid touch to the flower, which is a delightful contrast to the gold. It becomes a plant of handsome stature when mature. (A. Waterer before 1917).

'**Mrs. Lammot Copeland**' (*wardii* x 'Virginia Scott'). 5', 0ºF, L, 4/3-4/3-4. Leaves are large. Clear yellow blooms, 3 1/2" across, are carried in 15 flower truss. (Larson 1971).

'**Mrs. Lindsay Smith**' ('George Hardy' x Duchess of Edinburgh'). 6', 0ºF, M-ML, 3-4/2/3. Plant habit is upright, open, sometimes inclined to droop. Leaves are large, light green in color. Large flat flowers are white, with some red spotting on upper lobe, in a large upright truss. (M. Koster & Sons 1910) A.M. 1933.

'**Mrs. Lionel de Rothschild**' see 'Lady de Rothschild'.

'**Mrs. Mary Ashley**' (*campylocarpum* hybrid). 4', 5ºF, EM, 3/3/-. Salmon pink flowers are shaded cream. Round leaves and compact growth create a nice plant that looks much like 'Unique'. (W. C. Slocock intro, reg. 1958).

'**Mrs. O. B. Watson**' (contains *ponticum*). 5', -5ºF, M, 4/3/3. Deep green leaves and delicate lavender flowers with a rich purple splotch characterize this plant. (Grown in the Portland, Oregon area since 1965).

'**Mrs. P. den Ouden**' ('Atrosanguineum' x 'Doncaster'). 5', -15ºF, EM-M, 2-3/3/3. The plant habit is quite compact and it blooms very prolifically with deep crimson flowers. (H. den Ouden & Son 1912).

'**Mrs. P. D. Williams**' (parentage unknown). 5', -10ºF, L, 3/2/3-4. Upright as young plant, later tends to sprawl, needs staking until sturdy at maturity. Smooth, very dark green leaves, with a very narrow base, mature to medium large size. Mid-sized flowers are ivory white with a large tawny brown blotch, in a tight rounded truss. This variety has occasionally been confused with 'Mrs. J. C. Williams' in some nurseries. (A. Waterer before 1925) A.M. 1936.

'**Mrs. Philip Martineau**' (parentage unknown). 6', -5ºF, L, 4/2/3. Growth habit is loose and straggling. Large leaves are medium green, and flowers are rose pink fading to lighter pink, blotched light yellow. The truss is rounded and quite large. (Knap Hill Nursery Co. before 1930) A.M. 1933, F.C.C. 1936.

'**Mrs. Powell Glass**' ('Catalgla' x *decorum*). 5', -20ºF, ML, 3/2/3. Foliage is dark green, with pure white blooms in a lax truss. Plant should have been registered 'Anne Glass'. Synonym, 'Anne Glass'. (Gable 1958).

'**Mrs. R. S. Holford**' (parentage unknown). 5', -15ºF, ML, 2-3/2/3. Habit is upright and rounded, with medium-large, medium green leaves. 2 1/2" flowers are rosy salmon, held in a tight truss. (A. Waterer 1866).

'Mrs. T. H. Lowinsky' (exact parentage unknown: a combination of *catawbiense, maximum* and *ponticum*). 5', -15ºF, L, 4/3/4. This is the plant that is generally grown under the name of 'Mrs. Tom H. Lowinsky', which is a different plant and may not be in cultivation. It is a medium compact plant with very dark green, glossy leaves. Vigorous growing. White flowers open from lavender buds to show an extremely striking orange brown blotch. It flowers well and is an adaptable, easy plant. (A. Waterer before 1917).

'Mrs. Tom H. Lowinsky' (*griffithianum* x 'Halopeanum' ['Halopeanum' = 'White Pearl' which is why this is sometimes listed as a hybrid of 'White Pearl']) 6', 5ºF?, EM, -/-/-. The true 'Mrs. Tom H. Lowinsky' is probably not in cultivation, and the plant that is grown around the world under this name is actually 'Mrs. T. H. Lowinsky'. This plant would be white with little or no blotch. (Cross probably by A. Waterer; Lowinsky intro. about 1900, but probably lost from cultivation).

'Mrs. Walter Burns' ('Standishii' x *griffithianum*). 6', 0ºF, EM-M, 3/3/3. Medium sized leaves, dark green, on a sturdy, upright plant. Flowers are light pink, more intensely colored along the petal edges, and with a deep pink blotch at the base of the upper petals. (Lowinsky) A.M. 1931.

'Mrs. W. C. Slocock' (*campylocarpum* hybrid). 4', -5ºF, EM, 3/3-4/3-4. A rounded shrub, compact in habit, with apricot flowers fading to buff. Quite appealing. (Slocock) A.M. 1929.

'Mrs. W. R. Coe' (*fortunei* ssp. *fortunei* hybrid). 6', -5ºF, ML, 3/4/3. Foliage is large, shiny dark green. Flowers are a bright intense pink, crimson in the throat, 4" wide and held in a huge, dome-shaped truss. (Dexter before 1943).

'Mrs. W. R. Dykes' ('Carl Mette' x 'Prinses Juliana' [note: 'Prinses Juliana' is supposed to be the correct parent. However no rhododendron by that name is listed, though there is a 'Princess Juliana']). 5', -10ºF, ML, 3/3/3. Strong rose red flowers appear above foliage of matte citrus green. It has been sold as 'R. W. Dykes' and is also incorrectly listed as 'Mr. W. R. Dykes'. (C. B. van Nes & Sons before 1930).

'Multimaculatum' (*ponticum* hybrid). 5', -25ºF, ML, 2-3/3/4. A super hardy hybrid that is good where you just can't grow other rhododendrons. The vigorous plant has white flowers with red spots. (J. Waterer before 1860).

'Muncaster Mist' (*campanulatum* x *floribundum*). 4', -5ºF, EM, 4/4/4. Lavender blue flowers with darker markings form a conical, compact truss. The plant has compact, dense stature. (Ramsden grower, Pennington-Ramsden reg. 1964).

'Mundai' ('Nobleanum' x 'Unique'). 5', -5ºF, E, -/-/-. Magenta pink flowers are a very vibrant contrast to the somewhat rounded pale green foliage. (Boulter 1964).

'Muriel Pearce' ('Anna' x 'Fusilier'). 6', 10ºF, EM, -/-/-. Foliage is medium sized and narrow. 3 1/2" wide flowers are shaded rose generously spotted with red, and are carried in a good-sized truss of up to 15 flowers. (Lem, Pearce 1973).

'My Lady' ('Forsterianum' selfed). 3', 15ºF, E, 4/3-4/3-4. Habit is compact and rounded, very symmetrical, with medium-sized leaves, glossy dark green, with a wrinkled puffy texture and a distinctive midrib in back. Flower is very open and flat, the color white blushed pink, pale yellow in the throat, set in an open truss. (Sumner 1971).

'My Pet' (unknown parentage). 2', 0ºF, 3/3/3. An attractive dwarf plant with many branches. The deep green rounded leaves profusely cover the plant. In flower, it is a mass of yellow with each flower having a small red blotch for accent. (Whitney, Sather 1976).

'Myrtifolium' (*minus* var. *minus* x *hirsutum*). 3', -15ºF, L, 3/5/4. For heat and sun tolerance this is an extremely good plant. The plant is dense and well clothed in leathery little leaves that are a rich matte green in summer. It has beautiful, deep bronze red foliage all winter. It flowers very late in the season with small medium pink flowers. (exhibited 1917). Note: there is a species by the same name.

'Mystic' ('Barclayi' x *williamsianum*). 3', 5ºF, EM, -/-/-. Absolutely clear pink, campanulate flowers on a super shrub. (Gen. Harrison hyb. 1950, intro. 1957).

'Namu' (*fortunei* ssp. *discolor* x 'Mrs. Horace Fogg'). 6', -15ºF, M, 4/4/4. Roseine purple flowers with 6-7 lobes bloom in large trusses of 13-14 on this hybrid. (H. L. Larson 1983).

'Nancy Evans' ('Hotei' x 'Lem's Cameo'). 3', 5ºF, M, 5/4/3-4. A visual delight. These orange red buds open to amber yellow, then become rich golden yellow while retaining some of the amber hues on the outer edges. Not only that, it has a very large calyx that gives an almost hose-in-hose effect. Free flowering, rounded plant habit. (Brockenbrough 1983).

'Nantucket' (*catawbiense* hybrid). 4', -15ºF, ML, -/-/-. Bright pink flowers appear in upright trusses all over this hardy plant. Large leaves are slightly convex and are lustrous green. It is a robust grower that makes an attractive plant in the garden. (Mezitt hyb. 1965, Weston Nurseries intro. 1990).

'Naomi A.M.' ('Aurora' x *fortunei* ssp. *fortunei*). 5', -5ºF, M, 4/3/3. Pink with yellow undertone. Like all hybrids in the 'Naomi' group this will become a magnificently full shrub, covered from top to ground with sweetly scented flowers. This clone out of the 'Naomi' group was named just 'Naomi' until it received an Award of Merit. It is now known as 'Naomi A.M.' (Rothschild 1926) A.M. 1933.

'Naomi Astarte' ('Aurora' x *fortunei* ssp. *fortunei*). 5', -10ºF, M, 4/4/3. Large leaves with round ends, on a fairly compact plant. Soft pink flowers shade inward to yellow, darker yellow in throat. (Rothschild 1926).

'Naomi Carissima' ('Aurora' x *fortunei* ssp. *fortunei*). 6', -10ºF, EM-M, 3/3/3. Pale pink mixed with creamy white. (Rothschild 1926).

'Naomi Early Dawn' ('Aurora' x *fortunei* ssp. *fortunei*). 6', -10ºF, EM-M. 3/3/3. Pale pink. (Rothschild 1926).

'Naomi Exbury' see 'Exbury Naomi'.

'Naomi Glow' ('Aurora' x *fortunei* ssp. *fortunei*). 6', -10ºF, EM-M, 4/4/3. Large foliage, rounded at both ends, on a somewhat compact plant. Large flowers, clear glowing pink, in a rounded truss. (Rothschild 1926).

'Naomi Hope' ('Aurora' x *fortunei* ssp. *fortunei*). 6', -10ºF, EM-M, 4/3/3. Pink with a mauve tinge. (Rothschild 1926).

'Naomi Nautilus' ('Aurora' x *fortunei* ssp. *fortunei*). 5', -5ºF, M, 4/4/3. Flowers are rose flushed pale orange, with soft greenish yellow in throat. One of the finest of the 'Naomi' group. Certainly the best of the group for foliage and plant. (Rothschild 1926) A.M. 1938.

'Naomi Nereid' ('Aurora' x *fortunei* ssp. *fortunei*). 6', -10ºF, EM-M, 4/4/3. Lavender and yellow. Foliage very similar to 'Naomi Nautilus'. (Rothschild 1926).

'Naomi Pink Beauty' ('Aurora' x *fortunei* ssp. *fortunei*). 6', -10ºF, EM-M, 4/4/3. A deep pink. (Rothschild 1926).

'Naomi Pixie' ('Aurora' x *fortunei* ssp. *fortunei*). 6', -10ºF, EM-M, 4/4/3. Growth habit more or less compact; large leaves with round ends. Large, brilliant pink flowers have rich crimson stain in throat. The bloom lasts a long time. Trusses are rounded. (Rothschild 1926).

'Naomi Stella Maris' ('Aurora' x *fortunei* ssp. *fortunei*). 6', -10ºF, EM-M, 4/4/3. Buff cream with shades of lilac pink. (Rothschild 1926) F.C.C. 1939.

'Naselle' ('Big Sam' x 'Lem's Cameo'). 4', EM, 10ºF, 5/4/4. This well proportioned plant is compact and broadly branched, amply covered with parsley green, elliptic foliage. Large blooms, 6-lobed, 15 per truss, of China rose shading to maize yellow, have burnt orange spotting within. The new growth is pale maroon. (J. Elliott 1987) A.E. 1992 Northwest.

'Nathan Hale' (parentage unknown). 5', -5ºF, ML, -/-/-. Leaves are medium to large. Fragrance is a bonus with this plant. 7-lobed blooms, to 3 1/2" across, are rose colored with a darker rose patch, carried in a ball-shaped truss. Synonym, HS #10. (Dexter hyb., Schlaikjer reg. 1973).

'Neat Feat' (*minus* var. *minus* Carolinianum Group tetraploid x 'Watchung'). 3', -15ºF, M, -/-/-. Deep reddish purple buds open vivid purple. Scaly leaves. (Delp 1994).

'Neat-O' (*campanulatum* x *yakushimanum* 'Koichiro Wada'). 3', 5ºF, EM, 4/5/4. Light rose flowers, spotted in the throat, form rounded trusses in groups of 25. A tight, rounded plant covered with elongated, dark green foliage sueded with indumentum below. (Goheen 1983).

'Nectarine' (['Coronis' x *griersonianum*] x 'Margaret Dunn'). 4', 0ºF, M, 4/3/3. An unusual nectarine flower color. Long, narrow leaves are matte olive green. (Brandt before 1958).

'Negrito' ('Oratorium' x 'Hachmann's Feuerschein'). 3', -15ºF, ML-L, -/-/-. Strong red flowers, with darker red spotting on the dorsal lobe, are accentuated by yellow anthers. Broad, rounded leaves are glossy green. (Hachmann hyb., Stuck reg. 1988).

'Nelda Peach' (Unnamed peach colored hybrid x 'Lem's Cameo'). 2', 0ºF, M, 4/4/4. Large, openly funnel shaped 7-lobed flowers, light yellowish pink with reddish orange speckling, have pinkish margins and open from strong yellowish pink to large ball shaped trusses of 14. Elliptic forest green leaves cover the mounding plant. (W. Robertson hyb., J. Davis 1987).

'Nepal' (*catawbiense* var. *album* x [*wightii* x *fortunei* ssp. *fortunei*]). 6', -25ºF, M, 4/4/4. Sparkling white flowers emerge from rose pink buds. Leaves are dark green with a slight wave. (Leach 1972).

'Nereid' (*neriiflorum* x *dichroanthum*). 2', 0ºF, ML, 3/4/3. Growth habit is very compact, with small, dark green, roundish oblong leaves. Flowers are bell shaped, peachy salmon orange, only an inch wide and long, in a flat-topped truss. (Wilding 1934).

'Nestucca' (*fortunei* ssp. *fortunei* x *yakushimanum*). 3', -10ºF, M, 4/3-4/3-4. A beautiful white flower with green-brown in the throat. Compact plant habit with good foliage, although it does tend to grow freak foliage at times which contains nothing but the midrib and a very narrow, a rather strange looking blade. (Hanger, C. Smith 1960) P.A. 1950.

'Newburyport Beauty' (open pollinated Dexter hybrid). 5', -15ºF, ML, -/-/-. This hybrid and 'Newburyport Belle' were crossed by D. Leach to create 'Rio' and 'Normandy'. The flowers are lavender pink. Synonym, 'Fowle No. 18'. (Grown by Fowle Nursery, named by Wister, Scott Hort. Fndn. intro. before 1980).

'Newburyport Belle' (parentage unknown). 4', -15ºF, ML, -/-/-. Light purplish pink flowers have a gold blotch made of yellow and green spotting. Domed trusses hold 16 flowers. This plant is free flowering and well branched. Synonym, 'Fowle No. 19'. (Dexter hyb., H. Fowle raiser, Scott Horticultural Foundation reg. 1985).

'Newcomb's Sweetheart' ('Pink Walloper' x *decorum*). 4', 0ºF, M, 4/4/4. Fragrant flowers of light pinkish mauve darken with age to orchid pink. They are edged with solferino purple, blotched in roseine purple. Their openly funnel shaped corollas have 6 lobes which are held in ball shaped trusses of 11. This plant is broader than tall. (L. L. Newcomb hyb. 1968, reg. 1981) C.A. 1983.

'New Comet' ('Idealist' x 'Naomi'). 4', -10ºF, M, -/-/-. Rounded trusses of beautiful blooms, yellow flushed with a very soft pink. (RHS Garden, Wisley 1956) A.M. 1957.

'New Hope' (*yakushimanum* x 'Kiev'). 3', -5ºF, EM, -/-/-. Foliage is medium to large and narrow. Flowers are dark pink, fading lighter to center, with darker pink spotting and on the outside, carried in a rounded truss of up to 10. (Bovee before 1963, Herbert 1976).

'New Patriot' (['PJM' x *dauricum* pink form] selfed). 3', -20ºF, EM, -/-/-. Trusses of 8 flowers open from deep red buds to vivid purplish red flowers with white anthers. The color extends down the stems. Kelly green leaves change to copper brown in the fall. (Mezitt hyb. 1979, Weston reg. 1988).

'New Romance' ('Lady Bligh' x 'Loderi Venus'). 5', 0ºF, ML, -/-/-. Rose pink buds open to very long lasting white flowers with no stamens. A dense bush with leaves persistent for 3 years. (Henny 1965).

'Nicholas' (*ponticum* hybrid). 5', -10ºF, ML, 4/2/3. The picture of this in <u>Rothschild Rhododendrons</u> makes it a much desired rhododendron. The flowers are plum purple with a white center, giving it a delightful two toned appearance. The foliage is sometimes a bit yellow, but is better with shade. It appears that there is more than one clone of this plant being grown. The one commonly grown in the U.S. is more reddish with a white center instead of the plum purple with white. (Rothschild 1965) A.M. 1965.

'Nicoletta' ('Fantastica' x ['Hachmann's Ornament' x 'Furnivall's Daughter']). 1.5', -15ºF, ML, -/-/-. Flowers bloom rosy pink with a conspicuous dark red blotch. Over time the background ages to white. Trusses of 16-19 funnel shaped flowers have wavy lobes. (Hachmann 1977, Stuck reg. 1991).

'Night Editor' (form of *russatum*). 4', 5ºF, E, 3/4/3. A great selection. The flowers on this plant are a superior dark violet. The leaves, which are curved down on the margins, look like miniature green tubes. It is a most unusual and interesting plant, well worth a spot in your garden if you want something nice and different. (Sheedy 1981).

'Night Sky' ('Blue Steel' x 'Russautinii'). 2', -10ºF, EM-M, -/-/-. Trusses are of 5 deep violet blue flowers, paler in the throat. Lanceolate leaves, sparsely scaly, decorate this plant. (J. P. C. Russell 1983).

'Night Watch' ('Cup Day' x 'Purple Splendour'). 5', -5ºF, M, 4/3/4. Similar to 'Midnight', this plant has flowers more lavender than soft red-purple with heavy, very dark spotting on the upper lobe and center. Foliage is pointed, glossy forest green. (K. Van de Ven before 1982).

'Nile' (*catawbiense* var. *album* x *wardii*). 6', -20ºF, M, 3-4/3-4/3-4. Formerly called 'Sahara'. Very bright yellow with vibrant red coloring deep in the throat. Foliage is rounded and large and hangs down. A great addition for that hardy yellow requirement. (Leach intro. 1973, reg. 1983).

Hybrids ~

by Davis

by Brockenbrough

'Paprika Spiced'

R. 'Horizon Snowbird'

R. 'Nelda Peach'

R. 'Ruth Mottley'

. 'Horizon Monarch'

R. 'Nancy Evans'

R. 'Tequilla Sunrise'

R. 'Scarlet Wonder'

Hybrids ~ by Hobbie

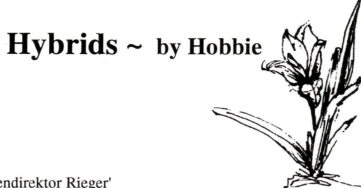

R. 'Aksel Olsen'

R. 'Gartendirektor Glocker'

R. 'Lissabon'

R. 'Bremen'

R. 'Royal Pin

R. 'Besse Howells'

'Lavender Queen'

R. 'Holden'

Hybrids ~ by Shammarello

R. 'Spring Parade'

'Cheer'

R. 'Vernus'

Hybrids ~
by Rothschild

R. 'Crest'

R. 'Crest'

R. 'Lionel's Triumph'

R. 'Leo'

R. 'Naomi Nautilus'

R. 'Repose'

R. 'Alpine Glo

R. 'Exbury Naomi'

R. 'Lady de Rothschild'

R. 'Alpine Glow'

'Nimbus' ('Snow Queen' x 'Cornish Loderi' or 'Snow Queen' x 'Venus'). 6', 0ºF, ML, -/-/-. The RHS 1958 Register lists the parentage as 'Snow Queen' x 'Venus'; the RHS Year Book 1966 lists 'Snow Queen' x ?; then the RHS Year Book 1968 lists 'Snow Queen' x 'Cornish Loderi'. To further complicate matters, were they thinking of 'Loderi Venus' or just 'Venus'? 'Venus' is a red which would not likely produce (though it could) this white rhododendron. A very light growing white, beginning as cream buds with a blush of pink. Floriferous. (Knap Hill Nurseries 1935, exhibited 1949) A.M. 1965, F.C.C. 1967.

'Nobleanum' (*caucasicum* x *arboreum*). 4', -10ºF, E, 2/2/3-4. One of the first man made hybrids. Flowers are rich rose with a flush of white inside. Foliage is dark green with tan indumentum. (Waterer, Knap Hill about 1835) A.G.M. 1926.

'Nobleanum Album' (*caucasicum* x *arboreum*). 4', -10ºF, E, 2/2/3-4. A white form of the above. (Knap Hill, originated in 1800's).

'Nobleanum Coccineum' (*caucasicum* x *arboreum*). 5', 0ºF, VE-E, 2/2/3-4. Plant inclined to be leggy, with upright new growth. Medium to large, narrow leaves seem to roll. Medium sized scarlet flowers in a small round truss. (A. Waterer 1835).

'Nobleanum Venustum' (*caucasicum* x *arboreum*). 5', 0ºF, VE-E, 2/2/3-4. Growth habit is slightly open and spreading, with medium large, narrow leaves which appear to roll. Medium sized, rose pink flowers in a small rounded truss. (William Smith, Surry, England, 1829) A.G.M. 1969, A.M. 1973.

'Noble Mountain' (*yakushimanum* x 'Rodeo'). 3', -5ºF, M, 4/4/4. Frilly, 5-lobed flowers of moderate purplish pink with heavy dark red spotting are held in trusses of 15. Dark olive green leaves cover this lovely dense plant. (Peste hyb. 1979, S. Johnston reg. 1986).

'Nodding Bells' (Red *catawbiense* hybrid x [*forrestii* ssp. *forrestii* Repens Group x *griersonianum*]). 2', -15ºF, EM, -/-/-. This interesting plant has spreading, downward-arching growth habit. Bell shaped, open flowers are cherry-red in color. (Amateis, not registered).

'Nofretete' ('Professor Hugo de Vries' x *insigne*). 6', 0ºF, L, -/-/-. Sanguine red flowers and deep forest green foliage are the distinguishing characteristics of this German hybrid. (Bruns 1961, Herbst intro. 1983).

'Norman Behring' ('Nova Zembla' x *yakushimanum* 'Pink Parasol'). 3', -25ºF, L, -/-/-. Flowers of light mallow purple, darker edges, yellow-green spotting, 5-lobed with openly funnel shaped corollas, are held in domed shaped trusses of 18. Leaves with grayed orange indumentum beneath form a plant wider than tall. (Rudy Behring hyb. 1974, reg. 1986).

'Normandy' ('Newburyport Beauty' x 'Newburyport Belle'). 3', -20ºF, ML, 4/4/4. Bright pink flowers of light texture have darker edges and orange spotting. It is a broad, rounded plant with dark green leaves. (Leach 1966, reg. 1983).

'Norman Gill' ('Beauty of Tremough' x *griffithianum*). 6', 5ºF, ML, 4/3/4. Medium large leaves on vigorous plant. White flowers, very large, with red blotch, in a tall truss. (R. Gill & Son) A.M. 1922, A.M. 1936.

'Norman Shaw' (*fortunei* ssp. *discolor* x 'B. de Bruin'). 5', -5ºF, L, -/-/-. Phlox pink flowers are held in nice, compact trusses. Plant eventually grows tall but maintains a neat appearance. (Rothschild intro. 1919) A.M. 1926.

'Norseman' (parentage unknown). 5', -5ºF, M, 4/3/3-4. This Lem hybrid is known for its striking fluorescent rose pink flowers. A truly exceptional color. The foliage is fairly long, and an interesting flat green. It tends to curl up on the edges to make a cup shaped leaf. An unusual hybrid. (Lem, Elliott 1974).

'Northern Star' (*fortunei* ssp. *discolor* x 'Lodauric Iceberg'). 5', -5ºF, L, -/-/-. Large compact shrub with fragrant funnel shaped white flowers, cinnamon colored anthers. Fragrant. (Hydon Nurseries 1967).

'Nosutchianum' (*williamsianum* x *Kalmia latifolia*). 4', -5ºF, M, -/-/-. This is a very unusual bigeneric hybrid between a rhododendron and a kalmia. The lovely light pink, rounded flowers with stamens turning to white, show the influence of both parents. The foliage, also about half way between kalmia and rhododendron in appearance, is deep green, relatively small, with a distinct curve, somewhat like kalmia. Since it was such an unusual hybrid, it was said by friends of Haldan Lem that "no such" hybrid could occur. Someone jokingly added a Latin ending to "no such", hence the name 'Nosutchianum'! (Lem hyb. before 1960, not registered).

'Nova Zembla' ('Parsons Grandiflorum' x hardy red hybrid). 5', -25ºF, M, 3/3/4. Here is true hardiness in a red. Certainly a plant to grow in more difficult areas. It is a vigorous grower with good foliage. The extremely showy red flowers make a real display in the spring. (M. Koster & Sons 1902).

'Noyo Brave' ('Noyo Chief' x *yakushimanum* 'Koichiro Wada'). 3', 0ºF, EM, 4/4/3-4. Leaves are medium to large. 2 1/2" flowers are a lively bright pink, dulling as they age, with a very small glowing red blotch, and held in a well-rounded truss of up to 22. (C. Smith hyb. 1963, reg. 1977).

'Noyo Chief' (hybrid of *arboreum* ssp. *nilagiricum*). 5', 10ºF, M, 3-4/4-5/4. The outstanding foliage is glossy, deep green and deeply ribbed. Flowers are showy, translucent red. This was also grown under the name of *R. zeylanicum*. (Reuthe, Brandt, Bowman 1965) C.A. 1971.

'Noyo Maiden' (*yakushimanum* 'Koichiro Wada' x 'Noyo Chief'). 3', 5ºF, EM, 4/4/4. This wide spreading, dense and compact plant is beautifully foliaged with well-proportioned dark olive green leaves which are heavily indumented and held for 3 years. Abundant pure white flowers open from clear pink buds into round trusses of 15-19. (C. Smith 1983).

'Nuance' ([*catawbiense* var. *album* x {*neriiflorum* x *dichroanthum*}] x *fortunei* ssp. *discolor*). 6', -15ºF, ML, 4/3-4/3-4. Leaves are medium sized. Flowers are of heavy substance, up to 2 3/4" across, lovely pale orange-yellow blushed purplish pink, and with greenish yellow dorsal spotting, held in a 14-flower truss. (Leach 1973).

'Nymph' (*forrestii* ssp. *forrestii* Repens Group x 'Largo'). 1', 5ºF, E, 3/3/2-3. Low, spreading growth habit. Dark green leaves, deep red flowers. (Aberconway hyb. 1936, Lord Aberconway intro. 1946).

'Oceanlake' ('Blue Diamond' x 'Sapphire'). 30", -5ºF, EM, 4/4/4. Deep violet blue flowers make a charming display on this small leaved hybrid. The foliage turns interesting bronze tones in winter. Will take sun. (Wright Sr. & Jr. 1965).

'Odee Wright' ('Idealist' x 'Mrs. Betty Robertson'). 4', -5ºF, M, 4/4/3-4. A compact grower with waxy green leaves. Deep clear yellow trusses are large and exceptionally beautiful. (Wright Sr. & Jr. 1964).

'Odoratum' (*ponticum* x *nudiflorum*). 4', -15ºF, ML, 2/3/3-4. This old azaleodendron should not be overlooked. It is especially good for its very delightful fragrance. The flowers are orchid lilac. (Thompson before 1875).

'Oh Canada' ('Lem's Cameo' x 'Jalisco' x 'King of Shrubs'). 4', 5ºF, ML, -/-/-. Rich yellow flowers, having a chestnut colored splotch in the throat, are held in ball shaped trusses. It has bronzy new growth. (Canadian hyb., grown by Riverwood Gardens, New Zealand).

'**Oh! Kitty**' (possibly a 'Cotton Candy' hybrid). 4', 0ºF, M, 4/4/4. Originally grown as 'Miss Kitty', this plant has strong currant red buds opening to strong pink, fragrant, funnel shaped flowers which have a currant red throat. The flowers are large, to 6" across. They are composed of 5 wavy lobes, and are held in groups of 17 to form impressive dome-shaped trusses. The leaves are elliptic and convex. Although registered under this name, the plant can still be found grown under both names. (Fred Minch hyb. 1973, reg. 1988).

'**Oh-Too**' ('China' x 'Goldbug'). 4', -5ºF, ML, 4/3/3. Here is a most interesting multicolored flower. The bud appears to enclose a red flower, then it bursts forth as a light red flower which gradually matures to a yellow color with a salmon throat and red spotting. There are up to 14 flowers in each ball shaped truss. The rounded plant branches well and has glossy, moss green leaves. (W. Elliot hyb. 1964, Sather 1976).

'**Old Copper**' ('Vulcan' x 'Fabia'). 5', -5ºF, L, 4/3-4/4. Late in the spring when most rhododendrons are finished blooming for the year, 'Old Copper' shows its large orange trusses. Foliage is perky and attractive. It is said to be a variety that does well in hotter climates. (Van Veen Sr. before 1964).

'**Old Port**' (*ponticum* hybrid). 5', -15ºF, M-ML, 3/3-4/3-4. There are two different plants being grown under the name of 'Old Port'. The most common one has very glossy, deeply ribbed leaves and a medium purple flower with a deeper blotch. It is a very vigorous plant. This form is supposedly not the true, original form, yet it is more widely grown. The true name of this plant may be 'William Downing,' according to correspondence from Per Sorensen in New Zealand. As of this writing, I have not seen the true 'William Downing', but its brief description fits this more commonly grown 'Old Port,' which also appears to be registered under the name of 'Whitney Purple'. The second, and supposedly true form, is a deeper wine purple without a distinct blotch. Its foliage is also glossy, but smoother than the other form. It is vigorous, but not quite as much so as the first. (A. Waterer 1865).

'**Old Spice**' (*decorum* x 'Azor'). 4', -5ºF, ML, 3/3/3. Foliage is large. Beautifully scented, phlox pink flowers, which shade to apricot, are large in size, to 3 1/2" across, and are carried in a truss of up to 12. (Lancaster 1961).

'**Ole Olson**' (*campylocarpum* var. *elatum* x *fortunei* ssp. *discolor*). 5', 0ºF, ML, 3/3/3. The plant habit is open and upright, with medium sized, medium green leaves. Flowers are 3 1/2" wide, pale yellow, in a loose truss. 'Old Olson' is presumed to be same plant. (Gable before 1950).

'**Olga**' ('Mrs. Lindsay Smith' x 'Dido'). 3', -10ºF, ML, -/-/-. A very lovely flower of light yellow orange flushed red. (Slocock Nurseries 1982) H.C. 1982.

'**Olga Mezitt**' (*minus* var. *minus* Carolinianum Group x *minus* var. *minus*). 3', -15ºF, EM, 4/3-4/4. Leaves are mahogany in the winter and bright, light green in the summer. They are just part of what makes this plant appealing! Small, tight balls of clear pink cover every terminal of this plant during bloom. (Mezitt hyb. 1958, Weston Nurseries reg. 1983).

'**Olin O. Dobbs**' ('Mars' x 'Purple Splendour'). 4', -15ºF, M, 5/3/3. Very deep, waxy red-purple flowers have tremendous substance and are so "perfect" that it is hard to believe they are real. The plant buds young. It is much like 'Mars' in growth and plant habit. The trusses are large, compact and a perfect conical shape. (Dobbs hyb. 1955, Greer reg. 1979).

'**Olive**' (*moupinense* x *dauricum*). 4', -15ºF, VE, 3/3/3. One of the earliest to burst forth with a display of orchid pink flowers in the early spring. Very worthwhile for this reason. Hardy, vigorous grower. (Maxwell) A.M. 1942.

'**Oliver Cromwell**' (*griersonianum* hybrid). 3', -10ºF, M, -/-/-. A great orange red that blooms prolifically in a protected area. (Reuthe).

'**Oliver Twist**' ('Charles Dickens' x *yakushimanum*). 3', 0ºF, EM, -/-/-. A semi-dwarf plant, as wide as tall, with a mounding habit. It has leathery, matte forest green foliage with slight beige indumentum. Leaves are held for 3 years. This hybrid has masses of clear fuchsine pink, ruffled flowers. (Lancaster reg. 1968).

'**Olympic Knight**' ('Fabia' x unknown hybrid). 5', 5ºF, M-ML, 3/3/3. This truss is dark red with a prominent black-red blotch shown on the upper petal of each flower. The foliage is attractive. (Clark before 1958) P.A. 1960.

'**Olympic Lady**' ('Loderi King George' x *williamsianum*). 3', -5ºF, EM, 3-4/4/4. The compact, spreading plant is nicely shaped and covers itself with large, white, cup-shaped flowers. (Ostbo before 1950, Clark 1958) A.M. 1977.

'**Omega**' (? *catawbiense* x unknown rose colored hybrid). 5', -20ºF, ML, -/-/-. Light ruby red flowers with red-brown or yellow-green markings on a light background are characteristic of this hybrid. (Seidel 1912).

'**One Thousand Butterflies**' ('Lem's Cameo' x 'Pink Petticoats'). 5', 0ºF, ML, 5/3/3. Giant balls of pink fade to almost cream towards the flowers' centers, and bursting out from the center of each flower is a bright red blotch resembling a butterfly. It is most attractive and sought after. (Lofthouse 1975, reg. 1981).

'**Ooh Gina**' ('Golden Belle' x 'Lem's Cameo'). 4', 0ºF, ML, 4-5/4/3-4. Frilled pink flowers with a rose margin and a red blotch in the throat display themselves in a rounded ball truss. From its parent 'Lem's Cameo', it gets bronzy new growth, which sets off its lovely green, medium sized foliage. What's more, it has a good low growth habit. A distinguished plant. (Burlingame hyb. 1976, reg. 1983).

'**Ooh-La-La**' (*yakushimanum* x 'Pink Petticoats'). 3', 0ºF, EM, 4/4/-. Deep forest green foliage, pale gray-green and tomentose when young, held for 3 years, clothes a broad, mounding plant with decumbent branches. Flowers of 6 frilled lobes open neyron rose then fade to white. They form spherical trusses of 22-26 flowers. Synonym, 'Hot Pants'. (J. Lofthouse hyb. 1966, reg. 1981).

'**Opal Fawcett**' (parentage unknown). 5'?, 0ºF?, M-ML, 4/4/4. Leaves are quite large. Flowers of opalescent character are very pale pink fading to white, up to 3 1/2" across are held in a 16-flower truss, and slightly fragrant. (Ostbo, Fawcett 1959) A.E. 1958.

'**Orange Honey**' ('Blondie' x 'Catalgla'). 5', -20ºF, L, -/-/-. Flowers of salmon pink, similar to those of 'Mary Belle', are held in trusses of 18. This plant has a rather open habit and attractive foliage (Pride 1977).

'**Orange Marmalade**' (*yakushimanum* x 'Mrs. Lammot Copeland'). 3', -5ºF, M, 4/4/4. Delightful, lax orange trusses have a slight salmon pink hue after emerging from dark red buds. Eventually the flowers turn a rich amber yellow. Formerly known as 'Orange Bells'. (Larson hyb. 1969, raised by Davis, reg. 1983).

'**Orangengold**' (*dichroanthum* ssp. *scyphocalyx* x unknown hybrid). 4', -10ºF, M-ML, -/-/-. Yellowish orange, 5-lobed flowers have brown markings. The bicolor tones are accentuated by light orange outside petal surfaces and wavy petal edges of orange-pink. Trusses are loose, flat-topped and contain 8-13 flowers. The foliage has silvery white indumentum beneath. (Wieting hyb. about 1970, Schmalscheidt reg. 1987).

'**Orange Sherbet**' ('Tahiti' x 'Catalgla'). 5', -20ºF, ML, -/-/-. Light pinkish orange flowers held in loose trusses decorate this vigorous hybrid. Orangish red new growth provides interest. (Pride before 1990).

'Orangina' (*dichroanthum* hybrid). 3', -5ºF, M, -/-/-. The rosy orange tones of the petal edges of these flowers are melded with yellow throats and small yellow gold markings. Large, lax trusses hold as many as 15 campanulate flowers. Foliage is bright green, plant habit is broadly round. (D. G. Hobbie hyb., H. Hachmann 1989).

'Orchard Gold' ('Honey Glow' x 'Crest'). 5', 5ºF, M-ML, -/-/-. Riverwood Gardens in New Zealand says this is *wardii* x 'Ivan D. Wood', so its parentage is questionable. Funnel shaped flowers, with 7 deeply indented lobes, uranium green, deeper towards the center, are held in trusses of 10. Elliptical leaves. (Mrs. G. Grant hyb. 1976, Mr. & Mrs. L. A. Grant reg. 1988).

'Orchard Road' ('Pacific Queen' x *wardii*). 5', 5ºF, M-ML, -/-/-. Riverwood Gardens says this is *wardii* x 'Ivan D. Wood', so there is question as to the correct parentage. Trusses are of 9 funnel shaped, 7 lobed flowers, with solferino purple edges which merge to pastel mauve. Hairless, elliptic foliage covers this hybrid. (The Grants reg. 1988).

'Oregon Queen' (*occidentale* x *macrophyllum*). 5', -10ºF, ML, 2-3/3/3. This is an interesting, light pink azaleodendron that originated in the wilds of Oregon where *occidentale* and *macrophyllum* grow in harmony. (1958)

'Ornatum' (*viscosum* x *ponticum*). 3', -20ºF, ML, -/-/-. Two forms of this azaleodendron exist. One has dark scarlet flowers, the other deep yellow with orange spots. Like most of this type, the foliage is thin and crinkly. (Gowan 1832).

'Osmar' (*williamsianum* hybrid). 3', -10ºF, EM, -/-/-. Loose trusses are made of 4-8, campanulate, lilac and light pink flowers. Deep green, recurved, almost orbicular foliage graces this hybrid. (Raised in UK pre-1965, van Gelderen, de Wilde intro. 1975, Royal Boskoop Horticultural Society reg. 1988).

'Ostbo's Low Yellow' (Possibly a 'Fabia' hybrid plus several other species. Probably a third or fourth generation hybrid). 3', 0ºF, M, 4/3/3-4. The flowers are one of those difficult to describe combinations of cream, apricot and yellow which change daily. The buds first show as apricot pink, and as the flowers emerge and change, the palette swirls until finally the flowers become a creamy yellow with a deeper apricot pink center. The plant is terrific. It is compact, with attractive, deeply veined leaves, about 4 1/2" by 1 3/4" wide. It buds young and heavily. Good for hybridizing. (Ostbo 1960) P.A. 1960.

'Ostfriesland' ('Madame de Bruin' x *forrestii* ssp. *forrestii* Repens Group). 3', -5ºF, M, 3/3/3. Like so many of Hobbie's superior Repens Group hybrids this has a spreading habit with many scarlet bells. (Hobbie 1949).

'Oudijk's Favorite' (*augustinii* hybrid). 3', -10ºF, EM, 3-4/3-4/3. Violet flowers profusely cover the entire plant in early spring, creating a tight ball of color. Winter foliage is showy bronze. (Fa. Le Feber & Co., Boskoop, intro. 1958, reg. 1965) S.M. Flora Nova (Boskoop) 1958.

'Oudijk's Sensation' ('Essex Scarlet' x *williamsianum*). 4', -10ºF, EM, 3-4/3/3. Leaves are widely elliptic, somewhat heart-shaped, and sharply pointed. Broadly funnel-form flowers, to 3" long, with wavy edges, are dark pink, fading lighter inside, spotted darker on upper lobes, and set in a 5-7 flower truss. (Hobbie, Le Feber 1965) G.M. 1960, S.M. 1958, 1961.

'Ovation' ('Tony's Gift' x 'Lady Bligh'). 5', -5ºF, ML, -/-/-. Pale purplish, phlox pink flowers with a dorsal spotting of cardinal red highlight this tall and well-branched plant. (Delp before 1990).

'Ovation' ('Mars' x *haematodes*). 4', -5ºF?, M, -/-/-. This German hybrid is considered to be an excellent plant. The plant is compact, has good foliage, and has bright red flowers in abundance. There are two plants named 'Ovation'. (Nagel hyb. 1968, intro. 1983).

'Oz' ('Fabia' x *catawbiense* var. *album*). 3', 5ºF, M, 3-4/3-4/3-4. Orange spots are spread around a field of lemon yellow which gradually turns to carmine rose on the edges. Well branched, with a dense plant habit. (Lem hyb., Barefield reg. 1980).

'Pacific Glow' ('Loderi Venus' x *strigillosum*). 6', 10ºF, E, 4/4/4. Leaves are medium to large. 6-lobed flowers are a clear unmarked pink with darker pink throats, carried in a ball-shaped truss up to 17. (Larson, Jack reg. 1979).

'Pacific Gold' ('Mrs. Lammot Copeland' x yellow hybrid). 3-4', 0ºF, M, -/-/-. Yellow flowers burst from orange red buds in mid season. New growth has a reddish cast to the green. (Larson hyb., raised by Davis, reg. 1982).

'Pacific Queen' ('Fawn' x 'Dido' x 'King of Shrubs'). 5', 5ºF, ML, 4-5/4/4. Trusses of jasper red flowers. (Mrs. R. J. Coker 1980).

'Pacific Sunset' (['Peach Lady' x 'Tally Ho'] x 'Malemute'). 4', 10ºF, M, -/-/-. Grows to a width greater than its height. The plant is coated with dark green, narrowly oblong foliage. Lax trusses hold wavy edged flowers of carmine pink. The yellow shaded throat is accented by dorsal spotting of brick red. (J. Elliott hyb. 1978, reg. 1989).

'Painted Lady' (['Dido' x 'Lem's Goal'] x ['Corry Koster' x 'Mrs. G. W. Leak']). 5', 10ºF, M, 4/3/3. Medium green foliage forms a dense background for peach flowers held in upright trusses. The blooms are enhanced by a warm yellow center and orange spotting which forms a flare on the upper petal. (Lem before 1960, Newcomb).

'Painted Star' ('Meadowbrook' x 'Anita'). 5', -5ºF, ML, -/-/-. Not much has been written about this hybrid. It has cream-colored flowers which are reddish in the throat. (Hardgrove before 1950).

'Pale Perfection' (*catawbiense* hybrid). 5', -15ºF, ML, 2/4/3. Leaves are medium sized and narrow. Light pink flowers, up to 2 1/2" across, have a distinctive dark green blotch, and are held in a truss of up to 13 blooms. (Wyman, Ticknor 1967).

'Paloma' ('Ruby F. Bowman' x *floccigerum*). 6', 0ºF, M, -/-/-. Red spotting is visible on pink flowers which have darker pink margins. A tall, rapid grower. (Goheen 1966, reg. 1986, Bulgin intro. 1983).

'Pamela Louise' (*fortunei* ssp. *fortunei* x unknown). 5', -10ºF, M, -/-/-. Large, lilac pink flowers have a nice fragrance. Similar to 'Naomi'. (Hydon Nurseries 1974).

'Pana' ('Oh My!' x 'Red Brave'). 4', -15ºF, L, -/-/-. Strong red and purplish pink flowers, some having white throats, are spotted deep yellow green. (Delp 1992).

'Panama' (['Fanfare' x *catawbiense* white] x [{*dichroanthum* x *griersonianum*} x {*fortunei* ssp. *discolor* x 'Corona'}]). 5', -15ºF, ML, 3/3/3. Dark spotting on cardinal red flowers. Leaves are yellow green. (Leach 1962, intro. 1976, reg. 1983).

'Pania' (*dichroanthum* hybrid). 4', 5ºF, EM, -/-/-. A compact grower with a spreading habit which becomes covered with a profusion of salmon blooms. (New Zealand Rhododendron Association intro. before 1982).

'Papaya Punch' ('Hotei' x 'Brandt's Tropicana'). 4', 0ºF, EM, 4/3/2-3. The spreading plant is clothed in matte green foliage. Rosy yellow buds open to dome-shaped flowers of light yellowish-pink with a wide margin of orange yellow. Blooms have a vivid yellow flare in each lobe completing the tropical effect. (Brockenbrough hyb. 1971, Kesterson reg. 1986).

'Paprika Spiced' ('Hotei' x 'Brandt's Tropicana'). 3', 0ºF, M, 5/3-4/3-4. An appropriately named, exciting plant. The pale creamy yellow flowers are surrounded by an explosion of paprika red spots! A faint hue of pink is present on the back of the upper lobe. (Brockenbrough hyb. 1971, Nelson reg. 1984).

'Paracutin' ('Britannia' x 'Tally Ho'). 4', 5ºF, ML, 4/3-4/3-4. Bright cardinal red flowers cover this attractive plant. Large green foliage has a light coating of tan indumentum. This is a very showy plant when in flower. (Brandt 1968).

'Parker's Pink' (parentage unknown). 5', -25ºF, ML, 2/3/3. Foliage is large. Nicely scented flowers, to 3 1/2" across, are dark pink fading white in the center. They are heavily spotted with red and are held in a 12-flower truss. Synonym, Parker's #1 (Dexter hyb. before 1943, Vossberg intro. 1959, New York Chapter ARS reg. 1973) A.E. 1973 Northeast.

'Parson's Gloriosum' (catawbiense hybrid). 5', -25ºF, ML, 2/2/3. Hardy, hardy, hardy is how to describe this old English hybrid. As it is so hardy and vigorous growing, it still remains popular after all these years. The plant is compact but upright growing, and has deep green leaves. The cone shaped trusses are orchid lavender with a shading of pink. (A. Waterer, Parsons about 1860).

'Party Girl' ('Whitney Late Red' x 'Loderi King George'). 5', 0ºF, L, -/-/-. A heavy-textured, light pink flower, accented by rose margins and an orangish throat blooms on this hybrid. Fragrance exudes from the trusses of 12 flowers. It is a broad, rounded plant covered with narrow, glossy green foliage. (Peste hyb. 1970, Peste reg. 1983).

'Party Pink' ('Mrs. Furnivall' x catawbiense var. album). 5', -20ºF, ML, 4-5/4-5/4-5. Widely elliptic, medium sized leaves are carried on this well-branched, broad plant. Funnel-shaped flowers, to 3", are purple-pink, shading paler toward the throat, with distinctive yellow spotting, and held in a rounded truss up to 18. (Leach 1973) C.A. 1981, A.E. 1982, S.P.A. 1983 Great Lakes.

'Passion' ('Caractacus' x 'Hugh Koster'). 7', -15ºF, ML, -/-/-. An upright grower which grows equally wide. The plant produces full trusses of vivid purplish red blooms. Each flower has a white throat and dorsal markings of moderate reddish orange. (Hachmann hyb. 1959, Stuck reg. 1988).

'Passionate Purple' (impeditum hybrid). 2', -10ºF, EM, 3-4/3/3. The compact plant has very small, rounded foliage accentuated by many electric purple blossoms. (Thompson before 1990, not registered).

'Patricia' (selected seedling of campylogynum var. charopeum). 1', 5ºF, ML, 3/3/3. Leaves are small, typical of species, and flowers are reddish purple. A very pretty plant with charming flowers. Susceptible to rust. (Caperci 1960).

'Patricia's Day' (yakushimanum x dwarf yellow). 3', 0ºF, M, -/-/-. Soft lavender flowers are veined deeper pink-lavender. (J. Waterer, Sons & Crisp 1975).

'Patty Bee' (keiskei 'Yaku Fairy' x fletcheranum). 18", -10ºF, EM, 5/4-5/4-5. Small foliage densely covers this well-branched plant. Clear yellow flowers, to 2" across, are carried in a 6-flower, lax truss. One of the very best of the dwarf yellow hybrids for both appearance and tolerance of heat and sun. (Berg hyb. 1970, reg. 1977) A.E. 1984, A.M. 1989 (Wisley Trials), S.P.A. 1985 Northwest.

'Paula' (elepidote rhododendron, unknown parentage). 3', -5ºF, EM, -/-/-. A compact grower with mauve buds which open to reveal tubular pink flowers highlighted with a kiss of gold. (Mezitt hyb., Weston Nurseries intro., Weston reg. 1987).

'Pauline Bralit' (fortunei ssp. fortunei x catawbiense low white form). 5', -10ºF, M, 3/4/4. An interesting blend of red, pink, white and fragrance! Buds of dark red open white but retain a slight pink edge on two upper lobes, accented by orange rays emanating from the throat. It's a winner! (Mezitt 1958, Weston intro. 1965, reg. 1963).

'Paul Lincke' ('Glamour' x strigillosum). 4', 5ºF, E, 4/3-4/3-4. Medium sized, deep green leaves frame bell-shaped bright red flowers held in a tight sturdy truss. (Seabrook 1963).

'Paul R. Bosley' (fortunei ssp. fortunei x catawbiense). 4', 0ºF, M, -/-/-. The large foliage is dark green and recurved. It densely covers the compact, upright plant. Large trusses are composed of medium pink flowers, each having a red blotch. (Paul Bosley, Sr.).

'Paul Vossberg' (maximum x thomsonii). 4', -10ºF, L, 3-4/4/4. R. thomsonii predominates with cardinal red flowers enhanced by a very dark blotch. The plant is rounded and as wide as tall. (Vossberg hyb. about 1960, Knippenberg intro. 1975, reg. 1984).

'Pawhuska' (['Palmer' x 'Loderi King George'] x 'Madame Masson'). 5', -5ºF, ML, 4/4/4. In the language of the Osage Indian, 'Pawhuska' means "white hair" and it fits beautifully. Large, glossy foliage clothes this exquisite hybrid without fail. Round, full trusses of very white flowers have a soft ray of yellow shooting out of the center and up the dorsal lobe. Very attractive. (Bowhan before 1980).

'Peace' (rigidum var. album x concatenans). 3', -10ºF, EM, 4/3/3-4. Lax trusses of nodding bells form perfect circles at the tops of the upright stems. (Aberconway hyb. 1934, intro 1946) A.M. 1946.

'Peach Blend' (keiskei x mucronulatum 'Cornell Pink'). 4', -5ºF, E, -/-/-. A small leaved selection displaying pink flowers with centers of yellow. (Weston Nurseries intro.).

'Peaches and Cream' (['Nereid' x fortunei ssp. fortunei] x 'Russell Harmon'). 6', -10ºF, ML, -/-/-. Soft combinations of pink and yellow converge in the throat with an accent of deep red spots in a yellow field. (Leach hyb., Pride intro. 1970). see 'Peach Surprise'.

'Peach Lady' ('Nereid' x fortunei ssp. discolor). 4', -5ºF, ML, 3/3/3. Great name. Peach colored flowers are edged in light rose and even have a yellowish eye. The only thing missing is fuzz. A good plant for that hot, sunny location. (Lancaster 1958).

'Peach Nugget' ('Vulcan' x 'Sun Devil'). 3', 5ºF, M, -/-/-. A low, rounded plant, densely covered in narrow foliage. Unusually shaped flowers are a soft pastel peach. (Lansing Bulgin intro.).

'Peach Pleasure' (parentage unknown). 5', -10ºF, EM, -/-/-. This hybrid has compact habit and is covered with glossy, bright green foliage. Pink buds open to expose light yellow flowers which have an orange flare, resulting in a truss with a peach glow. (Sold by Roslyn Nursery 1994).

'Peach Satin' (['Belvedere' x 'Jasper'] x 'Mary Drennen'). 4', 0ºF, L, 4/4/4. Apricot flowers maintain an aura of orange throughout the life of the bloom, looking like a pastel painting. Leaves are heavily textured with deep veining. (Larson hyb., Clint Smith intro. before 1990).

'Peach Surprise' ([{'Jalisco' x 'Loderi'} x decorum] x ['Dot' x 'Fawn']). 5', -5ºF, M, 4/4/4. Peachy, creamy flowers profusely cover this medium to large plant. It is not unusual for it to have multiple buds on each stem, each producing masses of flowers. The bud scales are an attractive red and the buds develop to a very large size early in the fall, as if to say "I can't wait until spring to flower". The foliage is an interesting olive green and is smooth and shiny. This has also been sold under the name of 'Peaches and Cream'. (Greer 1988).

'**Pearce's American Beauty**' (possibly 'Mrs. C. S. Sargent' x 'Dr. H. C. Dresselhuys'). 6', 0ºF, VL, 4/4/-. Deep beet red flowers, with yellow green spotting concentrated at the center, are held in flat, ball shaped trusses of 18. (Pearce intro. about 1938, Watson reintro. & reg. 1983).

'**Pearce's Treasure**' (parentage unknown). 1', -5ºF, M, 3/4/4. The low and spreading habit make this a nice groundcover. Small, rounded leaves hide the stretching branches on which delicate red flowers are produced. (Sold by Hammond 1994).

'**Pearl Diver**' ('Ice Cream' x 'Moser's Maroon'). 4', -10ºF, M, -/-/-. Pale pink, frilly flowers have yellow spotting in the throat. (George, Hydon Nurseries 1965).

'**Peekaboo**' (['Carmen' x 'Moonstone'] x *elliottii*). 2', -5ºF, EM, 3/4/3-4. Here is a cute dwarf red from the Whitney collection. The lovely rounded leaves are spring green. (Whitney not registered).

'**Peeping Tom**' (*wardii* x 'Mrs. Furnivall'). 4-5', 0ºF, M, 4/3-4/3. The narrow leaves are about 3" long. Flowers are white, with a deep purple blotch, to 2 1/2" across, held in a compact truss of up to 12. (Wright Sr. & Jr. 1965).

'**Peggy Bannier**' (unknown x 'Antoon van Welie'). 5', -5ºF, M, 4/3/3. Rose colored flowers stand tall in large, pyramidal trusses of up to 22 flowers per truss. The vigorous plant has light green foliage. (van Nes reg. 1961) A.M. 1960.

'**Peggy Zabel**' (parentage unknown). 6', -5ºF, EM, -/-/-. This upright grower has attractive foliage which appears tinged with bronze when new. Fragrant flowers are creamy yellow and held in ball-shaped trusses. (Bohle, Jim & Cannon, Cliff hyb., Briggs Nursery reg. 1990).

'**Peking**' ([*catawbiense* var. *album* x 'Hawk' Group] x ['LaBar's White' x 'Crest']). 5', -15ºF, ML, -/-/-. Leaves are medium sized. Brilliant green-yellow flowers have darkish red spotting and blotch. The 2 1/2" blooms are held in a 15 flower truss. (Leach 1973).

'**Pematit Cambridge**' (*pemakoense* x 'Blue Tit'). 2', -10ºF, E, 3-4/3-4/3-4. Pale powder pink trusses abound on this prolific bloomer. Leaves are 1" long and very deep green. (Reuthe reg. 1981) H.C. 1981.

'**Pematit Oxford**' (*pemakoense* x 'Blue Tit'). 18", -10ºF, E, 3-4/3-4/3-4. Deeper purplish pink flowers appear on a plant slightly smaller than 'Cambridge'. (Reuthe about 1980).

'**Penelope**' (*griersonianum* x 'Dragonfly'). 4', 0ºF, VL, -/-/-. Scarlet red flowers with dark spots are framed by very attractive dark green foliage. (Waterer, Sons & Crisp 1935, Rothschild intro. 1950).

'**Penheale Blue**' (*concinnum* var. *pseudoyanthinum* x *russatum*). 4', 0ºF, EM, -/-/-. A vigorous growing plant with growth that is more wide than tall. Small foliage is dark green, turning reddish bronze in winter. Small, deep violet blue flowers are tightly held in compact trusses of twenty. (Lt. Col. N.R. Colville reg. 1975) A.M. 1974, F.C.C. 1981.

'**Penjerrick**' g. (*campylocarpum* var. *elatum* x *griffithianum*). 6', 15ºF, EM, 4/3/3. Long, medium green leaves are held on an upright plant. Tubular bell-shaped flowers of heavy substance are white, soft yellow, or pink in a loose truss. (S. Smith) A.M. 1923.

'**Pennywise**' ('Mars' x *yakushimanum* 'Koichiro Wada'). 4', -5ºF, ML, -/-/-. Foliage is medium to large. Crimson rose colored blooms, up to 2" across, are carried in a ball-shaped truss of up to 17. (Reese 1977).

'**Peppermint Stick**' ('Moser's Maroon' x *yakushimanum*). 30", 0ºF, ML, -/-/-. Leaves are rather long and narrow. White flowers are edged red. They grow to 2 1/2" and sport white, star-shaped throat blotches with yellowish brown spotting. They are held in a 21-flower truss. (Lancaster, McGuire 1973) C.A. 1974.

'**Pepperpot**' ('Goldbug' x unnamed orange Lem hybrid). 3', 5ºF, EM, 4/3-4/3-4. Foliage is small to medium. Small yellow flowers, to 1 1/2", are generously spotted with red inside, less outside. The blooms are carried in a lax truss of up to 10. (Elliott 1977).

'**Pera**' (*pemakoense* x *racemosum*). 1', -5ºF, E, 3/3-4/4. Good, vigorous plant habit, compact and twiggy. Small leaves are oblong and rounded. Prolific blooms, to 1 1/2" wide, are lilac pink, and held in groups up to 6 in a flat top truss. (Lem before 1958).

'**Percy Wiseman**' (*yakushimanum* x 'Fabia Tangerine' selfed). 3', -10ºF, M, 4/4/4. Compact plant with dark green foliage. Trusses are formed of peach-yellow flowers which gently fade to white. (J. Waterer, Sons & Crisp 1970) H.C. 1977.

'**Perdita**' (*souliei* x 'Lady Bessborough'). 5', -5ºF, M, 3-4/4/3-4. This delightful hybrid is a clone of 'Halcyone'. The plant is well formed and flowers generously, covering itself with graceful flat-topped trusses. Flowers are pastel pink, cup-like, and wide open. The influence of *souliei* is apparent. (Rothschild) A.M. 1948.

'**Perfectly Pink**' ('Babylon' x unknown). 6', -5ºF, E, 4-5/4/3. Gigantic trusses of soft, perfect pink are enhanced by a ring of deep maroon red in the center. The edges of the flowers roll back making a beautiful truss. The glossy leaves are up to 10" long, forming a ring of excellent foliage under the delightful trusses. Very heavy stems are strong enough to support the weighty trusses. (Greer 1988).

'**Perfume**' (*fortunei* ssp. *fortunei* x unknown). 5', 0ºF, M, 3-4/ 3-4/4. Spicy fragrance fills the air when this beauty is in flower. Large, lax trusses are light pink with faint red spotting. Some shade required for best performance. (Whitney, Sather intro. 1986).

'**Persia**' ('Mrs. Furnivall' x *catawbiense* var. *album*). 5', -20ºF, ML, 4/4/3. Reddish purple flowers have bold, yellow-green spotting. It is a free flowering and a nicely shaped plant, almost conical in appearance. (Leach 1953, intro. 1975, reg. 1983).

'**Peste's Fire Light**' ('C.I.S.' x 'Fabia'). 3', 0ºF, M, -/-/-. An upright grower with a rounded habit, covered by shiny, olive green foliage. Strong red buds open to light yellowish pink flowers which have red spotting. The blooms have wavy margins, and form lax trusses. (F. Peste hyb. 1975, Sharon Peste Johnston reg. 1986).

'**Peter Alan**' (['Blue Peter' x 'Purple Splendour'] x 'Blue Perfecta'). 4.5', 0ºF, M, 4/4. Glossy, deep green foliage densely covers this vigorous grower. The broad, upright plant has purplish blue flowers which are accented with a darker eye. (Peter Girard hyb. 1972, intro. 1977) "Best Blue" award 1982, Great Lakes Chapter, ARS.

'**Peter Behring**' ('Nova Zembla' x *yakushimanum* 'Mist Maiden'). 3', -25ºF, L, -/-/-. A compact plant with small, narrow, elliptical foliage which displays golden brown indumentum. Funnel shaped flowers of light magenta have rosy red accents on the outer petals, and deep greenish yellow spotting inside. Ball-shaped trusses are formed by groups of 14 blooms. (Rudy Behring 1972, reg. 1986).

'**Peter Faulk**' (*strigillosum* x unknown). 3', 10ºF, VE, 4/3/3. An early, vibrant red bloomer. The long, slender leaves are covered with hairs and indumentum. One of the nicer *R. strigillosum* hybrids. (Faulk hyb. before 1950, Hanson raised, Johnson reg. 1981).

'Peter Koster' ('George Hardy' x 'Doncaster' hybrid). 5', -5ºF, ML, 2/3/3. Foliage is flat. Magenta red flowers with lighter shade on edges form a good solid truss. (M. Koster & Sons 1909).

'Peter Tigerstedt' (brachycarpum ssp. tigerstedtii x catawbiense album 'Glass'). 6', -25ºF, ML-L, -/-/-. White flowers with violet freckles are held above dark green foliage on this upright and spreading hybrid. (Marjatta Uosukainen, Finland).

'Peter Vermuelen' ('Scintillation' x 'America'). 4', -25ºF, M, -/-/-. Strong stems support shiny, deep green foliage on a plant of mounded habit. Perky pink flowers are held in ball shaped trusses. (Vermeulen).

'Phalarope' (pemakoense x davidsonianum). 3', -10ºF, E, 3/3/4. A superior, easy to grow plant with soft orchid pink blooms. (Cox 1968) P.C. 1968, A.M. 1983.

'Pheasant Tail' ([eriogynum hybrid x 'Fabia'] x [yakushimanum x 'Britannia']). 3', -5ºF, -/-/-. Pink flowers with a lighter pink center. (J. Waterer, Son & Crisp 1975).

'Phipps' Yellow' (parentage unknown, believed to be a 'Golden Star' hybrid). 4', -5ºF, M, -/-/-. Also sold under the name 'Phipps' 32', this mounding plant produces strong yellow flowers. The shiny foliage is light green and nicely accents the richly colored blooms. (Phipps, Woodard).

'Phyllis Ballard' ('Nereid' x fortunei ssp. discolor). 5', -5ºF, L-VL, 3/3/3. Each lawn green leaf is highlighted by a yellow midvein and leaf stem. Exceptionally late, bronzy orange flowers are worth the wait. (Ostbo before 1958) P.A. 1956.

'Phyllis Korn' ('Diane' x 'Gomer Waterer'). 5', -15ºF, M, 4/4/4. Upright, well branched plant, flowers white with currant red blotches. Excellent ratings, excellent plant! Synonym, 'Karl Korn'. (Korn 1969, Shrauger 1981).

'Pia Lehmann' (spinuliferum x cubittii). 4', 15ºF, EM, -/-/-. Flowers, 4 to a truss, are pale yellow fading white. The petal margins are reddish and the flower is spotted pink and yellow in the throat. (George 1964, Hydon Nurseries 1978).

'Piccadilly' ('Loderi King George' x 'Socrianum'). 5', 0ºF, ML, -/-/-. Soft magenta flowers are of good size and substance. (Stevenson, Hydon Nurseries 1976).

'Pickering' (['Catalgla' x {fortunei ssp. fortunei x campylocarpum}] x unknown). 6', -5ºF, ML, -/-/-. Leaves are medium to large. Generous-sized 3" flowers are cream-flushed-pink, with a clear yellow throat. They are held in a 10-flower truss. (Herbert hyb. 1953, reg. 1977).

'Pieces of Eight' ('Virginia Richards' x unknown). 5', 0ºF, EM, -/-/-. Flowers are large, to 4 1/2" across, 7 lobed and scented. The yellow blooms are spotted light orange on 3 dorsal lobes, and are held in a 10 flower truss. Leaves are medium to large. (Frederick 1977).

'Pieces of Gold' (parentage unknown). 3', 0ºF, EM, -/-/-. Foliage is large. Fragrant, 7-lobed flowers, to 4" across, are ivory colored, with chartreuse centers and brown spotting on the dorsal lobe. The blooms are carried in a rounded truss of up to 10. (Frederick 1977).

'Pikeland' (keiskei x campylogynum). 1', -5ºF, EM, -/-/-. Small leaves and blooms which are only 1 1/4" across. The flowers are light pink, with deeper pink edges and spots. Trusses are held at branch tips in groups of 6, each containing as many as 7 flowers. (Herbert 1976).

'Pilgrim' (fortunei ssp. fortunei x 'Gill's Triumph'). 5', -5ºF, M, 4/4/3. This rapid growing plant has a sturdy and open-growing habit and is clothed with long, narrow dark green foliage. Flowers are huge, clear pink, sparsely marked darker and held in large rounded truss. (Johnston before 1925) A.M. 1926.

'Pillar' (unknown lepidote). 4', -15ºF, EM, -/-/-. A small leaved hybrid with an upright growth habit, the appearance otherwise resembles 'PJM'. (Weston Nurseries intro.)

'Pillow Party' (minus var. minus Carolinianum Group x dauricum) 3', -25ºF, E, 3/3/3. This plant lavishly displays small and charming blushed white blooms. It is a compact and restrained plant that exhibits beautiful jade green foliage. (Briggs 1988).

'Pineapple Delight' ('Hotei' x 'Brandt's Tropicana'). 3', 0ºF, M, 5/4/3-4. Funnel-shaped, yellow flowers with a slight buff colored cast are held in rounded trusses. Dark green foliage covers this plant which achieves a rounded form, equally as wide as tall. (Brockenbrough hyb. 1971, Kesterson intro., reg. 1983).

'Pink Bountiful' ('Essex Scarlet' x williamsianum). 3', 0ºF, M, 4/4/4. A plant with vigorous, compact habit, covered with leaves of medium matte green. Freely produced, campanulate-shaped flowers are wine paling toward center and in throat. (Hobbie, LeFeber intro. 1974, Slocock Nurseries 1976) H.C. 1974, A.M. 1975.

'Pink Cameo' ('Boule de Neige' x red catawbiense hybrid). 5', -20ºF, EM, 3/3/3. Hardiness is an outstanding attribute of this good foliaged Shammarello hybrid. The flowers are a lovely flesh pink with a deeper pinkish blotch. (Shammarello intro. 1958).

'Pink Cherub' (yakushimanum x 'Doncaster'). 3', -5ºF, M, 4/4/4. Dainty rose pink flowers have fuchsia edges and lighter, almost white, centers. The plant is very floriferous, has rounded habit and dull, dark green leaves. (Waterer, Sons & Crisp 1968) A.M. 1968.

'Pink Cloud' (parentage unknown). 5', -10ºF, EM, -/-/-. Leaves are medium sized. Ruffled, scented blooms, to 3 1/2" wide, are medium pink with a dull yellow blotch, and are held in a 16 flower ball truss. (Whitney before 1960, Sather 1976).

'Pink Drift' (calostrotum x scintillans). 18", -10ºF, EM, 4/4/3. This is a super-cute little dwarf, accented with small, strongly aromatic, cinnamon-bronze foliage. Pinkish plum flowers are freely produced in neat clusters. (H. White, Sunningdale Nursery 1955).

'Pink Flair' (red catawbiense hybrid x 'Boule de Neige'). 5', -20ºF, M, 3/3/3. Shammarello hybrids are known for hardiness. These pastel pink flowers have conspicuous red blotches. Leathery, dark green foliage is displayed on a compact, bushy plant. (Shammarello 1972).

'Pink Flourish' ('Catalgla' x [{decorum x griffithianum} x catawbiense hybrid]). 3', -25ºF, M, 3/3/3. Leaves are medium to large. Pale pink flowers, to 3 1/2" wide, are colored deeper pink on outside and edges, and accented with a small yellow brown blotch. They are carried in a 15 flower truss. (Leach 1960).

'Pink Fluff' (racemosum x davidsonianum). 3', 5ºF, EM, 4/3/3. This rivals the very best of the davidsonianums for flower color. Flowers open light pink and turn to the clearest deep pink possible. Much like davidsonianum 'Ruth Lyons' only more compact in growth. Very hard to propagate. Flowers profusely. (Greer 1979).

'Pink Fondant' (['Mars' x 'Catalgla'] x wardii). 5', -15ºF, ML, 4/3/-. Attractive habit with dark green, recurved foliage. Light, rose pink flowers are held in upright trusses. (Gable hyb., Pride intro. 1970).

'Pink Frosting' (*catawbiense* var. *album* x *yakushimanum* 'Koichiro Wada'). 2', -15ºF, M, 4/4/4. Foliage is medium sized with a thin indumentum, covering a plant of compact habit which spreads to a width greater than its height. 2" wide flowers are light pink, darker on outside, held in a truss up to 14. (Leach 1963).

'Pink Globe' (*catawbiense* Gable's red selection x [*griersonianum* x *fortunei* ssp. *fortunei*]). 6', -15ºF, ML, -/-/-. Medium sized foliage covers this upright growing plant. 3 1/2" rosy pink flowers have a small red blotch, held in a 12 flower truss. (Nearing 1973).

'Pinkie Price' (['Meadowbrook' x *fortunei* ssp. *fortunei*, or reverse] x sibling of same cross). 6', -10ºF, ML, -/-/-. Foliage is medium sized. Flowers, up to 3 3/4" across, are deep pink, fading outward to white, with 2 green blotches, and held in a truss up to 10. (Phipps 1973).

'Pink Jeans' (sport of 'Jean Marie de Montague'). 4', -5ºF, EM, 4/4/4. The buds are red opening to a strong purplish red at the rim, then shading to yellow-white at the center. There is strong red spotting on the ventral half and a rose red star in the throat. This attractive flower is held in groups of 8-10 to form a domed truss which is supported by dark green foliage. A handsome plant. (Briggs intro. 1984, reg. 1989).

'Pink Magic' (*minus* var. *chapmanii* x *ciliatum* pink form). 2', -10ºF, M, -/-/-. Forming a shrubby mound, twice as wide as it is high, this plant is densely covered with attractive, small glossy green leaves. Large quantities of purplish pink, tube shaped flowers with speckled brown throats are produced on the spreading limbs, creating a magical display. (Dr. A.E. Kehr 1994).

'Pink Mist' (*racemosum* hybrid). 18", 0ºF, M, 3/3/-. A dwarf selection with red stems supporting small green foliage. Tiny, two-toned flowers are pink and white creating a muted effect. (sold by Kelleygreen 1993).

'Pink Parasol' (selected seedling of *yakushimanum*). 30", -15ºF, EM, 4/4/3-4. Growth habit and foliage are typical of species. White flowers open from vibrant deep purplish pink buds. (Leach 1968).

'Pink Pearl' ('George Hardy' x 'Broughtonii'). 6', -5ºF, M, 3/3/3. The standard to which all pinks must be judged. A strong growing plant with large conical trusses holding soft pink blooms which pale to blush at the base. A parent of many hybrids, this plant continued to earn awards for over half a century. (J. Waterer) A.M. 1897, F.C.C. 1900, A.G.M. 1952.

'Pink Pebble' (*callimorphum* x *williamsianum*). 3', -5ºF, M, 3/3/3. Dainty pale pink bells are companion to lovely, rounded leaves. (Gen. Harrison reg. 1954) A.M. 1975.

'Pink Perfection' (parentage unknown, believed to be *griffithianum* hybrid or 'Pink Pearl' x 'Cynthia'). 5', 0ºF, ML, -/-/-. Not to be confused with a vireya of the same name. This hybrid has pale pink flowers, tinged lilac, in a rather open truss. Foliage is supported by reddish petioles on a leggy bush. (R. Gill, Cornwall before 1900).

'Pink Petticoats' ('Jan Dekens' x 'Britannia'). 5', -5ºF, EM, 4/3/2-3. Huge, frilly, rose trusses are of utmost perfection. Its downward curling leaves are longer than wide and are an attractive medium green. (Lofthouse 1966) C.A. 1971.

'Pink Sherbet' (*yakushimanum* (Exbury form) x unknown). 3', -5ºF, M, -/-/-. Formerly called 'Pink Ice'. Reddish pink flowers, which fade to almost white, are held in ball-shaped trusses. Plant habit is excellent, like most "yak" hybrids, rounded, very full and densely covered with elliptical foliage which exhibits the attractive woolly indumentum underneath. (Larson 1969, Davis reg. 1983).

'Pink Snowflakes' (*racemosum* x *moupinense*). 2', 0ºF, E, 4/4/3. 'Pink Snowflakes' is a little plant with shining, glossy green leaves and beautiful bright red flower buds that make the plant extra attractive all winter. In early spring the plant is covered with light pastel pink to white flowers, which have touches of deep pink for added interest. Each flower has a spot of red purple in the throat. The new foliage is bronze red. (Scott 1968).

'Pink Tipp' (unknown elepidote rhododendron). 5', -10ºF, M-ML, -/-/-. This hardy plant has petite white flowers, tipped pink, and a compact habit. (Pride, sold by Carlson 1994).

'Pink Tufett' (*yakushimanum* 'Koichiro Wada' x 'Vanessa' FCC). 2.5', 0ºF, M, -/-/-. Medium pink, bell shaped flowers open from rose red buds. Medium green foliage, which exhibits a slight copper indumentum underneath, covers this dense, compact plant that is handsomely branched. (Bovee before 1965).

'Pink Twins' (*catawbiense* red x *haematodes* hybrid). 4', -15ºF, ML, 4/3/3-4. Trusses hold 15 uniquely ruffled, shrimp pink, hose-in-hose flowers. Emerald green leaves are accented by yellow petioles, as they cover this plant which reaches a width greater than its height. (Gable 1935, Gable Study Group reg. 1991).

'Pink Walloper' ('Anna' x 'Marinus Koster'). 6', -5ºF, M, 4-5/4-5/4-5. Huge satin pink trusses make a thrilling display. Large, deep green leaves with reddish petioles cover this sturdy plant. Its new growth stems are often larger than a finger; they have to be large to hold the weight of its fabulous trusses! Dr. Frank Mossman discovered this hybrid of Halfdan Lem's during one of his many trips to visit Mr. Lem. 'Pink Walloper' and 'Lem's Monarch' are the same plant. (Lem before 1960).

'Pinnacle' (pink *catawbiense* hybrid x pink *catawbiense* hybrid). 6', -20ºF, M-ML, 4/3/3. Plant habit and form are excellent, with good foliage. Vibrant pink, 2" flowers with delicate citron-yellow blotch are carried in profuse cone-shaped trusses. (Shammarello 1955).

'Pioneer' ('Conemaugh' x *mucronulatum*). 4-5', -25ºF, VE, 4/3-4/4. There is disagreement on the parentage of this rhododendron. It can be found listed as above, as *racemosum* x *mucronulatum* (which is 'Conemaugh'), and as 'Conemaugh' x unknown. I guess the choice of parentage you want to accept is up to you! 'Pioneer' is an upright growing, multiple stemmed plant. Its small leaves are semi-deciduous to deciduous. The heavy bloom of rose pink flowers are truly enjoyed during its early blooming period. Since there is another plant named by Aberconway as 'Pioneer', this plant should properly be known as 'Gable's Pioneer'. (Gable before 1946, not registered).

'Pioneer Silvery Pink' ('Pioneer' x unknown). 4', -20ºF, E, -/-/-. A more clear pink than 'Pioneer' (Gable), this plant blooms 2 weeks later. The autumn foliage is red on this heat tolerant hybrid. (Hoogendoorn before 1985).

'Pipaluk' ('Dr. Stocker' x *williamsianum*). 3', -10ºF, E, -/-/-. Flowers quite readily with pink bells fading to white when fully open. (Gen. Harrison 1968).

'Pipit' (*lowndesii* x *lepidotum*). 1', 0ºF, EM, 3-4/3/1. Small flat faced flowers are a light creamy pink. Very small leaves. A natural occurring hybrid which is difficult to grow, but worth the effort. (Cox 1970).

'Pirouette' (*yakushimanum* 'Koichiro Wada' x 'Pink Petticoats'). 4', -10ºF, M, 4/4/4. Large ball-shaped trusses of up to 28 flowers appear rose in bud but open to white, delicately flecked pink. Compact plant habit with good foliage. (Lofthouse 1973).

'PJM' (*minus* var. *minus* Carolinianum Group x *dauricum*). 4', -25°F, E, 4/4/4. This hybrid is cold hardy as well as tolerant of heat and sun. Its small, rounded leaves are green during the summer and mahogany colored in winter. 'PJM's early, bright lavender pink flowers are beautiful against its dark colored winter foliage. (E. V. Mezitt hyb. before 1960, Weston Nurseries intro.) P.C. 1967, A.M. 1972.

'PJM Checkmate' (same as above). This is the most dwarf form of the available 'PJM' clones. (Weston Nurseries).

'PJM Compact' (as above). The same cheery flowers on a more compact growing habit.

'PJM Elite' (as above). Flowers are slightly deeper pink than 'PJM.' (E. Mezitt 1939, Weston Nurseries 1987).

'PJM-K' (as above). An attractive habit with the same lavender-pink flowers. (Knuttel Nursery).

'PJM Regal' (as above). Strong lavender flowers bloom a little earlier than 'Elite'. (E. Mezitt 1939, Weston Nurseries 1987).

'PJM Victor' (as above). This form has deep lavender flowers and in the fall and winter it presents even darker purple foliage than other 'PJM' forms. (E. Mezitt 1939, Weston Nurseries 1987).

'Platinum Pearl' ('Trude Webster' x *fortunei* ssp. *discolor*). 6', -10°F, ML, 4/4/4. Reports from California and Georgia stated that it stood up to cold and other adverse conditions without fail. It is a strong growing plant that forms huge flower buds early in the fall. Each pearl pink flower is made more showy by a dark rose blotch at the base of the flower. The foliage is large, leek green, and appears on sturdy stems that are able to hold up those huge 'pearlescent' trusses. Best grown in light shade where the foliage develops to its utmost perfection. (Greer 1988).

'Pleasant Dream' (parentage unknown). 6', 0°F, L, 3/3/3-4. Foliage is medium to large. Ruffled flowers are a generous 5" wide, and scented. Color is pink, with a shading of yellow, displaying a little orange blotch. Flowers are held in a 10 flower truss. (Whitney, Sather 1975).

'Plum Beautiful' ('Purple Splendour' x 'A. Bedford'). 5', -5°F, ML, 4/3/3-4. The flowers on this rhododendron are just plain "plum beautiful". They burst forth a delightful plum purple with a deep black-purple flare. Foliage is medium large and glossy green, covering a plant which has attractive habit. (Greer 1988).

'Plum Duff' (unknown Coker cross). 5', -5°F, M?, -/-/-. Dense and bushy, this hybrid has trusses of clear lavender pink, delicately scented flowers. The matte grayish green foliage needs protection from too much direct sun. (sold by Riverwood Gardens 1994).

'Point Defiance' ('Anna' x 'Marinus Koster'). 6', -5°F, M, 5/4-5/4-5. This is a clone from Halfdan Lem's 'Walloper' group. Its large succulent flowers have pink picoteed edges which become lighter pink and finally white in the flower center. (Lem, Point Defiance Rhodo Garden, Tacoma 1970).

'Point Fosdick' (parentage unknown). 4', 0°F, EM, 4/4/4. Bronze colored new foliage is just one appealing thing about this plant. The flowers are an interesting fuchsia-plum that is hard to describe. It grows quite compact and is always attractive. (Larson).

'Polar Bear' (*diaprepes* x *auriculatum*). 6', -5°F, L-VL, 3/3/4. Large, fragrant white flowers have a green throat. The vigorous, heavy growth rapidly creates a large plant. A great garden plant as its icy white flowers appear late and provide a beautiful lily-like aroma! (Stevenson 1926) F.C.C. 1946.

'Polaris' (*yakushimanum* 'Koichiro Wada' x 'Omega'). 3', -15°F, M, 4/4/4. This charmer displays carmine red buds that open to a light fuschia-purple at the flower rim, with colors blending to lighter purple at the center. Very floriferous, even as a young plant. This is a low, compact plant with dense foliage. The leaves are elliptical and very hairy. It is sun and wind tolerant. (H. Hachmann hyb. 1963, G. Stuck reg. 1983).

'Polarnacht' ('Turkana' x 'Purple Splendour'). 3', -10°F, ML, -/-/-. Dark elliptic leaves cover a bush that is almost twice as wide as tall. The funnel-shaped, frilled flowers are beet-root purple and the dorsal lobe is spotted deep red. The flowers are held in trusses of 12-14. (Hachmann hyb. 1976, Stuck reg. 1988).

'Polly Clarke' (['Socrianum' x 'Rima'] x 'Crest'). 5', 5°F, M?, -/-/-. Delicate yellow flowers open from darker buds to form trusses of 10. (George 1964, Hydon Nurseries 1978).

'Polynesian Sunset' (probably a *dichroanthum* hybrid). 5', 0°F, L, 4/2-3/3. Crepe textured, large, tumbling trusses are enjoyed at the end of spring. Shades of orange, peach and apricot are fluidly blended in this bright flower. Medium toned, dense green leaves recurve and twist about, developing an interesting three dimensional form. (Whitney about 1963, Sather reg. 1976).

'Pom Pom' ('Katrina' x 'Lem's Cameo'). 5', 0°F, M, 4-5/4/4. The name describes it well! Each rounded truss is like a large "pom pom" of warm, vibrant rose pink. Since its parents are an apricot and a purple, the resultant color is most beautiful, but hard to describe. Overall it is a vibrant rose pink; yet it has yellow tones in the stamens and throat, as well as some light pink in the center and some purple on the edges. Each flower has a calyx of light pink. And there's more to cheer about: attractive plant habit and luxurient deep green leaves! (Thompson hyb. about 1985, intro. Thompson Nursery 1996).

'Ponticum Variegatum' (a selection of *ponticum*). 4', -15°F, M-ML, 2/4/4. Sometimes called 'Silver Edge'. Distinguished by its variegated foliage, leaves are long and narrow with silvery margins and irregular leaf tips. The flowers are orchid pink. (From England?).

'Pontiyak' (*ponticum* x *yakushimanum*). 3', -5°F, ML, 3/3/4. Rolls Royce, Mercedes, and Cadillac will be in line for their hybrids, too, when they see this one! Compact with a rounded habit, this plant has delicate pink flowers forming flat, small trusses. The foliage has slight indumentum. (sold by Kelleygreen 1994).

'Popacatapetl' ('Elizabeth' x 'Compactum Multiflorum'). 3', -5°F, E, 3/3/3. Bright rose, waxy flowers have darker spotting on the upper lobes. This shrub is bushier and slightly more dwarf than 'Elizabeth'. (Reuthe 1981) H.C. 1981.

'Popeye' ('Lodauric' x 'Purple Splendour'). 6', -10°F, ML, 4/4/3. Trusses are rounded, compact and composed of white flowers with a very prominent dark purple eye. The trusses are neatly surrounded by spinach green leaves. Olive Oyl would be delighted! (Mossman hyb., Greer intro.).

'Porzellan' ('Mrs. J. G. Millais' x *yakushimanum* 'Koichiro Wada'). 3', -10°F, M, 4/4/4. White flowers with a yellow flare decorate this plant. Deep olive green foliage covers a widely branched, rounded bush. (Hachmann 1982).

'**Potlatch**' ('Thor' hybrid). 3', 5ºF, M, 3-4/4/4. Dense, thick foliage with indumentum surrounds very large trusses of bright scarlet flowers. (Clark before 1960).

'**Powder Mill Run**' (*yakushimanum* x 'Mars'). 3', -5ºF, ML, -/-/-. Leaves are large and narrow. Flowers are deep pink, shading to white in the center, and held in a good-sized ball truss of up to 24 blooms. (Bagoly before 1968, Herbert 1976).

'**Powell Glass**' (natural white variant of *catawbiense* from 'Catalgla' seed). 5', -15ºF, M, 3/3/4. This is a fifth generation plant derived from *catawbiense* seed. It is presumed to have stabilized, so that new plants grown from its seed would continue to be white. The foliage is attractive on this vigorous plant. (Amateis 1961).

'**Powerhouse**' (['America' x 'Dr. V. H. Rutgers'] x *maximum*). 4', -20ºF, L, -/-/-. Dark reddish buds open to wavy edged flowers which display blended colors of reddish purple and light purple, accented by visible red veins on the reverse surface. The yellowish green foliage is densely held on the compact plant. (Delp 1993).

'**Praecox**' (*ciliatum* x *dauricum*). 4', -5ºF, E, 3/3/3. Rosy lilac flowers are framed by round, shiny leaves. Upright growth habit. (Davis 1860) Commended 1861, A.G.M. 1926.

'**Prairie Fire**' ('Cornubia' x 'Red Olympia'). 5', 5ºF, M-ML, 3/2-3/3-4. Narrow, dusky green foliage covers this upright growing plant to form a framework for the plentiful, fire-red flowers. Considered to be very heat tolerant. (Korth before 1985).

'**Prairie Gold**' (['Eldorado' x *leucaspis*] x 'Lemon Mist'). 2', 15ºF, E, 4/3/3. Leaves are quite small. Small yellow flowers, to 1 1/2" across, bloom at ends of branches from 3 buds containing 4 blooms each. (Scott 1976).

'**Prawn**' ('Lady Bessborough' x 'Tortoiseshell Wonder'). 5', -5ºF, L, -/-/-. Shrimp pink, lax trusses top this slender, upright plant. (Slocock, Goldsworth Nursery reg. 1966).

'**Prelude**' (*wardii* x *fortunei* ssp. *fortunei*). 5', -5ºF, M, 4/3/3. Buttery primrose yellow trusses grace this worthy hybrid. Its parent, *fortunei* ssp. *fortunei*, gives this plant vigorous growth, and it displays the glossy green foliage of *wardii*. (Rothschild 1942) A.M. 1951.

'**President Lincoln**' (*catawbiense* hybrid). 6', -25ºF, ML, 2/3/3. This hardy, adaptable plant is not to be confused with 'Abraham Lincoln', which is red. Lilac toned lavender-pink flowers with a bronzy blotch form a tight dome shaped truss. (S. Parsons before 1871).

'**President Roosevelt**' (*arboreum* hybrid). 4', 0ºF, EM, 4/4/3. Variegation, visable in both the flower and foliage, is the most predominant feature of 'President Roosevelt.' The frilly truss is red, fading to white in the center, while the green foliage has golden accents along the midrib. Tends to break off easily at the root ball. (Originated in Holland, Mesman [Boskoop] intro. before 1930).

'**Pridenjoy**' ('Lem's Cameo' x 'Kubla Khan'). 4', 0ºF, EM, -/-/-. Large, rounded trusses of soft yellow flowers are held upright above deep green foliage. Each bloom, appearing from a red bud, is gently flushed with pink and highlighted by vivid red spotting on the dorsal lobe. (L. Newcomb hyb. 1979, reg. 1987).

'**Pride of Leonardslee**' (*fortunei* ssp. *fortunei* x *thomsonii*). 6', 0ºF, EM, 3/4/3. Medium green, softly glossy leaves, of medium size, cover a sturdy, upright, rounded plant. Deep pink flowers shade to mauve, in a loose, open-topped truss. Rather slow to set buds. Usually called 'Luscombei' in the U.S.A. (Luscombe 1880, Loder intro.).

'**Pride of Split Rock**' (*racemosum* x unknown). 3', -15ºF, M, -/-/-. While the parentage of this hybrid is uncertain, it is believed to be a hardy form of *racemosum*. Its flowers are bright pink, in racemes. The small leaves are dark mahogany red in winter. (Origin unknown, possibly N.W. Pennsylvania).

'**Prima Donna**' ('Idealist' seedling x 'Jalisco' selfed). 4', 5ºF, M, -/-/-. Chartreuse green flowers with a brown blotch in the throat complement this nice compact plant. (J. Waterer, Sons & Crisp 1970).

'**Prince Camille de Rohan**' (*caucasicum* hybrid). 5', -15ºF, EM, 3/3/4. This has very ruffled flowers which are light pink with a deep reddish-pink blotch. The foliage is slightly twisted and tends to be light green, often with areas of the leaf that are even lighter green. (J. Verschaffelt 1865).

'**Prince of McKenzie**' ('Elizabeth' x 'Earl of Athlone'). 3', -5ºF, EM, -/-/-. Waxy, scarlet red flowers are held in trusses of up to 6. Plant has large, rounded leaves on downward hanging branches. (Phetteplace reg. 1983).

'**Princess Alice**' (*edgeworthii* x *ciliatum*). 3', 15ºF, M, -/-/-. An abundance of long, narrow white flowers with a pink line down the back of each lobe are held above fuzzy, deep green foliage. (Veitch intro. 1862) F.C.C. 1862.

'**Princess Anne**' (*keiskei* x *hanceanum*). 2', -10ºF, EM, 4/4/3. A beautiful yellow flower with a slight greenish cast. Foliage turns various shades of bronze depending on the weather. Compact plant habit. Was also known as 'Golden Fleece'. (Reuthe 1974).

'**Princess Elizabeth**' ('Bagshot Ruby' hybrid). 6', -15ºF, ML, 3/3/4. A large growing hybrid with deep crimson red flowers. The trusses are tight and tall, making a showy flower. Plant is vigorous, with large bullate, green leaves. (Waterer, Sons & Crisp 1928) A.M. 1933.

'**Princess Juliana**' (*griffithianum* hybrid). 6', 5ºF, EM, 3/3/3. While this hybrid is inclined to fertilizer sensitivity, it is otherwise vigorous and grows to form a wide plant. Soft rose pink flowers, fading to white, are held in a tight truss. (Otto Schultz 1890, Van Nos intro. 1896) A.M. 1910.

'**Princess Mary of Cambridge**' (unknown, but contains *catawbiense*). 5', -25ºF, ML, 3/3/4. This plant has beautiful flowers which have rose pink edges and a white center. It is fairly rapid growing and is very hardy. The plant that was commonly grown in the U.S. as 'Madame Wagner' is actually 'Princess Mary of Cambridge'. (Waterer before 1871).

'**Privot**' (probably the same parentage as 'Mary Fleming'). 3', -15ºF, EM, -/-/-. This hybrid could be a twin to 'Mary Fleming', but it is slightly different. It produces masses of small, salmon pink, cream and white flowers and it has a compact habit. (sold by Briggs about 1994).

'**Prize**' ('Boule de Neige' x red *catawbiense* seedling). 4', -20ºF, ML, 3/2/3-4. Leaves are medium sized and narrow. Clear shrimp-colored pink blooms, to 2" across, with a yellow brown blotch, are carried in a globular truss. (Shammarello 1955).

'**Prodigal's Return**' (parentage unknown). 5', -5ºF, M, 3-4/3-4/3-4. Good, clear, deep yellow flowers. Medium long shiny green foliage. (Nelson, not registered).

'**Professor Amateis**' ('Everestianum' x 'Van Nes Sensation'). 3', -15ºF, ML, -/-/-. The rounded habit plant is covered with medium large foliage. Soft-pink, open bell-shaped flowers are held in a neat mid-sized truss. (Amateis, Baldsiefen reg. 1971).

'Professor Hugo de Vries' ('Pink Pearl' x 'Doncaster'). 5', -5ºF, ML, 3-4/3/3. A hybrid which is much like the familiar and beautiful 'Pink Pearl' except that it is a darker shade of pink. The conical trusses hold funnel shaped, rosy flowers which have a reddish brown ray. The foliage is good. (L. J. Endtz & Co.).

'Professor J. H. Zaayer' ('Pink Pearl' x red *catawbiense* hybrid). 5', -5ºF, ML, 3/2/3. Large, light green, twisted leaves, on a vigorous, sprawling plant. Light red flowers form a dome-shaped truss. (L. J. Endtz & Co.).

Progres' (parentage unknown, may be *caucasicum* hybrid). 4', -10ºF, VE, -/-/-. Trusses are composed of 9-12 flowers, light to darker rose pink with a purple blotch. This broad, compact plant has dark foliage. Synonym, 'Le Progres'. (Sold in Denmark, Germany, U.K., origin unknown).

'Promise of Spring' (*strigillosum* x *arboreum*). 5', 5ºF, VE-E, 4/4/3-4. Fluorescent rose flowers are exhibited on a plant well clothed with leaves which are much longer than wide. Showy early color. (Lofthouse 1973).

'Prostigiatum' (*saluenense* ssp. *chameunum* Prostratum Group x *fastigiatum*). 6", -5ºF, EM, 4/4/3. Very slow growing, this dwarf plant has a low growing habit which makes it ideal for the rock garden. Deep purple flowers are held on erect stems. (E. J. P. Magor hyb. 1916, intro. 1924) A.M. 1924.

'Psyche' (*fortunei ssp. fortunei* 'Sir Charles Butler' x *williamsianum*). 3', -10ºF, EM, 3- 4/4/3-4. Pale pink flowers are held on a low growing, attractive plant. (Hobbie 1950).

'Ptarmigan' (*leucaspis* x *microleucum*). 1', -5ºF, EM, 4-5/3-4/3. Showy, pure white, small flowers cover this delicately branched plant. Its leaves, flowers and habit are nicely in scale to one another. 'Ptarmigan' will develop naturally into a finely textured mound, though it grows openly when very young. (Cox 1965) F.C.C. 1965.

'Puccini' (['Furnivall's Daughter' x 'Simona'] x 'King Tut'). 5', -10ºF, L, -/-/-. Funnel shaped flowers are light purple with a conspicuous blotch of orange-yellow to red. This hybrid has an erect, compact plant habit and is covered with mid green, glossy foliage, convex with brown hairs underneath. (H. Hachmann hyb. 1979, Stuck reg. 1991).

'Puget Sound' ('Loderi King George' x 'Van Nes Sensation'). 6', -5ºF, M, 4/4/4. Fragrant, large, pink ruffled flowers are loosely held atop this majestic rhododendron. Thick, glossy, deep green leaves attached to rosy leaf stems ornately clothe this vigorous growing plant. (Clark before 1958).

'Puncta' (*ferrugineum* x *minus* var. *minus*). 2', -15ºF, L, 2/3/3. Parentage is uncertain. Small clusters of late blooming pink flowers are partially concealed by new foliage which is scaly and aromatic. This plant is much like 'Wilsonii'. (Origin unknown, before 1835).

'Punctatum' This name has been used for several plants. Probably it has been used most often for the species plant that is still occasionally seen under the name *R. minus*, although it is actually the hybrid 'Myrtifolium'.

'Purest' (unknown). 2', -20ºF, EM, 4/3/3. Profuse white flowers, erect growth habit and dark green leaves yeild a very attractive plant. (Weston Nurseries intro. before 1980).

'Purple Elegans' (*ponticum* hybrid). 5-6', -15ºF, ML, 3/3/4. A rapid growing, dense plant with shiny, bright green foliage. It would make a great divider or hedge. Showy red purple flowers of good substance will stand sun and tough conditions. (Not registered).

'Purple Emperor' ('Moser's Maroon' x unknown). 6', -5ºF, ML, 2/2/3. Rich, dark red purple flowers have black spots on the upper petal. Plant habit is open. (Knap Hill Nursery intro. 1953) A.M. 1953.

'Purple Fuchsia' ('Mars' x 'Princess Elizabeth'). 4', -5ºF, M, -/-/-. Globe shaped trusses have fuchsia purple flowers with a darker eye. Foliage is medium green on this upright, well-branched plant. (Stephens before 1990).

'Purple Gem' (*fastigiatum* x *minus* var. *minus* Carolinianum Group). 2', -25ºF, EM, 3/4/3. A sister to 'Ramapo' which it resembles in foliage. However, the the leaves are slightly more rust colored and beautiful blue tones appear in the new growth. The flowers are deeper purple violet than 'Ramapo'. (Hardgrove 1958).

'Purple Heart' (unnamed hybrid x 'Purple Splendour'). 5', -5ºF, M, -/-/-. Trusses of violet flowers have a yellow-green blotch and markings. (J. Waterer, Sons & Crisp 1971).

'Purple Imp' (*rupicola* hybrid). 2', -15ºF, E, -/-/-. This vigorous grower has a spreading habit. It has violet flowers and glossy leaves, which are heat tolerant. (Nearing before 1960).

'Purple Lace' ('Britannia' x 'Purple Splendour'). 5', -5ºF, ML, 4/4/4. Large purple trusses have lacy, wavy edges. Deep, glossy green foliage is rough textured and very attractive. (From Boskoop via England).

'Purple Splendour' (*ponticum* hybrid). 5', -5ºF, ML, 4/3/3. Still the darkest purple, the black blotch makes it look even darker. Domed-trusses of wavy edged flowers sit above dense, deep green foliage. Does well in either sun or shade, but should be planted where it has good drainage. (A. Waterer before 1900) A.M. 1931.

'Purpureum Elegans' (*catawbiense* hybrid). 5', -25ºF, ML, 2/3/3. Don't let the rating of this plant deter you. While it may not be a 'Trude Webster', it is hardy and adaptable to unfriendly climatic conditions. The flowers are blue purple. It is a good plant with nice foliage. (H. Waterer before 1850).

'Purpureum Grandiflorum' (*catawbiense* hybrid). 5', -20ºF, ML, 2/3/3. Good looking growth habit combines with with large downward curving leaves to create a stately plant. Flowers are medium purple, with a golden yellow-orange blotch. (H. Waterer before 1850).

'Pygmalion' (parentage unknown). 5', -5ºF, ML, 3/2/3. An award winning English hybrid which displays crimson red flowers with a showy black blotch in the center. The plant is clothed with dark olive green foliage. (Waterer, Sons & Crisp) A.M. 1933.

'Pygmy' ('Moonstone' x 'Carmen'). 1', 0ºF, EM-M, 4/3/3. Growth habit is low and widely spreading. Entire plant becomes nearly covered with dark red, bell-shaped flowers in loose trusses. (Skonieczny not registered).

'Pyrex' (*haematodes* x *facetum*). 3', 0ºF, M, 4/3/3. Volatile scarlet, flat topped trusses form on a connoisseur's plant. Very different. (Reuthe 1945).

'Quala-A-Wa-Loo' ('Else Frye' x *johnstoneanum*). 30", 15ºF, E, 4-5/3/3-4. Leaves are fairly small. 3 1/4" flowers are yellow with a red dorsal blotch, held in a smallish 5-flower truss. (Anderson, Braafladt 1979).

'Quasar' (*wardii* x 'Idealist'). 5', 10ºF, EM, -/-/-. Leaves are medium sized. Flowers are clear yellow with a dark red blotch in the throat, to 2 3/4" across, held in truss up to 8. (Short 1978).

'Quaver' (*leucaspis* x *sulfureum*). 3', 10ºF, E, 3/4/3-4. Attractive foliage plant that has woolly, round, deep green leaves. Creamy primrose yellow flowers put on an early display. (Rothschild 1950) A.M. 1968.

'Queen Alice' (*yakushimanum* x 'Alice'). 4', -5ºF, M, 4/4/4. A rounded plant with splendid foliage, silvery when young, it develops to be flat green with light indumentum. Large cherry red buds open to rosy pink flowers. Each bloom in the large truss has a lighter throat with yellow spotting. (Briggs Nursery reg. 1993).

'Queen Anne's' ([*brachycarpum* x *catawbiense*] x unnamed white *fortunei ssp. fortunei* hybrid). 5', 0ºF, EM, 4-5/3-4/3-4. Leaves are on the large side. Pale lavender flowers, fading to white, have interesting stamens which resemble petals. The flowers have no markings at all, and are set in well-shaped trusses of up to 13 flowers. (Skinner 1979).

'Queen Elizabeth II' ('Idealist' x 'Crest'). 5', -10ºF, M, -/-/-. Gigantic clear yellow flowers, almost 5" across, grace this tall growing, statuesque plant. Trusses contain about 12 flowers. (Crown Estate, Windsor 1967) A.M. 1967.

'Queen Mary' ('Marion' x 'Mrs. C. S. Sargent'). 5', -15ºF, M, 3/4/4. Habit is sturdy, with fine glossy foliage having the look of leather. Flowers are a lovely rose pink. (Felix & Dijkhuis, Boskoop 1950) F.C.C. 1948.

'Queen Nefertiti' ('Loderi Venus' x 'Anna'). 5', 10ºF, M, 4/4/4. The Nile never had it so pretty. Light rose flowers have darker edging and light spotting. (Beck hyb. 1959, raised by Flora Markeeta Nursery, Korth reg. 1977).

'Queen of Hearts' (*meddianum* x 'Moser's Maroon'). 6', -5ºF, ML, 4/3/3. The beautiful black-red flowers are borne in a well rounded truss. The elongated, round leaves are bright green with a yellow mid-vein and partially yellow leaf stem. The remainder of the leaf stem and the tight buds are deep red. A great foliage plant affecting a bold appearance. (Rothschild 1949) A.M. 1949.

'Queen of McKenzie' ('Idealist' x 'Crest'). 3', -5ºF, M, 5/4/3. Magnificent canary yellow flowers have deeper yellow in the throat with a red brown blotch. Nice green leaves are held on an almost round, upright plant. (Bowhan intro., Phetteplace reg. 1983).

'Queen of Sheba' (parentage unknown). 4', -10ºF, M, 4/4/-. A very rare specimen with dark, glossy green leaves and beautiful white flowers. (Lem before 1960).

'Queen's Wood' (*souliei* x *aberconwayi*). 3', -5ºF, EM, -/-/-. Delicate flat bells hang in gentle groupings of white, suffused very pale pink. (Findlay, Crown Estate Commissioners reg. 1972) A.M. 1972.

'Quinella' ('Britannia' x 'May Day'). 3', 0ºF, M, 3/3/3. Brilliant red flowers. Because of their extremely large calyx, they appear to be double. Leaves are fairly narrow and matte green. (R. Henny before 1958).

'Racearound' (*racemosum* open pollinated). 5', -15ºF, EM, -/-/-. This appears to be a cross of *racemosum* and an evergreen azalea, thus an azaleodendron. The open growth habit supports attractive red foliage in the fall. The profusely blooming deep pink flowers cover the limbs in spring. It looks much like 'Ria Hardijzer', but it has slightly lighter pink flowers. (Cross before 1985).

'Racil' (*racemosum* x *ciliatum*). 3', -5ºF, E, 3/2-3/3. The young plant has open growth, becoming compact later. Leaves and flowers are small. The shell pink flowers are profuse, 3-4 to truss. Cuttings root easily. Susceptible to rust. (N.S. Holland 1937).

'Racilina' (seedling of *racemosum*). 5', -15ºF, E, -/-/-. This slow growing plant with an open growth habit and small foliage prefers a shady location. Blush pink flowers are abundant in early spring. (Sold by Weston 1993).

'Radium' (*griersonianum* x 'Earl of Athlone'). 5', 5ºF, ML, 3-4/3/3-4. Growth habit is upright and more or less open. Leaves are somewhat glossy and medium-large. Geranium scarlet flowers are set in large, loose trusses. The plant is easily rooted. (Crosfield 1936).

'Radistrotum' (*calostrotum* ssp. *keleticum* x *calostrotum* ssp. *calostrotum*). 2', -10ºF, ML, -/-/-. This hybrid has a creeping habit and aromatic, elliptical foliage. Saucer-shaped flowers are rich purple. (G. Arends).

'Rainbow' (a lost hybrid named 'Anthony Waterer' x *griffithianum*). 6', 0ºF, M, 4/3/4. This hybrid is also shown as 'A. W. Hardy' x *griffithianum*, however it is possible that 'A. W. Hardy' and 'Anthony Waterer' are the same plant. 'Rainbow's' tall upright appearance is a result of its thick, vertically directed, narrow-angle branches. Trusses are edged in deep pink with white centers and are somewhat floppy. Foliage is slightly rough textured, but is glossy and quite attractive. Always a popular plant. (W. C. Slocock about 1928).

'Ramapo' (*fastigiatum* x *carolinianum*). 2', -20ºF, EM, 3/4/4. This outstanding hardy dwarf grows well in sun or partial shade, although it will maintain a more compact form in full sun. In shade it will be quite a bit taller. It is well-suited for use in a low border or rock garden, and is notable for the pleasing foliage color changes throughout the year, especially the dusty blue new leaves. Tiny, inch-long flowers are lively, pinkish violet. The plant blooms abundantly. (Nearing 1940).

'Ramona' ('Huntsman' x *neriiflorum*). 6', -15ºF, ML, -/-/-. Flat trusses of deep red complement this plant. (Ramsden, Pennington-Ramsden 1964). Note: There is another unregistered plant that was apparently developed in the Eastern U.S. that uses this same name. It is probably a *catawbiense* hybrid and it has rosy pink flowers.

'Rangoon' ('Fanfare' x 'Gertrude Schale'). 3', -15ºF, E, 4/3/-. Leaves are medium sized. 2" flowers, medium to dark red, are held in truss of up to 8. (Leach 1973).

'Rasputin' ('Danamar' x 'Purple Splendour'). 4', -15ºF, L, -/-/-. This plant, with a habit reaching wider than tall is densely covered with attractive foliage. Deep purple flowers with a red blotch are held in trusses of 11-14. (Hachmann hyb. 1976, Stuck reg. 1988).

'Ravels' ('Leah Yates' x 'Pink Twins'). 4', -10ºF, ML, -/-/-. Leaves are long and narrow. Blooms to 3 1/2" across are pink, with darker pink veins and a yellow green blotch, and are held in a 12 flower truss. (M. Yates 1977).

'Ravenna' ('Scarlet Blast' x [{*catawbiense* var. *album* x *yakushimanum*} x {'Fanfare' x 'Gertrud Schale'}]). 4', -20ºF, ML, -/-/-. A broad growing, densely foliated plant with mid-sized, vivid red blooms held in lax trusses. (Leach 1991).

'Razorbill' (*spinuliferum* x unknown). 3', 10ºF, EM, 4/3/3-4. A hardy flowering plant with rosy pink, tubular flowers. This most unusual and attractive flower is produced in profusion. (Cox 1976) P.C. 1976, A.M. 1978.

'Razzle Dazzle' ('Mrs. J. G. Millais' x 'Cheyenne'). 6', -5ºF, ML, 4/3/3-4. The large trusses "dazzle" with showy, deep pinkish-maroon flares on the upper petals of each flower. Additional "razzle" is provided as the flowers open to display deep pink, picotee petal edges which are a delightful contrast to the lighter pink flower centers. Foliage is medium sized, fern green, and clothes the plant completely. Habit is somewhat open, creating a statuesque plant. (Greer 1988).

'Redberth' ('Mars' x *yakushimanum* 'Koichiro Wada'). 3', -5ºF, ML, -/-/-. Leaves are variable in size and shape, though generally large. Flowers, to 3" across, are red with minimal spotting and are carried in a good sized truss of up to 20 flowers. (Reese 1976).

'Red Brave' ('America' x 'Mars'). 5', -25ºF, M, -/-/-. Well-proportioned, stately, dome-shaped, deep red flowers are exquisitely accented by white stamens. This rounded plant displays medium-sized, sage green leaves, held for 3 years, on its well branched and bushy form. (O. Pride).

'Red Carpet' ('America' x *forrestii* ssp. *forrestii* Repens Group). 2', -10ºF, EM, 3-4/4/3-4. Although each truss contains but four blooms, the free flowering nature of the plant makes for a great show. Blossoms are deep cardinal red with darker veining and an almost black edging. (Hobbie 1945, Schmalscheidt reg. 1983) A.M. 1983.

'Red Cloud' ('Tally Ho' x 'Corona'). 5', 5ºF, ML, 3/3/3. Open growth habit, with medium green, somewhat large leaves. 3 1/2" wide flowers are claret rose to scarlet inside, in a generously flowered, open, dome-shaped truss. Easily rooted. (R. Henny 1953) P.A. 1953.

'Red Delicious' ('Jean Marie de Montague' x 'Leo'). 5', -5ºF, ML-L, 4/4/4. An exceptionally true red, showing virtually no blue undertone. The stunning flowers light the plant in glowing color. The rounded trusses are medium sized and appear above dark fir green leaves which are elliptic in shape, each leaf being 3 times longer than wide. The well behaved plant shows branching and growth habit of the same excellence as the flower and foliage. (Greer 1988).

'Redder Yet' (possibly a seedling of 'America'). 5', -25ºF, ML, -/-/-. Leaves are medium sized and narrow. Red flowers, to 2 1/2" across, have slight brown spotting, and are carried in rounded trusses of up to 18 flowers per truss. (Leach, Pride 1979).

'Red Devil' (*haemaleum* x *sanguineum* ssp. *didymum*). 2', 0ºF, M, 4/4/3. An almost black-red flower is surrounded by dark green leaves about 2" long. Tight, compact growth and good form. (Fawcett).

'Red Dragon' (*thomsonii* x *griersonianum*). 5', -10ºF, M, -/-/-. Loosely formed trusses of bright scarlet red appear on a plant with tall growing potential. (Aberconway 1943).

'Red Eye' ('Anah Kruschke' x 'Purple Splendour'). 5', -10ºF, ML, 4/4/4. This hybrid propagates easily, stands sun, buds young, branches readily and does not mind heavy cutting for propagation. This is not a collector's item, but rather the kind of plant you can depend on year after year. The flowers are deep red purple with a most interesting "eye" blotch. When it first opens, the eye is green gold and little by little becomes red, an interesting contrast with the purple. The foliage is shiny, medium sized, and densely covers the plant, making a well clothed mound. (Swenson, Greer 1988).

'Red Frilled' (red *catawbiense* hybrid). 3.5', -15ºF, M, -/-/-. Achieving a height greater than its width, this plant is densely foliated with elliptical, glossy dark green foliage. Conical shaped trusses hold wavy edged, funnel-shaped flowers, light purple inside, rosy red outside, in groups of 12-15. (Mezitt, Weston Nurseries 1983).

'Red Glow' ('Halopeanum' x *thomsonii*). 3', -5ºF, EM, -/-/-. Bright strawberry pink flowers dance atop a tall, somewhat open shrub. (Loder 1949).

'Red Hot Mamma' ('Anne Hardgrove' x [{('America' x 'Blaze') x 'Red Brave'} No. 2 x 'Delp's C. L.']). 3', -15ºF, L, -/-/-. Trusses of 18 bright, vivid cerise flowers ard edged deeper red. (Ring, Delp 1994).

'Red Lion' ('Tally Ho' x *catawbiense*-Gable's red selection). 5', -10ºF, L, -/-/-. Leaves are large. Faintly spotted red flowers, to 2" wide, are held in a 10-flower truss. (Nearing 1973).

'Red Majesty' (*elliottii* x *strigillosum*). 5', 10ºF, E, 4/3/3. Leaves are elongated. Currant red, generously spotted flowers are about 3" wide. (Larson 1964).

'Red Olympia' ('Anna' x 'Fusilier'). 5', 5ºF, M, 4/3/3. This hybrid has huge red trusses of flowers which are heavily spotted on all lobes. Quite different from any other rhododendron. The leaves are 7" long by 2" wide, and are retained three years. It is sensational! (Lem, Pierce 1976).

'Red Paint' ([{'Fabia' x *haematodes*} x 'Earl of Athlone'] x 'Jean Marie de Montague'). 4', 0ºF, E, -/-/-. Leaves are long and narrow. Flowers, to 3" across, are a clear brilliant red, lightly spotted and in a ball-shaped truss up to 14. (Goheen, McNew 1974).

'Redpoll' (*forrestii* [close to *forrestii* ssp. *papillatum*] x 'Rocket'). 2', 0ºF, VE-E, -/-/-. Dome shaped plant with dense branching and large scarlet bells. (Hydon Nurseries 1974).

'Red Puff' ('Golden Horn' x *catawbiense* var. *album* Catanea). 2', -15ºF, ML, -/-/-. Leaves are medium to long and narrow on a decumbent growth habit. Red blooms, to 2" across, are speckled darker red, and held in 16 flower truss. (Nearing 1973).

'Red River' (*maximum* 'Mount Mitchell' x ['Mars' x 'Fanfare']). 5', -20ºF, L, -/-/-. The upright plant is covered with large, wavy margined leaves. Pyramidal trusses hold bright red blooms that shade to pink and become almost pure white at the center. A yellow dorsal flare is delicately spotted yellow green to provide added interest. (Leach hyb. 1967, reg. 1984).

'Red Rum' ('Barclayi' x *forrestii* ssp. *forrestii* Repens Group). 2', 0ºF, VE-E, -/-/-. Bright red, hanging bell-shaped flowers decorate a tight growing, dwarf plant. A very nice, early bloomer. (Crown Estate, Windsor 1994) A.M. 1974.

'Red Velour' (parentage unknown, probably similar to 'Jock'). 3', 5ºF, M, 3/3-4/4. A plant of compact habit with its many branches covered with very dark green foliage. Lax trusses hold velvety textured, red flowers with deep spotting. (Whitney hyb., Sather intro.).

'Red Velvet' ('Fusilier' x *williamsianum*). 30", 0ºF, M, 3-4/3-4/3. Here is a mounding habit plant with coral red flowers. It is attractive and similar to an improved 'Jock'. Good foliage. (Larson 1964).

'Red Walloper' ('Anna' x 'Marinus Koster'). 6', -5ºF, M, 4/4/4. Buds show a deep rose red. Flowers open rose, but gradually lighten through many delightful shades of pink to end a beautiful pastel pink. Good looking foliage. Will grow to be a strong plant of large stature. (Lem not registered).

'Redwax' (*haematodes* x 'May Day'). 30", 5ºF, M, 3/4/3. The waxy red flowers are beautiful against the deep green foliage. Leaves have heavy tan indumentum on the underside and also on the tops of the new foliage. A very pleasing plant for the small garden. (R. Henny 1962) P.A. 1958.

'Red Wood' (*insigne* hybrid). 6', -20ºF, ML, -/-/-. Glossy foliage is held on red stems, forming an exciting combination with the bronzy colored new growth. Large trusses are comprised of pale pink flowers, which mature to a creamy white. (Hobbie intro. between 1965-70).

'Reine Long' (*taronense* x 'Else Frye'). 5', 20ºF, E-EM, -/-/-. This hybrid is very fragrant. The large, round, open flowers are white, streaked rose, with a large yellow blotch, set in a loose truss of 4 or 5 flowers. (Bowman, Long 1964).

'Remo' (*valentinianum* x *lutescens*). 30", 10°F, EM, 3/2/3. Bells of bright deep yellow nod on a low growing, slender leaved plant, similar in habit to *R. lutescens*. (Stevenson intro. 1943).

'Rendezvous' ('Marinus Koster' x *yakushimanum* 'Koichiro Wada'). 4', -10°F, ML, -/-/-. Reddish blooms, accented by white throats and internal red spotting, fade to white. These flowers are held in trusses of 17-24 above deep green, indumented foliage. (Hachmann hyb. 1968, Stuck reg. 1985).

'Renoir' ('Pauline' x *yakushimanum*). 3', -10°F, M, -/-/-. No indumentum on this "yak", however, what it lacks in showy leaf it makes up in attractive light pink flowers with dark edges and crimson spotting. (F. Hanger hyb., RHS Wisley reg. 1963) A.M. 1961.

'Repose' (*lacteum* x *fortunei* ssp. *discolor*). 5', -5°F, EM, 5/4/3. Large trusses of up to 18 flowers of creamy white have a flush of green. Plant size and habit is much like that of *R. lacteum*. (Rothschild intro. 1950, exhibited by Slocock) A.M. 1956.

'Reuthe's Purple' (form of *lepidotum*). 1', 0°F, EM, 4/4/3. An extremely compact plant habit supports elliptical, aromatic foliage which has densely scaly undersides. Flat-faced, deep purple flowers are held in small clusters. (G. Reuthe raiser, reg. 1967) A.M. 1967.

'Reve Rose' (*forrestii* ssp. *forrestii* Repens Group x 'Bow Bells'). 30", -5°F, EM, 3/4/3-4. This beautiful little dwarf has bright green leaves, about 1 1/2" long. The rose-colored flowers, to 1 3/4" across, are set in a rather loose truss of up to 5 flowers. (Brandt 1951).

'Revlon' (*cinnabarinum* 'Roylei' Group x 'Lady Chamberlain'). 5', -5°F, M, 4/3/3. A slender, tall, upright plant. Clusters of pendulous bright carmine red bells have an almost waxy texture. (Rothschild) A.M. 1957.

'Ria Hardijzer' (*racemosum* x 'Hinodegiri'). 30", -5°F, EM, 4/4/4. A bright show is made by numerous vibrant pink round trusses on this evergreen azaleodendron. Its red stems bear shiny small leaves, and it flowers young and heavily. A cheerful planting is made by pairing this with 'Hardijzer's Beauty'. (Hardijzer 1965) S.M. 1958, G.M. 1961, H.C. 1969, A.M. 1974.

'Rigging Slinger' (['Virginia Scott' x 'Alice Franklin'] x *yakushimanum*). 3', -5°F, EM, 4/4/4. Combinations of rose, pink and cream cover this gorgeous plant in large, round trusses. The compact growing plant has heavily indumented, very attractive foliage. (Larson hyb., Clint Smith intro.)

'Rik' (*racemosum* x *keiskei*). 2.5', -15°F, E, -/-/-. Bright red stems and leaves cover this beautiful little plant the entire winter and give way to lovely white flowers with pink edges in the spring. (Yavorsky 1987).

'Ring of Fire' ('Darigold' x 'Idealist'). 4', 0°F, ML, 4/4/4. Many flowers are described as having a margin of a certain color, and, although it's true, sometimes the color is not very prominent. In this case, 'Ring of Fire' means what it says! The golden yellow flowers have the most vibrant orange red edging of any plant! Nice, dense foliage and a compact growth habit are an added bonus. (Thompson hyb. about 1975, Greer intro. 1984, Thompson reg. 1990).

'Rio' ('Newburyport Beauty' x 'Newburyport Belle'). 3', -20°F, M, 3-4/3/3. Appealing trusses hold up to 16 flowers of salmon pink with a yellow throat. A very broad plant, it is twice as wide as tall. Shiny yellow green leaves are held 2 years. (Leach 1968, reg. 1983.)

'Ripe Corn' ('Goldsworth Orange' x 'Exbury Naomi'). 4', -10°F, M, -/-/-. Flowers are corn yellow with a hint of pink. (Slocock 1966).

'Riplet' (*forrestii* ssp. *forrestii* Repens Group x 'Letty Edwards'). 2', -5°F, EM, 4/4/3. Frilled, sweet, rose pink flowers cover this low growing, heavy stemmed plant. Halfdan Lem, the hybridizer, named this semi-dwarf 'Replet' after its parents *forrestii* ssp. *forrestii* Repens Group and 'Letty Edwards'. Somehow it was registered as 'Riplet', and the name will now stay that way. One form has a considerable amount of yellow in the flower, which becomes stronger the longer the flower is out. It literally glows! (Lem 1962) P.A. 1961, A.M. 1987.

'Riverwood Cream' (*griffithianum* x 'Crest'). 5', 5°F, ML, -/-/-. This upright growing plant has sweetly scented, satiny, cream colored blooms which form large trusses. Produced by grafting so the availability is limited. (Riverwood Gardens, New Zealand).

'Riverwood Regency' ('Ivan D. Wood' hybrid). 4.5', 5°F, L, -/-/-. The full, wide plant habit is covered with dense, medium green, oval foliage. Flowers of ivory cream are held upright in huge trusses. (Riverwood Gardens, New Zealand intro. 1995).

'Robert Allison' ('Caroline' x *fortunei* ssp. *discolor*). 5', -10°F, ML, 4/3/4. Large, waxy green foliage covers this vigorous, upright plant habit. Flowers are 3 1/2" wide, scented, pink with a golden throat, and held in a flat truss. It is a prolific bloomer and easily propagated from cuttings. Synonym, 'Gable's Pink #2'. (Gable hyb. 1938, Gable Study Group 1991).

'Robert Keir' (*lacteum* x 'Luscombei'). 5', -5°F. E, -/-/-. Large pale yellow flowers are flushed pale pink. (Stevenson 1951) A.M. 1957.

'Robert Korn' ('Diane' x 'Gomer Waterer'). 5', -10°F, M, 3-4/3/3. The large creamy flowers are held in upright trusses above attractive foliage. It is a vigorous growing, upright shrub. (Robert Korn hyb. before 1980).

'Robert Louis Stevenson' ('May Day' x 'Jester'). 2', 0°F, L, 4/4/3. Small, bright blood red flowers appear after all the other small reds. Glossy, forest green leaves set off the flowers. (Seabrook 1967).

'Robert Seleger' (*keleticum* hybrid). 1', -5°F, EM, 3/3/3. Rose purple flowers and tiny leaves combine to make this a real beauty. Free flowering and very attractive. (Hobbie about 1960).

'Robinette' (could contain a hybrid from the Repens Group and *williamsianum*). 3', -5°F, M, 3/4/3-4. This compact grower has curving, dark green foliage. Rosy red flowers sit atop this delightful shrub. (sold by Aasland Nursery about 1990.).

'Robin Leach' ('Catalgla' x ['Adriaan Koster' x *williamsianum*]). 3', -20°F, E, 3-4/3/3. Growth of this hybrid is much wider than tall. It is very densely foliated with ovate leaves that are medium green and turn sharply downward. Flowers, to 3" across, are open, bell-shaped, with faint red spotting and dark brown anthers. They are carried in a 7-flower, somewhat full rounded truss. (Leach 1972).

'Robin Redbreast' (*houlstonii* x *orbiculare*). 4', -5°F, M, -/-/-. Scarlet buds open to rosy pink bells. Foliage is somewhat rounded and very nice. (Williams 1933).

'Rochelle' ('Dorothea' x 'Kettledrum'). 4', -10°F, ML, 4/4/4. Leaves are large. Slightly scented flowers, to a generous 4" across, are rose colored with a strawberry blotch, and are carried in an outstanding truss. (Nearing, Baldsiefen 1969).

'Rocket' ('Cunningham's White' x red *catawbiense* seedling). 5', -15°F, M, 3/4-5/5. Foliage is medium sized, thick and heavily veined, giving this plant a full-bodied appearance. Frilled flowers, about 2 1/2" wide, are vibrant pink, blotched scarlet and are set in a cone-shaped truss. (Shammarello intro. 1955).

'**Rockhill Ivory Ruffles**' ('Yellow Rolls Royce' x 'Skipper'). 5', 10ºF, EM-M, 4/3/3. Ivy green leaves cover the well-branched habit of this upright growing plant. Wavy edged flowers are creamy yellow and have a primrose yellow throat accented with red spotting. (Brotherton reg. 1983).

'**Rockhill Parkay**' ('Yellow Rolls Royce' x 'Skipper'). 5', 10ºF, EM-M, 4/3/3. An upright grower selected from the same cross as above. Flowers are held in ball-shaped trusses. The blooms display a sulphur yellow throat shading to creamy white lobes, accented with a red eye. (Brotherton reg. 1983).

'**Rockhill Sunday Sunrise**' ('Yellow Rolls Royce' x 'Skipper'). 5', 10ºF, EM-M, -/-/-. Stiff branches on this upright grower are clothed with ivy green leaves. Flowers are primrose yellow with a red blotch visible in the throat. (Brotherton reg. 1983).

'**Rocky White**' ('Catalgla' x *fortunei* ssp. *fortunei*). 5', -10ºF, M, -/-/-. A well-branched, broad growing plant clothed in sage green leaves, offset by copper tinted new growth. Buds of lavender open to expose fragrant, white flowers which have an initial tinge of lavender. (C. Herbert).

'**Rococo**' ('Boule de Neige' x *fortunei* ssp. *fortunei*). 5', -25ºF, EM, 3/4/-. Leaves are medium-large and narrow. Fluted, ruffled flowers, to 2 1/4" across, are lilac pink, with deeper pink edging and yellow green dorsal rays, carried in a 12-flower truss. (Gable, Leach 1964).

'**Roedhaette**' (*sanguineum* ssp. *didymum* x *williamsianum*). 3', -5ºF, M, 3/3/3. Large, open, bell-shaped flowers are a bright rosy red. Held on long stems, the flopping petals resemble 'elf hats', inspiring the German namesake. Rounded foliage is gentle emerald green with a slightly convex curl. (Hobbie).

'**Rollie**' ('A. Bedford' x fragrant pink hybrid). 6', -15ºF, ML, 4/4/4. Large, intricate flowers are produced on this vigorous growing plant. The blooms have pink petals lined with yellow highlights radiating from the center. A maroon blotch accents the upper edge of the petals. (R. Mulkie 1990).

'**Romany Chai' g.**' ('Moser's Maroon' x *griersonianum*). 5', 0ºF, ML, 2/2/3. The mature plant is fairly dense, upright, and has large dark green leaves. Thin textured, scarlet red flowers, with some spotting, are set in a loose truss. The same cross was made by Knap Hill Nursery and named 'Empire Day', formerly known as 'Romany Chai' var. 'Empire Day'. (Rothschild before 1932).

'**Romany Chal**' ('Moser's Maroon' x *eriogynum*). 6', 5ºF, ML, 3/3/3. Of upright and sturdy growth habit, this hybrid also has large, dark green leaves. Flowers are a rich dark maroon scarlet, set in rounded trusses. Prefers shady location. (Rothschild before 1932) A.M. 1932, F.C.C. 1937.

'**Roma Sun**' ('Loderi King George' x 'Ostbo Y3'). 6', 0ºF, M, -/-/-. Leaves are quite large. Large, ruffled flowers are fragrant, yellowish pink in color. Petal edges are deeper pink, as are outer petal surfaces. Flowers are held in a truss of up to 10. (Bovee, Sorenson & Watson-The Bovees Nursery 1976).

'**Roman Holiday**' ('Chionoides' x 'Goldsworth Orange'). 5', -10ºF, EM, -/-/-. Striking white flowers with a dark red flare open from delicate pink buds. (L. Bulgin intro. before 1990).

'**Romeo**' (red *catawbiense* seedling x 'America'). 6', -20ºF, ML, 3/3/3. Leaves are medium sized. Blood red blooms, with darker red blotch, up to 2 1/2" across, are carried in a globular truss. (Shammarello 1972).

'**Ronald Otto Delp**' ('Lodestar' x 'Mary Belle'). 4', -15ºF, L, -/-/-. Trusses are made of 16 mauve flowers with soft yellow throats, and flares which have deep purplish red spotting. (Delp 1992).

'**Rosamundi**' (*caucasicum* hybrid). 4', -5ºF, VE-E, 2/3-4/3-4. There is much confusion about this rhododendron. The most common spelling of the name is the one above, but it can also be found spelled 'Rosa Mundi' and 'Rosamundii'. The flower color is described as darker than 'Christmas Cheer', with which it is often confused; however, the plant most commonly in cultivation under this name has very light pink flowers, generally beginning to flower about a week later than 'Christmas Cheer'. The leaves on 'Rosamundi' are smoother than those of 'Christmas Cheer', and it has slightly lighter buds. It is a compact plant with an attractive appearance. This same plant is grown in many places in Europe under the name of 'Jacksonii', although 'Jacksonii' should be a more two-toned pink. (Standish & Noble in the 1800's).

'**Rosa Regen**' (*astrocalyx* hybrid). 4', -5ºF, M, 2-3/4/4. The upright growing, compact plant has shiny, dark green foliage. Deep pink buds open to reveal frilled yellow flowers, with darker centers and a rose colored margin. (Hobbie before 1970).

'**Roseann**' ('Loderi Venus' x 'Britannia'). 5', 5ºF, M, 4/3-4/3. Medium rose pink flowers have a slight flared marking in the throat. Foliage is a medium green with a distinct red leaf petiole. (R. Henny about 1955) P.A. 1956.

'**Rose Elf**' (*racemosum* x *pemakoense*). 18", 5ºF, E, 3/4/3-4. Here's a great little bush that flowers as if there were no tomorrow. Often there are six or eight flower buds per stem which open to a delightful pastel orchid pink. Jade green leaves are numerous on a bushy, multiple stemmed plant. In full sun exposure, the leaves become bronze toned. 'Rose Elf' can be used to form a bushy low border and is also well suited to rock gardening and bonsai culture. (Lancaster about 1950) P.A. 1954.

'**Rose Haines**' (*fortunei* ssp. *fortunei* hybrid). 5', 0ºF, M, 3/3/3. This upright growing plant will assume a habit wider than it is tall. Heavy petals of purple gather around a light green throat to form large flowers. These blooms are gathered into trusses of 9-11, and held above dark green foliage. (C. English Jr. hyb., C. R. Burlingame intro. 1967, reg. 1977).

'**Rose Lancaster**' ('Tally Ho' x *yakushimanum*). 4', 5ºF, ML, -/-/-. Leaves are medium to large and narrow. Clear pink flowers, to 3" across, are held in a rounded truss of up to 30. (Lancaster hyb. before 1960, Goheen 1977).

'**Rosemarie**' (lepidote hybrid of unknown parentage). 3', 5ºF, M, -/-/-. A small leaved variety producing outstanding, large blue-violet flowers. (Sold by Carlson 1995).

'**Rose of China**' ('Tally Ho' x *fortunei* ssp. *discolor*). 4', 0ºF, L, 3/3/3. Campanulate flowers, 4" wide, are pure, clear rose pink. Sun tolerant. (Lem hyb., Lancaster intro., reg. 1958).

'**Rose Point**' ('Dido' x *williamsianum*). 3', 0ºF, EM, 3-4/4/3-4. Large, open-face flowers are pastel pink with a touch of salmon orange. Round, attractive leaves show the influence of its parent *williamsianum*. There were several plants propagated out of this cross and this is one of the best. (Lem, Pierce, Elliott 1980).

'**Rose Scott**' ('Else Frye' x [*johnstoneanum* x *cubittii*]). 4', 15ºF, E, -/-/-. Leaves are medium sized and narrow. Fragrant blooms are fairly large, to 4 1/2" across, and of strong substance. Color is white, with fuchsine pink blotches and flares. A flat truss of up to 7 flowers is formed. (Scott 1977).

'Roseum Elegans' (*catawbiense* hybrid). 6', -25ºF, ML, 2/3/4. You can depend on this hybrid in any sub-zero climate. The rosy lilac flowers are rated down because of their smaller size, however, they are still beautiful and delightful. This hybrid also succeeds in hot climates. The foliage is medium olive green and is produced in abundance on a vigorous plant. (A. Waterer before 1851).

'Roseum Pink' see 'English Roseum'.

'Roseum Superbum' (*catawbiense* hybrid). 6', -20ºF, ML, 2/3/4. Plant habit is very much like 'Roseum Elegans', vigorous and upright as a young plant, then more spreading, with good foliage. Rose-lilac flowers are small, in a dome-shaped truss. Easy to root and grow. (A. Waterer before 1865).

'Roseum Two' (selection of 'English Roseum'). 6', -20ºF, ML, 2/3/4-5. This is a very strong growing plant with light pink flowers. While the flowers are not outstanding, this hybrid is still exceptionally dependable in the garden. It will grow to a large plant with good foliage, usable for screening. (Wells about 1980?).

'Rosevallon' (form or possible hybrid of *neriiflorum*). 2', 5ºF, EM, 3/5/3. An excellent foliage plant! The compact and somewhat spreading plant has oblong foliage, dark green on top and with undersides of a striking red-purple. Flowers are bright red. (Crown Estate, Windsor, exhibitor, Crown Estate Comm. reg. 1975) A.M. 1975.

'Roslyn' ('Purpureum Elegans' x 'Everestianum'). 6', -10ºF, ML, 4/3/4. Leaves are large. Ruffled flowers, to 2 1/4" across, are of a purplish violet color, shading to a paler center, carried in 12-flower truss. (Vossberg 1973) A.E. 1973.

'Ross Maud' ('Fusilier' x 'Unique'). 3', 5ºF, EM, -/-/-. Bright rose flowers are held in ball shaped trusses above the compact shrub. (Bramley 1975).

'Rosy Dream' (*yakushimanum* x 'Britannia'). 2', 0ºF, M, 3-4/4/3-4. Cardinal red buds open to funnel-shaped spinel red flowers with paler throats that are displayed in domed trusses of 12-16. The plant is twice as wide as it is tall, and the olive green leaves are indumented silver, aging to cinnamon. (Larson hyb. 1969, Davies reg. 1986).

'Rothenburg' ('Diane' x *williamsianum*). 4', -10ºF, EM, 3/4/3-4. Light yellow flowers appear on a rounded plant which has glossy, green foliage. (Bruns 1971).

'Rouge Aureum' (a seedling of *aureum*, possibly *aureum* x *yakushimanum*). 2', -20ºF, M, 3-4/4/3-4. A young and consistent bloomer. This dense mound produces large flowers of pink, with a lighter center. Originally introduced as 'Rouge Chrysanthum', which is the old name for *aureum*. (Seedling from Caperci before 1965, Greer intro. 1973).

'Royal Beauty' ('Lady Rosebery' x *cinnabarinum* Roylei Group). 5', 10ºF, M, 4/3/3. The deep rose colored flowers hang in bells. This plant is upright and graceful. (Digby 1936, intro. 1953).

'Royal Blood' (*elliottii* x 'Rubens'). 4', 0ºF, L, -/-/-. Magnificent trusses of up to 35-40 flowers of bright cardinal red, covered with dark red spotting, engulf this fine hybrid. It is truly beautiful. (Hanger, RHS Garden, Wisley about 1954) A.M. 1954.

'Royal Coachman' (['Essex Scarlet' x *eriogynum*] x ['Tally Ho' x 'Sunshine']). 5', 5ºF, ML, -/-/-. Flowers are brilliant red with all-over darker spotting. (Waterer, Sons & Crisp 1975).

'Royal Decree' ('Helene Schiffner' x 'Elizabeth'). 3', 10ºF, EM, -/-/-. Forming a mound nearly as wide as tall, this plant is densely foliated with heavily textured leaves. Deep red buds open to similar color flowers that shade more purple in the center. The corolla is rimmed with deep purple and accented with yellowish gray on the dorsal lobe. (L. Bulgin hyb. 1979, reg. 1989).

'Royal Dragoon' ([{*eriogynum* x 'Fabia'} x 'Mayday'] x ['Fabia Tangerine' x 'Mars']). 4', 5ºF?, M, -/-/-. Flower is dark blood red. (Waterer, Sons & Crisp 1975).

'Royal Flush' (*cinnabarinum* x *maddenii*). 6', 5ºF, M, 4/3-4/3-4. Superb, tubular pink and orange flowers have heavy substance. The upright growing plant is somewhat sparsely clad with shiny green leaves, as is typical of subsect. Cinnabarina species and hybrids. (Williams before 1950).

'Royal Pink' ('Homer' x *williamsianum*). 3', -15ºF, M, 4/4/4. This foliage is round and dense showing its *williamsianum* background. The plant is round and tight making a perfect semi-dwarf shrub. To top it all off, it has terrific, clear pink flowers that are in a tight ball truss, unusual in *williamsianum* hybrids, which normally have floppy trusses. What more could you desire of a plant: hardiness, good foliage, showy trusses, vigorous growth and heavy budding. (Hobbie, LeFeber 1964) S.M. 1958, G.M. 1960.

'Royal Purple' (unknown). 4-5', -15ºF, ML, 3/3-4/4. A tough, attractive hybrid with deep shiny green leaves. The flowers are showy with their deep purple color which is lit with a bright yellow eye. (White, RHS reg. 1958).

'Royal Star' ('Moser's Maroon' x unknown). 4', -5ºF, M, 3/3/3. Medium green recurved foliage covers a plant of compact habit. Deep purple flowers with darker blotch are held in large, round trusses. (Donald Hardgrove).

'Royal Windsor' ('Jutland' x 'Royal Blood'). 3', -5ºF, M, -/-/-. Rich crimson flowers with darker spotting are in trusses of up to 24. Long, narrow, dark green leaves clothe this delightful plant. (Crown Estate, Windsor 1975) A.M. 1975.

'Roy Hudson' (*burmanicum* x *nuttallii*). 5', 15ºF, E-EM, -/-/-. Leaves are medium sized and narrow. Highly scented blooms, to 3 1/2" across, are white with yellow throat. Clusters of terminal buds open to 8 flowers in each bud. (Kerrigan 1977).

'Royston Red' (*forrestii* ssp. *forrestii* Repens Group x *thomsonii*). 3', 0ºF, E, 4/4/4. Very attractive, bright blood red flowers give color before most other rhododendrons bloom. Excellent round leaves adorn this compact, sturdy plant. (Grieg before 1960, not registered).

'Roza Stevenson' ('Loderi Sir Edmond' x *wardii* KW5736). 5', -5ºF, EM, -/-/-. Flowers, almost 5" across, are deep lemon yellow, darker yellow in bud. Round, shiny foliage. This plant has also been known as 'Roza Harrison'. (J. B. Stevenson before 1968, reg. RHS 1969) F.C.C. 1968.

'Rubens' (parentage unknown). 3', -5ºF, ML, 3/2/3. White stamens are very showy against a background of deep red. (Waterer before 1865).

'Rubicon' ('Noyo Chief' x 'Kilimanjaro'). 5', -10ºF, EM, 5/4/3-4. Fantastic cardinal red flowers have black spotting on the upper lobes. Anthers are white and add to the attractiveness of the truss. Plant has wonderful, glossy green leaves with deep veining. A superior plant. (Gordon, New Zealand, reg. 1979).

'Ruby Bowman' (*fortunei* ssp. *fortunei* x 'Lady Bligh'). 5', -5ºF, M, 4/4/4. Long lasting, large trusses are rose pink with flower centers shaded a deeper pink. Flat, long leaves grace the plant. 'Ruby Bowman' will become a formal plant of substantial size. (Bowman hyb. 1941, Druecker intro. 1953) P.A. 1951.

'Ruby Hart' (['Carmen' x 'Elizabeth'] x *elliottii*). 2', 0ºF, EM, 4-5/4-5/4. Dark red flowers appear on this fine dwarf plant. It has the deepest and most glossy green foliage possible and is a compact, well clothed plant. (Whitney, Sather 1976).

'Rudolph's Orange' ('Fabia' x 'Temple Belle'). 4', 0ºF, ML, 3/3/3. Leaves are small. 2" wide flowers are light orange in color, shaded pink inside and out, and are held in a lax truss of up to 6. (R. Henny, Caperci 1976).

'Rudy's Candy' ('Azor' x 'Corona'). 4', 0ºF, ML, 3/3/3. Large leaves surround the 3" wide flowers which are two-toned, deep pink outside and are carried in a 17-flower truss. (Henny, L. Henny 1969).

'Ruffles' (*catawbiense* hybrid). 5', -15ºF, ML, 3/3/3. This aptly named hybrid flaunts ruffled orchid flowers in later May. The foliage has a light hue to it, a result of its apple green leaves pendulously held from straw colored petioles. (unknown not registered).

'Russautinii' (*russatum* x *augustinii*). 5', -10ºF, EM, 4/2-3/3. Outstanding, deep blue flowers cover this lepidote hybrid. 'Russautinii's' form is more typical of *augustinii* than *russatum*. Foliage often spots in winter, but is nice in summer. (Ramsden intro. 1937).

'Russell Harmon' (*maximum* x *catawbiense*). 6', -25ºF, L, 4/3/3. Great, high trusses of magenta pink are formed from flowers in groups of up to 25. It is very hardy and attractive, although it does have an open growth habit. (LaBar hyb. 1950, LaBar's Rhododendron Nursery intro.).

'Russellianum' (*catawbiense* x *arboreum*). 6', -10ºF, EM, 2-3/3/4. Flowers are pale to rosy crimson to almost red. This is probably a grex; therefore, there are probably several forms of this old hybrid. It shows vigorous growth with an abundance of long, narrow leaves. Also known as 'Southamptonia'. Plants of this hybrid that are 50' tall exist in older gardens of Europe. (Russell 1831).

'Rustic Maid' (*russatum* x 'Blue Diamond'). 30", -5ºF, EM, 4/3/3-4. Deep lilac blue. Really a terrific plant when in flower; what a vibrant color! (Ingram intro. 1945).

'Ruth A. Weber' ('Marchioness of Lansdowne' x 'Old Port'). 4', -5ºF, ML, 3/3/4. Bright purple with slightly darker spotting on the upper lobes. Nice, spherical trusses of up to 17 flowers and dark green leaves. (Weber 1974).

'Ruth Davis' (*yakushimanum* x *metternichii*). 2.5', -10ºF, M, -/-/-. This low grower spreads to be wider than tall. Glossy, dark green foliage surrounds cherry ice buds that open to white flowers. The rear side of the bloom retains a blush of pink until fully open. Spherical trusses are formed. (Gable hyb., Ross B. Davis, Jr. reg. 1978).

'Ruthie B' (parentage unknown). 3', 0ºF, EM, -/-/-. A well rounded, densely foliaged plant with medium-sized, smooth textured jade green leaves. The double, yellow, funnel-shaped flowers are held in lax trusses. It buds at 4 years. (Whitney, Sather before 1990).

'Ruth Mottley' (peach hybrid x 'Lem's Cameo'). 3', 0ºF, M, -/-/-. Flat, elliptical leaves cover the frame of this upright growing plant. The peachy flowers are a strong purplish pink at the edges with dorsal spotting of brilliant orange. (W. Robertson hyb. 1975, J.A. Davis reg. 1989).

'R. W. Dykes' see 'Mrs. W. R. Dykes'.

'Sacko' (*russatum* x 'Moerheim'). 2', -10ºF, M, -/-/-. The compact plant has a spreading habit and is covered with small, dark, slightly scaly foliage. This hybrid is highly regarded for its profusion of bluish-purple blooms held in rounded trusses. (A. van Vliet hyb. 1970, Royal Boskoop Hort. Soc. reg. 1988) A.M. Boskoop 1977.

'Saffron Queen' (*xanthostephanum* x *burmanicum*). 4.5', 20ºF, EM, 4/3/4. Growth habit is upright and open. Leaves are medium size, narrow and glossy, lanceolate to oblanceolate in shape. Small funnel-shaped flowers, sulphur yellow with darker spotting on upper petals, are held in a lax truss of 8 to 9 flowers. (C. Williams intro. 1948) A.M. 1948.

'Sagamore Bayside' (unknown hybrid from subsect. Fortunea). 5', -5ºF, M, -/-/-. An upright growing, well-branched plant with matte olive green foliage. Frilled, fragrant flowers are light purplish pink with a yellowish green accent stripe down the center. (Grown by Dexter after 1920, unknown hybridizer, Scott Horticultural Foundation intro. about 1955, Tyler Arboretum reg. 1983).

'Sagamore Bridge' (unknown hybrid from subsect. Fortunea). 6', -5ºF, M, -/-/-. Broad and rounded in habit, the plant supports olive green foliage and it freely produces flowers. The heavy textured, purplish pink blooms are flushed with a dull yellow cast, and held in groups of 14 to form upright, rounded trusses. (Dexter hyb. before 1943, Scott Horticultural Foundation intro. 1950, reg. 1980).

'Saint Breward' (*impeditum* x *augustinii*). 3', -15ºF, EM, -/-/-. A compact grower, a plant wider than tall is formed. Tight ball trusses are composed of violet blue flowers numbering over two dozen. (Magor hyb., intro. Gen. Harrison 1962) F.C.C. 1962.

'Saint Merryn' ('Saint Tudy' x *impeditum*). 30", -5ºF, EM, 3-4/3/3. Blue violet funnel-form flowers appear on a compact, hardy plant. (Harrison 1970) A.M. 1970.

'Saint Minver' (*russatum* x 'Saint Breward'). 3', -10ºF, E, -/-/-. This hybrid has blue violet flowers and dense, small foliage. (Gen. Harrison reg. 1973).

'Saint Tudy' (*impeditum* x *augustinii*). 3', -5ºF, EM, 3/3/3. The flower is violet blue, paler in throat, funnel-form, with slightly wavy margins, and grows on a vigorous, upright, and compact, free-flowering plant. (Magor, Harrison 1961) A.M. 1960, F.C.C. 1973.

'Salute' ('Essex Scarlet' x *forrestii* ssp. *forrestii* Repens Group). 3', -15ºF, M, 3/3/3. 'Salute' is a vigorous growing plant with a relatively open, leggy habit. Dark green foliage, characteristic of the Repens Group, provides a background for the blood red flowers that open from lighter buds. (Hobbie).

'Sammetglut' ('Mars' x 'Nova Zembla'). 5', -15ºF, M, 3-4/3/3-4. In form a rounded plant with a spreading habit, this hardy hybrid is densely covered with hairy, dark green foliage. Large trusses of bright, cardinal red flowers have conspicuous peach anthers. This combination is well reflected in the German name which means 'Velvet Glow'. (Hachmann hyb., Stuck reg. 1983).

'Samoa' ([*catawbiense* var. *album* x *yakushimanum*] x ['Fanfare' x 'Gertrud Schale']). 5', -20ºF, EM, 4/4/3. Densely covered with rough, elliptical foliage, this plant grows to be wider than tall. Vivid red flowers have faint dorsal spotting. (David Leach hyb. 1962, reg. 1985).

'Sandling' ('Lady Bessborough' x *souliei*). 5', -5ºF, M, 3/3/3. Very attractive, frilly, soft pink flowers with faint amber coloring in the throat are held in compact trusses. (Hardy, Sandling Park) A.M. 1965.

Hybrids ~ by Leach

R. 'Rio'

R. 'Casanova'

R. 'Persia'

R. 'Small Wonder'

R. 'Dolly Madison'

R. 'Trinidad'

R. 'Normandy'

R. 'Ravenna'

R. 'Lodestar'

Hybrids ~

by Phetteplace

by Spady

by Jim Elliot

R. 'Crater Lake'

R. 'Honsu's Baby'

R. 'Wickiup'
R. 'Frontier'

R. 'Nasalle'
R. 'Gala'

R. 'Lady Luck'

R. 'Robinette'

by Berg

R. 'Honey Bee'

R. 'Wee Bee'

R. 'Ginny Gee'

'Noyo Brave'

R. 'Nestucca'

R. 'Molly Smith'

R. 'Livonia Lindsley'

by Cecil Smith

Hybrids ~

by Van Veen

by Wright

R. 'Van'

R. 'Old Copper'

R. 'Autumn Gold'

R. 'Evening Glow'

by Lofthouse / Cavender

R. 'Vancouver, USA'

by Larson

R. 'Lemon Marmalade'

Hybrids ~

R. 'Oh! Kitty'

R. 'Skookum'

by Minch

by Goheen

R. 'Neat-o'

R. 'Amigo'

R. 'Bergie Larson'

R. 'Blue Ja

'Sandwich Appleblossom' (elipidote hybrid, probably containing subsect. Fortunea). 6', -10ºF, M, -/-/-. Growing as high as wide, this well-branched shrub can reach dimensions of seven feet. The dense form is covered with large, matte green leaves in addition to fragrant flowers of purplish-pink. The blooms are deeper in color at the margins fading to lighter tones in a throat accented with strong greenish yellow spots. (Dexter hyb., Heritage Plantation reg. 1988).

'Sandy Petuso' (['America' x 'Nova Zembla'] x ['Mars' x 'America']). 5', -20ºF, ML, -/-/-. An upright growing plant with a spreading habit, its many branches are covered with large, green foliage. Dark buds open to reveal fiery red flowers held in full trusses. (Sold by Roslyn 1994).

'Sapphire' ('Blue Tit' x impeditum). 30", -5ºF, EM, 3/3/3-4. This bushy dwarf hybrid has pert dusty green leaves. The pleasing round shape is created by numerous short stems clad with small leaves whose margins are rolled downward. Light blue flowers are in scale with the plant's size. (Knap Hill Nursery before 1958).

'Sappho' (unknown). 6', -15ºF, M, 3/2/4. The plant habit is open-growing and sturdy, with a tendency toward legginess. Leaves are medium sized, somewhat narrow and olive green. Flowers are white, in the mid-size range, and have a very conspicuous, very dark, purplish-black blotch. Trusses are compact and rounded. (A. Waterer before 1867).

'Sarita Loder' (griersonianum x 'Loderi' g.). 4', 5ºF, ML, 4/3/3-4. Very large, tubular funnel shaped flowers are deep crimson in bud and open to a rich, rose salmon. The flowers have good substance. Long, pointed leaves clothe a plant with upright, open, formal appearance. (Loder 1934) A.M. 1934.

'Sarled' (sargentianum x trichostomum var. ledoides). 2', -10ºF, ML, 4/3/2-3. While many of the dwarf forms bloom early, this is refreshingly late. Creamy white, daphne-like flowers appear in tight little ball shaped trusses. (Ingram) A.M. 1974.

'Satan's Fury' ('Vulcan' x 'Sun Devil'). 3', 5ºF, -/-/-. Densely covered with long, narrow, dark green foliage, this compact plant grows to be equally as broad as high. Ruffled flowers are held together in groups of 11 to form dome shaped trusses. The blooms are cardinal red, shading to a grayish rust colored center with spots of similar color on the dorsal lobe. (Bulgin hyb. 1980, reg. 1988).

'Satin Gold' ('Shah Jehan' x yakushimanum). 3', -5ºF, M, 4/4/4. Great "yak" foliage persists on this neat, rounded plant which has soft yellow flowers, each containing a small, bright red eye. (Brandt before 1965).

'Sausalito' (calophytum pink form x 'Loderi Venus'). 6', -5ºF, E, 4/4/4. Leaves are quite large; 4" flowers are bright pink, blotched bright red on the upper lobe, in a 14 flower truss. (J. Henny about 1968, The Bovees reg. 1974) P.A. 1967.

'Scandinavia' ('Betty Wormald' x 'Hugh Koster'). 3', 0ºF, ML, 3/2/3. Large, dome shaped trusses of dark crimson have black spotting. There is a slight reddish coloring to the branches and leaves. (Koster & Sons before 1950) A.M. 1950.

'Scarlet Blast' ('Mars' x ['Mars' x catawbiense var. rubrum]). 3', -20ºF, M, -/-/-. Plant habit is broader than tall, with foliage open, not too dense. Leaves are elliptic, curving downward, dark green. Open bell-shaped flowers are dark red, shading lighter, blotched light pinkish yellow and with a few darker orange-yellow spots, and held in a tight truss to 17 flowers. (Leach 1972).

'Scarlet Glow' (red catawbiense seedling x red catawbiense seedling). 5', -15ºF, ML, 2/3/3. Leaves are medium size and narrow. Flowers are 2" wide, brick red, and held in a conical truss. (Shammarello 1972).

'Scarlet King' ('Ilam Alarm' x griersonianum). 5', 10ºF, M-ML, 4/3/3-4. An introduction from New Zealand, good for warmer climates. Rich scarlet trusses form on a handsome shrub. (Stead, New Zealand, intro. 1950, RHS reg. 1958).

'Scarlet Romance' ('Vulcan' x 'Chocolate Soldier'). 4', -25ºF, L, 3/3/3. A spreading habit provides this plant with a width nearly twice its height. The red flowers open to form large, rounded trusses. (Melquist).

'Scarlet Wonder' ('Essex Scarlet' x forrestii ssp. forrestii Repens Group) 2', -15ºF, M, 4/4-5/4. Here is a low, exceptionally compact, floriferous hybrid with dense glossy green leaves that have a delightful texture. The plant will stand more sun and exposure than most. This will be a plant you will enjoy 12 months of the year, especially when it explodes into a mass of brilliant scarlet red flowers. (Hobbie hyb. before 1960, Le Feber intro., Hobbie reg. 1970) H.C. 1970, S.G.M. 1960, G.M. (Boskoop) 1961.

'Schamenek's Glow' (yakushimanum x smirnowii). 3', -10ºF, ML, 4/4/3-4. Leaves are medium large. Flowers, to 3 1/2" in width, are pale pink to white, with a chartreuse blotch, and are held in a ball shaped, 12 flower truss. (Schamenek, Tietjens 1976).

'Schneebukett' ('Mrs J. G. Millais x 'Bismarck'). 6', -10ºF, ML, -/-/-. A mounding plant with elliptical, glossy green foliage. Ball-shaped trusses hold many white flowers, each having a prominent red blotch. (Hachmann hyb. 1965, Stuck reg. 1983).

'Schneekoppe' (carolinianum x ciliatum). 3', -15ºF, ML, 4/3/3. A rarity in the U.S., this compact plant has narrow, green foliage and upright white trusses which have slight cast of blue. (Sold by Kelleygreen 1994).

'Schneekrone' ('Humboldt' x yakushimanum 'Koichiro Wada'). 3', -15ºF, M, -/-/-. This rounded plant has many branches covered with deep green, slightly hairy foliage. Buds, rose in color, open to reveal white blooms flushed with pink and delicate red spotting. (Hachmann hyb. 1968, Stuck reg. 1983).

'Schubert' (griffithianum hybrid. 4', -5ºF, M, -/-/-. A vigorous growing, bushy plant having fringed, pale orchid flowers with a lighter blotch. (M. Koster & Sons before 1958).

'Schuylkill' (probably natural hybrid of catawbiense x decorum). 30", -5ºF, EM, -/-/-. The foliage is medium large. It has 3 1/4" flowers that are pink fading to creamy white. Each has a darker pink center, stripes and spotting. Flowers are carried in a rounded truss of up to 18. (Herbert 1978).

'Scintillation' (unknown). 5', -15ºF, M, 4/4/4-5. The foliage is deep shiny green. It curls interestingly and has a heavy, waxy texture. The strong growing plant has large stems, providing the strength to support its large flowers. The flowers are a beautiful pastel pink and have flared markings in the throats. These start out as a rich, dark pink becoming burnished after the flower has been out for some time. Extra hardy. (Dexter, Vossberg 1973) S.P.A. 1991 Northeast.

'Scott's Starbright' ('Else Frye' x dalhousiae var. rhabdotum). 4', 15ºF, EM, 4-5/3/3. Bright primrose yellow buds, striped berry red, open to white wavy edged, moderately scented flowers. The blooms are accented by soft yellow spotting, external red stripes, and are held in flat trusses. Oblong foliage has scaly petioles. (Scott hyb. 1968, reg. 1992).

'Sea Shells' (unknown parentage, likely to contain *forrestii* ssp. *forrestii* Repens Group). 3', 0ºF, M, 4/4/4. Of rounded habit and covered with dark, glossy, rounded foliage. The coral pink flowers have a creamy yellow center. The vibrant colors of the fresh blooms fade to a delicate, swirling appearance of the inside of a sea shell. (Grown by Aasland before 1990). Note: there is a registered *R. campylocarpum* cross named 'Sea-Shell'.

'Sea-Tac' ('Moser's Maroon' x *williamsianum*). 30", 0ºF, E, 3/3-4/3-4. Foliage is small, and flowers are dark red, up to 2 1/2" across, held in a 7-flower truss. (Larson 1958, reg. 1977).

'Seattle Gold' ('Diva' x 'Lady Bessborough'). 6', 0ºF, M, 3-4/3/3-4. Highly colored petioles suspend slender, long leaves from the boughs of this large plant. 'Seattle Gold's' flower is a deep warm yellow. (Lem, McClure before 1958).

'Seattle Springtime' (*leucaspis* x *mucronulatum*). 3', 5ºF, E, 3/2/3. Growth habit is open, and small leaves are medium olive green. Flowers are 2 1/4" wide and white flushed with amaranth rose. (Mulligan 1954).

'Second Honeymoon' ([*wardii* (Barto form) x 'Devonshire Cream'] x *wardii*). 4', 5ºF, M, 4/3/-. The plant is compact and has heavy, dark green foliage. Its yellow flowers each have a red blotch. Same cross as 'Honeymoon'. (Whitney before 1970).

'Sefton' (*catawbiense* hybrid). 4', -15ºF, ML, 3/2/3. Large plum maroon flowers, in a fairly large truss are held on a plant with spreading growth habit. This plant benefits from pinching and pruning to prevent a straggly appearance. (A. Waterer 1881).

'Senator Henry M. Jackson' (*yakushimanum* x 'Mrs. Horace Fogg'). 3', -5ºF, M, 4/5/5. Typical of many "yak" hybrids, this super plant is compact and has that great, deep green, indumented foliage. Perfect trusses of pure white cover this profuse bloomer. Note: This name will probably change to 'Senator Jackson'. (Larson hyb., Fisher intro. about 1985).

'Senegal' (*keiskei* x *minus* var. *minus* Carolinianum Group). 3', -15ºF, EM, -/-/-. A rounded, mounding growth habit is clothed in small, narrow foliage. Flowers open a pale greenish-yellow, lightly flushed with orange. They mature to a uniform pale yellow. (Leach 1985).

'Senko Blue' (parentage unknown). 6', -15ºF, M, 3/3/3. This is a fast grower, densely covered with lush green foliage. Lavender-blue flowers are held in upright, dome-shaped trusses. (sold by Hammond).

'Senora Meldon' (*augustinii* 'Lackamas Blue' x 'Blue Diamond'). 4', 0ºF, M, 4-5/4-5/4. Small, wisteria blue flowers, with a few green spots, grow in clusters to 5" wide. It is an upright, well-branched, densely growing plant with rich aromatic, emerald green leaves. It blooms profusely and reliably, beginning at a young age. (Goheen 1993).

'Senorita' ('Loderi King George' x 'Ostbo's 43' No. 2). 5', -5ºF, ML, -/-/-. Leaves are large. The ruffled, lilac pink flowers are also large, to 4" wide. They have reddish purple edges, yellowish pink throats with yellow brown spotting and are held in a truss up to 14. (Bovee 1960).

'Senorita Chere' (*yakushimanum* x 'Mars'). 4', -15ºF, M, 4/4-5/4. Buds of delicious red open to rose flowers which mature to light rose. Tight trusses with an exceptional number of flowers cover this plant in profusion. Compact growth habit and a cover of heavy green leaves make this a good looking plant year around. (Greer, Boltman 1988).

'September Song' ('Dido' x 'Fawn'). 4', 0ºF, M, 4-5/4/4. Magnificent orange trusses cover this hybrid with a color rarely seen in rhododendrons. It buds young and freely and has great foliage that is olive green, medium sized and about three times as long as wide. It's a good compact growing plant which will grow wider than tall. (Phetteplace hyb., Greer raised and intro. 1988).

'September Snow' (*leucaspis* x *edgeworthii*). 2', 15ºF, E, 4/4/4. A very compact plant with rounded, fuzzy foliage. Fragrant, white flowers are held in trusses of 4-6. Called 'September Snow' because it flowers in September in New Zealand, which is equal to March conditions in the Northern Hemisphere. (B. W. Campbell 1981).

'Serenata' ('Russell Harmon' x [*dichroanthum* x {*fortunei* ssp. *discolor* x *campylocarpum*}]). 5', -15ºF, ML, 4/4/-. Leaves grow obliquely at a 45º angle. Flowers, up to 2 1/2" across, are light orangey yellow with a strong orange spotted dorsal blotch. The blooms have heavy substance and are carried in a truss of up to 17 flowers. (Leach 1964).

'Serendipity' (*yakushimanum* x *aureum*). 1', -25ºF, M, 4/4/4. Low growing and spreading, this plant is densely covered with dark green foliage. Pale yellow, campanulate flowers are held in flat trusses. (Potter 1972).

'Seta' (*spinuliferum* x *moupinense*). 5', 5ºF, E, 4/3/3. In the early spring, before there is much color, 'Seta' bursts forth in full splendor. The flowers are light pink with deep candy pink on the back of the tubular flowers. (Aberconway 1933) A.M. 1933, F.C.C. 1960.

'Seven Stars' ('Sir Joseph Hooker' x *yakushimanum*). 3', -5ºF, M, 4/4/3. Dull green leaves clothe this compact plant, which needs shade or the foliage will burn. Very light pink, almost white, flowers are borne profusely. (Crown Estate comm. 1966) H.C. 1965, A.M. 1967, F.C.C. 1974.

'Sevenac' ('Britannia' x *hanceanum*). 3', -5ºF, EM, -/-/-. If this cross is accurately reported, it would be one of only a handful of lepidote x elepidote hybrids. It is offered by Hydon Nurseries, Surrey, England. Compact with scarlet red flowers. It has to be interesting. (sold by Hydon about 1980).

'Seville' see 'Madrid'.

'Shaazam' ('Pink Twins' x 'Leah Yates'). 4', -10ºF, ML, -/-/-. Foliage is medium size. Seven-lobed flowers, to 3 3/4" across, are neyron rose in color. They shade lighter towards the edges and sport a yellow blotch. The truss is ball shaped and holds up to 10 flowers. (Yates, M. Yates 1977).

'Shah Jehan' ('Day Dream' x 'Margaret Dunn'). 4', -5ºF, ML, 3-4/3/3. Compact plant habit and rounded leaves give this hybrid an appearance somewhat like 'Unique'. Flowers are a warm chrome yellow, paler at the outer edges, with burnt orange spotting on the throat. A very attractive rhododendron. (Brandt 1965).

'Shalimar' (Dexter hybrids, open pollinated). 5', -5ºF, ML, -/-/-. Leaves are large. 7-lobed flowers are a generous 4 1/2" wide, slightly scented, pale lavender pink, are held in a ball-shaped truss of up to 12 flowers. (Vossberg, Schlaikjer 1974).

'Shalom' ('Anna' x 'Antoon van Welie'). 5', -5ºF, ML, -/-/-. Foliage is of medium size; 3 1/2" flowers are white shaded rose, with a darker rose flare, carried in a 16-flower flat truss. (Lem, Hess 1974) C.A. 1973.

'Shamrock' (*keiskei* dwarf form x *hanceanum* 'Nanum'). 1', -5ºF, E, 3-4/4/4. The plant is extremely compact and wider than high. The flower color, chartreuse, and the blooming time, around St. Patrick's Day, go right along with its name. (Ticknor 1978).

'Sham's Candy' ('Pinnacle' x 'Pink Cameo'). 5', -20ºF, ML, 3/3/3. Leaves are medium sized and narrow. Deep pink flowers, to 2 3/4" across, have a yellow green blotch and are held in a conical truss. (Shammarello 1976).

'Sham's Juliet' ('Boule de Neige' x *catawbiense*). 4', -20ºF, ML, 3/3/3. A brown blotch floats in a sea of apple blossom pink. Leaves are olive green and plant is compact. (Shammarello reg. 1972).

'Sham's Pink' ('Boule de Neige' x red *catawbiense* seedling). 4', -20ºF, ML, 3/2/3. Foliage is medium sized, pea-green. 2 1/2" wide flowers are rosy pink, with darker edges and a light red blotch, held in a rounded truss. (Shammarello 1972).

'Sham's Ruby' ('Kettledrum' x 'America'). 3', -20ºF, ML, 3/3/3. Flowers of strong purplish red have a faint blotch of deeper tone. Valued for its hardiness, it forms an upright, broad semi-dwarf shrub. (Shammarello hyb. 1943, intro. 1961, reg. 1976).

'Shanghai' (['Mrs. Furnivall' x *catawbiense* var. *album*] x unnamed seedling). 6', -10ºF, ML, 4/3/3-4. Leaves are medium sized and narrow. Pale pink flowers, to 3 3/4" across, are edged darker pink, with strong spots of orange-yellow to greenish yellow on dorsal lobe, held in a ball truss of up to 18. (Leach 1973).

'Shapiro Starbright' ('Vulcan' x 'Slocock 24'). 3', -5ºF?, L, -/-/-. Clear red buds open to funnel shaped, frilly red flowers with brighter red edges. Almost immediately shading to near white, the blooms are held in domed trusses of 13-15. (Shapiro hyb. 1965, reg. 1993).

'Shawme Lake' (parentage unknown). 5', -5ºF, E, -/-/-. Of upright growth habit and decorated with large, rose lavender flowers which have a darker flare. The blooms are held in slightly loose trusses. (Dexter pre-1943).

'Sheila Ann' (probably a hybrid of *sanguineum*). 3', 5ºF, L, 3/3/3. This hybrid has the deepest black red flower and is an attractive plant. Good foliage. (Caperci 1969).

'Shilsonii' (*thomsonii* x *barbatum*). 4', 0ºF, VE-E, -/-/-. Deep scarlet, waxy flowers have faint dark brown markings. The plant is tall, arboreal and has leaves which are small and rounded. (Gill 1900) A.M. 1900.

'Shirlandy' ([*brachycarpum* x 'Crest'] x 'Scotty D'). 2', -5ºF, L, -/-/-. Wavy edged flowers display a blend of colors from yellowish pink to reddish orange to pale yellow. The funnel-shaped blooms have a throat with red spots which fades to light greenish yellow. (Delp 1994).

'Shirley' (*yakushimanum* Exbury form x 'Thomaleum'). 3', 10ºF, M, -/-/-. This is A rounded compact plant sheathed in deep olive green leaves that have a yellowish white, felted indumentum. Dusty-rose buds open to reveal pink flowers that fade to white. This creates an interesting show as new buds are opening pink while the trusses have matured to white. (A. P. Johnson 1986).

'Shirley Rose Lent' (*strigillosum* x *praevernum*). 5', 10ºF, VE, -/-/-. Leaves are long 'and quite narrow. Flowers, to 2 1/4" in width, are deep, dark pink, with even darker spots on upper lobe. They are carried in a well-rounded 13 flower truss. (Nelson, Heller 1977).

'Shooting Star' (*hippophaeoides* var. *hippophaeoides* Fimbriatum group x *racemosum*). 3', -5ºF, E, 3-4/3-4/4. A rapid growing little hybrid that flowers very heavily, covering itself with long spires of lavender pink flowers. Like its parent *R. racemosum*, it grows long stems, supporting the racemes. These are best cut back after blooming to maintain compact plant habit. They can also be cut while flowering, giving a super cut flower. The leaves are small, 3 to 4 times as long as wide. This young flowering plant grows easily, propagates well, and is sun tolerant. (Greer 1988).

'Show Boat' (*yakushimanum* 'Exbury' x 'Tumalo'). 4', -5ºF, M, 4/4/3. Compact, rounded, and well branched, 'Show Boat' has an excellent plant habit. Rounded leaves have a very light coating of buff indumentum. The flowers are pink in bud, opening into pure white with a yellowish green blotch in throat. An all-around good plant. (Phetteplace 1975).

'Show-Off' ('Moonstone' x 'Carolyn Grace'). 4', 5ºF, M, 3/4/3-4. Growth habit of this plant is compact and mound-like with small, dark green leaves. Flowers are cup-shaped, to 2 1/2" wide. The clear pale yellow blooms are set in a lax truss. (Wright 1963).

'Shrimp Girl' (*yakushimanum* x 'Fabia Tangerine'). 3', 0ºF, M, 3-4/3-4/3-4. This plant has good foliage and a compact habit, with soft rose flowers. (Waterer, Sons & Crisp Ltd. 1970).

'Siam' (*catawbiense* var. *album* x *yakushimanum*). 4', -20ºF, ML, 4/4/4. Shiny leaves have nice indumentum below. Buds are light purple pink opening first to soft pink, then becoming a beautiful white. (Leach hyb. 1952, intro. 1975, reg. 1983).

'Side Step' ('Laetevirens' x *minus* var. *minus* Carolinianum Group *album*). 3', -20ºF, ML, -/-/-. A compact, wide growing plant with small foliage. The white flowers appear in May. (Mezitt hyb. about 1985, Weston Nurseries intro. about 1990).

'Sierra Sunrise' ('Mrs. Horace Fogg' x 'Point Defiance'). 6', 0ºF, ML, 5/4/3-4. This is a large-growing, handsome plant, with dark green, pointed leaves that curve upward from the midrib. Large, ruffled flowers, rosy-pink shading slightly darker to edges, have a small reddish blotch, and are set in foot-tall, conical trusses. (Lofthouse 1975).

'Siesta' ('Britannia' x *yakushimanum*). 3', -15ºF, M, 4/4/3. Light indumentum covers the underside of the foliage. Flowers begin as pink buds opening to soft pink and aging to white. (Elliott).

'Sigismund Rucker' (parentage unknown). 4', -15ºF, ML, -/-/-. This mounding plant is densely covered with curving, elliptical, dark green leaves. Medium-sized, rounded trusses hold rich, cherry ice colored blooms with a black flare. (A. Waterer) F.C.C. 1872.

'Signal Horn' ('Atrosanguineum' x 'Goldsworth Yellow'). 5', -15ºF, ML, -/-/-. Leaves are large. Blooms, to 2" across, are rosy pink accented by darker pink edging and a distinctive spotted red blotch. The flowers are held in a lax truss of up to 8. (Nearing 1973).

'Sigrid' ('Marinus Koster' x 'Pilgrim'). 5', 5ºF, L, -/-/-. Foliage is medium size and narrow. 3" wide flowers are pink fading paler, with darker pink outside and edging, held in a 12-flower truss. (Laxdall 1977).

'Silberwolke' (*yakushimanum* 'Koichiro Wada' x 'Album Novum'). 3', -15ºF, ML, 4/4/4. The rounded plant is covered with dark green foliage. The flowers are very light purple inside with yellow green spotting, the reverse side is shaded darker. (Hachmann hyb. 1963, Stuck reg. 1983) A.M. Boskoop 1982.

'Silky Gold' (['Seattle Gold' x 'Autumn Gold'] x 'Bonito'). 5', 0ºF, L, 4/3/3. Here is an upright grower with rugged, deeply veined foliage and flowers of contrasting very soft, pastel hues of yellow. (Larson hyb., Clint Smith intro.).

'Silver Jubilee' ('Mrs. W. C. Slocock' x 'Coronation Day'). 5', 5ºF, M, -/-/-. Flowers open chartreuse green, and mature to white lightly washed in green. Crimson spotting accents the inner throat. (George hyb. 1967, Hydon Nurseries reg. 1978).

'Silver Lady' (*yakushimanum* x *smirnowii*). 3', 0ºF, M, 4/4/4. A free flowering hybrid with both flowers and foliage resembling the *yakushimanum* parent. Leaves have a very pronounced indumentum. Rose colored buds burst open to reveal white flowers. (Horstmann, Wieting 1989).

'Silver Sixpence' (['Fabia' x {*fortunei* ssp. *discolor* x *eriogynum*}] x ([{*fortunei* ssp. *discolor* x unknown} x *griersonianum*] x [*wardii* x *yakushimanum*])). The exact order of parentage is unknown. 3', -5ºF, M, 5/4/4. White flowers have a blush of rose and light yellow spotting in the throat. Silvery foliage is another plus on this beautiful English hybrid. (Waterer 1975).

'Silver Skies' (*yakushimanum* 'Koichiro Wada' x 'Medusa'). 3', -5ºF, M, -/-/-. Dark buds open to reveal magenta pink flowers with darker margins. The dark green foliage is attractively indumented. (Fujioka 1990).

'Simmon's Classic' (elepidote hybrid, possibly *R. wardii* and other species). 3', 0ºF, M, 3-4/4/3. This plant with a spreading but rounded habit, has many branches cloaked in glossy, forest green leaves. Upright, lax trusses hold yellow blossoms with scarlet spotting inside. (Whitney hyb., Briggs 1989).

'Simona' ('Harvest Moon' x 'Letty Edwards'). 6', 0ºF, M, 4/4/4. Light, rose pink flowers are held in groups of a dozen to form rounded trusses. The blooms are edged with a creamy yellow pink and blotched with a vibrant ruby red. As the flower ages, it becomes more cream colored. A very beautiful and vigorous hybrid with attractive deep green leaves. (Hachmann hyb. 1964, Stuck reg. 1983) G. M. 1987.

'Singapore' ('Fanfare' x 'Gertrude Schale'). 3', -15ºF, M, -/-/-. Leaves are of medium size. Red flowers, to 2 1/4" across, sport a pearly overlay and are held in a truss of up to 13. (Leach 1973).

'Sir Charles Lemon' (probably a selected *arboreum* ssp. *cinnamomeum*). 5', 5ºF, EM, 4/5/3. A real accent plant. Extra handsome foliage has bright cinnamon brown indumentum. New leaves are beautiful as they unfold white. Excellent pure white flowers are a real bonus. Plant it where you can view it all year. (Aberconway 1937).

'Sirius' (*crassum* x 'Magnificum'). 3', 0ºF, ML, -/-/-. Slender, upright growth is highlighted by apricot pink bells. (Reuthe intro. 1949) P.C. 1973.

'Si Si' (*yakushimanum* x 'Gold Mohur'). 4', -5ºF, L, -/-/-. Flowers are light pink to yellowish pink, and have greenish yellow throats. There is a bright red dorsal spot, and outer petal surfaces are strong pink. (Delp 1995).

'Skipper' ('Fawn' x 'Indian Penny'). 5', 0ºF, EM, 5/3/3. Foliage is large. Flowers are huge, to 5" across, empire yellow in color, shading deeper yellow to throat, and are in trusses of up to 14 flowers. (James, Thompson 1972).

'Skookum' ([*yakushimanum* x 'Mars'] x 'America'). 3', -20ºF, M, 4/4/4. The rounded habit supports many branches covered with matte, dark green foliage. The dome-shaped trusses hold flowers of strong red with visible white filaments. (Larson hyb., Fred Minch raiser, reg. 1986).

'Skookumchuck' ([*yakushimanum* x Mars'] x 'America'). 3', -15ºF, M-ML, 4/4/4. A sister cross to the above 'Skookum', this hybrid is more vigorous growing and will achieve a larger size at maturity. It produces bright red flowers that stand out against dark green, leathery leaves. (Larson hyb., Fred Minch raiser about 1986).

'Skyglow' (parentage unknown, probably a hybrid of subsect. Fortunea). 5', -5ºF, L, 3/2/-. The growth habit and leaf color are poor. The leaves are medium size. Flowers are 6-lobed, to 3" wide, peach colored, edged pink, and have a pale greenish yellow blotch. The scented blooms are carried in a flat truss of up to 12. Synonym, Dexter #9. (Heritage Plantation 1977).

'Sleepy' (*yakushimanum* x 'Doncaster' selfed). 3', -10ºF, M, 4/4/4. Cute little plant with compact habit and pale lavender-pink flowers. (Waterer, Sons & Crisp 1970).

'Small Fry' ('Carmen' x 'Moonstone'). 2', 0ºF, E-EM, 3-4/4/4. Bright red stems hold glossy, dark green foliage and rose red flowers. A great low grower. (Hill hyb., Fisher intro.).

'Small Gem' (*pemakoense* x *leucaspis*). 18", -5ºF, E, 3/3-4/4. A real cutie which shows both of its parents. The plant looks like *pemakoense* and the flower looks like *leucaspis*. It buds heavily and at a very young age. The buds, showing a touch of pink, open white, retaining just a kiss of soft pink. A bonus is the deep brown anthers contrasting with the white petals. (Frisbee before 1960).

'Small Wonder' ('Fanfare' x ['Prometheus' x *forrestii* ssp. *forrestii* Repens Group]). 18", -15ºF, EM, 4/4/3-4. Narrow leaves are small to medium in size. 2" wide flowers are red with lighter colored centers, and are held in a 7-flower globular truss. (Leach 1972).

'Smokey #9' ('Burgundy' x 'Moser's Maroon'). 6', -5ºF, ML, 3-4/3/3. 'Smokey #9' has many extravagant features. It exemplifies the showy hybrid Halfdan Lem always pursued in his hybridizing. Heavily veined, fir green leaves veil this large rhododendron. Interesting flower buds have recurved bracts that have a "leafy" look until they open to expose deep purple trusses. This hybrid is one to be enjoyed throughout the year. Unfortunately, the plant becomes leggy with age. (Lem before 1960).

'Sneezy' (*yakushimanum* x 'Doncaster'). 3', -10ºF, M, 4/4/4. This plant has compact habit and flowers of soft pink, with darker margins, and a dark red blotch on each upper petal. (Waterer, Sons & Crisp 1970).

'Snipe' (*pemakoense* x *davidsonianum*). 2', -5ºF, EM, 3/3-4/3. Flowers are light orchid pink. The twiggy branching habit is upright growing. (Cox 1978) A.M. 1975.

'Snow Cap' (*souliei* x ['Loderi White Diamond' x *williamsianum*]). 4', -5ºF, M, 3/3/3. Both leaf buds and new growth stems are chalk yellow. The leaves also have a chalky cast to the underside and are quite flat and somewhat pendant. Flowers are abundant and pure white. (Whitney, Sather 1976).

'Snow Lady' (*leucaspis* x *ciliatum*). 30", -5ºF, E, 3-4/4/4-5/4. The right name was picked for this plant. In flower it might remind you of new fallen snow. Its soft, fuzzy green leaves dress it like a real lady. Flowers well in deep shade. Much appreciated because it buds easily and blooms early. (Lancaster 1958) P.A. 1955.

'Snow Queen' ('Halopeanum' x 'Loderi'). 5', 5ºF, M, 4/2/2-3. One of the best pure snow white flowers you will find. Needs shade for the foliage; however, reported to do well in hotter climates. It is difficult to propagate, so it is rare. (Loder 1926) A.M. 1934, A.M. 1946.

'Snow Sprite' ('Snow Lady' x *moupinense*). 1', 5ºF, E, -/-/-. A compact grower that reaches a width equal to its height. Glossy green leaves are decorated with pure white campanulate flowers. (B. F. Lancaster & R. Whalley reg. 1969).

'Snow's Red' (parentage unknown). 4', -15ºF, M, -/-/-. Vigorous in growth and with an upright habit, this hybrid produces true scarlet flowers in abundance. It is currently acclaimed to be one of the best reds for the Northeast. (Sold by Roslyn 1994).

'Snowstorm' (*yakushimanum* x 'Cary Ann'). 3', -5ºF, M, -/-/-. Flowers are white with rose spotting. It is a vigorous grower with dark green foliage. (Lofthouse 1973).

'Snow White' (*griffithianum* x *fortunei* ssp. *fortunei*). 6', 0ºF, EM, -/-/-. Tall growing, and open in habit. The fragrant, white flowers are flushed with pink before maturing to pure white. (Lowinsky 1923).

'Soft Satin' ('Seattle Gold' x *yakushimanum*). 3', -5ºF, M, 4/5/3. Flowers are creamy in color with a sheen of satin. Leaves are small and dark, and the plant growth is compact. (Brandt before 1965).

'Soldier Palmer' ([*eriogynum* hybrid x 'Fabia'] x [*yakushimanum* x 'Britannia']). 3', 0ºF, -/-/-. Rich brick red flowers are spotted red on this compact plant. (Waterer, Sons & Crisp 1975).

'Soldier Sam' (*dichroanthum* x 'Dido'). 3', -10ºF, M, -/-/-. A magnificent, showy calyx gives an almost hose-in-hose look to these yellow-orange flowers which are tinged red on the outside. Very prolific bloomer. (Reuthe 1985).

'Solidarity' (*yakushimanum* x 'Jean Marie de Montague'). 3', -15ºF, M, -/-/-. This plant was originally listed as being a hybrid of 'Sefton' x *yakushimanum*. Without doubt it is a hybrid of 'Jean Marie de Montague' as its foliage and flower buds look much like this parent. It is faster growing than many R. *yakushimanum* hybrids, often pushing heavy growths of 6-10" long each year. The flower buds first open red, quickly becoming pink and eventually almost white. 'Jean Marie de Montague' has produced some outstanding hybrids such as 'Hallelujah' and 'Halfdan Lem'. 'Solidarity' deserves to join the "famous" hybrids from both of its outstanding parents. (Schannen 1990).

'Sonata' ('Purple Splendour' x *dichroanthum*). 3', 0ºF, L, 3-4/3-4/4. This is one of those hard to describe combinations. Tubular flowers of orange red are edged with claret. The plant grows as a dense mass of slender, dark green leaves and is excellent for a sunny location. (Reuthe 1949) H.C. 1959.

'Sonatine' ('Mars' x *yakushimanum* 'Koichiro Wada'). 2.5', -10ºF, ML, 4/4/4. Forming a plant twice as wide as tall, new growth appears with a silvery covering. Flowers are strong purplish-red fading to white in the throat, with the dorsal lobes marked with strong yellowish-green. (Hachmann hyb. 1968, Stuck reg. 1988).

'Songbird' (*russatum* x 'Blue Tit'). 3', -5ºF or hardier, E-EM, 3-4/4/4. There are many small "blue" rhododendrons, sometimes so many it is hard to separate them all; however, this one will stand out for its bright purple blue flowers which seem to glow. The foliage is glossy green and the plant super compact. (Horlick 1954) A.M. 1957.

'Sonic Ray' ('Vulcan' x 'Sun Devil'). 3', 5ºF, M, -/-/-. An upright grower, the vivid red buds open to reveal deep pink flowers, darker at the base. (Bulgin 1988).

'Sophisticated Lady' ('Firebird' x 'Autumn Gold'). 4', 0ºF, M, -/-/-. Mid-sized and well-branched, this lady is finely clad in lush green foliage. Apricot buds open, exposing multi-color flowers in shades of lilac, peach and yellow. (Bulgin).

'Southamptonia' - see 'Russellianum'.

'Southern Cross' (*fortunei* ssp. *discolor* x 'Lodauric Iceberg'). 5', -5ºF, L, -/-/-. This nicely scented, blush-white flower has a bronze throat. (George, Hydon Nurseries 1955) H.C. 1969.

'Southland' (*minus* var. *chapmanii* x *keiskei* prostrate form). 1.5', -10ºF, M, -/-/-. A compact grower that stretches to a width greater than its height. The salmon colored flowers bloom in profusion and are very tolerant to both heat and drought. (Kehr 1994).

'Souvenir de Anthony Waterer' (parentage unknown). 4', -10ºF, L, -/-/-. Salmon red with an orange yellow eye. (Waterer probably early 1900's or before).

'Souvenir de Dr. S. Endtz' ('Pink Pearl' x 'John Walter'). 5', -10ºF, M, -/-/-. Reuthe says, "An improved 'Pink Pearl'". Dome shaped trusses of bright pink with dark crimson spotting. (Endtz intro. 1927) A.M. 1924, A.G.M. 1969, F.C.C. 1970.

'Souvenir of W. C. Slocock' (*campylocarpum* hybrid). 4', -5ºF, M, 3/3/3. Rounded, compact primrose yellow flowers open apricot. Similar to 'Unique' in its habit and flower, as it is a compact and attractive plant. (W.C. Slocock & Co. Ltd. before 1935) A.M. 1935.

'Spanish Lady' ('Evening Glow' x 'Lamplighter'). 5', -5ºF, ML, 4/3-4/4. Warm reddish orange flowers have a golden glow. A heavy budding plant with long and fairly narrow pine green leaves. Quite vigorous, compact and easy to grow. (Harold & Morna Stockman hyb. 1972, intro. Greer 1988, Stockman reg. 1992).

'Sparkler' ([*eriogynum* hybrid x 'Fabia'] x [*yakushimanum* x 'Britannia']). 4', 0ºF, M, -/-/-. Plant of compact habit and prolific flowering. Flowers are rose colored. (Waterer, Sons & Crisp 1971).

'Sparkling Burgundy' ('Purple Splendour' x *macrophyllum* 'Seven Devils'). 5', 10ºF, M, 3/3/3. An upright, open growth habit is topped with ivy green leaves. Dome-shaped trusses are composed of bell-shaped, lilac flowers with darker violet spotting. (Mossman hyb. 1973, Brotherton reg. 1983).

'Spellbinder' ([*maximum* x 'Russell Harmon'] x [*calophytum* x *sutchuenense*]). 6', -15ºF, E, 3-4/4/4. Foliage is very large. 3 1/2" wide flowers are light lilac pink, with dorsal red spots, darker pink outside, carried in a ball truss to 16. (Leach 1975).

'Spice' see 'Dexter's Spice'.

'Spinulosum' (*spinuliferum* x *racemosum*). 4', 5ºF, E, 4/2-3/3. Light pink buds open into dark pink flowers creating an interesting two-toned appearance. Flowers are borne in feathery pom-pom like trusses and also bloom up and down the stems. Puts on long growth characteristic of its parent *racemosum*. (R. B. G. Kew 1926) A.M. 1944.

'Spitfire' (*griffithianum* hybrid). 6', 0ºF, EM-M, -/-/-. Growth habit is very fine and compact. Flowers are deep, dark crimson red with dark brown blotch. (A. Kluis 1946).

'Springbok' (*griersonianum* x *ponticum* seedling). 4', 0ºF, ML, -/-/-. This open growing plant has large trusses of vivid carmine pink, spotted with crimson. (George 1963).

'Spring Dawn' (pink *catawbiense* hybrid x 'Mrs. Charles S. Sargent'). 5', -20°F, EM, 3/3/3. The strong rosy pink flowers glow with a warm golden yellow blotch that puts life into the flower. Known to do well in the more adverse "non" rhododendron growing areas. It is a vigorous growing plant with attractive foliage. (Shammarello before 1960).

'Springfield' ('Umpqua Chief' x 'Fawn'). 5', 5°F, L, 4/3/3-4. A salmon orange shade that is not duplicated by any other rhododendron is found here. The flowers are very flat faced and the edges roll backwards making a bold truss. Long, narrow fir green leaves clothe this upright plant. (James, Greer 1979).

'Spring Fling' (plant from the 'Lapponicum' Series x *russatum*). 30", -10°F, E, 4/3-4/3-4. Dark electric blue flowers completely cover this super little plant. It has a compact growth habit and is well-clothed with small, deep green leaves which turn reddish bronze in winter. Propagates well and grows easily, but should be planted in a location with excellent drainage. (Greer 1988).

'Spring Frolic' (*catawbiense* var. *album* x *yakushimanum* 'Koichiro Wada'). 3', -25°F, EM, 4/4/4. Medium sized leaves back the deep pink buds. These open to white flowers which reflect the *yakushimanum* parentage, as does the truss. (Leach 1972).

'Spring Glory' ('Cunningham's White' x red *catawbiense* hybrid), 5', -15°F, EM, 3-4/3-4/4. A vigorous growing plant that does well in sun or shade. Pink flowers have a deeper pink marking. If you like pinks with deeper blotches, such as the popular 'Mrs. Furnivall', you will also like this flower. Plant habit is compact. (Shammarello 1955).

'Spring Parade' (red *catawbiense* hybrid x 'Cunningham's White'). 4-5', -20°F, M, 3/2/3-4. Clear scarlet red covers this plant when it is in full flower. Each truss is in the shape of a round globe. The dark green leaves are recurved. (Shammarello 1960).

'Spring Snow' (*aureum* x *metternichii* var. *pentamerum*). 30", -5°F, E, -/-/-. Foliage is small. White flowers, to 2" in width, are lavender pink on the outside, held in a 10 flower truss. (University of Washington Arboretum, Mulligan 1977).

'Spring Song' ([*racemosum* x *keiskei*] x *keiskei*). 2-3', -10°F, E-EM, -/-/-. Flowers are light yellow, fading to salmon apricot. (Hardgrove 1951).

'Spring Sun' ('Adriaan Koster' x *williamsianum*). 3', 0°F, ML, 3/3/3. Pert yellow flowers and delicate, rounded foliage are found on this plant. A very neat appearance. (Hobbie).

'Springtime' (Klupenger) see 'Williams'.

'Spun Gold' ('Mrs. Lammot Copeland' x 'Mary Drennen'). 3', 0°F, ML, -/-/-. This upright grower has a habit as broad as it is tall. The well-branched structure is densely covered with matte green leaves. Campanulate flowers of amber yellow are held in lax trusses. Each bloom is accented with red freckling on the dorsal lobe. (Larson hyb., W. Robertson, intro. 1980, reg. 1983).

'Staccato' ('Shrimp Pink' hybrid). 4', -15°F, EM, 3-4/3-4/3-4. Wide and upright in growth, 'Staccato' is dressed with lush green summer foliage that turns to shades of mahogany in winter. Semi-double flowers are deep, silvery pink. (Weston Nurseries intro.).

'Stacia' (*fortunei* ssp. *fortunei* x 'Everestianum'). 5', -15°F, ML, -/-/-. Leaves are medium to large. Fragrant blooms, to 3 1/4" across, are cobalt violet, fading toward the throat, with a dim blotch of uranium green. The 6-lobed flowers are held in a 12 flower truss. (Druecker 1976).

'Stadt Essen' (*williamsianum* x 'Louis Pasteur'). 3', -10°F, ML, 3/3/-. This compact plant is densely covered with round, green foliage. The flowers are clear pink fading lighter inside. (Hobbie 1978).

'Stan Kubas' (parentage unknown). 3', 0°F, EM, -/-/-. A great, free flowering plant with vibrant red bells hanging in neat clusters. Foliage is narrow and dense and the plant is round. (Kubas before 1985).

'Stanley Davies' (parentage unknown). 4, -10°F, ML, 4/4/3. The broadly mounding habit displays dense, dark green foliage. Fiery red blossoms have darker markings and form compact trusses. (Davies of Ormskirk, England 1890).

'Stanley Rivlin' (*yakushimanum* x 'Royal Blood'). 3', 0°F, M, -/-/-. Purple mauve petal edges surround a deeper center. (Hydon Nurseries 1972).

'Starbright' see 'Greer's Starbright', 'Scott's Starbright', or 'Shapiro Starbright'.

'Starbright Champagne' (['Yaku Sunrise' x 'Hansel'] x 'Lem's Cameo'). 4', 0°F, EM, -/-/-. An unusual star shaped flower, each petal is long and pointed! The flowers are a dark champagne color with a dark purple throat. Great foliage on a dense, very rounded growing plant, makes this a delight in the garden. (Frank Fujioka hyb. 1983, reg. 1995).

'Starburst' ('Moser's Maroon' x 'Purple Splendour'). 6', 5°F, L, 4/2-3/3-4. A golden blotch surrounded by white makes a magnificent display on a deep red purple flower. The foliage is deep green with red stems. Plant habit is upright and somewhat open. Has also been called 'Royal Star', although there is another plant by that name. (Greer 1988).

'Starcross' (*fortunei* ssp. *discolor* x 'Lodauric Iceberg'). 5', -5°F, L, 4/3-4/3-4. Large, compact trusses are of fragrant, creamy pink flowers. (George, Hydon Nurseries reg. 1967).

'Stardust' ('Unique' x 'Crest'). 4', -5°F, M, 4/4/3-4. A yellow 'Unique'! All the attributes that make 'Unique' so appealing are present on this slightly larger growing plant. (Sold by Fisher about 1980).

'Starlet' ('Diva' x *williamsianum*). 30", 5°F, EM, 4/4/3-4. Leaves are small to medium. 4" wide flowers are rose colored, held in a loose 6-flower truss. (Lem, Fawcett 1963) P.A. 1963.

'Star of Spring' (parentage unknown). 5', -5°F, EM, -/-/-. Leaves are medium to large. 3 1/2" flowers are clear pink, fading to white, with red spotting. The 6-lobed flowers are held in a truss of up to 13. (Hardgrove about 1960, Royce 1979).

'Starry Night' see 'Gletschernacht'.

'Stars and Stripes' (unknown elepidote hybrid). 3', M, -5°F, -/-/-. This hybrid from Whitney Gardens has a most unusual flower, rose colored, covered with dots of deeper red all over the inside of each flower. It is a compact grower and buds exceptionally heavily, flowering beautifully each year. (Whitney hyb. before 1970, Sather intro. about 1990).

'Star Sapphire' (*augustinii* x *minus* var. *minus* Carolinianum Group). 3', -5°F, EM, -/-/-. An upright growing plant with large bluish flowers. (Hardgrove before 1958).

'Star Trek' (*davidsonianum* Exbury form x *davidsonianum* 'Ruth Lyons'). 4', 5°F, E, 4/3-4/4. Clusters of 3-5 purple flowers at each terminal are held on very erect branches with dark green, 2 1/2" leaves. This plant has been sold as *R. davidsonianum* Bergie form. (Childers reg. 1977).

'**Stephanie**' (unknown, probably contains *forrestii* ssp. *forrestii* Repens Group and *griersonianum*, plus other species). 3', 0ºF, M, 3/3/4. A light red with no other color in the flower. The leaves are small on a compact plant. (Whitney, Sather 1976).

'**Stephen Clarke**' ('Britannia' x 'Autumn Gold'). 4', -5ºF, M, 4/3/3-4. An upright grower, achieving a width greater than its height. Carmine buds open to coral pink flowers, with rose edges. The blooms mature to show yellow tones. (Mrs. J. H. Clarke hyb., S. Clarke reg. 1981).

'**Stockholm**' ('Catalgla' x *decorum*). 5', -20ºF, EM, 3/3/4. Medium sized foliage. Flowers are white, to 2 1/4" across, with 2 small rays of greenish yellow spots on the dorsal lobe. They are carrried in ball shaped trusses of up to 14. (Hobbie, Leach 1974).

'**Stoplight**' (*griersonianum* x 'Cornubia'). 6', 10ºF, EM, 3-4/2/4. Leaves are large and narrow. 3 1/2" flowers are bright geranium red, lightly blotched, in a 13-flower truss. (R. Henny about 1950) P.A. 1951.

'**Strategist**' (*griffithianum* x 'John Waterer'). 6', -10ºF?, L, -/-/-. Tall conical trusses are comprised of pale pink flowers, with rose margins and yellow spotting in the throat. Bright green foliage is broad and covers the frame of branches. (J. Waterer before 1900).

'**Strawberry Cream**' (*flavidum* x 'Lady Rosebery'). 5', 0ºF, EM, 3/3/3. An upright plant with neat, glossy foliage. Large, unique flowers open pastel pink. See further description of this plant under 'Flip'. (Brandt hyb. before 1960, grown by Greer, Cox reg. 1993).

'**Strawberry Swirl**' (*caucasicum* x 'Nobleman'). 4', -15ºF, EM, -/-/-. A very attractive blend of rose with a darker blotch and peppermint pink stripes on the reverse. Plant is rounded, slightly broader than tall. (unknown hybridizer).

'**Suave**' (*edgeworthii* x *bullatum*) 5', 10ºF, EM, 4/3/3-4. One of the most fragrant of all rhododendrons, this plant covers itself with light pink and white flowers. When in flower, one plant will give the whole garden fragrance. Rough textured foliage is medium sized and quite attractive. (Ludwig Leopold Liebig before 1863).

'**Sue**' ('Loderi King George' selfed). 6', 0ºF, M, 5/3-4/3-4. 'Sue' is not actually one of the 'Loderi' group since it is down an additional generation. It does, however, have the very same 'Loderi' characteristics of plant habit, leaf, and flower. The colossal trusses are made up of fragrant flowers that are even pinker than 'Loderi Venus'. A magnificently beautiful rhododendron. (James before 1958).

'**Suede**' (*haematodes* x *bureavii*). 3', -10ºF, M, 3-4/4-5/3. Thick, orange red indumentum clothes the deep green foliage of this wonderful hybrid. Flowers are deep rose with brown speckles in the throat. (Judson reg. 1973).

'**Sugar and Spice**' (['Palmer' x 'Loderi King George'] x 'Madame Masson'). 5', - 5ºF, ML, 4/4/4. A fantastic hybrid from Tom and Emma Bowhan. The flowers are bright creamy white with a golden brown blotch, from creamy pink buds. Leaves are dark and slender. A very pretty plant with blooms that always look fresh and crisp. (Bowhan about 1980).

'**Sugar Daddy**' (a *decorum* hybrid). 5', 0ºF, EM, -/-/-. Stiff, upright plant habit with rounded trusses of pink fading to white, green in the throat. (Waterer, Sons & Crisp 1970).

'**Sugar Pink**' ('Trude Webster' x ['Fawn' x 'Queen of the May']). 6', -5ºF, M, 4/4/4-5. 'Sugar Pink' has the tallest truss of about any rhododendron, often over 1', and it has foliage to match. The flower color is a tantalizing cotton candy pink, looking good enough to eat. This hybrid has taken all the best traits of its parent 'Trude Webster'. The foliage is large, smooth and deep green. (Greer 1979).

'**Sugar Plum**' ('Moonstone' x 'Carolyn Grace'). 3', 0ºF, EM, 3/3/3. This plant has small foliage and 3" wide, deep pink flowers which are held in lax trusses of up to 8. (Wright, Sr. and Jr. 1963).

'**Sumatra**' ('America' x 'Gertrud Schale'). 2', -15ºF, M, 4/4/3. Deep cardinal red flowers are found in an open truss. Narrow, yellow green leaves grace the plant which is more broad than tall. (Leach intro. 1973, reg. 1983).

'**Summer Cloud**' (*yakushimanum* x *fortunei* ssp. *fortunei*). 3', -15ºF, ML, 4-5/4-5/4. A compact and spreading hybrid with pink buds that open to expose fragrant, white flowers. (Riverwood Gardens, New Zealand, intro. before 1994).

'**Summer Glow**' ('Summer Snow' x 'Scarlet Blast'). 6', -15ºF, VL, 4/4/4. This tall growing plant, even greater in width, is covered with long, narrow foliage. Vivid rose flowers shade to pale purplish-pink in the center. The interior is accented with light orange dorsal spotting, while the blossom's exterior is strong violet. (Leach hyb. 1971, reg. 1985).

'**Summer Rose**' (*maximum* x 'Romany Chai'). 5', -10ºF, VL, -/-/-. Leaves are medium large and narrow. Flowers, to 2 1/2" across, are darkish rose in color, with deep red dorsal spotting, and are carried in a ball-shaped truss up to 12. (Ticknor, Weston Nurseries 1979).

'**Summer Snow**' (*maximum* x [{*ungernii* x *auriculatum*}F2]). 5', -15ºF, VL, 3-4/3/4. Leaves are quite large. White, 6-lobed flowers, to 3 3/4" across, sport a small greenish yellow dorsal blotch, in an 11-flower truss. (Leach 1969).

'**Summer Summit**' (*maximum* x [*auriculatum* x *fortunei* ssp. *discolor*]). 7', -20ºF, VL, 3-4/3/4. Long, dark green, elliptical foliage densely covers this vigorous plant, which at maturity will achieve a stature greater than ten feet. The pink buds open to expose blooms of white with a shading of orchid at the base. They mature to a pure white with dark yellow dorsal spotting. (David Leach 1984).

'**Summertime**' (form of *maximum*). 6', -25ºF, L, -/-/-. A tall growing hybrid with long, dark green foliage. Flowers are white flushed with purple, and have a throat accented with yellow-green. (Crown Estate, Windsor reg. 1974).

'**Sundari**' (*augustinii* 'Tower Court' x *trichanthum* 'Tower Court'). 5', -5ºF, EM, -/-/-. Leaves are medium sized. Blooms, to 2 1/4" wide, are violet shading to a lighter center with throat spots of yellowish green. They are held in a rounded truss of up to 12. (Short 1977).

'**Sun Devil**' (probably a *wardii* hybrid). 4', -5ºF, M-ML, 4/3-4/3. Here is a plant which draws more than its share of admiration each spring when the voluptuous buttery yellow trusses warm the hearts of all who view it. The plant has a compact habit with leaves of deep bluish green that appear especially blue when new. It is more sensitive to fertilizer than most and will burn easily if overdone. Synonym, 'Sundance'. (Whitney hyb., Dr. Otis Burris raiser, Bulgin reg. 1989).

'**Sunny Day**' (parentage unknown). 4', 0ºF, EM, 4/3-4/3-4. Rounded in habit, this well-branched plant is foliated with smooth, elliptical leaves. Flowers open primrose yellow with red spotting. (Whitney hyb., Sather reg. 1985).

'**Sunset Bay**' ('Odee Wright' x 'Malemute'). 3', 5ºF, EM, -/-/-. A compact grower with year-round green leaves. Coral buds open to primrose yellow flowers with pink margins and a chartreuse green throat. (J. Elliott 1990).

'**Sunset Yates**' ('Pink Twins' x 'Leah Yates'). 4', -10ºF, ML, -/-/-. Leaves are medium to large. 3 1/4" flowers, colored in shades of neyron rose, boasting a large red blotch, are carried in a ball-shaped truss of 15. (Yates, M. Yates 1977).

'Sunsplash' (parentage unknown). 4', -15ºF, ML, -/-/-. An upright, spreading plant with striking, variegated foliage. The elliptical, matte green background is accented with gold markings. Dome-shaped trusses hold lavender blooms with a gold eye. (Sold by Whitney Gardens 1991).

'Sunspot' (['Darigold' x 'Lackamas Spice'] x [*croceum* x *wardii*]). 4', 0ºF, M, 3-4/3-4/3-4. A vigorous grower, forming a compact, rounded plant densely covered with dark green, rounded foliage. Blooms of warm yellow form large trusses. (W. Thompson before 1985).

'Sunspray' ('Alice Franklin' x 'Crest'). 6', -5ºF, M, 5/3-4/3. Imagine a rhododendron with flowers even yellower and larger than those of 'Crest', with better foliage, better habit, and you have 'Sunspray'. The full trusses are such a pure and true yellow that they would put a lemon to shame. Lovely, wide, 6" long leaves fully clothe the branches. (Swenson, Greer 1979).

'Sunup Sundown' ([*yakushimanum* x 'Fabia'] x [{'Fabia' x *bureavii*} x 'Crest']). 2.5', 0ºF, EM, -/-/-. This semi-dwarf is a compact grower spreading to a width much greater than its height. Intense red buds open to form trusses of rose flowers that fade to a delicate pink. (J. G. Lofthouse hyb. 1975, reg. 1982).

'Suomi' ('Linswegeanum' x 'Metterianum'). 3', -5ºF, VE, 3/3/3. A great early blooming red with dark, glossy green leaves. (Hobbie 1953).

'Supergold' ('Hotei' x 'Joanita'). 5', 5ºF, EM, 4/3/3. It has a pleasing growth form that supports attractive green foliage. The golden yellow flowers provide a warm glow of color. (J. G. Lofthouse 1983).

'Super Jay' ('Else Frye' x *johnstoneanum*). 30", 15ºF, E, -/-/-. Leaves are of a medium size. 3 1/2" flowers are white, with an orange dorsal blotch, carried in a small 5-flower truss. (Anderson, Braafladt 1979).

'Surrey Heath' ([*eriogynum* x 'Fabia'] x [*yakushimanum* x 'Britannia']). 3', 0ºF, M, 4/4/4. Flowers of rose pink with lighter edging appear on a tightly growing plant. (Waterer, Sons & Crisp 1975).

'Susan' (*campanulatum* x *fortunei* ssp. *fortunei*). 6', -5ºF, M, 4/4-5/4. A plant with excellent habit and glossy dark green leaves. Violet blue flowers are a real joy. Rapid grower. (J. C. Williams, W.C. Slocock, Ltd. before 1925) A.M. 1930, A.M. 1948, F.C.C. 1954.

'Swamp Beauty' ('Purple Splendour' x 'Loderi Superlative'). 5', 10ºF, ML, 4/4/3. Bronze red spots explode from the center of rosy pink, open flowers. Long, elliptic leaves make a nice collar around the upright truss. (Elliott reg. 1983).

'Swansdown' (*catawbiense* var. *album* x 'Belle Heller'). 5', -20ºF?, ML, 4/4/4. Leaves are medium large. 3" wide flowers are held in a large pyramidal truss of up to 20. Color is white, which may vary now and then to very pale pink, with a distinctive dorsal blotch of strong yellow spots. (Leach 1965).

'Sweet Lulu' ('Gosh Darn!' x 'Dead Ringer'). 3', -10ºF, L, -/-/-. Deep red buds open to moderate yellowish pink flowers with pale yellow throats and strong orange dorsal spots. (Delp 1992).

'Sweet Mystery' (*yakushimanum* hybrid). 3', -10ºF?, M, 4/4/4. Flowers of delicate pink, have brilliant rosy pink margins offset by a throat that fades to white. These blooms are held in full trusses above dark green, elliptical foliage. (Thompson before 1990).

'Sweet Simplicity' (*ponticum* hybrid). 5', -5ºF, ML, 2/3/3. This hybrid grows bushy, almost round. Shiny, medium large, dark green leaves are elliptic and slightly waved. Smallish ruffled flowers of flushed white, edged with pink, open from deep pink buds. A prolific bloomer producing round, average size, well-filled trusses. Cuttings root easily. (Waterer, Sons & Crisp before 1922).

'Sweet Sixteen' ('Jan Dekens' hybrid). 5', -5ºF, M, 4/3/3-4. The huge flowers are a light clear pink with a deeper pink picotee on the edges. Large curled leaves grace the plant, covering it with green. Difficult to propagate. (Whitney, Sather 1976).

'Sweet Sue' ([*facetum* x 'Fabia'] x [*yakushimanum* x 'Fabia Tangerine']). 2.5', 0ºF, ML, -/-/-. A vigorous upright grower that forms a plant wider than it is tall. Pink buds open to expose pale pink, bell-shaped flowers. The interior of the bloom is flushed with rosy shades while the margins are lighter, accenting the light freckling of scarlet. (Waterer, Sons & Crisp 1972) H. C. Wisley Trials 1982.

'Swen' (*yakushimanum* x 'Mars'). 4', -10ºF, M, 4/4/4. Growing equally wide as high, this plant is densely foliated with curved, dark green leaves having a reddish brown indumentum. Funnel-shaped flowers of vivid purple are held in ball-shaped trusses. Each bloom has a light center, accented by a white flare. (Willard Swenson hyb., Childers reg. 1977).

'Swift' (*mekongense* Viridescens x *ludlowii*). 2', -5ºF, M, -/-/-. A dwarf habit supports profuse yellow blooms with strong red spotting. The exterior of the flower is highlighted with intriguing red stripes. (Cox, Glendoick Gardens 1991).

'Sylvia V. Knight' ('J. H. Van Nes' x 'Bow Bells'). 5', 10ºF, EM, -/-/-. Leaves are medium sized. Pink flowers, to 3 3/4" across, have white flares on each lobe, and are held in a 10 flower truss. (Briggs, Knight 1979).

'Tacoma' (possibly *wardii*, *fortunei* ssp. *fortunei*, and other species). 5', 5ºF?, EM. -/-/-. This free flowering hybrid has a big and bushy growth habit. Large, creamy yellow flowers with slightly ruffled edges are produced in mid-season. The location of the origin is unknown, but it may have come from Australia where there is a town by that name. It also could have also come from Tacoma, Washington, but that is unlikely since this plant is unknown in the U.S. (Huthnance Nurseries, New Zealand, intro. about 1960).

'Tahiti' ([*maximum* x *catawbiense*] x [*dichroanthum* x {*fortunei* ssp. *discolor* x *campylocarpum*}]). 4.5', -15ºF?, ML, 4/3/3. Foliage is medium sized. Ivory colored flowers, to 3" across, have salmon orange edging and a russet blotch on the upper lobe. The flowers are surrounded by a conspicuous calyx. (Leach 1960).

'Tahitian Dawn' ('Lem's Cameo' x 'Skipper'). 5', 5ºF, M, 4/4/4. An upright grower with large, dark green foliage. Flowers are an intense shade of yellow, accented with tones of peach and apricot, held in rounded trusses. This plant was first released as a door prize for the 1991 National Convention in Oakland, California. (Alan Korth 1991).

'Taku' ('Tally Ho' x *yakushimanum*). 4', -5ºF, M-ML, 3-4/4-5/3-4. An exceptional plant for foliage, having pert leaves which are thickly covered with indumentum. The flowers are a medium shade of pink that lightens as the flowers age. (M. Clark 1992).

'Tally Ho' g. (*griersonianum* x *eriogynum*). 6', 10ºF, L, 4/3/3. Large, medium green, somewhat bullate leaves, with twisted margins, are held on a dense plant. This upright grower is easily rooted. Flowers, in a lax truss, are a bright huntsman red. (Crosfield 1933) F.C.C. 1933.

'Tanana' (*decorum* x *yakushimanum* Exbury form). 3', -10°F, EM, -/-/-. A compact grower with a widely branching habit. Evergreen foliage, held for 4 years, is matte olive green. Flower trusses are slightly flat topped, holding delicately scented white blooms, which have a freckling of yellowish green. (Childers 1979).

'Tanyosho' (*yakushimanum* x 'Vanessa'). 3', -5°F, M, 4/4/4. A compact plant with attractively indumented foliage. Beautiful trusses of pink fade to almost white on this very free flowering plant. (Bovee before 1965).

'Tapestry' (*catawbiense* hybrid). 4', -20°F, M, -/-/-. Low growing and spreading, the plant is densely covered with forest green foliage. This free flowering hybrid has ball shaped trusses of deep lavender accented by darker eyes. (Mezitt, Weston Nurseries about 1990).

'Tarantella' ('Oratorium' x 'Hachmann's Feuerschein'). 4', -15°F, ML, -/-/-. Funnel shaped flowers are deep red with wavy edges. The dorsal lobes are marked with a darker red, offset by the throat shading to white. It is a dense plant that will reach a width greater than its height. (Hachmann, Stuck 1988).

'Taurus' ('Jean Marie de Montague' x *strigillosum*). 6', -5°F, EM, 4-5/4/4. 'Taurus' is a magnificent shrub; it is vigorous and full in shape. Deep green, pointed leaves are held for 3 years. In winter, deep red buds adorn the branches. Globular trusses are made up of glowing red, campanulate flowers with black speckling on the upper petal. It is the same parentage as 'Grace Seabrook', but not a sister seedling. (Mossman 1972) S.P.A. 1990 N.W.

'Teal' (*brachyanthum* ssp. *hypolepidotum* x *fletcheranum*). 3', 0°F, M, 4/4/4. This beautiful little hybrid has abundant small, lime-green leaves. To add to its uniqueness, it has reddish, exfoliating bark. Flowers are bright sunny yellow, in trusses of 5-8, which cover the plant and give it the glow of the sun. (Cox 1977) A.M. 1977.

'Tea Party' (*yakushimanum* x 'Noyo Chief'). 5', -10°F, ML, 4/4/4. Rosy pink flowers are abundant and long-lasting. Attractive foliage covers this plant which has a well-branched, rounded growth habit. (Briggs 1991).

'Teddy Bear' (*bureavii* x *yakushimanum*). 3', 0°F, EM, 4/5/4. A compact grower with rounded habit, the foliage is shiny, dark green with a light dusting of reddish indumentum underneath. Delicate pink flowers are held in tight, rounded trusses. (Briggs 1991).

'Ted's Orchid Sunset' ('Purple Splendour' x 'Mrs. Donald Graham'). 5', -5°F, M, 3-4/3/3. Elegant orchid flowers have a sunset of deep bronze colors in the center. Very striking and unusual in color. Bronzy green leaves, fairly long and narrow are held on reddish stems. Quite a show stopper! (Fawcett before 1975).

'Telestar' ('Van Nes Sensation' x 'Purple Splendour'). 5', 0°F, ML, 4/3-4/3. Large, light orchid flowers cover this plant. The edges of the flowers are slightly deeper in color than the center of the petals, and there is an orange-green flare that originates in the base of the throat. The good foliage makes this an attractive plant in the garden during all seasons. (Lloyd Newcomb before 1990, not registered).

'Telstar' ('Pauline' x *yakushimanum*). 4', 0°F, M, -/-/-. A smaller growing plant with glossy, dark green leaves and a slow growth rate. Rose colored flowers fade to an almost white inside, accented by an upper throat marking of vivid oxblood red. (F. Hanger hyb., RHS Garden, Wisley reg. 1963).

'Tempest' ('Mars' x 'Fabia'). 5', -5°F, L, 4/3/3. Growth habit is upright on this late-flowering, exceptionally showy plant. The flowers, funnel-form to 3" across, are a good bright red, possibly one of the best shades of red you will ever see. These blooms are set in loose trusses of 8-10 flowers. (Wright Sr. & Jr. 1961).

'Temple Belle' (*orbiculare* x *williamsianum*). 3', -5°F, EM, 3/4/3. Lovely soft pink flowers are held in dainty loose trusses. The plant forms a globular mound of rounded leaves which are supported on pink-tinged petioles. This semi-dwarf is resistant to pests, as well as being attractive. (Royal Botanical Garden, Kew 1916).

'Temptation' ('Day Dream' hybrid). 4', 0°F, ML, 3/3/3. Creamy peach flowers have a darker center. An interesting display is provided by red bud scales, which persist through the winter when your other plants are looking dull. (Eichelser before 1975).

'Tennessee' ('LaBar's White' x ['Ole Olson' x 'Fabia']). 5', -15°F, EM, -/-/-. The upright growing plant has smooth, elliptical foliage. Strong, purplish pink buds open to reveal light pink flowers blushed with purple. The blooms mature to a more yellow shade of pink that is effectively accented by a dorsal blotch of bold red. (Leach hyb. 1959, reg. 1986).

'Tensing' ('Fabia' x 'Romany Chai'). 3', -10°F, L, -/-/-. Rose melts into orange in the throat of campanulate flowers held in large, handsome trusses. (Hanger, RHS Garden, Wisley 1963) A.M. 1953.

'Tequila Sunrise' (*yakushimanum* x 'Borde Hill'). 4', -5°F, M, -/-/-. Compact globular trusses hold 13 funnel shaped flowers. The blooms are strong purplish pink, flushed very pale pink at the bases with spots of bright red. (Hanger hyb., RHS reg. 1985) A.M. 1985.

'Tequila Sunrise' ('Mrs. Lamont Copeland' x 'Mary Drennen'). 4', 5°F, M-ML, -/-/-. The parentage of this plant has been misquoted as being a 'Lem's Cameo' hybrid. It is not, and the correct parentage is listed above. 'Tequila Sunrise' has a dense growth habit and is covered with shiny, deep green leaves. Flowers are orangey yellow, held in ball-shaped trusses. (Joe Davis before 1990).

'Terrific' (parentage unknown). 6', -20°F, M, -/-/-. A floriferous hybrid, the flowers are deep pink with yellow centers. This plant is strong and full growing with attractive, glossy foliage. (Leach, Pride intro.).

'Terry Herbert' (*minus* var. *minus* Carolinianum Group x *augustinii*). 4', -5°F, EM, -/-/-. Foliage is small. Flowers, to 2" wide, are clear orchid without markings. Buds are held at branch terminals in groups of 5, opening to form trusses which hold up to 12 flowers each. (Herbert 1977).

'Tessa' ('Praecox' x *moupinense*). 4', -5°F, E, 3-4/3/3-4. 'Tessa's' clear cameo pink flowers are often described as looking like trusses of 'Alice' in miniature. The flat-topped trusses make a fantastic show in the early spring when so little else is in flower. The foliage has interesting, downward curled edges and is deep emerald green when well fed. If planted where it gets winter sun, the foliage will turn a bronze brown tone. The somewhat open growth habit displays the unusual peeling cinnamon brown bark of the older branches. (Stevenson 1935) A.M. 1935.

'Tessa Bianca' ('Praecox' x *moupinense*). 3', -5°F, E, 3-4/3-4/3-4. White flowers have a pale pink flush on petal lobes, and a tinge of yellow in the throat. It is a compact plant with better foliage and plant habit than 'Tessa'. An extra fine plant and flower. (Brandt 1964).

'Tessa Roza' ('Praecox' x *moupinense*). 4', 0°F, E, 4/3/3. This plant is very similar to 'Tessa', except that the flowers are slightly darker pink with deeper carmine spotting. (Stevenson intro. 1953) A.M. 1953.

'The Bride' (*caucasicum* var. *album*, inbred). 6', -15°F, ML, 2/3/3-4. Flowers are white, yellow blotched. Plant has good growth habit. (Standish and Noble before 1850) F.C.C. 1871.

'**The General**' (red *catawbiense* seedling x red *catawbiense* seedling). 5', -20ºF, ML, 4/3-4/3-4. Leaves are dark green. Flowers are crimson, with a darkish red blotch, in an upright truss. (Shammarello 1955).

'**The Honourable Jean Marie de Montague**' (*griffithianum* hybrid). 5', -5ºF, M, 4/4/4. Practically every new red introduced must be judged against this plant to see if it is better, and few actually make the grade. 'Jean Marie' has bright red flowers and buds young. The thick, heavy foliage is sun tolerant, a deep emerald green unmatched by many plants. Although registered as 'The Honourable Jean Marie de Montague', it is often referred to as 'Jean Marie de Montague', or simply 'Jean Marie'. (C. B. van Nes & Sons before 1940).

'**The Master**' ('China' x 'Letty Edwards'). 5', -10ºF, M, 4/4/3-4. Deep maroon red accents the throats of pale shrimp pink flowers, held in a gigantic truss of 14. The plant is very vigorous and grows slightly wider than tall. Leaves are a dull, deep green. (Slocock Nurseries 1948) H.C. 1964, A.M. 1966.

'**Theo Light**' ('Conemaugh' x *drumonium*). 2', -15ºF, EM, -/-/-. The small foliage is held erect by eye-catching red stems. Dense flower heads hold white blooms blushed with pink. (Linc Foster before 1955).

'**The Queen Mother**' ('Halcyone' x *aberconwayi*). 3', -10ºF, M, 4/4/3-4. Magenta rose flowers pale to lovely silvery pink in trusses of 10. The three inch leaves are dark and slender. (Crown Estate, Windsor 1968) A.M. 1968.

'**Thomwilliams**' (*thomsonii* x *williamsianum*). 2', -5ºF, EM, 3/4/3. A dense, compact grower with a rounded growth habit. The rounded foliage is very tolerant to sun as well as being attractive. Loose trusses hold deep rose, bell shaped flowers that have a waxy appearance. (E.J.P. Magor intro. 1927).

'**Thor**' (*haematodes* x 'Felis'). 3', 5ºF, M, 4/4/4. Bright scarlet red flowers have a large calyx. The plant has good, compact habit and thick indumentum on the leaf undersides. A real improvement over 'May Day'. (Brandt 1962).

'**Thunder**' ('PJM' seedling). 3', -20ºF, EM, 3-4/4/4. A hybrid with an upright and spreading habit. It holds small, glossy dark green foliage with a pungent fragrance. Blooms of dark purplish pink are produced in profusion early in the season. Exceptionally heat tolerant, this plant enjoys full sun to encourage bloom color. (Mezitt hyb., Weston Nurseries reg. 1987).

'**Thunderhead**' (probably contains some *ponticum*). 5', -15ºF, ML, 3/3-4/3-4. Leaves are matte green and slightly curved. Flowers are quite a deep purple, somewhat like 'Purple Splendour', but without the blotch, which makes them appear lighter colored. They are slightly frilled. (Clark before 1958).

'**Thunderstorm**' ('Doncaster' hybrid). 4', -10ºF, M, -/-/-. White stamens become very conspicuous against the background of pure scarlet red flowers held in cylindrical trusses. (Slocock 1930) A.M. 1955.

'**Tiana**' ('Sappho' x *yakushimanum* Exbury Form). 4', -5ºF, M, -/-/-. A plant of upright, open growth habit that is dressed with dark green foliage. Ball shaped trusses are composed of white blooms with a unique, "butterfly" shaped, burgundy blotch inside. (R. Murcott hyb., W. Brack reg. 1989).

'**Tiara**' ('Golden Jubilee' x 'Loderi King George'). 4', 5ºF, E, -/-/-. Broad leaves encircle large, delicately scented white flowers with light green in the center. (Love reg. 1964).

'**Tickled Pink**' ('Unique' x 'Crest'). 4', 0ºF, EM, 3-4/3-4/3-4. A compact growing plant with wavy, twisting foliage. Rounded trusses hold creamy yellow flowers with a satiny appearance. The blooms have a deep yellow center accented with peachy pink edges. (C. Fawcett 1983).

'**Tidbit**' (*dichroanthum* x *wardii*). 3', 5ºF, M, 3/4/3-4. Buds of bright cherry red show the first color on 'Tidbit'. As the buds begin to open in the spring, flowers emerge a bright straw yellow with a touch of red at the base of the stamens. Shiny green, pointed leaves complete the display. (R. Henny before 1958) P.A. 1957.

'**Tiddly Winks**' ('Tidbit' x 'Idealist'). 4', 0ºF, M, 4/4/4. Sunny, deep lemon yellow flowers have a gigantic calyx on the back of each, giving the blossoms a hose-in-hose double appearance. Deep green, glossy foliage clothes the plant, forming a dense mound. Good vigor and habit make it a plant well worth growing. (Thompson 1988).

'**Tiffany**' ('Anna Baldsiefen' x *keiskei*). 30", -15ºF, M, 3-4/3/4. An extremely attractive plant with outstanding flower color. While primarily pink, the flowers also have a mixture of apricot and yellow in the throat. They are star shaped and reflexed. Good foliage. (Baldsiefen 1971).

'**Tiger**' (*dichroanthum* x 'Cremorne'). 3', -10ºF, M, -/-/-. Loose trusses are formed from flowers of orange-tinged red, with purple spotting. Leaves are to 3", on a compact, free flowering plant. (Reuthe reg. 1970) H.C. 1970.

'**Timothy James**' (*yakushimanum* x 'Fabia Tangerine'). 3', -5ºF, M, -/-/-. Light pink flowers with slightly deeper center, are speckled brown. (Waterer, Sons & Crisp 1971).

'**Tina Heinje**' (*yakushimanum* 'Koichiro Wada' x 'Kluis Sensation'). 3', -10ºF, ML, -/-/-. A compact growing plant with long, curving foliage. Intensely red flower buds open to dark pink flowers with a dark red eye. Trusses hold 14-15 flowers. (Heinje 1986).

'**Tinker Hill**' (red *catawbiense* x 'Lavender Charm'). 5', -5ºF, EM, -/-/-. Leaves are medium size and rather narrow. Nicely scented, 7-lobed flowers, to 4" wide, are rose colored with a red blotch, held in a truss of up to 13. (Herbert 1977).

'**Tinkle Bells**' (*williamsianum* hybrid). 2, -5ºF, M, 3/3/3. A rounded, compact plant densely covered with light green, rounded foliage. Bright red buds open to reveal delicate pink flowers. (Sold by Kelleygreen Nursery 1994).

'**Tioga**' ('Jalisco Elect' x ['Fawn' x 'Sarita Loder']). 5', 5ºF, ML, -/-/-. Leaves are medium size and narrow. Seven-lobed blooms, to 4" across, are primrose yellow, lightly spotted reddish brown, carried in a lax truss of up to 8. (James, Joslin 1974).

'**Tish**' ('Beckyann' x [*fortunei* ssp. *fortunei* Gable's cream form x 'Mount Siga']). 4', -5ºF, ML, -/-/-. Leaves are medium large. Scented, 6-lobed flowers, to 3 1/4" across, are yellow, a little deeper color in throat, with no markings, in a 10-flower truss. (Yates, M. Yates 1977).

'**Titian Beauty**' ([*eriogynum* x 'Fabia Tangerine'] x [*yakushimanum* x 'Fabia Tangerine']). 3', 0ºF, M, 3/3/3. Bright turkey red flowers are held on a plant with small leaves and erect, compact habit. (Waterer, Sons & Crisp reg. 1970).

'**Today and Tomorrow**' (*smirnowii* x *yakushimanum*). 3', -20ºF, EM, -/-/-. A plant of mounding habit which is densely covered with foliage of deep green upper surface and bronze indumentum below. Dark pink buds open to lighter pink flowers that fade to delicate white. (Mehlquist 1994).

'Todmorden' (['Pygmalion' x *haematodes* x 'Wellfleet'] x ['Pygmalion x *haematodes* x 'Wellfleet'], exact combination of parents is uncertain). 5', -15ºF, ML, 3-4/3/3-4. This Dexter variety was selected by John Wister. It is very nearly a bicolor of strikingly intense pink and white, with brownish spotting on the upper lobe. It's a vigorous, hardy plant with good foliage. (Dexter before 1945, Scott Horticultural Foundation 1983).

'Tofino' ('Lem's Cameo' x ['Jalisco' x {'Crest' x 'King of Shrubs'}]). 6', 0ºF, ML, -/-/-. An upright growing shrub which achieves a width equal to its height. Red buds open to form dome shaped trusses of light yellow flowers with rosy red markings. The foliage is heavily textured, glossy and dark yellow-green. (John Lofthouse 1983).

'Tokatee' ('Mars' x *williamsianum*). 30", 0ºF, EM, -/-/-. Foliage is small. Flowers, to 2 3/4" across, are deep pink shading lighter in throat, slightly spotted, held in a lax truss of up to 7 flowers. (Lancaster before 1965, Grothaus 1975) C.A. 1977.

'Tomeka' ([*dichroanthum* x *griersonianum*] x *decorum*). 5', 10ºF, M, 3-4/3-4/3. Leaves are long and narrow. 2 3/4" flowers are vermilion with an orange glow. Veins, dorsal spots and nectaries are all red, on blooms carried in a lax truss of up to 9. (James before 1960, Osborn 1979).

'Tom Ethrington' (['Virginia Scott' x 'Alice Franklin'] x *yakushimanum*). 5', 10ºF, E, -/-/-. Leaves are medium large. 8-lobed, scented flowers, to 3 3/4" across, are yellow, without blotch or spots, held in a 12-flower truss. (Larson 1979).

'Tom Everett' (parentage unknown, believed to be *fortunei* ssp. *fortunei* hybrid). 5', -10ºF, M, -/-/-. This compact, slow growing hybrid has a pleasing shape. Strong, reddish purple buds open to expose fragrant, wavy edged mauve flowers that fade to almost pure white. Trusses are dome shaped. (C. Dexter hyb., Scott Hort. Foundation reg. 1985).

'Tom Koenig' ([*racemosum* x *keiskei*] x *keiskei*). 30", -10ºF?, EM, 3/3/3. Leaves are small. Blooms reflect the *racemosum* parentage, but are larger and pale pink in color. (Nearing, Koenig 1969).

'Tony' ('Boule de Neige' x red *catawbiense* seedling). 4', -15ºF, M, 3/4/4. Glowing cherry red flowers and somewhat crinkly foliage decorate this handsome, low growing rhododendron. (Shammarello 1955).

'Too Bee' (*campylogynum* 'Patricia' x *keiskei* 'Yaku Fairy'). 1', -10ºF, EM, 5/4/4. Low growing, this plant will spread to a width twice its height. Foliage is small and rounded, accented by frilly, bell shaped pink flowers with rose spotting. (Berg hyb. 1972, reg. 1983) A.E. 1989, A.M. 1988.

'Top Banana' (probably a 'Hotei' hybrid). 3', 0ºF, EM, 4/4/3-4. Very similar to 'Hotei', except it blooms in late April and buds at a much younger age. A good yellow. It's a little more upright than 'Hotei' and it flowers more consistently. It has the same root rot tendency, therefore it needs good drainage. (Whitney hyb., Sather intro., reg. 1985).

'Top Brass' ('Crest' hybrid). 4', 0ºF, EM, -/-/-. A compact and densely foliated plant which produces blooms of bright yellow with an orange margin. (Whitney, Sather before 1990).

'Top Gun' ('Anah Kruschke' mutation). 5', -10ºF, ML, -/-/-. Parentage information comes from Wrights, although the registration records show "unknown, possibly *ponticum* hybrid." This is a vigorous growing, sun tolerant plant with a more compact growth habit than 'Anah Kruschke'. Blooms are pinkish purple and appear above lush dark green foliage. (Discovered at EBY Nursery, named and introduced by Wright's Nursery).

'Top Hat' (parentage unknown). 4', -5ºF, EM, 3-4/3/3. Bright, sunny yellow flowers appear on a plant of nice growth habit. It is compact and has semi-glossy, green leaves. Confusion exists between this and 'High Gold'. At one point, there was a mixup, and 'Top Hat' was being sold as 'High Gold'. 'Top Hat' is less upright in growth and does not have as shiny a leaf as 'High Gold'. (Whitney, Sather intro. before 1990).

'Topsvoort Pearl' (sport of 'Pink Pearl'). 6', -5ºF, M, 4/3/3. An interesting twist to 'Pink Pearl'. Large flowers are surrounded by a lovely, frilled mauve-red edge. Very showy. (Topsvoort Nursery, Holland before 1958).

'Torch' ('Britannia' x 'Sarita Loder'). 5', -5ºF, M, -/-/-. The red flowers have an orange flush and darker throat. Tall growing. This form of 'Torch' is listed in Bean's <u>Trees and Shrubs Hardy in the British Isles</u>. There is also another plant named 'Torch' listed in the RHS registry, the parentage of which is 'Ascot Brilliant' x *thomsonii*. (Slocock before 1950).

'Torlonianum' (possible parentage, *calendulaceum* x *catawbiense*). 5', -10ºF, ML-L, 3-4/2/2. This a hybrid between a rhododendron and deciduous azalea, making it what is called an azaleodendron. It is pinkish-purple with a very showy, yellow-orange blotch and has 12 funnel-shaped flowers to the dome-shaped truss. For an azaleodendron, its foliage is fair, though it does not hold too many leaves in winter. (M. Young before 1845).

'Tornado' (['Wilgen's Ruby' x 'May Day'] x 'Billy Budd'). 5', 5ºF, ML, -/-/-. This compact growing plant displays blooms of very true red above interesting foliage. Tolerant of both heat and cold, this plant is considered a favorite of all. (Research Station for Woody Nursery Crops, Boskoop, reg. 1979).

'Tortoiseshell Champagne' see 'Champagne'.

'Tortoiseshell Orange' ('Goldsworth Orange' x *griersonianum*). 4', -5ºF, ML, 4/3/3. Large, deep clear orange flowers. Growth is upright with elongated, slender leaves. (Slocock Nurseries 1945).

'Tortoiseshell Salome' ('Goldsworth Orange' x *griersonianum*). 4', -5ºF, ML, 4/3/3. Large biscuit colored blossoms are shaded with pink. (Slocock Nurseries 1946).

'Tortoiseshell Scarlet' ('Goldsworth Orange' x *griersonianum*). 4', -5ºF, ML, 4/3/3. It is similar to others of the 'Tortoiseshell' group but with orange-scarlet flowers. (Slocock Nurseries 1946).

'Tortoiseshell Wonder' ('Goldsworth Orange' x *griersonianum*). 4', -5ºF, ML, 4/3/3. Beautiful orange salmon and salmon pink combination flowers. (Slocock before 1945) A.M. 1947.

'Tottenham' (*ferrugineum* hybrid). 2', -20ºF, M, 3/3/3. A super bloomer, with pink flowers which are tubular with a flare at the end. They are held in loose trusses of up to 10. Leaves are very dark green with brown undersides, a result of the dense scales of this lepidote hybrid. (Moerheim mid 1900s).

'Tow Head' (*carolinianum* var. *album* x *ludlowii*). 1', -15ºF, EM, 3/4/3. Leaves are quite small, almost round, and scaly on both surfaces. Small flowers, to 1 1/4" across, are a brilliant greenish yellow, with orange dots on the dorsal lobe. They are held in a truss of up to 5. (Leach 1968).

'Towhee' (['C. P. Raffill' x 'Red Cap'] x 'Tally Ho'). 4', 5ºF, ML, 3/3/3. Leaves are medium sized and narrow. 3" wide flowers are clear bright red, in an open top truss of up to 10. (James 1958) P.A. 1956.

'**Tracigo'** (*yakushimanum* x *sperabile*). 3', 5ºF, M, 4/4/3. An upright grower which forms a rounded plant wider than it is tall. Foliage is dark green with a woolly orange indumentum below. The red buds open to dome shaped trusses of pink flowers with white interiors. (Dr. David Goheen 1983).

'**Traci Suzanne'** ('Blue Peter' x 'Loderi King George'). 6', 5ºF, L, -/-/-. Leaves are long and narrow. Flowers are fragrant, to 3 1/2" across, pale orchid in color, with most of the upper lobe spotted green, held in a rounded truss of up to 12. (Kaiser, Granston 1977).

'**Trail Blazer'** ('Mrs. Furnivall' x 'Sappho'). 5', -10ºF, M-ML, 4/4/3-4. The flower resembles that of 'Mrs. Furnivall', pink with a striking blotch, but this blotch has a more raspberry color. The plant is a vigorous grower; but, at the same time, it is well mannered and compact. (Wright Sr. & Jr. 1979).

'**Travis L.'** (unknown x 'Albatross'). 4', -5ºF, EM, 4/3-4/4. Growth habit is upright, with arching branches. Long, narrow leaves are smooth and dark green. Freely produced flowers, to 4 1/2" wide, are an open funnel form, ivory white and blotched very pale greenish-white. The slightly frilled blooms are held in a good-sized rounded truss of 8-12 flowers. (Cannon 1981).

'**Treasure'** (*forrestii* ssp. *forrestii* Repens Group x *williamsianum*). 2', -5ºF, EM, 3/4/3-4. As the name suggests, this lovely dwarf deserves a special spot where its worth can be discovered at close range. It would be perfect in a raised bed or rock garden and would make an excellent companion for 'Carmen'. Rounded, deep green foliage on this pleasingly prostrate plant makes 'Treasure' valuable even when not in bloom. Spring brings nodding flowers of burnt rose that are a joy. (Crosfield 1937).

'**Tressa McMurry'** (*occidentale* x *ponticum*). 3', 0ºF, ML, -/-/-. Although this parentage is listed, the plant does not look like an azaleodendron as the parentage would reflect. The plant looks more like a selection of *R. ponticum* 'Cheiranthifolium', and that is likely what it is. Narrow leaves are up to 3" long. Lavender pink flowers measure to 1 1/2" wide, each with a sienna-spotted blotch. Trusses hold up to 18 flowers. (McMurry 1978).

'**Trewithen Orange'** ('Full House' x *concatenans*). 4', -5ºF, M, 4-5/3-4/3. Pendulous flowers of deep orange-brown hang in loose clusters in mid season. Branches are erect and plant is narrow and tall. (Johnstone, raised at Trewithen before 1950) F.C.C. 1950.

'**Trilby'** ('Queen Wilhelmina' x 'Stanley Davies'). 5', -15ºF, ML, 3/4/4. Beautiful trusses are deep crimson with black marking. Matte green leaves are set off by red stems to beautify the plant even when it is not in flower. It is sun tolerant. (C.B. van Nes & Sons intro. before 1930).

'**Trinidad'** ('Calcutta' x 'Tahiti'). 4', -20ºF, ML, 4-5/4/4. Flowers have yellow ivory centers with a bright cherry red perimeter, in trusses of up to 14. A breakthrough for this flower color in this hardiness range. Plant is broader than tall and free flowering. (Leach reg. 1983).

'**Trinity'** ('Powell Glass' selfed x *yakushimanum* 'Koichiro Wada'). 30", -25ºF, ML, -/-/-. Foliage is medium sized. White, pink edged flowers, to 2 3/4" across, with dorsal spotting of light green, are carried in 14-flower truss. (Pride 1979).

'**Trojan Warrior'** (*catawbiense* hybrid). 4', -15ºF, ML, -/-/-. This is a low and compact grower that produces full trusses of bright red flowers. (Weston Nurseries before 1980).

'**Tropicana'** see 'Brandt's Tropicana'

'**Trude Webster'** ('Countess of Derby' x 'Countess of Derby'). 5', -10ºF, M, 5/4/4. This is the first plant to win the Superior Plant Award, the highest award possible for a rhododendron. Along with 'Lem's Cameo', it won from among more than 4,000 varieties which were eligible for an S.P.A. To see this plant in full flower is such an awe inspiring sight that it will not be forgotten. The trusses are absolutely gigantic, in a clear shade of pink. The foliage is large, wide and slightly twisted, making a perfect combination with the trusses. Good plant habit. A super plant and flower. (Greer 1961) S.P.A. 1971 Northwest.

'**Trula'** ('Belvedere' x 'Jasper'). 5', 10ºF, ML, 4/3-4/3-4. Foliage is of a medium size. 3" wide flowers are carried in a 10-flower truss. The blooms are yellow with green spotting on the dorsal lobe, and reddish orange on outside and edge. (Larson 1979).

'**Trumpeter'** ([red *catawbiense* hybrid x {*griersonianum* x Romany Chal}] x ['Mars' x *catawbiense* var. *rubrum*]). 5', -10ºF, ML, 3/3/3. Leaves are medium sized. 2 1/2" flowers have heavy substance, strong red color with darker red dorsal spots, and are held in a truss of up to 15. (Leach 1973).

'**Tudor Ruffles'** ('Naomi Hope' x 'Molly Coker'). 5', ML, 5ºF, -/-/-. This vigorous growing, bushy plant is covered with long, leathery leaves. Upright, full trusses are composed of ruffled white flowers with a crimson eye. (Riverwood Gardens, New Zealand, intro. 1995).

'**Turkish Delight'** (elepidote hybrid with parentage similar to 'Cynthia'). 4', -20ºF, M, 3-4/3-4/3-4. A delightful, medium growing plant with large pink flowers. Plant tends to be slightly open in habit. Possibly originated in Holland? (Sold by Greer about 1985).

'**Tuscany'** ('Mrs. Furnivall' x *catawbiense* var. *album*). 5', -20ºF, M, 4/4/3. A sister of the award winning 'Party Pink', this plant has an upright growth habit. The blooms appear soft pink accented by a red blotch. (David Leach 1991).

'**Tutu'** ('Mrs. Lindsay Smith' x 'C.I.S.'). 4', 5ºF, ML, -/-/-. Leaves are large. Flowers are a generous 4" wide, buff colored shading to empire yellow, carried in a loose truss of up to 9. (Parker 1971).

'**Tweedy Bird'** (['Darigold' x 'Lackamas Spice'] x 'Golden Anniversary #2'). 3', -5ºF, M, 4/3-4/3-4. Huge trusses hold flowers of vibrant yellow with a maroon throat. The blooms are further enhanced by maroon dorsal spotting and frilled edges. (Thompson about 1985).

'**Twilight Pink'** ([*fortunei* ssp. *fortunei* x 'Alice'] selfed x 'Comstock'). 4', -5ºF, M, 4/4/4. This is named 'Twilight Pink' because of the warm pink flowers that evoke images of the pink and apricot hues occurring at sunset. 'Twilight Pink' literally glows with beauty. The flower has a large calyx giving it a double appearance. The apple green leaves clothe the plant completely, making it desirable year around. It grows as a compact, yet sturdy mound, that does best when given some shade. (Greer 1988).

'**Twinkles'** (*racemosum* x *spiciferum*). 4', 0ºF, EM, 3/2/4. Growth habit is strong, and vigorous, tending to decumbency. Leaves are small, bicolor, dark green above and gray underneath. Very heavy bloomer, with small light pink flowers all along the stems. (Wright, Sr. & Jr. before 1958).

'**Twins Candy'** ('Pink Twins' x 'Cotton Candy'). 5', -5ºF, EM, -/-/-. Leaves are medium large. Large, 7-lobed flowers, to 4" across, are dark vibrant pink shading lighter pink to center, with upper 2 lobes spotted red, held in a ball shaped truss of up to 18. (Herbert 1977).

'**Tyee'** ('Esquire' x 'Idealist'). 5', 5ºF, ML, 3/3/3. Leaves are of a medium size. Primrose colored flowers, to 4" across, have uranium green throat, and are carried in a lax, 11-flower truss. (D.W. James 1960) A.E. 1960.

'Tyermanii' (*nuttallii* x *formosum*). 5', 20ºF, M, 4/2/3. An upright growing plant with glossy, dark green foliage and attractive bark. Lax trusses hold large, lily-like flowers. The blossoms are white with a yellow throat and have a strong, sweet fragrance. (Tyermann intro. 1925) F.C.C. 1925.

'Unique' (*campylocarpum* hybrid). 4', -5ºF, EM, 3/4-5/4. Smooth, oblong leaves, are so thick and dense on the rounded plant that it becomes a thick mound of clover green. In the spring, the buds show color of bright pink and open to beautiful, buttery cream. Older plants become so covered with flowers that every leaf is hidden. (W. C. Slocock Ltd. before 1934) A.M. 1934, F.C.C. 1935.

'Unique Marmalade' ('Orange Marmalade' x 'Unique'). 3', 0ºF, EM, -/-/-. A low growing, compact plant which is densely foliated with glossy, dark green leaves. Bright red buds open to reveal rosy pink flowers with an orange throat. The blooms have a wavy edge and a delicate spotting. (Davis 1990).

'Unknown Warrior' ('Queen Wilhelmina' x 'Stanley Davies'). 5', 5ºF, E-EM, 3/3/3-4. One of the first reds to bloom each spring, the flowers are a light but bright, dazzling red. Out of the same cross as the late flowering 'Britannia'. (C. B. van Nes and Sons before 1922).

'Valaspis' (*valentinianum* x *leucaspis*). 3', 10ºF, VE, 3/3-4/3-4. Showy, pale yellow flowers, in loose clusters of 4-5, bloom early in the season. Foliage is small and hairy with a bronze hue when immature. (Aberconway intro. 1935) A.M. 1935.

'Valley Creek' ('Essex Scarlet' x *fortunei* ssp. *fortunei*). 6', -5ºF, ML, -/-/-. Foliage is large. Slightly fragrant flowers, to 3 1/2" wide, are deep rosy pink, with a scarlet blotch in the throat. Blooms are held in a 10 flower truss. (Gable, Herbert 1976).

'Valley Forge' ('Atrosanguineum' x [*fortunei* ssp. *fortunei* x *williamsianum*]). 6', -5ºF, ML, -/-/-. Leaves are medium large. Deep rose colored flowers, to 2 1/2" across, with dark blotch in the throat, are held in 18-flower truss. (Herbert 1976).

'Valley Sunrise' (*occidentale* x 'Purple Splendour'). 4', 0ºF, M-ML, 4/3/4. An exceptional azaleodendron from Dr. Robert Ticknor at Oregon State University's North Willamette Experiment Station. It took years of experimentation to come up with this worthwhile hybrid. When it was first exhibited in the Portland show, it took the show by storm! That sensational orange blotch glowing against a background of orchid creates unbelievable eye appeal. (Ticknor 1982).

'Van' (*griersonianum* x 'Countess of Derby'). 6', -5ºF, ML, 3-4/4/4. Profusely blooming flowers are deep pink with a distinctive, darker center. Although a sister to 'Anna Rose Whitney', this plant is believed to be superior. The growth habit is more compact, it has smaller, prominently veined foliage, and it is hardier. This cross was originally made by Van Veen and is named 'Van' in his honor. A superior variety desired for its attractive foliage. (Van Veen, Sr. before 1950, grown by Griebnow, Greer intro. 1979).

'Vancouver USA' ('Hotei' x ['Crest' x 'Roman Pottery']). 4', 10ºF, M, -/-/-. This interesting plant was selected by the city of Vancouver, Washington to bear its name. It is an unusual creamy pink, with red spotting all over the flower, on the lower petals as well as the upper petals. Fir green foliage completes the display. (Lofthouse hyb. 1977, grown by Richard Cavender, named by Vancouver Parks & Recreation, reg. Cavender 1987).

'Vandec' ('Van Nes Sensation' x *decorum*). 6', 5ºF, EM, -/-/-. An upright and spreading grower that will obtain a size wider than it is tall. Thick leathery leaves cover the plant, providing a sturdy backdrop for the freely produced pale pink trusses composed of fragrant flowers. (Probably from New Zealand before 1982, sold by Riverwood Gardens 1994).

'Vanessa' ('Soulbut' x *griersonianum*). 3', 5ºF, L, 3/3/3. Warm pink flowers in lax trusses adorn this very broad plant, which produces an almost flat top. Long leaves are dark green with visible pubescence. (Aberconway intro. 1929) F.C.C. 1929.

'Vanessa Pastel' ('Soulbut' x *griersonianum*). 5', 5ºF, ML, 3/3/3. Flowers are soft cream with a flush of shell pink, deeper pink in the throat. Pointed leaves of moss green have reddish purple stems. (Aberconway 1946) A.M. 1946.

'Van Nes Sensation' ('Sir Charles Butler' x 'White Pearl'). 5', -5ºF, M, 4/4/4. Luscious, fragrant flowers are light orchid pink. Attractive foliage covers a full, strong plant. (C.B. van Nes & Sons before 1925).

'Van Veen' (*griersonianum* x 'Pygmalion'). 6', -5ºF, ML, 3/2/3-4. Leaves are medium large. The dark red blooms, up to 3" wide, are carried in a rounded, 7-flower truss. (Van Veen, Sr. 1956).

'Van Weerden Poelman' ('Charles Dickens' x 'Lord Roberts'). 5', -15ºF, ML, -/- /-. Large crimson flowers are held above attractive foliage. (H. den Ouden hyb. intro. 1925, reg. 1958).

'Veesprite' (*impeditum* x *racemosum*). 18", -10ºF, EM, -/-/-. Leaves are very small, with small flowers to match, only 3/4" wide. Blooms are Persian rose, held in terminal clusters of 5 flowers each. (Forster, Horticultural Research Institute of Ontario 1967).

'Veldtstar' (*fortunei* ssp. *discolor* x 'Lodauric Iceberg'). 5', 0ºF, ML, -/-/-. An open plant, this has large, compact trusses of pale pink flowers which have a slight red throat and some spotting. (George, Hydon Nurseries Ltd. 1967).

'Venetian Chimes' ([*eriogynum* x 'Fabia'] x [*yakushimanum* x 'Britannia']). 2', 0ºF, M, 4/3/3. Compact plant habit. Carmine rose flowers have brown markings on the upper lobe. (Waterer, Sons & Crisp 1970).

'Venice' ('Party Pink' x [*yakushimanum* x 'Mars']). 4', -20ºF, ML, -/-/-. This rounded plant grows equally as wide as tall. Spherical trusses hold pale, funnel shaped pink blooms, flushed darker with dorsal spotting of yellow. (Leach hyb. 1965, reg. 1983).

'Vera Elliott' ('Virginia Richards' x *fortunei* ssp. *fortunei*). 6', 0ºF, ML, -/-/-. Foliage is large. 7-lobed flowers are rose in color, lightly spotted with orange-red on the 3 upper lobes. The 4 1/2" blooms are carried in a lax truss of up to 10. (W. Elliott 1977).

'Vera Hawkins' ('Albatross' x 'Fabia'). 6', 5ºF?, ML, -/-/-. Porcelain rose flowers have veins and netting of a deeper shade. The blooms are accented with deep orange dotting and a thin overlay of pale yellow. The 4" flowers are held in a 12 flower truss. (Larson 1964).

'Verna Phetteplace' ('Lady Bessborough' x *yakushimanum* Exbury). 6', -5ºF, ML, 4/2/3. Leaves are medium large. Unique blooms have outsides of pink which bleeds through to shade the ivory insides to a delicate pink color. This is accented by a small red blotch. Flowers are to 3 1/2" across and are held in a ball-shaped truss of up to 15. (Phetteplace 1975).

'Vernus' ('Cunningham's White' x red *catawbiense* hybrid). 5', -25ºF, VE, 3/3/4. Foliage is medium large and pale pink flowers are about 2" across. This is one of the earliest bloomers. (Shammarello 1961).

'Veronica Milner' (*campylocarpum* x 'Little Ben'). 4', -5ºF, M, 4/4. An attractive plant offering vibrant green foliage and rose flowers. (E. J. Greig, Royston Nursery reg. 1961).

'Veronica Pfeiffer' ('Nova Zembla' x ['Catalgla' x 'Lady Bessborough']). 4', -20ºF, M, -/-/-. A well proportioned mid-sized plant with medium green foliage. The frilled flowers are light purple. (Behring 1986).

'Very Berry' ('Trude Webster' x 'Jean Marie de Montague'). 6', -10ºF, M-ML, 4/4-5/4-5. This showy, rose-red hybrid has magnificent, perfectly cone shaped trusses. Large, deep fir green leaves thickly cover the plant. Gigantic is the word to describe the leaves which are up to 10" long and the 1' tall trusses of bright glowing color. WOW! (Greer 1988).

'Vibrant Violet' (*impeditum* x *augustinii* 'Towercourt'). 3', 0ºF, EM, 4/4/4. The name says it all. Small, pointed dark green leaves are a beautiful backdrop for these very bright violet flowers. (Fujioka 1986).

'Vicki Reine' (parentage unknown). 5', -5ºF, ML, 4/3-4/4. Another of the popular two-toned flowers like 'Rainbow'. Deep rose red edges encircle a white center. Leaves are deeply veined, giving interesting texture to the foliage. (Clark 1972) C.A. 1971.

'Victor' see 'PJM Victor'.

'Victor Frederick' ('King of Shrubs' x 'Walloper'). 6', 5ºF, M, -/-/-. Large foliage with reddish petioles and stems give this delightful rhododendron a richly clothed appearance. Its flowers are large, to 5" across, warm red with a slight salmon cast. In the throat there is a darker red blotch around the entire center. The trusses are formed of up to 17 flowers. This is the same plant that was sold for years under the name of 'KSW', which stood for 'King of Shrubs' x 'Walloper'. (Lem before 1960, Sinclair 1974).

'Victoria's Consort' (compact white *catawbiense* hybrid x light yellow *catawbiense* hybrid). 4', -20ºF, ML, -/-/-. Vigorous and upright growing, this plant will remain more tall than wide. Large foliage is olive green; mauve flower buds open to reveal yellowish white blooms with a greenish yellow eye. (Mezitt hyb. 1971, Weston reg. 1987).

'Vida' (unknown, probably contains *decorum* and *wardii*). 6', 0ºF, ML, 4/3/3. This is a fine flowering plant, but it is very difficult to propagate. The buds first show as orange-yellow opening to clear deep yellow, unmarked by any spotting. It's a nice deep, butter yellow with slightly lighter edges. Good foliage. (Steinmetz 1964).

'Vincent Van Gogh' (elepidote hybrid of unknown parentage). 5', -10ºF, M, 4/2-3/3. Here is a variety that is seldom seen. It has an almost unbelievable flower, somewhat like 'Rainbow' only better. It has a very white center with a red picotee edge and red on the back side of the flower. Foliage is dark yew green. (M. Koster & Sons 1939).

'Vinebelle' ('Robert Allison' x *yakushimanum*). 5', -10ºF, ML, -/-/-. Tall growing, 'Vinebelle' will achieve a width equal to its height over time. Purplish pink buds open to reveal white flowers with olive green spotting. New leaves emerge buff colored, and mature foliage retains the buff indumentum underneath. (R. Forster hyb., Horticultural Research Institute of Ontario 1986).

'Vinecrest' ([{'LaBar's White' x *fortunei* ssp. *fortunei*} x *wardii*] x *wardii* Litiense Group). 3', -15ºF, M, -/-/-. Olive green foliage covers this plant of mounding, rounded habit. Peach flower buds open to reveal light yellow flowers which have small auburn rays. The blooms are held in groups of 12 per upright truss. (Ken Begg hyb., Horticultural Research Institute of Ontario 1986).

'Vinemark' (['America' x *yakushimanum*] open pollinated) 3', -15ºF, ML, -/-/-. Trusses have wavy edged flowers of heavy substance which open from light purple buds. The light lavender-pink flowers have a more deeply colored flare. Growth habit is dense and foliage is good. (R. Forster hyb., Al Smith, Horticultural Research Institute of Ontario reg. 1987.)

'Vinemount' ([{'Hassan' x (*dichroanthum* ssp. *scyphocalyx* x *kyawii*)} x 'Catalgla'] x 'La Bar's White'). 4', -15ºF, ML, -/-/-. Funnel-shaped, vivid, reddish-purple flowers have a pale yellow blotch on the dorsal lobe. (R. Forster hyb., Horticultural Institute of Ontario 1986).

'Vinewood' ('Sham's Ruby' x *williamsianum*). 2', -15ºF, M, -/-/-. Ball trusses are formed from purplish-pink flowers which are darker on the petal outsides. This low and mounding plant will achieve a width equal to its height. (R. Forster hyb., Horticultural Institute of Ontario 1988).

'Virginia Anderson' (*yakushimanum* 'Koichiro Wada' x 'Bow Bells'). 3', 0ºF, ML, 3-4/4/3-4. Leaves are medium sized. Blooms are deep pink, fading to white with red stripes on the outside. 3" flowers are held in a large truss of up to 20. (Bovee, Sorensen, Watson 1976).

'Virginia Leach' ([{*maximum* x *catawbiense*} x {*dichroanthum* x (*fortunei* ssp. *discolor* x *campylocarpum*)}] x [*catawbiense* var. *album* x {*dichroanthum* x *griersonianum*}]). 30", -15ºF, ML, 4/3/3. Leaves are of medium size. Flowers, to 3" across, are a vibrant greenish yellow, edged strong pink with a dim blotch of brownish orange spots, held in a tall pyramidal truss of up to 18. (Leach 1972).

'Virginia Richards' ([*wardii* x 'F. C. Puddle'] x 'Mrs. Betty Robertson'). 4', 0ºF, M, 4/4/4. A good healthy grower with flowers that open pink, turning to yellow with a crimson blotch. The flower is a color combination seldom seen. The plant has compact habit and dark, glossy leaves. (Whitney, Sather 1976).

'Virginia Stewart' ('Countess of Haddington' x *nuttallii*). 5', 25ºF, EM, -/-/-. Leaves are of medium size. Flowers are very fragrant, to 3 1/2" across, white in color with a yellow blotch, held in a flat truss of up to 7. (Kerrigan, Stewart 1975).

'Virgo' (['Antoon van Welie' x 'Professor J. H. Zaayer'] x 'Annie E. Endtz'). 6', -10ºF, ML, 3-4/3-4. A superior introduction from Holland, this is interesting because all three of the above parents are sisters out of the same cross. It worked to bring the best out of this blood line, producing a large foliaged plant with pinkish rose flowers which have a red-brown blotch. (P. van Nes 1961).

'Viscy' ('Diane' x *viscidifolium*). 5', -10ºF, ML, 3/3/3. Large, glossy foliage covers this wide and full plant. Orange-yellow flowers are brushed with dark red spotting. The blooms provide a warm feeling similar to its name, which means "whiskey" in English. (Hobbie about 1950).

'Vivacious' ('America' x 'Dr. Ross'). 4', -5ºF, ML, 3-4/4/4. Foliage is medium to large. Shaded red flowers, to 2 1/2" across, are carried in a ball-shaped, 10 flower truss. (Forster, Horticultural Research Institute of Ontario 1976).

'Voluptuous' ('Scintillation' x 'Mary Belle'). 5', -5ºF, ML, -/-/-. 'Voluptuous' derives its name from the huge, dome shaped trusses composed of fragrant, frilly flowers. The blooms open pink and are accented by a red flare. This densely branched mound has an upright habit and glossy, oblong leaves. (W. Brack hyb. 1976, reg. 1989).

'Voodoo' ('Britannia' x 'May Day'). 5', 5ºF, ML, 3/3/3. Foliage is of medium size, margins recurved. Cardinal red flowers, to 2 1/2", are held in a loose truss of up to 9. (R. Henny about 1952) P.A. 1952.

'Vulcan' ('Mars' x *griersonianum*). 5', -15ºF, ML, 4/4/4. This plant grows into a magnificent mound of green. The flowers are bright fire red. An excellent hybrid, there are several forms grown, the best of which is 'Vulcan's Flame'. For all practical purposes, it is impossible to tell them apart. (Waterer, Sons & Crisp 1938) A.M. 1957.

'Vulcan's Bells' ('Vulcan's Flame' x *williamsianum*). 3', 0ºF, M, 3/4/3-4. Rosy red flowers cover this densely foliaged mound. Leaves are round and pointed at the tips. An attractive, graceful plant. (Lancaster 1966).

'Vulcan's Flame' (*griersonianum* x 'Mars'). 5', -15ºF, ML, 4/4/4. This is the reverse cross of 'Vulcan'. In other words, 'Mars' was the seed parent (female) of 'Vulcan' and *griersonianum* was the seed parent of 'Vulcan's Flame'. To be truthful, this is so much like the best form of 'Vulcan', you probably can't tell the difference. It has bright red flowers that glow like a warm fire. Foliage is deep yew green with red stems. (Lancaster before 1955).

'Wagtail' (*lowndesii* x *keiskei* 'Yaku Fairy'). 1', 0ºF, EM-ML, -/-/-. This hybrid retains the attractive appearance of the species *lowndesii* while being more vigorous and easier to grow. A semi-deciduous variety, the growth habit forms a tight mat of somewhat shiny foliage. Many pale yellow flowers are produced during May. (Cox, Glendoick Gardens 1990).

'Walloper' ('Anna' x 'Marinus Koster'). 6', -5ºF, M, 4/3-4/3-4. It is a delicious deep pink with huge trusses. Large, vigorous foliage covers the plant, making a perfect combination with the fabulous trusses. This is often confused with 'Red Walloper', however this plant has red growth bud, while the true 'Red Walloper' does not. (Lem before 1960).

'Wally' (*minus* var. *minus* Carolinianum group *album* x *mucronulatum* 'Cornell Pink'). 5', -25ºF, E, 3/3/3. A vigorous grower, forming a wide, upright shrub. Dark green foliage is small and pointed, turning orange-yellow in the fall. Flowers are an outstanding shrimp pink color. This plant is also known as 'Vallya', which is Latvian for Wally. (Mezitt hyb. 1958, Weston Nurseries intro. before 1990).

'Walter Hunnewell' (parentage unknown). 5', -10ºF, ML, -/-/-. Flowers have a white center with ruby red rims. New growth is an effective complement, as it is red-stemmed. (W. Hunnewell hyb. about 1955, Weston reg. 1983).

'Waltham' ('Wilsoni', syn. 'Laetevirens' x *minus* var. *minus* Carolinianum Group). 2-3', -25ºF, M, 3/4/4. Delicate light pink flowers appear in small trusses on top of small, deep forest green leaves. Light, delicate stems form on this compact grower. (Ticknor, Weston before 1980).

'Warchant' ('Old Copper' selfed). 4', -5ºF, M, -/-/-. A spreading, well-branched plant with dark green foliage. Flowers are orange and each has a darker throat which serves as an effective accent. (Lansing Bulgin before 1990).

'War Dance' ('Mars' x 'Pygmalion'). 4', -10ºF, M, -/-/-. The low and spreading plant is densely covered with dark, matte green foliage. This plant is floriforous, producing vivid red flowers held in trusses of 17-21. Each bloom is accented with a black dorsal blotch in addition to freckling of the same color. (M. E. Hall hyb. 1970, E. J. Brown reg. 1979).

'Warlock' ('Romany Chal' x 'Purple Splendour'). 6', 0ºF, L, 4/2-3/3-4. Leaves are large. 3 3/4" flowers are dark reddish purple color, with deeply embossed black dorsal blotch and spotting, held in a flattish truss of up to 14. (Bledsoe 1976).

'Warm Glow' (*dichroanthum* hybrid x 'Vida'). 3', 0ºF, ML, 4/4/4. Leaves are medium sized and rather narrow. Flowers, to 2 1/2" across, are held in a lax truss of up to 12. Color is pale orange, darker in throat, minimal dark red spotting, and reddish orange on the outside. (Greer hyb. 1960, intro. 1976, reg. 1979).

'Warwick' (elepidote hybrid of unknown parentage which, like many Dexter hybrids, probably contains *fortunei* ssp. *fortunei*). 5', -20ºF, EM, 3/3/3. A wide growing shrub with slightly drooping foliage. Fragrant flowers of delicate mauve pink are held in full trusses. (C. O. Dexter before 1950).

'Water Cricket' ([{*griersonianum* x 'Siren'} x 'Fabia'] x 'Grosclaude'). 4', 0ºF, M, -/-/-. White flowers are flushed rose at petal juncture. (Waterer, Sons & Crisp 1975).

'Wayne Pink' (parentage unknown). 6', -10ºF?, ML, -/-/-. Foliage is large. Flowers are spiraea red in color, to 3 1/2" across, held in a large truss of up to 22. (Dexter, Knippenberg 1966).

'Weber's Pride' ('Lady Clementine Mitford' x 'Kate Waterer'). 5', -5ºF, M, 3/3/3. Very flat flowers are bright light plum with a striking orange blotch on the upper lobe. Foliage is light green and held on upright branches for 3 years. (Weber 1974).

'Wee Bee' (*campylognum* 'Patricia' x *keiskei* 'Yaku Fairy'). 1', 5ºF, EM, 4/4/4. A well branched dwarf, which achieves a mature size twice as wide as high. The small foliage densely covers the mounded plant. Leaves are thickly scaled on undersides. Yellowish pink buds open to form lax trusses of 3-5. The funnel shaped flowers are composed of vivid red lobes shading to strong pink in the throat. Each lobe has a ray of strong red through the center, making the bloom season very dramatic. (W. E. Berg reg. 1987) A.E. 1989.

'Wee Willie Winkie' (*yakushimanum* x 'Winsome'). 3', 5ºF, ML, -/-/-. A compact, rounded plant with foliage typical of R. *yakushimanum*. Trusses of rich pink flowers bloom best in sun or partial shade. (New Zealand intro., sold by Riverwood Gardens 1994).

'Weldy' (['Pygmalion' x *haematodes*] x *yakushimanum* Exbury form). 3', -15ºF, M-ML, -/-/-. The flowers are a blend of light and very pale purplish pink fading to almost white, wavy edged. Foliage with slight, wooly white indumentum coats a plant which grows equally as wide as tall. (Kehr, Delp 1992).

'Wendy' ('Cornish Cross' x *williamsianum*). 4', 5ºF, EM, 3/3/3. Cherry colored trusses make a showy display each spring. Rounded foliage is held on a compact plant. (Brandt 1961).

'Westbury' (parentage unknown). 4', -10ºF, M, -/-/-. This slow growing plant spreads to be more wide than tall. Flowers are appealing in both fragrance and texture. The frilled blooms are light purplish pink with darker edges. The throat is accented with yellowish green rays. (Dexter hyb., Tyler Arboretum reg. 1983).

'Westhaven' (selected seedling of *aberconwayi*). 4', -5ºF, M, -/-/-. Leaves are typical of species. Frilled flowers are white with sparse maroon spotting on upper lobe. The flat saucer shaped blooms, to 3 1/4" across, are carried in 15-flower truss. (McGuire 1972) C.A. 1978.

'Weston' (parentage unknown). 5', -10ºF, ML, -/-/-. Leaves are medium size. 2" flowers are rose with golden yellow spots on the dorsal lobe, and darker rose on the outside, in a 10-flower truss. (Dexter, Weston Nurseries 1980).

'Weston's Crescendo' (['PJM' x *minus* ssp. *minus* Carolinianum Group] x unknown). 2', -15ºF, M, -/-/-. A compact plant, more wide than tall. Buds are deep pink, opening to reveal purplish red blooms which mature to be pale orange yellow in color. (Mezitt hyb., Weston reg. 1988).

'Weston's Mayflower' (['Laetevirens' x *minus* var. *minus* Carolinianum Group *album*] x [hybrid of *minus* var. *minus* Carolinianum Group x 'Myrtifolium']). 2', -15ºF, M, -/-/-. A floriferous, compact plant. Slow growing, it forms a mound wider than it is tall. Small trusses of pink flowers are held above elliptical, dark green foliage. (Mezitt hyb. 1971, Weston Nurseries 1988).

'Weston's Pink Diamond' ('PJM' x *mucronulatum* 'Cornell Pink'). 5', -15ºF, E, 4/4/4. An upright growing, well-branched plant that is more tall than wide at maturity. Very glossy, yellow-green leaves provide a background for bright pink buds which open to reveal double fuchsia purple flowers. (Mezitt hyb. 1964, Weston Nurseries intro. 1977, reg. 1983).

'Wheatley' ('Westbury' x 'Meadowbrook'). 6', -15ºF, M, 3-4/4/4. Fragrant flowers are rosy apple blossom pink with a kiss of green in the throat. Large, vigorous foliage and strong plant habit. Considered to be one of the best in the East. (Phipps 1973, Vossberg intro., New York Chapter ARS 1973) A.E. 1973.

'Whisperingrose' (*williamsianum* x 'Elizabeth'). 3', 0ºF, EM, 3-4/4/4. 'Whisperingrose' delights the eye with the richness of carnation rose. This new plant grows in a compact shape to become a verdant mound of Irish green, decorated with rubescent buds of fuchsine red. The flowers are a solid color and form wide open bells which cover the plant from top to bottom. The leaves are small and round with wine red petioles. It is an easy plant to grow, propagates well and buds young. (Greer 1988).

'Whistle Punk' (*yakushimanum* x 'Gipsy King'). 3', -5ºF, E, 4/4/4. Tight, rounded shape in both plant and truss. Flowers are dark rose, fading to pastel pink. (Larson hyb. before 1970, Clint Smith intro.)

'White Bird' ('King Tut' x *yakushimanum* 'Koichiro Wada'). 30", -25ºF, ML, -/-/-. Foliage is medium sized. Flowers, to 2 1/4" wide, are white, faintly spotted green, held in a rounded truss of up to 14. Synonym 'Snow Bird'. (Pride 1979).

'White Dimples' (low white hybrid x white hybrid with yellow center). 3', -20ºF, ML, -/-/-. This dense growing plant is a very heavy bloomer. Buds of strong purplish pink open to white flowers with a yellow center. These flowers are held in ball shaped trusses in groups of twenty. (Mezitt hyb., Weston Nurseries, reg. 1987).

'White Gold' ('Mrs. J. G. Millais' x 'Cheyenne'), 5', -10ºF, ML, 4/3/4. Flowers on this plant are a pure stark white, rolled back at the edges, showing the blotch within. This dramatic blotch begins as burning orange deep in the throat, then widens and lightens into rays of golden yellow reaching out onto the upper lobe. Medium green leaves cover the plant well. Too much sun can cause leaf burn. (Greer 1979).

'White Gull' (*yakushimanum* open pollinated, a hybrid). 3', -5ºF, ML, -/-/-. Foliage is medium large. Flowers, to 2 3/4", are white with chartreuse dorsal spotting and are carried in a large truss up to 20. (Herbert 1979).

'White Mice' (*callimorphum* hybrid). 2', 5ºF?, ML, -/-/-. Mounding in habit, this plant is adorned with small, rounded leaves. The blooms, faring best in some shade, are delicate white, held in small clusters scattered over the plant. (New Zealand, Riverwood Gardens intro. 1995).

'White Mustang' (*calophytum* x 'Goldworth Yellow'). 6', -10ºF, EM, 4/4/3. This plant, clothed with long, elliptical foliage is synonymous with 'Debutante'. The flowers open white and are spotted with a delicate pink. (Rudolph & Leona Henny reg. 1964).

'White Pearl' (*griffithianum* x *maximum*). 6', 5ºF, M, 3/3-4/4-5. Tall conical trusses open with a touch of pastel pink which fades to pristine white. This is an extremely vigorous, upright plant with dark green, slightly rough textured foliage. It is an excellent choice for a large hedge planting, as it grows really fast. Also known as 'Halopeanum'. (Halope, Belgium 1896) A.M. 1906.

'White Peter' ('Blue Peter' selfed). 4', -25ºF, M, -/-/-. A compact growing plant, densely covered with wide, glossy, dark green foliage. White, wavy edged flowers, accented with a prominent maroon flare, are produced in profusion. Note the additional hardiness! (Mehlquist 1991).

'White Pippin' (*williamsianum* x 'Olympic Lady'). 2', 5ºF, ML, -/-/-. This semi-dwarf hybrid has shiny, rounded-elliptical leaves. Light greenish white, bell-shaped flowers are produced in loose trusses. Formerly called 'White Moonstone'. (H. L. Larson reg. 1983).

'White Queen' (*fortunei* ssp. *discolor* x *campylocarpum*). 5', -5ºF?, ML, -/-/-. Leaves are large. 7-lobed flowers of strong substance, to 4" wide, are white, spotted deep chocolate on upper lobes, carried in a 10 flower truss. (Herbert 1967).

'White Ruby' (parentage unknown). 6', -15ºF, M, 4/3/3. An upright growing plant with light green foliage. Fragrant flowers are white with ruffled edges and each has a prominent ruby red blotch. (Sold by Kelleygreen Nursery 1994).

'White Swan' (*decorum* x 'Pink Pearl'). 6', -5ºF, M, 4/3/4. Huge, perfect trusses of satin white are exceptionally showy. The plant is tall growing and has dusty green, concave leaves. (Waterer, Sons & Crisp) A.M. 1937, F.C.C. 1957.

'White Wedding' (*yakushimanum* 'Exbury' x *makinoi*). 2', -5ºF?, M, -/-/-. Leaves are small and heavily indumented. 2 1/2" flowers are pink fading to white, held 15 flowers to the truss, with 3 trusses per terminal. (Lofthouse 1970).

'Whitney Appleblossom' (parentage unknown). 4', 5ºF, M, -/-/-. Forming a mound at maturity, this plant offers medium pink, "appleblossom" flowers with red and gold spotting on the upper lobes. Foliage is deep green. (Whitney hyb., Sather intro. before 1990).

'Whitney Buff' (parentage unknown). 5', -5ºF, M, 4/4/4. A free flowering plant with an attractive growth habit. The large trusses are composed of unique buff colored flowers, surrounded by glossy green foliage. (Whitney hyb., Sather intro. before 1985).

'Whitney Dwarf Orange' (parentage unknown). 2', 0ºF, M, 3/3/3. A low growing, compact plant with flowers blooming in shades of salmon pink to orange. (Whitney hyb., Sather intro. before 1990).

'Whitney Dwarf Red' (parentage unknown). 3', 0ºF, EM, 3/4/4. Low growing plant with upright growth habit. Shiny green leaves and red buds make an attractive plant. Good red flowers. (Whitney before 1980).

'Whitney Peach Blossom' (parentage unknown). 3', 0ºF, EM, -/-/-. A tight and compact plant with matte green leaves. The frilled peach flowers are held in dome shaped trusses. (Whitney hyb., Sather intro. 1991).

'Whitney Pink' (parentage unknown). 3', 0ºF, EM, -/-/-. The mounding habit plant is densely covered with dark green leaves which have a light indumentum below. The funnel-shaped blossoms appear pink, fade to cream at maturity. (Whitney hyb., Sather intro. 1991).

'Whitney Purple' (*ponticum* hybrid). 5', -10ºF, M-ML, 3/3-4/4. A very dark eye stands out against the of blue-violet of the petals. Leaves are glossy and deeply ribbed. From all appearances, this is the same plant that is sold as 'Old Port'. (Whitney, Sather 1986).

'Whitney Tiger Lily' (parentage unknown). 3', 5ºF, EM, -/-/-. An upright growing plant that is well-branched and spreading. Medium green foliage is held on stems with a tone of bronze. The flowers are truly unique for a rhododendron. The pink blooms with red spotting have a very split calyx, strongly resembling a lily. (Whitney hyb., Sather intro. about 1990).

R. 'Burgundy Rose'

'Halfdan Lem'

R. 'Pink Walloper'

Hybrids ~ by Lem

R. 'Point
Defiance'

. 'Norseman'

R 'Riplet'

R. 'Victor Frederick'

R. 'Percy Wiseman'

R. 'Pink Cherub'

R. 'Surrey Heath'

R. 'Titian Beauty'

R. 'Dope

by Waterer

Hybrids ~

R. 'One Thousand Butterflies'

by Lofthouse

R. 'Pink Petticoats'

R. 'Sunup Sundown'

R. 'Lemon Float'

R. 'Canadian Sunset'

'Whitney Dwarf Red'

R. 'Oh Too'

R. 'Anna Rose Whitney'

R. 'Anne's Delight'

R. 'Sunny Day'

Hybrids ~ by Whitney

'Hurricane'

R. 'Stars & Stripes'

R. 'George's Delight'

R. 'Whitney Buff'

R. 'Wojnar's Purple'

Hybrids ~
by Mezitt

R. 'Scintillation'

R. 'Parker's Pink'

Hybrids ~
by Dexter

R. 'Years of Peace'

R. 'Pillow Party'

R. 'PJM'

R. 'Llenroc'

R. 'Lavender Princess'

R. 'Todmorden'

R. 'Accomplishment'

'Whitney's Best Yellow' (uncertain, believed to be a 'Hotei' hybrid). 5', -5ºF, EM, -/-/-. A compact grower with very possibly the richest yellow flowers of any rhododendron. Unfortunately, it is difficult to propagate; therefore, it is often hard to obtain. (Whitney, Sather before 1993).

'Whitney's Georgeanne' (parentage unknown). 3', 5ºF, ML, 3-4/3/3. Slightly lax trusses of salmon orange flowers are found on this plant with slender, small leaves and upright growth habit. (Whitney, Sather before 1985).

'Whitney's Late Orange' (probably contains dichroanthum and a late flowering member of the Fortunea subsection). 4', -5ºF, L-VL, 4/3/3-4. Similar to 'Whitney Orange', but it's a deeper orange and it flowers later in the spring. It is also more upright growing than 'Whitney Orange', with better shape. The solid Spanish orange flowers appear in a full truss and delightfully show themselves after most rhododendrons are through flowering. The sharply pointed leaves are a neat mistletoe green. Originally known as 'Whitney #58-22 Late Orange'. (Whitney, Sather before 1985).

'Whitney's Orange' (dichroanthum 'Sunningdale' x 'Diane'). 3', 0ºF, ML, 4/3/4. If you like orange, this is it. An absolute sensation! Tending to be low in growth habit, with decumbent branches, it is another hybrid with interesting rolling and curling leaves which are a light moss green. It should be used for further hybridizing. (Whitney, Sather 1976).

'Whittenton' (reputedly a hybrid of the Fortunea subseries). 6', -15ºF, M, -/-/-. Light purplish pink flowers on a vigorous plant. (Dexter, Wells intro., The Tyler Arboretum 1980).

'Wickatunk' (minus var. minus Carolinianum Group x mucronulatum 'Pink Panther'). 5', -15ºF, E, -/-/-. An upright grower reaching a height greater than its width, this plant has small foliage that is semi-deciduous in nature. The large, wavy-edged, double flowers are very showy bright pink, flushed with deep purple pink. (Lewis 1994).

'Wickiup' ('C.I.S.' x fortunei ssp. fortunei hybrid). 5', 5ºF, M, 4/3/3-4. This plant has one of those luscious multi-hued peach, orange, apricot and lemon flowers with a touch of cherry in the throat. A beautiful flower of unusual color. The foliage is good, too. A nice looking plant. (James Elliott before 1985).

'Wickiup's Sister' ('C.I.S.' x fortunei ssp. fortunei hybrid). 5', 5ºF, M, 4/3. More upright growing than 'Wickiup', the multi-hued fruit colored flowers have a more golden effect. An excellent accent plant to 'Wickiup' or it is equally as interesting on its own. (James Elliott before 1985).

'Wigeon' (carolinianum x calostrotum 'Gigha'). 2', -10ºF, M, 4/4-5/4. Reddish pink flowers have red spotting on the upper lobes, with short red stamens, in trusses of 3-4. A small plant with attractive leaves. (Cox 1982) A.M. 1982.

'Wilbar' g. (williamsianum x 'Barclayi'). 4', 5ºF, E, 3/3/3. Plant grows compactly, spreading wider than its height. Dark green, ovate leaves are complemented by deep rose pink flowers. (Aberconway 1938, intro. 1946).

'Wild Affair' ('Jean Marie de Montague' x 'Moser's Maroon'). 6', -5ºF, ML, 4/3-4/4. "Wild" is the word for the bright red flowers on this hybrid. Each flower lights up with a golden yellow blotch that makes the red flower glow. Foliage is large, it has an interesting twist, and the color is deep fir green. Plant growth is strong and needs some pinching when young to make a good compact plant. There are five registered rhododendron names that would make interesting conversation if planted in a row in the garden. They are 'Blind Date', 'Joy Ride', 'Wild Affair', 'Youthful Sin' and 'Blessed Event'! (Greer 1988).

'Wilgen's Ruby' ('Britannia' x 'John Walter'). 5', -15ºF, ML, 4/3/3-4. A very deep red with brown blotching. Good green foliage on a hardy plant. Imported from Holland and worth growing. (A.C. van Wilgen, Boskoop, 1951) F.C.C. 1951.

'Willbrit' ('Britannia' x williamsianum). 3', -10ºF, ML, 3-4/4/3-4. Light green foliage enhances the deep pink flowers with lighter edges. (Hobbie, Le Feber intro., Boskoop, reg. 1964). Gold Medal (Rotterdam) 1960.

'Williams' (parentage unknown). 5', -10ºF, L, 3-4/3-4/4. Pink with a prominent blotch. Much like 'Mrs. Furnivall', but blooms later. Klupenger's Nursery introduced this plant under the unregistered name 'Springtime'. It is also sometimes mistakenly sold under the name of 'Marchioness of Lansdowne'. (Probably from England in the early 1900's).

'Wilsoni' (carolinianum x ferrugineum). 3', -15ºF, L, 3/3/3-4. Not to be confused with species wilsonae. Rosy pink flowers on a compact dwarf. It's hardy and sun tolerant. Also known as 'Laetevirens'. (Probably originated in England before 1900, registered by RHS 1958).

'Windbeam' ('Conestoga' hybrid). 4', -25ºF, EM, 4/3/3-4. Very hardy apricot pink flowers change to light pink. Foliage is small and round. (Nearing intro. 1943) A.E. 1973.

'Windjammer' ('Sonata' x 'Lamplighter'). 3', 0ºF, EM, -/-/-. A densely growing plant covered with beautiful green foliage. Compact trusses are made of deep, coral-orange flowers which have dark spotting on the dorsal lobes. (Lansing Bulgin intro. before 1990).

'Windlesham Scarlet' ('Britannia' x 'Doncaster'). 4', -10ºF, L, 4/3/3-4. Nice, tight dome shaped trusses are bright cardinal red with black spots. Dull, dark green leaves clothe a plant of upright growth. (Fromow Nurseries 1968) A.M. 1968.

'Windsor Lad' (ponticum hybrid). 4-5', -10ºF, ML-L, 4/3/4. About the flashiest flower you will see, it is blue-purple with a golden eye that glows against the purple background. The foliage is narrow, and about medium length. A good looking plant. (Knap Hill Nursery before 1958).

'Wine Fuschia' ('Mars' x 'Princess Elizabeth'). 5', -5ºF, ML, -/-/-. This medium sized plant exhibits a spreading, rounded growth habit, cloaked in olive green foliage. Burgundy red flowers with a prominent dark-bluish eye are held in showy, ball shaped trusses. (Stephens before 1990).

'Winneconnet' (a hybrid of the Fortunea series). 6', -10ºF, M, -/-/-. Pale purplish pink flowers adorn this tall growing plant. (Dexter, Wells, The Tyler Arboretum 1980).

'Winning One' ('Lodestar' x 'Mary Belle'). 3', -10ºF, L, -/-/-. Soft yellow-pink flowers have a greenish yellow throat. The outside of the bloom is a blend of purplish red and purplish pink. Flowers are held in trusses of 12. The plant will grows as wide as tall. (Hinerman, Delp 1992).

'Winning Post' ('Marion' x 'Coronation Day'). 6', -5ºF, M, 4/4/3. Large trusses are made of bright rose red flowers. (Boulter, Australia, reg. 1978).

'Win Paul' (souliei x 'Diva'). 4', 0ºF, EM, -/-/-. Leaves are medium large. 3 1/2" flowers are clear pink, paler in the center, and are held in a ball shaped truss. (Larson 1971).

'Winsome' ('Humming Bird' x griersonianum). 3', 0ºF, EM, 3-4/4/4. The plant is compact with healthy looking, small, pointed foliage. It sets attractive, reddish flower buds that you will enjoy all winter. It flowers extremely heavily with beautiful, rosy cerise flowers. (Aberconway 1939) A.M. 1950.

'Winter Snow' ('Kimberly' x *aberconwayi*). 4', -10ºF, EM, 4/4/4. Pristine, snowy white trusses cover this plant in abundance. Each flower is lightly marked in the center with a small red marking. The flowers form a fairly tight upright truss, which is unusual for a smaller type hybrid. Hard edged, deep matte green, rounded leaves are small to medium sized and are slightly longer than wide. The vigorous growing plant branches readily and buds heavily. (Greer 1988).

'Winterset' (*mucronulatum* selfed). 6', -15ºF, VE, -/-/-. Small leaves, typical of the species. 2" flowers are pink with flesh colored undertone, held in a smallish truss of 5. (Grothaus, Brockenbrough 1976) C.A. 1975.

'Wintonbury' (*yakushimanum* x *fortunei* ssp. *fortunei*). 3', -15ºF, M, -/-/-. A compact grower with small, rounded foliage that displays bronze toned new growth. Light pink flowers create a soft color display. (Sold by Roslyn Nursery 1994).

'Wishmoor' (*yakushimanum* x 'Springbok'). 3', -5ºF, M, -/-/-. Lovely, 7-lobed bells of light primrose yellow are held in tight trusses of 14. Four inch leaves have a soft, velvety coating of indumentum. (Crown Estate, Windsor 1972) A.M. 1972.

'Wisp' (*williamsianum* x *irroratum* 'Spatter Paint'). 4', 0ºF, E, 4/4/4. Soft, sugary pink flowers in a slightly lax truss are touched with candy red spotting on all the petals. Showy and pretty! The leaves are rounded and larger than *williamsianum*. A profuse bloomer and a vigorous plant that would add charm to any garden. (Landregan hyb, seedling raised by Sheedy, Skei reg. 1986).

'Wisp of Glory' (parentage unknown, believed to be a *yakushimanum* hybrid). 4', 0ºF, M, -/-/-. Foliage is characteristically *yakushimanum*, forming an attractive backdrop for trusses of light purplish pink. (Clarke 1990).

'Wissahickon' (parentage unknown). 5', -15ºF, ML, 3-4/3-4/4. Bright rose flowers, with a deeper throat, have brownish green spotting. This vigorous growing variety is sun tolerant. A plant of very good reputation in the East. (Dexter not registered).

'Witch Doctor' (['Doncaster' x 'Nereid'] x 'Vulcan'). 4', 0ºF, ML, 3/3/3. The heavy spotting over the entire flower makes this exceptionally different. It is cardinal red and has an unusually large calyx on the back of the flower. The foliage is deep fir green on a plant that is attractive; but it can be open growing if it is in too much shade. (Lem, Elliott 1974).

'Witchery' ('Mars' x *eriogynum*). 5', -5ºF, ML, 4/3-4/-. A terrific fiery red. The flowers are so bright they glow. The new growth is covered with silvery tomentum which is a show in itself. (R. Henny before 1955).

'Wizard' ('Catawbiense Album' x 'Fabia'). 4', -10ºF, ML, 4/3/3-4. Apricot and yellow create a bicolor of super beauty. Streaks of yellow flare from the throat while each division of the petals is marked with apricot orange. The 'Catawbiense Album' in its parentage makes for hardiness not found in most yellow oranges. The sharp, pointed leaves are medium sized. (Lem 1961) A.E. 1959.

'Wojnar's Purple' (parentage unknown). 3', -20ºF, ML, -/-/-. This is a compact plant with widely spreading habit, densely covered in slightly rolled, emerald green leaves. Flowers are vivid reddish purple with darker margins and each has a darker flare on the upper lobe. (Wojnar hyb. before 1960, Mehlquist named, Brand reg. 1990).

'Woodchat' (*brachyanthum* ssp. *hypolepidotum* x *ludlowii*). 2', 0ºF, ML, -/-/-. Vivid yellow, bell-shaped flowers in groups of 3, form trusses held on long stalks above the low, compact growing plant. A unique plant. (Cox 1982) H.C. 1982.

'Woodcock' ('Elizabeth' x *hyperythrum*). 3', -10ºF, EM, 3-4/3-4/3-4. Rosy red flowers are one result of this interesting cross. The leaves are elongated and growth is compact and short. (RHS Garden, Wisley 1971) P.C. 1971.

'Woody's Friggin Riggin' ('Bern' x *yakushimanum*). 4', -5ºF, M, 3-4/3-4/3-4. A plant of compact spreading habit, with leaves showing light traces of the characteristic *yakushimanum* indumentum. Large trusses are composed of pastel pink flowers with a dark red eye. (Hybrid from the Seattle area about 1990).

'Wren' (*ludlowii* x *keiskei* 'Yaku Fairy'). 1', 0ºF, EM, 4/4/3. A most delicate, low growing plant. Flowers are yellow and stand erect, high above the plant, in little trusses of 3. (Cox 1971, reg. 1983).

'Wyandanch Pink' (parentage unknown). 5', -10ºF, M, -/-/-. A sun-loving, upright grower with very large, deep green, shiny foliage. Large, rose pink flowers have darker spotting on the upper lobe. (Dexter, Briarwood Gardens 1994).

'Wyanokie' ('Conestoga' hybrid). 3', -15ºF, M, 3/3-4/4. This hardy, small leaved, white flowered hybrid blooms very heavily. (Nearing about 1950).

'Wynterset White' (*catawbiense* hybrid). 5', -15ºF, M, -/-/-. Flowers open with a light tinge of lavender before maturing to form snow white trusses. Red bracts in winter provide a unique contrast to the shiny green foliage. (Wynterset Nurseries reg. 1990).

'Yaku Dawn' (*yakushimanum* x *pseudochrysanthum* x 'Peter Faulk'). 3', 0ºF, EM, -/-/-. A compact plant with intriguingly indumented foliage. Flowers are pastel pink with a darker margin. (Sold by Hammond 1994).

'Yaku Duchess' ('King Tut' x *yakushimanum* 'Koichiro Wada'). 3', -10ºF, ML, 4/4/4. Foliage is of medium size. 2 1/4" flowers are deep pink, blotched light pink, fading even lighter and carried in a ball-shaped truss of up to 15 flowers. (Shammarello 1977).

'Yaku Duke' ('King Tut' x *yakushimanum* 'Koichiro Wada'). 3', -10ºF, ML, 4/4/4. Foliage is large and rather narrow. Flowers, to 2 1/4" wide, are deep pink, light pink in throat, fading lighter, and held in a rounded truss of up to 14. (Shammarello 1977).

'Yaku Fantasia' ('Vulcan' x *yakushimanum* Exbury Form). 3', 0ºF, EM, 4/4/4. A mounded shrub, as wide as tall, which has rose colored, frilled flowers. These hold their color well throughout the extended blooming period. (Bulgin 1988).

'Yaku Frills' (*smirnowii* x *yakushimanum* 'Koichiro Wada'). 3', -10ºF, ML, 4/4/4. Leaves are medium sized and narrow. Pink in the bud, flowers open white and ruffled, to 2 1/2" across, in a 14 flower truss. (Lancaster 1968).

'Yaku Incense' ('Lackamas Spice' x *yakushimanum*). 4', -5ºF, M, 4/4/4. Although a "yak" is in its parentage, the foliage has no indumentum. Flowers are white with a slight blush and yellow green spotting. (Lancaster before 1965).

'Yaku King' ('King Tut' x *yakushimanum* 'Koichiro Wada'). 3', -10ºF, ML, 4/4/4. Foliage is of medium size. Flowers, to 2 1/4" across, are held in a good sized ball shaped truss of up to 18. Color is deep pink, blotched lighter pink, with the outside deeper pink, fading lighter. (Shammarello 1977).

'Yaku Picotee' ('Moser's Maroon' x *yakushimanum* 'Koichiro Wada'). 3', -10ºF, M, 4/4/3-4. Tight, ball shaped trusses of rose with white centers are on a plant that grows as wide as tall. Indumentum covers the undersides of the slender leaves. (Lancaster reg. 1968).

'Yaku Prince' ('King Tut' x *yakushimanum* 'Koichiro Wada'). 3', -10ºF, ML, 4/4/4. Leaves are medium large. Flowers, to 2 1/4" wide, are pink, blotched paler pink, with reddish orange spotting fading lighter, carried in a 14-flower rounded truss. (Shammarello 1977).

'Yaku Princess' ('King Tut' x *yakushimanum* 'Koichiro Wada'). 3', -10ºF, ML, 4/4/4. Flowers, to 2 1/2", are held in a ball-shaped truss of up to 15. The color is apple blossom pink, and accents are a rosy pink blush with greenish spots which fade lighter. Foliage is medium sized. (Shammarello 1977).

'Yaku Queen' ('King Tut' x *yakushimanum* 'Koichiro Wada'). 3', -10ºF, ML, 4/4/3-4. The leaves are medium in size. 2 1/2" flowers are carried in a rounded truss of up to 16 flowers. Color is pale pink with a dim yellow blotch, the outside strong pink fading to white. (Shammarello 1977).

'Yaku Sunrise' ('Vulcan's Flame' x *yakushimanum* 'Koichiro Wada'). 3', -10ºF, M, 4/4/4. Blossoms are rose colored with darker tones on the reverse of the petals and on the edges. Deep green leaves are recurved slightly. Plant habit is much more broad than tall. (Lancaster reg. 1966).

'Yates' Albino' (*catawbiense* red selection x 'Mars'). 4', -10ºF, ML, -/-/-. Leaves are large. Flowers, to 2 3/4", white, are sparsely spotted greenish yellow and are carried in a lax truss of up to 11. (Yates, M. Yates 1977).

'Yates' Best' ('Mrs. H. R. Yates' x *yakushimanum* 'Koichiro Wada'). 3', -15ºF, ML, -/-/-. Foliage is medium sized. Smallish flowers, to 1 3/4" wide, are pink in color, fading to white with minimal yellow spotting, held in a rounded, 12-flower truss. (Yates, M. Yates 1977).

'Yates' Hazel' ('Mrs. C. S. Sargent' x 'Mount Siga'). 5', -20ºF, ML, -/-/-. Leaves are medium large. 6-lobed flowers, to 3" across, are clear pink, spotted greenish yellow, with pale yellow throat, carried in a ball shaped truss of up to 12. (Yates, M. Yates 1977).

'Yates' Purple' ('Catawbiense Grandiflorum' x 'Purple Splendour'). 3', -5ºF, ML, -/-/-. Leaves are medium large. Flowers, to 2 1/2" wide, are purple with a darker purple blotch and spotting to the top of dorsal lobe, held in a 13-flower truss. (Yates, M. Yates 1979).

'Years of Peace' ('Mrs. C. S. Sargent' selfed). 5', -15ºF, M, 2-3/3-4/4. A vigorous growing plant with hardy, sun tolerant flowers of pink with upper petal spotting. (Mezitt, Weston Nurseries 1980).

'Yellow Creek' ('Sarita Loder' x 'Idealist'). 6', 5ºF, EM, 4/2/2. Growth habit is moderately open, with long, narrow, smooth leaves, light green in color. Primrose yellow flowers are 4" across, flat and flaring, held in a lax, dome shaped truss up to 10 flowers. (James 1961) P.A. 1962.

'Yellow Eye' ('Wyanokie' open pollinated). 4', -20ºF, EM, -/-/-. A vigorous growing plant with an upright habit. New growth has a red tinge. The spherical trusses appear yellow, but the large flowers are actually cream colored with a striking yellow flare. (Nearing before 1965).

'Yellow Fever' ('Mary Fleming' x 'Banana Boat'). 2.5', -10ºF, E, -/-/-. This dense evergreen hybrid, barely taller than it is wide, has matte green leaves which are slightly scaly on both sides. Light greenish yellow, funnel shaped flowers are tinged light pink. These mature to a heavier shade of purplish pink. (Lewis 1988).

'Yellow Gold' ('Apricot Gold' x 'Lem's Cameo'). 3', 5ºF, M, -/-/-. Of shrubby growth habit, this plant will achieve an equal height and spread. Funnel shaped flowers are light yellow with a touch of pink, and are held together in groups of a dozen to a truss. (K. van de Ven, Australia, hyb. 1979; Olinda Nursery reg. 1986).

'Yellow Hammer' (*sulfureum* x *flavidum*). 4', 5ºF, EM, 4/3/4. Very deep yellow, lantern-like flowers grace this plant. The upright growth habit can be trimmed easily, and the plant is said to make a good hedge. One of the few yellow rhododendrons that does well in sunny locations. (Williams before 1950).

'Yellow Pages' (parentage unknown). 4', 0ºF, M, -/-/-. Dome shaped trusses hold wavy-lobed blooms that open a vibrant yellow before mellowing with age. The plant achieves a greater width than height, and it has been documented to spread to 6'. (Wm. Whitney hyb. before 1960, Briggs Nursery reg. 1989).

'Yellow Petticoats' ('Hotei' x ['Pink Petticoats' x *wardii*]). 4', 0ºF, M, 4-5/3-4/3. Clear, deep yellow, frilly flowers are borne in great profusion on this compact plant. Dark green leaves create an excellent backdrop for the flowers and look good all year long, too. (Lofthouse reg. 1983).

'Yellow Pippin' ('Mrs. Lammot Copeland' x *yakushimanum*). 4', -5ºF, M, 3-4/3/3-4. Light yellow flowers are a surprise when they emerge from bright carmine buds. The center of each flower is darker yellow with faint chartreuse spotting. (Larson 1983).

'Yellow Rolls Royce' ('Crest' x 'Odee Wright'). 5', 10ºF, EM, 3-4/3-4/3-4. An attractive growth habit with glossy green foliage, nicely complemented by wavy edged, rich yellow flowers which have bright green accents. (George Clarke, Spady 1990).

'Yellow Saucer' ([*aberconwayi* x {*yakushimanum* 'Koichiro Wada' x 'Fabia'}] selfed). 4', 0ºF, M, 4/3/3. This is an upright growing plant that achieves a wide and spreading habit. The glossy, dark green foliage covers the plant fairly well, although it tends to be slightly open. Flattened funnel shaped flowers open yellow, mottled with a vibrant orange. They mature to lemon yellow with a small red spot on the dorsal lobe. (Smith 1983).

'Yellow Spring' (*keiskei* x *racemosum*). 1', -5ºF, EM, 3-4/3-4/3-4. Leaves are small. Inch wide flowers are pink, shading to a yellowish throat with yellow green spotting. Terminal inflorescences of 10 buds hold up to 5 flowers each. (Herbert 1976).

'Yeoman' (*forrestii* ssp. *forrestii* Repens x 'Choremia'). 18", 0ºF, EM, 3/3/2-3. Waxy, bright red bells form on a tempting little plant. Foliage is small and deep green. (Aberconway 1946) A.M. 1947.

'Youthful Sin' (*cinnabarinum* x *yunnanense*). 5', 10ºF, ML, -/-/-. An upright growing hybrid with small foliage and unique flowers, tubular shaped with a waxy coating. The violet blooms are held in pendulous trusses. (Lord Aberconway 1961) A.M. 1960.

'Yo-Yo' (parentage unknown). 18", -5ºF, EM, 3-4/3/3-4. Leaves are small. Red flowers, to 1 1/4" across, have dull purple spotting on upper lobe, held in a flat truss of up to 8. (Whitney, Sather 1976).

'Yvonne Opaline' ('Aurora' x *griffithianum*). 6', 5ºF, M, 3-4/3/3. This hybrid is tall growing and delightful. The *griffithianum* in its parentage makes it a large plant with large flowers. The buds open deep pink, gradually changing to deep rose on the back of the flower, with pale rose inside. (Rothschild before 1931) A.M. 1931.

'Zuiderzee' ('Mrs. Lindsay Smith' x [*campylocarpum* x unknown]). 3', 5ºF, M, 3/3/3. Pale yellow flowers have red spotting at the base. The very light green leaves require some shade to keep from burning. (Koster 1936) A.M. 1936.

'Zyxya' ('Barclayi Robert Fox' x 'Elizabeth'). 3', 5ºF, E, 3/3/3. Clear blood red flowers, unspotted, are quite large and form a 6-flower truss. (Harrison 1966) A.M. 1966.

DISTINCTIVE FEATURES CHART FOR HYBRIDS

Name	Hardy °F	Sun	Heat	Early	Late	Dwarf	Medium	Tall	Fragr.
A. Bedford		X						X	
Abigail			X					X	
Abraham Lincoln	-25		X				X		
Accomplishment	-15						X		
Aglo	-25	X					X		
Airy Fairy				X			X		
Aksel Olsen	-15					X			
Aladdin			X				X		
Albatross			X					X	X
Albert Close			X				X		
Albert Schweitzer	-15						X		
Album Elegans	-20	X	X	X			X		
Album Novum	-20	X	X				X		
Alena		X		X			X		X
Alice							X		
Always Admired	-15						X		
Amazing Grace	-30						X		
Amber Lantern				X					
America	-20	X					X		
Amor				X			X		
Anah Kruschke	-15	X	X	X			X		
Angelo			X					X	X
Angel's Dream									X
Anita Gehnrich	-15			X			X		
Anka Heinje	-15						X		
Anna							X		
Anna Baldsiefen			X				X		
Anna H. Hall	-25						X		
Anna Rose Whitney								X	
Anna's Riplet				X	X				
Ann Carey				X			X		
Anne Hardgrove				X			X		
Annie Dalton	-15						X		
Ann Lindsay	-15						X		
Antoon van Welie							X		
Applause	-20						X		
April Blush	-25		X	X					
April Fire			X				X		
April Gem	-25		X				X		
April Glow			X				X		
April Love	-25		X					X	
April Mist	-25		X				X		
April Rose	-25		X				X		
April Snow	-20						X		
April White	-25			X			X		
Arctic Dawn	-35		X						
Arctic Glow	-15			X			X		
Arctic Pearl	-25			X			X		
Argentina	-25						X		
Argosy				X				X	X
Arkle						X			
Arnold Piper								X	

Name	Hardy °F	Sun	Heat	Early	Late	Dwarf	Medium	Tall	Fragr.
Aronimink								X	
Arsen's Pink	-15			X	X				
Arthur Osborn				X	X				
Arthur Pride	-30			X			X		
Ashes of Roses	-15						X		
Astrid	-15						X		
Atlantis	-20			X			X		
Atrosanguineum	-20						X		
August Lamken					X				
Aunt Martha			X	X			X		
Austin H.							X		
Autumn Gold			X	X			X		
Avalanche				X			X		
Avocet	-15				X			X	X
Ayah					X		X		
Azma							X		
Azor					X		X		
Aztec Gold						X			
Baby Bear						X			
Babylon				X			X		
Bad Eilsen	-15				X				
Baden Baden	-15				X				
Bad Zwischenahn		X					X		
Bali	-20						X		
Bally Cotton					X				
Balta	-25			X			X		
Bambi							X		
Bambino							X		
Bandoola							X		
Bangkok	-15						X		
Barbara Behring	-25						X		
Barbara Houston					X		X		
Bariton							X		
Barnstable								X	X
Barry Rodgers					X				
Barto Ivory								X	X
Barto Lavender								X	X
Bashful Betty						X			
Beau Brummell				X	X				
Beaufort	-20						X		
Beautiful Dreamer				X			X		
Beauty of Littleworth							X		
Beechwood Pink	-15						X		
Beer Sheba					X				
Bellefontaine	-15				X			X	
Belle Heller		X					X		
Belle of Tremeer					X				
Bellvale	-25				X				
Belva's Joy					X				
Ben Briggs				X	X				
Bergie Larson					X		X		
Berryrose					X		X		

Name	Hardy °F	Sun	Heat	Early	Late	Dwarf	Medium	Tall	Fragr.
Besse Howells	-15							X	
Betty Arrington				X				X	
Betty's Belle			X				X		
Betty Sears							X		
Betty Wormald								X	
Bewitched				X			X		
Bibiani				X				X	
Big Deal	-20						X		
Big Savage Red	-20							X	
Bill Massey								X	X
Black Eye		X						X	
Black Magic					X		X		
Black Prince									
Black Prince's Ruby			X				X		
Black Satin	-20						X		
Black Sport					X			X	
Blanc-Mange					X			X	
Blanka	-15			X					
Blaze	-25						X		
Blitz			X	X			X		
Blood Ruby					X				
Blue Bird				X					
Blue Boy				X				X	
Blue Chip				X					
Blue Cloud							X		
Blue Diamond							X		
Blue Ensign	-15						X		
Blue Frost								X	
Blue Gown							X		
Blue Jay				X				X	
Blue Lagoon			X				X		
Blue Ridge	-15						X		
Blueshine Girl			X						
Blue Silver	-25		X				X		
Blue Star				X					
Blue Thunder			X						
Blue Tit			X				X		
Bluette							X		
Boddaertianum			X					X	
Bombay							X		
Bonfire							X		
Bonito				X				X	X
Bonnie Babe							X		
Bonnie Brae								X	X
Bo-Peep				X			X		
Boule de Neige	-25	X	X				X		
Boule de Rose	-20						X		
Boulodes								X	X
Bow Bells							X		
Brasilia							X		
Bravo!	-15		X				X		
Brenda Lee	-20						X		

	Hardy °F	Sun	Heat	Early	Late	Dwarf	Medium	Tall	Fragr.
Bric-a-Brac				X		X			
Brick Dust				X					
Bridal Bouquet							X		
Brigitte							X		
Brilliant				X					
Britalier					X		X		
Brookside							X		
Broughtonii Aureum		X	X				X		
Brown Eyes	-15		X					X	
Bruce Brechtbill							X		
Bud Flanagan					X	X			
Bulstrode Park								X	
Burma	-20							X	
Burning Love	-15						X		
Buttered Popcorn					X	X			
Buttersteep					X		X		
Cadis	-15	X	X		X			X	X
Cairo	-20							X	
Calcutta	-15			X		X			
California Gold				X		X			X
Calsap	-25					X			
Canada					X				
Canadian Beauty							X		
Canadian Lilac	-25				X				
Canadian Magenta	-25				X				
Canadian Sunset							X		
Canary							X		
Canary Islands	-20							X	
Candidissimum	-15		X				X		
Captain Jack			X				X		
Caractacus	-25		X				X		
Caramou	-15				X				
Carex		X						X	
Carex Blush		X						X	
Carlpi	-15		X		X				
Carmen					X				
Carol Amelia				X		X			X
Caroline	-15		X					X	X
Caroline de Zoete	-15					X			
Carousel	-15				X				
Casanova	-25					X			
Castanets							X		
Catalgla	-25						X		
Catawbiense Album	-25						X		
Catawbiense Boursault	-20						X		
Catawbiense Grandiflorum	-15						X		
Celeste			X				X		
Centennial Celebration	-15						X		
Chapmanii Wonder	-15	X	X				X		
Charles D			X			X			
Charles Dickens	-25							X	
Charles Thorold	-15			X	X				
Charlestown	-15							X	X

	Hardy °F	Sun	Heat	Early	Late	Dwarf	Medium	Tall	Fragr.
Charmaine						X			
Cherry Bright							X		
Cherry Float							X		
Chesapeake	-25						X		
Chesterland	-25			X				X	
Chiffchaff						X			
Chiffon						X			
Chikor						X			
China Doll								X	
Choremia				X			X		
Christmas Cheer				X			X		
Chrysomanicum						X			
Cilpinense				X		X			
Cinnamon Bear	-15						X		
Cliff Garland	-20			X	X				
Cliff Spangle	-20			X	X				
Cloud Nine	-15						X		
Colts Neck Rose	-25			X	X				
Compacta							X		
Conchita				X			X		
Concorde	-10						X		
Conemaugh	-15			X				X	
Conewago	-25			X				X	
Congo	-20							X	
Connecticut Yankee	-25				X		X		
Conroy							X		
Cookie							X		
Coral Reef					X		X		
Cornubia				X			X		
Coronation Day				X			X		
Cotton Candy							X		
Countess of Athlone							X		
Countess of Haddington					X			X	X
County of York	-15						X		
Court Jester						X			
Cowslip					X				
C. P. Raffill				X			X		
Cream Crest				X			X		
Creeping Jenny					X				
Crest								X	
Crete	-15						X		
Crimson Pippin					X				
Crossbill				X			X		
Cunningham's Sulphur				X			X		
Cunningham's White	-15						X		
Cupie						X			
Curlew						X			
Cutie	-15					X			
Cynosure								X	
Cynthia	-15							X	
Cyprus	-20						X		
Dainty Jean						X			
Dainty Maiden						X			

	Hardy °F	Sun	Heat	Early	Late	Dwarf	Medium	Tall	Fragr.
Dalkeith				X		X			
Dame Nellie Melba				X				X	
Damozel								X	
Daniela	-15						X		
Dan's Early Purple				X			X		
Daphnoides	-15						X		
David								X	
David Forsythe	-20						X		
David Gable	-15							X	
Debbie							X		
Debijo	-15						X		
Delta	-15				X	X			X
Deming Brook	-20						X		
Denali								X	
Desmit	-15						X		
Dexter's Appleblossom								X	X
Dexter's Apricot								X	X
Dexter's Brandy-Green								X	X
Dexter's Champagne	-15						X		
Dexter's Count Vitetti	-15						X		
Dexter's Cream								X	X
Dexter's Crown Pink					X			X	
Dexter's Giant Red					X			X	
Dexter's Glow					X			X	
Dexter's Horizon					X			X	
Dexter's Orchid	-15					X			
Dexter's Peppermint					X				X
Dexter's Pink Glory					X			X	X
Dexter's Spice					X			X	X
Dexter's Springtime					X	X			X
Dexter's Vanilla						X			X
Dexter's Victoria					X			X	
Disca								X	X
Diva								X	
Dixy Lee Ray								X	
Doctor Richard Anderson			X				X		X
Dolly Madison	-20						X		
Doncaster							X		
Dora Amateis	-15					X			
Doris Bigler	-15							X	
Dorothy Amateis	-15							X	
Dorothy Peste Anderson						X			
Dorothy Swift	-20				X				
Double Dip	-25					X			
Douglas McEwan								X	
Dover Rose								X	
Dr. A. Blok								X	
Dragonfly				X	X				
Dr. V. H. Rutgers	-15							X	
Duchess of York								X	X
Duet	-25							X	
Duke of York								X	X
Earlene	-15						X		

Name	Hardy °F	Sun	Heat	Early	Late	Dwarf	Medium	Tall	Fragr.
Earlybird	-15			X			X		
Early Brilliant				X			X		
Easter Dawn	-15			X				X	
Ebony					X				
Edith Pride	-25							X	
Edmond Amateis	-15							X	
Edna McCarty					X			X	
Edward Dunn					X			X	
Edward S. Rand	-15							X	
Edwin O. Weber							X	X	
Egret			X	X					
Eider			X	X					
El Alamein				X					
Elam	-20			X					
Eldorado			X		X				
Eleanore							X		
Elizabeth Lockhart					X				
Else Frye			X		X				
Elsmere	-25							X	
Emasculum			X				X		
EMS					X				
English Roseum	-25							X	
Enticement				X					
Erato	-15							X	
Ermine								X	
Ernie Dee					X				
Ethel					X				
Etta Burrows			X				X		
Euan Cox					X				
Euclid	-25							X	
Evelyn				X				X	
Evening Glow				X				X	
Everestianum	-15							X	
Everything Nice			X		X				
Exbury Calstocker			X					X	
Exotic								X	
Fabulous			X		X				
Faggetter's Favourite								X	
Fair Lady								X	
Fair Sky								X	
Fairy Mary	-15				X				
Faisa	-20				X				
Fanfare	-20							X	
Farewell Party				X				X	
Fastuosum Flore Pleno	-15							X	
Festivo						X			
Fiji	-20							X	
Fine Feathers			X		X				
Finlandia	-15				X				
Fiona			X		X				
Firedrake				X			X		
Firestorm	-25				X				
Flair	-15				X				

Name	Hardy °F	Sun	Heat	Early	Late	Dwarf	Medium	Tall	Fragr.
Floda	-20						X		
Flora's Boy						X			
Florence Archer				X	X				
For Pete's Sake	-15						X		
Fragrans Affinity				X			X		
Fragrantissimum								X	X
Francesca							X		
Frango							X		
Frank Baum				X			X		
Frank Galsworthy	-15			X	X				
Fran Labera	-15							X	X
French Creek	-15						X		
Frontier							X		
Fundy	-15							X	X
Gabriel	-15						X		
Gartendirektor Glocker						X			
Gary Herbert								X	X
General Anthony Wayne								X	X
General Eisenhower							X		
Genoveva	-20						X		
Germania	-15					X			
Gertrude Saxe	-25						X		
Giganteum	-15						X		
Gill's Crimson				X			X		
Ginny Beale					X				
Ginny Gee					X				
Gipsy King						X			
Glad Tidings						X			
Gladys Johnson								X	X
Glenfalloch Blue					X				
Gloxineum	-15						X		
Golden Bee					X				
Golden Fantasy							X		
Golden Gala	-20						X		
Golden Princess					X				
Golden Salmon	-15						X		
Goldfinch	-15					X			
Goldfort	-15					X			
Gold Moon							X		X
Goldsworth Yellow	-15					X			
Golfer	-15				X				
Gomer Waterer	-15	X					X		
Good News				X	X				
Goosander					X				
Graf Zeppelin	-15	X						X	
Grand Pre						X			
Grand Sight	-15					X			
Great Eastern	-15							X	
Great Smoky	-15							X	
Grenadier					X			X	
Gretchen	-15							X	
Grilse					X	X			
Grouse			X	X					

Name	Hardy °F	Sun	Heat	Early	Late	Dwarf	Medium	Tall	Fragr.
Guardian Fir				X				X	
Guy Bradour	-15							X	X
Guy Nearing								X	
Hachmann's Charmant	-15						X		
Hachmann's Feuerschein	-15						X		
Hachmann's Marlis							X		
Hachmann's Polaris	-15						X		
Halesite Maiden								X	X
Halfdan Lem								X	
Hallelujah	-15						X		
Hardijzer's Beauty							X		
Hardy Giant								X	
Harry Carter						X		X	
Hawaii	-25						X		
Hazel	-15					X		X	
Hazel Fisher				X	X				
Heatherside Beauty						X		X	
Heavenly Scent								X	X
Helen Child			X						
Helen Everitt	-15							X	X
Helen Scott Richey					X	X			
Helene Huber								X	X
Helios								X	X
Hellilkki	-35						X		
Henriette Sargent	-25						X		
Henry R. Yates						X	X		
Henry's Red	-25						X		
Hess Orange	-15						X		
Hill's Low Red						X			
Hindustan	-20						X		
Hobbie Salute	-15					X			
Hockessin	-25					X			
Holden	-15					X			
Honey Bee					X	X			
Hong Kong	-20						X		
Honore Hacanson							X		
Honsu's Baby			X	X					
Hope Braafladt								X	X
Horizon Lakeside								X	X
Horizon Monarch							X		
Hot Stuff						X			
Hudson Bay	-20					X	X		
Hugh Koster							X		
Hugtight						X			
Humboldt Sunrise							X		X
Humming Bird						X			
H. W. Sargent	-25						X		
Hydon Mist						X			
Hydon Snowflake						X			
Ice Cream					X			X	
Ice Cube	-20					X			
Ignatius Sargent	-25						X		
Igtham Gold			X					X	

	Hardy °F	Sun	Heat	Early	Late	Dwarf	Medium	Tall	Fragr.
m Cream								X	X
pi				X		X			
ca Chief	-20						X		
dependence Day	-15			X			X		
diana				X	X				
grid Mehlquist	-25						X		
trifast	-15					X			
ene Stead								X	X
abel Pierce							X		
anhoe							X		
ery's Scarlet							X		
ory Coast	-20						X		
ory Queen							X		
ory Tower	-25						X		
bberwocky		X		X					
cksonii	-15	X			X				
ipur		X			X				
lipeno					X				
ane Grant	-20						X		
ane Henny								X	
ane Mamot								X	
anet Blair	-15							X	
anet Scroggs								X	
ay Murray	-15							X	
ean				X				X	
ean Marie de Montague		X	X					X	
ennie Dosser				X				X	
erico	-20						X		
. G. Millais								X	
o Ann Newsome		X	X						
ock		X	X	X					
odi		X			X				
oe Paterno	-20							X	
ohn Coutts			X		X				
ohn Waterer	-15				X				
onathan Shaw			X		X				
oseph Dunn	-15				X				
osephine Everitt			X		X				
oshua	-25							X	
oshua Huddy	-15							X	
oy Ride								X	
uan De Fuca				X				X	
udy Spillane				X	X				
ulia Grothaus				X				X	
ulie Titcomb								X	
ulischka	-15						X		
une Pink	-15		X				X		
unifreude	-15				X				
utland g.				X				X	
Kaponga								X	
Kapunatiki								X	
Karin	-15					X			
Karin Seleger	-25				X				

	Hardy °F	Sun	Heat	Early	Late	Dwarf	Medium	Tall	Fragr.
Katherine Dalton	-15							X	
Kathryna	-15							X	
Kelley								X	
Ken Janeck	-15						X		
Kentucky Cardinal	-15						X		
Kettledrum	-20							X	
Kim					X				
Kimberly	-10						X		X
Kinglet		X					X		
Kingston							X		
King Tut	-20						X		
Kluis Triumph							X		
Kunming	-15						X		
LaBar's White	-20							X	
Lackamas Blue								X	
Lackamas Firebrand					X	X			
Lackamas Spice								X	X
Lady Alice Fitzwilliam								X	X
Lady Annette de Trafford	-15				X				
Lady Armstrong	-20						X		
Lady Bessborough							X		
Ladybird					X		X		
Lady Bowes Lyon	-15					X			
Lady Clementine Mitford							X		
Lady Grey Egerton	-15						X		
Lady Longman	-15						X		
Lady of Spain							X		
Lajka	-15							X	
Lalique							X		
Langworth	-15						X		
Lartag					X		X		
Last Chance							X		
Last Hurrah					X				
Laurel Pink	-20						X		
Laurie	-20		X				X		
Lava Flow				X	X				
Lavender Charm							X		
Lavendula	-15						X		
Leah Yates	-15						X		
Leeann			X				X		
Lee's Best Purple	-20		X					X	
Lee's Dark Purple	-15							X	
Lee's Scarlet			X		X				
Lem's Monarch								X	
Lem's Stormcloud	-15							X	
Leo			X				X		
Leonardslee Giles								X	
Leonore					X		X		
Lightly Lavender	-15							X	
Lillan Peste				X					
Limelight	-25						X		
Linda	-15						X		
Lisa	-15								X

	Hardy °F	Sun	Heat	Early	Late	Dwarf	Medium	Tall	Fragr.
Little Ben g.						X			
Little Bert						X			
Little Gem						X			
Little Joe						X			
Little Lou						X			
Little Miss Muffett						X			
Little Nemo						X			
Little Sheba						X			
Liz Ann						X			
Llenroc	-20		X				X		
Lodauric			X					X	X
Lodauric Iceburg			X					X	X
Loderi Group								X	X
Lodestar	-20							X	
Lois						X			
Looking Glass	-15						X		
Lucy's Good Pink	-15		X					X	
Luxor	-25							X	
Lydia								X	
Lynne Robbins Steinman	-25		X					X	
Macopin	-20						X		
Madah Jean								X	
Mdm. Carvalho	-15					X		X	
Mdm. Cochet						X	X		
Mdm. Jules Porges						X		X	
Mdm. Masson	-15							X	
Mdm. Wagner	-25							X	
Madras	-15						X		
Madrid	-20							X	
Magnagloss	-15					X		X	
Magnificat								X	
Maharani								X	
Mah Jong			X		X				
Malta	-25					X			
Mantou	-25					X			
Mannheim	-15					X			
Marchioness of Lansdowne	-15					X		X	
Margaret Falmouth			X					X	
Marge Danik	-25							X	
Maricee						X			
Marie Forte	-15					X			
Marietta	-15					X			
Marilyn Horne	-15					X			
Marine							X		
Mariner			X		X				
Marinus Koster							X		
Marion Street	-15							X	
Mars	-15							X	
Martha Isaacson			X		X				X
Martha Phipps							X		
Martha Robbins						X			
Martine						X			
Mary Belle	-15							X	

Name	Hardy °F	Sun	Heat	Early	Late	Dwarf	Medium	Tall	Fragr.
Mary Drennen					X			X	
Mary Fleming	-15						X		
Master Mariner					X	X			
Matilda	-15						X		
Maxecat	-25			X				X	
Maxhaem Yellow				X		X			
Maxine Childers				X		X			
May Schwartz				X	X				
May Time	-15						X		
Meadowbrook	-15							X	
Meadowgold			X			X			
Melrose Pink	-20	X						X	
Merganser						X			
Merry May White						X			
Mi Amor								X	X
Michael Rice	-15						X		
Michael Waterer	-15			X			X		
Midsummer	-15			X			X		
Mildred Fawcett							X		
Milestone	-15						X		
Millcent Scott				X			X		
Minas Maid	-15			X		X			
Minas Peace	-15			X		X			
Minas Rose	-15			X		X			
Minas Snow	-15						X		
Mini Brite	-15		X	X					
Minnetonka	-25						X		
Minterne Cinnkeys				X		X			
Miss Prim			X			X			
Moerheim	-15					X			
Mollie Coker							X		
Monaco	-20			X			X		
Monique Behring	-25						X		
Monsieur Guillemot				X			X		
Montchanin	-25					X			
Montego	-15						X		
Monterey	-25			X				X	
Moser's Maroon				X			X		
Moth					X				
Mother Greer						X			
Mother of Pearl							X		
Mountain Flare	-15						X		
Mountain Glow	-15					X			
Mountain Queen	-15					X			
Mount Everest			X				X		
Mount Mitchell	-25						X		
Mrs. A. F. McEwan							X		
Mrs. A. J. Holden				X			X	X	
Mrs. A. T. de la Mare	-15						X	X	
Mrs. Charles E. Pearson		X	X				X		
Mrs. Charles S. Sargent	-25	X	X				X		
Mrs. Davies Evans						X	X		
Mrs. Donald Graham					X		X		

Name	Hardy °F	Sun	Heat	Early	Late	Dwarf	Medium	Tall	Fragr.
Mrs. E. C. Stirling								X	
Mrs. Furnivall	-15						X		
Mrs. G. W. Leak								X	
Mrs. Horace Fogg								X	
Mrs. J. A. Withington III	-25						X		
Mrs. J. C. Williams	-15				X			X	
Mrs. J. G. Millais								X	
Mrs. Lammot Copeland					X			X	
Mrs. Lindsay Smith								X	
Mrs. P. den Ouden	-15							X	
Mrs. P. D. Williams					X			X	
Mrs. Philip Martineau					X			X	
Mrs. Powell Glass	-20							X	
Mrs. R. S. Holford	-15							X	
Mrs. T. H. Lowinsky	-15				X			X	
Mrs. Walter Burns								X	
Mrs. W. R. Coe								X	
Multimaculatum	-25							X	
Mundai			X					X	
Muriel Pearce								X	
My Lady					X			X	
My Pet						X			
Myrtifolium	-15	X	X		X		X		
Namu	-15						X		
Nantucket	-15					X			
Naomi Group								X	X
Nepal	-25							X	
Nereid					X				
Newburyport Beauty	-15							X	
Newburyport Belle	-15					X			
Newcomb's Sweetheart						X			X
New Patriot	-20							X	
Night Editor					X			X	
Nile	-20						X		
Nimbus							X		
Nobleanum				X		X			
Nobleanum Album				X		X			
Nobleanum Coccineum				X			X		
Nobleanum Venustum				X			X		
Noble Mountain						X			
Nodding Bells	-15					X			
Nofretete					X		X		
Norman Behring	-25				X	X			
Norman Gill							X		
Norman Shaw					X			X	
Northern Star					X			X	
Nova Zembla	-25							X	
Nuance	-15							X	
Nymph				X	X				
Oceanlake		X					X		
Odoratum	-15					X			X
Old Copper					X		X		
Old Spice							X		X

Name	Hardy °F	Sun	Heat	Early	Late	Dwarf	Medium	Tall	Fragr.
Olga Mezitt	-15						X		
Olin O. Dobbs	-15						X		
Olive	-15		X				X		
Omega	-20							X	
Orange Honey	-20				X			X	
Orange Sherbet	-20							X	
Ornatum	-20						X		
Pacific Glow			X					X	
Pale Perfection	-15							X	
Paloma								X	
Pamela Louise								X	X
Panama	-15						X		
Parker's Pink	-25							X	X
Parson's Gloriosum	-25						X		
Party Pink	-20						X		
Passion	-15							X	
Passionate Purple					X				
Patricia						X			
Patty Bee						X			
Paul Lincke			X			X			
Paul Vossberg				X		X			
Pauline Bralit								X	X
Peach Blend			X			X			
Peaches and Cream						X			
Peach Satin				X		X			
Pearce's American Beauty				X			X		
Peekaboo						X			
Peggy Zabel								X	X
Peking	-15								
Penelope				X		X			
Pera			X	X					
Perfectly Pink			X				X		
Perfume								X	X
Persia	-20						X		
Peter Behring	-25					X			
Peter Faulk			X			X			
Peter Tigerstedt	-25						X		
Peter Vermuelen	-25					X			
Phalarope			X			X			
Phyllis Ballard				X		X			
Pickering						X			
Pieces of Eight								X	X
Pieces of Gold							X		X
Pikeland				X					
Pillar	-15					X			
Pillow Party	-25					X			
Pink Cameo	-20					X			
Pink Drift			X						
Pink Flair	-20					X			
Pink Flourish	-25					X			
Pink Fondant	-15								
Pink Globe	-15							X	
Pink Mist					X				

R. 'Black Magic'

R. 'Senorita Chere'

Hybrids ~ by Greer

R. 'September Song'

R. 'Peach Surprise'

R. 'Black Eye'

R. 'Cheyenne'

R. 'Winter Snow'

R. 'Lydia'

R. 'Blue Lagoon'

R. 'Perfectly Pink'

R. 'Kimberly'

R. 'Lightly Lavender'

R. 'Mother Greer'

R. 'Greer's Cream Delight'

R. 'Olin O. Dobbs'

R. 'Mother Greer'

R. 'Razzle Dazzle'

R. 'Red Delicious'

R. 'Cream Glory'

R. 'Red Eye'

R. 'Kimbeth'

Hybrids ~
by Greer

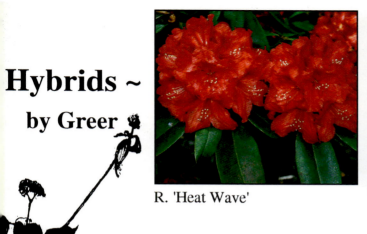
R. 'Heat Wave'

R. 'White Gold'

R. 'Wild Affair'

R. 'Very Berry'

R. 'Gold Medal'

R. 'Firewine'

. 'Greer's Starbright'

R. 'Everything Nice'

R. 'Grand Slam'

R. 'Sugar Pink'

R. 'Irresistable Impulse'

Hybrids ~ by Cox

R.'Curlew'
(below center)

R. 'Chikor'
(bottom center)

R. 'Wren

R. 'Eider'

R. 'Teal'

R. 'Egret

	Hardy °F	Sun	Heat	Early	Late	Dwarf	Medium	Tall	Fragr.
ink Parasol	-15						X		
ink Pearl								X	
ink Snowflakes			X	X					
ink Twins	-15						X		
ink Walloper								X	
innacle	-20							X	
ioneer	-25	X	X	X			X		
ioneer Silvery Pink	-20			X			X		
ipaluk				X			X		
JM group	-25	X	X	X			X		
latinum Pearl		X						X	
leasant Dream					X			X	X
oint Defiance							X		
olar Bear					X			X	X
olaris	-15	X					X		
olynesian Sunset					X		X		
onticum Variegatum	-15						X		
opeye								X	
owell Glass	-15							X	
raecox				X			X		
rawn				X				X	
resident Lincoln	-25	X	X					X	
ride of Leonardslee								X	
ride of Split Rock	-15						X		
rincess Anne					X				
rincess Elizabeth	-15							X	
rincess Juliana								X	
rincess Mary of Cambridge	-25	X						X	
rize	-20						X		
rofessor Amateis	-15						X		
rogres			X				X		
romise of Spring			X					X	
rostigiatum						X			
tarmigan						X			
uget Sound								X	X
uncta	-15			X	X				
urest	-20						X		
urple Elegans	-15	X	X					X	
urple Emperor								X	
urple Gem	-25	X	X				X		
urple Imp	-15		X	X			X		
urpureum Elegans	-25	X	X					X	
urpureum Grandiflorum	-20							X	
ygmy							X		
Queen Mary	-15	X							
Queen of Hearts							X		
Racearound	-15						X		
Racil				X			X		
Racilina	-15						X		
Radistrotum						X			
Rainbow								X	
Ramapo	-25	X	X				X		
Ramona	-15								X

	Hardy °F	Sun	Heat	Early	Late	Dwarf	Medium	Tall	Fragr.
Rangoon	-15			X			X		
Rasputin	-15		X	X					
Ravenna	-20						X		
Red Brave	-25							X	
Red Carpet						X			
Red Delicious				X				X	
Redder Yet	-25							X	
Red Devil						X			
Red Frilled	-15					X			
Red Lion				X				X	
Red Majesty					X			X	
Red Paint					X		X		
Redpoll				X	X				
Red Puff	-15						X		
Red River	-20				X				
Red Rum				X	X				
Red Walloper								X	
Red Wood	-20							X	
Reine Long								X	X
Reuthe's Purple					X				
Reve Rose					X				
Rik	-15			X	X				
Rio	-20					X			
Riplet					X				
Robert Allison								X	X
Robert Louis Stevenson				X	X				
Robert Seleger					X				
Robin Leach	-20			X		X			
Rocket	-15							X	
Rocky White								X	X
Rococo	-25							X	
Rollie	-15							X	
Romany Chal								X	
Roma Sun								X	X
Romeo	-20							X	
Rosamundi					X		X		
Rose Elf			X		X	X			
Rose of China					X		X		
Rose Scott					X		X		
Roseum Elegans	-25	X	X					X	
Roseum Superbum	-20	X	X					X	
Roslyn								X	
Rouge Aureum	-20					X			
Royal Blood				X	X				
Royal Flush								X	
Royal Pink	-15						X		
Royal Purple	-15						X		
Roy Hudson				X				X	X
Royston Red				X			X		
Ruby Hart					X				
Ruffles	-15							X	
Russell Harmon	-25				X			X	
Rustic Maid					X				

	Hardy °F	Sun	Heat	Early	Late	Dwarf	Medium	Tall	Fragr.
Sacko		X					X		
Sagamore Bayside								X	X
Saint Breward	-15						X		
Saint Merryn							X		
Saint Minver				X			X		
Salute	-15						X		
Sammetglut	-15							X	
Samoa	-20							X	
Sandwich Appleblossom								X	X
Sandy Petuso	-20							X	
Sappho	-15							X	
Sausalito				X				X	
Scarlet Blast	-20						X		
Scarlet Glow	-15							X	
Scarlet King			X					X	
Scarlet Romance	-25						X		
Scarlet Wonder	-15					X			
Schneebukett								X	
Schneekrone	-15						X		
Scintillation	-15							X	
Sea-Tac				X	X				
Seattle Springtime				X			X		
Sefton	-15							X	
Senegal	-15							X	
Senko Blue	-15							X	
Senorita Chere	-15						X		
September Snow				X	X				
Seta				X					
Shamrock				X	X				
Sham's Candy	-20							X	
Sham's Juliet	-20						X		
Sham's Pink	-20						X		
Sham's Ruby	-20						X		
Shanghai								X	
Shawme Lake				X				X	
Shilsonii				X			X		
Shirley Rose Lent				X				X	
Siam	-20						X		
Sierra Sunrise							X		
Siesta	-15						X		
Sigismund Rucker	-15							X	
Signal Horn	-15							X	
Sigrid				X					X
Silberwolke	-15						X		
Silky Gold				X				X	
Singapore	-15						X		
Skookum	-20						X		
Skookumchuck	-15						X		
Skyglow				X					X
Small Fry			X			X			
Small Gem			X			X			
Small Wonder	-15					X			
Smokey #9								X	

Name	Hardy °F	Sun	Heat	Early	Late	Dwarf	Medium	Tall	Fragr.
Snipe						X			
Snow Lady				X		X			
Solidarity	-15						X		
Sonata					X		X		
Songbird				X			X		
Southern Cross					X			X	X
Southland					X				
Souvenir de Anthony Waterer					X		X		
Spellbinder	-15			X			X		
Spinulosum				X		X			
Spitfire							X		
Spring Dawn	-20						X		
Springfield					X		X		
Spring Fling				X	X				
Spring Frolic	-25					X			
Spring Glory	-15						X		
Spring Parade	-20	X				X			
Spring Snow				X	X				
Spring Song				X	X				
Stacia	-15							X	X
Starburst						X	X		
Starcross						X	X	X	
Star Trek				X		X			
Stockholm	-20						X		
Strawberry Swirl	-15					X			
Sue								X	X
Sugar Pink							X		
Sumatra	-15				X				
Summer Glow	-15			X			X		
Summer Rose				X			X		
Summer Snow	-15			X			X		
Summer Summit	-20			X			X		
Summertime	-25			X			X		
Sunsplash	-15					X			
Sunspray							X		
Suomi			X			X			
Susan							X		
Tahiti	-15					X			
Tally Ho			X			X			
Tapestry	-20					X			
Tarantella	-15					X			
Taurus							X		
Tempest				X			X		
Tensing				X	X				
Tessa			X			X			
Tessa Bianca			X			X			
Tessa Roza			X			X			
The Bride	-15						X		
The General	-20						X		
Theo Light	-15				X				
Thomwilliams					X				
Thunder	-20					X			
Thunderhead	-15							X	
Tiara				X			X		
Tiffany	-15								
Tinker Hill								X	X
Tinkle Bells						X			
Tish						X			X
Today and Tomorrow	-20					X			
Todmorden	-15						X		
Tofino							X		
Tom Ethrington				X			X		
Tony	-15						X		
Too Bee					X				
Topsvoort Pearl							X		
Tottenham	-20					X			
Tow Head	-15					X			
Traci Suzanne					X			X	X
Treasure					X				
Trilby	-15						X		
Trinidad	-20					X			
Trinity	-25								
Trojan Warrior	-15					X			
Tropicana				X		X			
Turkish Delight	-20					X			
Tuscany	-20						X		
Tyermanii								X	X
Unknown Warrior				X			X		
Valaspis				X		X			
Valley Creek								X	X
Valley Forge							X		
Van		X					X		
Vandec								X	X
Van Nes Sensation								X	X
Van Veen							X		
Veesprite					X				
Venice	-20					X			
Vera Elliott							X		
Vera Hawkins							X		
Vernus	-25	X	X	X			X		
Veronica Pfeiffer	-20					X			
Very Berry							X		
Victor Frederick							X		
Victoria's Consort	-20					X			
Vinecrest	-15					X			
Vinemount	-15					X			
Vinewood	-15				X				
Virginia Leach	-15								
Virgo							X		
Vulcan	-15						X		
Vulcan's Flame	-15						X		
Wagtail					X				
Walloper							X		
Wally	-20		X						
Waltham	-25	X	X		X				
Warlock					X		X		
Warwick	-20							X	
Wayne Pink								X	
Wee Bee						X			
Westbury								X	X
Weston's Crescendo	-15					X			
Weston's Mayflower	-15					X			
Weston's Pink Diamond	-15			X			X		
Wheatley	-15							X	X
Whistle Punk				X			X		
White Bird	-25								
White Dimples	-20					X			
White Mice						X			
White Mustang							X		
White Pearl							X		
White Peter	-25					X			
White Pippin						X			
White Ruby	-15							X	X
White Swan							X		
White Wedding						X			
Whitney Dwarf Orange						X			
Whittenton	-15						X		
Wickatunk	-15						X		
Wigeon						X			
Wilbar			X				X		
Wild Affair								X	
Wilgen's Ruby	-15							X	
Wilsoni	-15					X			
Windbeam	-25					X			
Windlesham Scarlet					X			X	
Windsor Lad				X	X				
Winneconnet						X			
Winning Post						X			
Winterset	-15			X		X			
Wintonbury	-15					X			
Wisp			X			X			
Wissahickon	-15						X		
Wojnar's Purple	-20					X			
Woodchat			X						
Wren			X						
Wyanokie	-15					X			
Yates' Best	-15					X			
Yates' Hazel	-20						X		
Years of Peace	-15						X		
Yellow Eye	-20					X			
Yellow Fever			X		X				
Yellow Spring						X			
Yeoman						X			
Yo-Yo						X			
Yvonne Opaline							X		
Zyxya			X		X				

GLOSSARY

...rrant - Differing from the type form.
Acuminate - Elongated, tapering to a point.
Acute - Abruptly tapering to a point.
Agglutinate - An indumentum joined by adhesion.
Anther - The end of the stamen which bears pollen.
Apex - The tip or end.
Appressed - Lying close to or flat against.
Asexual - Without gender.
Auricle - Small, ear-like extension of the leaf at its base.
Basal - Relating to the base.
Bloom - A waxy coating.
Bullate - Puckered or blistered in appearance.
Calyx - The outer most part of the flower at its base.
Campanulate - Bell shaped.
Candelabroid - A truss with flowers appearing in tiers.
Ciliate - Fringed with hairs.
Clone - Asexual propagation of a particular variety.
Cordate - Heart shaped.
Corolla - The petals of a flower.
Cultivar - A horticulturally individual variety.
Cuneate - Wedge shaped.
Deciduous - Losing its leaves upon maturity or onset of autumn.
Detersile- An indumentum which completely sheds eventually.
Dimorphic - Occurring in two forms.
Dissected - Segmented by deep cuts.
Dorsal - Pertaining to the upper surface of a leaf.
Eglandular - Without glands.
Elepidote - Without scales.
Elliptic - Oval, rounded on the ends.
Entire - Not toothed or cut.
Epiphytic - Growing on plants but not parastically.
Exserted - Protruding, as anthers beyond the corolla.
Fastigiate - With branches erect and near together.
Ferruginous - Rust colored.
Filament - That to which the anther is attached.
Floccose - Having soft wool or tufts of hairs.
Floriferous - Bearing flowers, usually meaning readily.
Genus - A group of species closety related. (Pi. Genera)
Glabrescent- Shedding hair.
Glabrous - Smooth, hairless.
Glaucous - Having a waxy bloom, usually whitish or grayish.
Grex - All the seedlings of a particular cross.
Hose-in-hose - A double corona (a flower within a flower).
Hybrid - Offspring of two different plants, usually the same genus.
Indumentum - A woolly or hairy covering on leaves or stems.
Inflorescence - The flower arrangement of a plant.
Lanceolate - Tapered at the end like a lance.
Lax - Open, loose, as a truss.
Lepidote - Bearing scales.
Linear - Very narrow and elongated.
Lobe - The rounded division of a flower.
Mucro - The abrupt tip of a leaf, ending in a small point.
Mutation - A variation in the normal appearance.

N.E.F.A. - North East Frontier Agency of India.
Node - The location of the origin of a leaf on a stem.
Oblanceolate - Graduating from the base to broadest at the apex.
Oblong - More or less parallel tapering at both ends.
Obovate - Egg shaped.
Orbicular - Circular.
Oval - Elliptical.
Ovary - That portion of the pistil which bears the seeds.
Ovate - Egg shaped, broadest at the base.
Pedicle - The stalk supporting an individual flower.
Persistent - Not deciduous, remaining attached.
Petal - The parts dividing the corolla.
Petiole - A leaf stalk.
Pistil - Female flower organ; ovary, style, stigma.
Pollen - Male spores or grains produced by the anthers.
Pubescent - Covered with short, soft, fine hairs.
Raceme - Inflorescence occurring along the leaf axis.
Rachis - The principal stalk for an inflorescence.
Rotate - Wheel shaped.
Rufose - Rust colored.
Rugose - Covered with wrinkles.
Scabrous - Rough to the touch.
Scale - Tiny plate or disc-like structures on rhododendrons.
Scurfy - Covered with scales.
Sessile - Without a stalk.
Sport - Mutant, mutated branch.
Stamen - The filament and anther - the male organ of a flower.
Style - That part connecting the ovary and stigma.
Terminal - At the end.
Tomentose - Covered with short, dense hairs.
Truss - A flower cluster.
Viscid - Sticky.
Whorl - Positioned around the stem in a circle.

PLANT AWARDS

A.E.	—	Award of Excellence (American Rhododendron Society)
A.G.M.	—	Award of Garden Merit (English)
A.M.	—	Award of Merit (English)
C.A.	—	Conditional Award (American Rhododendron Society)
F.C.C.	—	First Class Certificate (English)
G.M.	—	Gold Medal (Dutch)
H.C.	—	Highest Commendation (English)
P.A.	—	Preliminary Award (English)
P.C.	—	Preliminary Commendation (English)
S.C.C.	—	Second Class Certificate. Used before 1888 and discontinued. (English)
S.M.	—	Silver Medal (Dutch)
S.P.A.	—	Superior Plant Award (American Rhododendron Society)

BIBLIOGRAPHY

American Rhododendron Society and Rhododendron Species Foundation. Iconographia Cormophytorum Sinicorum, Vol. III.
Rhododendrons of China. Translated by Judy Young and Dr. Lusheng Chong. Portland, Oregon: Binford & Mort, 1980.
American Phytopathological Society The. Compendium of Rhododendron and Azalea Diseases.
American Rhododendron Society, The. American Rhododendron Hybrids, 1980.
American Rhododendron Society, The. Fundamentals of Rhododendron and Azalea Culture.
American Rhododendron Society, The. Rhododendrons for your Garden, 1961.
American Rhododendron Society, The. Rhododendron Information, 1967.
Bailey, Liberty Hyde Bailey, Ethel Zoe, initial compilers. Hortus Third. Revised and expanded by the staff of the Liberty Hyde Bailey Hortorium, 1978.
Cox, Peter A. Dwarf Rhododendrons, 1973.
Cox, Peter A. The Larger Species of Rhododendron, 1979, & 1991.
Cox, Peter A. The Smaller Rhododendrons, 1985.
Cox, Peter A. & Keneth N. E. Encyclopedia of Rhododendron Hybrids.
Cullen, J. Notes from the Royal Botanic Garden, Edinburgh, Vol. 39, No. 1, 1980.
Cullen, J. Chamberlain, D.F. A Preliminary Synopsis of the Genus Rhododendron, 1978.
Fletcher, H.R., PhD., D, Sc., F.R.S.E., V.M.H. (Royal Botanic Garden, Edinburgh). The International Rhododendron Register, 1958.
Leach, David G. Rhododendrons of the World. 1961.
Philipson, W. R. Notes from the Royal Botanic Garden, Edinburgh, 1973.
Reiley, Edward H. Success with Rhododendrons and Azaleas.
Rhododendron Society, London. The Species of Rhododendron, 1930.
Salley & Greer. Rhododendron Hybrids: A Guide To Their Origins, First Edition 1986, Second Edition 1992.
Schmalscheidt, Walter. Rhododendron und Azaleenzuchtung in Deutschland 1989.
Van Veen, Ted Rhododendrons in America, 1969.
Washinton State University Cooperative Extension. How to Identify Rhododendron and Azalea Problems.

Periodicals and Year Books:
American Rhododendron Society. Quarterly Bulletin, Portland, Oregon, 1947, on ward.
Royal Horticultural Society, London. Rhododendron & Camellia Year Book 1954-1971.
Royal Horticultural Society, London. Rhododendrons, 1972-1973.
Royal Horticultural Society, London. Rhododendrons with Magnolias & Camellias, 1974-1995.
Royal Horticultural Society, London, The. The Rhododendron Handbook, 1980.

For More Information —

We invite you to join the
American Rhododendron Society

This educational and enjoyable organization issues four colorful journals each year
highlighting species and hybrid rhododendrons and azaleas. There are local chapters
spread over the rhododendron growing areas of the United States, Canada and Europe.

The A.R.S. Seed Exchange offers seed not otherwise available.

There are national and regional conferences which offer an opportunity to learn more
about rhododendorns and azaleas.

Contact —
American Rhododendron Society
P.O. Box 1380
Gloucester, VA 23061

Also offering useful information and plants —
Rhododendron Species Foundation
P. O. Box 3798
Federal Way, WA 98063-3798

If you are interested in azaleas consider also —
Azalea Society of America
P.O. Box 34536
West Bethesda, MD 20827-0536

GREER GARDENS

Display Garden & Mail Order Nursery

Our catalog describes, prices over 3000 plants

Azaleas
Rhododendrons
Japanese Maples
Dwarf Conifers
Bonsai Materials
Flowering Trees & Shrubs
Perennials

Fine Horticultural Books

Justly Famous for the Rare and Unusual

1280 Goodpasture Island Road
Eugene, OR 97401-1794
U.S.A.
Phone (541) 686-8266